The Cambridge History of Latin America is a large scale, collaborative, multi-volume history of Latin America during the five centuries from the first contacts between Europeans and the native peoples of the Americas in the late fifteenth and early sixteenth centuries to the present.

Ideas and Ideologies in Twentieth Century Latin America brings together chapters from Volumes IV, VI, and X of *The Cambridge History*. Each chapter is accompanied by a bibliographical essay.

D1533478

IDEAS AND IDEOLOGIES IN
TWENTIETH CENTURY LATIN AMERICA

The following titles drawn from
The Cambridge History of Latin America edited by Leslie Bethell
are available in hardcover and paperback:

Colonial Spanish America

Colonial Brazil

The Independence of Latin America

Spanish America after Independence, c. 1820–c. 1870

Brazil: Empire and the Republic, 1822–1930

Latin America: Economy and Society, 1870–1930

Mexico since Independence

Central America since Independence

Cuba: A Short History

Chile since Independence

Argentina since Independence

Ideas and Ideologies in Twentieth Century Latin America

IDEAS AND IDEOLOGIES IN TWENTIETH CENTURY LATIN AMERICA

edited by

LESLIE BETHELL

St. Antony's College, Oxford

Published by the Press Syndicate of the University of Cambridge
The Pitt Building, Trumpington Street, Cambridge CB2 1RP
40 West 20th Stree, New York, NY 10011-4211, USA
10 Stamford Road, Oakleigh, Melbourne 3166, Australia

The contents of this book were previously published as parts of volumes IV,
VI, and X of *The Cambridge History of Latin America,* copyright ©
Cambridge University Press, 1986, 1994, 1995

First published 1996

Printed in the United States of America

Library of Congress Cataloging-in-Publication data applied for.

A catalog record for this book is available from the British Library.

ISBN 0-521-46341-6 hardback
ISBN 0-521-46833-7 paperback

CONTENTS

PREFACE

The Cambridge History of Latin America is a large scale, collaborative, multi-volume history of Latin America during the five centuries from the first contacts between Europeans and the native peoples of the Americas in the late fifteenth and early sixteenth centuries to the present.

Ideas and Ideologies in Twentieth Century Latin America brings together chapters from Volumes IV, VI and X of *The Cambridge History*. This, it is hoped, will be useful for both teachers and students of Latin American history and of contemporary Latin America. Each chapter is accompanied by a bibliographical essay.

Part One

1

THE MULTIVERSE OF LATIN AMERICAN IDENTITY, c. 1920 – c. 1970

INTRODUCTION: CONTEXTS FOR IDENTITY

In the twentieth century the term 'identity' has been heavily worked to denote linkage between culture and society. Although the word keeps losing its edge, new generations periodically resharpen it. The term is so loose that one can apply it to anything from mankind at large[1] to a single person seeking self-knowledge via psychotherapy. Artists, poets, historians, anthropologists, philosophers and politicians entertain versions of identity even when not consciously in quest of it or not confident of the term's utility. This chapter will consider identity primarily with reference to national societies, to aggregations of national societies (Latin America), and to sub-national societies or groups. Two distinctions are important. First, identity, which implies linkage to or manifestation of collective conscience, is not the same as 'reality', a word widely used in Latin America to mean historical, socio-geographic factors that might be recognized as creating a circumambient reality. Both terms fluctuate between a descriptive, empirical meaning and a prospective or promissory one. 'Reality' may signify what 'really' exists or else, in a quasi-Hegelian sense, a 'higher' reality to be ascertained as a *sine qua non* for pursuit of the historic vocation of a people or nation (e.g., essays of interpretation of the 'Peruvian reality'). Identity is not 'national character' as diagnosed by detached socio-psychiatry but collective awareness of historic vocation. Reality starts with environment, identity with tacit self-recognition.

Identity, a human universal, assumed special accents with the rise of modern nations. Germany was a strategic case. As its leaders, thinkers, musicians and artists began to envision a German 'nation', they were

[1] See Ernst Cassirer, *An Essay on Man: An Introduction to a Philosophy of Human Culture* (New Haven, Conn., 1944), Part II, ch. 6.

3

driven to explore wellsprings of identity in ethnicity, folk culture and philosophic premises of history and religious faith. Germany has been called the first 'underdeveloped' country, implying that its advent on the world stage required not merely political *sagesse,* military prowess, and economic weight but affirmation of collective selfhood. Because England and France became (somewhat unwittingly) the first 'developed' countries as the industrial age dawned, their intelligentsias were more at home with political and economic matters than with the portentous metaphysical interests of Germans. In philosophizing, moreover, the English and French tended to conflate their national ideals with recipes for mankind at large. This produced a body of Enlightenment thought which in its more glib and self-serving aspects encountered head-on challenge from German romanticism. By the early nineteenth century this German rejoinder was a powerful solvent on mind and sensibility in England and France.

The lessons that the German analogy holds for Latin America and, more concretely, the ultimate influences of German ideas upon the region are examined later in the chapter. For the moment an illustration will show how present-day thinking on identity still falls under the shadow of the Enlightenment versus romanticism construction or, as in the case at hand, empiricism versus holism. In a collective work published in 1987, eight historians addressed the topic of colonial identity in the Atlantic world using six case studies (three of which were Brazil, Spanish America and the British Caribbean) to compare the formation of distinctive patterns in the period 1500 to 1800.[2] This comparative project required divorcing identity as 'self-definition and self-image' from the story of political independence and asking why some colonies had more 'success' at achieving psychological as well as political autonomy. The authors pursued their inquiry in a detached Anglo-empirical spirit rather than the empathic, holistic tradition of romanticism. The introductory chapter for example endorsed a quest for positive indicators of the 'process of identity formation' and cited such possible deterrents as the lack of printing presses in Brazil for three centuries or the absence of universities in the British West Indies until the 1950s. Identity is thus seen, as it was in the Enlightenment, as manipulable by technological and institutional innovation.

Scholars from the region itself had already addressed two of these cases

[2] Nicholas Canny and Anthony Pagden (eds.), *Colonial Identity in the Atlantic World, 1500–1800* (Princeton, N.J., 1987).

with different premises and purposes. Antônio Cândido, one of Brazil's foremost literary historians and critics, sees the absence of presses and gazettes in colonial Brazil not as inhibiting collective identity but as shaping it. Given an illiterate society, sacred oratory with its spoken word adapted to baroque arabesques and symbolism, was an ideal genre.[3] The Barbadian poet and historian Edward K. Brathwaite believes the distinctive spoken language of the present-day West Indies to be an emergent *nation language,* a form of 'total expression' that provides the keystone for regional identity. His colleagues at the School of Education, University of the West Indies, Brathwaite finds, have set out the grammar and syntax of the nation language but cannot connect it to literary expression. The whole school system, he holds, imposes a Victorian set of literary attitudes and responses that block creativity. The crux of the matter lies still deeper. The language issue lies not simply in lexicon, phonetics and subject matter but is rooted, Brathwaite argues, in the English capitulation since Chaucer to iambic pentameter. Caribbean life – the African legacy; the oral, communal expression of the people – is alien to the English language as parochially practised in England. 'The hurricane does not roar in pentameter.' Nor do the drums pulse to it. What the storm *does* roar in and what people *do* dance to – the young literati of the 1940s found out from their traditional calypsos – is a dactylic beat. This discovery provides academic nomenclature to legitimate everyday facts of life. Until then the disinherited must use the emergent nation language as a 'forced poetics' that perpetuates their culture while disguising self and personality. For literati and universities, one might venture, identity is not their invention but their belated recognition of social circumstance.[4]

The critical significance of language, or discourse, cannot receive central attention in this chapter.[5] Enough has been said, however, to suggest that the nature of our eight historians' concern with publication and universities (a reflection perhaps of modern academic anxiety) may not be wholly consistent with the understandings of this chapter. More germane to present purposes is the 'existential' commitment expressed as follows by W. H. Auden: 'In contrast to those philosophers who begin by considering the *objects* of human knowledge, essences and relations, the existential

3 Antônio Cândido, 'Oswald viajante', in *Vários escritos* (São Paulo, 1970), pp. 51–6.
4 Antônio Cândido, *Literatura e sociedade* (São Paulo, 1965), pp. 110–11; Edward Kamau Brathwaite, 'English in the Caribbean', in L. A. Fiedler and H. A. Baker, Jr. (eds.), *English Literature: Opening Up the Canon* (Baltimore, Md., 1981), pp. 15–53, and *Roots* (Havana, 1986).
5 For a general treatment, see Richard M. Morse, 'Language in America', in *New World Soundings* (Baltimore, Md., 1989), pp. 11–60.

philosopher begins with man's immediate experience as a *subject,* i.e., as a being in *need,* an *interested* being whose existence is at stake.'[6] This 'existential' gambit is inviting, for it treats collective experience as a project or adventure. This informal inquiry can be launched in such a spirit, by placing Latin America alongside two other civilizations that confronted the industrial West in the nineteenth century – namely, Japan and Russia. This is not done in the empirical vein of meticulous 'comparative history' but simply to help sketch out a set of questions more useful for present purposes than the ones more frequently posed in academic circles.

Japan had for centuries acquired civilizational ways from the Chinese. Fruitful adaptation brought self-knowledge and, when the time came, an impressive capacity to select what was needed from the West with few confusions of purpose. The germ of Tokyo University was an institute of 'barbarian learning' designed to translate Western texts that seemed useful for the Japanese national project. This project was preceded by a scholarly movement to free Japan from the formalism and pedantry of the Chinese Confucian tradition (although not at the expense of the tradition itself) attended by evocations of Japanese spirit and esthetic. Such evocations have been likened to the quest by German romantics of the same period for an unbridled release of domestic tradition.[7]

In the case of Russia there had been longer direct exposure to the West than in Japan, notably via the construction of St Petersburg in 1703–12. As in Japan there was awareness of a domestic civilization that required decisions on what was to be 'protected'. The Russian generation of Slavophiles and Westernizers defined the dichotomy, with the former dreaming of an ideal pre-Petrine Russia and the latter of an ideal West. Westernizers complicated matters with their 'Russian rehash' of Western ideas, however, while Russian nationalists sent for study to Germany succumbed to a crypto-Francophilism more fanatical than even the chauvinism of the Parisian boulevards.[8] In any case the dialectic was established as clearly in Russia, allowing for clandestine cross-overs, as in Japan.

How Latin America fits into our summary comparison hinges on how the notion of an original culture is handled. The Japanese recognized a domestic culture to which exogenous elements were to be selectively

---

[6] Quoted in Mitzi Berger Hamovitch (ed.), *The Hound and Horn Letters* (Athens, Ga., 1982), p. xiv.
[7] See Marius B. Jansen, *Japan and its World, Two Centuries of Change* (Princeton, 1980), ch. 1.
[8] Nicolas Berdyaev, *The Origin of Russian Communism,* trans. R. M. French, new ed. (Ann Arbor, Mich., 1960), ch. 1; Isaiah Berlin, *Russian Thinkers* (Harmondsworth, 1979), pp. 114–49.

assimilated, while Russian nationalists envisioned recovery of pre-Petrine rural communalism and non-Western Christianity. Nineteenth-century Latin America, in contrast, was not a single nation, while its fragmented parts shared the culture and religion of the Iberian peninsula, by then a 'backward' region of Western Europe. For Russian critics the societies of England and France may have represented soulless atomism, but for modernizing elites in Latin America these European leaders were paragons. And, if such elites regarded their Ibero-Catholic heritage as déclassé, all the more so were the hundreds of Afro-American and Amerindian communities that were stigmatized by past or present bondage. Whatever opposed the progress of the urban, Europeanized world was to be effaced. Consider the military campaigns against 'natives' and backlanders under General Roca in Argentina and under the Mexican dictator Porfirio Díaz in Sonora and Yucatan and the Canudos war in Brazil. Even 'judicious sociologists' like Carlos Octavio Bunge and Alcides Arguedas were agreed that 'nothing could be expected of the degraded aboriginal people'.[9]

Japanese engagement with Western science and culture was controlled and methodical, as instanced by the institute for 'barbarian books', the 'learning missions' sent abroad in the 1870s to identify 'realistic' national models for selective emulation, and the temperate enthusiasm for European institutions and manners during the 1880s that led to a permissive if not uncritical 'new Japanism'. On the other hand, many Russians, whether Europeanizers or Slavophiles, felt after 1848 that socialism would never regenerate bourgeois 'equilibrium' in the West and that Russia's 'primitive' collectivism offered possibilities for direct transition to modern socialism. Latin American elites, in contrast, apart from intransigent conservative factions or occasional free spirits, were prepared neither to question the implications of Western technology, rationalization and imperialism nor to promote broad consensus on matters of national culture and tradition. In his early writings, the Mexican philosopher Leopoldo Zea held that for Latin America the nineteenth century was in effect a 'lost century'.[10]

There were of course Latin Americans, individual pensadores and occasionally a national 'generation', who made signal contributions toward devising an agenda for their country or their continent. The point is that they were often adrift when it came to identifying *domestic* ingredients to be

[9] See José Luis Romero, *Latinoamérica: las ciudades y las ideas* (Buenos Aires, 1976), p. 311.
[10] See Leopoldo Zea, *The Latin-American Mind*, trans. J. H. Abbott and L. Dunham (Norman, Okla., 1963).

appropriated and adapted. The classic example is Domingo Faustino Sarmiento (Argentina, 1811–88), whose reflections on the life and times of the Argentine caudillo Facundo in *Civilización y barbarie* (1845) seemed to pit liberal Europe as filtered through Buenos Aires against the 'barbarism' of the pampas.[11] Read searchingly, Sarmiento's essay goes well beyond this formula, especially when combined with the notes on his 1846–7 travels to Europe and the United States when he discovered Europeans themselves to be barbarous if compared to American frontiersmen. The general point, however, is that well-to-do classes throughout Latin America, including their 'enlightened' and reformist spokesmen, freely applied the term 'barbarian' not, as did the Japanese, to foreigners but to groups within their own countries who were assignably 'native': Indians, mestizos, Afro-Americans, or dirt farmers of Iberian descent.

The decisive rebuttal to Sarmiento came from José Martí (Cuba, 1853–95) who, if he did not excel Sarmiento in his gift for social portraiture, was a more adept analyst of social process and the exigencies of nationhood. In an incisive passage in 'Nuestra América' (1891) he challenged those who mistook the struggle between 'false erudition and Nature' as one between 'civilization and barbarity'.[12] 'The native halfbreed has conquered the exotic Creole . . . The natural man is good, and he respects and rewards superior intelligence as long as his humility is not turned against him.' The tyrants of Latin America climb to power by appealing to disdained native elements and fall by betraying them. 'Republics have paid with oppression for their inability to recognize the true elements of their countries, to derive from them the right kind of government, and to govern accordingly.' 'To govern well, one must see things as they are.'

Martí's contribution to defining the identity issue was to democratize it. Nationalism had taken hold in Latin America but without the romanticist implication of rootedness in the people. Until the early twentieth century, pensadores, essayists and historians seemed agreed that cultural questions were a province of diagnosis and prescription reserved for intellectuals. The idea that people at large were the bedrock of national identity was incongruous in default of sustained, pluricentric, multi-ideological popular movements such as had shaped political awareness

---

[11] Domingo F. Sarmiento, *Life in the Argentine Republic in the Days of the Tyrants*, trans. Mrs Horace Mann (New York, 1961); and see Joseph T. Criscenti (ed.), *Sarmiento and his Argentina* (Boulder, Co., 1992) and Tulio Halperín Donghi et al. (eds.) *Sarmiento, Author of a Nation* (Berkeley, 1994).

[12] José Martí, *Our America*, Philip S. Foner (ed.) (New York, 1977), pp. 86–7.

and political process in Western Europe, most significantly the Protestant Reformation and the proletarian revolution. Thinkers, theologians, ideologues and politicians might supply doctrine and tactics for these diversely composed movements, but their roots were in widespread feelings and aspiration. Save for its African population, the United States was settled by émigrés from the two 'revolutions', thus internalizing them. Latin America, however, resisted them. The mother countries barred Protestantism at the gates, along with its messages concerning modern individualism. Europe's later proletarian 'revolution', which took forms from government paternalism through a gamut of socialisms all the way to anarchism, syndicalism and terrorism, made only tentative incursions because of the limited scope of industrialization in Latin America, the lasting efficacy of elite 'conciliations', and a permanent reserve army of workers. However much the pensadores may have kept abreast of progressive thought in Europe, the people whom they claimed to 'think for' were blocked from forming coherent movements that might have given inspiration, definition and support to the critiques made by the intelligentsia.

The identity question therefore consists not entirely of a consensual act of portraiture by sensitive observers but also of a popular voice, featuring the disinherited, that pursues outlet in the generalized discourse of society. For two reasons the identity search came later in Latin America than in Western Europe and the modernizing world, achieving full momentum only in the twentieth century. First, it was only by the 1910s and 1920s that there occurred a conflation of intellectual and popular outlooks as exemplified in letters and visual arts in Mexico, modernist manifestoes in Brazil, socio-political dialogues in Peru, ethno-literary pronouncements in Haiti and diverse manifestations elsewhere. Secondly, with regard specifically to the pensadores, we have argued that their assurances of prior European identity were in the last century too problematic, and their confidence for sustaining critical exchange with ideologies of the industrial West too insecure, to favour a coming-to-terms with world currents. They acquiesced in regnant prescriptions for 'progress' and ruefully confessed their domestic retardation. Here again the early twentieth century was a renovative moment. For suddenly the vanguard voices of Europe, attuned to earlier prophetic cries of the Baudelaires and Nietzsches, were raised in cacophonous condemnation (or even condemnatory exaltation) of the rationalist, scientistic and menacingly dehumanizing premises of the Western enterprise.

In Europe vanguardism, or modernism[13] had antecedents as an attitude both critical and celebratory of 'modernization'. One might call modernism a cognitive assault on the contradictions of modernity. In its golden age (1910–30) modernism, particularly from its Parisian arena, finally made its impact on Latin America, but not in a merely tutorial role. For Europe now experienced the crisis of nerve associated with technification, commodification, alienation and rampant violence as these found expression in Marxian contradictions, Spenglerian decadence, Freudian invasions of the subconscious, and of course, industrialism and the First World War. This seeming collapse of evolutionary assumptions gave Latin Americans leverage for dismissing presumed determinisms of their past and for inventing a new 'reality' and a new future. Europe now offered pathologies and not simply models. Disenchantment at the centre gave grounds for rehabilitation at the rim. Latin America had to produce its own Rousseaus and Herders at the same time that it was keeping up with the Picassos and Joyces.

Over the years many have claimed that Latin American high culture was derivative from metropolitan sources in the nineteenth century and suddenly responsive to indigenous or *indigenista* leads after 1920. Almost the reverse is true. What made the Latin American *prise de conscience* of the 1920s possible was not the artists' and intellectuals' stubborn appropriation of 'native' subject matter but their bold acrobatics to retain intellectual footing amid the disintegration of Western rationales and received understandings. With the centre now unstrung, views from the periphery earned respect. Alejo Carpentier (1904–80) was to discover the world as polycentric and Jorge Luis Borges (1899–1986) to find that it has no centre at all. As the Mexican novelist Carlos Fuentes puts it, 'the Western writer can be central only in recognizing that today he is ex-centric, and the Latin American writer only in recognizing that his eccentricity is today centered in a world without cultural axes.'[14]

A newspaper article of 1925 by José Carlos Mariátegui, 'Is There a Hispanic American Thought?', illustrates how his generation had begun to dissolve the polarities of intellectual life on the 'periphery'.[15] During three and a half years of exile in Italy (1919–23), Mariátegui directly

---

[13] I use 'modernism' in the European, North American (and Brazilian) meaning to designate twentieth-century vanguardism, not the Spanish American *modernismo* that was akin to symbolism and Parnassianism.

[14] Carlos Fuentes, *La nueva novela hispanoamericana*, 6th ed. (Mexico, D.F., 1980), p. 32.

[15] José Carlos Mariátegui, '¿Existe un pensamiento hispano-americano?' in *Temas de nuestra América*, 2nd ed. (Lima, 1970), pp. 22–6.

experienced both the decadence and the promise of Europe. Here he found Marxist analysis of social and economic domination an eye-opener and learned to admire how modernism, especially surrealism, could shatter the solid bourgeois world into absurd fragments. It was to a degree the modernist impulse that led him to extract Marxism itself from positivist armature giving its scientific message mythic force, translating its categories into praxis and relativizing its pretension to universal evolutionism.

In 1925 Mariátegui sensed that his query about Hispanic American thought was germinating in the 'nerve centers of the continent', although he felt that the true question was whether there existed a *characteristically* Hispanic American thought. He chided the Argentine socialist Alfredo Palacios, who had proclaimed the hour at hand for 'radical emancipation' from European culture. Europe had been the lodestar, wrote Palacios, but the Great War showed its culture to contain the seeds of its own decay. Palacios, Mariátegui felt, had led youthful tropical temperaments to exaggerate the prospects for Latin American thought. It was a tonic, he said, to call 'our America' the future cradle of civilization or to proclaim, as José Vasconcelos had in his motto for the National University of Mexico, that: 'Through my race the spirit will speak.' But it was an error to predict the imminent demise of European hegemony. The West was in crisis but far from collapse; Europe was not, 'as is absurdly said, exhausted and paralytic'. 'Our America' continued importing ideas, books, machines and fashions. Capitalist civilization was dying, not Europe. Greco-Roman civilization had long since perished, but Europe went on. Who could deny, Mariátegui asked, that the society of the future was being shaped in Europe or that the finest artists and thinkers of the age were European? He therefore acknowledged a French or German thought but not yet a Hispanic American one, which instead was a 'rhapsody' of European motifs. One might in the countries of the Río de la Plata speak of a spirit of 'Latinity', but it awoke no recognition from autocthonous peoples of the continent.

The purpose of this chapter is not to provide an inventory of trends and genres but to review and selectively illustrate various tactics, whether deliberate or unwitting, for establishing recognition of shared identity. An impressionistic glance from the 1920s to the 1960s suggests three distinctive categories of expression or analysis that carry forward the lines of inquiry set forth by Mariátegui, presented here as modernism, the 'neo-naturalist' novel in conjunction with the 'identity' essay, and philosophy plus history of ideas. Cultural history in an academic vein would assign Latin American modernism to the 1920s, the identity essay to the 1930s and 1940s, and history of ideas to the 1940s and 1950s. Such pigeon-holing, however, omits the tangled antecedents, both New World and European, of these expressive forms and forecloses appreciation of their persistence after the assigned decades.[16] The narratives of the Latin American literary 'boom' of the 1960s, for example, clearly bear the mark of these antecedents. In the twentieth century, cultural expression in Latin America has acquired a heavier retrospective concern, and the logic of exposition requires overrunning the designated decades. The chronological ladders of literary history matter less than the cumulative impact of self-recognition.

First, then, we sketch the career of modernism in three locations during the 1920s and 1930s. The first two of these locales are not countries – the usual reference point for literary histories – but cities. This is because modernism found its Latin American crucibles in urban settings just as it did in Europe (Paris, Vienna, Milan, Berlin). Unlike, say, romanticism or realism, which managed a broad geographic palette, modernism required the arena where mind and sensibility awoke to specifically *modern* features of the Western world view: velocity, simultaneity, collage, inversion, free association, catachresis, the cult of machines and rationality – but not to the exclusion of 'primitive' evocations. The two cities chosen are São Paulo, the burgeoning financial and industrial capital of South America, and Buenos Aires, its earlier commercial and cultural capital.[17]

In São Paulo, founded in 1554, a city whose colonial traces had vanished, whose population had leaped from 65,000 to 580,000 in thirty years, whose streets were thronged by Italians, Syrians and Japanese, whose sky was perforated overnight by smokestacks, the imagination was challenged not to understand but to see, not explain but apprehend. It was assigned an act of *cognition*.[18] Buenos Aires in contrast entered the post–First World War era of national and cultural assertion precisely as its citification and

---

[16] Stabb traces the identity essay from 1890 and could certainly have dropped at least as far back as Sarmiento's *Facundo*, while Abellán traces the history of the American 'idea' back to 1492. Martin S. Stabb, *In Quest of Identity: Patterns in the Spanish American Essay of Ideas, 1890–1960* (Chapel Hill, N.C., 1967); J. L. Abellán, *La idea de América, origen y evolución* (Madrid, 1972).

[17] Jorge Schwartz compares Paulista and Porteño avant-gardism in *Vanguarda e cosmpolitismo: Oliverio Girondo e Oswald de Andrade* (São Paulo, 1983), while Raúl Antelo examines the Paulistas' reception of Spanish American vanguardism in *Na ilha de Marapatá (Mário de Andrade lê os hispano-americanos)* (São Paulo, 1986).

[18] See Nicolau Sevcenko, *Orfeu extático na metrópole: São Paulo, sociedade e cultura nos frementes anos 20* (São Paulo, 1992).

Europeanization had come under question. A note of decadence, of ominous warning was sounding in both high and popular culture. So accepted was the cosmopolitan ethos that commonplaces of domestic history and culture assumed a mythic cast, as in the nostalgic Argentine *gauchismo*. Brazilians might exalt their *bandeirantes,* or colonial path-finders, as did modernist poet Cassiano Ricardo in a dithyrambic account of their exploits or modernist sculptor Victor Brecheret in a monumental public statue; yet the *bandeirante,* historically quite as venerable as the gaucho, had not faded into a mythic past but was exemplary for pioneers of a dynamic future. He was a flesh-and-blood hero, unlike Ricardo Güiraldes's oneiric, 'shadowy' gaucho in *Don Segundo Sombra* (1926), who concludes the most renowned work of Argentine fiction of the 1920s by fading from sight as a man, leaving the observer's meditation cut off from its source, his lifeblood flowing away. Here inquiry probes beyond 'reality' to a domain of enigma or paradox. The challenge is not cognition but *decipherment.* If the Brazilian 'anti-hero' of Mário de Andrade's *Macunaíma* (1928) finally goes off to muse alone as a star in the vast firmament, it is not because the old life has evanesced but precisely because it is all too tenacious, too real, in a land 'sem saúde e com muita saúva' – with no health and lots of ants.[19]

Mexico, our third instance, is a case of modernism manqué because the putative modernist moment coincided with a revolution. Although in retrospect the Mexican Revolution seems not to have been a full-dress socio-political *renversement,* it did at least convert Mexico City into a radiant, innovative centre by what was then interpreted as a collective act of vision and volition. The revolution itself became a 'modernist' event by working lightning reversals and expansions of sense and sensibility. Under its inspiration the painterly imagination fused Aztec deities, the late-medieval *danse macabre* (rediscovered by José Guadalupe Posada), German expressionism, and Montparnasse cubism, not to mention Renaissance muralism and Spanish ecclesial baroque. The *revolution,* Octavio Paz has said, had no programme. It was a gigantic subterranean revolt, a *revelation* that restored our eyes to see Mexico. Thus Mexicans in the modernist age such as Paz's representative list of painters and writers (Rivera, Orozco, López Velarde, Azuela, Guzmán and Vasconcelos) were less concerned with inversion, collage, or geometric reduction than with retrieval. Diego Rivera, after a dozen years in Paris (where he won stardom as a cubist)

---

[19] Ricardo Güiraldes, *Don Segundo Sombra,* trans. Harriet de Onís (New York, 1966); Mário de Andrade, *Macunaíma,* trans. E. A. Goodland (New York, 1984).

returned to Mexico, adopted a dynamic, even orgiastic fauvist manner, and, at his best, escaped the clutch of official ideology to capture the germination and sheer materiality of plants, people and machines. Orozco and Siqueiros developed a home-grown expressionism, in Siqueiros's case with ideological baggage similar to Rivera's, in Orozco's with moral and personal accents. In Mexico, the modernist agenda was not the *cognition* of São Paulo or the *decipherment* of Buenos Aires but a task of *propaganda* in the original sense of a duty to spread the 'good tidings'.[20]

Historically, the modernists seem a focal point of the 1920s. However, the interpretation of their early messages (Oswald de Andrade) or the cumulative influence of their unfolding work (Borges) took time, even decades. Only the quasi-modernist Mexican muralists won instant fame. Years later, in 1942, Mário de Andrade, playfully known as the pope of Brazilian modernism, poignantly recounted the fate of avant-gardism.[21] He recalled the exaltation of the 1920s, the infatuating rediscovery of Europe and Brazil, the festive impulse to demolition, the dance on the volcanoes: 'Doctrinaire, intoxicated by a thousand and one theories, saving Brazil . . . we consumed everything including ourselves in the bitter, almost delirious cultivation of pleasure.' Yet looking back from Brazil's Estado Novo (1937–45) and a second global war he felt that while joyously trying to serve his time and country he had succumbed to a vast illusion. More was needed than to break windows, joggle the eternal verities, or quench cultural curiosity: not mere political activism, not explosive manifestoes, but greater anxiety about the epoch, fiercer revolt against life as it is.

This statement, while highly personal, betokens a general Latin American transition. For reasons related to the collapse of the international economy, to authoritarian threats at home and abroad, to ominous murmurs of the dispossessed, and to ennui with hermetic or meretricious features of vanguardism, the modernist flame was wavering, to reassert its inspiration only a generation or more later. If fiction, poetry and the arts were exemplary vehicles of modernism, a shift in primacy occurs in the 1930s and 1940s as conspicuous novelists leaned toward a world of commonsensical yet menacing phenomena while essayists derived cues from

---

[20] See Dawn Ades, *Art in Latin America: The Modern Era, 1820–1980* (New Haven, Conn., 1989), chs. 6–7; Octavio Paz, *Sombras de obras* (Mexico, D.F., 1983), pp. 163–79; Olivier Debroise, *Diego de Montparnasse* (Mexico, D.F., 1979).

[21] Mário de Andrade, 'O movimento modernista', in *Aspectos da literatura brasileira*, 4th ed. (São Paulo, 1972), pp. 231–55.

philosophy, history, ethnography and psychology to solidify their grounds for speculation. One might pair them as neo-naturalists (such as Rómulo Gallegos, José Américo de Almeida or Ciro Alegría) and neo-pensadores (such as Mariátegui, Price-Mars or Samuel Ramos). The former, however, moved beyond Zolaesque canons and even, paradoxically, anticipated the 'marvellous realism' of the 1960s while the latter laid partial claim to empirical science, but a science leavened by post-positivist philosophy and modernist wit.

The late 1940s and 1950s created fresh context for intellectual endeavour, now conducted with an eye to such external circumstances as the aftermath of the Spanish Civil War, the Second World War, and the incipient Cold War and to such domestic trends as the advent of populist politics and the developmentalist alliance between the state and new industrial groups. The mid-1940s saw the appearance of reformist, constitutional regimes, while rapid urbanization, the growth of middle sectors with a supposed stake in a stable order, and the by now canonical imperative of development 'from within' seemed to brighten possibilities for revolutionary change. Modernist extravagance seemed whimsical and dated save for monumental products like Mexican murals or Brazilian architecture, absorbable to the purposes of mushrooming bureaucracies. Imaginative writers tended private gardens unless they found occasions for political statement (Pablo Neruda, Miguel Angel Asturias) or enticed the growing audience for 'best sellers' (Manuel Gálvez, Erico Veríssimo, Jorge Amado) or consolidated their careers around research and institutional service (Jorge Basadre, Sérgio Buarque de Holanda).

Various circumstances contributed to endow the identity question with a less nationalistic, more speculative dimension: the effect of the Spanish Civil War in incorporating the Hispanic world to global politics; the modernization of Spanish academe and the transatlantic migration of many of its finest scholars; the effect of the Second World War in assimilating Latin American countries to a purported democratic partnership and in subsequently prescribing their global economic role. Just as modernism had played its part in shaping sensibilities in the 1920s, so in the late 1940s and 1950s philosophy, and particularly the schools of phenomenology and existentialism, played a part – inconspicuously for a general public – in rehabilitating the intellectual image of the American continents. Latin American philosophers anticipated social scientists by two decades in professionalizing their discipline with a vocabulary that made explicit certain promptings of the modernists and raised to higher planes of generalization the reconnoitering of indigenists, novelists, and essay-ists. What is more, the Germanic style that caught on gave cachet to Latin American philosophizing while slighting the Anglo American analytic vein in favour of a holism more consonant with Iberian precedents.

The next three sections of this chapter, then, examine modernism, the novel and essay, and philosophy as moments of a *prise de conscience* that took shape in Latin America in the 1920s and, in shifting modes and guises, still continues. These three moments are not strictly consecutive nor confined to specific decades, nor are they the sole intellectual beacons of their periods, nor are they walled off like 'disciplines' (some writers are identified with more than one of them: Vasconcelos, Mariátegui, Martínez Estrada, Mário de Andrade). The point is that activity in these areas made distinctive contributions to the identity quest broadly defined. Moreover, they have heuristic uses, for if we liken them to Whitehead's three stages of mental growth they suggest ways of understanding how minds, from many angles and suppositions, may reach tacit recognition of shared experi-ence.[22] Whitehead's initial stage of 'romance' – here, Latin American modernism – is a first apprehension when subject matter has the vividness of novelty, and its possibilities are 'half-disclosed by glimpses and half-concealed by the wealth of material'. Knowledge is *ad hoc* and piecemeal. Emotion flares up in the transition from bare facts to awareness of unex-plored relationships. The stage of 'precision' – here the novelists and essayists – subordinates breadth of relationship to exactness of formula-tion. It provides grammars of language and science along with a mode of analysis that digests facts as they accumulate. Finally comes the stage of generalization – analogous to the philosophic contribution – which rekin-dles romanticism but now with benefit of orderly ideas and apposite technique. Whitehead's stages are familiar in common experience where, however, they forever spin in cycles and nested minicycles. For present purposes the three stages are applied not as a grand evolutionary scheme but to treat cultural history on the 'periphery' less as an importation of models than as domestic gestation.

In what follows certain outcomes of our three 'stages' will be traced up to the 1970s, and the envoi will briefly consider two notable develop-ments from the late 1950s to the 1970s, namely, the invasion of academic social science and the literary 'boom'. The simultaneity of these occur-rences rescues us from what might have seemed an evolutionary process. By the 1960s social scientists had recognized the determinative effects of

---

[22] Alfred North Whitehead, *The Aims of Education* (New York, 1949), pp. 28–52.

international economic and political forces and were producing a body of 'dependency' theory that assimilated Latin American to modern Western history, assigning it lugubrious prospects. (More 'radical' exponents preached a doctrine of revolutionary voluntarism to upset the logic of economic domination they had so persuasively set forth.) The literary imagination, on the other hand, was not so much appalled by forces of *domination* as it was captivated by the *resistance* of local societies to the dictates of 'development', whether of foreign or domestic origin. Hence its fascination with the colonial or aboriginal past, with mythic recurrence or 'eternal return', and with an ethos of 'marvellous realism'. What Antonio Gramsci was for the sociologist, Mircea Eliade represented for the novelist. The social science and literary 'booms' formed a new generational *prise.* But while the scientists distantly echoed nineteenth-century positivism (though with a self-conscious modernization of language), artists and writers were captivated by tensions and contradictions of a new baroque age, often mediated by modernist mentors who were now accorded belated or posthumous acknowledgement. Without Borges, Fuentes claims, 'there simply would have been no modern Hispanic American novel'[23] – and indeed Borges himself both inspired and helped to shepherd the whole transition from the 1920s to the 1980s.

This dichotomy arose clearly in the 1960s, when social scientists, whatever the provisos and shadings of their analyses, *rationally* perceived Latin America as 'inserted into' schemes of metropolitan domination, manipulation and desacralization. The writers for their part, however 'leftist' their political sympathies might in some cases be, *instinctively* 'marvelled at' the intransigence of their societies to the invasion of Western rationalism, capitalism, and political mandates. How do we bridge these divergent visions? One might suppose the possibility, the multiple possibilities, for dialectical engagement if not, in any facile sense, for 'synthesis'.

MODERNISM

São Paulo: Modernism as Cognition

The opening salvo of modernism in Brazil was Modern Art Week, occurring in São Paulo city from 11 to 17 February 1922.[24] This was in fact the

---

[23] Fuentes, *La nueva novela*, p. 26.
[24] General treatments include Wilson Martins, *The Modernist Idea: A Critical Survey of Brazilian Writing in the Twentieth Century*, trans. Jack E. Tomlins (New York, 1970) and John Nist, *The Modernist Movement in Brazil* (Austin, Tex., 1967).

only self-styled modernist movement in Latin America, the analogue in Spanish America being vanguardism. Modern Art Week was celebrated by young writers and artists in the Parisian-style municipal theatre as if mocking the stale Europhilism for which it stood. The event – eight days of public exhibits and three days of 'festivals' (lectures, readings, concerts) – was calculated to scandalize the public, and in this it fully succeeded. Although the participants included a few from Rio de Janeiro – such as Ronald de Carvalho, Manuel Bandeira, and the elder statesman Graça Aranha, author of *Canaã* (1902) – most were Paulistas including, to cite names that have lasted, the sculptor Brecheret, painters Anita Malfatti and Di Cavalcanti, writers Guilherme de Almeida and Menotti del Picchia, and the two stars to be discussed shortly, Oswald de Andrade and Mário de Andrade.

Because Modern Art Week was taunting, carnivalesque and outrageously vanguard, the sessions provoked catcalls, even fistfights. Years later Mário de Andrade wrote of this moment that: 'Given its character as a risky game, its extreme spirit of adventure, its modernist internationalism, its raging nationalism, its gratuitous antipopulism, its overbearing dogmatism – it revealed an aristocracy of the spirit.'[25] The initial impression of Paulista modernism as a prank or *boutade* obscured recognition of the decade preceding Modern Art Week when modernist notions took shape, from foreign examples and domestic messages, within a small cenacle as instanced by Oswald's tidings from his first Parisian visit of 1912, the 1913 exhibit of the young Lithuanian expressionist Lasar Segall (destined to be one of Brazil's finest artists), daily meetings of a coterie in the bookstore O Livro, and the controversial expressionist show of Anita Malfatti in 1917. In other words, Paulista modernism did not capitulate in mimetic fashion to Parisian dada, cubism and the like. Marinetti's futurism, originating in industrial, 'unpoetic' Milan, did have a vogue on the eve of Modern Art Week, perhaps because its gospel of automation and sheer movement was congenial to São Paulo. But Paulista cognoscenti were sceptical, and Marinetti, whom Mário de Andrade disliked, alienated Brazilians on a later visit, not the least for his fascist sympathies.

Modern Art Week, then, was not an eye-opener for initiates and in this differed from the New York Armory Show of 1913. Although two-thirds of the latter was given to pioneering American trends, the Europeans received the acclaim, especially cubists and fauvists, who caused shock,

---

[25] Mário de Andrade, 'O movimento modernista', p. 236.

bemusement and awe.[26] In São Paulo the purpose of the Week was not to mystify a parochial bourgeoisie with Europe's latest *divertissements* but to use these as explosives to demystify the foundations of a class-based system of literary production and to achieve artistic expression of national scope. São Paulo's modernists were concerned less with stylistic novelty than with mastery of the artistic media. The Brazilian musicians, Guiomar Novaes and Villa-Lobos, may have performed European composers, but the music of Villa-Lobos himself swept all before it. As Mário de Andrade later wrote, beneath the *blague* and raillery lay three central objectives: permanent freedom for esthetic research, renovation of the Brazilian artistic intelligence and stabilization of a national creative consciousness on a collective rather than individualist base. To oversimplify: the Armory Show helped American artists catch up to Europe; Modern Art Week helped art itself catch up to the idea of Brazil.

One may ask why upstart industrial São Paulo hatched this sophisticated movement rather than Rio, Brazil's cultural and publishing headquarters. Mário's answer was that while Rio, as seaport and political capital, had an inborn vocation for internationalism, coffee and industry had given São Paulo a more modern spirit and more vibrant foreign connection. Rio retained a dose of folkloric 'exoticism' with an interfusion of urban and rural cultures. São Paulo was a burgeoning metropolis perched on its plateau with a large hinterland that was more *caipira* (bumpkin) than exotic. Rio, successively the seat of a viceroyalty, an empire and a republic, immured by fanciful mountains that left it facing toward Europe, was an *imperial* city. São Paulo had from the start turned its back on the sea and followed an inland vocation, first *bandeirismo,* then the westward march of coffee, and finally industry in quest of markets. São Paulo is an *imperialist* city. Its very modernity betokened a certain innocence. In 'malicious' Rio, wrote Mário de Andrade, an exhibit like Anita Malfatti's 'might have caused a public stir but no one would have been carried away. In ingenuous São Paulo it created a religion.'[27]

Modern Art Week was one of four events in 1922, centennial year of Brazilian independence, that denounced the status quo from quite different angles. The other three, all based in Rio, were: the Copacabana revolt of the *tenentes,* young officers claiming national renovation and social

---

[26] See Milton W. Brown, *The Story of the Armory Show,* 2nd ed. (New York, 1988); Eliane Bastos, *Entre o escândalo e o sucesso: a Semana de 22 e o Armory Show* (Campinas, 1991).

[27] Mário de Andrade, 'O movimento modernista', p. 236.

justice; the creation of the Centro Dom Vital and the review *A Ordem* to mobilize the church's programmes of indoctrination and political action; and the founding of the Communist Party. Modernism, particularly in its iconoclastic, heroic years of 1922–30, seems removed from the social and political *engagement* of these initiatives unless we abandon the narrowly avant-gardist meaning of Brazilian modernism, as Lafetá does, and prolong the movement to the early 1940s.[28] Lafetá divides modernism into an aesthetic project, which seeks to renovate the means of expression and break with traditional language, and an ideological project, which delves into national consciousness seeking specifically Brazilian expression. These projects are not mutually exclusive. Single writers might pursue both in shifting combinations; or single works might bridge the two. As collective expressions, however, the aesthetic project was foremost at the outset, began yielding to the ideological in the late 1920s, and lost primacy in the 1930s.

The early phase, with a cast of Paulistas and Cariocas including Antônio de Alcântara Machado, Sérgio Milliet, Sérgio Buarque de Holanda and Di Cavalcanti, was marked by Mário de Andrade's esthetic orientations, the irreverence and audacity of the review *Klaxon* (1922), and a pilgrimage to Minas Gerais as a preamble to a collective discovery of Brazil. Soon Oswald de Andrade showed his genius for composing verbal *affiches* with the Brazilwood Manifesto of 1924, a charge that Europe had profited long enough from Brazilian exports of sugar, coffee and rubber and that now Brazilian poetry must go on the list. His Anthropophagic Manifesto of 1928 along with an anthropophagic review co-edited with Alcântara Machado and Raul Bopp radicalized and primitivized the Brazil-wood thesis. To be sure, Oswald took cues from fauvism, futurism, and above all dadaism. In 1920 Francis Picabia had even published a 'Manifeste Cannibale Dada' in Paris and co-founded the review *Cannibale* with Tristan Tzara. But Oswald's Anthropophagy was far from imitative. For Brazilians cannibals were a historical reality, not a *divertissement*. That is, once one accepts the Tupi as the original Brazilian, his cannibalism is no longer savage, exotic, or an anthropological curiosity. It now becomes the Indian ritual *ingesting* of the strength and power of enemies and eventually of European invaders. The modernists needed precisely this lesson to handle the cultural relation between Brazil and Europe (hence Oswald's *bon mot*, 'Tupi or not Tupi'). They could now repudiate the clumsy binomial be-

---

[28] João Luiz Lafetá, *1930: A crítica e o modernismo* (São Paulo, 1974).

tween mimicry of Europe and a 'native' culture cut from whole cloth. Cannibalism recognized both the nutritive property of European culture and a transformative process of appropriation. Brazilians might chuckle at the *boutades* of French modernism; but for guidance on 'primitivism', language, and culture they turned to sixteenth-century mentors such as Montaigne, Rabelais and the Pleiad poets, who had been at a point to forge French culture rather than cleverly embellish it.[29]

Brazil-wood and anthropophagy show points of mutual reinforcement between the esthetic and ideological projects. If Oswald moved toward 'ideological' issues in the late 1920s, Mário de Andrade remained true to his linguistic-literary priority, for he was obsessed by the search for a 'de-geographized' Brazilian language (i.e., not compiled of picturesque region-alisms) adequate for expressing the cosmos of the Brazilian people.[30] He went beyond 'aesthetics' in the narrow usage, however, when he rejected naturalist technique, which merely ratified a vision of Brazil that was implicit in cultural preferences of the oligarchy. Although closely atten-tive to politics, Mário was not an activist, because he accepted as the precondition for action not a grand design but new grammar and lexicon. The success of modernism in stripping discourse to its elements therefore made the arts a testing-ground for reinventing politics.

The early benchmarks for Lafetá's 'ideological' project were almost coin-cident with those of Oswald's manifestoes. The two movements that passed, in Antonio Candido's terms, from 'aesthetic to political national-ism' were Verdeamarelismo or Green-and-yellowism (the national colours) in 1925 and Anta, named for the Brazilian tapir, in 1927. Key players in both groups were Cassiano Ricardo, Guilherme de Almeida, Menotti del Picchia and the notorious Plínio Salgado. Salgado joined the modernists from the start bringing with him an addiction to nationalism and a conservative familial Catholicism refreshed by the Catholic revival in Rio. He wrote two creditable political novels (*O estrangeiro*, 1926, and *O esperado*, 1931), but the quality of his literary efforts declined as his political interests took focus. A trip to the Near East and Europe in 1930

---

[29] Erdmute Wenzel White, *Les années vingt au Brésil: Le modernisme et l'avant-garde internationale* (Paris, 1977); Michael Palencia-Roth, 'Cannibalism and the New Man of Latin America in the 15th- and 16th-century European imagination', *Comparative Civilizations Review*, 12 (1985): 1–27. Maggie Kilgour examines the cannibal theme in Western literature from Homer and Ovid to Coleridge and Melville in *From Communion to Cannibalism: An Anatomy of Metaphors of Incorporation* (Princeton, 1990).

[30] Edith Pimentel Pinto assembles the notes Mário gathered throughout his life for a 'modest grammar' of Brazilian speech in *A Gramatiquinha de Mário de Andrade: texto e contexto* (São Paulo, 1990).

gave him sympathetic awareness of fascism, and by 1932 he was leading Brazil's Integralist party.[31]

After 1925 modernism spread elsewhere from the São Paulo–Rio axis. In places the Paulistas' example was overshadowed, as in Recife where Joaquim Inojosa shepherded a nascent modernist movement that soon yielded to a northeast school of regionalism inaugurated by a manifesto in 1926. Its members found a sociological expositor in Gilberto Freyre (see below) and produced a crop of novelists in the 1930s who won renown immediately in Brazil and more gradually overseas. In later years, specifically in *Região e tradição* (1941), Freyre perhaps magnified the significance of regionalism just as in the early years he had been dismissive of Paulista modernism. In any case the northeast novelists, discussed in the next section, richly exemplify the 'ideological' option of the period, with one of them, Graciliano Ramos, mastering the 'rare equilibrium' needed to imbue familiar schemes for representing reality with the conquests of the avant-garde.[32]

Of the mainstream modernists the two who have best stood the test of time are Oswald de Andrade (1890–1954) and Mário de Andrade (1893–1945). Unrelated by family, they were comrades in the heroic years of modernism, then drew apart but continued respecting and finding sustenance in each other's example.

Oswald's public self was iconoclastic and Rabelaisian. He was the dandy, the enfant terrible, the self-styled 'clown of the bourgeoisie'.[33] Save for an excursion to Amazonian Peru, Mário never left Brazil, while Oswald plunged into modernist Paris as early as 1912. He was impatient with Mário's professorial inclinations and his devotion to cultural intricacies. Oswald rendered his poems and narratives, his perceptions and prescriptions, in a telegraphic style of explosive vignettes. His life and works, Antônio Cândido observes, betoken an eternal voyager, 'the transitive esthetic of the traveller' who composed a divinatory vision from swiftly seized fragments. His conformist bourgeois casing is stripped off by the search for plenitude through a ceaseless redemptive journey. Oswald's Pau-Brasil poems of 1925 open with a series of poetic

---

[31] Hélgio Trindade treats Salgado's career from modernism to politics in *Integralismo* (*o fascismo brasileiro na década de 30*) (São Paulo, 1974), parts 1, 2.

[32] Lafetá, *1930*, p. 156; Joaquim Inojosa, 'O movimento modernista no Norte', in *Os Andrades e outros aspectos do modernismo* (Rio de Janeiro, 1975), pp. 218–39.

[33] For interpretations of Oswald, see Antônio Cândido, *Vários escritos* (São Paulo, 1970), chs. 2–4 and prefaces by Haroldo de Campos and Benedito Nunes in Vols. 2, 6, and 7 of Oswald's *Obras completas* (Rio de Janeiro, 1972).

abstracts of the colonial chroniclers, retrieving their direct language and Kodak vision. In one of his telescoped poems, 'Mistake of the Portuguese', Oswald echoes Montaigne to show the arbitrariness of opposing roles: A pity it was raining when the Portuguese arrived, making him clothe the Indian! – On a sunny day the Indian would have disrobed the Portuguese.

Other poems were quite as synoptic. The recruit who swore to his sweetheart that even if he died he would return to hear her play the piano, but he stayed in Paraguay forever. Or the slave who leaped into the Paraíba river with her daughter so the baby wouldn't suffer. Or the 'feudal lord': 'If Pedro II / Comes around / With a big story / I'll lock him up.' The poems and manifestoes address several historical themes: the church–state apparatus that moulded Brazilian civilization, patriarchal society and its moral standards, messianic dreams, the rhetoric of Europhile intellectuals, an indianism that camouflaged the outlook of the colonizer and the frustrations of the colonized. Not only did Oswald posthumously inspire Brazil's internationally known Tropicália movement of the late 1960s, but he also anticipated the motifs that were, at that same moment, to attract academic historians. Of Oswald's fiction his two most notable books were *Memórias sentimentais de João Miramar,* published in 1924 (where prose and poetry merge in a cinematic technique that renders the routines and vapidities of the coffee bourgeoisie on transatlantic tour) and *Serafim Ponte Grande* (1933).[34] The latter, an even more radical text, has been called a non-book, an anti-book, a fragment of a great book, and finally 'a great non-book of book fragments'.

Antônio Cândido observes that *Serafim* is the counterpart to Mário de Andrade's *Macunaíma* (considered below). Each narrative takes the reader on a 'mythological' journey into acute cultural trauma, with the parochial Paulista bourgeois immersed in sophisticated Europe on one hand and the Amazonian 'native' in industrial São Paulo on the other. Both situations required grotesque, erotic and obscene language of Rabelaisian gusto to smash the literary equilibrium of Brazil's *fin de siècle,* the universe of Machado de Assis where stylistic excess took the chastened forms of sentimentality, pathos and grandiloquence. Facing the asynchronous collision of what the world took as civilization versus primitivism, Oswald and Mário put their anthropophagic principles to the test in an act of

---

[34] 'Sentimental Memoirs of John Seaborne', trans. Ralph Niebuhr and Albert Bork, *Texas Quarterly,* 15/4 (1972), 112–60; *Seraphim Grosse Pointe,* trans. Kenneth D. Jackson and Albert Bork (Austin, Tex., 1979).

devoration. This meant that the noble savage of Indianist novels must yield to the bad savage whose need for marrow and protein required expropriation of the enemy's cultural past.[35] For Oswald, however, *Serafim* was another turning-point. Written from 1925 to 1929, it reached print only in 1933. By then he had discovered that intellectuals had been playing ring-around-the-rosy. Short of cash, ignorant of Marx, yet anti-bourgeois, he had become a bohemian. But he was now ready to join the Proletarian Revolution. Happily he did not succumb. He broke with Marxism in 1945 and returned to anthropophagy, the base for a new career in philosophy which might reveal, he hoped, why the recent war had done little to solve the world's abiding problems.

Mário de Andrade's first book of verse in the modernist vein was *Paulicea desvairada* (1922), or 'hallucinated city' (São Paulo).[36] Although he had abjured his early 'metrical' poems, his verse, while now 'free', was suffused with assonance, internal rhymes, and classic metrical effects. He rejoices in the splintered vision of modernism but is on some counts a willing hostage to tradition. He is, for example, unabashedly lyrical about São Paulo; his point of reference is not the inhuman urban dynamism of the futurists but explicitly his own 'self'. Mário dedicates the book to his 'beloved master', Mário de Andrade, and his 'Most Interesting Preface' insists that he sings in his own way. In the book's first line São Paulo is the 'commotion of my life'. Even with its physical identity effaced by business and industry, São Paulo sweeps the observer into an age-old carnivalesque setting of grey and gold, ashes and money, repentance and greed. The poet's world is not one that *he* has decomposed as an imagist or surrealist might; nor is it one that has fallen into pieces *on its own*. It is rather a self-given mystery that he feels challenged to apprehend through fused vision, objective and private, and through a harlequin figure symbolizing ancient myth and lonely self, revelry and sorrow, foolery and wisdom. Hence a strong hint of romanticism in his verse.

Mário de Andrade confessed that in the chit-chat of his 'interesting' preface one scarcely knew where *blague* left off and sobriety began. He even parodied his own avant-garde by founding a school of 'Hallucinism' at the start of the preface and disbanding it at the end. He confessed to being

[35] Antônio Cândido, *Vários escritos*, pp. 84–7; Haroldo de Campos, 'The Rule of Anthropophagy: Europe under the Sign of Devoration', *Latin American Literary Review*, 14/27 (1986), 42–60.

[36] Mário de Andrade, *Hallucinated City*, bilingual ed., trans. Jack E. Tomlins (Kingsport, Tenn., 1968). Telê Porto Ancona Lopez traces Mário's intellectual development in *Mário de Andrade: ramais e caminho* (São Paulo, 1972).

old-fashioned and scolded those who poked fun at Rodin or Debussy only to kneel before Bach and African sculpture or even cold squares and cubes. Being placed in Brazil, 'outside' history, offered Mário a more serene vantage point to contemplate the art of all epochs than was enjoyed by those at the 'centre', who felt appointed to dethrone and remake. He felt no call to denigrate Parnassians and other immediate predecessors, for he was constructing a past, not merely a future, which helps explain his refusal of futurism. His challenge was that of the Indian church builders of colonial Mexico who in the space of a generation had to retrace the logic of European architectural development since primitive romanesque. We marvel at how far Mário travelled when we learn that as late as 1916 this young man of middle-class Catholic upbringing was asking his archbishop's permission to read the indexed Balzac, Flaubert and the Larousse dictionary.

Narrowly ideological accounts of Mário's intellectual journey portray a somewhat artless mind groping among incongruous influences – family Catholicism, positivism, Jules Romains's unanimism, liberalism, nationalism, Freudianism and several strains of Marxism – without finding a prescription for more than political reformism. Gilda de Mello e Souza warns, however, that Mário's intellectual positions, taken at face value, do little to explain his creative power. In his mythopoeic 'rhapsody' *Macunaíma* (1928) she discovers two obsessions that permeated and unified his life work: to understand the nature of music (he was a trained musicologist) and to analyse the creative process of the common people.[37] Musical analogies gave access to a 'reality' that mocked the intellective faculty, while fascination with the mind, culture and expressive resources of common folk not only helped stitch together his Catholicism, unanimism, and Marxism but foretold the recognition in Brazil, decades later, of 'conscientization' as therapy for a 'pre-political' citizenry.

In *Macunaíma,* Mário created a Brazilian folk hero (without precisely intending to), a persona of shifting ethnic identity who meanders throughout Brazil and across the centuries. Morally, he was a representative man, holding to neither a heroic code nor a diabolic anti-code. A conspicuous trait was his indolence (*preguiça*), an impediment to economic 'progress' but, by affording leisure for creativity, a prerequisite for 'civilization'. The text draws on Mário's vast knowledge of lore, culture, psychology, language and books without becoming a whimsical bricolage. He controlled

[37] Gilda de Mello e Souza, *O Tupi e o alaúde* (São Paulo, 1979).

his materials by principles of musical composition derived from close knowledge of the intricate process by which a popular talent without viable traditions appropriates and ingeniously reworks Iberian, Indian and African ingredients to find a voice of its own. By Aristotelian 'imitation of action' the author hoped to elucidate the task of the Brazilian artist or intellectual. Thus *Macunaíma* entwines scholarly and popular sources in leading the hero through a fanciful geography that 'corrects' shifting historical disparities between penury and affluence, archaism and technology, to produce 'co-existence'.

As founding director of São Paulo's municipal Department of Culture (1934–7) Mário had a brief chance to translate his understanding of education, Brazilian traditions and the permeations between popular and highbrow culture into a public programme.[38] This experience exemplified how Mário navigated the transition from the esthetic to the ideological years, always keeping his concern with language and art as a context and source of coherence for his concern with 'politics', that is, the polis. Oswald in contrast had no way to organize his vision, to convert lightning into a steady glow, to cultivate the delicate filaments between art and politics. With the advent of the bureaucratic Vargas era he could not, like Mário, find a platform, however cramped, from which to pursue tasks *pro bono publico* of administration, pedagogy and research. He finally took refuge by writing two remarkable messianic theses in a vain attempt to obtain a professorship.

In an interview of 1974 Antônio Cândido spoke of this genial pair as two dialectical forces – Mário the 'revolutionary' and Oswald the 'terrorist' – and as two outstanding sources for contemporary Brazilian literature.[39] Who was the more important? Oswald if one seeks language that breaks with traditional mimesis, but Mário if one seeks language for a Brazilian view of the world. In time of existential trouble as in the late 1960s and early 1970s Oswald plays a more agglutinative role, finding a climate wherein to survive culturally. At a moment offering constructive socialist possibilities Oswald's example suffers eclipse because Mário more clearly embodies the notions of service, collectivity, and search for the people. The historical moment continues to determine the reputation of each.

[38] See Carlos Sandroni, *Mário contra 'Macunaíma'* (São Paulo, 1988), pp. 69–128; Joan Dassin, *Política e poesia em Mário de Andrade* (São Paulo, 1978).
[39] Antônio Cândido, 'Entrevista', *Trans/form/ação*, 1 (1974), 20–22.

Buenos Aires: Modernism as Decipherment

The modernist agenda for Argentina was different from that for Brazil. Here was a country without the sprawling tropical geography and 'primitive' ethnicity of Brazil. It was a flat, traversable territory with nearly a quarter of its population corralled in an Anglo-French capital city. Even though industrialism had taken only preliminary hold, Argentina alone in Latin America – save perhaps for its miniature replica Uruguay and its western neighbour Chile – seemed to have crossed the threshold of Western modernization. 'Rich as an Argentine' was a byword in Paris. There were tensions and predatory forces in Buenos Aires as in any Western city; but the south European provenance of much of its proletariat and petty bourgeoisie did not pose such problems of assimilation as plagued Mexico, Peru, and even Brazil. Argentina's formative era seemed to have passed, as had been acknowledged in the second part of the national epic by José Hernández, the *Vuelta* ['Return'] *de Martín Fierro* (1879), when the defiant gaucho resignedly accepts the encroachment of 'civilization'. In this setting Marxism could take a conciliatory cast in the revisionist version of Juan B. Justo (1865–1928), the acknowledged Marxist pioneer of Latin America who translated volume one of *Kapital* and edited the socialist daily *La Vanguardia*. Argentine writers were not more 'cosmopolitan' than their Paulista counterparts, but their sense of a completed phase of history, their acceptance of Buenos Aires as a sub-equatorial Paris or London, the lack of challenge from 'exoticism' and problems of survival, allowed them to cast their inquiry in more familiar Western terms.[40] Borges went so far as to dismiss the passionate identity question in saying that 'being Argentine is either a fatality, in which case we cannot avoid it, or else a mere affectation, a mask'.[41] His first book of verse (*Fervor de Buenos Aires*, 1923) was, like Mário de Andrade's *Hallucinated City* of the previous year, an urban paean; yet while Mário's city was the 'commotion of my life' – or, a force not yet appropriated – for Borges the streets of Buenos Aires were in his opening lines simply 'mi entraña' (my entrails).

---

[40] For Buenos Aires in the 1920s: Christopher Towne Leland, *The Last Happy Men: The Generation of 1922, Fiction and the Argentine Reality* (Syracuse, 1986); Beatriz Sarlo, *Una modernidad periférica: Buenos Aires, 1920 y 1930* (Buenos Aires, 1988); Francis Korn, *Buenos Aires, los huéspedes del 20* (Buenos Aires, 1974).

[41] Jorge Luis Borges, 'El escritor argentino y la tradición', in *Discusión* (Buenos Aires, 1969), pp. 151–62.

To savour directly the ethos of urban Argentina in the 1920s and 1930s – a haunting sense of creole-immigrant identity fused with assurance of having entered the Western mainstream, yet darkened by hints of impending *débâcle* – one turns to the tango culture. The tango was not, save when packaged for export, a 'ballroom' dance. Nor was it a samba that suspended social hierarchy and engulfed onlookers in a shared world, where 'schools' and *blocos* are communal and incorporative, and whose cues come from social reference points, not the private psyche.[42] The musical origins of tango culture may have been African or creole while its social origins were along the river and in the outskirts (*arrabales*) of Buenos Aires. As a child Borges had known the *arrabal* poet Evaristo Carriego and his tango lyrics, and he devoted an early book to this modest bard of the urban poor. Later he renounced the tango as it entered its international phase of 'sentimentality' with Enrique Discépolo and Carlos Gardel. For him, vicariously perhaps, the tango was the vivacious, erotic dance of the harbour's brothels. Yet despite Borges it found its unique destiny only in the mid-1920s, not as a dance but as a lyrical, generally male outpouring of private fantasies that offsets an elusive social reality. This version neither adjusts to the world nor creates surrogate *communitas* but exalts interior images. As a confessional act it resists collectivization; it is not sung in chorus nor danced by groups. The singer yearns for a mythic past, for childhood, a mother, a *barrio,* and for a time that was loving and luminous. Composers from proletarian, anarchist backgrounds strike an occasional note of social protest, but generally an overriding fatalism precludes coming to grips with society. The singer is moved not by war but by the bereaved mother, not by the desecration of rural life but by the bird that sings no more. Instead of seeing vagabonds and delinquents as a social product, he bemoans a private destiny. Usually unmarried and without fixed employment, the narrator lacks the elemental ties that yield social knowledge by involvement. His stereotyped women abandon or betray him, and the dance itself, which had once exalted carnality, becomes a mechanical exercise that levels the sexes in dispirited routine.

In *Radiografía de la pampa* (1933) the poet Ezequiel Martínez Estrada (see below) analysed the dissociation between private imagination and public reality that the tango so compellingly rendered as 'pseudo-structures' pervading the whole of city culture and society. The literary

[42] Compare Julio Mafud, *Sociología del tango* (Buenos Aires, 1966) and Roberto DaMatta, *Carnavais, malandros e heróis* (Rio de Janeiro, 1979; Eng. trans., Notre Dame, Ind., 1991).

world exemplifies his theme in the somewhat mythicized antagonism between the Florida and Boedo groups. Their differences were couched as a rarefied debate over pure versus engaged art that did little to illuminate the situation of writers struggling for expression in Argentina. If we believe Borges the whole episode was a sham literary feud cooked up between the chic downtown set of Calle Florida and the 'proletarian' set of Boedo.[43] Disingenuously, Borges claimed he would have preferred Boedo affiliation, 'since I was writing about the old Northside and slums, sadness, and sunsets'. But he learned that he was a Florida warrior and it was too late to change, although a few, like Roberto Arlt, managed dual alliance. 'This sham,' Borges continued, 'is now taken into serious consideration by "credulous universities".'

Leónidas Barletta, a loyal Boedista, claims that the split was fundamental and would serve for decades to distinguish between the 'asphalt' writers and the *poetas de gabinete,* between those who understood the Russian Revolution and those who refused to, between those pledged to art for revolution's sake and those to revolution for art's sake. From the other camp Córdova Iturburu recalls that many Boedistas, like Barletta himself, were apolitical in the early years and that what divided the groups was at first not politics but the commitment of one to Russian and French naturalist novels and of the other to 'the task of achieving an expression in tune with the times'.[44] The Florida or *Martín Fierro* group insisted that a literary review should no more deal with politics than it does with horse races and women's fashions, and that if literature is not taken as a profession, it will remain mired in superannuated naturalism.

The critical point is not the historical importance of the feud but the disembodied nature of the debate. It lacked the engagement with circumstances of the esthetic and ideological projects in São Paulo. Suffice it to compare the *Martín Fierro* manifesto (1924) with the Paulista Pau Brasil manifesto of the same year. The former inveighed against the 'hippopotamic impermeability of the honourable public', the professor's 'funereal solemnity', the mimetism of Argentine high culture, the fear of equivocation that causes desperate reliance on libraries. New sensibility was needed. The Hispano-Suizo was finer art than a Louis Quinze chair. One could find a lesson of synthesis in a marconigram without throwing out the family

[43] Jorge Luis Borges, 'An Autobiographical Essay', in *The Aleph and Other Stories, 1933–1969* (New York, 1971), pp. 164–5.

[44] Leónidas Barletta, *Boedo y Florida, una versión distinta* (Buenos Aires, 1967); Córdova Iturburu, *La revolución martinfierrista* (Buenos Aires, 1962).

album. The emancipation of language begun by Rubén Dario did not preclude using Swiss toothpaste. '*Martín Fierro* has faith in our phonetics, our vision, our ways, our hearing, our capacity to digest and assimilate.'[45] In the Pau Brasil manifesto Oswald de Andrade did not state the issue; he rendered it: 'Carnival in Rio is the religious event of the race. Brazilwood. Wagner submerges before the Botafogo samba schools. Barbarous and ours. Rich ethnic formation. Vegetable wealth . . . Poetry still hidden in the malicious lianas of knowledge . . . Yet the lessons exploded. Men who knew everything were deformed like inflated balloons . . . There'd been inversion of everything, invasion of everything . . . The agile theatre, son of the mountebank. Agile and illogical. The agile novel, born of invention. Agile poetry . . . Let's divide: Imported poetry. And Brazilwood poetry. Exported.'[46]

The point is not that Argentine writers were blasé or deracinated but rather that the world, above all the urban world wherein they lived, instilled a curious set of ambivalences: a sense of irrecoverable or mythic past and a sense of a present in disarray or decadence; a sense of national achievement, whether cultural or economic, that was eminently 'respectable' for South America yet a haunting sense that the success was illusory; a groping for local identity and destiny that seemed condemned to find issue in international discourse and imagery. While such tensions did not lend themselves to public manifestoes, their very indeterminacy might elicit shafts of vision from the gifted writer. The Spanish surrealist Ramón Gómez de la Serna, conspicuous in the tertulia life of Madrid, marveled at the dedication of literary life in Buenos Aires.[47] The writer, he found, lived in absolute solitude; he might venture out for a testimonial or a new exhibition but immediately returned to his handsome estancia or his rented room. As a prime example of such a 'writerly' writer he singles out Macedonio Fernández (1874–1952) 'who has lived sixty years without being seen, feigning to be an old man to justify his retirement – which began when he was sixteen – when he's the precursor of everyone'. In his 'Autobiographical Essay' Borges later claimed that Macedonio impressed him more deeply than any other man. His philosophic bent, his belief that our world is a dream world and that truth is incommunicable, his vision

[45] Reprinted in María Raquel Llagostera (ed.), *Boedo y Florida* (Buenos Aires, 1980), pp. 7–9.
[46] Oswald de Andrade, 'Manifesto of Pau-Brasil poetry', *Latin American Literary Review*, 14/27 (1986), 184–7.
[47] Ramón Gómez de la Serna, *Retratos contemporáneos escogidos* (Buenos Aires, 1968), pp. 59–83, 189–212.

both splintered and radiographic – such traits made him a home-grown modernist before his time and an alleged influence on Borges, Bioy Casares, Marechal, Cortázar, and others. Some wonder, however, whether he was a true 'precursor' or simply a native son, inexplicably attuned to the wavelength of marconigrams, who never crossed the charmed circle of irremediably private imagination.

One might select any of several writers as illuminating the Argentine outlook and *mise-en-scène* of the 1920s and 1930s: the mystical dialectic of redemption that hovers in Güiraldes's *Don Segundo Sombra* (1926); the poetry of Oliverio Girondo, tracing a sure flight from the absurd domain of quotidian objects in *Veinte poemas para ser leídos en la tranvía* (1922) to *En la masmédula* (1954), a book said to penetrate the vertigo of interior space; the obstinate counterpoint of Eduardo Mallea (1903–82) between the prevarications and philistinism of 'visible' Argentina and a subterranean promise of selfhood and moral commitment in the 'invisible' one; or *Adán Buenosayres* (published in 1948 but begun in the 1920s) by Leopoldo Marechal which follows classical and Joycean models to render Buenos Aires as the arena for an Odyssean spiritual quest starting among the Martinfierristas of the 1920s and including a Dantean descent to the infernal Cacodelphia, a probable spoof on Mallea's 'invisible' Argentina. As with São Paulo we will juxtapose two representative if arbitrarily chosen figures as a shorthand device: Jorge Luis Borges (1899–1986) and Roberto Arlt (1900–42). The fact that they are clumsily accorded Florida and Boedo affiliation respectively spices the contrast; it doubles the counterpoint as it were.

The phasing of Borges's early travels deeply affected his mental development and his influence on the Porteño literary scene of the 1920s.[48] At fifteen he went to Europe with his family; here the war trapped them, and he returned only at age twenty-one. That is, he was uprooted precisely as he was asserting intellectual control and experiencing the disenchantment of late adolescence. Hence the identity of Argentine culture, and above all Buenos Aires, remained for him an almost mythic premise. He could even wonder in later years whether he had really left the English books and walled garden of his early home. What had he ever done but 'weave and unweave imaginings derived from them?' The European sojourn was important in two ways. First, it placed 'Georgie' (his nickname) in Switzerland, a wartime sanctuary where he could calmly ponder the harbingers of

---

[48] Emir Rodríguez Monegal, *Jorge Luis Borges: A Literary Biography* (New York, 1978), parts 2, 3.

the modern condition: De Quincey, Heine, the French symbolists, Whitman, Schopenhauer, Nietzsche. When he came to German expressionism he was prepared to read its revolutionary messages in context and to appreciate its advantages over other modernisms like cubism, futurism, surrealism and dadaism. Second, the family's move to Spain in 1919 initiated him to an active, inventive literary community via the tertulias of Gómez de la Serna and Rafael Cansinos-Asséns. 'Georgie' began publishing essays and poems and became identified with ultraism, a movement with international linkage. It drew from Mallarmé and French modernism but also from creationism, launched in 1914 by the precocious Chilean Vicente Huidobro (1893–1948) and epitomized in his lines: 'Why do you sing of the rose, oh poets? / Make it bloom in the poem! / The poet is a little god.' In a Borges pronouncement of 1921, ultraism was to reduce the lyric to primordial metaphor; suppress connective or redundant language; eliminate ornament, confession proof and sermonizing; and fuse images to enhance their suggestive power.

By the time he returned to Buenos Aires in 1921 Borges had, from inside the whale, assimilated the unfolding designs of Western literature and, as a poet, begun to contribute to immediate outcomes. Barely more than a youth, he had the experience and serenity to assume leadership in the renovation of Argentine letters. His poems in *Fervor de Buenos Aires* (1923) showed, however, that the return to origins was a litmus test for what might be artificial in the tertulias of Madrid. Borges, said his French translator, ceased being an ultraist with his first ultraist poem. So deep are the personal meanings of *Fervor* that Borges much later confessed to feeling that throughout his life he had been rewriting that one book. Emblematic of such meanings was his poem 'Fundación mitológica de Buenos Aires' wherein he 'discovers' that the city actually had a beginning, for he had judged it to be eternal like water and air. The poem suspends history, leaving space for private mind and collective memory to take hold. The primeval setting of monsters, mermaids, and magnets that bedevilled ships' compasses, where the explorer Solís was devoured by Indians before his own men, co-exists with the immigrant grinding out a *habanera* on the first hand-organ and with a political claque for Yrigoyen. A solitary tobacco shop perfumes the desert like a rose, and a whole block of Borges's *barrio,* Palermo, materialized beneath dawns and rains. This vision is startlingly akin to Freud's treatment of Rome when a year later, in *Civilization and its Discontents* (1930), he likened the mind itself to the Eternal City, conceived as a psychic entity with a copious past where 'nothing that has come into existence will have passed away and all the earlier phases of development continue to exist alongside the latest one'. Taking Buenos Aires as a microcosm and not a fragment, finding it haunted by dark and timeless omens, Borges was to rise above schools and manifestoes to accept vocation as a master cryptographer and theoretician of enigma.

If Borges, born in the last year of the old century, linked the strenuous present to a mythicized past, Roberto Arlt, born the first year of the new one, epitomized in his life and writings the dissolution of both history and community. Borges traced his forebears to the conquistadors, a lineage bolstered by the solid Victorian stock of his English grandmother. Arlt's home was one of ethnic improvisation. His father came from Prussia, spoke German, was bohemian, improvident, and authoritarian with his son. His mother was from Trieste, spoke Italian, read Dante, Tasso, Nietzsche and romantic novels, and was drawn to occult sciences. From this household Arlt became the first Argentine to write of the immigrants and lumpen from within, to render them fit subjects of literature. His subject-matter and his appeal to a mass public made Arlt an ideal candidate for Boedo. His caustic *aguafuertes,* or chronicles of daily life, in *El Mundo* delighted hundreds of thousands of readers, while Borges's bi-weekly book page in the women's magazine *El Hogar* was squeezed aside and finally dropped. Yet Arlt was taken up by the patrician Güiraldes, who corrected his chaotic Spanish, introduced him to Proust's work, made him his secretary, and published chapters of his first novel in *Proa.*

Arlt like Borges entertained fixations that led him into a universe of his own, possessing its inner logic and not submissive to fads in style or ideology. For Borges, as he matured as a poet and spinner of tales, a (perhaps *the*) central preoccupation shone forth as the philosophic challenge of distinguishing appearance from reality. To pursue this obsession required finely honed language and abstractions; yet his very success at imposing linguistic and conceptual control, at achieving what David Todd calls 'semantic ascent' above commonplace reality, led to a realm of inherent contradiction where the subject-matter of paradox displaces the subject-matter of consensual 'experience'. This of course generates a paradox regarding the persona of Borges himself. For once he addresses ultimate reality in an epistemological or ontological sense he lies open to charges of estheticism, elitism, and effete cosmopolitanism launched by persons whose own grasp of 'reality' is, on philosophic grounds, unexamined and sheerly tactical.

Arlt's reality consisted only of the urban society of his time and place, and specifically those reaches wherein he moved. Yet so intense was his rendering of it that he transcended the premises of naturalist fiction to arrive, like Borges, at a domain of paradox. Arlt divided his social universe into three parts – the lumpen, the petty bourgeoisie, and 'los ricos' – with class identification determined not by wealth, power and prestige but by the disposition for humiliation. An avid reader of Dostoevsky, Arlt was captivated by the underground man, overwhelmed and isolated by a society he cannot understand. Diana Guerrero observes that to the extent he lives out this abasement as guilt because it keeps him from being an effective social being he accepts it, but without renouncing the conviction of his superiority.[49] The victim is cynical and derisive; he flaunts his precious humiliation, precious because it alone yields reference points in a society from which he is isolated. The petty bourgeoisie suffers this degradation in its most excruciating form. The lumpen (vendors of newspapers and Bibles, brothel attendants, thieves, murderers and the like), caged in a world of boredom and ferocity, head irreversibly down the path to dehumanization. 'Los ricos', like the lumpen, live beyond the pale of petty-bourgeois legality but also beyond reach of humiliation. Their life therefore becomes unimaginable, and Arlt's fiction discloses only the elegant façades of their mansions. So remote is this world that the petty bourgeois has no more hope of reaching it than does the lumpen, which means that proletarian ennui and terror are in fact the repressed truth of petty bourgeois existence.

The petty bourgeois situation is therefore defined by an impressive hypocrisy, that is, the impossibility of being non-hypocritical, of recognizing, publicizing and suffering the torture of one's degradation. To acknowledge the contradiction between their situation and their professed values would mean slipping down the class ladder. Reflecting on his novel *Los siete locos* (1929), Arlt described his characters as *canaille* and as sad, vile and dreamy. They are interconnected by a desperation sprung not from poverty but from the bankruptcy of civilization. They move ghostlike in a world of shadows and cruel moral choices. 'If they were less cowardly they'd commit suicide; with a bit more character they'd be saints. In truth they seek the light but do so wholly immersed in mud. They besmirch what they touch.'[50] Marriage is the classic defeat in the Arltian world because it sentences one to daily petty-bourgeois routine. Hence such

[49] Diana Guerrero, *Roberto Arlt, el habitante solitario* (Buenos Aires, 1972).
[50] Roberto Arlt, *The Seven Madmen*, trans. Naomi Lindstrom (Boston, 1984). See also David Maldavsky, *Las crisis en la narrativa de Roberto Arlt* (Buenos Aires, 1968).

incidents of resistance as the groom who betrays his wife on their wedding day or the man who resorts to homicide during coitus to forestall violence by the partner. It is a world pervaded by fearful symmetries. The prostitute who goes home to her man wipes off her make-up; the 'honest' housewife who welcomes her man home applies it before he arrives. Throughout his narratives runs the theme of betrayal, as in the popular culture of the tango and *sainete*. The immigrant world reinforces it. Children of immigrants pose another symmetry; they not only betray the new *patria* by assuming the ideals of their parents but betray those same ideals in accepting the new *patria*. Arlt's writing thus throws a bridge from Porteño tango culture to the Dostoevskyan alienation of urban man in the West. His paradoxes and labyrinths, sprung from the lives of Buenos Aires, taken with those of Borges, sprung from frontiers of epistemology, form a fearful symmetry.

Mexico: Modernism Manqué

Mexico forces us into a more permissive approach to modernism than we have so far used. Because Brazil and Argentina experienced no 'revolution' in the 1920s, and entertained no revolutionary expectations, we have until now considered writers whose visibility was at the time modest. Only hindsight shows Borges or Oswald de Andrade to have been framing messages for future times of trouble. Once revolution occurs, however, it too becomes a 'modernist' event by working lightning reversals and expansions of sense and sensibility. In Mexico, furthermore, revolutionary discourse and imagery brought forth indigenous elements that European modernism prized as 'exotic'. Yet by chronological accident, Mexico's modernist generation was somewhat young to assume cultural leadership. The immediate seniors who did assume it might experience fresh illuminations (José Vasconcelos, Alfonso Reyes). Or else, like the novelists, they might *seem* to innovate by sensitively reporting private versions of the 'happenings' which had swept them up. We thus face three considerations: first, cultural manifestations of the Revolution (notably novels, chronicles, and mural painting); second, the reception of Western modernism in the 1920s; third, transactions between the revolutionary impulse and the modernist temper.

To orientate our reflections it may help to contrast the nearly contemporaneous Mexican and Russian Revolutions. Modernist innovation in the arts chronologically bracketed the Russian Revolution, lasting from the 1880s to the Stalinist 'great change' after 1928. Marked by such liberative, partly mystical movements as Prometheanism, sensualism and apocalypticism, this 'profound cultural upheaval' was neither initiated nor immediately curtailed by Bolshevism.[51] It lent an aura of mixed apprehension and spiritual fulfillment to the dream of social transformation that had flickered in urban circles since the 1860s. Once the political whirlwind struck, apocalyptic spirits sensed the onset of final catastrophe while cubo-futurists accepted the Revolution without demur. As early as 1920, Zamiatin's novel, *We,* chillingly anatomized the imminent society by demonstrating the implications of wholly rationalized social life. In contrast, Mexico's first generation of 'revolutionary' novelists, imbued from youth with liberalism, positivism and naturalism, spent their mature lifetimes readjusting their ideological blinders in simply trying to glimpse the facts and ironies of the case at hand.

Russia had a thirty-year modernist flowering of world importance that withered after 1928 under a regime obsessively concerned to control thought and expression. In Mexico, newly hatched modernist impulses of the 1920s in literature, if not in painting, showed ambivalence to the Revolution; their fruition still lay ahead. The golden age of the Revolution under Cárdenas (1934–40) coincided with the Stalinist great purges, but while the Soviet Union was smothering intellectual inquiry and esthetic experiment, Mexico averted relapse into caudillist rule. Writers exiled in the 1920s returned to publish critical memoirs. Socialist education was prescribed for public schools, and the vocabulary of pre-Leninist Marxism was popularized, in this case expanding rather than shrinking the realm of public discourse. The rise of a 'triumphalist' state in the post-Cárdenas decades did not inhibit arts and letters from steady growth in maturity, diversity and imagination. The central challenge to Soviet artists was not to create culture for a new society, whose programme was officially defined, but to find a place for the arts of the past.[52] In Mexico, however much the state has promoted an official culture, the intellectual is challenged to appropriate a cultural past as the precondition for national 'identity'.

For post-revolutionary Mexico Enrique Krauze has identified three intellectual generations that overlapped in the 1910s. Two were Porfirian. The younger of these centred on the Ateneo group, a motley assortment of

[51] James H. Billington, *The Icon and the Axe* (New York, 1970), pp. 474–532.
[52] Boris Thompson, *The Premature Revolution: Russian Literature and Society, 1917–1946* (London, 1972), p. 76.

artists, literati and intellectuals who began meeting in 1910. While noted for humanism, spiritualism, anti-positivism and reverence for the classical tradition, their intellectual break with the previous century was by no means decisive. The ateneístas were dispersed in the early revolutionary period and when they reappeared it was rarely in leadership roles, Vasconcelos being the outstanding exception. The recipes for institutional change in the 1917 Constitution are less traceable to the ateneístas than to political economists of the positivist generation that preceded them.

Krauze's 'revolutionary' Generation of 1915 (born 1891–1905) came of age when the Revolution was a *fait accompli*.[53] They arrived without mentors or bookish vocations, obedient to the call of action and of imposing order. They included Vicente Lombardo Toledano, labour leader and eclectic socialist; Daniel Cosío Villegas, editor, historian, economist, publisher; Samuel Ramos, philosopher, essayist, public functionary. In the 1930s this generation found solidarity with exiled intellectuals from Spain whose professionalism greatly advanced the institutionalization of academic life. The poet and essayist Ramón López Velarde (1888–1921), who was navigating *con brio* the transition from Spanish American Modernism to Western modernism, was cut off in mid-career and required posthumous resurrection.[54]

Instead of dispersing this generation as it had the ateneístas, the Revolution kneaded it in a common effort to build what the Porfiriato had denied or the violent years had destroyed. Many who might have been complacent office holders or 'pure' intellectuals or alienated reformers were thrust into public roles of improvisation and reconstruction. Talent was commandeered to overhaul legal codes, establish banks, devise economic policy, found publishing houses and vanguard reviews, rebuild education from rural cultural missions to the university, create research centres, or excavate Indian cities. Within this kaleidoscopic endeavour the vanguard message was muted. *Estridentistas* led by Manuel Maples Arce introduced the new esthetics (dadaism, creationism, futurism) but left no monuments. The *agoristas* were perhaps more experimental but even less memorable.

Of greater esthetic projection than the groups mentioned were the *contemporáneos*. Considered slightly junior to Krauze's 'revolutionary' generation, they included among others Jaime Torres Bodet, Carlos Pellicer, José Gorostiza, Salvador Novo, Xavier Villaurrutia and the acerbic essayist Jorge

[53] Enrique Krauze, 'Cuatro estaciones de la cultura mexicana', in *Caras de la historia* (Mexico, D.F., 1983), pp. 124–68; see also his *Caudillos culturales de la Revolución Mexicana* (Mexico, D.F., 1976).
[54] See Guillermo Sheridan, *Un corazón adicto: la vida de Ramón López Velarde* (Mexico, D.F., 1989).

Cuesta.[55] As they matured they found bureaucratic or diplomatic niches, with Torres Bodet eventually becoming Mexican secretary of education and director general of UNESCO. While still students the future *contemporáneos* reinvented the Ateneo de la Juventud under its original name but fell short of their predecessors' idealism. Isolated in private worlds, they became a generation rather than a functional group. They left their mark on the narrative, essays and theatre, but their special achievement was poetry drawn from personal realms populated, in Paz's phrase, 'by the ghosts of erotism, sleep and death'. Gorostiza, perhaps the most striking of the poets, has been likened to Rilke, Valéry and Eliot in the quality of his inspiration. The *contemporáneos* loosely corresponded to the 'aesthetic' current in São Paulo or to Florida in Buenos Aires; but in Mexico the 'ideological' or Boedista position was commandeered by a culturally triumphant state, with the paradoxical result that the enthusiasm of Europeans and Americans for Mexican muralism, novels and folk art gave foreigners a hand in defining Mexican identity (*lo mexicano*). 'One of the greatest tragedies of the Revolution,' writes Luis Villoro, 'perhaps lies in the fact that the moment of greatest revolutionary advance failed to coincide with the moment of generosity and optimism of its intelligentsia.'[56]

The crowning irony, Guillermo Sheridan reminds us, was that because bureaucratic nationalists regarded the *contemporáneos* as elitist, Europeanizing and sometimes even 'effeminate', one of the latters' 'most eloquent displays of patriotism would be the careful, energetic, and of course futile battle against these restrictive and anecdotal conventions.' The moment when the group (or *grupo sin grupo*) founded their review *Contemporáneos* (1928–31) was precisely when they drifted apart. The journal suffered from indecisive eclecticism, wavering between European avant-gardism and Mexican nationalism. Its great merit, Sheridan comments, derived 'more from the quality of its collaborators than from the journal's ability to amalgamate them'. The nationalists had the universalists at a clear disadvantage. The latter found it more difficult to ignore being publicly caricatured by Rivera and Orozco than it was for the Florida clique to dismiss the taunts of Boedo. In 1932 a published interview with the 'ambiguous and inscrutable' Gorostiza ignited a polemic by manipulating

---

[55] Oscar Collazos (ed.), *Los vanguardismos en la América Latina* (Barcelona, 1977), pp. 105–22; Guillermo Sheridan, *Los Contemporáneos ayer* (Mexico, D.F., 1985); Paz's essays on Pellicer, Gorostiza and Villaurrutia in Luis Mario Schneider (ed.), *México en la obra de Octavio Paz* (Mexico, D.F., 1979), pp. 242–77.

[56] Luis Villoro, 'La cultura mexicana de 1910 a 1960', *Historia Mexicana* 10/2 (1960), 206.

his words into a seeming 'act of contrition' aimed at 'rectifying' his alleged Europhilism. It took time for the *contemporáneos* to win the recognition that a protégé, Octavio Paz, accorded in 1966 when he stated that 'in a strictly intellectual sense nearly all that's being done now in Mexico owes something to the Contemporáneos, to their example, their rigor, their zeal for perfection'.[57]

The challenge here was not, for the moment, to parse meanings of modernity and to surmise their import for a recalcitrant 'colonial' ethos. For in Mexico the dikes of tradition had cracked and rapid change had set in. The times required not the vatic cries and cryptic images of vanguardism but keen reportage and diagnosis for which an earlier generation from the naturalist tradition was trained. The future was to be inferred from leaders and events, not gleaned from random clues of private imagination. The two writers to receive special attention here were both born before 1890. The first, Martín Luis Guzmán, was plunged into the Revolution from the start, and its subsequent course yielded his prism on the world. The second, Alfonso Reyes, by his loyalty to Western humanism and his aloofness from quotidian events adopted a macrocosmic view that assimilated Mexican to Western culture rather than a prismatic one that probed particulars of time and place. Both were sympathetic to modernism. In his travel chronicles of 1916–18 Guzmán wrote of his entrancement by vorticism, imagism and Rivera's Parisian cubism, and Reyes, while ambassador to Argentina and Brazil in 1927–38, was early to recognize Borges's genius and became an *aficionado* of Brazilian Anthropophagy. They learned lessons from modernism without adopting its tactics.

Martín Luis Guzmán (1887–1976) grew up in a rural town near Mexico City where he occasionally glimpsed Porfirio Díaz moving at the summit of greatness, resplendent in ceremonial uniform or else mysteriously garbed in black.[58] When he was eleven Guzmán's family moved to Veracruz, cradle of the Reform laws. There he read Rousseau, Hugo, and Pérez Galdós and in school succumbed to liberalism and the Mexican civic ideal personified in Juárez. Later as a student in Mexico City he repudiated the positivist apologia for the regime and began to frequent the Ateneo. In May 1911 he demonstrated for Madero, baptizing his political career. By now the guidelines for Guzmán's life as a writer and publicist were in place: classic liberal principles, a vague but committed vision of an emer-

---

[57] Paz cited in Sheridan, *Contemporáneos*, p. 21.
[58] Guzmán recalled his life in 'Apunte sobre una personalidad', in *Academia: Tradición, independencia, libertad* (Mexico, D.F., 1959), pp. 11–51.

gent Mexico, and fascination with the thoughts and instincts of great leaders. Since the age of fourteen, moreover, he had shown a journalist's vocation. His intellectual shortcomings were offset by his passion, grasp of human character and reportorial skill.

The diagnosis that would inform his future writings Guzmán set forth from exile in Spain in *La querella de México* (1915).[59] Here he offered no such pathology of economic institutions as those of Wistano Luis Orozco, Andrés Molina Enríquez, or Luis Cabrera. The deeper cause of Mexico's distress, he assumed, was a 'penury of spirit' reflected, first, in the mimicry and dilettantism of intellectuals who had never cultivated philosophy and science, studied national history, or analysed social problems and, second, in the apathy and moral obtuseness of the Indians, whose spiritual desperation pre-dated the trauma of Spanish conquest and stemmed from the superstition, terror and cannibalism of Aztec society. Two impulses to renovation, national independence and the Reform, were extinguished under the Porfiriato when the creoles turned away from history and the work of construction. The country lived in 'the shadow of the caudillo', a phrase that became the title of Guzmán's novel *La sombra del caudillo* (1929). When revolution came the creoles sacrificed their own hero, Madero, and renewed the chaos of warring factions, each clamouring for foreign recognition instead of cultivating morality for leadership. How could one redeem the Indian while the creole was unregenerate? 'We seem to have intelligence in surfeit. What lacks is virtue.'

His journalist's eye, his friendship with revolutionary leaders, and above all his moral vision explain Guzmán's fascination with single actors and lend his writings a Thucydidean accent. *La sombra del caudillo* is in part a roman à clef based on events and figures of the mid-1920s. *El águila y la serpiente* (1928) is a memoir of Guzmán's own experience from Madero's death in 1913 to his exile in 1915, yet composed with such dramatic craft and illumination of character that it assumes imaginative force in the tradition of Sarmiento and da Cunha.[60] On the surface the camera's eye of authorial narration links the book's kaleidoscopic episodes. Deeper unity arises from the tension between Villa and Carranza projected against the mute, anonymous mass of peasant soldiery. Ideologies, lofty political aims, the claims of history fade before primordial instinct and fugitive passion. The collective soul is only dimly sensed. The human

[59] *La querella* was extended in newspaper articles from New York (1916–18): Martín Luis Guzmán, *La querella de México: A orillas del Hudson; otras páginas* (Mexico, D.F., 1958).
[60] *The Eagle and the Serpent,* trans. Harriet de Onís (Garden City, N.Y., 1965).

mass moves as one body, swaying, weaving, stumbling, murmuring, fused by a secret filament – a huge reptile crawling drunk and sluggish along the cavernous street of an empty city. The observer must jerk free to escape a crushing sense of physical and moral oppression.

Actors are stripped to psychic essentials. In confronting Carranza, Villa opposes the amoral instincts of a child to the picayune, selfish scheming of an old man. Villa is half-tamed and feline. His pistol is an extension of his hand; bullets spurt from the man, not the gun. He is incapable of etiquette, yet tenderness may at times dim his glittering eyes. He marvels at such simple life processes as the mystery of sleep. When in a paroxysm of wrath Villa orders 170 prisoners slaughtered, Guzmán risks his own life to argue why it is wrong. As to a child he explains that he who surrenders renounces the chance of killing others. Villa leaps up, issues the counter-order, and when it arrives in time, wipes the sweat from his brow. Later he mumbles thanks 'for that thing this morning, that business of the prisoners'. Carranza, a Porfirian-style figure whom Guzmán recalls with ambivalence, assumes a benign, patriarchal air. In an ancient tradition he has mastered the art of village politics, of pitting opponents against followers, of premeditated corruption, of fanning passions, intrigues and bad faith. Impervious to noble ideals, bereft of magnanimity, he prizes flattery over actions, servility over talent in his subordinates. He is in short a stubborn old man with all the ruses and pettiness of senility.

With Guzmán as with Mariano Azuela, 'father' of the revolutionary novel, the point of interest is not the author's disenchantment or pessimism but the fact that he painfully sets aside ideology and reduces his subject to directly experienced elements. While Guzmán's prose therefore has some of the naturalist power of a Zola, his feat of psychic reduction is akin to the vanguardist pulverization of received forms. To seize the meanings and possibilities of the Revolution Guzmán gradually ceased fitting it to his early political categories. Villa became for him emblematic as an amoral or pre-moral figure, arisen from the disinherited masses and unshaped by fancy ideological or moral codes. 'Primitive' instinct and his elemental, sometimes contradictory convictions informed his future society.[61] In search of the essential Villa, Guzmán went on to write the five-volume *Memorias de Pancho Villa* (1938–40) using an autobiographical first person and Villa's own pungent language in a valiant effort to suspend

---

[61] Larry M. Grimes, *The Revolutionary Cycle in the Literary Production of Martín Luis Guzmán* (Cuernavaca, 1969), p. 72.

judgement and recreate the psyche and self-vindication of the subject himself.[62]

Alfonso Reyes (1889–1959), barely twenty when the Ateneo was founded, was Guzmán's colleague in the group. But while Guzmán sought to recover an eclipsed liberal tradition and to penetrate a discrete Mexican 'reality', Reyes addressed the general case of a society that had 'arrived late at the banquet of civilization'. The challenge he took on was not redemption from the authoritarian uses of positivism but the place-ment of Mexico within occidental culture. Of the four Ateneo luminaries it has been said that Vasconcelos was driven to rebuild the world, Antonio Caso to contemplate it, Henríquez Ureña (the 'Socrates' of the group) to explain it, and Reyes to illuminate it. These missions may at later mo-ments, particularly during the flight of the ateneístas after the outbreak of revolution, have seemed diaphanous. Yet in the long run they offer co-ordinates for the *derniers cris* of vanguardism. Reyes at an early age began to trace paths for the 'moralization' of Mexican society and culture relying on classical studies and the Spanish *siglo de oro,* with reinforcement from French and English letters, current strains of philosophy and literary theory, and fresh appreciation of Mexican culture itself. The agenda did not centre on local 'problems' of race, politics and poverty. The issue was to assimilate thinking in Mexico to the canons and experience of the West. His generation, his temperament, his upbringing did not seduce Reyes toward the short-circuits of vanguardism. He addressed not outcomes but premises of Western civilization, in particular the branch that included Mexico.

Guzmán, we saw, entered the political maelstrom as a *maderista* in 1911. Reyes, however, was the son of General Bernardo Reyes, the entre-preneurial governor of Nuevo León and a loyal, if reformist, Díaz sup-porter. On 9 February 1913, the general was killed before the National Palace leading a counter-revolution that soon brought death to Madero. Refusing the offer of Provisional President Huerta to become his secretary, Alfonso left Mexico in poverty and remained abroad until 1938. Years later Alfonso recalled his father as a hero who was amused by tempests and displayed such sterling virtues as vitality, loyalty, moderation and a pru-dence matched by bravura. His death, 'an obscure equivocation in the

---

[62] *Memoirs of Pancho Villa,* trans. Virginia H. Taylor (Austin, Tex., 1965); see also Christopher Domínguez, 'Martín Luis Guzmán: El Teatro de la política,' *Vuelta, Revista Mensual,* 11/131 (1987): 22–31.

moral clockwork of our world', was a spilling of aging wine.[63] This libation gave Alfonso a quarter century of Wanderjahre and with it the life and outlook of a universal writer. While Guzmán looked for nobility in the cadres of new leadership, Reyes found it in the old. Although he saw Don Porfirio and his coterie as insulated from the democratic era by a wall of glass, an abyss of time, filial piety allowed him to discern heroism in the old order and, by extension, the more distant past.

The treatment of philosophy later in this chapter examines the notion of 'anabatic recovery', that is, an 'upstream' expedition from local circumstances to outlooks of the contemporary West and thence, against the current of time, to the sources of Western thought. The clench of immediacy impels and shapes the campaign making it, in Ortega's term, a 'perspectival' assault on the citadel of Western culture. Reyes did not conduct an 'anabasis'. He began his journey with a genealogy already in mind; his mission was to illuminate, not assault and reinterpret. As a penniless expatriate in 1913 his brief stay in the Paris of Picasso and Gertrude Stein did not yield him, as it had Oswald de Andrade a year earlier, a foothold within dissolving ideas and images. Reyes soon moved to Spain where he joined the cenacle of the proto-surrealist Ramón Gómez de la Serna, as would Borges a few years later. But Ramón's catachrestic *greguerías* (shocking oxymoronic one-liners) were for him less a symptom of modernism than a reprise of Quevedo, Goya and the history of Spanish alienation. Spain's ambivalent relation with the Rest of the West from its own version of the classical, Christian tradition drew Reyes to Menéndez Pidal, Unamuno, Ortega, Juan Ramón Jiménez and the Generation of 1898 and its successors, who had revived the eighteenth-century debate between Hispanism and modernity. Reyes required this context not to 'invent' a Mexican identity but to discover Mexico's presumptive place in the scheme of things. Just as he rejected vanguard reversals of the rules, so later would he chide the phenomenologists for their claim to have given philosophy a fresh start.

In Spain, freed of constraints of his homeland, Reyes laid the foundations for his life work. He assembled his impressions of contemporary Spain in *Cartones de Madrid* and recreated the Spaniards' pristine view of Tenochtitlán in *Visión de Anahuac;* he secured scholarly command of the ancient and the Spanish classics; he wrote *El suicida* to develop a diffuse

[63] Emmanuel Carballo, 'Alfonso Reyes a la luz de una fecha', in Margarita Vera Cuspinera (ed.), *Alfonso Reyes, homenaje de la Facultad de Filosofía y Letras* (Mexico, D.F., 1981), pp. 383–7; Barbara Bockus Aponte, *Alfonso Reyes and Spain* (Austin, Tex., 1972), p. 11.

humanist's credo from the mystery of the suicidal impulse; he composed a dramatic poem, *Ifigenia cruel,* of autobiographical inspiration whose protagonist rejects the rancour and persecutions of her homeland in favour of freedom and autonomy. What remained was to round out his American experience.

After serving the Mexican legation in Paris, Reyes regained a diplomatic post in Spain in 1920. Then in 1927 he was named ambassador to Argentina, serving there until 1930, in Brazil until 1936, and in Argentina again until 1938. Reyes has been scolded for not publicizing these national literatures throughout Hispanic America. He did, however, publish penetrating commentary on the Argentine temperament and was thanked by Borges for having rescued him from being simply the son of Leonor Azevedo. In the case of unknown Brazil, Ruedas argues that even so keen a mind as Reyes's was unprepared to orchestrate the memory of Machado de Assis, the cacophonic modernism of São Paulo, and the telluric fiction of the northeast. Nor indeed was Brazilian literature ripe for exportation despite the war whoops of the Brazil-wood manifesto. What Reyes did do was to reflect on nuances of Brazilian social life, learn an unaccented Portuguese, and publish a literary newsletter named *Monterrey* after his native city (1930–7), which tried neither to introduce Mexicans to Brazilian literature nor vice versa.[64] As in all his writings Reyes was concerned with neither expository journalism nor intellectual formulas but with luminous understandings.

When Reyes finally returned to Mexico in 1938, his connections with the Spanish intelligentsia and his sympathy with Spanish culture equipped him ideally – given the Republican sympathy of the Cárdenas government – to create a mecca for émigré Spanish intellectuals. He became president of the Casa de España, and when it became the Colegio de México in 1940 he continued as its director until his death in 1959. However much the Colegio itself may later have succumbed to bureaucratization and government co-optation, here was a moment when, after a long interregnum, the humanist, Americanist messages of the best Spanish thought could find transatlantic assimilation.

Reyes was a prolific, multifarious writer like Andrés Bello or Sarmiento or Martí or Eugenio María de Hostos whose life work evades easy synthesis. Others, like Machado de Assis or Mariátegui or Borges or Octavio Paz,

---

[64] Jorge Ruedas de la Serna, 'La misión brasileña de Alfonso Reyes', in Cuspinera, *Alfonso Reyes,* pp. 195–210; Manuel Ulacia, 'A antropofagia de Alfonso Reyes', *O Estado de São Paulo* (literary supplement), 10 June 1989.

are perhaps more layered and complex than the first group, but their psychic obsessions flash more clearly; they drop conspicuous, though never facile, clues to the enigmas that await deciphering. If there is a key to Reyes, it lies embedded in his passion for Greek culture, traceable from his early Ateneo years through the classical studies of his last two decades in Mexico. The Roman example of juridical uniformity and use of urban centres for spreading 'civilization' had been prominent for Spanish colonial jurists. The ateneístas rejected this outlook of privilege in favour of Greek *sophrosyne:* search for an inclusive Mexican culture, thought unfolding without dogmatisms, freedom for creativity, disciplined love of reason and beauty, and a dynamic equilibrium of contrasting views.[65] Throughout his life Reyes held true to the Greek precedent, in part as inspiration for a Mexican ideal, in part as the source for an outlook transmitted to Mexico in a version less distorted than it had been in northern Europe by the religious and scientific revolutions. In a sense Reyes was an *arielista,* but one whose classical, Mediterranean understandings delved to origins, not tinctured as were Rodó's by the fears and forebodings of *fin de siècle* Paris.

FICTION AND THE ESSAY

Naturalism and its Pathetic Fallacies

The foregoing treatments of Brazil, Argentina and Mexico in the 1920s reveal tension between two ways of appropriating experience. Of the writers discussed, Borges pursues a covert search for epistemological foundations while at the other extreme Martín Luis Guzmán conducts a frontal assault on phenomena as directly presented. The rest flourish in zones of transaction: Mário de Andrade, caught between nostalgia and iconoclasm, lucid visions and patient research; Oswald de Andrade, who employs oxymorons of the vanguard esthetic to overturn hallowed verities of Brazilian history; Roberto Arlt, who chronicles petty bourgeois life while alert to Dostoevskyan reversals; and Alfonso Reyes, who explores the Iberian and classical past to fix co-ordinates for the here and now of a 'new world'. Yet for reasons suggested earlier the aesthetic emphasis of the heroic modernist years was shifting toward an ideological or broadly explicative emphasis in the late 1920s. This makes the identity essay an obvious

---

[65] Ernesto Mejía Sánchez, 'Alfonso Reyes y el mundo clásico', and Paola Vianello de Córdova, 'Alfonso Reyes y el estudio de las culturas clásicas', in Cuspinera, *Alfonso Reyes,* pp. 105–46.

attraction, not simply because of its diagnostic uses but because its authors were more critical of the status quo and more respectful of aspirations of the disinherited than had been the earlier pensadores.

First, however, let us consider the novelists of the mid-1920s to mid-1940s. Of these, a significant number became recognized by their stylistic taste for naturalism or their penchant for the land, regionalism or indigenism. To call them 'neo-naturalists', however, is misleading insofar as this implies reprise of a literary mode of the 1880s and 1890s that had in turn reflected European fashion. For while European naturalism was a step in a logical sequence from romanticism and realism to symbolism and modernism, in Latin America it offered fresh tools for an ancient inquiry. French and English authors, that is, were less concerned with local 'identity' than with credible versions of the social universe at a moment when scientific ratification was a *sine qua non*. Naturalism was for them a transitory phenomenon. Latin American literature, however, was heralded at the era of European conquest by an early brand of naturalism ('natural history') or – in that dawning age of science, imperialism, journalism, censuses and bureaucratic reports – the attempt to decode a strange environment from self-given phenomena. By the eighteenth century the broad question of 'American' identity was voiced and, after independence, preoccupation with the attributes of discrete nationhood. In the 1880s these concerns meshed with the European vogue of naturalism, but as something more than a mimetic episode or an ephemeral response to the procession of 'styles' at the centre.

The 'eternal return' of naturalism is illustrated below for Brazil. But first, the relation of transatlantic naturalism to realism deserves attention. In Europe realism avoided 'romantic' subjectivity and idealism but stopped short of the determinism that gave naturalism its reputation for moral aloofness. Martín Luis Guzmán fits the looser category. If he failed to adopt the shock methods of modernism or count on historic precepts of Western humanism, neither did he choose clinical naturalism for organizing his world. Trusting what he saw and knew, he took his chances along the frontiers between documentation and fiction, psychological portraiture and moral judgement, the journalistic and the empathic eye. Much the same could be said of Mariano Azuela, whose *Los de abajo* (1915), originally subtitled 'Views and Scenes from the Present Revolution', established him as the founder of the Mexican revolutionary novel. Although he admired Zola for books as 'chaste as any treatise on medicine', Azuela called not him but Balzac the 'greatest novelist of all times' for having raised testimony on popular life to the realm of high art.[66]

As the 1930s drew near, a new wave of fiction came into sight: the Colombian José Eustasio Rivera's *La vorágine* (1924), the Brazilian José Américo de Almeida's *A bagaceira* (1928), and the Venezuelan Rómulo Gallegos's *Doña Bárbara* (1929) followed by the Ecuadorian Jorge Icaza's *Huasipongo* (1934) and the Peruvian Ciro Alegría's *El mundo es ancho y ajeno* (1941). While these newer authors remained faithful to the hallowed domestic tradition of 'natural history' they also, in part unwittingly, encouraged subversion of the original aim of naturalism. Characterized as *novelas de la tierra* (novels of the earth or land), their narratives became criticized for allowing geographic space to cancel interior space. 'Wild nature came to the fore', wrote Emir Rodríguez Monegal, 'and to such a degree dominated the human actor, moulding and determining him, that his individual character nearly disappeared, or was reduced . . . to the role of an archetype: the sign or symbol of something, but not a person'. Only in the 1960s and 1970s, with the acceptance of 'marvellous realism' in Latin American fiction, he continued, could we appreciate that 'these works establish deep linkage between the marvelled narratives of the first explorations and discoveries of America and the novel (frankly mythic) of a Rulfo, a García Márquez, a Vargas Llosa'.[67] One example among many is *Don Goyo* (1933) by the Ecuadorian novelist Aguilera Malta.[68] The folk hero Don Goyo predicts the ruin of his community of mangrove cutters by the invasion of whites. In this confrontation the actors are mechanized and unmotivated, propelled by lust, fear and a quest for idyllic pleasure. Humans are likened to objects (a woman's hips become a canoe on the river) while human behaviour is projected onto an angry, muttering nature (the mangroves overhear human lovers; trees have intercourse with the river). Don Goyo is finally killed by a mangrove tree, as though by intention, and only then does he achieve vitality as his corpse topples from

---

[66] Eliud Martínez, *The Art of Mariano Azuela* (Pittsburgh, Pa., 1980), pp. 88–9; Stanley L. Robe, *Azuela and the Mexican Underdogs* (includes bilingual text) (Berkeley, 1979); Adalbert Dessau offers ideological analysis in *La novela de la Revolución Mexicana*, trans. Juan José Utrilla (Mexico, D.F., 1972).

[67] Emir Rodríguez Monegal, *El boom de la novela latinoamericana* (Caracas, 1972), pp. 49–50. For up-to-date treatises on 'regional' novels, see Carlos J. Alonso, *The Spanish American Regional Novel* (Cambridge, Eng., 1990) and Doris Sommer, *Foundational Fictions: The National Romances of Latin America* (Berkeley, 1991).

[68] Demetrio Aguilera Malta, 'Don Goyo', trans. E. E. Perkins, in Angel Flores and Dudley Poore (eds.), *Fiesta in November: Stories from Latin America* (Boston, 1942), pp. 120–228.

a canoe and descends the current, laughing in triumph over the now submissive river and its sharks. Yet as John Brushwood has pointed out, the author avoids full surrender to the naturalist 'pathetic fallacy' by stylizing and distilling the course of events and by 'persistent intercalation of the nonliteral' to sustain Don Goyo's movement between man and legend.[69]

For the moment, then, we are left with a paradox. The discussion above of Guzmán and Azuela suggests that their personal, open-ended 'realism' was an *ipso facto* renunciation of modernist experimentalism and iconoclasm.[70] Yet it now appears that 'naturalism', a clinical and methodical brand of realism, opens the door to what is inexplicable and mythic. Thus realism appears pragmatic and commonsensical with naturalism being prescriptive and mythopoeic. This would mean that Latin American neo-naturalism of the 1930s deviated from the Zolaesque prototype and became instead an episode on the path from modernism to the complex narratives of the 1950s during a brief interval when the need for social description and political protest loomed large. By the beginning of the 1940s naturalist ideological protest loses primacy. Social and political malfeasance is now traced to an urban point of origin, not to the feudal periphery, and ascribed to human nature rather than to regional geography. 'For this new line,' wrote Rodríguez Monegal, 'Manichaeism is a political charge more than a virtue; protest becomes a burden; true denunciation is presented as a narrative, not in emotionally charged speeches; the supernatural blends intimately with the quotidian.'[71] For him the emblematic figure of the post-naturalist transition was Ciro Alegría, who published his best book in 1941 and then nothing of note before his death a quarter century later. A contemporary of Onetti and Lezama Lima, Alegría felt himself trapped, his critic surmised, between his rich thematic repertoire and a solid, two-dimensional technique before a literature about to move from, as it were, *Uncle Tom's Cabin* to *The Sound and the Fury*.[72]

[69] John S. Brushwood, *The Spanish American Novel: A Twentieth-Century Survey* (Austin, Tex., 1978), pp. 96–101. See also Roberto González Echevarría's treatment of *Doña Bárbara* in *The Voice of the Masters: Writing and Authority in Modern Latin American Literature* (Austin, Tex., 1988), ch. 2, and for Brazil José H. Decanal, *O romance dos 30* (Porto Alegre, 1982).

[70] For Azuela's mannered attempts to adopt a modernist esthetic in his later career see Martínez, *Art of Mariano Azuela*.

[71] Emir Rodríguez Monegal, *Narradores de esta América*, Vol. 1 (Buenos Aires, 1976), p. 172; 'The New Novelists', *Encounter*, 25/3 (1965), 97–109.

[72] Rodríguez Monegal, *Narradores*, pp. 166–74; also Antonio Cornejo Polar, 'La novela indigenista: una desgarrada conciencia de la historia', *Revista Lexis*, 4/1 (1980): 88; Julio Rodríguez-Luis, *Hermenéutica y praxis del indigenismo: la novela indigenista de Clorinda Matto a José María Arguedas* (Mexico, D.F., 1980).

Naturalism as reportage or as 'scientific' interpretation clarifies aspects of the identity question that concern us. Our clues thus far proffered as to the historical role of naturalism in Latin America, however, are somewhat disparate. For example: (1) because the Americas have been a 'new world' for half a millennium they are of permanent interest as an arena for 'novelties' to be meticulously reported; (2) Latin American writers of the 1880s and 1890s were influenced by the rationale and technique of Zolaesque naturalism; (3) political and ideological pressures of the 1930s opened a space propitious for neo-naturalist fiction, often in the form of novels of the land that might retrieve the foundation myths implied in (1) above; and (4) while naturalism claimed clinical authority more strict than that of realism, this gave its narratives a transhuman scientific warrant which paradoxically resembled the *deus ex machina* of the marvellous realism that won literary cachet in the 1940s.

Various authors wove these strands into patterns; an obvious example is Alejo Carpentier, who often expatiated on the matter. His key books for present purposes are his first novel, *¡Ecue-Yamba-O!* (written 1928, published 1933), and his *El reino de este mundo* (1949).[73] The former, featuring themes of social justice and Afro Cuban culture (the book's title means 'Lord, Praised Be Thou' in ñáñigo dialect), was a product of time and place for its elements of social realism and 'indigenism', seasoned however by modernist hints of cubism, futurism and especially surrealism. Citing Juan Marinello, González Echevarría remarks that in *¡Ecue-Yamba-O!* Carpentier portrays Afro Cubans from the inside and outside simultaneously, causing a 'crack' at the centre of the novel, or cleavage between the black world and a white perception of it. Carpentier experienced his curative revelation on a trip to Haiti with Louis Jouvet's theatre company in 1943. Here direct contact with Afro-Caribbean religion and with the monuments erected by Henri Christophe inspired him to break with cosmopolitan sur*realism* in favour of a 'marvellous *realism*' (or magic *realism* from the Afro viewpoint) having roots in communal faith, myth and identity. *El reino de este mundo,* a story immersed in the ordeal of Haitian independence, was the initial fruit of this conversion. In later novels he expanded and emancipated his American theatre to develop, wrote Rodríguez Monegal, 'the contrast between the magic of the American topography or the "marvellous" quality of its history and the products of a European superculture that pursues and even oppresses its human actors'.

---

[73] *The Kingdom of this World*, trans. Harriet de Onís (New York, 1957).

Carpentier's successive discussions of his ideas did less to dissolve his original contradictions than to orchestrate his several realities – socialist realism, surrealism, magic realism (which discredits causation), and marvellous realism (which celebrates the unwonted, or *lo insólito*) – to yield a 'real' matrix for imaginative reconnaissance.[74]

Carpentier's fiction and pronouncements help place realism and naturalism in literary context. It remains, however, to demonstrate that naturalism *tout court* has had its own career and that it is known to appear in relatively unadulterated form. In her *Tal Brasil, qual romance?* [If such is Brazil, what is its novel?] Flora Süssekind makes this case for Brazil, which witnessed three flowerings of naturalism in the 1880s/1890s, the 1930s and the 1970s.[75] Her premise is that the naturalist aesthetic flings the cloak of science across the abiding quest for New World identity. In representing a national reality it seeks mimesis that admits no doubts or divisions, even to the point of sacrificing stylistic felicity. Insofar as it grows from a sense of uprootedness and orphanhood, however, the mimetic fixation may be of emotive origin. A writer's goal is therefore not necessarily 'tal Brasil, qual romance?' but may be 'tal Brasil, tal romance' ('as is Brazil so *must* be its novel'). Carried to its logical conclusion, the argument leaves us to assume that the great nay-sayers of Brazilian identity – who like Machado de Assis or Oswald de Andrade or Guimarães Rosa accept the fragmentation of Brazil on the one hand and its universal attunements on the other – become literary foundlings without progenitors or disciples.

Examining three successive moments of naturalism allows underlying premises to be distinguished from shifting technique and sensibility. Thus to explicate the 1930s requires knowledge of the other two moments, for each shares the photographic imperative. The 'photographer' assumes that he faces a coherent subject and must perform as a mere lens, even though he himself is part of the subject portrayed. In all three periods writers vow to report without distortion or preconception and perform a 'visually' mimetic act. Their critical verbs are see, examine, discern and portray. They propose to cancel the reader's role as interpreter by connecting the reader directly to the evidence. Science and literature merge in a linear vision. Comparing the three moments of naturalism, however, reveals that three disparate political diagnoses have been smuggled in under the pretence of objectivity. In the

[74] Emir Rodríguez Monegal, 'Lo real y lo maravilloso en *El reino de este mundo*', in Klaus Müller-Bergh (ed.), *Asedios a Carpentier* (Santiago, Chile, 1972), pp. 101–32; Roberto González Echevarría, *Alejo Carpentier: The Pilgrim at Home* (Ithaca, N.Y., 1977), ch. 2.
[75] Flora Süssekind, *Tal Brasil, qual romance?* (Rio de Janeiro, 1984).

1880s the things that are 'seen' yield a deterministic view of biological heredity and a presumption against socialism as a political remedy. In the 1930s they dismiss heredity, posit social dialectic and predict structural change or revolution. In the 1970s our informant is no longer the white-coated physician of the early period nor the decadent patriarchal heir of the middle one but the heroic, marginalized news reporter with his hopes pinned to democratic insurgence via denunciation.

While remaining faithful to direct reportage and the quest for national-ity, the regionalist novels of the 1930s, especially the novels of the northeast (Jorge Amado, José Lins do Rego, and with qualifications, Graciliano Ramos), abandon the pathology of individuals in favour of the fortunes of economic enterprises. Interest turns from individuals and their genes to the self-made man and his manipulation of factors of production. Titles that once identified persons (*Bom crioulo, A normalista*) now feature crops and enterprises (*Cacao, Usina, São Bernardo*). Romans-fleuves are favoured for handling inter-generational socio-economic forces, while 'cycles' of novels echo the economists' new cyclical version of Brazil's economic development. The nostalgic sociologist Gilberto Freyre and the Marxist economic histo-rian Caio Prado Junior (scion of Paulista entrepreneurs) both published influential works in the 1930s – *Casa Grande e Senzala* (Eng. trans. *The Masters and the Slaves*) and *Formação do Brasil Contemporâneo, Colônia* (Eng. trans. *The Colonial Background of Modern Brazil*) respectively – that gave academic support for the transition from the patriarchal fazenda to the industrial *usina* that the novelists identified (see below).

From the three successive episodes – the 1880s/90s, the 1930s and the 1970s – the limits and confusions of Brazilian naturalism become clear. 'Tal Brasil, tal romance' contains a fatal ambivalence. Does naturalism truly enjoin unmediated replication of Brazil? Or does it, unlike open-ended realism, imply replication and imposition of Zola, European litera-ture, or Western science? Does it reproduce a recognized foreign model or an unrecognized Brazil? If we assume that the naturalist intention is to replicate Brazil, we must ask whether Brazil is truly unitary or whether it is fractured by race, class, power, wealth and group outlooks, as indeed Euclides da Cunha found it to be. Naturalism admittedly draws energy from these divisions and is far from the genre of static national-character portraiture. Where it finds 'unity' is in a future condition (aryanization, economic development, revolution, or democratic consensus) and in the patterned forces at work to produce it. Naturalism finds redemption over the generations in precisely those fractures within its own diagnosis that yield spiralling self-correction and fresh openings instead of circularity and frozen identity. In each period, moreover, an occasional writer, classed as a naturalist on formal grounds, makes a private breakthrough to broader currents of sensibility. The obvious case in the 1930s is Graciliano Ramos, who called his diverse writings an unfolding series rather than a cycle, who was not driven to anchor his writerly instincts in documentary form, who refused to taxonomize his fictional characters, and who never sacrificed his art to political circumstance.

The Search for Causality: Mariátegui, Price-Mars, Prado

The term 'identity essay' usually implies compact, eclectic, interpretive texts that characterize aspects of a people's history and outlook.[76] It may further imply a piece of writing that is opinionated, impressionistic, aphoristic, or simply an exercise in literary charm. From the proper pen, however, one essay is more persuasive than a treatise. Octavio Paz instances Ortega y Gasset, whom he calls a true essayist, perhaps the best in Spanish and master of a genre that resists easy synopsis. The example is apropos because Ortega's probings into Hispanic identity were a beacon for New World essayists of the 1920s, 1930s and beyond. The essayist, writes Paz, needs the art of suspension points. When he becomes categorical, as Ortega often does, he must add a pinch of salt. He does not systematize but explores. His prose flows fresh, never in a straight channel, always equidistant from the treatise and the aphorism, two forms of congealment. The essayist should bring us treasures and trophies but never a map. He does not colonize, he discovers.[77]

The essayists to be discussed here, successors in a sense to the pensadores, were freer than their forerunners to challenge the social outlook and political convictions of elites and less encumbered in making overtures to modernized philosophy and social science. Moreover, all were in various ways responsive to the modernist climate in literature and the arts, which helped season the new social sciences with expressive concerns. In fact, it is precisely the blend of instrumental and expressive orientations (or to use José Lezama Lima's more elegant pairing: the search for causality

---

[76] For the Spanish American essay: Stabb, *In Quest of Identity;* Peter Earle and Robert Mead, *Historia del essayo hispanoamericano* (Mexico, D.F., 1973). In *O caráter nacional brasileiro*, 4th ed. (São Paulo, 1983) Dante Moreira Leite examines national character in Brazilian writings using social-science rather than literary criteria.

[77] Octavio Paz, 'José Ortega y Gasset: el cómo y el para qué', in *Hombres en su siglo* (Barcelona, 1984), pp. 97–110.

versus search for imaginative or mythic form) that guides the three groupings offered.

First comes a trio of differing ages though each published his most famous book in the same year, 1928. They are: José Carlos Mariátegui (Peru, 1894–1930), Jean Price-Mars (Haiti, 1876–1969), and Paulo Prado (Brazil, 1869–1943). All three started with a view of countries whose beginnings had been exploitative and sanguinary and whose 'emancipatory' nineteenth century had been largely a mirage. Their nations were not yet nations. They shared an evolutionary view of history but feeling that their own societies were blocked at inception by the incongruent forces unleashed by European conquest. They therefore look to problems and causes, urging more productive, egalitarian societies equipped to rejoin history. While each writer had comparable diagnostic intentions, they identified central blockages differently for each country. Mariátegui found his central target in Peru's economic exploitation and the land question, Price-Mars in Haiti's racial intolerance, and Prado in the abulia or, in the medieval term, 'spiritual dryness' of all classes of Brazilians.

Both Mariátegui and Price-Mars achieved their reputations with books of seven essays: *Siete ensayos de interpretación de la realidad peruana* and *Ainsi parla l'oncle*.[78] Both helped to launch, or were later invoked by, international movements, respectively Third World Marxism and negritude, although as the latter movement took shape, Price-Mars hoped that Black people would be absorbed to, not differentiated within, mankind. Thus he argued the assimilation of Haitians to the human condition while Mariátegui demonstrated the peculiar historical conditioning of Andean America. The paradox was that Price-Mars required cultural specificity to clinch his universalist argument, while Mariátegui invoked universal principles to show the uniqueness of his case.

When their books appeared Price-Mars, a generation older than Mariátegui, was a pillar of the Haitian establishment. A physician, former inspector general of public instruction, and minister to Paris, he had published an indictment of the Haitian elite (*La vocation de l'élite*, 1919) for having provoked the U.S. occupation of 1915 and for being guilty of *bovarysme collectif* at a time when Mariátegui, at the threshold of his 'radical-

---

[78] José Carlos Mariátegui, *Seven Interpretive Essays on Peruvian Reality*, trans. Marjory Urquidi (Austin, Tex., 1971); see also Jesús Chavarría, *José Carlos Mariátegui and the Rise of Modern Peru, 1890–1930* (Albuquerque, 1979); José Aricó (ed.), *Mariátegui y los orígenes del Marxismo latinoamericano*, 2nd ed. (Mexico, D.F., 1980). Jean Price-Mars, *So Spoke the Uncle*, trans. Magdalin W. Shannon (Washington, D.C., 1983); see also Jacques C. Antoine, *Jean Price-Mars and Haiti* (Washington, D.C., 1981); *Témoignages sur la vie et l'oeuvre du Dr. Jean Price Mars 1876–1956* (Port-au-Prince, 1956).

ization', had been reporting the doings of Lima's high society under the sobriquet 'Juan Croniqueur'. The latter's political activity and his European interlude would soon form his socialist explanation of why the Peruvian elite had not, in four centuries, assumed its appointed economic function. Price-Mars had attributed his country's woes to the 'puerile vanity' of his elitist peers in promoting the 'rancid' idea that 'the Gauls are our ancestors'. As for his country's heritage, he wrote, 'eight-tenths of it is a gift from Africa'. For Peru, Mariátegui came to see the 'Indian problem' as a false issue.

Born to an impoverished family, crippled in childhood and forced to work at fourteen, Mariátegui knew the belly of the Peruvian monster, and during his European exile (1919–23) he moved into the larger belly of the Western one. The secret of his intellectual *prise* lies in his Italian sojourn. He had arrived thinking of Marxism as 'confused, heavy, and cold'; only in Italy did he have the 'revelation'. A clue to the fragmentation of his opinions in Europe is his fascination with modernist art. Surrealism particularly intrigued him for splintering the solid bourgeois world to expose its meretricious ideals.

Mariátegui's changed outlook owed much to the vitalist Marxism that he absorbed under Croce, whose denial that Marxism had laid bare the iron laws of history inspired the young Peruvian; for Croce, Marxism was persuasive as praxis but not as science. Mariátegui then proceeded to Croce's own teacher, Labriola; to Sorel and Pareto; and to Marxist sympathizers like Gramsci, Gobetti and the Russian revolutionaries. Post-war socialist journals and congresses steered Mariátegui toward revolutionary communism rather than revisionism. His choice was braced by the fascist march on Rome (1922), which symbolized for him the political bankruptcy of capitalism and recalled the attitudes of South American elites. The task, he saw, was no longer to 'catch up' with Europe but to expose the crepuscular spirit of bourgeois life and to embrace the cause of *el hombre matinal,* of peoples receptive to a 'multitudinous myth' wherever it could be found.

Mariátegui thus questioned whether Peru had really experienced a national history as a sequential transcending of stages. What aggravated the problem was that 'progressive' spokesmen construed the unassimilability of the vast indigenous population as a challenge for educational policy, humanitarianism, or 'human rights'. By suspending the ethnic definition of the 'Indian problem' he linked it directly to the 'land question', shifting it from a problem of tutelage to a revolutionary agenda. The solution did not lie, he felt, in a mystical 'Zionism' of servile races, Indian or black. Although Indian militants might win leadership over their fellows, an autonomous Indian state would not be a classless society but one with all the contradictions of a bourgeois state. Only the struggle of Indians, workers and peasants, he wrote, allied with the mestizo and white proletariat against the feudal, capitalist regime could permit the unfolding of indigenous racial characteristics, and institutions with collective tendencies. This might eventually unite Indians of different countries across present boundaries that divided ancient racial groups and lead to political autonomy for their race. Meanwhile, as long as vindication of the Indian is kept on a philosophical or cultural plane, he felt, or idly discussed in the pseudo-idealistic verbiage of a liberal bourgeois education, the economic base of the problem would be disguised.

The starting point of Price-Mars was not the 'land question', for impoverished though the Haitian masses might be, the country had experienced its 'agrarian revolution' with the expulsion of the French and become a nation of peasants. The economic issue was not land but fiscal and social exploitation and cultural oppression. *Ainsi parla l'oncle* opens with the question, 'What is folklore?' For Price-Mars the term 'folklore' (coined in 1846) had less innocuous connotations than it may for modern readers; for him it referred to the realm of belief, not to exotic practices and colorful artifacts. His insistence on folklore reflected his conviction that the root cause of Haitian stagnation was that its heritage was a broken mirror yielding a 'reduced image of human nature'. His argument responded in part to the cultural nationalism provoked by the U.S. occupation, but in larger measure to the general Western view, shared by the Haitian elite, that African and Afro-American culture was primitive and barbarous. *Ainsi parla l'oncle* was in part occasioned by Price-Mars's 1915 encounter in Paris with Gustave Le Bon, whose books had for years influenced Latin American intellectuals who deplored race mixing. Price-Mars took him to task and Le Bon challenged him to write the book. For Mariátegui not only did the ethnic argument offer no foothold for political diagnosis but, when it came to the Afro-Peruvian, he felt he had brought fetishistic sensualism to Catholic worship, 'exuding from every pore the primitivism of his African tribe', while he corrupted the Indians with his 'false servility and exhibitionist, morbid psychology'.

For Price-Mars, Haitian rehabilitation must find its ethnic premise. Because the elite 'donned the old frock of Western civilization' after 1804, ignoring or suppressing the African transplants and syncretisms of the people, Price-Mars accused them of denying their country the binding force of shared symbolism so conspicuous in the Greco-Roman world and in modern Africa. Hence the importance of Haitian creole, that promised to be the vehicle for a national literature. Or of voodoo – ridiculed by sensationalist travellers as fetishism or even cannibalism – which Price-Mars defended as a religion that reached no less mystical heights than did Christianity. Language and faith betokened a new social form arising from confused mores and beliefs. At the moment it was a mere chrysalis, yet to which 'philosophers and brave men pay heed'. Price-Mars traced Haitian culture to the highest African civilizations. If one were to compare Africans with Europeans and Americans, he wrote, one would not find the former to be the closest to barbarism or the farthest from a higher social ideal. Mariátegui, in all the sufferings of his short life, perhaps never experienced the humiliation of Price-Mars when, as a Black intellectual heading the Haitian mission to the St Louis World's Fair of 1904, he visited the Deep South of the United States. *Ainsi parla l'oncle* expresses visceral emotion in closing with the ancient adage: 'There is nothing ugly in the house of my father.'

Mariátegui and Price-Mars built from reputable contemporary sources: neo-Marxist thought and racial anthropology respectively. The inspiration for Paulo Prado's *Retrato do Brasil, ensaio sobre a tristeza brasileira*[79] (Portrait of Brazil, Essay on Brazilian Sadness), the third of the 1928 landmarks, is more diffuse. Scion of a Paulista family of planters, politicians, and entrepreneurs, Prado was drawn to life in Europe and exhibited, contemporaries remarked, traits of dilettantism and neurasthenia. He won credentials as a historian, however, under the tutelage of João Capistrano de Abreu and was a discerning patron of São Paulo's vanguardist movement of 1922. Prado's *Portrait of Brazil* reveals little of the modernity of Mariátegui and Price-Mars and little of the modernism of the Paulista avant-garde. His text requires two readings, both linking it to less fashionable modes of enquiry. On the first, it shows affinity to late-positivist essays that deplored the anaemia and languor of mixed-race populations. A closer reading brings to light a more venerable, Catholic frame of reference.

The first chapter, 'Luxúria' (lust), describes tropical seductiveness and scenes of 'pure animality'. Documents told Prado that one-third or more of the cases brought to the Holy Office in Bahia in 1591–2 featured shame-

---

[79] Paulo Prado, *Retrato do Brasil*, 5th ed. (São Paulo, 1944). Darrell E. Levi gives a family history in *The Prados of São Paulo, Brazil: An Elite Family and Social Change, 1840–1930* (Athens, Ga, 1987), esp. pp. 130–37 for Paulo.

less sins of 'sexual hyperesthesia'. The second chapter addresses the more tyrannical passion of 'Cobiça' (covetousness). Here Prado evokes visions of El Dorado and Potosí that 'volatilized' the social instincts and anarchic individualism of deportees, castaways and mutineers. Emblematic were the *bandeirantes,* he felt, whose energy and ambition lacked mental or moral basis. 'What wealth, holy Lord, is that' – in Prado's quote from Pombal – 'whose possession brings on the ruin of the State?'

The third chapter, 'Tristeza' (sadness), is the hinge of the book and will detain us again later. It opens with the classic contrast of the morally hygienic spirit of the New England and Virginia colonists with the despotic, demoralized life of the Portuguese in Brazil. Sexual excess (*post coitum animal triste*) and the mirage of easy wealth stamped the Brazilian psyche with abulia and melancholia. A chapter on Romanticism claims that in the era of independence Brazil's 'sickness' was displaced to the new ruling and intellectual classes as a pathological *mal romântico* that found central loci in the new law schools of Recife and São Paulo. In Europe, Prado felt, romanticism was a passing fashion, while in Brazil it created *tristeza* by its 'concern with human misery, the contingency of events, and above all . . . the desire for happiness in an imaginary world'. In a 'Postscriptum' Prado confesses that he disregarded the *bovarysme* of São Paulo (a key term for Price-Mars as well) and composed his book (in contrast to Mariátegui) as an impressionist version of the forces of history without cubic masses of data and chronology. Only mental images were to remain. His national history was rooted not in the ubiquitous racial conflict of the Americas but in the intimacy of miscegenation. While denying Gobineau's presumption of racial inequality, however, he saw the 'hybrid vigour' of race-crossing as limited to the early generations.[80] The closing off of social opportunities condemned the population to somatic deficiency and congenital indolence – qualities that, ironically, preserved the unity of Brazil's vast territory. For the four republican decades after 1889, Prado concludes, politicians had danced on this bloated and atrophied body. The two solutions he envisioned were war, which might bring a 'providential hero', or revolution, which might banish the chimeras of the colonial past.

Thus far Prado's argument has been presented *ad literam.* What follows is perhaps a reading more adequate to the text and to the author's subjacent intentions. We may start by comparing the first sentence of Prado's book with that of Mariátegui's *Siete ensayos* (which affirms that the schism

---

[80] See Georges Raeders, *O inimigo cordial do Brasil: o Conde de Gobineau no Brasil* (São Paulo, 1988).

in Peruvian history is best seen as economic, thus demolishing at a stroke the specious *indigenismo* of the elite) and with Price-Mars's *Ainsi parla l'oncle* (whose 'What is Folklore?' was to be answered by a critical inventory of Haitian oral traditions, legends, songs, riddles, customs, ceremonies and beliefs – thus ripping off the *masque blanc* from the *peau noire* long before the terms were coined). Here is Paulo Prado's initial sentence: 'In a radiant land lives a sad people.' First, note that he speaks of 'a sad people' and not 'three sad races', the phrase from the Brazilian poet Olavo Bilac used as a title of a book on racial identity and national consensus in Brazilian literature by the U.S. literary historian of Brazil, David Haberly.[81] Prado sees Brazil not as an ethnic mosaic but as a nation that collectively experiences, as we have noted, a state of spiritual dryness. Second, Prado's sentence implicitly refers us to the first salvo of Rousseau's *Social Contract:* 'Man was born free, and he is everywhere in chains.' Rousseau addressed a state of external oppression, Prado a state of soul. From these clues we recognize that Prado's first two chapters, 'Lust' and 'Covetousness' – two of the deadly sins – point toward theological and moral issues that transcend the fixation of commentators on genes, race, heredity, sanitation and scientific determinism.

As the book's subtitle indicates, Prado's third chapter, 'Sadness', is his pivot. Sadness does not figure in the modern repertory of the seven capital sins; its nearest equivalent is sloth. Yet the genealogy of sloth shows that it merges with medieval acedia, which once counted as a 'deadly' sin and included both mental or spiritual states (listlessness, loathing, slackness of mind) and qualities of behaviour (torpor, negligence, idleness).[82] By the late Middle Ages, with the spread of moral theology to the common folk, acedia lost its theological force, yielding primacy in the roster of capital vices to sloth and to an emphasis on 'external' manifestations of indolence. By the time of the Renaissance, acedia and its theological component of *tristitia* were secularized under the atmospheric term 'melancholy'.

Prado's attempt to recover the moral premises of Brazil's Catholic society, inspired by his reading of sixteenth-century Inquisition documents, was part of a project of fellow Paulista modernists who had recognized the significance for Brazil of Europe's transition from the late Middle Ages to early modernity. The difference was that while Prado sought, perhaps

---

[81] David T. Haberly, *Three Sad Races: Racial Identity and National Consciousness in Brazilian Literature* (Cambridge, Eng., 1983).

[82] See Siegfried Wenzel, *The Sin of Sloth: Acedia in Medieval Thought and Literature* (Chapel Hill, N.C., 1967), pp. 60–63, 164–5 for 'spiritual dryness'.

subconsciously, the medieval therapy for *tristitia,* his younger cohorts Mário de Andrade and Oswald de Andrade looked ahead to Montaigne, Rabelais and a Renaissance therapy. Prado, that is, held to *tristitia* as a theological, 'internal' aspect of acedia while Mário and Oswald addressed 'external' or behavioural aspects. Thus Mário adopted the Portuguese word *preguiça* (from the Latin *pigritia*) or 'indolence' to designate a Brazilian lack of firm character or aptitude for modern, disciplined life, but also praised it as idleness propitious for cultivating the arts and as a tropical antidote to a technified, consumerized society.[83] Oswald gave an even more positive accent to *ócio* ('leisure', from the Latin *otium*), stressing its denials in the forms of *negócio* ('business', from *nec-otium* or *not-leisure*) and *sacerdócio* (from *sacerdotium* or 'priesthood'). Oswald's 'way out' was the transition from technical to natural life, or from civilization to culture.[84]

Paulo Prado's 'way out' returns us to historical origins and to the corrective for acedia. His therapy was perhaps confusedly expressed. But surely it prefigures the contribution of his compatriot Paulo Freire, whose conscientization would, a generation later, challenge the passive *tristitia* of the people with psychological and even theological empowerment, presenting a culturally and sociologically rooted version of 'education' in contrast to the utilitarian and manipulative 'schooling' of the industrial West. Freire's starting point was surely one sad people, not three sad races.

Balancing Myth and Evidence (1): Martínez Estrada, Paz, Ortiz, González

The next group of four essayists (who have, or had, many other literary roles) entertain hopes for their homelands comparable to those of the first group but are driven less to cope or remake than to contemplate the self-givenness of identity itself. Identity becomes as much a processual structure as a goal. Two of the writers, Ezequiel Martínez Estrada (Argentina, 1895–1964) and Octavio Paz (Mexico, 1914–), display rich literary, philosophic and historical understandings, and a prose that leads them on voyages of interior discovery and to private acts of communion. No less than Paz's Mexican pilgrimage, Martínez Estrada's Argentine X-ray draws

---

[83] Mário de Andrade, 'A divina preguiça' (1918), in M. R. Batista et al., *Brasil: 1° tempo modernista – 1917/29* (São Paulo, 1972), pp. 181–3. Mário's *Macunaíma* was published in 1928, the year of the three books under discussion. The first utterance of the hero as a tot appears on the first page as 'Ai! que preguiça!' – 'Ay, what laziness!' or 'Aw, what a drag!'

[84] Oswald de Andrade, *Do Pau-Brasil à antropofagia e às utopias* (Rio de Janeiro, 1972), pp. 157–64.

him into a labyrinth of solitude. Fernando Ortiz (Cuba, 1881–1969) and José Luis González (Dominican Republic, b. 1926) are more sociable guides (as befits Antilleans). They welcome us to the tour, point out the everyday environment of objects, vegetation, crops and people of diverse colours and professions. But as these objects or persons take on symbolic or mythic force we see patterned dimensions and movements that had escaped us. Here as in the labyrinths lie mysteries. Cuba's two main export crops take on the persona of a man and woman; the *ajiaco* or stew pot becomes a symbol of Cuba and a four-storeyed house the image of Puerto Rico: or we suddenly discover that the voices of a very modern Cuba are implicated in meanings, still audible, of a fourteenth-century Spanish poet. Problems and causes and certainly 'solutions' are more evident on these sunny isles than in the labyrinths of solitude. But as we squint into the sunlight we sense a move from linear to recurrent time.

In 1933 the Argentine poet Ezequiel Martínez Estrada published *Radiografía de la pampa,* claiming new territory for the identity essay.[85] Here the Indo- and Afro-American components of society were absorbed or inconspicuous; they could not, as in Peru or Haiti, dictate agendas for national therapy, such as agrarian reform or racial tolerance. Indeed, for several decades Argentina had seemed to be solving the chronic regional problems of poverty, social oppression and educational neglect. It was reckoned as prosperous, modern, or in a later term, developed. Yet by the 1920s premonitions were afloat in cosmopolitan Buenos Aires, as seen in the discussion of Borges and Arlt. For Martínez Estrada, who had published six books of poetry by 1929, the calamitous political and economic events of 1929–32 forced him from evocations to diagnosis. Yet even though Argentina might be moving toward exclusion from the club of Western nations, neither was it germinating an exotic identity as an arrested enclave. Martínez Estrada had come to see Argentine history to be static and not evolutionary and to feel that the country had never come to terms with that history nor even with its prehistory ('the Pleistocene still held fully sway'). At the same time he felt that Nietzsche, the voice for a new civilization in the West, spoke directly to Argentine society with his notions of collective resentment, will to power, and society's fear of the individual.

To translate Nietzschean premonitions for the Argentine setting Martí-

---

[85] Ezequiel Martínez Estrada, *X-Ray of the Pampa,* trans. Alain Swietlicki (Austin, Tex., 1971). See Peter G. Earle, *Prophet in the Wilderness. The Works of Ezequiel Martínez Estrada* (Austin, Tex., 1971).

nez Estrada turned to domestic history and to those who could help him read it.[86] Important cues came from the French-born, humanely sceptic director of the National Library, Paul Groussac. For a year and a half the poet browsed through some 400 books but accumulating them as lived experience, not as data. Later he would devote strategic volumes to three Argentines whose lives and writings he found emblematic: Sarmiento, José Hernández and W. H. Hudson. This trio was balanced by three Europeans who taught him to interpret collective life: Spengler by his symbolic readings, the Freud of *Totem and Tabu* as a diagnostician of tumult in the social psyche, and Simmel, whose *Sociology* was his 'control book' for the configurationist method. Another European mentor – perhaps even more important than these three, for Martínez Estrada devoted a 900-page book to him – was Balzac, who saw history as the morphology of the facts and learned, as Martínez Estrada would later do, from J. K. Lavater (1741–1801), a Swiss poet, mystic, physiognomist, and influence on Stendhal who claimed to divine the soul's imprint on the human face.

In his commemorative interview Martínez Estrada provided 'exegeses' of the six parts of his book. The first deals with Trapalanda, the Indians' promised land that became the Argentines' illusory, 'impossible' country from the conquest to the present. The deceived intruder invents a false Arcadia to expunge the traces of his failure. 'He wants what he has not and wants it as what was denied.' Part two is a study in solitude, a term that harks back to the *soledades* of classic Spanish poetry. Martínez Estrada feels solitude to emanate from space and time: from space because here was a ' "new" world petrified in its fossils, savagery, panoramas of an astral scale', and villages strewn like aerolites; and an emanation from time because here time worked in reverse in that Spain's mission was to conquer a relic, the emblematic sepulchre of Christ, rather than to confer life on a *new* world. In 1500 the Spaniards reverted to existence as of the year 700. The German, Gallic, Italian and Saxon peoples saw them sclerotic and rupestrine, a true 'American' people because no other race was so qualified for maintaining the primordial barbarism of America.

In 1950 Octavio Paz closed his *Labyrinth of Solitude* with a 'dialectic of solitude': the 'nostalgic longing for the body from which we were cast out', an evocation of purification rites, spiritual combat and finally grace or communion. Martínez Estrada's 'solitude' lacks this theological accent

---

[86] See Martínez Estrada's reflections on the silver anniversary of *Radiografía* in his *Leer y escribir* (Mexico, D.F., 1969), pp. 131–6.

and refers to dismemberment by isolation and the chimerical boundaries of empire. America for him was without historicity. Unlike Napoleon on Saint Helena, its caudillos could not record the history they had made but wrote only autobiographies. Common to both Argentine and Mexican solitudes was passivity or disillusionment before history. In *Children of the Mire* Paz contrasts the Spanish with a 'modern' poet, to remind us that the aesthetic revolution of Góngora's *Soledades* reflected his refusal of commerce, industry and the conquest of America. Góngora *reorients poetry because he cannot change life.* Rimbaud's poetry, on the other hand, spills over into action. His verbal alchemy urges human nature to 'multiply the future'. He aims to provoke new psychic states (religions, drugs), liberate nations (revolutions), transform erotic relations, throw a bridge to utopia. Rimbaud *changes poetry so as to change human nature.*[87]

The third part of *X-Ray* deals with 'primitive forces', divisible into telluric, mechanical and psychic. To a degree Martínez Estrada sees them as energies that for Sarmiento produced the face-off between barbarity and civilization. He admired his mentor's telluric sense of the scout and trail guide of the pampas but failed to share his conviction that encroachment by the state brought tidings of civilization. For Martínez Estrada civilization and barbarity were centrifugal and centripetal forces in equilibrium. Barbarity found refuge in the new regime to await its opportunities during economic crisis or episodes of ruffianism. Europe's troops, ships, diplomats and gold were impotent against Rosas but all-powerful against Sarmiento and the new presidents. The nationality that Rosas achieved with land the new presidents built with bricks and iron. Gauchos became day labourers and public life was formally organized; but the nation did not exist. The telluric provinces of the caudillos became suburbs of the national capital. As the sum of public powers the state became the arsenal of violent impulses retired from circulation. It kept huge armies of employees and soldiers, producing university graduates like paper money – without control or solvency. The strength of the state lay in its having weakened all else. The country became a dumping ground for the detritus of civilization: telephones and journalism, cars and movies, books and textiles. Man, a passive vegetable, confronts a world of objects that is born, multiplies and dies.

For its author Buenos Aires, successor to metropolitan Spain, was the

[87] Octavio Paz, *Children of the Mire*, trans. Rachel Phillips (Cambridge, Mass., 1974), p. 113. Paz rehearsed his treatment of solitude in 'Poesía de soledad y poesía de comunión' (*El Hijo Pródigo*, 1943) reprinted in his *Primeras letras (1931–1943)* (Mexico, D.F., 1988), pp. 291–303.

book's keystone: the enemy in the house who devours, subverts, corrupts. Here and in *La cabeza de Goliat* (1940) he portrays Buenos Aires as Argentina's oneiric fantasy that became the capital not of the nation but only of itself, like the teratological creature that does not live for the species. Originally caudillos divided the land around cabildos as points of control and settlement. Later the railroads divided it into tariff zones, not to create a circulatory system but to irrigate a phantasmal body. For Porteños, who felt they lived on Europe's periphery, to look at their 'interior' or heartland meant not the pampas but Europe. Argentine railway cars placed in motion from London were pounds sterling producing pounds sterling, not vehicles producing wealth.

Such musings led Martínez Estrada to adopt 'pseudo-structures' for diagnosing the national malady. These he saw as false forms not in accord with environment, life, or national mission. Lacking inborn instincts Argentines took on a borrowed crust. Thus, religion became a formula and not a faith, a private belief and not a social force, a public cult and not a source of freedom. Or, if laws are not inscribed on a people's soul, a state based on force of law is a false one. Or, Argentina adopted cars and planes merely for touring with no constructive function; they became problems, not solutions. Or, some countries 'make history, some live it, and others falsify it; we write it'. Or, Argentine women now appear worldly with their short hair, exposed thighs and pencilled eyes; yet beyond the aphrodisiac shell lies an incorruptible vestal. And finally, the tango could not escape the author: a narcotic performance bereft of flirtation, resistance and possession, and emptied of directing will.

The device of pseudo-structures goes beyond familiar explanations of evolutionary blockage or mimesis on the periphery. It aims toward psychology and therapy, that is, toward converting the immediate objects, characters, and *mise-en-scène* dear to historians, essayists and anthropologists into symbolic markers. Thus while the book appears on the surface to be steeped in minutiae of national culture, it is indeed an X-ray that lights up common structures. As the author put it, one consults the radiologist, not the photographer, when the problem is glandular, not cutaneous. Instead, then, of treating Argentina as a breakaway success story, he absorbed it into a common American history. There was, he surmised, an 'ethnic, somatic and mental South American commonality that lends a similar atmosphere to half a continent'. Nothing binds these nations, which share no high ideals of confraternity. The supremacy of nature over the inhabitants and of environment over will isolates human events, forcing them to float unrelated in a halo of irresponsibility. The southern countries submit to northern centres of economic energy ruled by the unknown lender and calibrated to profit, not public need. South America served as Europe's suburban real estate: 'we are all defending the owner's possessions while intoxicating ourselves with the clandestine liquors he sends us: gold, magazines, movies, weapons'. A generation later 'dependency theory' would be removed from the cultural armature where Martínez Estrada had placed it, causing appreciable restriction of its cognitive scope.

X-Ray delivered a powerful message to the next Argentine generation as instanced in a tribute by H. A. Murena, who in 1954 praised it as the 'exact and dramatic description of the illness by the patient himself', who as a physician relates without concessions the genesis, growth and prognosis of a cancer in his own body. Placing Martínez Estrada in the company of three other prophetic Argentine writers (Borges, Mallea and Leopoldo Marechal), Murena accords him the extra tribute of heralding the rise of a new conscience in the Americas at large.[88] At the end of his life (he died embittered in 1964) Martínez Estrada, released from a bleak job in the post office, tested his hemispheric vocation (1959–62) by giving seminars on Latin America at the National University of Mexico and spending two years in Cuba, where he composed a lengthy study of Martí as a revolutionary but where, despite his admiration for Fidel Castro, he was never invited to meet him.

Save perhaps for Mariátegui's *Seven Essays* the best known Latin American essay in the twentieth century may well be Octavio Paz's '*El labirinto de la soledad*', published in 1950 and revised in 1959. *The Labyrinth of Solitude* has similarities to *X-Ray* (for one thing both authors were poets), although Paz stated in an interview of 1975 that he had not yet read *X-Ray* in 1950.[89] An explicit link is their Nietzschean inspiration. Martínez Estrada was influenced by his theory of collective resentment, as discussed above, while Paz claimed he could not have written *The Labyrinth of Solitude* without Nietzsche's guidance, especially *The Genealogy of Morals*. 'Nietzsche taught me to see what was behind words like virtue, goodness, evil. He guided me in exploring the Mexican idiom: If words are masks,

---

[88] H. A. Murena, 'La lección a los desposeídos: Martínez Estrada', in *El pecado original de América*, 2nd ed. (Buenos Aires, 1965), pp. 95–119.

[89] The expanded edition of the English translation, *The Labyrinth of Solitude* (New York, 1985), contains three complementary writings and one interview by Paz: 'The Other Mexico', 'Return to the Labyrinth of Solitude', 'Mexico and the United States', and 'The Philanthropic Ogre' (trans. L. Kemp, Y. Miles and R. P. Belash). The reference to Martínez Estrada is on p. 331.

what is behind them?'[90] More broadly, both authors drew deeply from history, philosophy, sociology and literature. On the matter of history, Martínez Estrada felt that Spain at the conquest reverted to an early medieval phase that gave it no purchase for taming the American environment, whereas Paz reminded readers that Spain was not simply a caste-ridden society but had adopted a universalist tradition before the Counter Reformation, synthesizing the strands at least in the realm of art. As for literature, the lesson of Balzac was critical for Martínez Estrada while Paz, who used poets widely, gave a sketch of Sor Juana Inés de la Cruz as an emblematic figure that would eventually inform his masterful *Sor Juana or, The Traps of Faith* (1982). Both men were fully cognizant of psychology, Martínez Estrada as an admirer of Freud's *Totem and Tabu* and Paz as a critical reader of the Mexican philosopher Samuel Ramos, who in 1934 had published an influential study of Adlerian derivation to explain the Mexican 'inferiority complex' and the Frenchification of Mexican elite culture. Ramos, Paz declared, 'dwells on psychology; in my case psychology is but a way of reaching moral and historical criticism'.[91]

As discussed earlier, Martínez Estrada and Paz both gave prominence to the solitude theme with its implications of expulsion and pilgrimage. Paz develops it with reference to the myth of the Fisher King – as found in Sir James Frazer and in T. S. Eliot's *Waste Land* – and to the search for grace through jungles, deserts, or underground mazes. While Martínez Estrada exempts 'Saxon' Americans from this ordeal – for they defied and conquered environment – Paz finds all Americans to be prisoners of solitude. 'If the solitude of the Mexican is like a stagnant pool', he writes, 'that of the North American is like a mirror. We have ceased to be living springs of water.' A dimension available to the Mexican and not to the Argentine was Aztec civilization. In Mexico Paz feels, 'the ancient beliefs and customs are still in existence beneath Western forms'. Modern man, he observes, was exiled from eternity, where all times are one, to chronometric time that lacks all particularity. The Mexican fiesta, whether Indian or Catholic, suspends clock and calendar time for a moment so as to reproduce an event, not celebrate it. Myth permits man to emerge from solitude and rejoin creation. In Mexico, myth reappears in human acts and intervenes in its history, opening doors of communion. If North Ameri-

[90] Earle, *Prophet*, pp. 106–9; Paz, *Labyrinth*, p. 351.

[91] Samuel Ramos, *Profile of Man and Culture in Mexico*, trans. Peter G. Earle (New York, 1963); Paz, *Labyrinth*, pp. 330–32. For Ramos and his antecedents, see Henry C. Schmidt, *The Roots of Lo Mexicano: Self and Society in Mexican Thought, 1900–1934* (College Station, Tex., 1978).

cans see the world as something to be perfected, Mexicans see it as something to be redeemed.

Other parallels might be traced. Martínez Estrada's pseudo-structures, meaning a false form over natural environment and declared missions, correspond to the recurrent masks in *Labyrinth* that must be torn off if Mexicans are to live and think in an 'open' solitude where transcendence awaits; they are not simply to reach out to fellows but become 'contemporaries of all mankind'. Or, the two writers shared a similar sense of the immersion of their lands in the Americas. Martínez Estrada saw Argentina as still captive of the primitive, telluric forces of the southern Americas that undermined the futile incursions of civilization from without, whether Europe or North America. While Paz also feels Mexico to be symptomatic of Spanish America, his meditation starts by directly comparing Mexico with the United States. He takes the latter not loosely as a northern industrial country but as a specifically New World country with a version of solitude that helped him pose questions to ask of Mexico.

These two works move the identity essay from the realm of national 'problems', assumed to be curable by enlightened intervention, to a search for national psyche whose continuous disclosure lies in the inscrutable realm of historical process.

A book of a style and spirit quite different from the two just examined is *Contrapunteo cubano del tabaco y azúcar* published in 1940 by Fernando Ortiz.[92] It contains a general statement of his thesis on the counterpoint of tobacco and sugar with a lengthy appendix on the 'ethnography and transculturation' of the two crops that expanded with each edition. Again we have a book that needs two readings. On the first reading, we recognize that the starting point is not Caribbean history conceived as a political and cultural invasion of an exotic periphery. Instead, Ortiz features two crops (one indigenous, one transplanted) that define the native landscape of every Cuban. He starts with an experienced Cuban 'reality' still to be specified rather than with conflictive impositions upon it. He deduces his story of Cuba not from ideologies of control and exploitation but from biotic requirements of two forms of vegetation. Tobacco and sugar are defined not as the currency of capitalist exchange but as products of Cuban soil that in themselves dictate institutional arrangements and ways of life.

[92] Fernando Ortiz, *Cuban Counterpoint, Tobacco and Sugar* (New York, 1970). See Gustavo Pérez Firmat, *The Cuban Condition: Translation and Identity in Modern Cuban Literature* (Cambridge, 1989); Antonio Benítez-Rojo, *The Repeating Island: The Caribbean and the Postmodern Perspective*, trans. James E. Maraniss (Durham, 1992), ch. 4.

Ortiz builds from the land and its fruits (as did the early Marx and Engels in the *German Ideology*), not with human contrivances.

There is, then, a lucid and poetic ingredient in Ortiz's counterpoint because it originates in nature and not from maleficent forces. From germination to human consumption, he observes, tobacco and sugar are radically opposed. One grows from cuttings, the other from seeds; one is needed for its stalk, the other for its foliage; sugar is ground for juice, tobacco is dried out; one is white and odourless, the other dark and aromatic. This duet rested on a foundation that Mariátegui would have called economic infrastructure. Ortiz was aware that for tobacco and sugar the same four factors are present: land, machinery, labour, and money. He saw the implications of skilled immigrants versus slaves; small holdings versus plantations; a universal market for tobacco and a single one for sugar; national sovereignty against colonialism. In short, sugar passed into distant, corporate, all-powerful hands while tobacco 'created a middle class, a free bourgeoisie' without the extremes of slaves and masters, proletariat and rich.

Structural-economic determination was not, however, fundamental for Ortiz. In fact there was perhaps *no* 'foundation' to his argument. And here begins the second reading of *Cuban Counterpoint,* taking a clue once more from opening sentences. If Mariátegui dismissed any plane save the economic for interpreting the schism caused by the Spanish conquest, Ortiz drew on a jovial Spanish poet of the Middle Ages, the Archpriest of Hita (c.1283–c.1350), who personified Carnival and Lent in unforgettable verses, cleverly imbuing the assertions and rebuttals of their satirical contest with the 'ills and benefits that each has conferred on mankind'. Like Paulo Prado he had recourse to the Iberian tradition. But unlike Prado, who found clues in persistent 'sinful' categories of moral behaviour, he called to mind the 'mocking verse' of the *Libro de Buen Amor* (1343) with its Battle of the Lord Flesh-Season and the Lady Lent serving as his precedent 'to personify dark tobacco and "high yellow" sugar.' Lacking authority as a poet or priest to conjure up creatures of fantasy, wrote the disingenuous Ortiz, he had merely set down 'in drab prose, the amazing contrasts I have observed in the two agricultural products on which the economic history of Cuba rests'.[93]

In his examination of Ortiz's thought and sensibility Gustavo Pérez

---

[93] Juan Ruiz (Archpriest of Hita), *The Book of True Love,* trans. Saralyn R. Daly (bilingual ed.) (University Park, Pa., 1978).

Firmat attempts to show that his appreciation of Cuban culture and society depends less on historical ingredients and stages than on the processual formation of the nation's vernacular underpinning. His key notion is 'the fermentation and turmoil that *precedes* synthesis', his two key terms being 'transculturation' (translational displacements that generate vernacular culture) and *ajiaco* (a metaphor for the outcome of displacements). The word *ajiaco* itself – a simmering stew – is onomastic, for it combines the African name for an Indian condiment (*ají* or green pepper) with the Spanish suffix *-aco*. The *ajiaco* is never finished, changes incessantly with fresh ingredients, has no core of flavour and substance, and changes in taste and consistency depending on whether one dips from the bottom or the top. It is not the *crisol* or 'melting pot' of North America, taken from the metaphor of metal foundries, with its outcome of fusion. Here the image is unending *cocción* (literally concoction), implying indefinite deferral or a 'no-ser-*siempre*-todavía' (a state of always not yet). The idea is caught in the difference between the words *cubanidad,* implying defined civil status, and *cubanía,* an open-ended spiritual condition of desire which is given even to those who simply want it. Indeed Ortiz's own work is a prime example of his metaphor, a vast body of texts all falling short of finality and synthesis, creating doubt whether one is reading *about* Cuba or *experiencing* Cuban culture first hand. *Cuban Counterpoint* with its proliferating appendices is an outstanding case. All this, Pérez Firmat suggests, refers back to Ortiz's original counterpoint between the European *contrapunto,* or initial 'point', furnished by the debate between Carnival and Lent in the *Libro de Buen Amor* and the *contrapunteo,* or '*counter*point', of Cuba. As he sensed it, history itself is thus a constant simmer, not an itinerary, nor even a dialectic.

Ortiz's engaging manner of pictorializing invisible forces at play in a complex and changing society (national identity in motion we might call the effect) invites comparative reference to a similar use of technique forty years later by the Dominican-born Puerto Rican, José Luis González in his essay 'El país de cuatro pisos' (1980).[94] He in effect arrives at the simmering *ajiaco* of Ortiz, but in Puerto Rico the succession of Spanish and varied forms of U.S. domination since the nineteenth century has been too asphyxiating to allow the blossoming of a spirit equivalent to *cubanía*. González therefore addresses prevalent versions of Puerto Rican 'national culture' in the traditional Hispanic and modernizing American interpreta-

[94] José Luis González, *Puerto Rico: The Four-Storeyed Country,* trans. G. Guinness (Princeton, 1993), ch. 1.

tions as masks for elite ideologies.[95] The reason is that in the absence of a popular independence movement the formation of a nation was left to political and juridical arrangements that produced a national culture dichotomously defined by the dominant class. Popular culture was disparaged as 'folklore' while the group González sees as culturally most important, the Afro-Puerto Ricans, were held to be virtually insignificant.

The stratification of cultural vision leads González to the corrective metaphor of Puerto Rico as a house of four storeys. This device suspends the search for a static national identity by presenting four socio-cultural ingredients in historical order, with a popular, mestizo and above all Afro-Antillean society at the bottom. Above it lies a stratum of expatriates from the Spanish American independence wars enlarged by Europeans and a subsequent 'mezzanine' of Corsicans, Majorcans and Catalans. Next comes the U.S. occupation that provides, especially in the 1930s to 1950s, an alternative to the classic Spanish model for 'guided identity'. And finally comes the fourth floor, constructed from late-blooming U.S. capitalism welded to the opportunist populism of contemporary Puerto Rico. At first this architectonic structure may seem to elaborate the basic dualism of oppressors and oppressed. The question however is not who is on top but what upholds the structure. In addition, these 'floors' do not compose a fixed portrait but represent forces of living history that have operated, some in neglected or clandestine fashion, through the centuries. For González a critical point came in recent years when pseudo-industrialization and the pseudo-autonomous political formula reached a dead end, with marginalization of citizens, the demoralizing false beneficence of the colonial power, the rise of delinquency and criminality and institutionalized demagogy.

Here the structural metaphor of González takes on some of the fluidity of Ortiz's *ajiaco*. He feels that the dismantled culture of the Puerto Ricans 'on top' is replaced not by a somewhat discredited Americanization but by the rise of and permeation by the ever more visible culture of Puerto Ricans 'from below'. Similarly, the elitist myth of the stalwart Hispanic peasant (*jíbaro*) yields to the reality of the Afro-Antillean populace. Puerto Rico's 'special relationship' with the United States having lost its mystique, the 'simmering' process extends outward to the neighbouring Antil-

---

[95] The Puerto Rican identity controversy was shaped for a generation by Antonio S. Pedreira's *Insularismo* of 1934 (3rd ed.; San Juan, 1946), who cast the antagonism of Hispanophiles and Americanizers in Spenglerian and Orteguian terms of culture versus civilization. In lieu of their insular oscillation between Madrid and Washington he urged his countrymen to set out to fish in deep waters even though, as in the faraway past, a Dutch pirate might lurk there. Juan Flores offers a 'new reading' in: *Insularismo e ideología burguesa* (Río Piedras, 1979).

les as well as vertically in the island society. French and English can be seen not simply as imperial languages but as Antillean or creolized ones that serve the needs of decolonization. Recovery of its popular culture implies a re-Caribbeanization of Puerto Rico, to give it a custom-made regional identity rather than a 'Latin' or 'Anglo' American one that is ready-made.[96]

Balancing Myth and Evidence (2): Freyre, Buarque de Holanda

In his preface to the fifth Brazilian edition of Sérgio Buarque de Holanda's *Raízes do Brasil* the distinguished critic Antônio Cândido names three books that awakened his generation to the 'gust of intellectual radicalism and social analysis' created by the 1930 Revolution and not wholly snuffed out by the Estado Novo (1937–45). They were *Casa-Grande e Senzala* (1933) by Gilberto Freyre, *Raízes do Brasil* (1936), and *Formação do Brasil contemporâneo* (1942) by Caio Prado Júnior, appearing successively when Cândido's group were students in the *ginásio, curso complementar* and *escola superior*.[97] The first two books are discussed here as being in the essayist vein of this section (despite the immense length of Freyre's major works).[98]

Gilberto Freyre (1900–87) embeds complex and controversial meanings in his writings. Some of the intricacy derives from the biographic fact that he left his ancestral home in Pernambuco at eighteen to enter Baylor University in Waco, Texas. In 1920 he made a leap nearly as bold to enter the Master of Arts programme at Columbia University, which removed him from a stronghold of primitive Baptism, Jim Crowism and lynching to a sophisticated intellectual environment (with its nearby Harlem, of course). Recognized as a precocious *litterateur,* Freyre was soon familiarizing Brazilian readers with Mencken, Sandburg, O'Neill, Dreiser, Sinclair Lewis, Amy Lowell, Charles Beard, and more. It was a post-Whitman, post-W. D. Howells cast that stopped short of Eliot, Pound and the modernists. This youngster from a traditional region was thus immersed in the non-traditional but racist society of Texas, then exposed to a cosmo-

---

[96] Historical and ideological critiques of 'El país de cuatro pisos' include Juan Flores, 'The Puerto Rico that José Luis González built', *Latin American Perspectives,* 11/3 (1984), 173–84, and Manuel Maldonado Denis, 'En torno a "El país de cuatro pisos": Aproximación crítica a la obra sociológica de José Luis González', *Casa de las Américas,* 23, 135 (1982), 151–9.

[97] Antônio Cândido's preface to *Raízes* is reprinted in his *Teresina etc.* (Rio de Janeiro, 1980), pp. 135–52.

[98] For a collective study of Prado, see Maria Angela d'Incao (ed.), *Historia e ideal: ensaios sobre Caio Prado Júnior* (São Paulo, 1989).

politan city, a taste of literary life, and a world-class university that inculcated Deweyan social thought and fine points of bibliography and documentation. Although in New York his mentor, Franz Boas, assured him that innate racial differences did not exist, he was perplexed, after a three-year absence from Brazil, why some mulatto Brazilian sailors he ran into on Brooklyn Bridge seemed 'caricatures of men'.[99] He completed his education by reconnoitering Europe. By now, however, his American years had stamped his mind.[100]

José Lins do Rego described Freyre's return to Recife in 1923 after nearly six years of absence. It seemed a 'marriage' with his native land in a fiesta of light and colour; his first chronicles were carnivalesque, reflecting certain tension between the down-to-earth American culture that had shaped his mind and the tantalizing Brazilian one that now beckoned him to his origins. Such ambivalence was to mark his career as he wavered between intuition and research, between literary and scientific readings of history. His profuse writings, while usually informed, intelligent and provocative (even his clichés are in a way his own), do not always fulfill his intellectual claims. He spends hundreds of pages to demarcate his academic territory and justify his procedural mannerisms, showing less concern with the searching European debates since the Enlightenment over art versus science than with the bureaucratization of knowledge in American curricula as he experienced it. His book *Como e porque sou e não sou sociólogo* (*How and Why I am and am not a Sociologist*) (1968) is a self-justifying autobiography rather than an intellectual voyage, with such chapters as 'Why I'm More Anthropologist than Sociologist' or 'Why I'm a Writer without Ceasing to be Somewhat Sociological'.[101]

Ineluctably Freyre deleted his frontier between social science and literature, which he regarded as curricular categories rather than distinct modes of sensibility. He produced two novels, or 'seminovels', to assure dual control of his enlarged domain (*Dona Sinhá e o filho padre*, 1964, and *O outro amor do doutor Paulo*, 1977) followed by a study of 'heroes and villains' in Brazilian novels as 'socio-anthropological' types.[102] His boosters call Freyre's oeuvre an *histoire-fleuve;* liken him to Tolstoy, Balzac and Joyce;

[99] Gilberto Freyre, *The Masters and the Slaves,* trans. Samuel Putnam, 2nd Eng. ed. (Berkeley, 1986); pp. xxvi–xxvii.
[100] *Gilberto Freyre: sua ciência, sua filosofia, sua arte* (Rio de Janeiro, 1962).
[101] Gilberto Freyre, *Como e porque sou e não sou sociólogo* (Brasília, 1968).
[102] Gilberto Freyre, *Heróis e vilões no romance brasileiro* (São Paulo, 1979). The 'seminovel' *Dona Sinhá* is translated as *Mother and Son* (New York, 1967). See Edilberto Coutinho, *A imaginação do real: uma leitura da ficção de Gilberto Freyre* (Rio de Janeiro, 1983).

call him a poet; and hail him as a founder of meta-literature. Such plaudits are less explicable by his not inconsiderable literary gifts than by the remarkable self-invention and projection of his persona. The secret of Freyre's distinction lies beyond squabbles over his scholarship, his complex politics, his paeans to Brazilian civilization, his insouciant view of historical process, or his ambiguous portrayal of paternalism, slavery, race, sex and women. He commits the cardinal academic sin of enjoying his vocation.

On cognitive grounds an obvious starting point is Freyre's preference for an empathic 'Proustian' sociology of Brazil as against an 'objective' Durkheimian one rooted in 'social facts'.[103] Freyre adapts the two names to his own ends. Having little affinity with either writer, he misunderstands them. Proust's process of recollection was more sensitive than Freyre's, for it brought back experience as a whole rather than cataloguing it. (Proust's world of memory was released by a single *petite madeleine* soaked in tea. Freyre would have described sixty Pernambucan sweetmeats and a dozen types of maté.) If Proust penetrates far beyond mere atmospheric musings, Durkheim casts off gracefully from the realm of data. Freyre confesses that the latter's 'Israelite' background may add a Cleopatra's nose to his work but with no hint of the implications. He overlooks Durkheim's contributions to morals and the nature of civilizations; or his constructs of mechanical and organic solidarity, critical for elucidating Freyre's loose notions of social structure; or his clues to 'abnormal' social organization in pre-industrial societies set forth in his preface to the second edition (1902) of *Division of Labor.*[104]

If Freyre has such blind spots, what accounts for his influence and acclaim? A kindred spirit is perhaps Edmund Burke, whose conservatism, historical idealism and style give him lasting appeal. Despite Marx's charge that Burke was a cant-monger and sycophant in the pay of oligarchs, Burke's message that England is a partnership between the living, the dead and those to be born still stirs hearts in a manner that *Capital* cannot.[105] Freyre in his turn was attacked by progressives of the 1960s and pseudo-progressives of the 1980s. Yet his national vision is one that many Brazilians endorse in their (increasingly rare) self-conceited moments: 'The secret of Brazil's success in building a humane, Christian and modern

---

[103] Gilberto Freyre, *Sociologia,* 4th ed.; 2 vols. (Rio de Janeiro, 1967), Vol. 1, pp. 70–72.
[104] See Durkheim and Marcel Mauss, 'Note on the notion of civilization', *Social Research,* 38/4 (1971), 808–13.
[105] M. M. Bober, *Karl Marx's Interpretation of History* (New York, 1965), pp. 83–4.

civilization in tropical America has been her genius for compromise.' While the British, as no other people, have had this genius in the political sphere, Brazilians extend it, Freyre adds for good measure, to the cultural and social realms.[106]

Freyre touches imaginations in Brazil and elsewhere by eschewing academic sobriety in favour of long-winded, ingratiatory, often saucy inventories of contraband information. When in 1969 he recalled Freyre's impact on his teenage generation of the mid-1930s, Antonio Candido suspended his later political misgivings to recapture the non-conformist intent that infused 'the uninhibited composition of *Casa-Grande e Senzala* with its candor in treating the sex life of patriarchalism and the decisive importance ascribed to the slave in forming our most intimate mode of being'. Future generations, he imagined, might not understand 'the revolutionary force, the liberating shock of this great book'.[107]

Later on as a 'participant observer' Cândido defined concisely the two poles between which Freyre's reputation has swung ever since. As a young professor and critic in the early 1940s he gave an interview that confessed distaste for the cultural sociology practiced by 'our master', whose recent works had fallen 'into the most lamentable social and cultural sentimentalism, into conservatism and traditionalism'.[108] This prescient critique took fifteen or more years to be widely endorsed, although Cândido himself was never perplexed in reconciling the 'liberating' with the 'patriarchal' Gilberto, while his nuanced appreciation of Gilberto's work goes well beyond these two succinct opinions. Now that Gilberto has departed, leaving a still-charismatic oeuvre, it remains to sift political considerations, which (justifiably) irritated many contemporaries, from qualities that account for his esprit and power to captivate and for the predictable longevity of his major works. The enigma lies in Freyre's fascination with antagonisms and transformations that yield no solidary historical pattern. The *saudosismo* (nostalgia, longing) he is accused of may not be mere longing for a past beyond retrieval, but also recognition that the past was not, within its cultural tradition, what it might have been. Otherwise it would not have suffered the entropy he describes. Freyre saw the evil of colonial Brazil – flogging, mutilation, tyranny – conveying it with more force than he did

---

[106] Gilberto Freyre, *New World in the Tropics* (New York, 1963), p. 7. In a lively post-modern essay Vasconcelos urges that Freyre's readers rise above criticism polarized in the purely ethical terms of 'well written perverse sociology' versus 'badly written subversive sociology'. Gilberto Felisberto Vasconcelos, *O xará de Apipucos* (São Paulo, 1987).

[107] Cândido, *Teresina etc.*, p. 136.

[108] Mário Neme (ed.), *Plataforma da nova geração* (Porto Alegre, 1945), p. 39.

the putative good. Yet while he calmly documents the planter's wife serving her husband the gouged eyeballs of his *mulata* mistress in a dessert dish of blood, he elsewhere claims that Brazil's secret for building a humane, Christian civilization had been a genius for compromise. For him the Brazilian monarchical example corrected excesses of the patriarchal plantation tradition.[109]

In *The Waning of the Middle Ages* Huizinga had set himself precisely Freyre's problem of a culture that was drifting without guideposts toward modernity, in his case northeast Europe in the early Renaissance where the chivalric code still prevailed.[110] Modern scholars, wrote Huizinga, fix on new forms of political and economic life that emerged in the fifteenth century. Chroniclers of the time, however, had focused on superannuated feudal habits with their 'heroic rules'. Huizinga was more concerned with this inertial mind-set than with the Renaissance awakening. The contemporary actors, he felt, were drawn to a 'symbolistic attitude' rather than to a causal or genetic one. He wrote of course about a European society 500 years before his own and, as a Dutchman, knew what was to happen. Freyre described a society bearing pre-modern traits that was not five centuries behind him but only two. Like Huizinga he was a historian, but vicariously an actor as well. Neither he nor his society had completed the transition from the symbolist to the causal attitude. He proudly confessed having used symbolic figures such as the plantation boy or the upwardly mobile law student.[111] The third book of his main trilogy finishes by mythicizing past, present and future. 'The period recalled in this essay', he wrote, speaking of the 1860s–1910s, 'represented in Brazil the supersession of the myth of the King by the myth of a Republic founded on an abstractly Positivist motto: Order and Progress.'[112]

If Gilberto Freyre suggests one of Huizinga's medieval chroniclers, his contemporary, Sérgio Buarque de Holanda (1902–82), takes the path of Huizinga himself. Both pursue the secret of Brazil, but Gilberto evokes its image while Sérgio inserts the nation into Western historical process and prescribes for its extrication from traditional politics. One, in an American spirit of anthropological pluralism, celebrates Brazilian patriarchal culture; the other uses his European training to explore the tension be-

---

[109] Freyre, *New World,* p. 205.

[110] Johan Huizinga, *The Waning of the Middle Ages* (Garden City, N.Y., 1954), chs 3, 4, 15.

[111] Freyre, *Como e porque,* pp. 68–9.

[112] Gilberto Freyre, *Order and Progress: Brazil from Monarchy to Republic,* trans. Rod W. Horton (Berkeley, 1986), p. 405.

tween patriarchalism and the encroachment of Western liberalism. In the categories of art historian Heinrich Wölfflin, Freyre's was a baroque or painterly mentality that explored variations on a central theme while Sérgio Buarque followed a classical or linear search for tectonic strength.

Sérgio's interest in history was kindled in secondary school by his prolific mentor Afonso d'E. Taunay. Yet his early inclinations were more cultural than historiographical. In São Paulo and after 1921 in Rio he joined the modernists' iconoclastic rediscovery of Brazil. He plunged into literature and journalism with only perfunctory attention to his law studies. In 1929 he went to Germany for *O Jornal* of Rio where he interviewed writers, including Mann, and composed Portuguese subtitles for *The Blue Angel* and other films. Rio had prepared him well for what he called the 'worldly bohemian euphoria' of late Weimar.[113] Now, however, he was ready to absorb history and sociology from Meinecke (whose lectures he attended), Kantorowicz, Sombart and particularly the example of the departed Weber. As it did for Mariátegui in Italy a few years earlier, the European sojourn orientated his life work. He came home in 1931 with a 400-page manuscript bearing the alternative titles 'Teoria da América' and 'Corpo e alma do Brasil' that would yield two chapters for his seminal *Raízes do Brasil* (1936). Evincing a shift in priorities from literature to history, *Raízes* was the cornerstone for his career as a historian.[114] In *Os monções* (1945) and *Caminhos e fronteiras* (1957) he counterpoises the image of penurious, expansionist, *mameluco* Brazil to that of Freyre's coastal, seigneurial society. His magisterial *Visão do paraíso* (1959) examines the 'baroque' mind-set of Portuguese explorers and settlers subtly contrasting it with the Spaniards. His introduction to the *Obras* of Azeredo Coutinho (1966) reviews economic antecedents to Brazilian independence. As editor of the first seven volumes of the *História geral da civilização brasileira* (1960–72) he assembled a composite history of Brazil from Iberian and Amerindian origins to the advent of the Republic, writing Volume 7 on the late Empire himself. Because *Raízes* so concisely set out theoretical

---

[113] Francisco de Assis Barbosa collected Sérgio Buarque's European dispatches of 1929–30 in *Raízes de Sérgio Buarque de Holanda* (Rio de Janeiro, 1989); see also Assis Barbosa's 'Formación de Sérgio Buarque de Holanda', prologue to the Spanish version of Sérgio's *Visão do paraíso*, trans. Estela dos Santos (Caracas, 1987).

[114] Buarque de Holanda, *Tentativas de mitologia* (São Paulo, 1979), pp. 29–30, and 'Corpo e alma do Brasil', *Espelho* (Rio de Janeiro), March 1935 (reprinted in *Revista do Brasil*, 3/6 (1987): 32–42). Sérgio's literary criticism of 1940–41 appears in *Cobra de vidro*, 2nd ed (1978) and his studies from the 1950s of colonial literature in Antônio Cândido (ed.), *Capítulos de literatura colonial* (São Paulo, 1991).

formulations that anticipate his future interests, it claims attention in what follows.[115]

Sérgio Buarque's *Raízes* like the books by Mariátegui and Price-Mars consists of seven essays. Although *Casa-Grande* had appeared three years earlier, Sérgio seldom refers to Freyre in his text. The first two chapters of *Raízes* actually fit with many of Gilberto's ideas, although 'influence' is difficult to attribute given the hefty manuscript that Sérgio brought from Germany in 1931. As for personal relations, Gilberto recalled in 1982 that he and Sérgio had been 'bohemian' comrades in Rio of the 1920s and that as editor of the classic José Olympio series of 'Brazilian Documents' his maiden introduction in 1936 to Volume 1, Sérgio's *Raízes,* praised the author's analytic skill, interpretive flair and glee in shedding intellectual light.[116] It may well be that the two budding intellectuals' search for Brazilian identity from afar, in the United States and Germany, led to certain triangulations.

A few reflections from *Raízes* may be cited that mesh with, though come to a finer point than, Gilberto's diffuse vignettes. Sérgio starts with hierarchy and social organization. In colonial Brazil both were nebulous. Hierarchy was imported not as a rigid principle but as a ceaseless calculus of privileges, which paradoxically made Iberians pioneers of the 'modern mentality'. Long before the advent of 'revolutionary ideas' they were sensitive to irrationality and social injustice. 'Everyone knows', writes Sérgio, 'that Portuguese nobility was never rigorous and impermeable.' Porous hierarchies went with a weak capacity for social organization. Solidarity grew from sentimental bonds, not from calculated interests, while routinized labour was unacceptable because it prized achievement external to the person of the worker. Brazilian life accented the affective and passionate at the expense of discipline, to which African slaves added a honied, insinuating tone. The *senzala* morality penetrated administration, the economy and religious belief. The very creation of the world seemed understood as an 'abandonment, a languishing (*languescimento*) of God'. Such traits were the opposite needed for a people on the path to political modernization. Lacking discipline and organization on one hand and the hallowed principle of feudal loyalty on the other, the only recourse was to

[115] Maria Odila Leite da Silva Dias presents an introduction to Sérgio's historiography with representative texts in *Sérgio Buarque de Holanda* (São Paulo, 1985). Assis Barbosa gathered evocations of his career, including texts by Sérgio, in a special number of *Revista do Brasil,* 3/6 (1987).

[116] Gilberto Freyre, 'Sérgio, mestre de mestres', *Folha de São Paulo,* 11 May 1982 (reprinted in *Revista do Brasil,* 3/6 (1987): 117).

sheer obedience as notably imposed by Jesuit schooling. 'Today,' wrote
Sérgio in 1936, 'simple obedience as a principle of discipline seems an
outworn, ineffective remedy and thence, inevitably, the constant instability of our social life.'

The chapter 'Trabalho e aventura' treats the Portuguese adoption of
'adventure' in preference to 'work'; yet, implicitly challenging Freyre's
long-term cultural determinism, Sérgio describes Englishmen of the early
modern period as being no less given than Iberians to indolence, prodigal-
ity, and the good life. It was the Dutch occupation of northeast Brazil that
revealed the historic rupture between Brazil and the 'new' North Atlantic.
Yet, Sérgio asks, could Dutch Protestants found a society on the dissolvent
principles they encountered? What they lacked in plasticity they had to
excess in entrepreneurial spirit, capacity for work and social cohesion. As
adventurers weary of persecutions, however, they sought impossible fortunes without striking roots in the land. The Portuguese achievement had
been to efface, wittingly or not, the distinction between themselves and
their new world. 'Their weakness was their strength.'

Sérgio's analysis is thus far roughly compatible with Gilberto's save
that he relies on political sociology in a broad European sense and Freyre
on anthropology in the condescending, atheoretical American one. The
former looks for exit from political tradition, the latter for celebration of
cultural tradition. They divide at the nineteenth century, where Gilberto's *Mansions and Shanties* traces vegetative change from patriarchalism
to semi-patriarchalism while Sérgio treats the mid-century as a missed
opportunity to liquidate the colonial heritage of servile labour and exploitation of the land. The 1850s, Sérgio shows, might have been a benchmark with the incursion of corporations, banks, telegraphs and railroads.
Yet two mentalities lingered, traditional versus rational, corporeal versus
abstract, parochial versus cosmopolitan. Patriarchalism formed an indi-
visible whole whose members were linked by sentiments and duties,
never by interests and ideas, whereas in political theory, Sérgio held, the
birth of the state requires suppressing the family order and producing
citizens responsible to public laws. Here he recalls Antigone representing
the family and Creon the abstract, impersonal polis, noting that in
Brazil Antigone was still alive and obstinate. 'New' elites, transplanted
from fazendas to cities, favoured 'intelligence' and 'talent' – love of sono-
rous phrases and ostentatious erudition – over the concerns of James
Madison (whom Sérgio cites from Charles A. Beard) who disparaged
moral and religious motives in favour of reconciling divergent economic

interests. The forced improvisation of an urban bourgeoisie meant that attitudes once peculiar to the rural patriciate now extended to all classes. Modernization gave fresh impetus, as it were, to patriarchal culture.[117]

To define the human substrate of Brazilian society Sérgio advanced his disputed notion of the 'cordial man'. By cordiality he meant neither the calculated leniency of patrons soothing their workers nor elaborate rituals of politeness (e.g., English or Japanese) that disguised or repressed private feelings. Brazilians, Sérgio felt, were averse to ritualism. Social life liberates the cordial man from rationalizing his world and from fearing to live with his own self. Cordiality, he argues, dictates preferences whereas democratic benevolence aims to balance off and neutralize egoisms. While the 'humanitarian' ideal of greatest welfare for the greatest number subordinates quality to quantity, cordiality loses force beyond a narrow circle and fails to cement extended forms of social organization. Nor is cordiality per se a source of good principles, for 'social crystallization' requires an innate normative element. Thus does Sérgio define Brazil's challenge of political organization.

Gilberto and Sérgio both started from a loosely defined premise of patriarchalism. For Freyre this was the subject of his trilogy, 'History of Patriarchal Society in Brazil', that demonstrates the extraordinary assimilative capacity of Brazilian society while tracing the decadence of its once-vigorous patriarchal substructure. Freyre's entropic treatment of social change was redeemed in part by his futuristic vision of 'messianic' cities such as Brasília and Goiânia (*cidades-esperança*); or his multi-ethnic image of modern Brazil (anticipating by decades the U.S. shift from the melting-pot myth to that of cultural pluralism, or from *e pluribus unum* to *ex uno plures*); or his 'tropicology' theory that shifts 'development' calculus from an industrial-non-industrial binomial to one that juxtaposes Western rationalism and tropical functionalism.[118] What Gilberto never managed was to visualize historical process that would connect his account of the past with his luminous hopes for the future.

If Gilberto was an imagist, Sérgio was an architect. While he too relished the savour of time and place, his forte was the X-ray that probes from historicism to history, from empathy to analysis. Thus in carrying Brazil's

---

[117] Sérgio's theory of elite 'intelligence' perhaps draws from the *medalhão* of Machado de Assis in 'Education of a Stuffed Shirt' (*The Psychiatrist and Other Stories* (Berkeley, 1963), pp. 113–22). For a later treatment of Sérgio's 'improvised' bourgeoisie, see Roberto Schwarz, *Ao vencedor as batatas* (São Paulo, 1977), especially his discussion (pp. 42–43) of the novelist José de Alencar and the 'fables that owe their symbolic force to a world wherein Brazil found no place'.

[118] For example, Freyre's *Brasis, Brasil, Brasília* (Lisbon, 1960).

story to the nineteenth century he stripped the obsolescent *casa-grande* image to the category of 'cordiality', subsuming patriarchalism to a general case of interpersonal relations.[119] Similarly with democratic liberalism, he did not linger over political niceties of the *Federalist* papers but went straight to Bentham for a statement of utilitarian individualism.[120] Instead of leaving him with a moribund culture that faced a modern one powerless to be born, this strategy allowed Sérgio a dialectic construction. His conclusion fits Spengler's notion of 'historical pseudomorphosis', designating cases where an old culture blankets the land so heavily that a young culture cannot achieve expressive form or even self-consciousness.[121] The young soul is cramped in former moulds; its feelings stifle in senile works and, lacking creativity, it can only hate the distant power. For Sérgio the old soul was embedded in the national psyche and the young one was an inevitable part of the immediate future. Rather than composing a linear transition, they were both by the nineteenth century fully present and engaged.

Sérgio's historiography was of a piece with his political commitment. In his closing essay of *Raízes* on 'Our Revolution', he neither forecast the tropical utopia of Freyre nor did he, in the cavalier manner of Paulo Prado, propose War or Revolution as solutions. As a historian he accepted processes at work. The options of fascism or domestic Integralism were dubious. He was attracted to features of Marxism but in the spirit of a Brazilian 'anarchist mentality', not of Muscovite discipline. Rapid urbanization was converting rural Brazil into colonies without the climate for industrial liberalism. At times, he ventured, political personalism might be more salutary that the declamatory slogans of liberal democracy. On the other hand, *casa-grande* patriarchalism was evaporating to leave behind the culture of *cordialismo* as possible articulation between natural sentiment and dogmatic liberalism. Sérgio refused to discount the positive example of Brazil's second empire (1840–89) wherein the mechanism of the state functioned 'with a certain harmony and stateliness (*garbo*)'. This nuanced analysis – true to history, open to possibility – did not inhibit decisive political commitment. He formally protested against the Vargas dictatorship (1945); was a founder of Esquerda Democrática, soon the Partido Socialista Brasileira (1946); resigned his professorship at the University of

---

[119] For the 'modernization' of cordiality, see Roberto DaMatta, *A casa e a rua* (São Paulo, 1985), pp. 55–80, and *Carnivals, Rogues, and Heroes*, ch. 4.
[120] For the persistent blockage of liberalism in Brazil, see Wanderley G. dos Santos, 'Liberalism in Brazil: Ideology and Praxis', in M. J. Blachmann and R. G. Hellman (eds.), *Terms of Conflict: Ideology in Latin American Politics* (Philadelphia, Pa., 1977), pp. 1–38.
[121] Oswald Spengler, *The Decline of the West*, 2 vols. (New York, 1939), Vol. 2, ch. 7.

São Paulo to protest against the military government's dismissal of faculty members (1969); was a founder of the Centro Brasileiro Democrático (1978) and at the end of his life the Partido dos Trabalhadores (1980). Rarely are creative intellect and coherent political stance so securely matched.

Lezama Lima: History as image

Although of the essayists so far discussed only three were primarily literary figures, all were attuned to literature and expressive arts, and all were adept with metaphor and analogy. At the same time the group were versed in or conversant with history, philosophy, social thought and theory, and even social science, the literati no less than the others. Far from being 'impressionists' they were deeply informed eclectics, aware of pitfalls in exploring terrain that was vaguely or unwarrantably mapped and of the idées reçues of presumptive readers schooled under the sign of positivism. Cognizant of history, they tried to balance the lessons of vanguardism in the arts against new European cues for the study of society. But neither arts nor sciences were yet institutionalized or commodified in Latin America. The intellectual enjoyed a private pasture. For the three writers first examined, the balance of their enquiries tipped toward the challenge of explaining history, not rendering it, and therefore toward the problem of causality, not reconstruction through images. For the next six the scales were closer to equilibrium. And for the one to be considered now the balance tipped sharply toward an imagistic strategy.

In 1957 the Cuban poet, novelist and essayist José Lezama Lima (1910–76) gave five lectures in Havana, published as *La expresión americana,* in which he suspended the search for causes so as to convey more directly the historic meanings of hemispheric America.[122] Lezama had founded several influential literary reviews; he was an established poet who wrote with hermetic density, reviving without replicating the Spanish baroque; and he was germinating his masterpiece *Paradiso* (1966; Eng. trans. 1974) where in the words of Mario Vargas Llosa, 'the history of humanity and of traditional European culture appears summarized, deformed into caricature, but at the same time poetically enriched and assimilated within a

---

[122] The edition used here is that of 1969 published in Santiago, Chile. The only critical edition, however, is the Portuguese translation by Irlemar Chiampi (*A expressão americana,* São Paulo, 1988), which contains a valuable introduction and notes that are freely utilized here.

great American narrative'.[123] Lezama's literary genius was complemented by a vast repertoire of history, metaphysics and esoterica, always subordinate, however, to the expressive purpose of his account. *La expresión americana* appeared in 1957 at the critical threshold of Latin America's (misnamed) literary boom and its (precipitate) social science boom. A fork in the path, reconciled or glossed over by previous essayists, was coming into evidence. Instinctively, Lezama made his choice for imagistic (though not impressionistic) historiography.

With this said, the starting point is not the philosophic reach of Lezama's miniature New World symphony but, as Julio Cortázar wrote in a luminous chapter on Lezama, his innocence, an American innocence, insular in both literal and extended senses.[124] Lezama was integrally Cuban. He found foreign names to be unspellable, while his foreign quotations were 'orthographic fantasies'. Argentine intellectuals thought he lacked formal correctness as did Cuban sophisticates with their deodorant style. Between Lezama and a Europeanized writer, Cortázar continues, lies 'the difference between innocence and guilt'. The latter carries a frightening tradition as a succubus. 'Why write, if everything has, in a way, already been said?' If a new slice of the invisible appears – symbolism, surrealism, or the *nouveau roman* – Europeans put aside their guilt for a moment. But slowly they feel European again and each writer retains the albatross around his neck. Meanwhile, Cortázar continues, 'Lezama wakes up on his island with a pre-adamite happiness, without a fig leaf, innocent of any direct tradition. He assumes them all, from the Etruscan interpreting entrails to Leopold Bloom blowing his nose in a dirty handkerchief, but without historical compromise . . . ; he is a Cuban with only a handful of his own culture behind him and the rest is knowledge, pure and free, not a career responsibility.'

Because of his agile command of European ideas one might be tempted to call Lezama derivative. But that would explode his whole notion of what America is about and cancel his innocence. From intimate experience Lezama knew what he wanted when, at the start of *La expresión americana,* he avoided the search for causality to accept the contrapuntal historical vision offered 'by the *imago,* by the image participating in history'. Then

---

[123] Cited in D. W. and V. R. Foster (eds.), *Modern Latin American Literature*, 2 vols. (New York, 1975) 1, 479.

[124] Julio Cortázar, *Around the Day in Eighty Worlds* (San Francisco, 1986), pp. 82–108. The English edition reproduces the selection of the French edition (1980) which in turn draws from texts published in *La vuelta del día en ochenta mundos* and *Ultimo round* (Mexico, D.F. and Madrid, 1967 and 1969).

came the choice of how to identify his images or myths. One guide might have been T. S. Eliot, save that he was neo-classic *à outrance,* unconcerned with new myths as a pessimistic critic of what he took to be a crepuscular era. An alternative was the German literary critic E. R. Curtius, who surmised that old myths must all be reinvented (if indeed they deserved it) to offer their enigmas in a new guise. Lezama chose the latter as the European who liberated him. 'If a culture cannot create an imaginative form . . .', he wrote, 'when it suffers the quantitative burden of the millennia it will be grossly indecipherable.'

This leads Lezama in his opening chapter 'Myths and Classic Fatigue' to a distinction between two forms of recall: recollection and memory. Recollection is a product of the spirit while memory is plasma of the soul, ever creative and spermatic; with it we *memorize* from the roots of the species. 'Even the plant harbours the memory that allows it to acquire its plenitude of form.' Citing Ludwig Klages he recalls that the year of Goethe's death (1832), whose last words were 'More light!', was the year the phosphorous match was invented. 'It is difficult,' wrote Lezama, 'to disregard the wee chronological tribute of the discovery of the match. Not in vain did Germans consider routines of memorization [e.g., of dates] as forms of *Witz,* of ingenuity.' Faulty memory accounts, he felt, for the terrible American complex involving belief that expression is not an immanent form but a problématique to be resolved, forgetting that the plasma of his own autochthony fills a space equal to Europe's.

Having set the terms for his evocations, Lezama moves toward three historic phases of American expression: 'baroque curiosity', 'romanticism and the fact of America', and 'birth of creole expression'. These were conceived in historical sequence for ease of exposition, with 'history' making them interactive. Drawing on scholars of the baroque, Lezama defined American baroque as 'counter-conquest' rather than 'counter-Reformation'.[125] Its three components were internal *tension, plutonism* (an original fire that breaks fragments to recompose them), and a plenary, not degenerative, style that acquires new tongues, furnishings, forms of life and curiosity, a mysticism in new modes of prayer, and taste in food that all give off a way of life, refined and mysterious, theocratic and self-

---

[125] For the twentieth-century revival and 'modernization' of the 'American' baroque see: José Lezama Lima, *Esferaimagen / Sierpe de Don Luis de Góngora / Las imágenes posibles* (Barcelona, 1970); Haroldo de Campos, *O sequestro do barroco na formação da literatura brasileira* (Salvador, Bahia, 1989) and 'Lezama e a plenitud pelo excesso', *O Estado de São Paulo,* Caderno 2, 10 July 1988; Severo Sarduy, *Nueva instabilidad* (Mexico, D.F., 1987); Alejo Carpentier, *Concierto barroco* (Havana, 1987).

absorbed, vagrant yet entrenched in essences. American baroque was not frustrated or doctrinaire or self-censored but an outlook of the late seventeenth and eighteenth centuries that became 'a firm friend of the Enlightenment', even drawing on antecedent Cartesianism. Lezama adduces two eighteenth-century artists of popular origin as examples of the vitality and metamorphoses of baroque: First is the Indian or mestizo José Kondori from the Peruvian lowlands and purported sculptor of the genial portal of San Lorenzo church (1728–44) in Potosí. Lezama takes his art to represent a Hispano-Indian synthesis in 'an occult and hieratic form' that betokens a 'pact of equality'. Second is the Brazilian sculptor Aleijadinho (Antônio Francisco Lisboa, 1738–1814) whose art culminates 'the American baroque, uniting in grandiose form the union of Hispanic and African cultures'.

For his central figure Lezama calls up Sor Juana Inés de la Cruz (1651–95), who turned her baroque vision toward a quest for universal science that approximates the Enlightenment. She was the first American poet, he believed, to achieve primacy in the Hispanophone world, and even though she apologized that her remarkable poem 'First Dream' imitated the *culteranista* Spanish poet Góngora, Lezama calls this 'a charming act of humility more than a literary truth'. Octavio Paz, whose biography of Sor Juana appeared a quarter century after Lezama's essay, concurs in his praise of 'First Dream' but is less euphoric about the baroque, particularly if seen as a wellspring of American culture. He feels that its 'plethoric and inflated forms . . . faded at their frenetic peak, attracted by the void. The baroque festival is an *ars moriendi.*' Sor Juana's ideal of multi-faceted yet connected knowledge, Paz argues, was unattainable in New Spain, where she was unaware of the intellectual revolution that was transforming Europe. Even so, her baroque poem negates the baroque and 'prefigures the most modern modernity'.[126] Here the two interpretations join. Whether by her intuition of the vitalities of her immediate culture (Lezama) or by her prophetic sense of how to leap beyond the constrictions that bound her (Paz), both poets acclaim Sor Juana as a 'modern' poet who anticipated Rilke, Valéry, Gorostiza, and, Paz insists, Mallarmé.

Because his essays are not a textbook Lezama jumps from baroque to romanticism, omitting the Enlightenment and classicism. The obvious messages of liberalism, rationalism, guided education, empiricism, anti-

[126] Octavio Paz, *Sor Juana or, The Traps of Faith,* trans. Margaret Sayers Peden (Cambridge, 1988), pp. 147, 381, 419; 'First Dream' in *A Sor Juana Anthology,* trans. Alan S. Trueblood (Cambridge, Eng., 1988), pp. 166–95.

mysticism, and 'development' did not concern him. These would all float into the Latin American ideological *ajiaco* and receive lip service and intermittent acquiescence from those in power. What concerned Lezama was the Americanization of a culture that New World baroque foreshadowed. This would necessarily happen in the nineteenth century with romanticism as the mainspring but not the romanticism of literati, nor even the romantic figure of Bolívar, who 'is marginalized once he draws near the promised land and pulls back at naming a reality'. Lezama's romantics were not in the mould of Napoleon or Rousseau or Victor Hugo. He resolved to see the era as decisively formative yet represented by heroes whose lives were decisive failures, and not as with Bolívar contingent ones. He needed to encapsulate history as lived out and of course found romanticism suffused with tensions between individual and society, private vision and academic 'reality', the beauty of forests and ugliness of trains that invade them. Lezama wished to capture the grand romantic tradition of 'the dungeon, of absence, of the image, and of death'. From this he points to an American reality 'whose destiny is composed more of possible absences than of impossible presences', a tradition wherein lay 'the achieved historical fact' with José Martí as its grand master.

For the romantic moment Lezama selected three figures: Fray Servando Teresa de Mier, Simón Rodríguez, and Francisco de Miranda, all of them 'romantic by frustration', all of them embittered and one killed by the events of national independence and all of them actors on the vast transatlantic stage. Fray Servando embellished the American political tradition with: the conjecture that the Virgin of Guadalupe appeared not on the cape of the humble Indian Juan Diego but on that of Quetzalcóatl who was in fact the apostle St Thomas; a sweeping condemnation of the achievement in America of a backward and ignorant Spain; an assertion that the Laws of the Indies contained a Magna Carta for governance in the Americas; his shift from the English to the U.S. political model but always envisioning a constitution derived from norms of behaviour and not doctrinal law. Fray Servando's travels and exiles (to Spain, France, Italy, Portugal, England and the United States) and his detentions, imprisonments, and escapes resist enumeration. So fantastic were his perambulations that a parodic novelist was needed to catch the flavour of his life. In *El mundo alucinante* (1969) the Cuban writer Reinaldo Arenas alleged that between prison terms Fray Servando met Simón Rodríguez, Bolívar, Napoleon, Humboldt, Lady Hamilton, Chateaubriand and Madame de Staël;

that he escaped prison off the Veracruz coast by gnawing open his iron chains; that he reported seeing twenty-nine carloads of black people fed into a train furnace in the United States (a country where every breath of air was taxed) as they were 'the closest thing to coal'. At the end Fray Servando's portrait of Mexican president Guadalupe Victoria becomes entangled in a vignette of Fidel Castro.[127]

Lezama likens Fray Servando to Fabrice del Dongo in Stendhal's *The Charterhouse of Parma* who was forever in headlong flight during the Napoleonic wars. But the comparison goes deeper. Lezama makes much of *paisaje* (landscape) as space wherein a new destiny unfolds and a native romantic spirit takes root in American soil. Stendhal too, Brombert tells us, gave landscapes a prime role as concrete figurations of his lyricism, notably at the unique site of the Dongo castle with its sublime lake and rolling hills: not a picture-book setting but transfigured into 'a world of revery and energy'. As fugitives both heroes needed space to secure freedom and vision for enriching themselves and reconstructing their world. Persecution thus brings liberation.[128] The Mexican baroque world had deteriorated so slowly, writes Lezama, that few were aware of it. 'Fray Servando is the first who decides to be persecuted, for he has sensed that another emerging landscape is seeking him out, one that no longer relies on the great arch that united Hispanic baroque and its enrichment in American baroque.' The new one intuits the opulence of a new destiny, an image or island, arising from portolanos of the unknown to foster the freedoms of the native landscape, now liberated from dialogue with a ghost. In Fray Servando's transition from baroque to romanticism Lezama finds occult American surprises. 'He thinks he breaks with tradition when he in fact exalts it. Thus when he believes he has departed from what is Hispanic he rediscovers it within himself, now enhanced. To reform within the old order, not breaking but retaking the thread, is what is Hispanic.'

Lezama's second paragon is Simón Rodríguez (1771–1854) – not, significantly, Bolívar, but his tutor. Bolívar called Rodríguez his 'only universal teacher', who shaped him toward 'freedom, justice, the great and the

[127] Edmundo O'Gorman's prologue and chronology in *Fray Servando Teresa de Mier* (Mexico, D.F., 1945), pp. vii–lix; Seymour Menton, *Prose Fiction of the Cuban Revolution* (Austin, Tex., 1975), pp. 100–4.

[128] The Stendhalian prison restores heroes to their own selves, or allows them to discover and even create them. 'The prison thus assumes a protective and dynamic role. It liberates one from the captivity of social existence.' See Victor Brombert, *Stendhal: Fiction and the Themes of Freedom* (Chicago, Ill., 1976), pp. 152, 173.

beautiful'. Lezama attributed the influence of Rodríguez on Bolívar not to historical accident but to what both shared of a 'demonic and primigenial' spirit. Rodríguez's era may have led him to a disguised Rousseauan notion of pedagogy, 'but his virus was essentially Socratic' and carried him from the daimon of idea or logic to the passionate Eros of understanding. He contained something of the pedagogic Aleijadinho, being 'ugly, excessive and itinerant'; something of Swedenborg without his prophecies and theocracy; and something of Blake without his lyricism. He spent his old age wandering in poverty amid the Andes founding schools, opening shops for gunpowder, candles, or groceries, but never rediscovering his one great dialogue with the adolescent Bolívar. At the end he admitted: 'I, who wanted to make of the world a paradise for all, have made it a hell for myself.'

Of Lezama's three subjects he calls Francisco de Miranda (1750–1816) the first great American who constructed in Europe and the United States a frame appropriate to his life work. Yet his reversals of fortune, and his eventual demise indirectly caused by Bolívar, accorded him the destiny of Fray Servando in his dungeon and 'the fatal flight of Simón Rodríguez to the centre of the earth toward the lakes of protohistory'. Miranda's case was complex, for he became a friend of Washington and Hamilton, moved as a performer across the Europe of the French Revolution, of Pitt and Catherine the Great, and whom in 1795 the young Napoleon called 'a Don Quixote excepting that he is not crazy. That man has a sacred fire in his soul.' Then came the encounter with the young Bolívar, who 'attached his name to the first great calamity of Venezuelan independence'. More facile with pen than with sword, Miranda remained what he had always been, a plotter and conspirator rather than a man of action. 'Ruckus (*bochinche*), ruckus!' he exclaimed on his arrest by Bolívar, 'These people can only raise a ruckus.' Wherewith he departed for his final imprisonment. Like the others of Lezama's romantic trio, his ambitions exceeded his gifts – which is why Lezama found them exemplary.

Following his private version of the romantic moment Lezama addresses the birth of creole expression. Having written of illustrious prisoners, brave exiles, fugitive misanthropes and untamable heroes, he counterposes a submerged current that raises verbal altars for fresh lustre and smashes the gloomy mansion of the metropolis. Here he introduces another trio composed of Martí, Rubén Darío and César Vallejo, who plunge verbal shafts into the detritus of inefficacy and dead lexicon. These true Americans compose their words to acknowledge the new *paisaje* and its need for expression in vivid molecules (*corpúsculos coloreados*). 'Every American contains always a quiet Gongorism that explodes his discourse, yet in comfort, not tragically like the Spaniard.' From the literary stars Lezama turns to the people, whose role as architects of America was finding recognition. For the birth of America 'the stoicism of Quevedo and the scintillation of Góngora find popular roots. They engender a creole culture of superb resistance in ethical matters and a keen sense for language and for discriminating the sources of independence.'

The anonymous *corrido* now becomes an exemplary expression of creole culture. Whereas the European *romance* celebrated Carolingian or Mozarabic historical feats, the informal *corrido* of America limits itself, as in Mexico, to the defence of the city plaza, the shadow of execution, and most notably the broadsides and the tears of love in the provinces, or, as in Argentina, reaches a plenitude of tenderness in the maternal image of the ombu tree on the boundless pampas. Goya had symbolized weapons as a theology wherein defeat was accompanied by clouts of a sulfurous broom. To combat that tragicomic world in collapse, he reached beyond his prancing genius toward the rays of Enlightenment. The Mexican engraver, who always accompanies the *corrido,* has no theological world but only the dictates of circumstance. If he should say, with Paul Valéry, that events had no interest for him, he would be lost. In America the reaction to degenerescence was offset by a new *paisaje* that resisted concentration on death. José Guadalupe Posada converts uproar and bare facts into a skeleton that smiles. Finally, Lezama pays his delicate tribute to Martí, whose *versos sencillos* acquired tenderness in the *corrido*'s designs and spirals that intervened between *copla* and *romance*.

Lezama's final chapter unites his argument in his own allusive way. He starts off concerned less with American expression than with expression *per se*. Modernism, he says, begins with attention to 'something else': *faire autre chose, faire le contraire.* But after a decade the links to the past emerge. For Joyce, neo-Thomism was not late scholasticism but it revealed a creative medieval world. Stravinsky's voyage via Rimsky-Korsakov, ragtime and jazz back to Pergolesi was not a neo-classical discovery but a thread of tradition leading to the secret of music. The grand exceptions were Leonardo and Goethe, who are lessons for our age in requiring 'swift and intuitive knowledge of past styles, countenances of what remained creative after so many shipwrecks, and adequate placement in contemporary polemics'. Then came their successor, Picasso: 'No painter taught so many occult things, revived so many styles, projected on dead eras so many possibilities of re-encounters and beginnings.'

As Chiampi summarizes Lezama's 'parabolic' argument inspired by Picasso, 'the wealth of a culture depends on its capacity to assimilate, synthesize and renovate potential forms of other cultures. The American "summa", conceived via the paradigmatic modernity of Picasso, now requires, with the example of the Greeks facing the Egyptians and Persians, critical vision and precaution for selectivity in starting to incorporate influences.' This leads to Lezama's emphatic anti-Hegelian argument attacking the European view that nature is reducible to man, omitting *paisaje*. Accepting Schelling's dictum that 'nature is the visible spirit and the spirit is invisible nature', Lezama assumes that the 'spirit that reveals nature and man is *paisaje*'. He continues with vignettes from his earlier text of Havana Bay, the Andean baroque of Cuzco, the pampa of *Martín Fierro* (*paisaje* or nature?, he queries), and the line connecting Miranda's dungeon to Martí's death scene. All are forms of *paisaje* where the struggle of nature and man creates a cultural *paisaje* as man triumphs over nature. Thus Sor Juana's dream is night over the valley of Mexico when sleep converts scholastic dialectic into clues to secrets of *paisaje*. Lezama adds some reflections on three North Americans – Melville, Whitman and Gershwin – who each in his own way won emancipation from Hegelian historicism, thus placing Anglo America squarely into his hemispheric argument.

From what precedes Lezama extracts his idea of 'gnostic space', a space of and for knowledge. The notion is rooted in post-Kantian Romantic idealism, interpreted by Lezama as a challenge to Hegel's lectures on *The Philosophy of History* and Ortega's commentary thereon. The question is whether space passively awaits insemination by a world-historical Idea or Spirit without collaboration or whether it contributes to the intrusion of the Spirit. In Lezama's answer: 'In the American influence what predominates is what I dare to call open, gnostic space, where insertion of the invading spirit is recognized by immediate visual comprehension. The frozen forms of European baroque and every explicit manifestation of a damaged body dissolve in America in that gnostic space identified by its own breadth of *paisaje*, its surplus of gifts.' He continues: 'Why could the western spirit not penetrate Asia and Africa but did so totally in America? Because that gnostic space was awaiting a form of vegetative fecundation . . . the blessing of a temperature adequate to receive the generative particles.' What Lezama rejected in Hegel were his pronouncements that: 'Nature, as contrasted with Spirit, is a quantitative mass, whose power must not be so great as to make its single force omnipotent.' Or that, 'North America will be comparable with Europe only after the immeasurable space which that country presents to its inhabitants shall have been occupied, and the members of the political body shall have begun to be pressed back on each other.'[129] For Lezama the critical pressure was not between the spirit and nature or among communities of an imported civilization, but between people and nature to produce *paisajes*.

IDENTITY IN THE SHADOW OF PHILOSOPHY

In the 1940s and early 1950s the Latin American *prise de conscience* of the twentieth century leads to the realm of philosophy. For the historian this yields the opportunity not simply to pursue his usual assignment of relating cultural expression to large trends and events but also to ask how expressive crafts or academic disciplines come, by internal maturation, to artistic or intellectual control. With this last question in mind the Peruvian philosopher Francisco Miró Quesada traces the origins and fruition of the Latin American 'philosophizing project'.[130] He does so, not unmindful of historical context, but without giving primary focus to the political enthusiasms or class 'bias' of his subjects. His concern is not with philosophy as justificatory *response to* circumstance but with how, in Whitehead's sense, philosophy gained in precision for generalization as it became *immersed in* circumstance. He shows the intellectual quest for 'reality' or 'identity' to be not merely a matter of will-power or chance illumination but a technical enterprise as well.

The professionalization of philosophy in Latin America preceded that of the social sciences, which got fully under way only in the 1960s. Ironically, colonial Spanish America had produced reputable philosophers who sometimes attained metropolitan standards. The neo-scholasticism of the universities was an Iberian transplant; it began to yield to Enlightenment influences after 1760 and was discredited after independence. Overnight Latin America shifted from colonial status within the Ibero-Atlantic world, where its thinkers shared intellectual premises, to neo-colonial status in the modern Western world where they were to adapt maxims and methods derived from quite different understandings. This produced what Miró Quesada calls a *vivencia del desenfoque,* or 'bifocal coexistence'. The Ibero-Atlantic world, that is, had not internalized the Western 'revolution of values' that Louis Dumont, stressing its British version, traces from

---

[129] G. W. F. Hegel, *Lectures on the Philosophy of History,* trans. J. Sibree (London, 1894), pp. 84, 90.
[130] Francisco Miró Quesada, *Despertar y proyecto del filosofar latinoamericano* (Mexico D.F., 1974) and *Proyecto y realización del filosofar latinoamericano* (Mexico, D.F., 1981).

Mandeville to Adam Smith, or from Locke to Bentham.[131] When Latin Americans finally tried to join this 'revolution', its philosophic origins in the great religious and scientific revolutions had become veiled. By the early nineteenth century, Anglo-French definitions of individual, state and nation, of freedom, democracy and economic principles, of science, rationality and empirical demonstration were serenely argued without reference to the turbulent social and ideological contexts from which they had arisen. A new universalism had replaced that of the Roman Catholic Church. But unlike the Catholic order, the 'Enlightened' one failed to transplant its philosophic assumptions, insofar as these were culturally and historically rooted, to new host countries.

As we turn toward Latin America's philosophic renaissance in the 1940s, this background helps to keep three considerations in mind. First, when we recall the importance of philosophy as the foundation for ideology in Europe, we may assume that philosophic speculation would come to the fore in Latin America once it was recognized that here ideology was to answer conditions that were *sui generis*. Secondly, the scarcity of informed, systematic philosophic thought in Latin America for a century after independence is only partly attributable to the inadequacy or narrow professionalism of its institutions of higher learning. More importantly, it reflected the *pensador*'s inability to philosophize without clear, self-consistent knowledge of his society and without having recovered the logic of European philosophic thought since its Greek origins. That is, he could not simply 'join in' the flowing current of contemporary European philosophy. What would ultimately be required was, in Miró Quesada's term, an 'anabatic recovery' (*recuperación anabásica*) of that philosophy, a heroic upstream campaign or anabasis, to its sources. Thirdly, even though Latin American adaptations of European thought, notably positivism, might serve the purposes of dominant groups, one cannot conclude that intellectual activity was a reflex response to class interest. Whatever the political sympathies of a Latin American positivist or *científico*, the imported discourse of political or moral philosophy did not effectively serve domestic purposes of diagnosis and therapy. The multiple formulations in the 1970s of what is significantly called 'liberation philosophy' has required not so much a softening of the heart – the human heart is always a bit obdurate – as rigorous domestication of the philosophic enterprise and a less blinkered vision of the social facts of the case.

[131] Louis Dumont, *From Mandeville to Marx* (Chicago, Ill., 1977).

Miró Quesada gauges the renaissance of philosophy in Latin America by the contributions of three generations: the patriarchs, the shapers (*forjadores*), and a third wave of technically equipped thinkers who inherit a ready-made 'philosophical project'. To these a fourth generation that matured in the 1940s can be added; it has moved from what Francisco Romero called a 'normal' situation where academic conditions were in place for true philosophizing to a 'natural' one where both the activity and the conditions for pursuing it could be routinely assumed.

Save for Alejandro Deústua (Peru, 1849–1945) and Enrique José Varona (Cuba, 1849–1933), the patriarchs were born between 1860 and 1883: José Vasconcelos (Mexico, 1882–1959), Antonio Caso (Mexico, 1883–1948), Alejandro Korn (Argentina, 1860–1936), Carlos Vaz Ferreira (Uruguay, 1872–1958), Enrique Molina (Chile, 1871–1964) and Raimundo de Farias Brito (Brazil, 1862–1917). This generation initiated the 'anabatic recovery' of the Western tradition, although their notions of how philosophy might be acclimated to the American scene were vague or, as with Vasconcelos, more declaratory than analytic. Miró Quesada ascribes two qualities to the patriarchs: first, they were enamoured of Western ideas to the extent that they might accept the Bergsonian critique of positivism without understanding Bergson's reasoning; second, they were necessarily confined to spontaneous and isolated expressions of the philosophic enterprise.

While these features may loosely characterize the generation as a whole, they lose force when applied to leaders. As early as 1908, for example, Vaz Ferreira made a searching critique of William James' pragmatism in a series of six lectures.[132] And while he never brought his thought into a coherent 'system', his richly aphoristic *Fermentario* (1938) is a self-secure reconnaissance of many realms – society and psychology, science and metaphysics, religion and immortality – that holds the analytic, the speculative and the confessional in careful balance to place him, Alejandro Arias has said, in the tradition of Marcus Aurelius, Nietzsche and Unamuno. Of all Latin American thinkers, writes Francisco Larroyo, 'perhaps Vaz Ferreira has attained *l'esprit de finesse* in highest measure'.[133] Vasconcelos was quite different. In book-length treatises he dashed off a metaphysics

---

[132] Carlos Vaz Ferreira, *El pragmatismo, exposición y crítica* (Montevideo, 1909). In Chile, Enrique Molina produced a simultaneous critique of James; see Solomon Lipp, *Three Chilean Thinkers* (Waterloo, Ont., 1975), p. 107.

[133] Alejandro C. Arias, *Vaz Ferreira* (Mexico D.F., 1948); Francisco Larroyo, *La filosofía iberomericana*, 2nd ed. (Mexico, D.F., 1978), p. 124.

(1929), an ethics (1932), an esthetics (1935) and an organic logic (1945). As early as 1918 he had laid the basis for his 'system' in *Monismo estético* (Esthetic Monism). His most famous book was *La raza cósmica* (*The Cosmic Race,* 1925) which predicted that a 'fifth race' would produce ethnic fusion of scientific, spiritual, and aesthetic capacities permitting civilization to reclaim the tropics as its land of promise. Four 'races' – black, Indian, Mongol and white – had thus far forged world history in isolation. Because the white race had resisted miscegenation while taming nature, it was left to Ibero-Americans, with all the 'defects' of their civilization, to provide the cradle for a fifth race. 'The inferior races', wrote Vasconcelos, 'would become less prolific with education, and the best specimens will keep ascending an ethnic scale whose ideal type is not precisely the white but the new race to which the white himself must aspire so as to dominate the synthesis.' Aesthetic mating of the 'black Apollo' with the 'blond Venus' rather than brutal struggle for survival, Vasconcelos claimed (ignoring Darwin's attention to sexual selection), would determine a eugenic outcome, preserving the gifts of mestizos, Indians, and 'even the Negro', who 'surpasses the white in an infinity of spiritual attitudes'.

If this summary suggests a latter-day *pensador* clumsily navigating from social Darwinism to Bergsonian idealism, it is only a fragment of the truth. Vasconcelos by no means merely accompanied European fashions. His vocation led toward contact with the divine through sensual passion. Yoga and theosophy captivated him. Nietzschean exaltation took him to Hinduism, Buddhism to Pythagoras. Plotinus became his lodestar. Without being bookish, as he accused the *ateneístas* of being, Vasconcelos still felt that encounter with books could be redemptive, not benign or critical books but revelatory or prophetic ones. As secretary of education in the early 1920s he distributed Homer, Plato, Dante, Cervantes, Goethe and a dozen more classics in tens of thousands of copies to Mexican schools. In his turbulent public life he sought to incarnate his own mystical ideal, not to project it intellectually. He called himself a Tolstoyan Christian; Krauze calls him a creole Plotinus.[134]

---

[134] Enrique Krauze, 'Pasión y contemplación de Vasconcelos', *Vuelta,* 78 (1983), 12–19 and 79 (1983), 16–26; see also John H. Haddox, *Vasconcelos of Mexico: Philosopher and Prophet* (Austin, Tex., 1967). For other patriarchs, see Jack Himelblau, *Alejandro O. Deústua: Philosophy in Defense of Man* (Gainesville, Fla., 1979); Medardo Vitier on Varona in *La filosofía en Cuba* (Mexico, D.F., 1948), ch. 11; Enrique Krauze, 'Antonio Caso: el filósofo como héroe', *Revista de la Universidad de México,* 39 (nueva época), 29 (1983), 2–10; Solomon Lipp on Korn in *Three Argentine Thinkers* (New York, 1969), ch. 3; Lipp on Molina in *Three Chilean Thinkers,* pp. 101–41; Sylvio Rabello, *Farias Brito, ou uma aventura do espírito,* 2nd ed. (Rio de Janeiro, 1967).

The transition from the patriarchs, who devised personal versions of the philosophic enterprise, to the shapers, who erected consciously American foundations for it, was orientated by trends of largely Germanic origin, particularly phenomenology and existentialism, often filtered via France or via Ortega y Gasset and the Spaniards. German thought might from the start have been a source of creative energy for Latin America when we recall that Germany was in a sense, as we have said, the world's first 'underdeveloped' country, that its intelligentsia rejected the brittle pansophism of the Enlightenment, and that German thought was, by the dawn of the nineteenth century, probing more deeply than French and English into nationhood, ethnicity, culture, religion and historical process.[135] Latin America, however, received only echoes of this tradition through the eclecticism of Cousin, the anti-positivism of Krausism that caught hold in Spain, the Hegelian precepts that appealed to Cubans for justifying self-rule, the 'Germanist' school of Recife and Sergipe in Brazil, or finally, by the century's end, retailed versions of revisionist Marxism.[136]

The reception of Spengler's *Decline of the West* (1918–22) signalized the Germanizing of Latin American thought. Proof of European 'decadence' was precisely what Latin Americans needed to break loose from intellectual mimicry and to explore what cultural assertion at the periphery might now involve. By treating Europe as a world culture in decline, Spengler legitimized newly emergent cultures. Yet while his historical pronouncements might illuminate discrete New World situations, such as the Argentina of Martínez Estrada or the Andean realm of Victor Raúl Haya de la Torre, they failed to yield foundations for comprehensive, self-consistent philosophy. These larger guideposts arrived in two stages. First came the neo-Kantian, idealist reaction to positivism of the Marburg school, which began in Germany in the 1870s and reached Latin America in the early twentieth century. The second, decisive influence made swifter transit, arriving by the end of the First World War. This was a return to metaphysics featuring the philosophy of culture, the theory of values, and existentialism, all grouped around phenomenology, taken less as a philosophy than a movement.

Phenomenology poses large challenges to the historian of ideas in Latin America. On one hand, it was a shaping influence on existentialism and

---

[135] Cf. Marshall Berman, *All That is Solid Melts into Air* (New York, 1982), part I.
[136] See Leopoldo Zea, 'Alemania en la cultura hispanoamericana', in *Esquema para una historia de las ideas en Iberoamérica* (Mexico, D.F., 1956), pp. 59–89; João Cruz Costa, *Contribuição á história das idéias no Brasil* (Rio de Janeiro, 1956), pp. 296–330.

on the perspectivism of Ortega y Gasset which by the 1940s were in wide ascendancy in Latin America. On the other hand, phenomenology, both in the seminal writings of Edmund Husserl (1859–1938) and in extensive commentaries, is abstract, technical and almost bereft of illustration and analogies. Yet despite its eclipse by Marxism by the 1960s there were signs that phenomenology had influenced the case of Latin American thought. What follows is an attempt to suggest how the phenomenological outlook met ingrained habits of thought and conjunctural needs of the moment.[137]

First of all, phenomenology does not deal with concrete 'phenomena' or sheer facts but with the essence of things conceived apart from their existence. For the phenomenologist empiricism is not a philosophical pursuit, nor does he draw on the special sciences. He is no more concerned to marshal evidence for his findings than is the geometer to demonstrate the reality of a triangle. To non-philosophical sciences phenomenology ascribes a 'natural' or naive attitude that assumes an explainable world existing outside the consciousness of the subject. The mind roams at will through the world, dividing it into fields of inquiry, extracting laws or regularities. This naive attitude rests on canonical postulates while philosophy, Husserl insisted, requires a 'radical' attitude that dismisses all presuppositions. Philosophy is, in this sense, more rigorous than science. Descartes was a persuasive mentor becuase he had deduced scientific method from the single postulate of the *cogito*. Husserl eliminated even this postulate by assimilating the mind to its *cogitata* from the start (his *Cartesian Meditations* appeared in 1931). Husserl demanded special intuition: not the emotional intuitionism of Bergson but a disciplined, 'eidetic' intuition that 'brackets' the world as naively seen, reduces it to essences (*eidos* – essence), and culminates in the *epoché,* or suspension of judgement.

Thus phenomenology fights on several fronts: against empiricism and scientism, against scepticism and relativism, against mysticism and traditional metaphysics. What it proposes is appropriation of pure consciousness, the living stream of experiences: a primal apperception that suspends

---

[137] A concise introduction to phenomenology is the article, 'Phenomenology', by Husserl himself in the fourteenth edition of the *Encyclopaedia Britannica* (1929). A good anthology is Joseph J. Kockelmans (ed.), *Phenomenology: The Philosophy of Edmund Husserl and its Interpretation* (Garden City, N.Y., 1967); it provides keys to Husserl's thought, shows implications for human sciences, and traces the transition to existential phenomenology in writings by and about Heidegger, Sartre, and Merleau-Ponty. For phenomenology in Latin American legal thought, see Josef L. Kunz, *La filosofía del derecho latinoamericano en el siglo XX* (Buenos Aires, 1951), ch. 8 and Luis Recaséns Siches et al., *Latin American Legal Philosophy* (Cambridge, Eng., 1948).

the categories of subjective and objective and must undergird common sense and scientific inquiry. Four aspects of this 'radical' attitude concern the cultural historian. First, fusion of mind and object means that consciousness is consciousness-of-something: not a relation between mind and object but an act that confers meaning. In other words, consciousness is governed by intentionality, a neo-scholastic term that Husserl took from his mentor, Franz Brentano. The conscious process already harbours an intentional correspondence to objects. A second corollary is intersubjectivity. Because the world is available to everyone, the possibility of solipsism vanishes. Cultural objects, for example, refer back to the intentions that comprise them. Representations of the world cohere in mutual participation; the world coalesces where experiences intersect. Minds are thus unified, making subjectivity inseparable from inter-subjectivity.

In the third place, phenomenology neither pursues preexisting truths nor aspires to construct a system. Rather, the epoché immerses the conscious ego in the flux of experience. That is to say, it suspends awareness of what does or does not exist to reveal the world as a correlate of consciousness. Like art, philosophy thus conceived brings truth into being through attentiveness and wonder. Its task is not progressive construction but ever-renewed parturition or experiment, given that complete 'reduction' or epoché is unattainable. Finally, there are implications for history. There is, for phenomenology, no Hegelian Idea or evolutionary law to be unveiled. Instead, an ego renders the social world as a circumference of alter egos – past, present, and future – for whom living space is not a geographical notion but a home, and language not a grammatical system but a vehicle of intentions. Human situations are not resultants of ideological or economic forces but constellations of shared, intentional behaviour toward nature, time and death. If Marx said that history does not walk on its head, neither, Merleau-Ponty reminds us, does it think with its feet. Phenomenology addressed the body *in toto,* not its extremities. From this follows a concern with historicity, or the ceaseless interplay between cultural tradition and the activity of participants that yields its sediment.

We may assess the significance of phenomenological thought for Latin America on two planes. First, it is in some respects consistent with the venerable neo-scholastic heritage of the Iberian world. The notion of intentionality, derived from Aristotle, softens the hard, self-sufficient world of science, while the comprehensive reach of phenomenology, from a self-given or presuppositionless foundation, echoes the claim of Catholic thought to universalism and self-legitimation. Positivism too had appealed as an inclusive system: yet phenomenology, while claiming even greater procedural rigour, lacks the evolutionary implication that classed Latin America at an inferior stage of 'development'. In the second place, phenomenology met conjunctural needs. Its historicism legitimized the *pensadores'* search for identity and supported the vague but persistent notion of a Latin American civilization. Moreover, its 'aestheticism' struck a chord with an important domestic concern (cf. José Vasconcelos, *Monismo estético*, 1918; Brazil's J. P. da Graça Aranha, *A estética da vida*, 1921; Alejandro Deústua, *Estética general*, 1923; Antonio Caso, *Principios de estética*, 1925; Samuel Ramos, *Filosofía de la vida artística*, 1950). The conception of art or constant parturition relieved the sense of unilateral dependence on metropolitan intellectual authority.

The brand of existentialism that spread in Latin America derived from phenomenology through the early Heidegger, Sartre and Merleau-Ponty. Although there are affinities between the two, distinctions are possible. Existentialism has no pretension to systematic rigour; its subject matter is human existence, not consciousness; it rejects Husserl's eidetic reduction that suspends the naive attitudes of the special sciences; and, instead of justifying beliefs by intuitive perception, it aspires to awaken adherents to a special way of life or 'authentic existence'.[138] For the cultural historian, however, the significance of both modes of thought for Latin America bears strong similarities.

For understanding how and why existential phenomenology was internalized in the Ibero Atlantic world and not simply received as an 'influence', the pivotal figure is José Ortega y Gasset (1883–1955).[139] His importance has little to do with his pronouncements on Latin America, which were relatively few, nor with the controversial question of his originality as a philosopher. Partisans of Unamuno scored their point in likening him to Charles, the Spanish ruler who was First of Spain and Fifth of Germany. Our interest in Ortega here is that at the outset of his career he saw Spain's ambivalence toward European modernization to require philosophic explication, not economic or political recipes. His use of German thought was crafted to this end. His sources and findings were diffused in his *Meditaciones del Quijote* (1914) and later via the *Revista de Occidente* (1923–

---

[138] Herbert Spiegelberg, 'Husserl's Phenomenology and Sartre's Existentialism', in Kockelmans, *Phenomenology*, pp. 252–66.

[139] For the formation of Ortega's thought: Julian Marías, *José Ortega y Gasset: Circumstance and Vocation*, trans. Frances M. López-Morillas (Norman, Okla. 1979); Philip W. Silver, *Ortega as Phenomenologist: The Genesis of 'Meditations on Quixote'* (New York, 1978); Fernando Salmerón, *Las mocedades de Ortega y Gasset*, 3rd ed. (Mexico, D.F., 1983).

36) and his disciples who emigrated to Latin America after 1936. For Latin Americans who recognized their situation as analogous to that of the Iberian peninsula, Ortega demonstrated uses of philosophic thought which, at face value, seemed amorphous and unanchorable. What he attempted was, in effect, to link the psycho-historical specificity of a Martín Luis Guzmán to the inclusive Western humanism of an Alfonso Reyes.

It is loosely said that while Miguel de Unamuno (1864–1936) urged the Hispanization of Europe, Ortega preached the Europeanization of Spain. The simplification is considerable. Ortega felt that to become truly a Spaniard, to understand Spain, meant becoming a technical philosopher. This would produce a fresh European philosophy with unexpected Spanish accents. To shut the windows, to resort to Spanish mysticism, could only prolong the 'Tibetanization' of Spain. The country would remain a cistern, a repository of European flotsam, and not become a spring, or source of interpretation. Assimilating European *ciencia* (science) was not to 'catch up' but to overcome *inconsciencia,* or unconsciousness of one's own history.

Ortega was aware of the implications of his thought for Latin America and once told Alfonso Reyes that he would enjoy being known as Ortega 'the American' in the style of Scipio 'Africanus'. Ortega visited only Argentina, however, and resisted involvement with the rest of America. His essays on that country assimilated it to the hemispheric case and to the Hegelian notion that the Americas as a whole, Argentina and the United States alike, were primitive and immature.[140] When it came to the New World he spoke not as a Spaniard but also as a European. He was Ortega Americanus *malgré lui,* not because of his American writings (which were not without insight) but in spite of them. Ortega's lesson for America lay in his 'perspectivism' or 'circumstantial thinking' which bore traces of phenomenology but was far from a replica. Indeed, Ortega's German education had been at Marburg under the influence of Hermann Cohen, Paul Natorp, and pre-Husserlian neo-Kantianism. It was only in 1913, three years after his return to Madrid, that two disparate books were published to wrench him into intellectual maturity. One was Husserl's *Ideas,* which struck him by its innovative method but straightaway impelled him to go farther. He later wrote that he emerged from phenomenology without having entered it and that 'phenomenology was not a philoso-

---

[140] Zea, 'Ortega el americano' in *Esquema*, pp. 93–120. See Ortega's essays, 'Hégel y América', 'La pampa . . . promesas', and 'El hombre a la defensiva' in Vol. 7 of *El espectador* (Madrid, 1929), pp. 11–21, 193–264. Also Peter G. Earle, 'Ortega y Gasset in Argentina: The exasperating colony', *Hispania*, 70, 3 (1987), 475–86.

phy for us' but 'a piece of good luck'. The other book was Unamuno's *Tragic Sense of Life,* whose shocking imagery and 'palpable hits' in demonstrating the opposition between reason and life disclosed still vital mainsprings of Spanish thought. Ortega now accepted to strike out alone without support from his own generation.

Discussion of Ortega's perspectivism commences with his pronouncement that 'I am I and my circumstance, and if I do not save it, I do not save myself.' The two initial I's are the clue. The first designates a personal, internal reality that is not of the senses. The second 'I' is a dynamic part of circumstance. In contrast to Husserl's 'surrounding world' (*Unwelt*), Ortega's 'circumstance' contains the human organism as an ingredient. He thus disallows both subjectivism, which leads to the sceptical position that truth cannot exist if the only viewpoint is individual, and rationalism, which holds that because truth exists it requires a supra-individual viewpoint. Nor does Ortega accept Husserl's reduction, for by bracketing reality it suspends the 'natural attitude', or *living* perception, and turns to contemplate perception itself. Ortega asks that each person contribute his own irreplaceable truth, that he not adopt an imaginary retina. There *is* a reality, but a profound one from which appearances spring, not the 'laminated' reality of positivism that reflects surfaces. The latent, true reality is offered only in perspectives. The issue, then, is not the 'destiny of man' but concrete destinies requiring reabsorption of circumstance, humanization of life and conversion of the world 'out there' into a true, personal world. Later Ortega was to deride the existentialism of Parisian boulevards for the 'gratuitous' choice it imposed. One's fate, one's tragic fate – he believed – was proposed, not imposed. One cannot choose one's fate; one chooses whether to be faithful to it.

While the generation of the patriarchs might acknowledge the new Husserlian and Orteguian currents, they were not positioned to give them understanding reception. In 1934 Antonio Caso bravely produced a book on the philosophy of Husserl, whom he praised for vindicating the role of intuition in apprehending essences. The book was perhaps his weakest effort, for 'it is really Bergson whom he understands, not Husserl'.[141] In 1939 Alfonso Reyes, who bore something of the relation to contemporary Europe that a Renaissance humanist bore to seventeenth-century philosophy, wrote an appreciative essay on Alejandro Korn and his disciple, Francisco Romero, yet disparaged the German sources that shaped the

---

[141] Patrick Romanell, *Making of the Mexican Mind* (Lincoln, Nebr., 1952), p. 83.

passage between the two. From his humanist outlook he dismissed Scheler and Heidegger and regarded Husserl's phenomenology as a flickering spark that cast no light.[142] What follows starts with the transition from Korn (an exemplary patriarch) to Romero (an exemplary *forjador*), then examines the pedagogic and philosophic contributions of the Spanish *transterrado*, José Gaos, and his Mexican disciple Leopoldo Zea. These representative cases illustrate – far from exhaustively – the disciplinary ripening and mutual engagement of intellectual abstraction and self-given *realidad*.

Alejandro Korn (1860–1936) was a 'patriarch' not so much for his writings, which never reached achieved form, as for his public life, teaching and example of a mind at work.[143] His gift was wholeness of understanding. He saw no split between technical philosophy and social conscience or between foreign influence and domestic intelligence. For him philosophy was not airy speculation nor assimilation of exotic theories but congruent expression of mental attitude. Korn is often lumped with Latin American anti-positivists, but as Francisco Romero has said, he experienced on his own the European philosophic renovation: 'not an echo but a correspondence'. Nor did he accept conventional charts of periods and influences. The *Bases* (1852) of Juan Bautista Alberdi, if they came with English utilitarianism and economic determinism, he affirmed to provide a sturdy positivist foundation that anticipated Comte, Spencer and even elements of Marx while being consonant with the needs of Argentina. Alberdi's synthesis served three generations. The task at hand, Korn felt, was not to discredit Alberdi's argument but to imitate his genius in identifying durable bases for synthesis under changed conditions. If, for example, creation of wealth had preoccupied Alberdi, the current challenge was distribution. But unlike the facile interpreters of 'national character', he did not mechanically apply world thinkers to the national case. He conflated the particular and the general. The chairs he held were ethics, metaphysics, gnosiology and history of philosophy, while his centre, founded in 1929, was not a 'centre for studying Argentine Reality' but the Kantian Society of Buenos Aires. Faithful to Miró Quesada's 'recuperación anabásica', he recapitulated European philosophy since the Greeks.

---

[142] Alfonso Reyes, 'Korn y la filosofía argentina', in *Obras completas*, Vol. 9 (Mexico, D.F., 1959), pp. 166–71.

[143] Alejandro Korn, *El pensamiento argentino* (Buenos Aires, 1961), pp. 233–60. (The 1983 edition bears the original 1936 title, *Influencias filosóficas en la evolución nacional*.) See also Francisco Romero et al., *Alejandro Korn* (Buenos Aires, 1940); Lipp, *Argentine Thinkers*, ch. 3.

Korn's concern was that the scientific pretension of positivism was too restrictive for current needs. He thought science to be an ordering of partial and abstract features of reality. Philosophy on the other hand should address how values are distilled, in biological, social and cultural clusters, from the promptings of single persons. The cornerstone of philosophy is axiology, opposing subjectivity to the objectivity of science. Because universal values are illusory, they must be rooted in the autonomy of human personality which, unlike science, can assess the circumstantial value of real objects; they must bend before the normative conscience. Metaphysics, traditionally linked to philosophy, becomes an independent exploration of the unknown, a necessary but impossible venture that is never satisfied but can reveal contradictory aspects of reality and make us conscious of our power and impotence. Korn, in sum, orchestrates science and metaphysics to axiology, freedom, and ultimate arbitration by human beings.

These premises, rooted both in Argentine needs and in the course of Western philosophy, gave Korn his Ockham's razor for testing winds of change from wherever they might blow. As for his compatriots, José Ingenieros (1877–1925), he felt, fought to rescue positivism by intellectual fireworks without abandoning scientistic dogmatism, while Ricardo Rojas (1882–1957) urged a 'nationalist restoration' considered not as nostalgia for past glories but as palingenesis of peoples' inborn energies. For him, a more coherent contribution was that of Juan B. Justo (1865–1928), who translated Marx and founded the Socialist Party. Argentine socialists recognized, Korn believed, that the social problem was less economic than ethical, while beneath their profession of Marxism lay the influence of Le Play, Schmoller and Leo XIII. This outlook was therapy for the pragmatic persuasion that converted conscience to a biological function, excluded *telos* from the cosmic process, and gave ethics a utilitarian cast.

Korn's Argentine concerns shaped his views on Western philosophic currents and made him impatient with mere fads. He deplored Spengler's *payasadas* (clowning) that allowed positivists to give a mystical cast to scientific determinism. Without denigrating the psychiatric research of Freud, he charged him with having reinvented the wheel of sexuality, constructed long ago by Plato, Pascal and Darwin. He mistrusted Keyserling's introduction of the oriental comparison with its 'esoteric penumbra'. 'The voyage to the Orient is fruitful providing one returns.'

He was more dismissive of Jamesian pragmatism than were his contemporaries Enrique Molina (Chile) and Carlos Vaz Ferreira (Uruguay). Yet the country of Emerson, Josiah Royce and Dewey was certain to chart a lofty path: 'For now it's imperative to find philosophic inspiration there.' Bergson was a decisive influence for having opened free space within determinism; yet Korn was disappointed that he had neither implanted a theoretical base nor produced an ethics. Croce was appealing mainly for his spirited attacks on scientism and rationalism.

The German tradition Korn spoke of with more deference and less assurance. His contemporaries, he wrote, paid homage to Kant, still regarded as 'influential', supposing him to be a nebulous metaphysician (even though Kant had demolished rational metaphysics) and unaware that German philosophy was a string of revolts against Kant. We have not heard, Korn remonstrated, that the up-to-date philosophy in Germany is the latest attack against the great thinker; we do not know what, after all this, is left standing. As of 1927 it was hard to detect a dominant German trend or genial figure. Dilthey appealed most to Korn but was still 'an unknown savant.' He liked Rickert's work on the limits of science but not his theory of values. He was attracted to the German Catholic tradition that challenged the dominant Protestant culture but felt unprepared to navigate the waters of modern German philosophy: 'only my friend Francisco Romero I feel can move with ease in this labyrinth.' As for himself, he found academic philosophy insipid. To commune with high German culture still meant turning to Kant and Goethe. 'The last German philosopher is Nietzsche', wrote Korn. 'He gave philosophy its axiological orientation.'[144]

Francisco Romero (1891–1962), who met Korn in 1923 and became an informal disciple, fulfilled the mentor's expectation that he would master the abstruse German contribution. Like Korn he addressed the state of philosophy in Latin America, the task of *recuperación anabásica,* and his duties as teacher and intellectual publicist but also managed to make contributions, notably his *Teoría del hombre* (1952), that were fully ripened. If Korn won continental recognition as an exemplary foe of positivism, Romero won acclaim as the dean of Latin American philosophers or, in Miró Quesada's view, the leader of the *generación forjadora.* His reputation rests on his having advanced and unified the explorations of Korn,

[144] Risieri Frondizi, Korn's compatriot, reexamined axiology in *What is Value?, An Introduction to Axiology,* trans. Solomon Lipp (Lasalle, Ill., 1963).

with firmer grounding in contemporary, especially German, thought and greater aptitude for synthesis.[145]

Romero assumes from the start that a Latin American contemplates European philosophy from a vast amphitheatre; whatever his intellectual limitations, they do not include the blinkers of regionalism and dogmatism. Here time lies open no less than space. The certainties of the positivist, Darwinist, nationalist age had crumbled. The modern age was one of psychological insecurity at both the centre and the rim of 'civilization'. For all alike, the future stretches indiscernibly ahead. To penetrate that future takes us to history, not as deterministic schema nor as blind flux nor as haphazard relativism but via 'ontological historicism' that assumes consciousness of the past for reconceiving the present. To demonstrate historicity Romero offers the metaphor of a river whose waters may flow peaceably along its bed or nearly dry up or overflow into adjacent canals or flood to convert the whole valley into its bed; or finally its surface may freeze leaving the liquid mass to flow silently beneath. Similarly history, although channelled by the inner nature of man, may at times seem to flow of its own accord. Microvisions supplement the panoramic one. 'Man seems wrapped in a subtle medium that is his conception of the world', not as conscious knowledge but as something lived, immediate, or almost unconscious.[146] A race, an epoch, a people each has a world view, as do social classes, human types, single persons; and these are often juxtaposed and blended. From this premise Latin Americans can claim partnership in the work of philosophic reconstruction.

A key to Romero's thinking, as for Husserl's, is intentionality. In its modern use this scholastic term has two general meanings: first, it designates ascent from the animal level, where the world is experienced passively as engulfing the subject, to an intentional level where man converts his amorphous milieu into defined objects that provoke reaction. Secondly, it designates the transition from associationist psychology, which explains mental life as a mix of impressions derived from sense experience, to consciousness of a subject-object relationship that involves the ego with the world as participant. To this Romero adds a further division. First is the self-centred intentionality of the *psyche* prevailing over the *individual;* sec-

---

[145] Born in Spain, Romero came to Argentina in 1904. Important here are his *Filosofía contemporánea*, 3rd ed. (Buenos Aires, 1953), *Papeles para una filosofía* (Buenos Aires, 1945), *El hombre y la cultura* (Buenos Aires, 1950), *Sobre la filosofía en América* (Buenos Aires, 1952), and *Teoría del hombre*, 2nd ed. (Buenos Aires, 1958) (*Theory of Man*, trans. William F. Cooper (Berkeley, 1964)). For discussions see Lipp, *Argentine Thinkers*, ch. 4, and Miró Quesada, *Despertar*, chs. 5, 6.

[146] Romero, *Filosofía contemporánea*, pp. 130–31.

ond is the 'disinterested' interest (or *spirit*) that seeks correspondence between human energy (the *person*) and value itself, thus projecting intentionality toward the objective and universal. This signifies a distinction between immanence, or enclosure in a particular reality, and transcendence, a spilling over of the self yet without abandoning the original centre. For Romero, the early modern religio-philosophic revolution (Luther, Descartes, Hobbes) implanted immanentism by making the individual the sole depository of knowledge, belief, and sovereignty. This atomizing of the medieval heritage was arrested by the romanticist inspiration of the nineteenth century, a corrective renewal for philosophy in the early decades of the twentieth. In the socio-political realm, however, Romero felt the crisis still to be acute, as evidenced by his pathology of the leading traits of Western culture: intellectualism, activism and individualism.[147]

Romero closed *Teoría del hombre* by applying intentionality and transcendence to what he considered the three major world cultures which above all others possess dignity and universality and confer on man a sense of destiny: India, China and the West. (Jewish culture he regarded as inseparable from Western.) The substrate of Indian culture he took as the undivided whole from which all beings arise, making private existence a passing instance that finds meaning only as it merges with the universal. Indian culture is non-temporal, disvaluing time. Central to classical Chinese culture is the social complex, a family with infinite predecessors, governed by ancestors and sanctified as the nexus with the supernatural. This culture is 'eternalist', paralysing time in the shadow of an ancestral past. Alone of the three, Western culture possesses historicity and allies with time in its 'throbbing consecutiveness' to achieve demands of the spirit. Whatever it may learn from others, it alone rescues the individual from realities that surpass him and seem to overflow with meaning. If citizens of other cultures abandon theirs to join ours, it is because the West, whatever its stains and crimes, alone acknowledges what is genuine in single beings. The others deny the historicity of man as a self that is strengthened and purified in the spiritual quest for universality. Man is born when he confers objectivity on the world through judgement; other cultures disparage and even annul the privilege of judging.[148]

One of Romero's uses for philosophy, then, particularly its modern

---

[147] Romero, *Teoría del hombre*, chs. 6, 7; Lipp, *Argentine Thinkers*, pp. 114–16, 122–25, 138–45; Miró Quesada, *Despertar*, pp. 147–53.

[148] Romero, *Teoría del hombre*, ch. 12; also his chapter 'Temporalismo', in *Filosofía contemporánea*, pp. 25–49.

German variants, was to map the broad lineaments of world cultures. In so doing he smoothly assimilated the Latin American tradition (as he had the Jewish) to Western culture, and although he kept abreast of Latin American currents, he made no heroic attempt to develop a cultural category for them. Or perhaps he did so by implication when, as discussed above, he praised the philosophic achievement of contemporary Europe but detected crisis in the socio-political realm, where he found intellect unsupportive of values, activism lacking a mission, and individualism frustrated by inadequate political organization. In addressing Latin America one surmises that instead of enquiring into local 'identity' he was asking how a subculture might, from unique resources, contribute to therapy for the whole.

There were literati of Romero's approximate generation who addressed directly the question of Argentine 'identity', sometimes in the context of a larger America, such as Ricardo Rojas or Eduardo Mallea, and sometimes taking cues from contemporary philosophy, such as Martínez Estrada, Carlos Alberto Erro, or the Spanish maestro himself, Ortega y Gasset, in a few casual sketches. Yet conditions were not propitious for assimilating identity to a canon of philosophic interpretation. First, Argentine identity swung within a multi-ideological political arena among the disparate poles of Amerindian origins, the Hispanic heritage and the diluvial immigration of modern times. Second, although there was no local dearth of philosophic talent, it lacked a roof under which to assemble for common endeavour (Romero in fact resigned all his academic positions in the Peronist years, 1946–55).

In Mexico circumstances were more favourable for Miró Quesada's awakening of the Latin American philosophic 'project'. Here the Revolution had struck roots, matured and seemingly translated the disparate hopes of the 1920s into a domestic cultural agenda. The muralists had apotheosized the Indian substrate of national culture, whose architectural monuments and ethnic descent were everywhere visible, while the influx of Italians, Central Europeans and Japanese to the South Atlantic zone had no parallel here. Doubts as to whether a 'revolution' had indeed occurred lay ahead. Two further factors enhanced philosophic receptivity in Mexico. The first was that the Revolution was premature to have absorbed the modernist élan. Older hands retained intellectual mentorship (Reyes, Caso, Vasconcelos and the slightly younger Samuel Ramos) and could adapt to new situations within the large philosophic vistas of an earlier period. The second was the exodus of Spanish intellectuals to Mexico in the late 1930s. They came with professional competence in arts, letters and sciences as well as sports and the mass media. Of the 20,000, or perhaps many more, exiles who arrived in Mexico, 650 appear in a roster of those with high professional accomplishment.[149] The anti-dictatorial politics of humanists and social scientists placed them to relegitimize the central Iberian component of Spanish American culture that had been so problematical, above all in Mexico, since independence. As Europeans, moreover, they could expand the question of transatlantic identity to its hemispheric dimension.

Although Spanish intellectuals and professionals were received throughout Spanish America, a critical mass came to Mexico, generally because of President Lázaro Cárdenas's policy of offering asylum to Spanish republicans and specifically through the efforts of Mexican scholars, conspicuously Alfonso Reyes and Daniel Cosío Villegas (1898–1976), to arrange accommodation for their Spanish colleagues. The Casa de España, founded in 1938, provided a base, transformed two years later into El Colegio de México. Here we limit ourselves to the consequences for philosophy in Mexico of the Spanish *hegira*, and, of the fifteen or twenty philosophers among the 650 professionals, we will focus on José Gaos, whose pedagogical genius and mentorship of the Hiperión group made him responsible, or at least a catalyst, for opening a new chapter in the exploration of 'identity'.

José Gaos y González Pola (1900–69) was born in Gijón, Spain. Unlike Francisco Romero, who came to Argentina as a youth and absorbed New World flexibilities, Gaos arrived in Mexico in 1938 with the full baggage of his European career. A disciple of Ortega and a militant in the Socialist Party, he became professor of philosophy at the Central University of Madrid in 1932 and rector in 1936. Memoirs by Mexican disciples and his own 'confesiones' convey something of his enigmatic character.[150] To start with an outrageous epithet, Uranga calls him, in the slang term from North American English, a 'jerk'. Far from a slur on Gaos's mental acuteness, this is an affectionate judgement by a salacious creole of his gachupín professor who had assumed the full weight of tradition and ancestral formal structures and had accepted his lot as condemnation. Gaos's father, he once told Uranga, had wished him to be a notary. 'And now you see me here as a professor. Am I in any way better off?' Resigned

---

[149] Salvador Reyes Nevares (ed.), *El exilio español en México, 1939–1982* (Mexico, D.F., 1982); José Luis Abellán, *Filosofía española en América (1936–1966)* (Madrid, 1967).

[150] José Gaos, *Confesiones personales* (Mexico, D.F., 1959); Emilio Uranga, *¿De quién es la filosofía?* (Mexico, D.F., 1977), pp. 177–223; Oswaldo Díaz Ruanova, *Los existencialistas mexicanos* (Mexico, D.F., 1982), pp. 103–54.

and sceptical, he seemed like a cameraman in the historical morgue of philosophers, empathizing with the specimens. He enviously congratulated anyone who abandoned philosophy, as when Marx boxed up Hegel's books and forgot them forever. A victim of congenital nihilism, his life was governed by regimen in his teaching, his voluminous writing and translating, his exercise (swimming), eating, loving and drinking. He much preferred Heidegger to Husserl but studied the latter assiduously to master the secrets of phenomenology. He had neither the spark of an original philosopher nor the literary fluency of a master essayist. He died as he had lived, in harness, presiding over a doctoral examination.

Wherein then lay the genius of Gaos? First, he was a magisterial lecturer. Second, he commanded every important philosopher and philosophic system since the Greeks. Third, he was implacable in his exegesis of philosophic texts. Fourth, his easy familiarity with Western philosophy, including contemporary versions, and his having wrestled with the Orteguian circumstances of a marginalized, 'retarded' Spain equipped him to fathom Mexican and American dilemmas at first glance. It was he who called the Spanish newcomers *transterrados* instead of refugees or exiles (*desterrados*) – i.e., transplaced, not displaced – for this 'morphological extension, this transcendence of Spain in America made him think that he had not been exiled but simply transported to another place in the same land that had watched him suffer'.[151] Finally, his scepticism and avoidance of systemic philosophizing left his disciples space for free speculation. They did not form a school (some rejected their mentor's German existentialism in favour of the French brand), but they *were* a group, who might consort with neo-Kantians but raised the hackles of neo-Thomists and neo-Marxists. Gaos's proselytes included such soon-to-be recognized Mexican philosophers and intellectual historians as Luis Villoro, Rafael Moreno, Pablo González Casanova, Francisco López Cámara, Edmundo O'Gorman, Bernabé Navarro and José Luis Martínez; the Peruvian philosopher Augusto Salazar Bondy and the Puerto Rican historian Monelisa Lina Pérez-Marchand. In striving to meet the interests of his students Gaos desisted in seminars from directly addressing Mexican autognosis or identity but dropped back to the eighteenth century, to the critical moment of the Enlightenment impingement, when foreign ideas no longer came from without in the heads of immigrants or visitors but from within in the

---

[151] Uranga, *¿De quién?*, p. 190; also José Gaos, 'Los "transterrados" españoles de la filosofía en México', in his *Filosofía mexicana de nuestros días* (Mexico, D.F., 1954), pp. 287–323.

heads of native importers. One case favoured a colonial outlook, the other an impulse of independence and national personality.[152] Some years later economists would propose an analogous contrast, for a subsequent period, between development from without and development from within.

The purpose of this section has not been to review the discipline of philosophy as practised in Latin America but to highlight practitioners whose training assisted them to lay foundations and shape an agenda for the 'identity' question, whether in national or in continental terms. At this point the achievement of Leopoldo Zea (1912–) deserves special attention as the favoured disciple of Gaos, who remarked that if Zea had not existed Gaos would have had to invent him to justify himself as a professor.[153] Others of Zea's peers may have made more ingenious speculative flights, but it is Zea who devoted his life to developing underpinnings for the ideological and political quest for Latin American self-awareness and autonomy. Because of his unpretentious, often didactic language, his largely tactical use of philosophic luminaries, and his concern with historical matrix, philosophers on the 'cutting edge' tend to belittle his conceptual acumen. On the other hand, North American historians, as *soi-disant* empiricists, chide him for not being exhaustive and even-handed in tracing intellectual trends of the last century and for allowing his vision of the future to skew his account of the past. Finally, activists who commend his argument for 'liberation' (mental, political, economic) fault him for lacking engagement and specificity. Zea can be accused, that is, of failing to see the forest for the trees, of failing to see the trees for the forest, and of failing to convert the forest into ridgepoles and rafters. To the purists he would respond that he uses Hegel as a source of ideas, not a text for exegesis. He reminds the historians that empirical dismemberment of history impedes (sometimes purposely) ideological reconstruction. To activists the answer is that the task of recovering half a millennium of hemispheric history differs from crafting instrumental prescriptions for time and place.

Zea staked his claims with his influential books on Mexican positivism (1943–4), which provided scaffolding for his subsequent study (1949) of the 'two stages' of nineteenth-century Spanish American thought. In them he formulated premises for extending his analysis to the Americas, to the

---

[152] 'Lo mexicano en filosofía', in Gaos, 'Los "transterrados" ', pp. 325–57.
[153] See Miró Quesada, *Proyecto y realización del filosofar latino-americano*, pp. 141–83; Tzvi Medin, *Leopoldo Zea: ideología, historia y filosofía de América Latina* (Mexico, D.F., 1983); Solomon Lipp, *Leopoldo Zea: From Mexicanidad to a Philosophy of History* (Waterloo, Ont., 1980).

West, and finally to the world. Despite later shifts in perspective and intellectual sources, Zea has been in Isaiah Berlin's terms a hedgehog, not a fox. The two points of departure for his unified mission are interlocked. First was his general attraction to the themes of historicism and liberation, for which he found elements in his highly selective use of Hegel, Ortega, Scheler, and Mannheim as well as Vico and Croce, with an early, somewhat fortuitous existentialist (largely Sartrian) parenthesis. Hegel and his notion of a *reality* to be *realized* remained important although with Zea's proviso that 'I back off from Hegel the moment he deifies the spirit'. The ancillary point was his division of Latin American thought into the two stages of romanticism and positivism. For Europeans this was a natural split, but it had not yet been applied systematically to Latin America. Moreover, the point of Zea's transplacement of the 'two stages' from Europe to America was not to certify the 'mental emancipation' of Latin America (a term he used somewhat ironically) from the scholastic and authoritarian proclivities of the colonial centuries but to demonstrate that Latin Americans could not, by faddish importations, deny their unassimilated past. Here was his Hegelian inspiration: a dialectical capacity to assimilate and not deny or eliminate the past, without which history becomes serial repetition. These two points – historicism, or recognition of a given people's inescapable immersion in history, and liberation, or the assimilation or 'digestion' of history – laid a foundation for his global adventures in ideology.

Because Zea's ideas had structure, breadth and flexibility, and reflected the temper of the times, he was able to mount a series of undertakings in the late 1940s and early 1950s having hemispheric projection. He founded the Hiperión group dedicated to identifying the logic of Mexican history from the premises of existential phenomenology and including such promising figures as Emilio Uranga, Jorge Portilla, Joaquín Sánchez MacGregor and Luis Villoro. This initiative led Zea to organize a series of short, widely read books on *México y lo mexicano* whose authors included mentors such as Alfonso Reyes, José Gaos, Silvio Zavala and Samuel Ramos and other Spanish Americans such as Mariano Picón Salas (1901–65) and Rafael Heliodoro Valle (1891–1959). Beyond this Zea began identifying intellectual historians throughout Latin America whose contributions would expand the search for authentic history to continental scope. Published in the Tierra Firme collection of the Fondo de Cultura Económica, the volumes he solicited created a lasting benchmark for the history of ideas in America. Later came the founding of the

Co-ordinating Centre at the National University of Mexico for interconnecting Latin American studies programmes throughout the region. Such programmes, Zea recognized, were routine in metropolitan curricula but not in the region itself, thus denying it elements for a comprehensive view of the subject.

In the 1960s the configuration of Zea's ideas shifted somewhat. On the surface it seemed that he was accepting a 'Third World' diagnosis lifting the notions of dependency and liberation from a rejuvenated Marxism and from writings of Marcuse, Fanon and even Che Guevara. He was not, however, echoing the *dernier cri*. The two now consecrated watchwords he had already treated explicitly in the introduction ('Sentimiento de dependencia') and first section ('La emancipación mental') of *Dos etapas del pensamiento en Hispanoamérica* (1949). He in fact held close to his original course, although conflating his search for Latin American identity with that for a philosophy pure and simple of man wherever he exists. In this his trajectory was close to that of Brazil's Mário de Andrade who, from grounding in folklore, popular music, ethnology, psychology and literature, had worked toward the universal from knowledge of Brazil and its regional fragments. Zea's base, in contrast, was philosophical, extending far beyond the purview of technical concerns but with little attention to the gambits of the burgeoning social sciences, to the visions of 'boom' novelists, or – as his critics insist – to details of microhistory.

Politically, Zea has held to a loose, relatively non-combative position that Medin calls 'nationalist, social, anti-imperialist neo-liberalism' in the most idealistic tradition of the Mexican Revolution. Any radicalism he may seem to endorse is tempered by humanism. His socialism means social justice, not abolition of private property. His liberty implies solidarity, a balance of sacrifice and benefit, radicalism within reformism. On one hand, he adheres to the finest flowering of Mexico's revolution. On the other hand, he remains alert to the grand dialectics of Hegel and Marx. If Hegel's history as dialectical liberation informs his analysis, however, he criticizes Hegel's Eurocentrism in defining the trajectory and beneficiaries of the Spirit. Similarly, in discussing Marxism he distinguishes between liberation of workers by their own promptings and effort, as a subject of history, and their external liberation by leaders and parties, as an object of history. This subject-object split applies also to his analysis of relations between the United States and Latin America or between the industrial world and the Third World. By Western calculus Latin America is still, as Hegel long ago declared it to be, prehistoric. For Zea, its only entry into history is by its own *toma de conciencia* a moral ideal and not a convergence of 'objective' interests. To be prisoner of the facts means to accept them. Because the will to change them is subjective, objectivity means for Zea the identification of subjective projects that converted history into 'reality'. Thus, paradoxically, objectivity creates a metahistory to supersede a 'real' history that can no longer continue and is therefore 'unreal'.

Why Zea runs afoul of orthodox historians is obvious. With fellow philosophers there are also problems, although again related to norms of a discipline. He has been charged, for example, with being a preacher and not a philosopher, with accepting the technically impoverished tradition of Caso, Vasconcelos and Ramos, and for not seeing that the force of philosophy lies in a neutrality that allows it to exercise the fierce weapon of Socratic criticism to unmask mystification. This professional critique focuses, however, on methods rather than on objectives. It seems excessive to demand that Zea practice Socratic deconstruction when his aim is to identify bases for nationhood in the tradition of Vico, Rousseau, Herder and Michelet.

In 1968–9 Zea began an exchange with the Peruvian philosopher Augusto Salazar Bondy (1927–74) that Cerutti calls 'one of the central links of current philosophic thought in Latin America'.[154] Both paid homage to their common mentor, José Gaos, and to his agenda for philosophy in Latin America.[155] Their arguments even overlap: both agreed that underdevelopment and external oppression had inhibited the flowering of philosophy in America. Both agreed on the derivative nature of domestic philosophizing, with Salazar Bondy however claiming that political and economic conditions were not suitable for 'originality' (fresh ideas and formulations) or for 'authenticity' (fidelity to circumstances at hand) – although he wavered on the second point. Zea replied that authentic philosophy is not a function of development. Developed and 'over-developed' countries, he argued, produce unauthentic philosophy in abundance when they universalize a vision of men who cannot recognize humanity in others, of liberty understood to apply only to a minority, and of a licence for violence justified by security and self-protection. 'Authenticity' can appear in any

[154] Augusto Salazar Bondy, *¿Existe una filosofía de nuestra América?*, 1968; 6th ed. (Mexico, D.F., 1979); Leopoldo Zea, *La filosofía americana como filosofía sin más*, 1969; 8th ed. (Mexico, D.F., 1980). Horacio Cerutti Guldberg traces the subsequent course of the debate in *Filosofía de la liberación latinoamericana* (Mexico, D.F., 1983), pp. 161–8.

[155] Cf. Gaos, *Pensamiento de lengua española* and *En torno a la filosofía mexicana*, 2 vols. (Mexico, D.F., 1952–3).

setting. As for 'originality', Zea insists that his previous explorations into *lo mexicano* and *lo americano* were not attempts to regionalize the philosophic enterprise but to use a favourable vantage point, given the narcissism of 'developed' countries, for constructing a philosophy 'for man wherever he be found.' He now advocated a philosophy of liberation that approached the universal via the Third World rather than in direct confrontation of *lo americano* with Europe.

In 1978 Zea gave his more recent formulations context by calling to mind three discredited historical projecs: the autochthonous *proyecto libertario* of Bolívar for a free union of American peoples, which soon collapsed with the unleashing of local power struggles; the conservative project, which sought to remedy chaos by restoring the colonial regime of order and social hierarchy; and the civilizing project, endorsed by Mora, Lastarria, Bilbao, Montalvo, Sarmiento and Alberdi, which pinned its hopes to positivist education, immigration and foreign investment, creating a pseudo-bourgeoisie subordinate to the West and rejecting historical roots and culture. Drawing on his personal brand of Hegelianism, Zea now asserts that the time has come for a new *proyecto asuntivo,* recognizing that the past can no longer be rejected but must be taken up or *assumed.*[156] Once assumed, or absorbed, it is then transcended and can be selectively negated in dialectical fashion, or affirmative negation. For this project Zea's disparate precursors include Bello, Simón Rodríguez, Bilbao, Rodó, Vasconcelos, González Prada, Reyes and Ugarte, but above all Martí, who most clearly defines a project of liberation to reinvigorate the Bolivarian ideal.

Throughout the period of the Cold War, Zea strongly resisted accepting the ideological dichotomization of the world. Whatever the perils and perplexities of the post-Cold War era that has dawned, it at least strengthens the basis for the ecumenical outlook that he has so fervently advocated across the decades. Moreover, the less structured, less predictable character of the current world scene may offer richer possibilities for intellectual transactions between the realms of speculative philosophy and political engagement.

TWO REALITIES: SOCIOLOGICAL AND MARVELLOUS

The deceptively sequential treatment of modernism → naturalism/essayism → philosophy now leads to the apotheosis of social science in

[156] Leopoldo Zea, *Filosofía de la historia americana* (Mexico, D.F., 1978), pp. 269–94. Also Zea, *The Role of the Americas in History,* trans. Sonja Karsen (Lanham, MD, 1991).

university curricula and of the Latin American novel (or more cautiously, narrative) for international readership. These coincident phenomena of the late 1950s and 1960s objectified a tension detectable in writings of an earlier period. Mariátegui, for example, was, in his own way, a Marxist and economic determinist yet took inspiration from surrealism and even the young Borges; Price-Mars, schooled in Paris in medicine and social science, became the apostle of myth and voodoo as the substrate of Haitian culture; the poet Martínez Estrada was deeply versed in historiography; Fernando Ortiz, a painstaking ethnographer, found his mentor in a medieval Spanish poet-priest. What follows investigates the branching apart of scientific and literary endeavour that was in some respects loosely joined.

The social science story centres on the career of sociology, social anthropology and aspects of history. (In the 1950s and 1960s São Paulo's so-called 'school of sociology' pioneered or rewrote whole sectors of the socio-economic and political history of Brazil.) Just as philosophy had its 'patriarchs' so sociology had exemplary pioneers, such as Andrés Molina Enríquez (Mexico, 1866–1940), Juan Agustín García (Argentina, 1862–1923), or Alberto Torres (Brazil, 1865–1917). They were succeeded by a generation of 'shapers' who as institution- and curriculum-builders tackled the challenges of theory and empiricism, pure and applied science, value-free science and ideology, European derivation and Latin American innovation.[157] The three names often identified as outstanding shapers are José Medina Echavarría (1903–77), Gino Germani (1911–79), and Florestan Fernandes (Brazil, b. 1920).[158] Two were, like Gaos, acculturated foreigners: Medina Echavarría, who came from Spain to Mexico (1939–46), then went to Puerto Rico (1946–52), and thereafter crowned his career in Chile; and Germani from Italy who became head of the Institute of Sociology at the University of Buenos Aires in 1955 and proceeded to put his stamp on the modernization of sociology in Argentina with influence throughout the Americas before capping his career at Harvard. Florestan Fernandes is ac-

---

[157] For case studies of the intellectual and institutional development of sociology since the mid-nineteenth century, see José Joaquín Brunner, *El caso de la sociología en Chile: formación de una disciplina* (Santiago, 1988); Juan Francisco Marsal, *La sociología en la Argentina* (Buenos Aires, 1963), and El Colegio de México, *Ciencias sociales en México* (Mexico, D.F., 1979). A special number of *Revista Paraguaya de Sociología*, 11/30 (1974) includes four critical studies of sociology in Latin America from c.1950 to the mid-1970s: Rolando Franco, 'Veinticinco años de sociología latinoamericana', (pp. 57–92) and country studies by Manuel Villa Aguilera (Mexico), Eliseo Verón (Argentina), and Carlos H. Filgueira (Uruguay).

[158] Joseph A. Kahl's study of Latin America's 'new sociology' focuses on Germani, Pablo González Casanova (Mexico), and Fernando Henrique Cardoso (Brazil): *Modernization, Exploitation and Dependency in Latin America* (New Brunswick, N.J., 1976).

claimed as the founder of the 'Paulista school of sociology' (a term he disowns) which produced a loosely Marxist counter-statement (with functionalist accents) to the previously conservative tenor of Brazilian social analysis and opened the way to a fresh historiography. Fernandes's disciple, Fernando Henrique Cardoso, was important in linking the work of the Paulistas to the continent-wide enquiries sponsored under Medina Echavarría at the UN Latin American Institute of Economic and Social Planning (ILPES) in Santiago, a collaboration notably realized in *Dependencia y desarrollo en América Latina* (1968) by Cardoso and Chilean sociologist Enzo Faletto.[159]

Among Medina's abundant contributions, not so much to modernizing as to intellectualizing sociology in Latin America, are his two broad but concise synopses of the foundations of sociology and its role in Latin America: one on the theory and technique of sociology (1941) at the threshold of his Latin American career and the other on the sociology of Latin American economic development (1964) after he had edited the path-breaking sociology collection of the Fondo de Cultura Económica, directed the Centro de Estudios Sociales at the Colegio de México in the 1940s, and thereafter, in Chile, acquired a comprehensive vision of Latin America, thanks to his leadership role in the UN programme (CEPAL and ILPES) and the Latin American Social Sciences Faculty (FLACSO).[160] Grounded in wide knowledge of European, American and Latin American social thought and science against a mature philosophic background, Medina wrote in a spirit of critical sympathy without sectarian rancour, with respect for adjoining fields of inquiry, affirming sociology as an autonomous yet interdependent domain. However divergent the starting-points of Comte and Weber in physical science and in neo-Kantian historicism, they coincided, Medina held, in endorsing empirical science and method as applied to social data. A philosopher's destiny, Medina believed, was *concentration,* or addressing the integral social realm (*lo social*); the sociologist's was to handle *dispersion,* or the 'most fiercely concrete phenomena'. Yet if division of labour was proper for the sciences, any given problem should be examined as a whole. He even felt that subtle and complex 'secrets of the age' were best fathomed by Picasso, Miró or Klee.

Gino Germani sharply tilted the balance of influences and intellectual commitments that composed Medina's hopes for a scientific sociology.

[159] *Dependency and Development in Latin America,* trans. Marjory M. Urquidi (Berkeley, 1979).
[160] José Medina Echavarría, *Sociología: teoría y téchnica,* 1941; 3rd ed. (Mexico, D.F., 1982); *Consideraciones sobre el desarrollo económico en América Latina* (Montevideo, 1964).

Although versed in German philosophy, he found its 'culturalist' or 'spiritualist' character that had flourished in Latin America earlier in the century to be quite indefensible. Former controversies over the discipline he dismissed as obsolete. By now, he argued, sociology was accepted as a 'positive' discipline, with empirical research conjoined with theory in a relationship expressible in concrete, operational terms. The social scientist no longer need rely on pre-existent data but could for certain purposes use experimental methods, given the technification, standardization, routinization and specialization of his profession. As befitted an industrial world, social research had graduated from artisanal to industrial methods, while schools of sociology were replacing occasional chairs of *cátedras* isolated in law faculties.[161]

Like Medina, Germani was attracted to U.S. contributions that had raised sociology to 'the highest level in the field of methodology and research techniques' and had infused Durkheim, Weber and Simmel with 'the vigorous Saxon empirical tradition'. Medina, however, (whom Germani admired) had seen the United States as a unique case marked by a fluid social structure, a frontier tradition, a prosperous economy, and massive immigration. He saw it not so much as a comprehensive model but as a source of discrete instruments such as the social survey, community study, case method, interview and life history, and he cautioned against the fetishism of quantification. Germani, unlike Medina, spoke for a 'scientific sociology' of judgemental neutrality that might have roots in discrepant ideologies but would be self-corrective given the renovative action of a scientific community. It was not the 'scientism' *per se* of Latin America that explained current weaknesses, he felt, but the incomplete institutionalization of science itself. Germani, who from his youth in Italy had opposed fascism (in both its left and right forms) and professed a strong political liberalism, was charged by the right for challenging their mystique of social solidarity and by the left for advocating an 'American' sociology without exploring the 'imperialist' messages it concealed. His 'second exile' to Harvard in 1966 coincided with the appearance of a re-Europeanized 'critical sociology' under diverse neo- and post-Marxian influences carried forward by Pablo González Casanova, Orlando Fals Borda, Fernando Henrique Cardoso, Aníbal Quijano, John Saxe-Fernández and others.

---

[161] Gino Germani, *La sociología en la América Latina*, 2nd ed. (Buenos Aires, 1965); *La sociología científica*, 2nd ed. (Mexico, D.F., 1962); *Argentina: sociedad de masas*, 2nd ed. (Buenos Aires, 1966).

Although his direct and innovative influence on the profession was largely limited to Brazil until the 1960s, Florestan Fernandes was, through his reputation, writings, or disciples, possibly the foremost preceptor of 'critical sociology' on a continental scale. If Medina was the *problematizador* of the new sociology and Germani the pilot from scientism to functionalist science, Fernandes – the only Latin American of the three – aimed to re-theorize the field from grass roots rather than from foreign paradigms wherein he too was thoroughly schooled. In his autobiography Fernandes attributes the shaping of his sociological vocation to an 'apprenticeship' when, at age six, he was forced to find employment at the lumpen fringe of an urban society composed of sharks and sardines.[162] When eventually he found his way to the Faculty of Philosophy of the University of São Paulo, he found no secure foothold, as Medina and Germani had, in the received wisdom of international social science. Occasional foreign professors were true mentors, such as Jean Maugüé who deepened his understanding of Hegel and Marx, or Roger Bastide who guided his early research on race relations, or Herbert Baldus who introduced him to ethnology and became a lifelong friend, or Donald Pierson who encouraged him to take São Paulo as a sociological laboratory. But for the most part foreign professors made unfulfillable cultural demands and presented an eclectic panorama of ideas that seemed unrelated to Brazil, a training that required random ingestion and tended to substitute 'intellectual artificiality' for 'cultural parochialism'. To Fernandes they seemed 'less concerned with the organism of the patient than with the brilliance of the operation'.[163] Still, there were advantages to an academic bill of fare that was too heterogeneous to be copied and forced consumers to make their own syntheses. It became apparent to Fernandes that while the Faculty could not offer the 'right' system one might at least learn architectonic principles for building one and recognize that Marx, Durkheim, and Weber were not reconcilable in simple additive fashion.

Fernandes formulated his politico-scientific position carefully during his formative years and asks those who read his writings of the 1940s and 1950s to see behind his apparent empirical critique or 'experimentalist' sociologism a firm, gradual intention to dissolve the inhibitions of 'a

---

[162] Florestan Fernandes, 'Em busca de uma sociologia crítica e militante', in *A sociologia no Brasil* (Petrópolis, 1977), pp. 140–212. Many facets of Fernandes's personal, academic and intellectual career are examined in Maria Angela D'Incao (ed.), *O saber militante: ensaios sobre Florestan Fernandes* (Rio de Janeiro and São Paulo, 1987).

[163] For a complementary reminiscence by Claude Lévi-Strauss of his period as a young visiting professor at the University of São Paulo, see his *Tristes Tropiques* (New York, 1964), pp. 106–8.

society as oppressive and repressive as the Brazilian'. To have linked his socialist tenets to his position as a sociologist at this time would have exceeded the bounds of the 'scientific sociology' that was accepted by the power elite as a misunderstood positivist sociologism. Meanwhile he cultivated his private determination to bind Engelsian materialist sociology to a pathology of present society and to the collapse of capitalism as foretold by Rosa Luxemburg. Instead of devoting his initial research to this agenda, however, he selected two themes that led to the human bedrock of Brazil: the Tupinambá Indians on the eve of European conquest and black–white relations since slavery. The Tupinambá taught him the 'folk philosophy' of their society where those who had nothing to divide shared their own persons with others. Here Fernandez acquired his primary 'wisdom about man, life, and the world'. His second understanding arose from his work with Bastide on blacks and whites in São Paulo. In the early 1950 few would have selected racism to spearhead an inquiry into industrializing São Paulo, where blacks were a small fraction of the population and race a subsidiary issue. Yet Fernandes's project forced him to reconstruct the region's economic history and its transition to capitalism; to interpret abolition as a revolution of 'whites for whites' that hastened consolidation of the urban, industrial economy; to juxtapose racial and social stratification, yielding the hypothesis of a transition from a society of 'estates' (*sociedade estamental*) to one of classes that created a 'bourgeois revolution'; and to identify mechanisms of control applied to all disinherited groups irrespective of race.[164] If his studies of the Tupinambá celebrated the sardines, his analysis of estates and classes indicted the sharks.

As substitute in 1952 for Roger Bastide in his sociology chair at the University of São Paulo and its occupant in 1955, Fernandes resolved to create a 'greenhouse' as a counter-institution within the establishment. The intent was to nurture a sociology 'made in Brazil' (as distinct from a 'Brazilian sociology') and to open 'political space' from which to influence the seat of academic power. While Fernandes's co-workers over the years were not united on doctrinal grounds, they shared a commitment to construct a sociology for developing lands from 'a descriptive, comparative, or historico-differential perspective'. They would not compete with

---

164 See Roger Bastide and Florestan Fernandes (eds.), *Relações raciais entre negros e brancos em São Paulo* (São Paulo, 1955) and Florestan Fernandes, *The Negro in Brazilian Society*, trans. J. D. Skiles et al. (New York, 1969). Fernandes's disciples, Fernando Henrique Cardoso and Otávio Ianni, extended the research on São Paulo to the southern states of Paraná, Santa Catarina and Rio Grande do Sul. See also Florestan Fernandes, *A revolução burguesa no Brasil: ensaio de interpretação sociológica* (Rio de Janeiro, 1975).

sociologists from metropolitan nations, yet would break with the eclecticism of foreign mentors. Although he enjoyed theoretical sociology and never abjured his faith in science, Fernandes felt obliged to descend from the Olympian heights of 'scholarship' and face the blind alley of dependent capitalism in a society that with no militant socialist movement could never duplicate the classic bourgeois revolution of Europe. The task was to revisit old questions but isolating Marxian 'specific differences' and demystifying a 'bourgeois conscience' that was 'dependent, ultraconservative, and profoundly pro-imperialist'. With a strong foundation in his earlier work he turned directly toward research themes that were at the crux of Brazil's impending crisis: entrepreneurship, labour, education, the state, political participation and internal relations.[165]

To trace Latin American sociology since the 1940s wholly through the careers and writings of eminent scholars would be to highlight theoretical concerns and to neglect the pragmatic, reductionist uses of their speculations by university communities. In the late 1950s universities began to expand at a dizzying rate. The professional curricula that for generations had validated the status and careers of upper-class sons as lawyers, doctors and engineers (or dentists and veterinarians for the less fortunate) were hopelessly inadequate for training the leadership and middle-management cadres needed to inflate and modernize public and private-sector bureaucracies at a time when 'development' was the order of the day. The academic solution was to create departments and faculties of social science on an emergency schedule. In the 1930s a few institutions, such as El Colegio de México and, despite the reservations of Fernandes, the University of São Paulo, had been well placed to adapt curricula to domestic society and culture. But the perceived need to apply 'science' to human affairs was now so urgent, and funding for academic staff and infrastructure so abundant after 1960s, that there was little time for judicious redesigning of foreign (notably U.S.) curricular models, much less for creative innovation *in situ*.[166] During the 1970s, the poet-economist Gabriel Zaid tells us, the caloric intake of Mexicans declined by 5 per cent; yet the budget for the National University increased by 600 per cent and that for regional universities by 1,400 per cent. For Zaid the implication was that the mere presence of a marginal population feeds the growth of bureaucratic pyra-

[165] Along with many colleagues Fernandes was removed from his university position by the military government in 1969, and regained it only in 1986. That same year he was elected to Brazil's congress/constituent assembly as a candidate of the Partido dos Trabalhadores (PT).

[166] See Florestan Fernandes, *Universidade brasileira: reforma ou revolução?* (São Paulo, 1975).

mids at the centre; simply by existing, destitute villages create a 'need' for contractors, tax collectors, amiable and well-informed tour guides, to say nothing of Mexican anthropologists holding foreign doctorates and expensively trained to document at grass roots level the nation's grievous socioeconomic asymmetries.[167]

Funding for academic expansion came largely from Latin American governments, often externally financed, that saw universities as a source of planners and technocrats and as a means of co-opting the allegiance of the new middle classes. Secondarily, support came directly from foreign governments and private foundations anxious to assist the 'evolutionary' progress of the region. Whereas previously the Kellogg and Rockefeller Foundations had tackled the generally non-controversial fields of medicine and agriculture, the younger Ford Foundation now moved into the social sciences while attempting to maintain the applied or practical intentions of its predecessors. Mounting campaigns against malaria or infertile soil, however, was not the same as devising remedies for school desertion, income concentration, and authoritarianism. Issues of culture and ideology caused the grantors to loosen their criterion of direct empirical relevance. The Ford Foundation won distinction by its strategic, hand-crafted programme of fellowships, research support, curriculum development and concern for human rights and its success at selling a pluralistic, or at least permissive, but essentially U.S. version of the social science enterprise to intellectual elites in Latin America.

The apparent paradox was that the North Americanization of the new social science establishments (with generous European and domestic accents to be sure) occurred precisely when large sectors of them were drawn to one or another brand of activist or intellectual Marxism, or else simply to the idea of Marxism. After its transplantation in the revisionist version of Juan B. Justo and the 'indigenous' version of Mariátegui, Marxism had fallen into disrepute as a result of disenchantment with Stalinism in the 1930s, the Allied war against fascism in the 1940s, and developmentalist hopes of the 1950s. Apart from the party apparatus, only such intellectual stalwarts as Caio Prado Júnior and Aníbal Ponce, along with the Cuban journal *Dialéctica,* kept alive its intellectual promise. Suddenly, with the economic polarization of national societies, the loss of faith in developmentalism and in the 'benevolence' of international capitalism and the stirring example of a 'fresh start' in Cuba, Marxism regained its initiative.

---

[167] Gabriel Zaid, *El progreso improductivo* (Mexico, D.F., 1979).

The joint hegemony of U.S. methods and Marxist interpretations in the social sciences was paradoxical but not illogical. According to Rolando Franco, 'Latin America had national schools for teaching sociology directed by Marxist socialists that, before the second half of the 1960s, differed in no way from the "functionalist" orientation professed at similar places with other objectives.'[168] As Dumont and Foucault have both held, Marxism did not represent an 'epistemic break' with Ricardian economics but was its logical culmination. Economics took priority for Smith and Ricardo, then assumed hegemony for Marx and Engels.[169] Both liberal empiricism and Marxian 'science' strove to unmask a social reality more concrete and definitive than the quasi-Hegelian Latin American 'reality' evoked by essayists and philosophers. Empiricists and Marxists alike arrayed the branches of inquiry in a hierarchy – whether a 'priapic' scale from hard to soft disciplines (i.e., economics to literature) or a Marxian ladder from infrastructure to superstructure. Because the essayists disregarded this scalar construction – or else like Lezama reversed it to favour an 'imagistic' strategy; or like Gabriel Zaid contrasted the voracity of economics with the veracity of poetry – Latin American and particularly U.S. social scientists found them 'soft' and 'subjective'. It is no surprise, then, to find fluent traffic between liberal empiricists and Marxists, for while their *politics* were poles apart their *ideologies,* in Dumont's sense of the term, were similar.[170] However much their therapies differed, both outlooks fixed on instrumental goals and both accepted a vision of Latin America as penetrated from above, for better or for worse, by a structure of capitalist domination that was reaching the taproots of society. A vision of the region as a family of nations created during centuries and even millennia by those at its taproots was more difficult to come by. Such a picture has begun to emerge since 1970, although more often as a jigsaw puzzle, given academic specialization and tribal narcissism, than as a vision.

This account of the professionalization of social science is selective and designed to assist contrast with the simultaneous literary 'boom' of the

---

168 Franco, 'Veinticinco años de sociología latinoamericana', p. 83.

169 Louis Dumont, *From Mandeville to Marx* (Chicago, Ill., 1983), pp. 147–8; Michel Foucault, *Power/Knowledge,* trans. C. Gordon et al. (New York, 1980), p. 76; Alan Sheridan, *Michel Foucault: The Will to Truth* (London, 1980), pp. 70–3.

170 In his chapter, 'A Comparative Approach to Modern Ideology and to the Place within it of Economic Thought' (in *From Mandeville to Marx,* pp. 3–30), Dumont defines ideology not in the derogatory sense but as 'the totality of ideas and values – or "representations" – common to a society or current in a given group'. In this, he means that England, France and Germany have held a common ideology since the seventeenth century in comparison to India, China or Japan.

late 1950s and 1960s. The pairing is devised not so as to characterize academic and literary phenomena as such but to probe their respective premises, or ideologies in Dumont's sense, and suggest their relation to broader Western context. The social scientists, for all their internal quarrels, drew energies from new or newly modernized universities; from unprecedented salaries, fellowships abroad and research grants; and from a common project of demystifying the colonial past, the pseudo-science of positivism and the slackness of belletrism and of blazing the paths for national development. Although the social sciences created a more sudden and compact explosion than did the literature of the period, it was not seen as a 'boom', given its rationality of purpose and its matter-of-fact management by governmental and philanthropic agencies.

The literary 'boom' was so called because of factors external to literature itself, such as the availability of expert translators for an international audience and campaigns by publishers to enrich the often lacklustre metropolitan literary menu of the period with exotic narratives. Rodríguez Monegal decorated his incisive account of the 'boom' with wittily chosen epigraphs to document ancient uses of the term and to trace the origins of the 'boom' itself to the late nineteenth century.[171] Authors like Borges and Asturias who began writing in the 1920s were now swept into visibility along with Mario Vargas Llosa, born in 1936. Although by now there exist elegant treatments of the literary generation born in the 1920s and 1930s, they often deal with 'influences' and 'idiosyncrasies'. Actually, to categorize a 'group project' is more difficult with novelists than with social scientists. 'Boom' yields no such generational handle as romanticism or naturalism. This becomes clear from leafing through any collection of mutually critical interviews with writers – for example, that of Rita Guibert.[172]

Since interviews offer few solid clues, two handles will be used in what follows but with no pretense of literary exegesis: marvellous realism and, in a non-technical sense, deconstruction. Magic realism and marvellous realism, which acquired currency during the boom, should be distinguished from each other, and both of them from surrealism and the fantastic, which date from modernism. Although surrealism might be called a modern invention, all have antecedents in past centuries of European arts and literature. At a still earlier period, when people 'believed in'

[171] Emir Rodríguez Monegal, *El Boom de la novela latinoamericana* (Caracas, 1972).
[172] Rita Guibert, *Seven Voices* (New York, 1973).

God and the devil, the supernatural and magic, such 'realisms' would not have had today's oxymoronic connotations. To define them loosely: magic realism refers to causality that is contrary to 'natural laws'. Marvellous realism refers to the extraordinary or unaccustomed (*lo insólito*) but is consonant with 'reality' and induces enchantment without the dread or presentiments of the fantastic. The fantastic evokes anxiety (fear) through intellectual anxiety (doubt). Surrealism projects spontaneous thought or images from the subconscious, free of convention and rational control.[173] None, not even magic or marvellous realism, was a Latin American creation. In its modernist guise the 'marvellous' appeared as an aesthetic category in André Breton's *Manifesto* of 1924, while in 1925 magic realism was the subject of a book by Franz Roh, a German; Pierre Mabille published *Le miroir du merveilleux* in 1940. In Latin America meanwhile Borges wrote a graceful landmark essay, 'Narrative Art and Magic' (1932),[174] and a few years later explored the fantastic vein. Preliminary but somewhat inconsistent formulations of magic realism were offered by Arturo Uslar Pietri in 1948 and Angel Flores in 1954. But the Latin American 'authority' became Alejo Carpentier (1904–80), starting with his 1948 statement and continuing to his collected interpretations in the early 1960s.[175] In retrospect it turned out that earlier fiction by Borges, Asturias and Arguedas or subsequent works by Rulfo, Roa Bastos, Vargas Llosa, Onetti and above all García Márquez had broken with the discourse of realism, infusing it in various manners with *lo maravilloso,* but it was Carpentier, with his highly readable texts, analytic essays and explicit concern with Caribbean or Latin American 'identity' who championed the cause.

Carpentier's trip to Haiti in 1943 led to the pivotal prologue to his novel *The Kingdom of this World* (1949) where he announced his discovery that 'the history of all America is but a chronicle of marvellous realism'.[176] After leaving Paris, where he had lived from 1927 to 1939, he lived till 1945 in

---

173 See Irlemar Chiampi, *O realismo maravilhoso: forma e ideologia no romance hispano-americano* (São Paulo, 1980).

174 Jorge Luis Borges, 'El arte narrativo y la magia', *Obras completas* (Buenos Aires, 1974). pp. 226–32.

175 For Mabille's influence on Carpentier, see Irlemar Chiampi. 'Carpentier y el surrealismo', *Revista Língua e Literatura,* 9 (1980), 155–74.

176 The prologue appeared separately in 1948 and then only in the novel's first edition; it was reprinted in Carpentier's *Tientos y diferencias* (Havana, 1966), pp. 95–9. See Emma Susana Speratti-Piñero, *Pasos hallados en El reino de este mundo* (Mexico, D.F., 1981); Alejo Carpentier, *Entrevistas,* ed. Virgilio López Lemus (Havana, 1985); González Echevarría, *Alejo Carpentier,* pp. 107–29; Alexis Márquez Rodríguez, *Lo barroco y lo real-maravilloso en la obra de Alejo Carpentier* (Mexico, D.F., 1982); Rodríguez Monegal, 'Lo Real y lo maravilloso'.

Cuba, then moved to Venezuela as a voluntary exile. On coming home to America he had plunged into colonial texts spending eight years in a passionate search to fathom the American world. In 1964 he observed that 'America seemed to me an enormous nebula that I tried to understand because I had the obscure intention that my work would unfold here, would become deeply American.' In what some call Carpentier's fullest definition of the 'marvellous' he relates how 'it arises from an unexpected alteration of reality (the miracle), from a privileged revelation of reality, . . . from a widening of the scales and categories of reality, as perceived with particular intensity by an exaltation of the spirit that leads it to an "ultimate state" (*estado límite*)'. Chiampi, who cites this interview, notes that Carpentier uses two sets of verbs: those like 'alter' and 'widen' denoting a modification of reality, and those like 'reveal' and 'perceive' that imply a mimetic function. This oscillation appears to be intentional, rendering the marvellous as both a perception that deforms the object and as a component of reality. Phenomenological and ontological positions are thus joined to resolve the apparent contradiction of 'deform' and 'exhibit'.[177]

Carpentier's famous 'prologue' criticized the emptiness of European modernism (although it had put him on his track). And if Europeans were also searching for alternatives to the formulae of 'Western' culture in primitivism, realm of the unconscious, Nietzsche or Bergsonian vitalism, for Carpentier these led only to general abstractions. The notable case was surrealism, which was for him never more than an artifice like certain oneiric writings or praises of folly of which he had tired. He felt the marvellous presupposed a faith. Those who are not Quixotes, he wrote, cannot throw themselves into the world of Amadís de Gaula. Unlike collective dance in America, that in Western Europe had lost magic or invocatory power. In Haiti thousands of men yearning for freedom had believed in the lycanthropic powers of Mackandal, a collective faith that produced a miracle at his execution. What Carpentier yearned for was to connect the realities of America to marvellous elements of the culture and not, as he felt surrealism did, to a universal logic. On all this he differs greatly from Borges, who dismissed Argentine identity as an unavoidable fatality or else mere affectation, and for whom magic and the fantastic were universals (as in his 1932 essay on magic). Indeed Borges could write a story of eleven lines, '*La trama*', which is universal, Argentine, realistic, magic, marvellous, fantastic, and − why not? − surrealist all at once. In

[177] Chiampi, *Realismo maravilhoso*, pp. 32−4.

the first paragraph Caesar, surrounded by assassins, sees Brutus among them and exclaims, '*Tú también, hijo mío!*' Nineteen centuries later a gaucho in southern Buenos Aires, attacked by other gauchos, sees his godchild among them and says quietly, '*¡Pero, che!*' 'They kill him and he doesn't know that he dies so that a scene may reoccur.'

Carpentier's commentaries are useful because he wrote from his French experience and with Gallic clarity (though not without contradiction and ambivalence) in reappropriating his Latin American origins. He created sophisticated publicity for the 'boom' of the sixties and the vitality of Latin American culture, much as writers and artists had done for Mexico half a century earlier. His pronouncements, however, do not yield direct access to such diverse texts, even if 'marvellous', as those of Rulfo, Guimarães Rosa and García Márquez. Indeed, his personal 'truth' lies in his novels, not his essays. Looking beyond technical literary analysis, however, Carpentier and others who joined him deserve their role in the arena of cultural history. For one thing, his case for marvellous realism lends vivid, non-intellectualized vocabulary and imagery to the abstracted identity quest and the balancing of localism and universalism discussed above for philosophers and sociologists. We can now relate Borges and Carpentier to the philosophic part of the inquiry by classifying the former as one who posits the 'defining qualities of man and history in a universal sense' and identifies magic, hallucination, and narrative not as embedded in specific cultures but as 'superficially dissimilar although homologous manifestations of being'. Carpentier on the other hand, like most Latin American artists and intellectuals, González Echevarría holds, adopted a polycentric Spenglerian and Orteguian view of world history that accommodates magic and the marvellous to cultural specificity.[178]

A further point is that marvellous realism translates into the sociological terms of enchantment and disenchantment. As originally proposed this Weberian polarity implied gradual intrusion, with modernization and industrialism, of an ethos of rationalization affecting all realms of personal and institutional behaviour. This is what Carpentier deplored in Europe and found therapy for in America. Here, despite poverty and caudillism, one still found cultural plurality, myth, eternal return, spontaneity and human rapport. In societies that had not since independence managed to universalize rationalization, where large countries seemed permanent Belgiums inserted into Indias, human communities that evinced aptitude for

[178] González Echevarría, *Alejo Carpentier*, p. 122.

the marvellous seemed fated to be permanent fixtures. They would not turn into the vanishing gypsy dancers of romantic Europe. When young Haitian modernists published a literary *Revue Indigène* in 1927, the title 'indigenous' did not mean 'native' American but referred to an alternative, non-rationalized culture, once called 'barbaric' or primitive. Moreover, because nations so constructed are anomalies in the West, they at times fall under the sway of homebred caudillos who confront the invasion of 'rational' commercialism and imperialism in 'marvellous' ways. Their careers became special narrative projects for Asturias, Carpentier, Roa Bastos, García Márquez, Fuentes and others.[179] If novelists accepted a permanent indigenous presence, developmental or Marxian social scientists found this premise difficult to reconcile with their evolutionary faith. But since the 1960s – while economics, political science and sociology remain ensconced for their instrumental importance (despite their grievous errors of diagnosis) – it would seem that social anthropology, ethnohistory, literary criticism, psychology, sociology of ideas and kindred fields have moved to the cutting edge of social studies. It seems also that the profession of the essayist, who knows how to synthesize gracefully without perspiring, has not fallen from fashion. Meanwhile, who knows what the poets and novelists have in store?

An important strategy that literary criticism offers for the study of Latin America remains to be mentioned. Marvellous realism, one must grant, has become shopworn and acquired too many connotations, from the empirical to the imaginative, for it to do much more than call attention or set a mood or inspire private visions. Like social science, however, literary study may offer schemas rather than themes, whose purpose is not to describe or savour phenomena but to demonstrate fresh ways of arranging them. The goal is not investigation or evocation but reconceptualization. As we saw, social scientists were bent on reconceiving society or, in a significant term used by some, demystifying it. Yet, irrespective of their political ideologies, they accepted (or at least pledged fealty to) the ground rules of science and empiricism. Their diagnoses, built on Western maxims and ideas, were certainly in commonsensical ways *critical,* but their prescriptions seemed drawn from a familiar Western armory, with whatever seasoning from local historical and cultural accents.

For all its looseness and heterogeneity, what marvellous realism suggested was that here were *different* societies, even though nestled in the

---

[179] Angel Rama, *La novela latinoamericana, 1920–80* (Bogotá, 1982), pp. 361–419.

bosom of the West. Once a novelist suspects that his job may not be primarily to *demystify,* which most serious writers can manage, but to *deconstruct* vocabulary and categories, then the game becomes a free-for-all. When available discourse fails to capture circumstances, artists sometimes excel at opening paths to recognition. To demystify is to draw aside a veil from a scene known to exist. To deconstruct is to examine elements of a bogus scene so as to recombine them in a cognitively more satisfying pattern. Although lacking the instrumental imperative of demystification, deconstruction enjoys more imaginative scope.

Here we may borrow five cases offered by the Peruvian critic Julio Ortega that illustrate ways in which talented authors, with different aims and tactics, succeed in dissolving familiar worlds.[180] He starts with the 'critical writing' of Borges whereby literature examines the functions of language so as to question its own function. Borges, in Ortega's view, approaches culture not as a monument but as a text. As did Joyce and Picasso he deconstructs the idea of a stable culture, 'the idea of information as a museum, as a hierarchical, exemplary, hegemonic monumentality . . . Within culture, the notion of "truth" thus becomes a formal operation that is no less fantastic than the literary act itself.' To abbreviate Ortega's other cases: The 'mythical writing' of Rulfo deconstructs a social life while constructing the ideological space of a social hell; in his 'colloquial writing' Cortázar deconstructs the genre of the novel itself and establishes a code for fresh dialogue; Lezama Lima uses 'poetic writing' to deconstruct the notion of referentiality in favour of the text as 'abundance of meaning'; and finally García Márquez using 'fictional writing' deconstructs history by shifting it to the 'critical consensus of popular culture'.

Examples now crop up to show that even the iron laws of liberal/Marxist economics are vulnerable to deconstruction which, if practised with high critical skills, is more persuasive and constructive than blunt academic refutation. Poet-economist Zaid relegates statistics to a bristling appendix and deconstructs them in the text with a 'biblical' parable that compares the indigent potter's six sons, who work hard from childhood and marry only when they can afford it, with the economist's six sons, who acquire tuition bills and mortgaged houses long before parasitic jobs are created for them in the 'pyramids'. Anthropologist Stephen Gudeman shows that

---

[180] Julio Ortega, *Poetics of Change: The New Spanish-American Narrative* (Austin, Tex., 1984), pp. 3–119.

the language of Colombian peasants is serviceable for their economic life, even though it contains no liberal/Marxist vocabulary (which would require deconstruction for them) to designate 'profit', 'capital', 'interest', or 'investment'. Anthropologist Michael Taussig shows how Andean peasants and tin miners instead of surrendering to commodity fetishism resist economic 'laws' by anthropomorphizing (or *re*constructing) their domination in the form of contracts with the devil, thus re-enacting the first historical moment of subjection. Finally, the Brazilian anthropologist Muniz Sodré confronts the premises of Western economics with a 'seduced truth' of African inspiration that, being symbolic, is also reversible. Once ritualized, truth is purged of univocal doctrinal meaning. Afro-Brazilian ritual arenas therefore expose reversibilities of the global society to replace, for example, the Western axiom 'exchange creates surplus' with the more venerable axiom that 'exchange is reciprocal' and requires restitution.[181]

CONCLUSION

We now come to a point where, in framing a conclusion, it is possible to suggest how the half century treated in these pages bears a relationship to developments in Europe since the Enlightenment, specifically the co-existence of literary and scientific establishments. While Latin America has accompanied these developments for two centuries thanks to individual *pensadores* or generational coteries or bookstores and newspapers or foreign travel by the privileged or somewhat problematic academic institutions (Mexico and Brazil even lacked universities in the nineteenth century), it has only since the 1920s boasted literary establishments of international calibre and linkage, and only since the 1950s has it groomed its cadres of social scientists. In *Between Literature and Science: the Rise of Sociology* Wolf Lepenies uses France, England and Germany to show that in the late eighteenth century no sharp division of literary and scientific works had yet occurred.[182] He identifies Buffon, whose *Histoire naturelle* attained 250 popular editions, as the last scholar whose reputation rested on stylistic presentation and the first to lose it because his research was

---

[181] Zaid, *Progreso improductivo;* Stephen F. Gudeman, *Economics as Culture: Models and Metaphors of Livelihood* (London, 1986); Michael T. Taussig, *The Devil and Commodity Fetishism in South America* (Chapel Hill, 1980); Muniz Sodré, *A verdade seduzida: por um conceito de cultura no Brasil* (Rio de Janeiro, 1983).

[182] Wolf Lepenies, *Between Literature and Science: The Rise of Sociology,* trans. R. J. Hollingdale (Cambridge, Eng., 1988).

erratic.[183] He was a prototype for Latin American *pensadores* of a century later whose world had not yet split into the 'two cultures'.

The encroachment of science, such as encyclopaedism or English economics, was countered by the romantic reaction, emphasizing the sanctity of the self and Wordsworthian lyricism in England, and in Germany historicity, community and the spirit. The tension between literature and science has lasted for generations, in England through such notable paired champions as Coleridge and Bentham, then Matthew Arnold and T. H. Huxley, then F. R. Leavis and C. P. Snow.[184] The German case is of special interest for Latin America. Dumont contrasts post-Enlightenment individualist or 'nominalist' England and France with the 'holistic' countries in the rest of the world.[185] His critical case is Germany, which offered the example of a peripheral culture making ideological adjustment to modernity as 'the first underdeveloped country'. Yet if German culture was 'holistic', it was early to accept Lutheran individualism, a pietist or internal individualism, however, that left intact the sentiment of global community unlike the modern nominalist brand. German culture was therefore favourable for mediation. Without referring to Latin America, Dumont opens conceptual space wherein to treat it alongside other world regions. His categories of nominalism and holism remind us, on one hand, of the shift in affiliation of Latin American elites after 1760 from Iberian to Anglo-French intellectual outlooks and, on the other, to the increasing 'visibility' of indigenous and African elements in the twentieth century. The 'premature' Latin American embrace of nominalism postponed a coming to terms with issues raised by the German critique of Enlightenment universalism until the reception of early twentieth-century German philosophy.

Octavio Paz has his own controversial interpretation of why the literature-science split failed to occur in Latin America after independence.[186] (In Europe the 'two cultures' were of course permeated by crossovers. The 'artist' Balzac took Buffon at face value as a 'scientist' and tried to do for human society what Buffon had done for zoology. Later, the 'scientists' Marx and Engels claimed to have learned more from Balzac

[183] Buffon, a man of imposing size, thought large mammals far more admirable than insects, a prejudice reinforced by his inability to use a microscope because he was short-sighted. Antonello Gerbi, *The Dispute of the New World*, trans. Jeremy Moyle, rev. ed. (Pittsburgh, Pa., 1973), pp. 15–20.

[184] John Stuart Mill, *On Bentham and Coleridge*, ed. F. R. Leavis (New York, 1962); Lionel Trilling, 'The Leavis-Snow Controversy', in *Beyond Culture* (New York, 1979), pp. 126–54.

[185] Dumont, *From Mandeville to Marx*, pp. 3–30, and *Essays on Individualism* (Chicago, Ill., 1986), pp. 76–132.

[186] Octavio Paz, *Children of the Mire*, chs. 5, 6.

than from economists and historians.) Paz's point, however, is that the Iberian world could not incubate modern literature because it had no modern age, 'neither critical reason nor bourgeois revolution', to provoke the process. Spanish romanticism was therefore superficial and sentimental, and Spanish America could only imitate Spain. The romantic 'urge to change reality' or 'unite life and art', Paz argues, was postponed in Latin America until the modernist age whose branching impulses were much the same as romantic ones: into magic or politics, into religious or revolutionary temptation. Because Paz feels that positivism in nineteenth-century Latin America was not the outlook of a liberal bourgeoisie interested in industrial and social progress, it was therefore 'an ideology and a belief', not a culture of science. He concludes that Europe's science-romantic binomial was postponed there for a century: 'Positivism is the Spanish American equivalent of the European Enlightenment, and modernism was our Romantic reaction.'

Antônio Cândido criticized Paz's argument *avant la lettre* when in his magisterial *Formation of Brazilian Literature* he pointed out the importance of the individual and of history in Brazilian romanticism, not wholly as a European imposition but as part of a domestic 'invention' of nationhood, identity and literature. Cândido confirms Paz, however, in noting that the possibilities opened by Brazilian romanticism were later 'carried to the extreme, as in Symbolism and various modernist currents'. González Echevarría explicitly criticizes Paz in holding that, while Latin America may not have produced romantics of German or English stature, the issues of modernity were vital dilemmas there too, and one must study their spokesmen in thought no less than in action. Through an analysis of Carpentier's *Explosion in the Cathedral* he shows how a modern-(ist) writer may project an analogy between the modernism of the eighteenth century and that of his own time, or 'a counterpoint between self-conscious modernities'.[187]

The two positions on romanticism just examined are not wholly antithetical, for both recognize affinities between romanticism and modernism; but for Paz the romantic impulse of Latin American modernists is a discovery

---

[187] Antônio Cândido, *Formação da literatura brasileira (momentos decisivos)*, 2nd ed.; 2 vols. (São Paulo, 1964), Vol. II, pp. 23–34; González Echevarría, *Voice of the Masters*, pp. 33–6, 171–72n. and *Alejo Carpentier*, pp. 226, 234. In *Sources of the Self: The Making of the Modern Identity* (Cambridge, Mass., 1989), chs. 21–4, Charles Taylor emphasizes the persistent engagement, far into the modernist age, of Enlightenment and romanticism: not as two 'styles' of sensibility but as an evolving contention between instrumental reason and the emergent freedom of the self-determining subject.

while for Cândido and González Echevarría it is a recovery. The critical point is that irrespective of the judgement on romanticism, the culture of science, which fuelled European romanticism in positive as well as hostile ways, was not yet available in Latin America to energize the dialectic. The Olympian Machado de Assis turned his back on the whole romantic-scientistic-naturalist farrago and went his way with Dante and Menippean satire. What this chapter has attempted is to characterize the (re)birth of romanticism in modernism, then the provisional rapprochement, in Charles Taylor's terms, between the 'emergent freedom of the self-determining subject' and 'instrumental reason', culminating in the Latin American version of the literature-science split that Lepenies documents for Europe. This is not a case of delayed replication of the metropolis. The Latin American setting makes a world of difference. What matters are analogies, which illuminate and assist interpretation of both arenas of the phenomenon. Earlier it was suggested that the instrumental guideposts of Latin American social science in the 1960s are no longer seen as determinative and are slowly yielding to recognition that peoples, not policies, determine outcomes. As for literature, Antônio Cândido speculates that the romantic agenda of regionalism, still a heavy influence on modernism (as evinced above by the three discrete urban locales of São Paulo, Buenos Aires and Mexico City) and on the novels of the 1930s and 1940s, has now given way to a 'super-regionalism' that absorbs cultural specificity into the discourse of universalism. Guimarães Rosa was the pioneer, followed by Rulfo, García Márquez, Vargas Llosa and many others.[188] The intellectual hegemony of scientism and romanticism may have drawn to a close – to create, *ça va sans dire,* new challenges.

---

[188] Antônio Cândido, 'Literatura, espelho da América?', paper for the conference 'Reflections on Culture and Ideology in the Americas', Oliveira Lima Library, Washington, D.C., 19–21 March 1993.

Part Two

2

POLITICAL IDEAS AND IDEOLOGIES IN LATIN AMERICA, 1870–1930

Political ideas in Latin America have been affected by two obvious though frequently unappreciated facts that distinguish the region from other parts of the 'non-Western', 'developing', or 'third' world with which it has often been compared. First, the culture of Latin America's governing and intellectual elites is integrally Western, that is, it has emerged within the broader confines of Western European culture, modified of course by the special characteristics Spain and Portugal imparted to their former colonies. Second, the nations of Latin America, with the exception of Cuba, gained their political independence at the beginning of the nineteenth century.

It is now common to refer to nineteenth-century Latin America as 'neo-colonial', which suggests a situation of economic and cultural dependence for nations that were politically independent. The implication is that independence was formal and superficial and that dependence was the deeper and more significant experience of the region. It is clear that the elites of nineteenth-century Latin America were tied to, even dependent on, Europe, and that their economic interests within the international capitalist system formed part of that tie. It is also clear that the bond with Europe was strengthened after 1870, with the burgeoning of the Latin American export economies. Less clear is that the circumstance of early political independence can be regarded as a superficial element in Latin American culture. On the contrary, the ideologies, political programmes and social theories of the nineteenth century, while intellectually 'European', were nonetheless distinctive and authentically 'Latin American', in part because they emerged in politically independent nations. To dismiss or downgrade these political and social ideas as 'imitative' or 'derivative', or as mere rationalisations for the economic interests of a dependent governing class, is to make insignificant what was regarded then as of great significance, and to distort our understanding of Latin American history.

THE LIBERAL HERITAGE

We begin this chapter with a discussion of liberalism, which in the newly independent nations formed the basis of programmes and theories for the establishment and consolidation of governments and the reorganization of societies. The distinctive experience of liberalism in Latin America derived from the fact that liberal ideas were applied in countries which were highly stratified, socially and racially, and economically underdeveloped, and in which the tradition of centralized state authority ran deep. In short, they were applied in an environment which was resistant and hostile, and which in some cases engendered a strong opposing ideology of conservatism. The years from the 1820s till about 1870, in contrast to the era that followed, were ones of ideological conflict and political confusion. They were also years in which the classic doctrines of liberalism underwent severe modification within this unique environment, a modification which followed changes within European thought itself.

As perceived by the contemporary elites of Latin America, the two decades following 1870 represented the fulfilment of liberalism. With the victory of the liberal forces over the empire of Maximilian in Mexico in 1867 and the abdication of Pedro II in Brazil in 1889, the remnants of the Old World monarchical system had succumbed to the New World system of republican, constitutional and representative institutions. The earlier American phenomenon of 'barbarous' regional caudillos finally yielded to a 'civilized' and uniform regime of law, most dramatically in Argentina but also in other nations. The liberal struggle to establish the secular state had been won, the result in Mexico of civil war and imposition of the Laws of Reform, and of more moderately enacted legislation in Argentina, Brazil and Chile. The obscurantist restraints of colonial society had given way to modern secular standards in education and in civil organization. 'Spiritual emancipation', the dream of early nineteenth-century liberals, was now a reality. Guided by the principles of free individual enterprise, the Latin American nations had entered the economic system of the civilized world. The resulting commercial prosperity and the growth of sophisticated, cosmopolitan, urban centres were for contemporaries only further signs that the liberal age had arrived.

What appeared the fulfilment of liberalism was in fact its transformation from an ideology in conflict with the inherited colonial order of institutions and social patterns into a unifying myth. In comparison with the first half-century following independence, the years after 1870 were years of political consensus. The classic liberal doctrines based on the autonomous individual gave way to theories construing the individual as an integral part of the social organism, conditioned by time and place and ever-changing as society itself changed. A theoretical conflict existed between classic or doctrinaire liberalism and the new concepts (often referred to loosely as 'positivism'), but it was a conflict that could be submerged in an era of consensus. However transformed, liberalism provided an almost universal heritage for the governing elites of the post-1870 years. Let us first, therefore, examine the principal elements of that heritage.

Republicanism and the American 'spirit'

Spanish American liberals of the mid-century decades were ambivalent toward Europe. Most shared the view of the Argentine, Juan Bautista Alberdi (1810–84) that their civilization was European and that 'our Revolution' in its ideas was no more than a phase of the great French Revolution. And yet, the New World held out hopes for human progress under free institutions, hopes which were continually being frustrated in the Old World. In short, there was a distinctive American 'spirit' separating the two worlds, at the heart of which was republicanism. Except in Brazil, political independence in the Western Hemisphere had entailed the rejection of monarchy, and Spanish American intellectuals throughout the century were sensitive to threats of monarchical restoration on their continent and to the ebb and flow of the republican ideal in Europe. This ideal was at its low point in the fifties and sixties, following the failure of the French and Italian republics in 1848 and the creation of the empire of Napoleon III. The brief presence of Maximilian of Hapsburg on a Mexican throne from 1864 to 1867 and the even briefer belligerence of monarchical Spain on the South American west coast in 1865–6 inspired an eloquent expression of Americanism, particularly by the Chileans José Victorino Lastarria (1817–88) and Francisco Bilbao (1823–65).

Both Lastarria and Bilbao had published notorious essays in the 1840s attacking the spiritual and social legacy of Spain in America. Lastarria excoriated the persisting feudal mentality and extolled utilitarian values that were consonant with the republican institutions Chile had adopted. Bilbao was more radical, calling for the 'de-hispanicizing', even the 'de-catholicizing', of Chile. Forced into exile, Bilbao spent the momentous years 1845 to 1850 in France, exposed to the growing republican movement, to the controversy over the role of the Church in education and, ultimately, to the Revolution of 1848 and its aftermath. He developed personal friendships with the liberal giants of the era, Felicité de Lammenais, Jules Michelet and Edgar Quinet. Quinet, himself an exile from Napoleon III's France, took a great interest in the young Chilean during the subsequent decade and encouraged the republicanism and the anti-Catholic mystical rationalism (tinged with freemasonry) which pervaded Bilbao's *América en peligro* (1862) and *El evangélico americano* (1864).

A year later, Bilbao died aged forty-two in Buenos Aires where he had published these tracts. His youth, his radical free-thinking views, and perhaps his unique cosmopolitanism, gave his writings wide currency among later generations. Bilbao's more moderate former teacher, Lastarria, struck similar themes and added others in *La América* (1865). For instance, he defended the 'liberal system' of republican North and South America against the 'ridiculous' recent notion that there existed a Latin race in Europe and America which shared a common destiny. For Lastarria, 'Latin' America was a Napoleonic idea designed to restore 'absolutism' in the New World.

The republican ideal was dramatically vindicated with the withdrawal of French troops from Mexico and the collapse of the Second Empire. The summary trial and execution of Maximilian and two Mexican Conservative generals in June 1867 was followed on 15 July by the declaration of Mexico's second independence by Benito Juárez, the embattled republican leader and hero of America. The Mexican victory evoked great enthusiasm among European republicans, thus removing much of the ambivalence Latin Americans had earlier expressed toward Europe. A principal agent of this new rapprochement of liberal Europe and America was the Spanish orator, republican propagandist, prolific publicist and statesman, Emilio Castelar. Though Castelar is today almost totally forgotten, his fame in Spanish America from 1870 to 1900 cannot be overestimated. He was the great Hispanic orator in an age of eloquence, and his verbose and elegant style was widely imitated in chamber and lecture hall. Since his employment as a politician after 1867 was sporadic, Castelar turned to journalism for a living, and for twenty-five years his fortnightly commentaries on Spanish and European politics filled newspapers (often the entire front page) in Buenos Aires, Lima, Mexico City and even New York.

As a pan-hispanist Castelar had reacted sharply to Bilbao's message of *desespañolización*. But the mood had now changed. Present at a Paris restaurant on 4 July 1867 when Domingo F. Sarmiento (1811–88) announced his candidacy for president of the Argentine Republic, Castelar toasted American democracy and the melding of the souls of Spain and America, as liberty triumphed on both continents. Sarmiento responded in kind with a tribute to Castelar's liberalism. The latter's prestige in America was further enhanced when he became president of the First Spanish Republic in September 1873. Castelar's policy of strong central government in the face of regional rebellions on the Left and the Right struck a responsive chord among those Latin American political leaders seeking a 'conservative-liberalism' in the years of consensus after 1870.

If the American spirit meant the advance of republican values and institutions, it also signified the plague of 'barbarous' caudillos who rose to power in the post-independence decades and whose power was sustained by charisma, by popular following, or by regional interests. In 1845 Sarmiento had evoked, even romanticized, the telluric force of the gaucho chieftain in his famous *Facundo: civilización i barbarie*. But Sarmiento was ambivalent toward this emanation of Americanism, for he also identified the march of civilization with the ascendancy of Buenos Aires, the city that faced outward toward Europe. After the gaucho tyrant, Juan Manuel de Rosas, had mastered Buenos Aires and triumphed over the provincial Facundo Quiroga, then 'the tyrant himself was superfluous' and fell in 1852 to the advance of liberal institutions.[1] Sarmiento was at heart a Buenos Aires centralist, an *unitario,* and it was fitting that he should as president of the Republic (1868–74) relentlessly pursue the last of the regional caudillos, Ricardo López Jordan of Entre Rios. 'Every caudillo carries my mark', announced Sarmiento proudly in the Senate.

Sarmiento's contemporaries in Mexico, Benito Juárez and Sebastián Lerdo de Tejada, also intervened vigorously in the provinces, following ten years of open civil conflict (1857–67), which had seen the strengthening of regional power centres such as Guerrero, San Luis Potosí and Yucatán. The government campaign to reduce provincial chieftains reached a climax in 1873 with the defeat and execution of Manuel Lozada, the long-time popular rebel and proto-agrarian reformer in the remote Sierra de Álica of Jalisco. Spanish American liberal governments after 1870 had no tolerance for 'Americanism' that took the form of regional and social challenges to central authority; and by 1880 Presidents Julio A. Roca of Argentina and Porfirio Díaz of Mexico could confidently proclaim the reign of 'peace and administration'.

The American spirit and its association with republicanism had by this

---

[1] D. F. Sarmiento, *Facundo,* ed. Alberto Palcos (Buenos Aires, 1961), 265.

time also made inroads in Brazil, the one Latin American nation to retain monarchical institutions. It was enunciated unequivocally in the Republican Manifesto of 1870, issued by a group of disaffected Liberal Party politicians and intellectuals. The Manifesto, which spawned a number of republican clubs and newspapers, grew from the internal political criticism, factional contention and call for reforms which accompanied the War with Paraguay (1865–70). Since the war allied Brazil with the republics of Argentina and Uruguay, it did much to make liberals aware of the ideological isolation of the Brazilian empire. This isolation was an important theme of the Manifesto. The restoration of the Republic of Mexico and the collapse of the European regime promoting monarchy in America clearly had an effect on Brazilians; the Manifesto, dated 3 December, was published only three months after the fall of Napoleon III. 'We are Americans', asserted the document. 'Our monarchical form of government is in its essence and practice contrary and hostile to the rights and interests of the American States.'

It should be noted, however, that in contrast with Spanish America, the most distinctive feature of the Brazilian republican movement, reiterated in the Manifesto, was its irrevocable tie to federalism. A republic had always meant the overthrow of an oppressively centralized monarchy and the establishment of provincial autonomy. In Spanish America, federalist challenges had to be made against already established centralist republics, not against monarchies. Despite this peculiarity, the growing republican cause in Brazil did much to enhance the sense of American solidarity among post-1870 liberals throughout the continent.

The decline of classic constitutionalism

A significant element of Latin America's liberal heritage was an enthusiasm for constitutional arrangements. Political independence had been achieved in the heyday of Western constitutionalism, the governing conviction of which was that a rationally conceived and written code of laws could effectively distribute political power and thus guarantee individual liberty, the mainspring of social harmony and progress. Constitutional liberals characteristically sought to limit authority by establishing legal barriers against the 'despotism' they associated with the colonial regime. In doing this they were guided by two variants of Enlightenment political philosophy, the natural rights of man and utilitarianism, variants which were theoretically in conflict but which had a common emphasis on the autonomous individual. The classic constitutional doctrines, though still persisting in some quarters in Latin America, had been seriously eroded as early as the 1830s and were in full decline by the 1870s.

The Argentine writers of the Asociación de Mayo and those of the Generation of 1842 in Chile derived their principal intellectual orientation from the broad European attack on the validity of the doctrines of natural rights and utility, doctrines now judged to be abstract, legalistic and of questionable universal application. Sarmiento acknowledged the new direction taken by the 'social sciences' in France after 1830. 'We then began', he wrote in 1845, 'to learn something of national inclinations, customs, and races, and of historical antecedents', and to abandon Bentham, Rousseau and Constant for the historians, Thierry, Michelet and Guizot, for Sismondi, and ultimately for Tocqueville.[2] Esteban Echeverría (1805–51), in his *Dogma socialista* (1839), was drawn to the precepts of Mazzini's Young Europe movement and the socialist 'religion of humanity' of Leroux; Alberdi, in his seminal essay, *Fragmento preliminar al estudio del derecho* (1837), cited Lerminier, the French popularizer of Savigny's comparative and historical approach to law. Law should be considered, said Alberdi, not as a 'collection of written documents', but as 'a living and continually progressing element of society'.[3]

In Chile Lastarria also mentioned Lerminier, but drew particularly from Quinet's introduction to his translation of Herder's philosophy of history. The laws of human progress and decadence can be found only in history, wrote Lastarria, not in nature.[4] *Sociabilidad,* as in Bilbao's *Sociabilidad chilena* (1844), became the key word of the day. Liberal reformers and constitution makers must be guided by the peculiarities of a country's historically conditioned social relations, not by abstract principles. In Mexico, this erosion of classic liberal doctrines appeared prior to the *Reforma* only in the essays of Mariano Otero, a minor figure. The Mexicans, by comparison with the Argentine and Chilean liberals, were peculiarly resistant before 1870 to new ideas from Europe.

The new orientation in Latin American social and legal thought was clearly reflected in the Argentine Constitution of 1853. Despite the acknowledged influence of the North American model on the document's form, much of its spirit was drawn from Alberdi's *Bases* (1852), written

---

[2] Sarmiento, *Facundo,* 118.
[3] J. B. Alberdi, 'Fragmento', *Obras completas* (Buenos Aires, 1886), I, 105.
[4] J. V. Lastarria, 'Investigaciones sobre la influencia social de la conquista i del sistema de los españoles en Chile' (1844), *Obras completas,* VII (Santiago, 1909), 25.

for the constitution makers from his exile in Chile. Applying the themes of his *Fragmento* of 1837, Alberdi called for originality in the Constitution; it should reflect the conditions of the people. The legalistic spirit of the Constitution of 1826 must be abandoned as out of harmony with the 'modern necessities of Argentine progress'.[5] Liberty is still the principal constitutional objective, but the new era demands more practicality and less theory. Constitution makers should be versed in economics, not just 'moral science'.[6] The Constitution of the newly consolidated Argentine nation must guarantee the expansion of commerce, the rise of a spirit of industry, the free pursuit of wealth, the entry of foreign capital and, most of all, immigration. These priorities were taken up and made specific in articles 25 and 67 of the document that emerged from the Convention at Santa Fe. Thus, the cult of material progress that engulfed the governing and intellectual elite between 1870 and 1914 was in harmony with the pragmatic spirit of the Constitution.

The precepts of the changing philosophy of law also worked to resolve the major constitutional issue of nineteenth-century Argentina: territorial organization. The Asociación de Mayo writers had sought to surmount the sterile conflict between federalists and *unitarios*. The ideals of the Buenos Aires *unitario* tradition and the interests of the provinces must be reconciled. In practice this reconciliation meant the adoption of the federal form of organization in 1853, along with a renewed commitment to make the city a federal district and thus the capital of the Republic. The opposition to federalization came principally from the province of Buenos Aires, which had monopolized the economic benefits of independence for half a century. When the Federal District was finally created in 1880, Alberdi saw the 'despotic power of evolution' and the 'natural progress of civilization' at work.[7] For him, the Colony had finally given way to the Republic. But the realization of the *unitario* dream also solidified the effective dominance of the city of Buenos Aires over the provinces. The theoretical federalism of the Constitution gave way to the realities of centralization.

In surveying the constitutions of the hemisphere in 1852, Alberdi singled out the Chilean code of 1833 (along with that of the United States) as a model of originality. One of the principal authors of this admirable document was Mariano Egaña, an aristocrat and frank political conserva-

[5] J. B. Alberdi, *Bases y puntos de partida para la organización política de la república argentina* (Buenos Aires, 1953), 14.
[6] *Ibid.*, 23.
[7] J. B. Alberdi, *La república argentina consolidada en 1880* (Buenos Aires, 1881), xiii.

tive, who had spent the years 1824–9 in Europe and had absorbed the ideas of Edmund Burke and the French traditionalists, Bonald and De Maistre. The final version of the Constitution modified some of Egaña's extreme proposals, such as an indefinitely re-electable president and an hereditary senate. Moreover, a reference was inserted to popular sovereignty. Yet the president still emerged as a monarch in republican dress, in concert with, but superior to, an oligarchic senate. Provision was made for the re-establishment of Church privileges and the entail of landed properties, both of which had been circumscribed in the Constitution of 1828. That a political liberal like Alberdi would praise this conservative document can be understood in part by the breadth of the reaction in European thought against the philosophy of natural rights and against the radical egalitarianism of the French Revolution. This change in philosophic premises could inspire both political liberals and conservatives. Alberdi's praise can also be understood as recognition of the prestige enjoyed by Chile's constitutional stability. The 'peace of Chile' seemed an enviable model for Argentina after a generation of civil war.

The Constitution of 1833 did engender much controversy in mid-century Chile, but it gradually diminished and yielded to consensus after 1891. Varied critics, including Lastarria, the historian Benjamín Vicuña Mackenna, and a future president, Federico Errázuriz, agreed that the document embodied a 'colonial reaction', guided by the authoritarian minister, Diego Portales, against the liberal spirit of the Revolution for Independence.[8] Their model was the Constitution of 1828, which could have implemented 'the great principle of social regeneration' and 'the democratic representative Republic'. However, since both critics and upholders of the Constitution of 1833 rejected the 'mechanistic' for the 'organic' view of society,[9] and since both adopted the historical philosophy of law, their positions were destined to merge. Moreover, both groups were part of the same narrow elite that showed pride in the country's peaceful economic growth and its victories in the War of the Pacific (1879–83). The Liberals could take satisfaction in the reforms of 1871–4, in particular the limitation of the presidency to one term. As one commentator in 1887 put it, 'the sickly and feeble plant of 1833' had 'grown into a

[8] J. V. Lastarria, 'Don Diego Portales. Juicio histórico' (1861), *Obras*, IX, 203; B. Vicuña Mackenna, *Don Diego Portales* (Santiago, 1937), 135–7 (1st edn 1883); F. Errázuriz, *Chile bajo el imperio de la constitución de 1828* (Santiago, 1861).

[9] The terms and phrases are Lastarria's, in 'Constitución de Chile comentada' (1856), *Obras*, 1, 193–6, 202–5.

gigantic fifty-year-old tree'.[10] With the shift of power from president to legislature following the Revolution of 1891, a benign Whig Interpretation emerged. The conservative Constitution was viewed by such liberal historians as Diego Barros Arana and Luis Galdames as an integral element in Chile's unique record of prosperity and peaceful evolution.

In Mexico, the liberal constitutionalist impulse was stronger and more persistent than in Argentina and Chile. The Constituent Congress of 1856–7 reacted sharply against the last government of Antonio López de Santa Anna (1853–5), whom it branded a conservative centralist dictator. The document that emerged from the Congress not only reaffirmed federalism, but also established a parliamentary regime based on a single-chamber legislature and a limited executive. Though the Constitution of 1857 served as the standard for the liberal and republican cause in the subsequent decade, it reigned only briefly, a few months in 1857 and from 1861 to 1863. Juárez was accorded formal dictatorial powers in 1864 to lead the struggle against Maximilian and the French. When the government's call for elections (*convocatoria*) came in August 1867, it included a series of 'reforms', particularly a presidential veto and the addition of a senate, designed to restore 'constitutional balance'. The phrase was that of Lerdo de Tejada, Juárez's chief minister and wartime deputy, who probably inspired the reforms. Their submission to a plebiscite, as proposed by the government, aroused strong opposition from defenders of the Constitution who regarded the procedure as arbitrary. For the next decade insurrection against the governments of Juárez and Lerdo could be mounted in the name of the Constitution, culminating in the successful rebellion of Porfirio Díaz in 1876.

Because it had been the banner of national defence against foreign intervention, the Mexican Constitution of 1857 acquired an aura of sanctity that was unique in Latin America. Yet by 1880 the defence of the pure Constitution had been decisively undermined. The influence of the historical school of law, through Edouard Laboulaye, a French adherent of Savigny, was apparent in the successful official campaign to reinstitute a senate. The Mexican Senate, like the Chilean Senate from 1833 to 1871, was designed to be not only a buttress against excessive democracy, but also an agent of centralization. Thus Porfirio Díaz, once in power, retained the Senate (adopted in 1874), despite the cry of his extreme constitutional-

---

[10] Cited in Simon Collier, 'Historiography of the "Portalian" period (1830–1891) in Chile', *Hispanic American Historical Review*, 57 (1977), 666.

ist followers to abolish it. A campaign further to reform the Constitution in the direction of 'stronger' government was launched by a self-styled new generation of intellectuals from 1878–80. Led by Justo Sierra (1848–1912), they combined the historical philosophy of law with new 'scientific' doctrines to provide significant support for an authoritarian regime that was to last thirty-five years. Though by no means dead, doctrinaire (or classic) constitutionalism in Mexico gave way to the imperatives of a new era of economic progress and political stability.

The supremacy of the secular state

The distinguishing element of the classic liberal programme in Latin America which set liberals apart from conservatives was the ideal of the secular state. The objectives of secularization and reform were theoretically in conflict with those of constitutional liberalism, since they entailed a strengthening rather than a weakening of governmental authority. Yet the decline of classic constitutionalism by the 1870s made this traditional conflict less apparent, and for intellectual and governmental elites the triumph of liberalism became synonymous with the advance of the *estado laico*.

A modern secular state was made up of free individuals, equal before the law and unrestrained in pursuit of their enlightened self-interest. They were first and foremost citizens whose primary loyalty was to the nation and not to the Church or to other corporate remnants of colonial society. As citizens they had a civil status that must be regulated and administered by the state. Vital statistics, fiscal processes, judicial procedure, education, even the calendar and births, marriages and deaths must be removed from Church control. Ecclesiastical wealth, whether in tithe income, real estate, or in mortgages, must pass from the 'dead hand' of the Church and be made a stimulus to individual enterprise. These objectives of secularization were enunciated by liberal writers and policy makers of the post-independence decades, for example the early reform governments of Bernardino Rivadavia in Buenos Aires (1822–3) and of Valentín Gómez Farías in Mexico (1833–4). Sarmiento's depiction of the colonial mentality of Córdoba in contrast with modern and liberal Buenos Aires, José María Luis Mora's (1794–1850) analysis of the corporate spirit in Mexico, and Lastarria and Bilbao's call for spiritual emancipation in Chile were classic early expressions of what came to be generalized assumptions in the period after 1870.

The liberal programme of secularization and anti-corporate reform was most clearly formulated in Mexico, where it engendered an opposing conservative ideology in the 1830s and 1840s, the creation of a conservative party in 1849 and a liberal–conservative civil war from 1854 to 1867. The liberal programme grew more radical as conservative opposition mounted. The moderate Ley Lerdo of 1856, forcing the Church to sell its real estate to tenants, was superseded by outright nationalization of all non-essential Church property in 1859. Freedom of worship, voted down as a constitutional article in 1856, was decreed by the Juárez government in December 1860, a year after another decree separating Church and state. These were essentially war measures, along with the secularization of cemeteries, marriage, vital statistics, and hospitals and the suppression of nunneries. Collectively known as 'La Reforma', the laws were incorporated into the Constitution in 1873, becoming a permanent part of the heroic liberal heritage.

Secularization in Argentina, Brazil and Chile came later and more gradually, but perhaps more decisively, than in Mexico. Following fifty years of relative peace, during which the Catholic Church enjoyed official status, the years 1870 to 1890 were marked by continual Church-state contention, national debates in the legislatures and the press, and successful passage of the standard reform measures. The pattern and timing of this activity ran parallel to the experience of European Catholic nations such as France, Germany and Italy, where the spirit of secular liberalism was sharpened by the intransigence of Pope Pius IX (1846–78) toward the modern world. After the publication of the Syllabus of Errors in 1864 and the pronouncement of Papal Infallibility in 1870, ultramontanism took on new life among national clergies; and Church–state confrontation was inevitable in Argentina, Chile and Brazil, as it was in Europe.

In each of the three countries the latent conflict was activated by an incident that touched on a characteristic issue. In Chile, the issue was Church control of cemeteries, brought into the open in 1871 when the bishop of Concepción refused public burial to Manuel Zañartu, a prominent army officer who had lived openly with a mistress for many years. In Brazil, the overt issue was the status of freemasonry, which had made broad inroads into imperial circles and had been tolerated by the ecclesiastical hierarchy, though now condemned by the pope. Beneath the masonic issue was another of greater political import, the close identification of the Brazilian Church with the Empire. Both issues were made public in 1872 when the bishop of Rio de Janeiro suspended a priest for preaching in a masonic lodge. There followed a vigorous anti-masonic campaign by Bishops Vital of Pernambuco and Macedo Costa of Pará. In Argentina, the confrontation came a decade later over the limits of state-controlled education, which had advanced rapidly since 1870. In 1884 the interim bishop of Córdoba forbade Catholic parents to send their daughters to a local public normal school whose directors were Protestant, an incident that led ultimately to a sixteen-year break in relations between the Argentine government and the papacy.

The bases of the secular state were laid down more peacefully and more decisively in Argentina, Brazil and Chile than in Mexico because reformers faced less resistance. Church establishments were weaker. Populations were sparser and lacked the reservoir of religious intensity of Mexican rural villages. Outside influences, both intellectual and social, were more prevalent. For example, it was the presence of an influential Protestant merchant community in Valparaíso that forced virtual abandonment of official intolerance in 1865 through a law 'interpreting' Article 5 of the Chilean Constitution. Toleration was scarcely an issue in Argentina and Brazil. One of the compelling arguments used in Argentina for instituting civil marriage and a civil register in 1884 was the inadequacy of the Church bureaucracy to contend with the influx of immigrants. In all three countries, the principal objectives of secularization could be achieved without an attack on Church property, the basis of bitter conflict in Mexico. In Chile and Argentina they could be achieved without a legal separation of Church and state. Separation did come ultimately in Chile in 1925, but never in Argentina, possibly the most secularized country in all Latin America. In Brazil, the separation of Church and state, along with other measures of liberal reform, was subsumed in the republican movement, given added intellectual support by positivism and decisively instituted within a year of the fall of the empire in 1889.

By 1890, then, the liberals, or *laicistas* as they were called in Argentina, had prevailed. The papacy, the national hierarchies and their conservative lay supporters temporarily acquiesced in the broad advance of the secular state. The passing of Church-related issues was further testimony that political consensus had been achieved among Latin American elites.

The vanishing ideal of a rural bourgeois society

One of the anomalies of the liberal legacy was the juxtaposition of political centralism and socio-economic individualism. While liberal constitutionalist opposition to centralized state authority weakened, the adherence to *laissez-faire* economics remained strong. At the heart of a liberal society was the enlightened individual, juridically equal to others and free to pursue his own interest. This interest was based on property, the right to which was regarded an extension of the individual's right to life itself. Thus, the sanctity of private property was upheld by both the doctrines of natural rights and of utility and became a virtually unquestioned liberal assumption.

In Latin America, as in other agricultural societies, liberals had placed their greatest hopes for social harmony and economic progress on the small property holder. The transformation of liberalism after 1870 from a reform-ist ideology to a unifying myth can be seen in part as the inadequacy of the ideal of the small property holder in countries made up of latifundia owners and dependent rural peoples, whether slaves, peons, hereditary tenants, or communal Indian villagers. In an era marked by the resurgence of export economies, the elites could and did conveniently hold to the formalities of liberal social philosophy while neglecting its earlier spirit.

The efforts of reformers were undercut by the limitations of liberal theory as well as by the realities of Latin American society. Liberals drew a distinction between corporate or legally entailed property and individual property. The former, a creation of society, could be restricted by lawmak-ers; the latter, predating society, could not. Influenced by the eighteenth-century 'Economists', especially Gaspar Melchor de Jovellanos, whose *Informe de ley agraria* (1795) was revered throughout the Hispanic world, liberals saw the central problem of society as removal of colonial legal and juridical privileges. These they regarded as obstacles to the realization of a 'natural' economic order. Though liberals frequently idealized the rural bourgeois of post-revolutionary France or the yeoman farmer of pre-Civil War United States, their theory provided no basis on which to resist the undue accumulation of land by individuals.

In Mexico, the main target of socio-economic reform from the 1830s through the 1850s was entailed ecclesiastical property, while in Chile it was the uniquely strong entailed estates of laymen, the *mayorazgos,* legally abolished in 1852. 'Privileged' Indian communal property also came un-der attack in Mexico and was left vulnerable to encroachment in the Constitution of 1857. Pre-1870 liberals, following Jovellanos, lamented excessive private holdings, particularly those that were uncultivated. How-ever, their successors, such as the Generation of 1880 in Argentina or the Porfirian elite in Mexico, acquiesced in, and indeed often benefited personally from, the rapid accumulation of private holdings which accompanied the expansion of commercial agriculture.

Thus, the liberal vision of a rural bourgeois society, permeated by the work ethic, faded after 1870. Not only did the efforts to put entailed property into circulation prove ineffective, but so did the cherished plans for colonization by European farmers. To be sure, Alberdi's dictum of 1852, 'to govern is to populate', inspired numerous Argentine colonization efforts, beginning with the prosperous Swiss settlements introduced by the government of Justo José de Urquiza in Santa Fe. In Chile, farming communities totalling some 3,000 people were established in the southern Llanquihue region, to the accompaniment of notable colonization essays by Vicent Pérez Rosales (1854) and Benjamín Vicuña Mackenna (1865).

Enthusiasm for colonization also ran strong in Mexico, though the loss of Texas and the war with the United States turned its focus away from the frontier to 'the already populated part of the Republic'. In 1849 Mora urged 'the fusion of all races and colors' as a means of curbing future Indian rebellions like those just experienced in Yucatán and the Huasteca. [11] Colonization ideas persisted in Mexico throughout the century but led to even fewer tangible results than in South America. In Argentina, the aging Sarmiento still envisioned a society transformed by European farmers when he uttered his famous plea in 1883: 'Let us be [like the] United States.' [12]

The small property holder was also idealized by the leaders of the Brazilian movement to abolish slavery. André Rebouças, in his *Agricultura nacional* (1883), saw 'rural democracy' resulting from 'the emancipation of the slave and his regeneration through landownership'. [13] Both Rebouças, from a poor mulatto background, and Joaquim Nabuco (1849–1910), from an aristocratic landowning family in Pernambuco, saw the economic and moral progress of the country held back by a decadent latifundia society resting on slavery. In his tract *Abolicionismo* (1883), Nabuco demonstrated the baneful influence of slavery on all aspects of Brazilian life. It made 'the air itself servile', he said. The revival of agriculture held a central place in his vision of a free Brazil. Was this revival to come through land reform that would accompany emancipation, producing a new class of

---

[11] Phrases from Mora's letter to Mexican foreign relations ministry (31 July 1849), Luis Chávez Orozco (ed.), *La gestión diplomática del Doctor Mora*, Archivo histórico diplomático mexicano, 35 (Mexico, 1931), 151–2.

[12] '*Seamos Estados Unidos*', the final sentence of the 1915 edition of *Conflicto y armonías de las razas en América*. The rendering of the sentence here is prompted by its context.

[13] Cited in Richard Graham, 'Landowners and the overthrow of the empire', *Luso-Brazilian Review*, 1 (1970), 48.

small landed proprietors, in part former slaves, in part European colonists, in part former owners? Or was the progress of agriculture to depend on the efforts of the existing landed class, once freed from the corruption imposed by slavery? Nabuco was ambivalent on this point prior to 1888. After emancipation and the downfall of the monarchy, he came increasingly, like many latter-day Spanish American liberals, to accept the rural status quo.

THE ASCENDANCY OF POSITIVISM

The political consensus of the late nineteenth century was upheld by a set of philosophic and social ideas that proclaimed the triumph of science in Latin America. This set of ideas is commonly referred to as positivism, though there is no accepted definition of the term. In its philosophic sense, positivism is a theory of knowledge in which the scientific method represents man's only means of knowing. The elements of this method are, first, an emphasis on observation and experiment, with a consequent rejection of all *a priori* knowledge, and, secondly, a search for the laws of phenomena, or the relations between them. We can know only phenomena, or 'facts', and their laws, but not their essential nature or ultimate causes. This theory of knowledge was not new in the nineteenth century, only its systematic formulation and the term positivism itself, both of which were the creation of Auguste Comte in his *Cours de philosophie positive* (1830–42). As a set of social ideas positivism shared the contemporary view that society was a developing organism and not a collection of individuals, and that the only proper way of studying society was through history. These characteristics of Comte's philosophy were, as John Stuart Mill put it in 1865, 'the general property of the age', which explains why the term has been subject to such widespread use and imprecise definition.[14]

If one considers positivism as the philosophic system of Auguste Comte, its original constructs were the Classification of the Societies and the Law of the Three Stages. Comte presented 'positive philosophy' as the interrelation of the various 'sciences of observation', regarding them as 'being subjected to a common method and as forming different parts of a general plan of investigation'.[15] This interrelation is hierarchical in form. In studying and classifying the sciences (or even a given science) one must move from the simpler, more general, more abstract and more independent to the more complex and interrelated. For example, one progresses

[14] J. S. Mill, *Auguste Comte and positivism* (Ann Arbor, 1961), 8.
[15] A. Comte, *Cours de philosophie positive* 5th ed. (Paris, 1907–8), 1, xiv.

from celestial to terrestrial physics (from astronomy to mechanics to chemistry), or from physics to physiology, and finally to social physics or sociology, the least perfected and most complicated of the sciences. This procedure is natural because in each of its conceptions the human mind passes successively through three stages, the theological (imaginary [*fictif*]), the metaphysical (abstract) and the scientific (positive). By extension, society itself also passes through these stages. The main problem Comte saw in the contemporary state of knowledge was that the theological and metaphysical methods, having largely disappeared in dealing with natural phenomena, 'are still, on the contrary, exclusively used . . . in all that concerns social phenomena'.[16]

Education of a new elite

In Latin America Comtean philosophy had its principal direct influence on the efforts to refashion higher education to meet the imperatives of the new era. Progressive modern economies and stable effective governments demanded a leadership imbued with a systematic mastery of modern science. The traditional universities, academies and professional institutes were deemed inadequate for the task. And yet in this age of consensus there was little disposition to abolish or even to renovate existing institutions, except in the unique circumstances of Mexico. Instead, new entities were created, centres of scientific preparation which ultimately came to influence the established schools.

In Mexico, the formal university structure was a casualty of the mid-century Reforma; and the focus of educational renewal became the Escuela Nacional Preparatoria, founded with the restoration of the Republic in 1867.[17] It was inspired by Gabino Barreda (1818–81), a professor of medicine who had attended Comte's lectures from 1848 to 1851 and who brought positivism to President Juárez's educational reform commission. The new school, which Barreda directed until 1878, replaced the ancient and esteemed Colegio de San Ildefonso and assumed the latter's role as the principal educator of Mexico's intellectual and governmental elite.

The agency for positivist education in Argentina was the Escuela Normal de Paraná, created in 1870 by President Sarmiento. The school far

---

[16] *Ibid.,* 12.

[17] The demise of the Real y Pontificia Universidad de Mexico, closed and reopened several times after 1834, finally came with the decree by Maximilian of 30 November 1865. This decree confirmed earlier liberal measures of 1857 and 1861. The present-day university, founded in 1910, was first proposed by Justo Sierra in 1881.

exceeded its intended role as the model provincial institution for teacher training. Taught by inspired pedagogue-philosophers such as José María Torres, Pedro Scalabrini and J. Alfredo Ferreyra, an unusual proportion of its graduates became national leaders. The Brazilian counterpart to these institutions was the Escola Militar, made a distinct entity in 1874. The positivist (and republican) orientation of the school was provided by Benjamin Constant (1836–91), its professor of mathematics who later served as Minister of Education in the first government of the Republic. The Chilean analogue, the Instituto Pedagógico of the University of Chile, was not established until 1889. Positivist educational philosophy was welcomed by the liberals Lastarria and Barros Arana as early as 1868, but its chief promoter was the latter's student, Valentín Letelier (1852–1919). Letelier began his reform campaign in 1879, and after an educational mission to Germany from 1882 to 1886, returned to found the Instituto and to become Chile's major intellectual and educational leader for the next thirty years.

Much of the study of Latin American positivism has been focused on the efforts to establish the Religion of Humanity and the Positivist Church, obsessions of Auguste Comte's 'second career' after 1848. Comte's French followers divided between religious or Orthodox Positivists, under the leadership of Pierre Lafitte, and philosophical or Heterodox Positivists, who, following Emile Littré, rejected Comte's religious schemes. While Heterodox Positivism was by its nature diffuse and difficult to identify as such, Orthodox Positivism was put forth by a small, coherent and clearly identifiable group of 'true' disciples of Comte, men like the Lagarrigue brothers, Jorge and Juan Enrique, in Chile, Miguel Lemos and Raimundo Teixeira Mendes in Brazil, and, somewhat later, Augustín Aragón in Mexico. Thus Orthodox Positivism, as a new religion, a new Church and as an elaborate cult, enjoyed much notoriety, but its impact on social and political thought was slight. As an educational philosophy in Latin America, positivism was clearly heterodox, and leaders like Barreda, Constant and Letelier shunned the Religion of Humanity.

Positivist influence can be discerned in three general characteristics of educational theory of the era: first, an emphasis on 'encyclopedic' learning of subjects placed in an ordered hierarchy; secondly, a growing bias toward scientific and practical as opposed to humanistic studies; and thirdly, an adherence to secularism and state control. Positivist educators believed that a uniform curriculum based upon systematic study of the sciences would encourage mental and social order and correct the anarchical influence of 'the disintegrating doctrines of the eighteenth century'.[18] In Comte's prescription for a 'universal education', one would study the several sciences in the order of their complexity and emerge with a sense of their interrelation.[19] Mathematics was the foundation, as Constant impressed upon generations of students at the Escola Militar; sociology was the capstone. The science of society could lead one to an understanding of the laws of development, a new way of studying history to replace what Letelier condemned as a mindless chronicle of names and events.[20]

The traditional humanistic and idealist orientation of higher education persisted but some positivist innovations did make headway by 1900. In Chile there was a successful campaign by Letelier and others to eliminate required Latin from the curriculum, an effort similar to one at the Paraná Normal School. In Mexico, controversy raged beginning in 1880 over the choice of logic texts for the National Preparatory School. The positivists finally prevailed, but not until the curricular reform of 1896, followed by the publication in 1903 of *Nuevo sistema de lógica* by Porfirio Parra, which marked the apogee of positivist educational thought in Mexico. A new enthusiasm for specialized technical and utilitarian studies, despite apparent conflict with the Comtean predilection for encyclopedic learning, became a permanent legacy of the age of positivism. Nonetheless, positivist-inspired pedagogy in Latin America retained the highly systematized and even authoritarian character of the master's thought, which may have inhibited free and original scientific inquiry.

Despite Auguste Comte's increasing sympathy after 1848 for the Catholic Church and despite his call for the disestablishment of schools from the state, positivist-inspired higher education did not depart from the traditional liberal goals of secularization and state control. Positivist doctrine could be variously interpreted to fit local conditions. In Mexico, reconciliation seemed to be its emphasis, beginning with Barreda's dramatic *Oración cívica* of 1867. In the aftermath of the Reforma, anticlericalism was muted, whereas it was more overtly expressed by positivist educators in

---

[18] The phrase is Barreda's in 'De la educación moral' (1863), *Opúsculos, discusiones, y discursos* (Mexico, 1877), 117.

[19] See Paul Arbousse-Bastide, *La doctrine de l'éducation universelle dans la philosophie d' Auguste Comte* (Paris, 1957).

[20] V. Letelier, 'El nuevo plan de estudios secundarios i la filosofía positiva' (1879), *La lucha por la cultura* (Santiago, 1895), 301. The positivist bias toward scientific education was actually a distortion of the pedagogical theories of Auguste Comte. He had intended that the sciences should not be introduced until the age of fifteen; before then instruction was to be in the arts and languages under maternal direction at home. But positivism had little impact on primary education and thus the balance in Comte's pedagogy was ignored.

Argentina, Brazil and Chile, men such as Luis Pereira Barreto, Constant and Letelier. The difference was more apparent than real, however. Heterodox positivists throughout Latin America, like the Frenchmen Littré and Jules Ferry, disregarded the idiosyncratic religious and social views of Comte's later years.

'Scientific politics' and authoritarianism

Though positivism was not explicitly a theory of politics, its precepts provided important assumptions for Latin America's governing elite. A concept of 'scientific politics' was formally expressed in Mexico and Chile, less formally so in Argentina and Brazil. The concept entailed a conviction that the methods of science could be applied to national problems. Politics was seen as an 'experimental science', based on facts. Statesmen should no longer be guided by abstract theories and legal formulas which had led only to revolutions and disorder. The new guides must be observation, patient investigation and experience. New value must be placed on the economic, the concrete and the practical.

Despite their hostility to political abstractions, which they judged the hallmark of the 'metaphysical' mentality, the advocates of scientific politics had a reverence for theory. Theory was the starting point for a science of society and served to co-ordinate observed facts. In the positive stage, Comte had said, the human mind is no longer concerned with the origin and destiny of the universe or with the search for essences, but instead works to 'discover by a nice combination of reason and observation, the effective laws [of phenomena]'.[21] Such laws were the increasingly scientific character of the human mind and thus of society (Comte's three stages), the 'fundamental notion of progress', and the historical relativity of institutions.

A tenet of scientific politics at its origin was that society should be administered, not governed by elected representatives. The idea was first expressed by Comte's predecessor and early collaborator, Henri de Saint-Simon, who, like Comte, sought a principle of order for a Europe disorganized by the 'metaphysicians and legists' and by the dogmas of the French Revolution. The new society would be industrial in character and Saint-Simon argued that *les industriels,* practical men of affairs who knew finance and who could prepare budgets, should be the new administrators. Comte also looked to the intervention of an elite, *savants* who saw the relation

---

[21] Comte, *Cours,* 1, 3.

between scientific and political analysis and could thus provide the leadership for social regeneration. These ideas in their modified Latin American form strengthened a leaning toward technocracy which went back at least to the eighteenth-century Bourbons.

Scientific politics stood in an ambivalent relation to political liberalism in Latin America, now transformed from an ideology into a myth. Its precepts were in large part a repudiation of classic liberal principles; indeed in Comte's formulation one might read 'liberal' for 'metaphysical' as the second stage of history. By 1870 the classic liberal faith in constitutional arrangements had already been eroded by the influx of social and historical theories akin to positivism. The authoritarian and technocratic strain of scientific politics added further to this erosion. Yet the advocates of scientific politics regarded themselves as liberals, or occasionally as 'new liberals' or 'conservative-liberals'. The confusion and reconciliation of theoretically contradictory terms was a characteristic of this era of consensus.

In Mexico the concept of scientific politics was elaborated by Justo Sierra and his collaborators in their newspaper *La Libertad* (1878–84). Guided by science, they said, the nation's leaders must repudiate a half-century of revolutions and anarchy, reconcile conflicting parties and strengthen government to meet the needs of the industrial age. Gabino Barreda had sounded this note briefly a decade earlier, interpreting Mexican history in Comtean terms. 'All the elements of social reconstruction are now assembled', said Barreda, 'all the obstacles overcome'. Independence has been vindicated, the Laws of Reform and the Constitution reign supreme; henceforth, our motto will be Liberty, Order and Progress.[22] But Barreda made it clear that Liberty was an accomplishment of the past, Order and Progress the task for the future. In his famous debate with José María Vigil, Sierra blamed disorder on the 'old' liberals of the Reforma. He compared them with the 'men of '93' in France, who believed that society could and should be moulded to conform with the rights of man, by violence and revolution if necessary.[23] Telésforo García (1844–1918), a Spanish-born entrepreneur and colleague of Sierra, summed up the themes of the debate in his widely read pamphlet, *Política científica y política metafísica* (1887).[24]

---

[22] Barreda, 'Oración cívica' (1867), *Opúsculos*, 105.

[23] *La Libertad*, 30 August 1878 (also J. Sierra, *Obras completas* [Mexico, 1948], iv, 158). Vigil's articles appeared in *El Monitor Republicano*.

[24] The pamphlet, first published in 1881 under another title, was a reprint of a series of articles in *La Libertad*, beginning 12 Oct. 1880. Though prompted by the educational debate of 1880, it also treated general political issues.

The most dramatic feature of scientific politics was *La Libertad's* frank appeal for authoritarian government. Especially notorious was the outburst of Francisco G. Cosmes (1850–1907). Society now rejects 'rights' for 'bread . . . security, order, and peace', asserted Cosmes. Rights have only produced distress. 'Now let us try a little tyranny, but honourable tyranny, and see what results it brings.'[25] Sierra's language was more muted, but his points were similar. *La Libertad* began to call itself a 'conservative-liberal newspaper'; it extolled contemporary European 'conservative republicans' Jules Simon and Emilio Castelar; it ran essays by Littré. It called for constitutional reforms, particularly a lengthened presidential term and a suspensive veto, 'to strengthen the administrative power'. The objective was a 'practical' constitution, not one that was 'utopian' and conducive to extra-legal dictatorship. Constitutional reform to strengthen government was an idea introduced by Juárez and Lerdo in 1867, as we have seen; in 1878 it was given added force by arguments from science. These arguments, along with the others constituting scientific politics, became quasi-official assumptions of the Díaz regime by the late 1880s.

As a new departure in political thought, the concept of scientific politics in Chile was less definite than in Mexico. Chile had no Reforma or French Intervention, no engrossing mid-century civil war to direct political ideas. Thus, the openness of Chilean intellectuals to changing currents of European thought was greater than in Mexico, and the grafting of new ideas onto old ones came more naturally and imperceptibly. The difference between Chile and Mexico was epitomized by the intellectual career of José Victorino Lastarria. This liberal leader of the Generation of 1842 is also credited with introducing Comtean positivism in 1868 and with first applying it to politics in his *Lecciones de política positiva* (1875). Therefore, scientific politics in Chile was not the dramatic statement of a post-civil war generation, and its relation to the liberal heritage was even more ambiguous than in Mexico.[26]

Though Lastarria's *Lecciones* was a lengthy treatise intended to establish the bases for a science of politics, it contained much that was reminiscent of his earlier writings. His critique of *a priori* knowledge, his depiction of the individual as moulded by society and of law as a reflection of historical circumstances were not new. Moreover, he maintained his faith in individ-

---

[25] *La Libertad*, 4 Sept. 1878.

[26] Lastarria's 'discovery' of positivism in 1868 might be compared with Gabino Barreda's first presentation of it in 1867. They were both of the 'older' generation, only one year apart in age. Barreda, however, was not politically oriented, either before or after 1867.

ual liberty, despite the anti-individualistic bias of positivism, and concluded that liberty was destined to increase with the progress of society.
Lastarria was more Comtean when he compared the Latin American nations to those in Europe that had received the 'French impulse'. They were
in a 'painful and anarchical transition' between metaphysical and positive
ideas because of the lingering tendency to impose 'revolutionary' doctrines
of rights and equality on societies not prepared to incorporate them. A
thorough anglophile, Lastarria extolled the 'positive spirit' of English
origin now in practice in North America.[27] He saw this spirit manifest in
semecracia (self-government), which for Lastarria had the status of a social
law, guiding his long campaign to gain for municipalities the autonomy
denied them in the centralist Constitution of 1833.

Lastarria's thought and practice (for example, as Minister of the Interior
in 1876–7) revealed the traditional tension within political liberalism
between the limitation and the strengthening of state authority. Lastarria
could be both an advocate of municipal freedom and an anticlerical reformer. Though his adoption of scientific politics reinforced his sympathy
for strong reformist government, his *Lecciones* did not contain the frank
apology for authoritarianism present in *La Libertad*. On a theoretical level
he was more explicit about the limits of state power than either the
Mexicans in 1878 or his younger colleague and fellow advocate of scientific politics, Valentín Letelier.

Social evolution was Letelier's supreme law. For him the science of
politics demonstrated 'how society is subject to continuous changes that
preserve or advance it, when reform rather than resistance is legitimate,
and what the norm is that must serve to guide all statesmen, be they
conservatives or liberals'. For example, the 'scientific statesman' (as opposed to a mere empiricist) would respond differently to a riot of fanatics
opposing freedom of thought than to a riot of workers seeking higher
wages. The first involves intolerance, a dying tendency in society, whereas
the second involves the pretensions of newly articulate classes. One be-
longs to the past, the other to the future.[28] Letelier looked upon liberty
and authority as relative principles, not the absolutes that had dominated
politics since the days of Portales. In addressing a convention of the
Radical Party in 1889, he told his colleagues that though liberty was at
this stage of history the 'organic principle' of our 'scientific philosophy'
and though specific freedoms must be upheld, we should not hesitate to

---

[27] Lastarria, 'Lecciones', *Obras*, 11, 54–9.
[28] V. Letelier, *De la ciencia política en Chile* (Santiago, 1886), 111, 83–4.

promote state authority over education, child labour, prostitution, social insurance and Church property. The end of politics is not to advance abstractions like liberty and authority, but to 'satisfy social needs in order to secure the improvement of mankind and the development of society.'[29] Letelier revealed clear admiration for 'responsible' authoritarianism and frequently cited Bismarck as a model. Also, it should be noted that his chair at the University was in the law and theory of administration.

The breach in the liberal establishment

Just as the fulfilment of liberalism seemed a reality and political consensus achieved, there occurred a significant breach in the liberal establishment of Latin America's four major nations: Argentina, Brazil, Chile and Mexico. The infusion of scientific concepts had enhanced the political consensus; yet the theoretical conflict that existed between classic liberalism and scientific politics was bound to emerge. Such a conflict can be discerned in the political events of 1889–93, which afford suggestive parallels in the four countries. The turbulent events of these years were closely related to economic and financial dislocations, and indeed these dislocations now provide the standard point of departure for interpreting them. The political turbulence, however, may also be examined as a significant moment in Latin American thought.

In 1895 Joaquim Nabuco published an essay on José Balmaceda, the Chilean president who was overthrown by a parliamentary and naval revolt in 1891, in which he implicitly compared the upheaval in Chile with contemporary events in Brazil.[30] Throughout 1890 and 1891 both countries experienced a mounting conflict between executive and congress. In Brazil, following the establishment of the Republic on 15 November 1889, two military presidents, Manoel Deodoro da Fonseca and Floriano Peixoto, clashed with the Constitutional Congress of 1890–1 and with its successor. Deodoro's resignation in favour of Floriano came three weeks after he had dissolved Congress on 3 November 1891. In 1894, after a civil war, the military finally withdrew from power and Prudente José Morais e Barros, the leader of the senate, was elected Brazil's first civilian president. In Chile, the parliament condemned Balmaceda for 'electoral

---

[29] V. Letelier, 'Ellos i nosotros o sea los liberales i los autoritarios', *Lucha,* 11, 30–1.
[30] J. Nabuco, *Balmaceda* (Santiago, 1914), 7. The work first appeared as a series of newspaper articles (January–March 1895), designed as a critique of the laudatory account by Julio Bañados Espinosa, *Balmaceda, su gobierno y la revolución de 1891* (Paris, 1894). The first Spanish edition was published the same year in Valparaíso.

intervention', particularly for the threat that he would impose a favourite as his successor and for decreeing a budget without its approval. The president closed the parliament twice during 1890 and reshuffled his cabinet several times to no avail. Civil war began early in 1891, ending with Balmaceda's resignation followed by his suicide on 19 September.

Argentina's dramatic events of 1890 ('El Noventa') also involved a challenge to presidential power, but one that emanated from beyond the legislature. On 26 July a 'revolution' broke out in downtown Buenos Aires and a momentary 'provisional government' was established under Leandro Alem, who had been a founder the year before of the Unión Cívica de la Juventud, a political club 'to co-operate in the re-establishment of constitutional practices in the country and to combat the existing order of things'. The existing order of things was the presidency of Miguel Juárez Celman. The revolt was suppressed but Juárez Celman was in turn forced by Congress to resign on 6 August in favour of his vice-president, Carlos Pellegrini. In Mexico, the events were less dramatic and well known. Instead of open conflict between branches of government, they consisted of a debate within the Chamber of Deputies (and the press) on an obscure constitutional amendment. The debate broadened to include the limits of presidential authority and reached a climax in November and December of 1893. It was preceded by a thinly disguised challenge to Porfirio Díaz in Justo Sierra's *Manifiesto* of the National Liberal Union, issued on 23 April 1892, overtly to promote the President's third re-election. The unsuccessful challenge to Díaz came from the *científicos,* a small group close to the government.

In all four countries the conflict entailed resistance to authoritarian leadership in the name of constitutional principles. Moreover, with the partial exception of Argentina, the resistance came from within the governing elite, even from some who were ministers. Since the assumptions of scientific politics and the dictates of historic constitutionalism had become intertwined, the challengers did not reject the principle of strong authority, despite open political conflict. From ambivalence in 1889, Letelier in Chile turned against Balmaceda in 1890, was briefly imprisoned and then championed the triumphant 'Revolution'. Its object, he said, was not to implant a parliamentary oligarchy, but rather to restore constitutional liberties *and* 'administration', of which the latter had become mixed with 'politics' under the personal tyranny of Balmaceda.[31]

---

[31] V. Letelier, *La tiranía y la revolución, o sea relaciones de la administración con la política estudiadas a la luz de los últimos acontecimientos* (Santiago, 1891). This was the initial lecture of Letelier's course in administrative law for 1891.

In Brazil, the positivist ideas that permeated the founding of the Republic tended to sharpen the conflict between authoritarianism and constitutionalism. Orthodox Positivists, like Lemos and Teixeira Mendes, expressing Comte's disdain for constitutional liberties, called for a 'republican dictatorship', just as Comte had welcomed Louis Napoleon's coup in 1851.[32] The heterodox Benjamin Constant, however, clashed with Deodoro before he died in 1891. Another opponent of the Provisional President was his Minister of Finance, Rui Barbosa (1849–1923), author of the draft constitution for the Republic. Barbosa's attack against Floriano was even sharper, both at home and as an exile in *Cartas de Inglaterra* (1896). The conflict in Brazil was complicated by the fact that it came in the wake of Pedro II's overthrow. Constitutionalist enthusiasm was exaggerated, as was a vain effort at political reconciliation, judging from the diverse makeup of the first republican ministries. Moreover, as Deodoro and Floriano became more 'dictatorial', nostalgia set in for the supposed constitutional balance achieved under the empire. It was this nostalgia that inspired Nabuco's massive biography of his father, a Liberal Party leader, and his essay on Chile. Both Brazil and Chile, he wrote, 'had [before 1889] the same continuity of order, parliamentary government, civil liberty, [and] administrative purity'. Only a 'Liberal League' of enlightened men could now save Latin America from further chaos.[33]

Letelier's ambivalence toward statism can be compared with that of Sierra in Mexico. In the main, Sierra's programme of 1892 seemed to epitomize the socially conservative, technocratic and economically oriented principles of scientific politics. However, he ended the *Manifiesto* by asserting that if 'effective peace has been acquired [since 1867] by the *strengthening of authority,* definitive peace will be acquired by its *assimilation with liberty'*.[34] He then proposed several constitutional reforms, particularly one to make judges irremovable, that is, appointed by the president for life, rather than democratically elected and thus subject to popular whim or presidential manipulation. In the 1893 debate on the measure, Sierra supported it with the arguments from 'science' he had used to support strong government in 1878. In the face of the dictatorial power acquired by Díaz in the intervening years, Sierra had turned constitutional-

---

[32] The Chilean positivist, Juan Enrique Lagarrigue, likewise supported Balmaceda. His brother Jorge, while in France, had addressed a pamphlet in 1888 to another would-be republican dictator, Boulanger.

[33] Nabuco, *Balmaceda,* 14, 219.

[34] *El Siglo XIX,* 26 April 1892. Italics added.

ist in hopes of limiting that power. He was opposed in this complex three-sided debate by both the defenders of the President and by the 'jacobins', defenders of the 'pure' or 'democratic' Constitution. These opponents labelled Sierra and his group *científicos,* a label they accepted with pride.[35]

The conflict in Argentina was similar to that in the other countries, but it also had unique national features. Scientific politics was not formally articulated, as in Chile and in Mexico, though many of its assumptions, stemming back to Alberdi and Sarmiento, became articles of faith among the liberal establishment.[36] The transition from liberal to positivist ideas was even more imperceptible than in Chile and the entanglement of the two by the 1880s even more complete. The practice, if not the theory, of authoritarian government took hold with the presidencies of Roca and Juárez Celman, enhanced by secularization policies, by the new economic and political centrality of the city of Buenos Aires and by the merging of the old parties into the single Partido Autonomista Nacional (PAN). The president became *jefe único del partido único,* branded the *unicato* by opponents.

The focus of resistance in 1889–90 was not Congress, as in Brazil or Chile, nor a definable inner circle like the Mexican *científicos.* The Unión Cívica included Alem, Aristóbulo del Valle and Bernardo de Yrigoyen, old Buenos Aires Autonomistas who resented the new centralism of the former provincials, Roca and Juárez Celman. Thus, they implicitly kept alive Argentina's peculiar constitutional question. The Unión Cívica also drew in former president Bartolomé Mitre, a principled old liberal who disliked the regime's corruption. The vague rhetoric of the Civic Union movement was constitutionalist, but it also had democratic overtones not present elsewhere.

The sealing of the breach was the work of Carlos Pellegrini (1846–1906), whose career and ideas epitomized the merging in practice of constitutionalism and scientific politics. A respected jurist and legislator, he was also a partisan of professionalism and administration; he became an expert in finance and as president (1890–2) established the Banco de la Nación in 1891. Pellegrini had been an uneasy participant in the *unicato,* an old porteño friend of Alem and del Valle who stayed in touch with them even during El Noventa. Yet he was a part of Buenos Aires high

---

[35] The phrase *los científicos* probably first appeared in an editorial in *El Siglo XIX* on 25 November 1893.

[36] Because of the early questioning of doctrinaire liberalism by Sarmiento and Alberdi, and because of the obsession with material progress and utilitarian values among the elite after 1870, there has been a tendency among Argentinians to regard positivism as of 'autochthonous origin', e.g. Alejandro Korn, 'Filosofía argentina' (1927), *Obras,* III (Buenos Aires, 1940), 261.

society and had been a founder of the Jockey Club in 1881. His prime concern was governmental continuity, which led him in 1892 to short-circuit the Civic Union by successfully proposing Luis Saenz Peña, the father of its candidate, Roque, as PAN candidate for president. Roque Saenz Peña withdrew from the race.

Political peace was quickly restored in all countries, facilitated by a fundamental agreement on economic and social values. The PAN remained in power in Argentina until 1916, Díaz in Mexico until 1911. The Chilean parliament continued supreme until 1924. The constitutional 'balance' established in Brazil by 1894 prevailed until 1930. A mood of reconciliation took hold in the aftermath of conflict. In Chile, the punitive measures enacted against adherents of Balmaceda were never put into effect. A general amnesty was declared in August 1894, and by 1895 Balmacedistas were returning to office. The Mexican *científicos* were co-opted by the Díaz regime. Justo Sierra was elevated to the Supreme Court in 1894, an appointment that must have seemed almost insulting to the defender of judicial independence. José Yves Limantour, the most famous *científico,* served as Díaz's finance minister until 1911.[37] In Argentina, the Mitre branch of the Civic Union movement became thoroughly reconciled with the governing PAN; in fact, its would-be candidate of 1892, Roque Sáenz Peña, was elected president in 1910.

The conflict nonetheless left significant legacies. Though the authoritarian impulse in scientific politics was temporarily thwarted (except in Mexico) by a resurgent 'constitutionalist' oligarchy, presidential power acquired new arms for future battles. One position in the Mexican debate was a defence of strong government on proto-populist grounds, the argument that Díaz was dedicated to attacking servitude in the countryside and the tyranny of the upper classes, both of which would only be strengthened by irremovable judges.[38] An interpretation of Balmaceda as a strong popular and nationalist leader, if not present in 1891, developed soon thereafter and had great impact on twentieth-century politics in Chile. Democratic ideas also appeared, most significantly in Argentina where the Unión Cívica split in 1892, producing the Radical party. The third group in the Mexican debate, the jacobins or doctrinaire constitutionalists, were

---

[37] Limantour was one of the original eleven signatories of the Liberal Union Manifesto of April 1892. He was appointed minister in March 1893 and thus did not participate in the debate.

[38] The position was argued in *El Siglo XIX,* principally by Francisco Cosmes, who split from his former colleague Sierra in a series of articles dated 14–30 December 1893. The irremovability measure passed the Chamber of Deputies but never left committee in the Senate.

ineffective in 1893, but did provide a precedent for the underground liberal clubs of 1900–6 and ultimately for the revolutionary movement of 1910. The term jacobin also appeared in Brazil, though its democratic import was questionable.[39] The breach in the liberal establishment was sealed and political unity restored, but the new ideas suggested that the consensus would not endure without future challenges.

Social evolution, race and nationality

After maturing for several decades, by the turn of the century positivism as a set of social ideas was in full flower in Latin America. There was little dissent among the elites from the conviction that society was an organism analogous to nature, subject to change over time. Among the numerous theorists of social evolution, it was Herbert Spencer who was most often cited by Latin Americans. He became the symbol of the age, though his actual influence was perhaps less than that of Auguste Comte, the other 'twin pillar' of positivism. Despite the appeal of Spencer's Law of Evolution and of his systematic use of biology as a model for social theory, his assumptions about socio-political organization were less congenial to Iberian traditions than were those of Comte. Spencer adhered to *laissez faire* and utilitarianism throughout his life, as manifested in his first work, *Social statics* (1850), and in one of his last, *The man versus the state* (1884). His envisioned Industrial Society, the culmination of human evolution, was individualistic, liberal and stateless (an idealized nineteenth-century England), though he saw these characteristics as the product of habit and instinct after centuries of natural adaptation and not as the product of man's rational choice.[40] Comte's ideal was a hierarchically organized and non-competitive collectivism in which state and society were one.

Despite their limited impact on political programmes, Spencer's ideas (more than Comte's) were an important component of the intense intellectual concern with Latin American society between 1890 and 1914. Spencer's evolutionary system was based on the development of particular societies, and his volumes were filled with a vast array of comparative data on specific customs, beliefs, rituals and ethnic characteristics. Thus, in a general way Spencer helped Latin Americans focus their attention on the peculiarities of their own society within the universal scheme. His thought had

---

[39] The Jacobin Club of Rio and a jacobin press supported Floriano in 1893, espousing an extreme republican (anti-monarchist) and xenophobic (anti-Portuguese) position.

[40] J. W. Burrow, *Evolution and society. A study in Victorian social theory* (Cambridge, 1968), 222–3.

an anthropological dimension that was lacking in Comte. Comte's system posited the progress of humanity (in an almost eighteenth-century sense) as the progress of the European white race.[41] His analogy for society in the Law of the Three Stages was the human mind, whereas Spencer's analogy in the Law of Evolution was all of nature.

One element of Spencer's evolutionary system, though not the major one, was race, which came to be a central preoccupation of Latin American social thought. Modern European racism seems to have sprung from at least two sources, both of which were relevant to Latin American theorizing but were difficult to separate by the 1890s. The first was the quest for national origins and peculiarities, as reflected in Romantic historiography, literature and philology. A 'race' was simply a nationality or a people developing over time, distinct from others by language, religion or geography. It was primarily a European grouping or its antecedent, for example the 'Aryan race' of Central Asia. In Latin America we encounter this sense of race occasionally before 1870, for example in Sarmiento's *Facundo*. The notorious racist views of the Frenchman, Count Arthur de Gobineau sprang partly from this source, fortified by an aristocratic revulsion for democracy, incipient mass society and the mixing of peoples.[42] Still another and more influential exponent of the historical sense of race was Hippolyte Taine, whose famous introduction to his history of English literature (1864) was widely read in Latin America.

A second source of nineteenth-century racism was empirical and anthropological, that is, the changing European attitudes toward primitive dark-skinned peoples which came from increased contact. Enlightenment ideals of the Noble Savage and of a universally attainable Civilization gave way to scientific evidence of the actual degradation of remote primitive peoples and to the resulting notion that only certain 'races', that is, human groups distinct from others by permanent inherited physical differences, were capable of becoming civilized.[43] A parallel idea in the development of the discipline of physical anthropology was 'polygenism', the initial creation of separate races, as opposed to the traditional 'monogenism' of biblical

---

[41] John C. Greene, 'Biology and social theory in the nineteenth century: Auguste Comte and Herbert Spencer', Marshall Clagett (ed.), *Critical problems in the history of science* (Madison, 1959), 427.

[42] Michael D. Biddiss, 'Gobineau and the origins of European racism', *Race*, 7 (1966), 255–70. Gobineau's major work was *Essai sur l'inégalité des races humaines* (1853–5). I use the term 'racism' to refer to theories that attributed social change, psychology, and behaviour exclusively to race, however defined. Thus, a theory could be racist without necessarily assuming the innate and permanent inferiority of non-whites, though most did include that assumption.

[43] George W. Stocking, Jr., *Race, culture, and evolution. Essays in the history of anthropology* (New York, 1968), 13–41.

Creation or the scientific monogenism of Charles Darwin's *Origin of Species* (1859) and *The Descent of Man* (1871). The racism inherent in polygenism proved compatible in practice if not in theory with social Darwinism, the survival of peoples (or races) best able to adapt in the struggle of life. Thus, the Latin American preoccupation with race was further strengthened by the Darwinist aspect of Spencer's thought and that of other influential evolutionary theorists such as Ludwig Gumplowicz and Ernst Haeckel.

The burgeoning science of psychology provided another dimension to nineteenth-century race consciousness, and much of Latin American racist thought took the form of an inquiry into social psychology. Taine was probably the initial inspiration for this genre, though by 1900 Latin Americans were more directly guided by Gustave Le Bon, 'the supreme scientific vulgarizer of his generation' and the most frequently read of European racial theorists.[44] Taine argued in 1864 that the historian as scientist must seek the 'elemental moral state', or 'psychology', of a people which lies beneath the surface of observable human artifacts, literary creations, or political documents. The visible or external man in history reveals an invisible or internal man. This psychology is produced by the action of three 'primordial forces', *le race, le milieu, et le moment*.[45] In Taine's historical scheme, race (defined as 'innate or hereditary tendencies' normally tied to 'marked differences in temperament and body structure') was only one determining element. However, it became predominant in Le Bon's *Lois psychologiques de l'évolution des peuples* (1894), in which the historical and the anthropological notions of race converged and became joined with numerous other themes of nineteenth-century social science.

'Race is the key, then climate, followed by history. All are complementary, but blood, the psychological heritage, is the mainspring of events. . . .' So wrote the Argentinian Carlos O. Bunge (1875–1918) in his *Nuestra América* (1903), a model Le Bonian essay that was heralded throughout Spanish America.[46] Le Bon emphasized the 'soul' of a race or people, which he equated with its 'mental constitution', or the moral and

---

[44] Robert A. Nye, *The origins of crowd psychology: Gustave Le Bon and the crisis of mass democracy in the Third Republic* (London, 1975), 3.

[45] H. A. Taine, *Histoire de la littérature anglaise* (6th edn, Paris, 1924), i, xxii–iii. Latin American *pensadores* were probably attracted to Taine in part because he seemed a perfect combination of the man of sciences and the man of letters. His *Histoire* was followed by *Sur l'intelligence* (1870), a key work in the development of scientific psychology.

[46] C. O. Bunge, *Nuestra América* (Barcelona, 1903), 20. The second edition (1905) was subtitled *Ensayo de psicología social*.

intellectual characteristics which determine its evolution. He saw these characteristics as virtually unalterable, constantly being reproduced by heredity. 'It is by its dead {and not by its living} that a race is founded' was his famous phrase.[47] He went on to classify and rank races psychologically, stressing that character was more critical than intelligence. Of his four categories, the only 'superior' races were the Indo-European, with the Anglo-Saxon sub-race clearly above the Latin. Character is derived from ideas that penetrate the racial soul and become permanent unconscious sentiments, such as Anglo-Saxon individualism, liberty and sense of duty as opposed to the Latin pursuit of equality and dependence on the state. He offered the Americas as proof of his psychological laws. The progress and stability of the North versus the 'sanguinary anarchy' and 'absolute autocracy' of the South were for him clearly the result of differences in European racial character.[48] Moreover, South America was only one instance of the Latin decadence that Le Bon saw as universal.

Le Bon's early career was in medicine and his approach to social science was diagnostic, a characteristic that also permeated Latin American thought. Numerous intellectuals saw themselves as 'diagnosticians of a sick continent.'[49] Their pessimism was derived not only from the Le Bonian conclusion that the Latin race was degenerate but also from the prevailing scientific strictures on racial mixture. Le Bon did recognize that the formation of new races, as in Europe, could come only from intermarriage. Mixture initially destroys the soul of the races and leads to a 'period of intestine struggles and vicissitudes', out of which gradually emerges a new psychological species. The result can be positive, wrote Le Bon, given certain conditions: races that interbreed must not be too unequal in numbers; their characters must not be too dissimilar; they must be subject to identical environmental conditions. While generally present in Europe and North America, these conditions have been clearly absent in Latin America, and the result is psychological instability.[50] The outlook was gloomy indeed for a continent that was both Latin and *mestizo*.

There was a cosmopolitan and hemispheric cast to the expressions of racial pessimism in Latin America. Three examples will suffice: Bunge's *Nuestra América* (1903); *Pueblo enfermo* (1909) by the Bolivian, Alcides

[47] G. Le Bon, *Lois psychologiques de l'évolution des peuples* (3rd edn, Paris, 1898), 13.
[48] *Ibid.*, 111–16.
[49] The phrase is from chap. 2 of Martin S. Stabb, *In quest of identity* (Chapel Hill, N.C., 1967).
[50] Le Bon, *Lois psychologiques*, 43–50. Countries in which the proportion of half-breeds is too large, he said, 'are solely for this reason given over to perpetual anarchy, unless they are ruled with an iron hand'. He cited Brazil as an example and quoted (p. 45) from Louis Agassiz.

Arguedas (1878–1946); and *Les démocraties latines de l' Amérique* (1912) by the Peruvian, Francisco García Calderón (1883–1953). All three works were first published in Europe and included laudatory introductions by distinguished European intellectuals.[51] Arguedas and García Calderón spent large portions of their lives in France; the latter actually wrote several of his works in French. Two of the essays surveyed all of Latin America, and the nationality of the authors is not obvious; the third, *Pueblo enfermo,* though an intensely Bolivian work, was intended (and often taken) to apply to Latin America generally.[52] All three works revealed in exaggerated form the tendency in Latin American thought to adopt European theories that were injurious to regional or national pride. Self-depreciation reached its peak in the age of positivism.

Hispanic America, wrote Bunge, is a racial 'Tower of Babel'. Unlike the Yankees, Spaniards in America are not a pure race, but 'mestizo-ized, indian-ized, and mulatto-ized Europeans'. Each racial stock has its own inherited psychological traits, and the 'national psychology' of each republic varies according to its peculiar racial amalgam. However, three fundamental characteristics constitute the 'spirit of the race': arrogance (of Spanish origin, traced back to the Visigoths), sadness (of Indian origin), and laziness. Scientifically analysed, arrogance and laziness are from the same root. 'In animals arrogance is the preservation instinct of the defenceless, in men, of the lazy.' Laziness, *la pereza criolla,* was for Bunge a 'parent quality' and to it he attributed the lack of imagination among the elite, the proclivity towards *caciquismo* in politics and, most of all, the disdain for work. 'Work is progress', asserted Bunge, 'laziness is decadence.'[53] The unrelieved pessimism of Bunge's racial characterology gave way to ambivalence in García Calderón. The decade between the publication of the two volumes saw the effects of a growing philosophic reaction against positivism and a new appreciation of the Latin spirit. Though García Calderón, as we shall see, was a leading spokesman for this new idealism, much of *Les démocraties latines* followed Bunge and Le Bon. For García, race was the 'key to the incurable disorder that divides [Latin] America'. He envisioned the 'brilliant and lazy' creole as the true American of the future, yet he

[51] The first two were published in Barcelona, the third in Paris. The introductions were by Rafael Altamira, Ramiro de Maeztú and Raymond Poincaré, respectively.

[52] See author's *advertencia* to second edition (1910), including comments by José E. Rodó (p. 8). The subtitle of the first two editions was *Contribución a la psicología de los pueblos hispano americanos.*

[53] Bunge, *Nuestra América,* 77. The second half of the essay was a more specific racial interpretation of politics, to be considered below.

seemed to preclude unity because of the absence of Le Bon's conditions for constructive miscegenation.[54]

Self-depreciation probably reached its extreme with Arguedas, and yet his *Pueblo enfermo* was more than facile racial theorizing in the manner of Bunge or García Calderón. It was also an evocative, though depressing, portrait of the regional cultures of Bolivia, which displayed another tendency of positivist sociology, the impulse toward factual description. For Arguedas, regional psychology seemed to be determined more by geography than by race. He depicted the character of the Aymara as harsh like his habitat, the *altiplano,* just as the 'dreamy, timid, and profoundly moral' Quechua reflected the 'mediterranean' environment of the Cochabamba valley.[55] However, when Arguedas moved from region to nation, from Indian to *mestizo* (*cholo*), race became the major determinant of character. He showed some sympathy for the abject, undernourished and exploited Indian, but only disdain for the *cholo*.[56] Though he attributed the numerous defects in national psychology – deception, passion for hollow oratory, lack of enterprise, intellectual sterility and so on – to the heavy infusion of Indian blood,[57] he did not identify these defects as Indian characteristics *per se*. Thus Arguedas's sociology revealed a tension between racial and environmental determinism, which was even more pronounced with other positivists for whom nationality was a major concern.

Though the racial pessimists did not emphasize remedies for Spanish America's social predicament, they did tend to perpetuate the traditional liberal panacea – European immigration. Bunge urged Europeanization 'through work'. García Calderón pointed to Basques and particularly Italians who were already transforming Argentina. Arguedas concluded that the profound defects in Bolivia's national character could only be altered by radical methods, like grafting in horticulture, and he proposed 'selected' immigration.[58]

The dictates of racial determinism were particularly agonizing for Brazil-

---

[54] F. García Calderón, *Les démocraties latines,* 337. Le Bon was the editor of the series in which García Calderón's volume was published.

[55] A. Arguedas, *Pueblo enfermo* (1909), 38, 79. It is significant that in discussing regional psychology *per se,* Arguedas referred to Taine (p. 68).

[56] Arguedas also wrote a proto-indianist novel, *Wata Wara* (1904), and a later version, *Raza de bronce* (1919). It should be noted that his antipathy toward the *mestizo* was more pronounced in the much-altered third edition of *Pueblo enfermo* (1937), where, for example, *psicología de la raza mestiza* was expanded and made a separate chapter. His change in attitude might have reflected his own frustrating experience in politics, which he (an aristocrat) claimed was dominated by *cholos*.

[57] Arguedas began his chapter '*el carácter nacional*' (pp. 91–2) by referring to Bunge.

[58] Bunge, *Nuestra América,* 98; García Calderón, *Les démocraties latines,* 339–40; Arguedas, *Pueblo enfermo,* 244.

ians, since Brazil had a population that by 1890 was approximately 15 per cent black and 40 per cent *mestizo* or mulatto. Many Brazilian writers, for example Silvio Romero and Raimundo Nina Rodrigues, accepted the indictment of miscegenation in evolutionary thought and endured the harsh social judgements of learned visitors like Gobineau and the American naturalist, Louis Agassiz. Yet by 1900 there was a growing tendency among other social theorists to counter extreme racial pessimism by rationalizing Brazil's multiracial society. They began to express the conviction that miscegenation and European immigration were leading inevitably to 'whitening' and thus to progress.

One such optimist was a young journalist, military engineer and ardent republican, Euclides da Cunha (1866–1909), whose bland positivism of the early 1890s was put to the test by a supposed pro-monarchist and religious rebellion of *sertanejos* (backlanders) at Canudos in Bahia. Sent by his newspaper, *O Estado de São Paulo* in 1897, Da Cunha witnessed the fierce resistance of the racially mixed rebels, and then their annihilation by overwhelming numbers of government troops supported by modern artillery. His journalistic assignment turned into *Os sertões* (1902), a massive narrative of the conflict, preceded by a full-dress scientific treatise on the 'sub-races' of the backlands and their successful interaction with a hostile, drought-ridden environment. Da Cunha's account revealed a profound contradiction between an acceptance of racism and social Darwinism and the empirical realization that the adaptive backlanders might be 'the very core of our nationality, the bedrock of our race'.[59] He theorized that the *mestizo* was psychologically unstable and degenerate, regressing always toward the primitive race, a 'victim of the fatality of biologic laws'. Canudos was the 'first assault' in a long struggle, 'the inevitable crushing of the weak races by the strong', a process (citing the Polish sociologist Gumplowicz) Da Cunha equated with the march of civilization. Yet he also spoke of the *sertanejo* as an 'ethnic subcategory already formed, an historic subrace of the future'. Being isolated from the coast for three centuries, it had been spared the exigencies of the struggle for racial existence and therefore could freely adapt to the environment. Thus Da Cunha distinguished between the 'rachitic' *mestizo* of the coast and the 'strong' *mestizo* of the backlands.[60] He seemed to surmount theory, how-

---

[59] E. Da Cunha, *Rebellion in the backlands* [trans. of *Os sertões*] (Chicago, 1944), 464; also author's note (from 1905 edn) on p. 481, where he explained the bedrock simile.

[60] Da Cunha, *Rebellion*, 84–9, xxix. Gumplowicz was an extreme social Darwinist who saw racial struggle as 'the motive force in history'.

ever, in describing the sheer courage, heroism and serenity of the last defenders of Canudos, 'beings on the lowest rung of our racial ladder'.[61] Without abandoning the scientific racism of his day, Euclides da Cunha introduced a new question into social thought, the ethnic or racial basis of national identity.

The question raised by Da Cunha was pursued intensely in late nineteenth-century Mexico, partly because of unique features of its recent history. The two great national movements, the Revolution for Independence and the Reforma, involved mass participation and social conflict; and many patriotic heroes, including Morelos and Juárez, were *mestizos* or Indians. Prior to the Reforma, the intellectual elite had tried to ignore the Indian and had espoused a creole sense of nationality. In an unusual mid-century essay, the scholar Francisco Pimentel (1832–93) had drawn a bleak picture of the degradation of the Indians, but his remedies were still those of the creole liberals: immigration, the whitening of the population and the elimination of the word race, 'in fact as well as in law'.[62] After 1870, the influx of evolutionary thought brought a new consciousness of race, but the conclusions were generally optimistic. For example, the theme of Justo Sierra's histories was the growth of the Mexican nation as an 'autonomous personality,' one element of which was racial mixture. We Mexicans, he asserted, are the offspring of two races, born of the Conquest, products of Spain and of the land of the aborigines. 'This fact rules our whole history, to it we owe our soul.'[63] Specifically refuting Le Bon's theories on the debilitating effect of miscegenation, Sierra demonstrated that the *mestizo* population had tripled in the nineteenth century and was the 'dynamic [political] factor in our history'.[64] Though he occasionally advocated immigration along with education as a social remedy, his ideal was not racial whitening. For him, national identity resided in the *mestizo*.

Another positive appreciation of racial mixture in Mexican society appeared in an austere study of 'Mexican sociology' by Andrés Molina Enríquez (1866–1940), a provincial judge who was outside Porfirian elite

[61] *Ibid.*, 440–1, including his moving portrait of a Negro captive who, as he approached his execution, became transformed from 'the wizened appearance of a sickly orangutan' to a 'statuesque masterpiece' of an ancient 'Titan'.

[62] F. Pimentel, 'Memoria sobre las causas que han originado la situación actual de la raza indígena de México y medios de remediarla' (1864), *Obras completas*, III (Mexico, 1903), 148.

[63] J. Sierra, 'Evolución política del pueblo mexicano', *Obras*, XII, 56 (1st edn 1900–2). It should be noted that *mestizo* for Sierra meant only Indian-white mixture, whereas for Da Cunha in Brazil it meant black-white or Indian-black-white.

[64] Sierra, 'México social y político. Apuntes para un libro' (1889), *Obras*, IX, 128–31. He cited a Le Bon article published the previous year in the *Revue scientifique*.

circles. Published in 1909 on the eve of Mexico's social upheaval, *Los grandes problemas nacionales* emphasized the problem of land and its maldistribution, thus making the work a famous (but little-read) precursor of revolution. Molina was an environmental determinist, citing Haeckel's theory of the unity of organic and inorganic matter. The selection and adaptation of organisms are the result of a struggle between the internal forces derived from 'vital combustion' and the external forces of nature. A race is simply a group of people who (through this process) adapt to similar environmental conditions and thus 'have acquired a uniformity of organization, indicated by a certain uniformity of type'. Though Molina went on to classify Mexican races scientifically, he admitted that any such classification was defective – largely because of the facts of Mexican history. His portrait of the *mestizo* was not always flattering, but on the whole, he accepted miscegenation as an inevitable and positive force. For example, he saw the greatest benefit of the 'republican form' to be civil equality, 'which has greatly favoured the contact, mixture and confusion of the races, leading to the formation of one single race'.[65]

In the absence of a large Indian or Negro population, the principal issue in Argentine social thought was not the effect of racial mixture on national identity, as it was in Bolivia, Mexico, or even Brazil. After the military conquest of the 'desert' (i.e., the Indian frontier) in 1879, Argentina's Indians became regionally isolated in the south and the north-west and were largely ignored by intellectuals and policy makers of the positivist era. The focus of social thought was rather the impact of the flood of European immigrants on a sparse creole population. The statistics themselves were dramatic. By 1914 about 2,400,000 immigrants, three quarters of them Spanish and Italian, had settled permanently in Argentina and 30 per cent of the total population was foreign-born. The concentration was most dense in the littoral provinces, and especially the Federal District. The 'new' Argentina, like Uruguay and southern Brazil, was ethnically a southern European province. Though rural colonization by Europeans had long been advocated by the elites throughout Latin America, the Argentine response to the reality of an urban immigrant tide was, at best, mixed.

[65] A. Molina Enríquez, *Grandes problemas*, 34–7. Molina also classified property from an evolutionary perspective, Indian communal property being a lower form than European individual titled property. His views influenced two post-1910 assumptions, (1) that all property was evolving toward the higher form and (2) that practicality dictated the temporary acceptance and legalization of communal holdings.

Concern with the character of the new society appeared as part of a remarkable scientific and cultural efflorescence between 1900 and 1915 which has remained unrivalled in modern Latin America. Positivist thought seemed to find its ideal milieu in *belle-époque* Argentina, nourished by the fabulous prosperity of the export economy, by the burgeoning of Buenos Aires as a sophisticated world metropolis and by a continuing consensus among the governing class. The cultural pretensions of the porteño elite found rich expression in the monumental Teatro Colón, planned in the late 1880s and finally completed in 1908. The establishment of the Universidad Nacional de La Plata in 1905, especially its Facultad de Ciencias Jurídicas y Sociales, was symptomatic of the special place occupied by social science in intellectual life. A series of important journals, beginning with the *Revista de derecho, historia y letras* (1898) and ending with the *Revista de filosofía* (1915), recalled the *Revue des deux mondes* and other major French intellectual journals of the late nineteenth century. The list of significant scientists, social theorists and their works is long and impressive.

The 'archetypal savant' of the positivist age in Argentina was Florentino Ameghino (1854–1911), a geo-palaeontologist whose prodigious research on the antiquity of man in the Río de la Plata region gained him world renown. In his famous declaration, *Mi credo* (1906), he espoused an absolute faith in science and in man's perfectibility; the pursuit of truth, he said, will become the 'religion of the future'. José Ingenieros called him a 'modern saint.' Ameghino's scientism was extreme, but it nonetheless inspired many who pursued the application of science to society.[66] Another star in the positivist constellation was José María Ramos Mejía (1849–1914), a pioneer in medicine (especially in psychiatry), who established a national tradition of medical engagement in social questions. His *Estudios clínicos sobre las enfermedades nerviosas y mentales* (1893) was followed by *Las multitudes argentinas* (1899), an application of Le Bon's crowd psychology, and by its sequel, *Rosas y su tiempo* (1907), which depicted the caudillo as an emanation of the masses.[67] Scientific rigour in legal and historical studies was championed by Juan Agustín García (1862–1923) in his *Introducción al estudio de las ciencias sociales argentinas* (1899). He

---

[66] F. Ameghino's works and correspondence were published in 24 folio volumes (La Plata, 1913–36). 'Mi credo' appeared in vol. xv, 687–719, the eulogy by Ingenieros in 1, 33–5. See also the oration by Ricardo Rojas, *Obras* (Buenos Aires, 1922), 11, (*Los arquetipos*), 197–237 ('Ameghino, el sabio').

[67] See J. Ingenieros, 'La personalidad intelectual de José M. Ramos Mejía', *Revista de filosofía*, 2 (1915), 103–58. Ingenieros received his psychiatric training under Ramos Mejía.

applied his precepts in *La ciudad indiana* (1900), a lasting study that emphasized economic interests and social structures in the development of colonial institutions.

We have noted the extreme sensitivity of Argentine social thought to varied and changing European ideas. Another characteristic in the positivist era was an almost exaggerated effort to establish an 'Argentine' sociology, built upon the ideas of the nineteenth-century *pensadores*. This paradox, that is, the dual Argentine tendency toward cosmopolitanism and cultural nationalism, was epitomized in the work of the most eminent of Argentine positivists, José Ingenieros (1877–1925). Besides his preoccupation with Argentine society, Ingenieros aspired (at least until 1915) to be a 'man of science', and he gained widespread European recognition as a psychologist, criminologist and psychopathologist. After 1915 he turned to philosophy and ethics. His works were a veritable encyclopedia of continental writers and their ideas. He was as well-travelled as any of his contemporaries. Nonetheless, he presented his studies of Argentina's sociological evolution as built upon premises of Echeverría, Sarmiento and Alberdi, and he wrote substantial essays on their thought.[68] He also edited an important series of Argentine classics entitled 'La cultura argentina', in which he included Sarmiento's unfinished *Conflicto y armonías*, forgotten since its appearance in 1883.

In his *Sociología argentina* (1913), Ingenieros tried to combine 'biological' and 'economic' sociology, that is, Spencerian social Darwinism and economic determinism (*economismo histórico*), especially as espoused by the Italian theorist, Achille Loria. Though Loria had rejected social Darwinism as elitist and *laissez faire*, Ingenieros was too eclectic to be troubled by such contradictions.[69] He depicted Argentine history as a struggle for existence among social aggregates, yet also as an economically determined evolution from indigenous barbarism to Spanish feudal dominion to an agrarian-pastoral (*agropecuario*) capitalism, and finally toward a 'progressive socialization of the great collective functions in the hands of the state'. Argentina shared this inevitable transition from capitalism to socialism

---

[68] First published in 1915–16, these essays were included by Ingenieros in the 1918 edition of *Sociología argentina*, reprinted as vol. VIII of *Obras completas* (Buenos Aires, 1957), 214–304.

[69] See A. Loria, *Contemporary social problems* (London, 1910), 104, 118 (1st edn 1894). Though Ingenieros frequently cited Loria, it is significant that he apparently ignored Loria's major theme, the effect of free land in history, especially in colonial areas. Loria's theory was important for Frederick Jackson Turner. See Lee Benson, 'Achille Loria's influence on American economic thought: including his contributions to the frontier hypothesis', *Turner and Beard* (New York, 1960), 2–40.

with other nations of the white race. Ingenieros was a pioneer socialist and was active politically until 1903; however, he gradually moved away from his socialist-inspired interpretation of Argentine society.[70]

Ingenieros viewed the recent European influx positively, perhaps in part because his own parents had been Italian immigrants. For Sarmiento in 1883, the great national evils had been the Spanish heritage and *mestizaje*, his remedies public education and immigration. Ingenieros perpetuated this view, asserting in his *Formación de una raza argentina* (1915) that while the first (colonial) immigration had been sterile, the second was consolidating a nationality. In the temperate zones, he wrote, there has been a 'progressive substitution of the aboriginal races of colour by white immigrant races, engendering new societies to replace the native ones'. The process was simply a struggle for life between species in a given environment, the most adaptable ones surviving. When species mixed, the strain 'better adapted to the dual physical-social environment' prevailed. He defined race as 'a homogeneous society of shared customs and ideals', a concept that was more historical than anthropological. Ingenieros portrayed the Argentines as a race of 'working and educated men' which now commanded the respect of Europe. An Argentine tradition does exist, he affirmed. It was born with nationhood itself and it was nourished by the ideals of 'our *pensadores*'. It is a tradition that points to the future, not to the past.[71]

By 1915, few major intellectuals shared the positive view of immigration held by Ingenieros. Instead, they sympathized with the growing xenophobia that was in part an elite reaction to hordes of European peasants and labourers, some of whom prospered in urban commerce and in the trades and professions. Immigrants became the scapegoat for urban social problems, and psychologists of the day identified immigrants as more prone to crime than lower class creoles. Since socialism and particularly anarchism grew along with immigration, the labour unrest of the 1900–10 decade was blamed on foreign extremists. The first immigrant restriction law was passed in 1902 following a crippling general strike,

---

[70] The phrase 'progressive socialization . . .', which appeared in the preface of the 1913 Madrid edition of *Sociología argentina* (p. 8), was omitted in the 1918 edition. The writings of Ingenieros present a bibliographical challenge because of his passion for publication and thus his tendency to reproduce earlier writings (with small revisions) in later publications. His *Sociología* went through many transformations, but the principal arguments first appeared in essays dating from 1898 to 1910.

[71] 'Formación' first appeared in Ingenieros' major journal *Revista de filosofía*, 2 (1915), 464–83, and then in the 1918 edition of *Sociología*.

another in 1910 after a bomb explosion in the Teatro Colón. One deputy attributed the crime to 'a dastardly, ignominious, foreign mind'. Among the supporters of the 1910 Social Defence Law were Ramos Mejía, whose hostility to immigration had appeared as early as 1899 in his *Las multitudes argentinas,* and Bunge, whose assessment of the benefits of immigration had changed sharply in the years since *Nuestra América.*

'Cosmopolitanism' came to be used in a new way, no longer referring to elite European cultural influences, but rather to the materialism and political radicalism of recent immigrants; and the response was nationalistic. Ricardo Rojas (1882–1957), in his *La restauración nacionalista* (1909), became the advocate of a new education in Argentine history and values as a way to lead future generations away from an 'ignoble materialism which has come to confuse for them progress with civilization'.[72] His contemporary, Manuel Gálvez (1882–1963) evoked the traditions of the creole provinces in *El diario de Gabriel Quiroga* (1910) and of Spain in *El solar de la raza* (1913). Though Gálvez's conclusions later turned extreme, at this stage they were still balanced. 'Modern Argentina', he wrote, '[though] constructed on a base of immigration, or cosmopolitanism, can and must preserve a foundation of *argentinidad*'.[73] Rojas and Gálvez both emphasized the revival of humanistic and spiritual values, and their resistance to immigrant influence drew from a new idealist challenge to positivism, to be considered below.

Immigration was not a major issue in Chilean social thought, principally because the influx of foreigners was small, generally middle class and mostly into the sparsely settled north rather than the central valley. The response of the elite (for example, Letelier) was generally benign, but one significant exception was Nicolás Palacios (1854–1911). His immensely popular *Raza chilena* (1904) espoused a biological racism in the manner of Le Bon (whom he quoted constantly) and drew from it unique conclusions on the role of racial mixture in nationality. The true Chilean race is *mestizo,* he said, combining the superior qualities of the Spanish *conquistadores* (traced to 'Gothic' origins in Scandinavia) and the fiercely independent Araucanian Indians. The recent entry of inferior 'Latin races' is harmful, and immigration (particularly Italian) should be curtailed. The peculiar version of racial nationalism Palacios espoused has had lasting influence in Chile.

[72] R. Rojas, *La restauración nacionalista. Informe sobre educación* (Buenos Aires, 1909), 64.
[73] M. Gálvez, *El solar de la raza* (5th edn, Madrid, 1920), 17–18n.

Social determinism and caudillo government

The racial and environmental determinism inherent in social thought from 1890 to 1914 sharpened and solidified a diagnosis of Latin American politics which had been developing since at least the 1840s. The early faith in the efficacy of constitutional arrangements had faded as law came to be regarded as a product of history and not as an emanation of reason. With the influx of Comtean positivism liberal doctrines and constitutional formulas were branded 'metaphysical'. After 1870 consensus-minded elites sought a remedy for disorder in scientific politics, a programme that would respond to social realities, strengthen government (often through constitutional reform), and ensure economic progress. Programmatic scientific politics and diagnostic social thought were not in conflict. They were merely variants within nineteenth-century positivism, the first derived principally from Comte, the second derived more from Darwin and Spencer. Whereas the latter tended to be more pessimistic and self-denigrating than the former, they both produced stereotypes about Latin American political behaviour which are still popularly accepted, particularly among foreigners.

Carlos O. Bunge argued that a nation's form of government must be construed as an 'organic' outgrowth of its racial and psychological heritage and not as an 'independent abstraction'. Arguedas quoted approvingly Le Bon's assertion that 'political institutions . . . are the expression of the stage of civilization of a people and they evolve with it'. If a country is organically monarchical or republican, wrote Bunge, 'its workshops, its laboratories, its arts, and its books are monarchized or republicanized'. In Latin America, where the regime of *caciques* is organic, all of life is 'caciquized'.[74] Independence was seen by the pessimists as premature, in part the product of exotic ideas, in part the personal creation of *caciques* or caudillos. Lacking any organic principle of institutional balance, the result was alternation between anarchy and despotism, the two sides of what Bunge called the 'American disease'. The caudillo was thus a natural phenomenon. For García Calderón, the great caudillos, such as Rosas, Portales and Díaz, were those who by 'interpreting the inner voices of [their] race' could impose political unity and advance material progress. Bunge, echoing a widely held view, referred to Porfirio Díaz as 'the

[74] Bunge, *Nuestra América*, 158; Arguedas, *Pueblo enfermo*, 207.

progressive cacique', one of the great statesmen of the century. 'He governs Mexico as Mexico must be governed.'[75]

The growing acceptance of the caudillo as a socially determined and natural political phenomenon appeared not only in popular essays but also in more elaborate histories. The most notable case was that of Juan Manuel de Rosas, whose federalist regime from 1831 to 1852 was substantially reinterpreted in works by Adolfo Saldías (1850–1914), the brothers José María and Francisco Ramos Mejía (1847–93) and by Ernesto Quesada (1858–1934). These authors purported to examine Rosas and federalism scientifically and thus to surmount the partisan passions that had led to a quasi-official *unitario* condemnation of the 'tyrant' in the years since 1852. José María Ramos Mejía claimed to be guided only by 'cold curiosity'; his approach would be that of 'an entomologist studying a new insect'. Saldías envisioned himself doing an 'autopsy' of the 'social body' in order to discover the 'nature of the foetus, which is Rosas'.[76] The revision of the Rosas era was also a more specific product of Argentine politics, particularly the mounting provincial opposition to the *unicato* and the democratic impulse in the Unión Cívica. In *El federalismo argentino* (1889) Francisco Ramos Mejía viewed that phenomenon as a natural legacy from the colonial past, not as an artificial implant of the era of independence. Saldías sought to understand why the masses had supported Rosas and thus to discover the course they had followed since Rosas's day. He concluded that the dictator was the 'incarnation of the sentiments, ideas and aspirations of the Argentine countryside'.[77]

The most significant and influential work of the revisionist movement was Quesada's lucid essay, *Rosas y su tiempo* (1898), the synthesis of his numerous monographs published after 1893. Quesada had studied in Germany and brought to his subject the standards and premises of German historical scholarship. For Quesada Rosas was simply a product of his times, 'no more, no less'; his 'tyranny' was no worse than the tyranny of numerous *unitario* chieftains. Since the Argentine masses lacked 'political

---

[75] Another important example of this interpretation was *La anarquía argentina y el caudillismo. Estudio psicológico de los orígenes argentinas* (Buenos Aires, 1904) by the physician turned social essayist, Lucas Ayarragaray (1861–1944). Though Bunge regarded *caudillismo* as a 'deformed' *caciquismo*, other writers, including Ayarragaray, did not distinguish between the two.

[76] José María Ramos Mejía, *Rosa y su tiempo* (3rd edn, Buenos Aires, 1927), I, xxxiii (1st edn 1907); A. Saldías, *Historia de la confederación argentina. Rozas y su época* (Buenos Aires, 1951), III, 497 (first published 1881–7).

[77] Saldías, *Historia*, III, 487. Both Saldías and Francisco Ramos Mejía were active in the Unión Cívica, and Saldías expanded and reissued his work in 1892.

education', liberal institutions could not function; the result was anarchy and petty dictatorship. Rosas provided the 'autocratic' leadership the masses demanded. His federalism was not localist; on the contrary, it brought unity and order out of chaos. By 1852, said Quesada, 'his historic mission had ended'.[78] Though Quesada avoided the overt psychological and racial theorizing of many of his contemporaries, his scholarship had the effect of reinforcing intellectual acceptance of caudillo leadership.[79]

As we have noted, a hostility toward classical liberal and democratic doctrines permeated deterministic social thought. By 1890 the label 'jacobin' was increasingly applied to those who believed that society could be transformed by the imposition of rational principles, replacing the comparable term 'metaphysical' of the 1870s. The new label was inspired by Hippolyte Taine's trenchant indictment of the jacobin mentality, first published in 1881 and subsequently popularized by Le Bon and others. For Taine jacobin 'psychology' was the bane of French politics from the Revolution of 1789 to the Commune of 1871. Its indestructible roots, he wrote, are 'exaggerated pride' and 'dogmatic reasoning', which exist beneath the surface of society. When social bonds dissolve (as in France in 1790), jacobins spring up 'like mushrooms in rotting compost'. Their principles, such as the rights of man, the social contract and equality, are the simplistic axioms of 'political geometry', espoused by the young and the unsuccessful and then imposed on a complex society by 'the philosophe legislator'. But, added Taine decisively, they are imposed in vain, because society 'is not the product of logic, but of history'.[80] Taine's diagnosis of French politics struck a responsive chord in Latin American sociologists, and it was universally cited in their writings.

The half-century long attack upon classical liberalism reached a climax in two works which represented the subtle but significant variants within positivist thought. The first, *La constitución y la dictadura* (1912), by the Mexican jurist Emilio Rabasa (1856–1930), marked the culmination of scientific politics, as enunciated by *La Libertad* in 1878 and reiterated by the *científicos* of 1893. Rabasa's work was a measured analysis of the defects

---

[78] E. Quesada, *Rosas y su tiempo* (Buenos Aires, 1923), 63. Cf. Sarmiento's interpretation of Rosas, cited by Quesada.

[79] Quesada made an intriguing comparison (*ibid.*, 149–53) between Rosas and Portales, citing the conservative Chilean historians Ramón Sotomayor y Valdes and Carlos Walker Martínez.

[80] H. Taine, 'Psychologie du jacobin', *Revue des deux mondes*, 44 (1881), 536–59, republished the same year in *Les origines de la France contemporaine* (*La révolution*, 11 ['La Conquête jacobine'], 3–39). In Latin America, see, e.g., J. E. Rodó, *Liberalismo y jacobinismo* (Montevideo, 1906), 72–8. Rodó emphasized jacobin 'intolerance'.

of the Constitution of 1857. 'We have placed our hope on the written law and it has shown its incurable weakness', he wrote. The jacobin legislators of 1856 severely restricted presidential authority in defiance of 'sociological laws'. The inevitable result, according to Rabasa, was the two dictatorships of Benito Juárez and Porfirio Díaz, which enjoyed popular sanction because they served 'to satisfy the needs of national development'. Rabasa's work has been attacked as an apology for Díaz in the wake of his overthrow in 1911.[81] Yet Rabasa maintained his faith in historic constitutionalism, the buttress of an enlightened oligarchy. 'The dictators have completed their task', he concluded. 'The constitutional stage must follow.' Rabasa's goal, like that of Sierra, was to bring the written and the real constitutions into harmony, to solidify the reign of political institutions and liberties in concert with strong and effective central administration.[82] It was an optimistic goal shared by the liberal establishment throughout Latin America.

The second work, *Caesarismo democrático* (1919), by the Venezuelan, Laureano Vallenilla Lanz (1870–1936), perpetuated the pessimistic diagnosis of politics in the tradition of Bunge, Arguedas, García Calderón and the Rosas revisionists. Vallenilla's focus was the civil strife unleashed by the Venezuelan revolution for independence, which he characterized (borrowing from Taine) as 'a state of spontaneous anarchy'. He identified in this anarchy an 'egalitarian and levelling democracy', which, as a natural American phenomenon, brought with it the necessity for strong government. Vallenilla excoriated the 'abstract principles of jacobinism' inherent in unworkable written constitutions and asserted that Venezuela could only be ruled effectively by a caesar who responded to 'the psychology of our popular masses', the mixed race of the interior plains (*llanos*). The two caesars Vallenilla singled out were the *llanero* chieftain José Antonio Paez, who exerted 'a personal power that was the concrete expression of the political instincts of our positive constitution', and Simón Bolívar. The latter's 'brilliant intuition as a sociologist' led him naturally to the concept of dictator for life, the 'Bolivian principle (*ley Boliviana*)'.[83] Vallenilla

---

[81] Most recently by Daniel Cosío Villegas (1898–1976), in *La constitución de 1857 y sus críticos* (Mexico, 1957). Cosío's passionate defence of the Constitution was directed against both Sierra and Rabasa, but particularly against the great influence Rabasa's work had in re-establishing an authoritarian presidency in the Constitution of 1917.

[82] Cf. E. Rabasa, *La constitución y la dictadura* (3rd edn, Mexico, 1956), 224–6, and Sierra, 'Evolución política', 395–6 (written in 1900).

[83] L. Vallenilla Lanz, *Caesarismo democrático: estudio sobre las bases soliológicas de la constitución efectiva de Venezuela* (2nd edn, Caracas, 1929), 281, 214. The book was made up of several studies originally published as early as 1911. Though Vallenilla acknowledged the uniqueness of Venezuelan society, he clearly meant his argument to apply to Latin America as a whole; see his references to Arguedas, Bunge and García Calderón (pp. 229–35).

could thus present the great Bolívar as a forerunner of the contemporary dictator, Juan Vicente Gómez (1908–35), whom Vallenilla served as minister and as editor of the official newspaper.

The late positivist interpretation of politics, as represented by both Rabasa and Vallenilla Lanz, was based on a conviction that the Latin American nations, following the dictates of history, race and social psychology, were unable to realize liberal and democratic principles as practised in the 'advanced' countries of Europe and particularly in the United States. Latin American positivists recognized that their society had unique features, but the limitations of evolutionary theory forced them to view that society as inferior on a unilinear scale of civilization. While Rabasa clung to the hope that an enlightened governing class and a strong central administration could bring stability and progress, Vallenilla saw the only solution in a charismatic leader who could respond to the instincts of the unruly masses. While Rabasa maintained a modicum of faith in liberal institutions, Vallenilla despaired of them altogether. The influence of both positivist conclusions, the one drawn from programmatic scientific politics and the other from diagnostic social determinism, persisted, but not without facing a fundamental challenge to the intellectual assumptions on which they were based.

THE NEW IDEALISM

In 1900, an Uruguayan litterateur, José E. Rodó (1871–1917) published a short essay which had an immense influence on Spanish American intellectuals for two decades and which has retained a symbolic importance to our day. Rodó's *Ariel,* dedicated to 'the youth of America', became the clarion call for a revival of idealism. By evoking a Latin American 'spirit' and identifying it with a revised sense of race, the essay inspired a reaffirmation of the humanistic values in Latin American culture and a resistance to the tide of pessimism in social thought. Moreover, *Ariel* included an indictment of the utilitarianism and democratic mediocrity of the United States, thus providing intellectuals with an easy basis for differentiating and defending 'their' America. They responded quickly to Rodó's appeal to reject the 'mania for the north (*nordomanía*)' that had prevailed, he said, since Alberdi's day, and to abandon 'the vision of a voluntarily delatinized America'. The 'mighty confederation', Rodó added, 'is realizing over us a kind of moral conquest'. Though he did not refer specifically to the Spanish American War, Rodó's essay was clearly a response to the shock produced by Spain's disastrous defeat in 1898. In short, 'from the moment of its appearance', it has been said, *Ariel* became 'the very symbol of Latinamericanism, defined for the first time'.[84]

The appeal of *Ariel* was in its timing and perhaps also in its elevated and abstract tone. For it lacked literary originality, philosophic depth and specific social or political analysis. Rodó's view of North American culture, though containing insights, was secondhand, based on *Del Plata al Niágara* (1897) by Paul Groussac and on a tendentious use of French travellers' accounts. Rodó drew his symbolism explicitly from Shakespeare's *Tempest*, though he modelled the essay itself more on Ernest Renan's philosophic drama, *Caliban, suite de 'la Tempête'* (1878). *Ariel* took the form of a year-end lecture by a venerated teacher ('Próspero') to a group of students, delivered beside a cherished statue of 'Ariel', symbol of spirituality, grace and intelligence. The antithesis of Ariel was 'Caliban', a symbol of materialism, 'sensuality and torpor'. In Renan's play, Caliban prevailed over Ariel and Prospero resigned himself to the victory. Rodó would not accept such a conclusion and began where Renan left off.

Though Rodó was heralded as the prophet of a new idealism, much of *Ariel* was cast in a positivist mould. In fact, the same was true of the writings of those intellectuals he directly inspired, often known as *arielistas*. Rodó's 'transitional' quality reflected one version of the continuing interaction between empiricism (positivism) and idealism (spiritualism) in nineteenth-century French thought. Auguste Comte and Victor Cousin (and some of their followers) promoted the notion of two sharply antagonistic philosophies, but they exaggerated the differences, which were based in part on a personal and academic rivalry. The thought of Renan and Taine, two of Rodó's mentors who are generally regarded as positivists, was in constant tension between science and metaphysics. Renan was plagued throughout his life by religious longings, Taine by the urge to abstract causes or essences in experience and thus to surmount the limitations of the positivist method.[85]

Rodó's principal intellectual guide in *Ariel* was probably Alfred Fouillée, whose prolific writings were specifically directed toward reconciling the values of philosophical idealism, especially liberty and free will,

---

[84] A. Zum Feld, *Índice crítico de la literatura hispanoamericana: los ensayistas* (Mexico, 1954), 292.

[85] W. H. Simon, 'The "Two Cultures" in nineteenth-century France: Victor Cousin and Auguste Comte', *Journal of the History of Ideas*, 26 (1965), 45–58; D. G. Charlton, *Positivist thought in France during the Second Empire, 1852–1870* (Oxford, 1959). Charlton characterizes Renan and Taine, along with Comte himself, as 'false friends of positivism', that is, of positivism as a theory of knowledge.

with the determinism of science.[86] Fouillée's central concept, the 'thought force' (*idée-force*), was an attempt to apply the scientific notion of force to mental states. Force is a fact of consciousness; conversely, every idea is a force that can be realized in action. Fouillée's influence was most apparent in Rodó's optimistic (and often overlooked) vision of an ultimate reconciliation between North American and Latin American values. 'All history', Rodó said, 'clearly shows a reciprocal influence between the progress of utilitarian activity and the ideal', and he pointed to Renaissance Italy as an example. Though he saw present evidence lacking, Rodó was confident that 'the work of North American positivism will in the end serve the cause of Ariel'. The energy of the United States will be transformed into higher values.

Rodó asserted in *Ariel* that 'we Latin Americans have an inheritance of race, a great ethnic tradition to maintain'; a decade later he went on to identify 'the idea and sentiment of race' with 'the communal sense of ancestry (*la comunidad del origen, de la casta, del abolengo histórico*)'.[87] Rodó was departing from anthropological or scientific racism and instead was reviving the historical conception of race. Did his 'inheritance of race' refer to national traditions or to the Hispanic past? Did it include indigenous and black culture? Or, was the inheritance more broadly 'Latin', a product of the humanistic and aesthetic ideals of Greco-Roman and Christian civilization? The message of *Ariel* was ambiguous in the extreme and thus became a point of departure for diverse tendencies in twentieth-century thought. Also unclear were the social and political implications of Rodó's appeal to America's youth. The tone of the essay was primarily elitist; it evoked aestheticism, a 'well-employed leisure', and 'Renan's wisdom of the aristocrat' against the tyranny of the mass. Rodó was clearly disturbed by the effects of urban immigration. Yet he recognized democracy (along with science) as one of 'the two props upon which our civilization rests' and agreed with Fouillée (against Renan) that the law of natural selection works in society toward the softening of hierarchies and the broadening of liberty.[88]

---

[86] The principal relevant work of A. Fouillée was *L'idée moderne du droit en Allemagne, en Angleterre, et en France* (1878); also *Le mouvement idéaliste et la réaction contre la science positive* (1896).

[87] J. E. Rodó, 'Rumbos nuevos', *El mirador de Próspero* (Montevideo, 1958 [1st edn 1913]), 26 (commentary on *Idola Fori* [1910] by the Colombian *arielista* Carlos Arturo Torres). Rodó also praised (p. 30) Rojas's *La restauración nacionalista* (1909) as promoting the new 'consciousness of race'.

[88] Rodó, *Ariel*, 6–7, 64–6. Rodó dismissed Nietzsche's 'anti-egalitarianism' as the product of 'an abominable, reactionary mentality'.

The new continent-wide idealism took nationally diverse forms, as exemplified by its experience in Argentina, Peru and Mexico. Argentine intellectual life from 1900 to 1920 was not only rich but remarkably complex. Though these years were the apogee of positivism, they were also marked by growing intellectual dissent, fed by changing European ideas, by political questions raised in the aftermath of El Noventa, and by a national soul-searching prompted by the influx of immigrants. Rodó's voice from across the Río de la Plata helped give focus to these varied national concerns. One early dissenter from positivism was the French-born historian and critic Paul Groussac (1848–1929). As a life-long disciple of Taine and Renan, he combined 'scientific' erudition with a strong critique of utilitarianism, both in North American and in Argentine society. Alarmed by immigrant values, he warned that 'material preoccupations may gradually dislodge pure aspirations from the Argentine soul, without which national prosperity is built on sand'.[89] The centennial of independence in 1910 abetted these sentiments and brought forth the essays by Gálvez, as we have noted, and also Rojas's *Blasón de plata* (1912).[90] The latter was followed by *La Argentinidad* (1916) and finally by *Eurindia* (1924), both of which sought Argentine cultural identity in a lyrical but ill-defined interplay between (European) 'exoticism' and 'Indianism'. However, the new idealism in Argentina had more than literary manifestations; it also took the form of significant political and educational departures, to be considered below.

Nowhere did Rodó's message have a more overt effect than in Peru, where a remarkable *'arielista* generation' or *'generación de novecientos'* emerged from the University of San Marcos in 1905. Its leaders were Victor Andrés Belaunde (1883–1966) and José de la Riva-Agüero (1885–1944), as well as Francisco García Calderón (see above). As students they first absorbed the dominant positivism of San Marcos, but soon embraced Rodó (our 'veritable spiritual director', said Belaunde) and also the idealism of Émile Boutroux and Henri Bergson, as taught to them by the philosophical dissenter, Alejandro Deústua. All three were aristocrats, Riva-Agüero from one of the great families of Lima, Belaunde from provincial Arequipa, where he nostalgically recalled the existence of a dignified

---

[89] P. Groussac, passage (1906?) quoted by A. Korn, *Influencias filosóficas en la evolución nacional* (Buenos Aires, 1936), 5. Groussac was defending the teaching of Latin in a report on secondary education.
[90] The *arielista* emphasis on race as ancestry was further evident in Rojas's subtitle: *Meditaciones y evocaciones . . . sobre el abolengo de los argentinos.*

'democracy of gentlefolk (*hidalgos*)'.[91] The elder Francisco García Calderón (also born in Arequipa) was a respected jurist and provisional president of the Republic in 1879.

The lives and thought of the three ultimately took quite different courses, but all began by seeking national renovation in a strong constitutional presidency, supported by a progressive and enlightened oligarchy. This ideal of scientific politics seemed to them embodied in the Civilista Party of Presidents Nicolás Piérola (1895–9) and José Pardo (1904–8). However, the *arielistas'* ambivalence towards rapid economic development and the materialism of the new 'plutocracy' of their day led them to advocate ethical and spiritual values and a tutelary political role for intellectuals.[92] García Calderón published *Le Pérou contemporaine* (1907), an ambitious (and unappreciated) sociological study. Riva-Agüero and Belaunde founded the ill-fated National Democratic (Futurista) Party in 1915 and then turned conservative and Catholic. Belaunde clung to traditional constitutionalism, and despite persecution and exile, pursued a distinguished career as law professor, founder of the Catholic University (1917), and finally as President of the United Nations General Assembly (1959). Riva-Agüero's idealism drew him to the colonial and Hispanic past; and beginning with *Perú en la historia* (1910), he became its leading interpreter and apologist. In politics he was increasingly isolated and in the 1930s even advocated Italian fascism.

At the age of twenty-three, García Calderón, along with his three brothers, left Peru for a diplomatic sinecure in Paris, not to return for forty years. He made an impressive debut as a protégé of Boutroux in French literary and philosophical circles, and until the end of World War I was a leading apostle of Americanism and of solidarity among the Latin races. Besides his numerous books and essays, García Calderón founded *La Revista de América* (1912–14), which he said 'belonged to the intellectual elite from across the sea'.[93] Though his goal was the autonomy of Ameri-

---

[91] V. A. Belaunde, *La realidad nacional* (Paris, 1931), 189–90; *Arequipa de mi infancia* (1960), as quoted in F. Bourricaud, *Power and society in contemporary Peru* (New York, 1970), 54–6. The family estates and brandy enterprise were ruined by the railroad, and Belaunde's father became a wool merchant.

[92] See F. García Calderón, 'La nueva generación intelectual del Perú' (1905), *Hombres e ideas de nuestro tiempo* (Valencia, 1907), 206–7, an explicit yet ambivalent expression of scientific politics.

[93] *Revistade América* (Paris), 1 (June 1912), 2; also *Creación de un continente* (Paris, 1913), a full exposition of Americanism. Contributors to the 20 issues of the *Revista* included Arguedas (Bolivia), Ingenieros and Gálvez (Argentina), Enrique Pérez (Colombia), Manoel Oliveira Lima and José Verissimo (Brazil), Alfonso Reyes (Mexico) and Ventura García Calderón, Francisco's brother.

can thought and letters, first, he wrote, we must absorb 'our [Latin] inheritance'. 'Imitation will prepare the way for invention'; and perhaps, he implied, Latin leadership will eventually pass to America. Even the eminent Poincaré was impressed and recommended García Calderón's *Les démocraties latines* (1912) 'to all Frenchmen concerned for the future of the Latin spirit'.[94] Yet García Calderón's Americanism, as we have seen, also had its pessimistic side, rooted in Le Bonian scientific racism; as such, it emphasized social disorganization and dictatorship stemming from the 'depressing' Iberian and Indian racial heritage. García Calderón surmounted this pessimism as his interests moved from sociology to letters, from Indian and *mestizo* Peru to the cosmopolitan Latin elite. By 1916 he could note the 'declining prestige of the biological notion of race', yet the persistence of 'the idea of race as a synthesis of the diverse elements of a defined civilization'.[95] In 1912 he still adhered to both concepts. So the elitist pan-Latin and pan-American ideal, as espoused by García Calderón, enjoyed its brief, significant moment, soon to be overwhelmed by world war and social revolution.

In Mexico, the main forum for the new idealism was the Ateneo de la Juventud, organized in 1909 as a study and lecture society by a philosophically minded group of young intellectuals. The principals of the Ateneo were Antonio Caso (1883–1946), José Vasconcelos (1882–1959) and Pedro Henríquez Ureña (1884–1946), who between 1910 and 1925 were to lead a profound cultural renovation in Mexican life. Henríquez Ureña, a native Dominican who settled in Mexico in 1906, was the catalyst of the group, giving it a cosmopolitan and Americanist orientation.[96] The Ateneo critique was directed at the positivist curriculum of the Escuela Nacional Preparatoria (ENP), long fixed by the Díaz regime. Yet the rebellious 'new generation' found implicit encouragement from the ever-flexible Justo Sierra, Minister of Public Instruction since 1905. In 1908 Sierra spoke in defence of Gabino Barreda, founder of the ENP, against attacks by 'intransigent' Catholics. Most of his oration upheld the school's state-controlled curriculum and Barreda's work as 'consummator (*completa-*

---

[94] R. Poincaré, preface to *Les démocraties latines*, 1. García Calderón and Poincaré submitted the preface in Dec. 1911, just before becoming President of the Council and Minister of Foreign Affairs.

[95] F. García Calderón, 'El panamericanismo: su pasado y su porvenir', *La revue hispanique*, 37 (June 1916), 1.

[96] From 1907 to 1911 Henríquez Ureña edited the important *Revista moderna* (Mexico), in which he included seven contributions by his friend García Calderón and an annotated Spanish version of the latter's 'Les courants philosophiques dans l'Amérique latine' in Nov. 1908, a month after its appearance in France. He also commented on Rodó's writings and in Aug. 1910 delivered an Ateneo lecture on Rodó.

dor) of the Reforma, the Juárez of mental emancipation'. However, Sierra's 'let us doubt' passages acknowledged changing conceptions in many scientific areas. Continual questioning of orthodoxies (whether scholastic or positivistic, he implied) was in the spirit of Barreda. Going a step further in 1910, Sierra announced that the new National University's Escuela de Altos Estudios would emphasize philosophy, the (metaphysical) 'why' of the universe, not just the (positivistic) 'how'. Moreover, he added (paraphrasing Fouillée), ideas must be turned into action; 'only thus can they be called forces.'[97]

The Ateneístas ranged wildly in their intellectual effort to break from positivism. In Kant and Schopenhauer they found the impetus to philosophic contemplation and aesthetic experience. Nietzsche inspired individual rebellion against slavish adherence to any doctrine. Like their mentor Sierra, they were attracted to the pragmatism and instrumentalism of James and to his assertion that 'the immediate experience of life resolves the problems that are most troubling to pure thought.'[98] Like Rodó and Groussac they also turned to the classics. Alfonso Reyes (1889–1959), a younger Ateneísta, called for a restoration of Latin, the key to literature, both of which had been 'erased' by the positivists as a sequel to the 'liberal reaction' against the Church.[99]

The Ateneístas and their *arielista* contemporaries were most directly guided by what Vasconcelos called the 'new French philosophy' of Boutroux and particularly of his student Bergson.[100] Boutroux emphasized contingency in the evolutionary process, thus undermining determinism. Bergson's distinction between precisely measured scientific time as space and 'real' time as experienced continuity or duration was for the Americans a liberating concept. Time as duration is perpetual movement, inherent in life itself, and it can only be sensed internally through 'intellectual sympathy' or 'intuition'. Intuition in turn is the basis of a 'vital impetus (*élan vital*)' in all of nature, a creative force that guides humanity to surmount all obstacles, 'perhaps even death'. García Calderón called Bergsonism 'the philosophy of young races' because it affirmed moral freedom and the

---

[97] J. Sierra, 'Homenaje al maestro Gabino Barreda en el Teatro Abreu' (22 Mar. 1908), *Obras*, v, 387–96; 'Discurso en el acto de inauguración de la Universidad nacional de México' (22 Sept. 1910), *ibid.*, 448 – 62.

[98] Passage quoted by Sierra, *ibid.*, 461.

[99] A. Reyes, 'Nosotros,' *Revista de América*, 20 (1914), 111. Reyes left Mexico in 1913 after the death of his father Bernardo, former war minister and state governor.

[100] J. Vasconcelos, 'Don Gabino Barreda y las ideas contemporáneas' (12 Sept. 1910), *Conferencias del Ateneo de la Juventud* (2nd edn, Mexico, 1962), 111.

value of struggle.[101] While accepting evolutionary theory, Bergson gave it a new and optimistic interpretation, which had great appeal to the new idealists of America.

Dramatic events in Mexico determined the ideas and careers of the Ateneo leaders, even though they may also be seen as part of a Spanish American intellectual cohort with common concerns and even some personal ties.[102] Two months after the pompous Centennial festivities of September 1910, occasion of the Ateneo lectures and the inauguration of the University, the country was engulfed in revolution. By June 1911 Porfirio Díaz had resigned, Francisco I. Madero was triumphantly proclaimed president, and popular rebellions dominated the regions. Among the Ateneístas, Henríquez Ureña and Reyes left Mexico, the former to return in the early 1920s, the latter not permanently until 1938. The apolitical Caso remained. During the chaotic years 1913–16, with the University in disarray, he was virtually the only major teacher of the new student generation, but he successfully managed to instil in it the humanistic and moral values of the Ateneo. Vasconcelos became a committed revolutionary with Madero and in the Convention of 1914–15 and then began his wanderings abroad as a new Ulysses. In Lima he compared the Latin American nations to the dispersed Greeks, in search of a Minerva to 'shape the soul of the great race of the future'. Our America, he told the Peruvians, 'is the creation of *mestizos,* of two or three races by blood and of all cultures by spirit'.[103] Vasconcelos was joining the Mexicanism of Sierra, *mestizaje* as the base of nationality, with the cosmopolitan Americanism of Rodó and García Calderón. He developed the theme more fully in the 1920s, thus bringing revolutionary Mexico into ideological contact with a new wave of social consciousness in Peru (see below).

The new idealism made some headway in Brazil between 1900 and 1915, but essentially the country followed political and intellectual rhythms distinct from those of Spanish America. The political system of the Old Republic (1889–1930) to a large extent inhibited the kind of democratic impulse we will encounter in Argentina, Mexico and Chile. After 1898 the 'politics of governors' prevailed, in which presidential elections were deter-

---

[101] F. García Calderón, 'La crisis del Bergsonismo' (1912–13), *Ideas e impresiones* (Madrid, 1919), 237, a lucid and discerning essay. The 'crisis' was Bergson's immense popularity after publication of *L'evolution créatrice* (1907), in the face of hostility by professional philosophers, especially Julien Benda. The *Revista de América* also carried articles on Bergson.

[102] It should be noted that Rojas, Gálvez, Belaunde, García Calderón, Caso, Vasconcelos and Henríquez Ureña were all born between 1882 and 1884.

[103] J. Vasconcelos, 'El movimiento intelectual contemporáneo de México' (1916), *Conferencias,* 120.

mined by agreement of São Paulo and Minas Gerais and, failing that, by intervention of a broker like the outlying Rio Grande do Sul. Between elections, local bossism (*coronelismo*) and a constitutionally sanctioned regional autonomy held sway. The ideal of effective liberal institutions on the national level was kept alive by an older group of former monarchists and 'historic' republicans, notably Joaquim Nabuco and Rui Barbosa. But its demise came in 1910 with Barbosa's presidential campaign, which failed despite the fact that he was idolized for his learning, his prolific writing and florid oratory, and for his juridical leadership at The Hague in 1907.

Among younger intellectuals, there was by 1910 a growing dichotomy between the cosmopolitan majority and a nationalist minority, represented by two contemporaries, Manoel Oliveira Lima (1865–1928) and Alberto Torres (1865–1917). From an old Pernambuco family and educated in Portugal, Oliveira Lima was a distinguished historian and Brazil's leading diplomat from 1892 to 1913. He was the 'civilized' face to the world of a race-conscious Brazil. He upheld an optimistic version of the whitening ideal of racial progress and an Americanism based on the equality of North and South; he also made overtures to the ideal of Latin solidarity.[104]

While Oliveira Lima served as an 'intellectual ambassador' abroad, Torres was a successful legislator, minister, governor and supreme court justice at home. He resigned in 1909, disillusioned with the political system, and in 1914 published his collected articles as *O problema nacional* and *A organização nacional brasileiro*. Torres was an idealist, probably touched by Bergson, but always self-consciously autochthonous in his analysis. He went further than Euclides da Cunha in repudiating scientific racism; for him, race was not relevant to national progress. He sought an organic society based on the 'value of man', and he spoke of an awakening 'primitive instinct'. The Brazilian elite, he argued, was alienated from reality by its fondness for verbal culture, European ideas and unworkable institutional formulas. Instead, he advocated a 'Brazilian solution', namely, increased central authority and the creation of a 'Coordinating Power', including a National Council of life-time appointees to set policy goals and resolve regional antagonisms. Though unappreciated in his own lifetime, Torres became an apostle for a 'spiritualist and nationalist' generation of the 1920s and 1930s in search of new political solutions.

[104] M. Oliveira Lima, 'A América para a humanidade', *Revista de América*, 9–10 (1913), 181–90, 257–75, an article that won the praise of the considerably younger editor, García Calderón. It was a Portuguese version of the final lecture given in the fall of 1912 on his multi-university U.S. tour: *The evolution of Brazil compared with that of Spanish and Anglo-Saxon America* (Stanford, 1914), 112–29.

Liberal democracy and the new idealism in Spanish America

The decade 1910–20 saw an intense but brief surge of liberal democracy in Spanish America. In Argentina it grew from the crisis of the early 1890s and was embodied in the Radical Party (UCR) under the leadership of Hipólito Yrigoyen. The Radicals developed strong middle-class support, urban and rural, but abstained from elections. Abstention was interpreted by the oligarchy as preparation for revolution, and the response was a movement within the governing PAN after 1900 to broaden the suffrage (and thus support for the PAN) through electoral reform. Carlos Pellegrini stated that the movement's objective was 'the restoration of representative government', which 'will allow us to organize ourselves to fight for our interests'.[105] An early reform measure in 1904, initiated by Minister of the Interior Joaquín V. González (1863–1923), was followed by the Sáenz Peña Law of 1912. The latter established compulsory voting for native-born Argentinians and the Incomplete List, by which representation from any jurisdiction would be divided two to one between the political parties running first and second. The modern party system had become a reality, but contrary to President Saenz Peña's expectations, Yrigoyen won the election of 1916. Once in power, the Radicals differed little from the 'enlightened' wing of the PAN. Radicalism was mainly political, rhetorically identifying itself with the national community while ignoring the immigrant masses and upholding the economic interests of the landholding elite.

Political democracy was reinforced by philosophical idealism and by the search for *argentinidad,* the roots and essence of national culture. One aspect of this search was a reaffirmation of the liberal tradition, the democratic, constitutional, secular and cosmopolitan ideas and programmes of Mariano Moreno (1810–13), Rivadavia, and the *pensadores* of the Asociación de Mayo. The liberal interpretation had a *unitario* and porteño bias, and it repudiated the Rosas revisionists, who had provided a rationale for charismatic authoritarian government. One lofty and discursive exposition of liberalism was *El juicio del siglo: cien años de historia argentina* (1910) by Joaquín González, who concluded that Argentina was 'a state worthy of exaltation as home and shrine of the qualities and ideals that most honour the human soul'.[106] More cogent were the essays of Alejandro Korn

---

[105] Letter to Miguel Cané (24 Mar. 1905), quoted in David Rock, *Politics in Argentina, 1890–1930; the rise and fall of radicalism* (Cambridge, 1975), 34. Pellegrini died a year later.
[106] J. González, 'Juicio', *Obras completas,* xxi (Buenos Aires, 1936), 216.

(1860–1936) on the development of Argentine philosophy, which were infused with a new appreciation of the metaphysics of Kant, and which ended with a trenchant critique of the narrow positivism of the Generation of 1880. Korn said the latter pursued an 'exclusively economic ideal', thus subverting the liberal principles of Alberdi.[107] The most influential interpreter of Argentine liberalism during this decade was Ingenieros, in his essays on the *pensadores* (see above), in his proposal for a 'new idealism founded in experience', and finally in *La evolución de las ideas argentinas* (1918), presented as a 'breviary of civic morality'. This detailed work portrayed Argentine history as the conflict between authoritarianism and liberty, 'two incompatible political philosophies' emanating from the 'Old Regime' and from the 'Revolution'. The Argentine experience, he implied, paralleled that of France.[108]

Liberal democracy in Argentine politics and the new idealism in thought converged in the movement for university reform, which began in Córdoba in March 1918, spread throughout the nation and had strong international repercussions. Its principal objectives, though often inconsistent, were student participation in university government, curricular reform to incorporate modern scientific and humanistic ideas, and reorientation of the university toward social change. The movement was student led, and though it engaged in confrontation politics and aggressive nation-wide organization (the Federación Universitaria Argentina), it won the support of the Yrigoyen government and of major intellectuals, such as González, Korn and Ingenieros. Persistent student rallies, protests and strikes at Córdoba first brought sympathetic government intervention, then a compromise effort to placate faculty conservatives and finally (after students had occupied university buildings), presidential accession to the reformers' demands in October 1918. The process was repeated, with less turmoil, at the Universities of Buenos Aires and La Plata. The Argentine student federation soon established contacts abroad; by 1920 similar reformist organizations had sprung up in Chile and Peru. In 1921 an International Student Congress met in Mexico City.

The ideology of university reform incorporated many of the ambiguities of the new idealism. One theme, articulated by the movement's major

---

[107] A. Korn published three essays between 1912 and 1914; he wrote the fourth (on positivism) in 1919. The four became the chapters of *Influencias filosóficas en la evolución nacional* (Buenos Aires, 1936).

[108] J. Ingenieros, 'Para una filosofia', *Revista de filosofia*, 1 (1915), 5; *Evolución de las ideas argentinas* (Buenos Aires, 1918), 1, author's preface.

theorist, Ingenieros, and by the student manifestos, was instrumentalist and democratic. The university should become 'an instrument of social action', whose mission was to transform the ideals of the 'higher culture' into 'scientific disciplines' in the service of society. The first Córdoba manifesto used the term 'scientific liberalism'. The reforms called for open admissions and outreach; 'popular universities' sprang up in Argentina and spread to Peru.[109] For the students Córdoba symbolized, as it had for Sarmiento in 1845, the jesuitical bastion of the 'colonial mentality'; the 'university as cloister' must give way to the 'university as laboratory'.[110]

The second reform theme was humanistic and elitist. The growth of professional and technical education, said Ingenieros, has killed the old university; what remains is a 'simple administrative mechanism (*engranaje*), a parasite of the specialized faculties'. The faculties can form the professionals, he continued; but the university of the future, with philosophy at its centre, must form men. Korn also argued this point vigorously at Buenos Aires, where he became dean in October 1918. There was an '*arielista* hue' to the Córdoba manifestos, an emphasis on the 'heroic destiny of youth'.[111] In the 'future university republic', announced the militant Cordobeses, the only professors will be 'the true builders of souls, the creators of truth, beauty and the good'. Favourite student reading was *El hombre mediocre* (1913) by Ingenieros (an analogue to Rodó's *Ariel*), which called on youth to be 'forgers of ideals' and which advocated an 'aristocracy of merit' to counteract social mediocrity. This theme had also been struck by José Ortega y Gasset during his influential visit to Argentina in 1916.[112] The inner contradictions of the Córdoba movement, the conflict between democracy and elitism, between social reform and humanism, were not confined to Argentina; they also appeared in Mexico and Peru.

Whereas the vehicle for democracy in Argentina was legislative initiative, electoral politics and university reform within a flexible and 'maturing' party system, in Mexico its vehicle was revolution against an ossified

---

[109] An analogous Universidad Popular Mexicana had been founded in 1913 by Ateneo leaders.

[110] J. Ingenieros, 'La filosofía científica en la organización de las universidades', *Revista de filosofía*, 3 (1916), 285–306, revised (and made more emphatic) as *La universidad del porvenir* (1920). The two principal Córdoba manifestos (31 Mar. and 21 June 1918) are in Gabriel del Mazo (ed.), *La reforma universitaria* (3rd edn, Lima, 1967), I, 1–8.

[111] F. Bourricaud, 'The adventures of Ariel', *Daedalus*, 101 (1972), 124. The different history and character of the several universities, e.g., ancient Córdoba and twentieth-century La Plata, must have contributed to the ambiguity in reformist ideology.

[112] A section of *El hombre mediocre* had appeared as 'Los forjadores de ideales' in F. García Calderón's *Revista de América*, 1 (1912), 105–19, 243–67. The book went through four editions by 1918. For J. Ortega's reflections, see 'Impresiones de un viajero' (1916), *Obras completas*, VIII (Madrid, 1962), 361–71.

dictatorship. In Argentina the liberal oligarchy came out of the crisis of 1889–92 strengthened at the expense of the executive, and it made concessions to democracy; in Mexico the *científicos* failed to limit the power of Porfirio Díaz. Moreover, the democratic arguments present in the debate of 1892–3 were suppressed. Democracy re-emerged after 1900 and culminated in Madero's abortive electoral challenge to Díaz in 1910 and then in his successful open rebellion. The movement drew inspiration from Mexico's liberal heritage of popular struggle against native conservatives, the Church and the French during the Reforma era; its symbol was Benito Juárez and its banner the Constitution of 1857. Madero's programme, 'effective suffrage and no re-election', like that of Yrigoyen, was narrowly political. Nonetheless, his fervent idealism galvanized wide support (including that of intellectuals like Vasconcelos), and his assassination in 1913 made him a martyr to democracy for contending revolutionary factions. The triumphant faction, the Constitutionalists under Venustiano Carranza, preserved Madero's restricted political focus without his degree of democratic idealism. The Constitution of 1917, except for its significant social articles not favoured by Carranza, reaffirmed the liberal formalities of 1857. Even the latter were modified, however, by a strengthened six-year presidency of positivist inspiration.[113] What emerged after 1917 was a broadly based but quasi-authoritarian revolutionary state, dedicated to the restructuring of society and to national development. Liberal democracy, after its brief resurgence, became a will-of-the-wisp in twentieth-century Mexico.

Chile also experienced a democratic and constitutional movement but it took place within a singular intellectual environment. There were few traces of *arielismo* or of French idealism in Chilean philosophy and letters between 1905 and 1920. One possible explanation was the strength of German influence in higher education and culture, beginning with Letelier's mission to Germany, which resulted in the establishment of the Instituto Pedagógico in 1889 (see above). For two decades the Instituto was staffed largely with German professors, whom Letelier and others deemed best able to guide Chilean education toward scientific ends.[114] The Instituto not only trained teachers but also, like the earlier Escuela Normal de Paraná in Argentina, the nation's intellectual and governmen-

[113] See discussion on Rabasa above.
[114] There was some opposition to the German professors, notably a series of articles on 'the German bewitchment' by Eduardo de la Barra in 1899. Letelier was rector of the university from 1906 to 1913.

tal elite. One Instituto product was Enrique Molina (1871–1964), the leading philosopher and educator of his generation. Molina remained attached to positivism and resistant to Bergson even longer than did Ingenieros.[115] *Arielismo* may also have been inhibited by the racial national-ism of Nicolás Palacios, which construed Chile's European roots to be Teutonic and not Latin. Palacios won high praise from Armando Donoso (1886–1946), the country's major literary critic and essayist of what elsewhere was the *arielista* generation. Donoso, who had studied with Molina and then in Germany, rejected Rodó's cosmopolitan Americanism, welcomed the replacement of French cultural influence by German, and urged younger writers to pursue national themes.[116] In short, exaltation of the 'Latin spirit' had little attraction for Chilean intellectuals.

Political democracy grew out of the multiparty parliamentary system that was dominated for the thirty years after Balmaceda by an extraordi-narily narrow oligarchy from the central valley. The democratic instru-ment was the Liberal Alliance, a coalition of younger dissidents from the Radical, Liberal and Democratic Parties, who were sensitive to the social dislocations brought by rapid urbanization and by periodic recessions in the nitrate industry. In 1915 the Alianza placed Arturo Alessandri, a successful lawyer from northern Tarapacá, in the Senate. Alessandri then led the Alianza to congressional victory in 1918 and to the presidency in 1920. The victory constituted a 'revolt of the electorate', to use the standard phrase, but it was a middle-class electorate; because of literacy qualifications only 8 per cent of the population voted.

Nonetheless, Alessandri developed a mass following. His triumph 'stu-pefied the rich and powerful classes', in part because it introduced a new political style, even more dramatically than had Yrigoyen's triumph in Argentina.[117] Politics were forced out of the gentleman's club and into the street; Alianza parades, slogans and inflammatory harangues replaced dig-nified discourse and bargaining among intimates. For genteel central-valley politicians Alessandri was an arriviste outsider, a power-seeking Italian adventurer.[118] As president he faced a hostile senate, but with

---

[115] Molina recalled his 'unjustified' opposition to Bergson, despite encouragement in 1912 from Bergson's German enthusiast Georg Simmel, in 'La filosofía en Chile en la primera mitad del siglo xx, *Atenea*, 315–16 (1951), 246–7.

[116] A. Donoso, *Los nuevos. La Joven literatura chilena* (Valencia, 1912), xi–xxiii.

[117] The phrase is from Ricardo Donoso, *Alessandri: agitador y demoledor* (Mexico, 1952), 1, 243.

[118] Ricardo Donoso (b. 1896), brother of Armando and a graduate of the Instituto Pedagógico, perpetuated this anti-Latin characterization: *ibid.*, 7–10. Alessandri was descended from an Italian 'puppeteer' who settled in Chile in the early 1820s.

military support he finally prevailed to institute a new constitution in 1925. The document abolished the parliamentary system in favour of a six-year directly elected president who could control his cabinet. It also separated Church and state, no longer a controversial issue, and advanced the concept of the social function of property. The surge of democracy in Chile broke the political monopoly of the old oligarchy, but it also fortified central state authority, as it did in Argentina and Mexico.

SOCIALISM, AGRARIANISM AND INDIGENISMO

Accompanying the democratic impulse was another and more fundamental challenge to the political and social consensus reestablished in the 1890s — socialism and agrarian radicalism. Though these ideologies made little headway during the nineteenth century, after 1900 their appearance was sudden and forceful in several countries, sparked by the quickened pace of socio-economic change — expansion of export economies and their integration into the international capitalist system, modest growth of industry and of an urban work force, and in some regions massive immigration. By 1920 the most significant of these radical departures were socialism in Argentina and Chile, indigenous agrarianism in Mexico and a unique ideology in Peru which included elements of both.

Socialist movements in Argentina and Chile were affected by the dissimilar conditions in which they developed. Urban workers in Argentina were largely immigrant; in Chile they were overwhelmingly native. The heart of Argentina's economy was a continually prosperous agricultural export sector, whereas Chile's was an unstable and declining mining enclave (especially after World War I), dominated by foreign capital. In contrast with Chile, intellectual and cultural cosmopolitanism throughout Argentine society reached its peak in the early twentieth century. Immigrant workers in Buenos Aires were fertile ground for an early proliferation of labour movements and competing socialist ideas. The Socialist Party, founded in 1895 by Ingenieros and by Juan B. Justo (1865–1928), was followed by a surge of anarchism, which dominated labour organizations from 1900 to 1910. Syndicalism appeared in 1906, grew rapidly, and captured the former anarchist workers federation, the FORA, in 1915. However, both the anarchists and the syndicalists were hindered by the lack of effective native leadership.

Chile's labour movement was initially smaller than Argentina's and it developed later, but it was both more unified and more radical. The

Federación Obrera de Chile (FOCH) began in 1909 as a small mutualist organization of railway workers, but its rapid growth was influenced by the militant Partido Obrero Socialista (POS), established in 1912 by Luis E. Recabarren (1876–1924). By 1919 Recabarren also led FOCH and brought in the nitrate workers. In 1922 Recabarren's POS became the Chilean Communist Party, affiliated with the Third International. By contrast, pluralism persisted in Argentina. The anarchists faded after 1920, having been the chief target of government repression. The syndicalists continued to compete for labour allegiance with a small Communist Party and with the firmly entrenched Socialists, who remained under Justo's leadership. Strikes and government reprisals were prevalent in both countries, reaching a crescendo in 1918–20; however, by the mid-twenties Chile had a comprehensive labour code, a development that came much later in Argentina.

Grounded in these conditions, socialist leadership and ideology differed sharply in the two countries. Recabarren, the soul of Chilean socialism, was a poor, self-taught typographer, devoted by trade to instructing his fellows. Though he became progressively more radical, his programme remained consistent. Private property should be abolished or made collective or communal. The proletarian struggle should simultaneously pursue two ends, economic gains through union organization and political power.[119] He was personally engaged in both and by the early 1920s not only led the Chilean Communist Party but also was elected a deputy from the nitrate region. Recabarren never became cosmopolitan, despite his travels and associations in Argentina, Spain and Russia, but remained a morally austere and ascetic figure who ultimately took his own life.

In contrast to Recabarren, Justo in Argentina was a surgeon of middle-class background who was drawn to socialism by his clinical contact with human suffering. He came to Marx late, only after a thorough preparation in positivism. Like Ingenieros, he adhered to biological evolution and, like the professors of Paraná, he saw 'socialist' implications in Comte.[120] He entered politics through the Unión Cívica and was, again like Ingenieros, guided by the national liberal tradition. Korn said of Justo that he was the first to go beyond 'Alberdian ideology'; by adding the idea

---

[119] The most elaborate exposition of Recabarren's ideas was in a series of articles published in *El despertar de los trabajadores* of Iquique (Oct.–Nov. 1912): 'El socialismo ¿Qué es y cómo se realizará?', *El pensamiento de Luis Emilio Recabarren* (Santiago, 1971), 1, 7–96.

[120] Justo's major work was *Teoría y práctica de la historia* (1909).

of social justice, he renewed 'the content of Argentine thought'.[121] Justo was committed to achieving socialism through non-violent parliamentary means, much in the manner of Jean Jaurès, the French leader who lectured in Buenos Aires in 1909 at Justo's invitation. By 1920 socialism had a solid though minor place in the intellectual and political establishment. Justo and Alfredo L. Palacios (1880–1965) had pushed piecemeal social legislation through congress, but the Party's programme remained moderate.[122] It approached workers as consumers, not as producers; it adhered to free trade; it made no distinction between foreign and native capital; it hesitated on the abolition of private property.[123] Since the Party never asserted effective control over workers, who were mostly non-voting foreigners, both socialism and the labour movement floundered in the years following 1920.

We have already seen that ideas in Mexico cannot be separated from the country's unique experience of social upheaval and extended civil conflict. Such is the case with socialism, which appeared in its anarchist form by 1910, but which was always less significant than the more indigenous agrarian ideology that became the radical centre of the Revolution. The leader of anarchism was Ricardo Flores Magón (1874–1922), founder of the newspaper *Regeneración* (1900) and of the Partido Liberal Mexicano (PLM) (1905). Hounded by Mexican and American authorities and encouraged by the IWW, the Flores Magón group moved from popular democracy to anarchism and broke with Madero's anti-re-electionist campaign of 1908–10. In 1906, the social content of the PLM programme was limited to the eight-hour day, a one-peso minimum wage, and the distribution of undeveloped land. By 1911 the programme's central provision was the abolition of the 'principle of property', from which spring the institutions of Church and state. Workers, continued the PLM manifesto, must 'take into their own hands the land and the machinery of production' so they can 'regulate the production of wealth for their own needs'.[124] The PLM

---

[121] See Korn's eulogy at Justo's death in 1928: *Obras completas* (Buenos Aires, 1949), 506–7. Korn was a socialist sympathizer from about 1915 but did not join the Party until 1931.

[122] The flamboyant and cosmopolitan Palacios was a Socialist deputy from 1904–8 and 1912–15, a law professor and dean at La Plata, a leading spokesman for university reform and a prolific publicist.

[123] See Justo's debate on property (1908–9) with the Italian sociologist, Enrico Ferri: *Obras,* VI (Buenos Aires, 1947), 236–49. Ferri called Argentine socialism an 'artificial flower'.

[124] The complete text of the programme, issued at Saint Louis on 1 July 1906, can be found in Arnaldo Córdoba, *La ideología de la revolución mexicana* (Mexico, 1973), 405–21; the manifesto issued at Los Angeles on 23 Sept. 1911 is in Juan Gómez Quiñones, *Sembradores. Ricardo Flores Magón and El Partido Liberal Mexicano* (Los Angeles, 1973), 120–5.

receded after 1911. Flores Magón remained in exile and finally died in a Kansas prison. However, several of his early adherents joined the agrarian and urban labour movements of the revolutionary decade, bringing anarchist ideas with them.

One such movement was led by Emiliano Zapata in Morelos. Through a decade of rebellion against Mexico City and a dogged adherence to their Plan of Ayala (November 1911), the Zapatistas more than any other faction influenced the direction of national agrarian reform. The Plan of Ayala was indigenous in that it sprang from the consensus of Zapatista peasant chiefs, was phrased inelegantly by a 'country intellectual' (Otilio Montāno) and made the Juárez nationalization decrees a precedent (article 9). Yet the Plan's anarchist images and its call for immediate takeover of property for the common welfare (article 6) were derived from the widely disseminated PLM manifesto of September.[125] The Zapatista programme within Morelos became increasingly anti-statist, anti-liberal and collectivist from 1914 to 1917, abetted by Antonio Díaz Soto y Gama, an ex-PLM intellectual. Article 27 of the Constitution of 1917, primarily the creation of Andrés Molina Enríquez, legalized the agrarian community (*ejido*) and made its lands inalienable. But the article also recognized the 'small [individual] property', reflecting the liberal assumptions of the constitution-makers and the ambivalence of Molina Enríquez on the place of communal property in the scheme of evolution. The reconciliation of the Zapatistas with the government of Álvaro Obregón in 1920 gave radical agrarianism an official status, but also provided the basis for its co-optation.

The most distinctive formulation of radical ideology prior to 1930 was in Peru, the other major 'Indian country' of Latin America. However, Peru did not experience revolution; thus radical ideas never achieved the official recognition (nor underwent the consequent modification) they did in Mexico. In Peru the new radicalism flowered in the 1920s, reflecting the late but dramatic development of export capitalism there. The new ideas, especially as expressed by José Carlos Mariátegui (1894–1930) and Víctor Raúl Haya de la Torre (1895–1979), were distinctive in that they were derived from both Marxism and from literary and philosophical idealism. Moreover, the university reform movement in Peru was a catalyst for radicalism, a function it did not serve elsewhere. Still another feature distinctive to Peru was the inspiration provided by Manuel González Prada (1848–1918), the unique iconoclast of Latin America's positivist

---

[125] For the text and a definitive analysis of the Plan of Ayala see John Womack, Jr., *Zapata and the Mexican Revolution* (New York, 1969), 393–403.

era. The Mexican rebels looked back to Juárez and the *reformistas,* the Argentine socialists to Echeverría and Alberdi, and Recabarren in Chile (less so) to Franciso Bilbao. None of these precursors, however, were so radical or so immediate as González Prada.

Descended from a pious, aristocratic family, González Prada had rejected traditional Peruvian society and its values on a deeply personal as well as a political and literary level. He was an atheist as a result of personal experience — he had fled a Catholic seminary as an adolescent and his older sister died apparently from excessive religious fasting and penitence (from 'fanaticism', he said) — and was fiercely anticlerical, partly under the influence of the ideas of Bilbao. His anticlericalism, however, became part of a broader indictment of a Peruvian elite that lacked national coherence or patriotism during the War with Chile, that ignored its depressed Indian population and that welcomed foreign economic exploitation. Through his speeches and essays from the late eighties — many of them published in *Páginas libres* (1894) and *Horas de lucha* (1908) — González Prada became the inspiration for a radical intellectual tradition in Peru as he moved from radical liberalism to libertarian anarchism and socialism in the years before his death in 1918. Some commentators emphasize to the point of exaggeration a direct link between the ideas of González Prada and those of Haya and Mariátegui.

The critical year for Peruvian radicalism was 1919. In January, Haya de la Torre, a leader of the Peruvian Student Federation (FEP), successfully turned the focus of the reform movement in San Marcos toward support for a general strike by textile workers for the eight-hour day. Out of this worker-student alliance came the Popular Universities (1921), and three years later the Alianza Popular Revolucionaria Americana (APRA), founded by Haya in Mexico City.[126] In July 1919 a coup by Augusto B. Leguía ended twenty-five years of rule by the Civilista oligarchy and initiated a decade of dictatorship devoted to economic modernization. In October Leguía sent Mariátegui, a journalist who sympathized with the strikers, into European exile, where for three years he was immersed in the intellectual and ideological ferment of post-war France, Italy and Germany. He returned determined to implant socialism in Peru. Though Mariátegui and Haya crossed paths for only a few months before Haya himself was exiled (1923–31), the two co-operated until 1927, when they

[126] González Prada had called for a worker-student alliance in 1905: 'El intelectual y el obrero', *Anarquía* (4th edn, Lima, 1948), 49–56. His name was attached to the Popular Universities in 1922.

split over whether APRA should become a party or remain an alliance. The split pointed up a fundamental difference between Haya, who was primarily a political organizer during the 1920s, and Mariátegui, who was primarily an ideologue.[127]

Mariátegui's writings from 1923 to 1930 combined an acute Marxist analysis of Peruvian history and culture with a religious vision of national regeneration through socialism. His major work established the complex coexistence of three economic stages, the indigenous or communal, the feudal or colonial, and the bourgeois or capitalist. With political independence, 'a feudal economy gradually became a bourgeois economy, but without losing its colonial character within the world picture'. The term 'colonial', as used by Mariátegui, meant both economically dependent on foreign capital and culturally dependent on traditional Hispanic values ('the spirit of the fief' as opposed to 'the spirit of the town').[128] He identified the oppressed class as the Indian rather than as the proletarian or worker, abstractly construed, and he saw the redemption of the Indian as the key to national revival. He rejected traditional 'westernizing' approaches to the 'Indian problem'. All such reform efforts, he said, have been and will continue to be subverted by *gamonalismo,* the pervasive system of local control imposed by the large landed estate, until the phenomenon itself is rooted out. 'The soul of the Indian' can only be raised up 'by the myth, the idea of the socialist revolution'. He must seek regeneration by looking to his past, to 'the highly developed and harmonious communistic system' of the Incas. 'The Indian proletariat awaits its Lenin.'[129]

Whereas Justo came to socialism from medical science, Recabarren from union organizing, and Flores Magón from law, Mariátegui came to it from avant-garde literature and art. Before becoming 'radicalized' in 1919, he was a dandyish columnist.[130] In Europe he was struck particularly by the ideas of Henri Barbusse, the novelist, and of Georges Sorel, the theorist of

---

[127] Ironically, Haya regarded himself primarily a theorist and Mariátegui helped organize the Peruvian Socialist Party (PSP) in 1928 and the General Confederation of Peruvian Workers (CGTP) in 1929.

[128] J. C. Mariátegui, *Siete ensayos de interpretación de la realidad peruana* (Lima, 1928); quotes from English edition (Austin, 1971), 6, 21. All of Mariátegui's longer works were compilations of previously published short articles and speeches. Those making up the *Siete ensayos* appeared mostly in 1925–6.

[129] Prologue to the militant *indigenista* Daniel Valcarcel's *Tempestad en los Andes* (1925), inserted as a note in *Siete ensayos* (Eng. edn, 29). Mariátegui quoted the Lenin phrase from Valcarcel.

[130] Mariátegui's heirs omitted his pre-1919 'stone-age' writings from his *Obras completas* (1959) as adding 'nothing to his work as guide and precursor of social consciousness in Peru' (Preface to each vol.). Yet it should be noted that Mariátegui's attachment to European literature persisted throughout his life, as revealed for example in the contents of *Amauta* (1926–30), his overtly *indigenista* journal.

syndicalism. Barbusse had just founded the International of Thought and the *Clarté* movement out of disillusionment with the War, which he regarded as the product of a dehumanizing and decadent bourgeois civilization. 'Politics is today the only great creative activity', wrote Mariátegui interpreting Barbusse. Intellectuals and artists must lead the poor to revolution, 'to the conquest of beauty, art, and thought' as well as to 'the conquest of bread'. Sorel made Mariátegui appreciate 'the religious, mystical and metaphysical character' of socialism and how man can be driven by 'myths', whether religious or revolutionary.[131] Sorel in turn idolized Bergson, whom he said demonstrated 'the illusion of scientific truths' as propagated by the positivists.[132] In a sense, Mariátegui was carrying to extreme anti-positivist conclusions the idealism that so affected the Peruvian *arielista* generation of 1905. He was drawn to Barbusse and Sorel just as García Calderón had been drawn to Boutroux and Bergson.[133] Thus Mariátegui has been called a 'radical humanist' as well as a socialist and an indigenous nationalist.

Mariátegui's vision of national regeneration was an extreme formulation of *indigenismo* (or *indianismo*), which was widespread in Mexico and Peru by 1920. As the origin of nationality, the Aztec and Inca civilizations must be better understood; and such understanding must be tied to redemption of the present-day Indian majority. *Indigenismo* became 'official' in Leguía's Peru as well as in Obregón's Mexico, though the constitutionally proclaimed protection of the Peruvian Indian was undermined by the regime's pursuit of road building and commercialization in the highlands. In Mexico, one product of rural upheaval was the government's Department of Anthropology (1917), directed by Manuel Gamio (1883–1960), a professional who put into practice the new theories of the relativity of culture and its separation from race. The 'forging of a nationality', he argued, must begin with scientific study of Mexico's diverse Indian groups, a new appreciation of native art and literature, and a reversal of the 'fatal foreignist orientation' of the nineteenth century. In his model project at the pyramid site of Teotihuacán, he tried to integrate archaeology with education of the local populace, always with an eye to the revival and preserva-

---

131 J. C. Mariátegui, *La escena contemporánea* (Lima, 1925), 201–2 (on Barbusse); 'El hombre y el mito' (1925), in *El alma matinal* (Lima, 1950), 28–9 (on Sorel). Mariátegui knew Barbusse personally and the latter paid him lavish tribute at his death. He was introduced to Sorel's thought in Italy.
132 G. Sorel, *Reflections on violence* (Glencoe, 1950), 162 (1st edn, 1908).
133 Mariátegui and other radicals of the 'Generation of 1919' repudiated the *arielistas* (or *futuristas*) and embraced instead González Prada, despite his atheistic anticlericalism: Mariátegui, *Siete ensayos* (Eng. edn), 184–5, 221–5; Luis Alberto Sánchez (b. 1900), *¿Tuvimos maestros en nuestra América? Balance y liquidación del novecientos* (2nd edn, Buenos Aires, 1955), 10–21. (The answer, of course, was 'no'.)

tion of native arts and culture.[134] His efforts, along with mural art and rural education on a national scale, were promoted by José Vasconcelos, who, as Obregón's Minister of Education (1921–4), was the great 'cultural caudillo' of the new Mexico.

Vasconcelos, however, was not an *indigenista* – beyond his sympathy for agrarianism and his conviction that the Indian must be truly incorporated into Mexican society. For Vasconcelos, nationality, whether Mexican or Ibero-American in the broader sense, resided in racial and cultural *mestizaje*. Whereas Mariátegui rejected past and present efforts to westernize the Indian, Vasconcelos maintained that 'the Indian's only door to the future is that of modern culture, his only road the one opened up by Latin Civilization.'[135] The educational programme of Vasconcelos included the wide distribution of European classics. He regarded the rural teachers of the 1920s as twentieth-century Franciscan friars. Though he tolerated Gamio's 'integral' approach to rural education, he did not believe Indians should be taught first in their native languages. Yet the ideas of both Vasconcelos and his contemporary Gamio, different as they were, retained the optimistic assumptions of evolutionary theory, in contrast to Mariátegui's radical and existential notion of Indian regeneration. 'In history,' wrote Vasconcelos, 'there is no turning back because all is transformation and novelty'. Expanding on his address of 1916 to the Peruvians, he envisioned America as the cradle of a 'cosmic race'. The influence of Vasconcelos was apparent in the concept of Indo-America, central to Haya de la Torre's APRA. In fact, it may be that much of Haya's pragmatic *indigenismo* and agrarianism bore a Mexican stamp.

THE EMERGENCE OF CORPORATISM

We conclude this chapter with a consideration of authoritarian or corporatist political ideas in the years prior to 1930. The term 'corporatism' has been used primarily as an analytical construct, 'a scholar's tool' for elucidating the distinctive structure of contemporary (post-1930) Latin American politics. As such, corporatism is differentiated from 'pluralism' and is defined as a system of interest representation by hierarchically

---

[134] M. Gamio studied at Columbia University under Franz Boas, receiving the Ph.D. in 1921. For his ideas, see *Forjando patria* (Mexico, 1916) and the introduction to his massive *La población del valle de Teotihuacán*, 2 vols. in 3 (Mexico, 1922).

[135] J. Vasconcelos, *La raza cósmica. Misión de la raza iberoamericana* (Paris, 1925), 13. Cf. Belaunde's critique of Mariátegui's *indigenismo:* while Mariátegui regards it as 'a supreme and ultimate value', I regard it 'as a step to something higher, *la peruanidad integral*'. See *La realidad nacional*, 198.

organized and non-competitive groups, recognized and regulated (if not created) by the state. Corporatism as a formal ideology, distinguished from corporatism as a system, has not been common in Latin America. Nonetheless, a variety of corporatist assumptions began to appear with some frequency in the thought and policy of the 1920s.

Corporatism was a response to, and yet often intertwined with, both liberal democracy and socialism; thus it appeared largely in political contexts we have already examined. Though contemporary European models were important, emerging corporatism drew even more from the positivist heritage, both scientific politics and deterministic social thought. Like positivism, corporatism was based on a hostility to the role of ideas in political organization, even though its advocates often regarded themselves as idealists. In a few cases corporatist formulations explicitly evoked precedents from the Spanish colonial system. Some prominent corporatist movements of the 1920s, for example in Mexico and Peru (APRA), were populist in orientation, that is, devoted to social reform and to mass participation. The social implications of others, such as in Brazil and Chile, were ambiguous. The least overt corporatist movement of the 1920s, in Argentina, was socially repressive.

In Mexico article 27 (property) and article 123 (labour) of the Constitution of 1917 gave legal recognition to agrarian and labour demands, but they also provided a basis for control, for bringing these militant groups into the revolutionary state. The constitutional rationale was provided by Andrés Molina Enríquez, responding in 1922 to two charges, that article 27 was 'radically communistic' and that the Constitution gave excessive power to the executive. Though Molina acknowledged that the 'spirit' of the Constitution was 'collectivist' as opposed to the 'individualist' spirit of 1857, he claimed this change merely reflected the Comtean concept (unknown in 1857) that societies were 'living organisms'. Moreover, the principle that property is vested originally in the nation, which in turn can grant property to individuals, is not new but merely a modern reaffirmation of the rights of the Spanish crown. As for executive authority, Molina maintained that the weakness of agrarian communities and of workers vis-à-vis landowners and industrialists made it 'indispensable that official action be exerted in their favour in order to balance the forces of the two sides' and to promote justice, as did the tribunals of the colonial era.[136]

---

[136] A. Molina Enríquez, 'El artículo 27 de la constitución federal', *Boletin de la Secretaría de Gobernación*, 1 (1922), 1–12. He said workers and peasants were like 'minors'. Cf. argument by Cosmes (1893) above, note 38.

Revolutionary governments were ambivalent toward urban labour. A Department of Labour was created in 1912 to mediate industrial conflicts and to encourage and guide workers' organizations. Over Carranza's objections, Department leaders tolerated the anarcho-syndicalist Casa del Obrero Mundial (House of the World Worker) and even persuaded the Casa to send 'Red Battalions' to fight the Villistas and Zapatistas in 1915. The Department also promoted organizations of textile workers, explicitly termed 'clusters (*agrupaciones*) of resistance' and not 'unions (*sindicatos*)', whose elected governing boards would represent labour interests before the government. According to a 1915 Department memo, the *agrupación* policy could 'put an end to the power of independent labor groups and their ability to conspire against legal authorities'.[137] Following a general strike in 1916, Carranza abolished the Casa, the most prominent independent group, and then sponsored a broad Regional Confederation of Mexican Labour (CROM) in 1918. The CROM, clearly under government tutelage from the start, claimed 300,000 members by 1920. The logic of policy toward peasants and workers led ultimately to their incorporation into the National Revolutionary Party (PRN) as two of three functional 'sectors'.

It should be added, incidentally, that one group clearly not incorporated was the Church, which strongly resisted the severe limitation of its educational role and property rights in the anticlerical articles 3 and 130 of the Constitution. The intense Church–state conflict of the late 1920s, which included a massive rebellion of religious peasants (*cristeros*) in the west, was a phenomenon unique to Mexico, a reenactment of the Reforma of the mid-nineteenth century.

'The Mexican Revolution is our revolution,' wrote the Peruvian exile Haya de la Torre in 1928. The early ideology of APRA may be construed in part as Haya's doctrinal elaboration of assumptions imbedded in what he called Mexico's 'spontaneous movement'. Haya envisioned the formation of an 'anti-imperialist state', an alliance of all those exploited by foreign capitalism, particularly North American. Because of a basically feudal structure, imperialism in Latin America, contrary to Lenin's theory, is the first, not the last, stage of capitalism. The anti-imperialist state will emerge from a single party (APRA), organized 'scientifically', not as a

[137] Cited in Ramón E. Ruíz, *Labor and the ambivalent revolutionaries: Mexico, 1911–1923* (Baltimore, 1976), 57. A new Ministry of Industry, Commerce, and Labour was created in 1916 under Plutarco Elías Calles, who later became the patron of CROM and as president (1924–8) the chief architect of the PRN, founded in 1929.

'bourgeois [liberal] democracy' but as a 'functional or economic democracy', in which classes will be 'represented according to their role in production'.[138] The key problem for Haya was the role of the national bourgeoisie, which he at times interpreted as among the exploited and at other times as tied to imperialism. As an ideologist and organizer out of power, challenged by doctrinaire socialists, Haya was obliged to confront the theoretical problem of the middle classes, one that could be conveniently ignored in Mexico. Haya disguised the confusion by presenting Aprismo as an autochthonous doctrine, free of 'mental colonialism' and 'Europeanism'.[139]

Corporatist themes were particularly apparent in the political ideas of the 1920s in Brazil. The strength and longevity of the Old Republic had the anomalous dual effect of inhibiting liberal democracy and socialism and yet inviting criticism of the republican system. Though positivism persisted in education and in social thought, it led increasingly to a 'sociological' emphasis that challenged intellectual cosmopolitanism and sought institutions in tune with Brazil's society and traditions. The combination of cultural nationalism, sociology and political criticism came forth in a powerful call for a 'new work of construction' by a dozen prominent intellectuals, writing in 1924 as 'the generation born with the Republic' who were overt admirers of Alberto Torres.[140] The most influential statement was by Francisco José Oliveira Vianna (1885–1951), a law professor and widely read social analyst, who attacked in familiar positivist terms the 'idealism' of the Constitution of 1890. He then went on to lament the absence of a 'regime of public opinion', or the kind of 'sentiment of collective interest' which is deep in 'genuine races' like the English. The heart of Brazil's constitution must be economic and social, not political. It must be responsive to land reforms in a country where 90 per cent of the people are rural dependants; to 'institutions of social solidarity', such as an efficient judiciary and strong municipal magistrates to restrain the will of local bosses; and to the diffusion of a 'corporative spirit'. The key to reform and to 'the architecture of the new political system', implied

---

[138] V. R. Haya de la Torre, *El antimperialismo y el APRA* (2nd edn, Santiago, 1936), 82, 149 (written in 1928, though not published till 1935). Haya's concept of the multi-class party was an expansion of his earlier alliance of workers and students.

[139] See passage from Haya (1928), cited by Bourricaud, *Power and Society*, 156. Haya was clearly referring to Mariátegui, who replied that APRA seemed too much like Italian fascism.

[140] Preface to *A margem da historia da república* (Rio de Janeiro, 1924). The collaborative work, delayed in publication, was prompted by the centennial of independence, as was the outpouring of cultural self-examination in the notorious 'Week of Modern Art' in São Paulo (1922).

Oliveira Vianna prophetically, was a strong national administration that would interact closely with the interests of groups.[141]

Corporatist ideas in Chile were remarkably varied: like Mexico they appeared in state labour policy, like Brazil in a major historical critique of political liberalism, like Argentina in admiration expressed for European fascism by elements of the military and the Church hierarchy. The labour code of 1924 recognized workers' organizations but subjected them to close government regulation. Passed suddenly and unanimously in 1924 under military pressure, the code was an amalgam of diverse projects that had divided Congress during the Alessandri administration. A major source of inspiration was German state socialism (or 'professorial socialism') of the Bismarck era, imbibed by Valentín Letelier and by Manuel Rivas Vicuña, an important Liberal intellectual and politician who was close to Alessandri. As early as 1906 Letelier had persuaded the majority of a Radical Party congress that legislation on social welfare and the organization of work was necessary 'to forestall the expansion of revolutionary (*de combate*) socialism'.[142]

Another response to the social and political turmoil of the twenties was *La fronda aristocrática* (1928) by Alberto Edwards Vives (1874–1932). Edwards attacked the fallacies of liberal ideals, as did Oliveira Vianna, but also the aristocracy, which he said reverted to its natural factious tendency with the breakdown of the Portalian system (1831–91). That system was based on strong central authority which restrained the aristocracy, on a sense of hierarchy and social discipline, and on moral and spiritual force, now undermined by bourgeois materialism. In short, it was a political regime 'in form', a phrase Edwards borrowed from Oswald Spengler. Such regimes depend for their existence on 'living organic elements', not on written constitutions. 'Liberty and organic are incompatible terms.'[143] Edwards predicted the decline of Chilean civilization unless some new Portales emerged. The book was an implicit apology for Carlos Ibáñez del Campo, Chile's military president (1927–31), whose authoritarian poli-

---

[141] Oliveira Vianna, 'O idealismo da constituição', *ibid.*, 137–60. Oliveira Vianna was a student of Silvio Romero and clung to much of scientific racism.

[142] Quoted in Luis Galdames, *Valentín Letelier y su obra* (Santiago, 1937), 378. On professorial socialism (or 'socialism of the chair'), including its concept of the state as an organ of moral solidarity, see Charles Gide and Charles Rist, *A history of economic doctrines* (2nd Eng. edn, London, 1948), 436–46.

[143] A. Edwards Vives, *La fronda aristocrática en Chile* (6th edn, Santiago, 1966), 272. Edwards's work also showed traces of the racial nationalism of Palacios. Both he and Palacios had a strong influence on the conservative historian, Francisco A. Encina.

cies were widely supported until the economic collapse of 1929. Edwards was briefly a minister under Ibañez.

Whereas corporatism in Mexico and Chile before 1930 was manifest in official policy, particularly towards labour, in Argentina it was confined primarily to movements of the dissident Right. After 1910, the creole elite increasingly branded working-class groups and ideologies as 'foreign', and there was little effort by Radical Party governments (1916–30) to patronize, co-opt, or regulate labour. Instead, ad hoc organizations condoned by the government sprang up, particularly during the general strike of January 1919, to defend property and wantonly to attack working-class neighbourhoods, in what became known as the 'tragic week (*semana trágica*)'. The most prominent of these groups was the Liga Patriótica Argentina, which followed up paramilitary repression with an ill-defined programme of 'practical humanitarianism' to achieve class harmony. Educational and welfare programmes for workers were instituted and there was even some discussion of organizing all productive members of society into functional corporations. However, the premise underlying the League's programme was 'seeing the world as it is', in other words, acceptance of a natural hierarchy of intelligence, culture and wealth.[144]

After 1923 the relatively benign League gave way to virulent 'nationalist', anti-liberal and anti-semitic groups, which recruited major intellectuals and reached a crescendo in the years 1927–30. One such intellectual was the poet Leopoldo Lugones (1874–1939), who turned from anarchism to fascism, lecturing on Mussolini in 1923, extolling military virtues in his 'hour of the sword' speech in Peru in 1924 and attacking electoral politics and liberal democracy in *La organización de la paz* (1925). Another recruit was Manuel Gálvez, whose suspicion of 'cosmopolitanism' in 1910 became by 1929 an appeal to authority, hierarchy and Catholic 'spirituality'. He even advocated 'a new revolution, founded on principles opposite to those which animated the French Revolution and its derivatives socialism and bolshevism'.[145] Both Gálvez and Lugones were associated with the bimonthly *La Nueva República* (1927–31), which called for a functional democracy based on the 'vital forces of society', and which supported the brief corporate state experiment of General José F. Uriburu in 1930.

[144] The long-time leader of the Liga was Manuel Carlés (1872–1946), a former teacher and conservative deputy.

[145] Gálvez, discussing 'dictatorships' in the Catholic journal *Criterio*, June 13, 1929, as quoted in Sandra F. McGee, 'Social origins of counterrevolution in Argentina, 1900–1932', unpublished Ph.D. thesis, University of Florida, 1979, 257.

Whereas the Liga Patriótica had made some attempt to broaden its base to include workers and lower middle class elements, the new nationalism was militantly elitist, presaging a basic conflict within future authoritarian movements in Argentina.

The emergence of corporatism in the 1920s revealed the persistence of an authoritarian tradition in Latin American politics, despite a heritage of liberalism. It had been fortified in the late nineteenth century by the scientific argument for strong government and by the positivist emphasis on social hierarchy and organic evolution. That political tradition was challenged, first by the constitutionalist movement of 1889–93, then by the democratic impulse of 1910–20 and finally by socialism and indigenous radicalism. However, the ideological consensus that had been achieved by the governing and intellectual elite by the late 1880s was strong enough to withstand these challenges. Ironically in fact, this consensus was reinforced by one aspect of the liberal heritage, the emphasis on the secular state. The alternative liberal ideal of constitutional limitations on central authority had been gradually eroded by the social, historical and racial theories which culminated in turn-of-the-century positivism. The consensus among the elite could also survive the idealist attack on the philosophic assumptions of positivism, in part because of the political and social ambiguities of the new idealism itself. Though authoritarianism may well have been the prevailing tendency of the years 1870 to 1930, this fact should not obscure our appreciation of the richness and diversity of the political ideas of the era.

3

ECONOMIC IDEAS AND IDEOLOGIES
IN LATIN AMERICA SINCE 1930

The history of ideas in Latin America is typically confined to the description of regional adaptations of European ideas. However, in the field of economic ideas in the period from the Depression of the 1930s to the debt and growth crises of the 1980s, first 'structuralism,' associated with the U.N. Economic Commission for Latin America (ECLA, or in Spanish, CEPAL), and subsequently 'dependency theory' were notably autochthonous, distinctly Latin American contributions to development theory. Moreover, they were widely embraced by theorists and policy-makers in the Third World at large. Although Marxism is treated and corporatism is discussed in brief compass, it is to the development of structuralism and dependency – arguably the most influential ideas ever to appear in Latin America – that this essay is principally devoted.[1] It deals with the diffusion of ideas, the formation of new ideas, and, necessarily, the independent rediscovery of ideas already developed elsewhere. Because they are sometimes inseparable in the Latin American context, it also occasionally treats policy as well as theory. The project is inherently a comparative one, since only by comparison can originality or distinctiveness be assessed. Genetic connections between ideas in Latin America and elsewhere will be indicated, as well as the independent rediscovery of identical or closely analo-

[1] Neo-classical and Keynesian ideas are not formally considered, except as necessary elements in the story of the advances and checks of structuralism and dependency – not because they are unimportant, but because there is little uniquely 'Latin American' about them. Also not treated is the contribution of the English-speaking Caribbean, where a related school of dependency developed in a slightly later period. There the issues were somewhat different (for example, greater population pressure on fewer resources); and problems of scale (and hence the urgency of integration) played a larger role. There also the debt to the neoclassical school was relatively greater. In the Caribbean the work of W. Arthur Lewis played a role similar to that of Raúl Prebisch in Latin America. On these matters, see Norman Girvan, 'The development of dependency economics in the Caribbean and Latin America: Review and Comparison', *Social and Economic Studies*, 22, 1 (March, 1973): 1–33.

gous propositions.[2] Finally, in social thought, it seems obvious that theory, if its tenets are assumed to be true and are not subject to empirical verification, slips easily into ideology, a set of propositions which implicitly justifies social values or social configurations. Both theory and ideology are part of the story.[3]

The central issue that economic theory and ideology addressed in Latin America in the period after 1930 was industrialization, both as fact (at first a consequence of the decline of export-led growth) and as desideratum (for ECLA, at least at the outset, a 'solution' to the problem of economic underdevelopment). In the early years, before 1949, with some notable exceptions, the process of industrialization was defended without the benefit of economic theory and a counterpart coherent ideology. The arguments were often limited in scope to special circumstances, sometimes inconsistent, and frequently apologetic. This was because, in part, they 'contradicted' neo-classical theory. In particular, they ran afoul of the Ricardian model of the international division of labour, still very much alive in the early years of the Depression of the 1930s, despite a surge of protectionism around the world in the previous decade.

In the 1930s the proponents of industrialization were almost exclusively the industrialists themselves, though by the Second World War they were joined by government spokesmen, at least in the four most industrialized countries – Argentina, Brazil, Mexico and Chile. ECLA, whose analyses legitimized and prescribed industrialization, reached the apogee of its influence in the decade after 1949. The defence of industrialization was now much more coherent and aggressive. But in the 1960s came the unpredicted failure of the industrialization process to maintain its momentum relative to population growth, and a failure of Latin American politi-

---

[2] I have avoided the temptation to set the problem in the framework of Thomas Kuhn's 'paradigms' or Imre Lakatos's 'scientific research programs', because the disputes over the applicability of the Kuhn and Lakatos models to the history of economic ideas would seem to make such an effort at the world-region level gratuitously problematic and polemical. See Thomas S. Kuhn, *The Structure of Scientific Revolutions,* 2nd edn (Chicago, Ill., 1970); Mark Blaug, *The Methodology of Economics: Or How Economists Explain* (Cambridge, 1980). One need not assert for economic thought, as Robert Merton has claimed for the natural sciences, that multiple independent discoveries are more the rule than the exception. Yet it is hardly surprising that such things happen: consider the contemporaneous and independent formulation of the theory of marginal utility in the 1870s by Karl Menger, Léon Walras, and Stanley Jevons. Inevitably, as Merton has noted, the *prioritätstreit* characterizes the social as well as the natural sciences. See Robert K. Merton, *The Sociology of Science: Theoretical and Empirical Investigation* (Chicago, Ill., 1973), pp. 289, 343–70, 394–5.

[3] Though many economic theorists have argued that the scientific project of economic analysis can be successfully separated from ideology, Ronald Meek is persuasively sceptical. See his *Economics and Ideology and Other Essays* (London, 1967), esp. pp. 196–224.

cal regimes to bring about the social changes advocated by ECLA. These facts put the agency's theses in jeopardy. The theory was reworked, and new consequences flowed from it: a school of dependency analysis, whose proponents had lost faith in the ability of the industrial bourgeoisies of Latin America to develop the region along Western lines, emerged from structuralism.

EARLY ADVOCATES OF INDUSTRIALIZATION

Industrialization in Latin America was fact before it was policy, and policy before it was theory. In the half-century preceding 1930, there seemed to be a rough correspondence between the fact of high-performance, export-led growth and the theory of comparative advantage, which 'justified' Latin America's specialization in raw materials production. This theory, originated by David Ricardo (1817), and elaborated by John Stuart Mill (1848), Alfred Marshall (1879), and others later, can be summarized as follows: (a) Given an absence of commerce between two countries, if the relative prices of two commodities differ between them, both can profit by trading such commodities at an intermediate price ratio (that is to say, both can gain even if one country produces both traded goods more efficiently than the other); (b) countries export commodities whose production requires relatively intensive use of factors found in relative abundance within their boundaries; (c) commodity trade reduces, if it does not eliminate, international differences in wages, rents, and other returns to factors of production; (d) among other things, the theory assumes the absence of monopoly power and the spread of the benefits of technological progress across the whole trading system.

In Latin America, an explicit articulation of the advantages of specialization in trade for the independent states could be heard over the course of the nineteenth century. Yet the refrain was repeated much more frequently in the decades after 1880, corresponding to the beginning of a half-century of unprecedented production of agricultural and mineral goods, to be exchanged on the world market for manufactures.[4]

A corollary, derivable from Ricardo, was that there are 'natural' and

---

[4] See, for example, Vicente Reyes Gómez, 'Si la depreciación del papel moneda en Chile debe considerarse como una causa o un efecto de la baja del cambio', *Revista Económica* (Chile), año 3, 14 (June, 1888), pp. 86, 88; Joaquim Murtinho, *Relatório apresentado ao Presidente da República dos Estados Unidos de Brasil no ano de 1899* (Rio de Janeiro, n.d.), p. xiii; V[ictorino] de la Plaza, *Estudio sobre la situación política, económica, y constitucional de la República Argentina* (Buenos Aires, 1903), pp. 49–50, 68–9. La Plaza served as president of Argentina, 1914–16.

'artificial' economic activities based on a country's factor endowments, and that 'artificial' industries should be discouraged because they result in misallocation of resources. In Brazil, for example, Joaquim Murtinho, the Brazilian Minister of Finance, would do nothing for 'artificial' industries in the financial crisis of 1901–2. Such was the policy that governments of the region generally followed until the latter years of the Depression of the 1930s, or even later. It was not a laissez-faire policy, however, since such regimes provided direct and indirect support (e.g., through artificially low exchange rates or through exchange rate deterioration) for their export industries and the interests behind them. Paying their costs in local currency and receiving 'hard' currencies for their exports, such groups profited by obtaining more local currency as its exchange value fell.

Nevertheless, in Chile, export-led growth, focussing on the nitrate boom before and after the War of the Pacific (1879–83), laid a foundation for a manufacturing sector, and a Chilean industrialists' association (SOFOFA) appeared as early as 1883. This fact was less unusual than that some Chileans favouring industrialization discovered and propagated the ideas of Friedrich List, the founder of the German historical school of economics. List found his Chilean paladin between 1880 and the First World War in the person of Malaquías Concha, who popularized List's argument that infant industries would eventually become competitive, as internal economies of scale and economies external to the firm developed over time.[5] At all events, Chile probably industrialized more fully in terms of structural change than any other Latin American country before the Second World War.[6]

List seems to have had little influence elsewhere, and before 1945 Latin American proponents of manufacturing tended to be apologetic, timid, and accommodationist; they sought a place in the sun *alongside* the traditional export industries. This was true, for example, of Alejandro Bunge and Luis Colombo in Argentina; of Roberto Simonsen, Alexandre Siciliano, Jr., and Octávio Pupo Nogueira in Brazil.[7] There were aggressive

---

[5] Malaquías Concha, 'Balanza de comercio', *Revista Económica* año II, 23 (March, 1889), pp. 327–8; Concha, *La lucha económica* (Santiago, 1910), pp. 25–7. List was also cited in the Argentine tariff debate of the 1870s and championed by Luís Vieira Souto in Brazil at the turn of the century.

[6] By the mid-1930s domestic suppliers produced 90 per cent of all manufactured goods consumed in Chile, and over 70 per cent of the durable consumer and capital goods. José Gabriel Palma, 'Growth and Structure of Chilean Manufacturing Industry from 1830 to 1935' (unpublished Ph.D. thesis, Oxford University, 1979), pp. 344–5.

[7] On the complementarity between industry and agriculture and the general defensiveness of industrialists, see Alejandro Bunge, *La economía argentina*, 4 v. (Buenos Aires, 1928–30); Luis Colombo (in note 15); Roberto Simonsen, *Crises, Finances and Industry* (São Paulo, n.d.), p. 6; Octávio Pupo

sallies, nevertheless; Brazilian industrialists tried to counter the charge of 'artificiality' by pointing to the apparent legitimacy of the coffee-roasting industry in the United States and the sugar-refining industry in England, for which domestic raw materials did not exist.[8]

By the 1930s, however, the Brazilians had discovered a theorist who, in their view, provided a scientific basis for industrialization. This was Mihail Manoilescu, the Rumanian economist, politician, and ideologue of corporatism, who recommended industrialization *à outrance* for agricultural-exporting countries. In his major economic study, *Théorie du protectionnisme* (1929) and in *Le siècle du corporatisme* (1934), Manoilescu made a frontal attack on the existing international division of labour, and argued that labour productivity in 'agricultural' countries was intrinsically and measurably inferior to that in 'industrial' countries – so categorized by the composition of their exports. Manoilescu did not hesitate to call agricultural countries 'backward', contending that surplus labour in agriculture in such nations should be transferred to industrial activities.[9] He denounced the international division of labour and the classical theories of trade which recommended to agricultural nations that they continue to channel their labour force into areas of what he considered inherently inferior productivity. New industries should be introduced as long as their labour productivity was higher than the national average. In a vulgarized version of his argument in *Le sìecle du corporatisme,* Manoilescu asserted that the average industrial worker produces ten times the value of an agricultural worker, and that agricultural countries 'are poor and stay poor' as long as they do not industrialize. Thus the international division of labour was basically a swindle: classical international trade theory 'justified' the exploitation of one people by another.[10]

In São Paulo, officials of the Centre of Industries corresponded with Manoilescu, and published *Théorie du protectionnisme* in Portuguese in 1931. In the early thirties three important industrial spokesmen – Simonsen,

Nogueira, *Em torno da tarifa aduaneira* (São Paulo, 1931), pp. 91–112, Alexandre Siciliano, Jr., *Agricultura, comércio e industria no Brasil* (São Paulo, 1931), p. 18; *Revista de Industria* (Mexico, D. F.), 1, 1 (November 1937): 3; *Revista de Economía* (Mexico, D. F.), 8, 10 (October, 1945): 6. Less defensive is Oscar Alvarez Andrews, *Historia del desarrollo industrial de Chile* (Santiago, 1936), perhaps because of the Listian heritage and Chile's relative success in industrializing by the mid-1930s.
[8] Pupo Nogueira, *Em torno,* p. 136; Siciliano, *Agricultura,* pp. 27–28; Simonsen, *Crises,* p. 88. In 1903 Serzedelo Correia had pointed to the 'artificiality' of the British cotton textile industry. Correia, 'As indústrias nacionais', in Edgard Carone (ed.), *O pensamento industrial no Brasil (1880–1945)* (São Paulo, 1971), pp. 42–3.
[9] Mihail Manoilescu, *Théorie du protectionnisme et de l'échange international* (Paris, 1929), pp. 61, 65, 184; *Le siècle du corporatisme: Doctrine du corporatisme intégral et pur* (Paris, 1934), p. 28.
[10] Manoilescu, *Théorie,* p. 184; *Le siècle,* pp. 28–30.

Siciliano Jr. and Pupo Nogueira – took Manoilescu's work to be proof of the legitimacy of their interests. Adding a touch of racism, Siciliano neatly adapted Manoilescu's theory by contending in 1931 that Brazil could not continue to rely on traditional exports, because of the lower wages that Africans and Asians would accept in competing agricultural activities, implicitly raising their labour productivities; thus agriculture in Brazil did not possess any intrinsic superiority to industry.[11] Manoilescu's theory as a 'scientific' rationale for Brazilian industrialization did not, however, survive the 1930s – chiefly because of the attacks by Jacob Viner and other neo-classical theorists on his work, and also perhaps because of his open adherence to fascism in the late thirties and his support for Germany in the Second World War. Manoilescu's ideas were slowly abandoned for more practical and circumstantial arguments. Simonsen, who frequently cited Manoilescu in the early 1930s, had ceased referring to the master by the time of the war.[12] Meanwhile, in 1944, Simonsen presided at an industrialists' congress which called for the 'harmonious' development of agriculture and industry, and even championed government aid to agriculture.[13]

The general absence of theoretical foundations for industrial development notwithstanding, Argentina, Brazil, and Chile had made rapid industrial advances in the 1920s. But after 1929 they faced a sustained crisis in export markets (the dollar value of Argentina's exports in 1933, for example, was one-third the 1929 figure); and despite the importance of industrialization in the 1920s, the following decade can still be understood as a period of significant structural and institutional change. In Argentina, Brazil, Chile and Mexico, convertibility and the gold standard were abandoned early in the Depression. The rise in prices of importables, because of a fall in the terms of trade and exchange devaluation, encouraged the substitution of domestic manufactures for imported goods, as did expansionary fiscal and monetary policies. By 1935 a North American economist would hazard that 'There is probably no major section of the world in which there is a greater industrial activity relative to pre-depression years than in temperate South America', that

---

[11] Siciliano, cited in Pupo Nogueira, *Em torno*, pp. 133; 3, 131 (on Manoilescu); Siciliano, *Agricultura*, pp. 12, 62; Simonsen, *Crises*, p. 58.

[12] In the debate between Simonsen and Eugênio Gudin on planning in 1945, it was Gudin, not Simonsen, who referred to Manoilescu, viewing him as a discredited charlatan. Roberto Simonsen and Eugênio Gudin, *A controvérsia do planejamento na economia brasileira* (Rio de Janeiro, 1977), pp. 108–9.

[13] Congresso Brasileiro de Indústria, *Anais* (São Paulo, 1945), I, pp. 225–6. What the Brazilian industrialist expected and received from Vargas was government control of the labour movement, in exchange for their acceptance of welfare legislation for workers.

is, Argentina, southern Brazil, and Chile.[14] When war came in 1939, manufactures in international trade became scarce again, permitting further industrialization to the extent that capital goods, fuel, and raw materials were available.

During the 1930s spokesmen for industry probably grew bolder, except perhaps those Brazilians who had initially followed Manoilescu. Note, for example, the themes chosen by Luis Colombo, the president of the Unión Industrial Argentina. In 1931, he supported a moderate and 'rational' protectionism, and defended the manufacturers against the charge of promoting policies inimical to the interests of Argentine consumers; in 1933, he even-handedly justified protection for both industry and agriculture; and by 1940 he was attacking the industrial countries as having themselves violated the rules of the international division of labour by developing large agricultural establishments, only choosing to buy abroad when convenient.[15] Industrialists pointed to the vulnerability of export-economies, which they more frequently dubbed 'colonial' than before. Gathering war clouds in Europe added another argument: domestic industries were necessary for an adequate national defence.[16] A basic characteristic of the period 1930–45 was an intensification of state intervention in the economy, in Latin America as elsewhere, and industrialists like other economic groups sought state assistance; they asked for subsidies, credits, and increased tariff protection. The state should, they argued, aid in 'economic rationalization', that is, cartelization, a theme of European industrialists in the thirties.[17]

In Argentina, Brazil, Chile, and Mexico, governments began to heed the importuning of manufacturers. State aid to industry in the form of development loans tended to converge in the early years of the war. The establishment of industrial development banks was an important symbolic act, as we shall see, but changes in tariff structures, which have not so far been thoroughly analysed, may have been more important for growth. The

---

[14] D. M. Phelps, 'Industrial Expansion in Temperate South America', *American Economic Review*, 25 (1935): 281.

[15] See Colombo's speeches in *Anales de la Unión Industrial Argentina*, año 44 (December, 1931), pp. 25, 27; ibid., año 46 (July, 1993), p. 37; *Argentina Fabril*, año 53 (Jan., 1940), p. 3.

[16] Unión Industrial Argentina, *Revista*, año 57 [sic] (May, 1946), p. 9. Alvarez Andrews, *Historia*, pp. 6, 328, 348; 'Necesitamos una política económica de industrialización' [editorial], *Revista de Economía y Finanzas* (Peru), 16, 92 (August, 1940), p. 128.

[17] Alvarez Andrews, *Historia*, pp. 327–8, 385; Pupo Nogueira, 'A propósito da modernização de uma grande indústria', *Revista Industrial de São Paulo*, año 1,6 (May, 1945), p. 18; 'Industrialización', [editorial], *Revista Económica* (Mexico, D. F.), 8, 10 (October, 1945), p. 6. In 1942, Enrique Zañartu Prieto defended 'autarky' in Chile, but in vague terms. See his *Tratado de economía política*, 2nd edn, (Santiago, 1946), p. 243.

reasons for such a shift by governments are clear in retrospect: a decade of wrestling with the intractable problem of reviving traditional export markets; the relative unavailability of foreign industrial goods over virtually a fifteen-year period (1930–45); and the fact that states (and particularly the officer corps) as well as industrialists began to consider the relation between manufacturing and national defence – a process that had already begun in Chile in the late twenties.

Governments, however, moved hesitantly and inconsistently toward addressing the problems of industry. In Argentina, Luis Duhau, the Minister of Agriculture, in 1933 proclaimed the necessity of producing industrial goods that could no longer be imported (for lack of foreign exchange), and he pledged his government's support for the process.[18] But in the same month the Argentine government supported the U.S. initiative for general tariff reductions at the Pan American Union Conference in Montevideo. Earlier that year Argentina had yielded to British pressure in the Roca-Runciman pact, a trade agreement favouring British manufactures in the Argentine market in exchange for a share of the British beef market for Argentina. As late as 1940, Finance Minister Pinedo's plan for the economic development of Argentina still distinguished between 'natural' and 'artificial' industries, implying that industrial development would occur in concert with the needs of the agricultural and pastoral sectors. By the time of the colonels' coup in June 1943, intervention for industrial development had become state policy, and an industrial development bank was created in 1944. Yet even at that point support for manufacturing was far from unrestrained: the ministry of agriculture still housed the department of industry, and the minister assured Argentinians that the development of manufacturing would not threaten, but would contribute to the growth of the country's 'mother industries', stockraising and agriculture.[19] In the next few years, however, the Perón government would demonstrably put the interests of industrialists above those of ranchers and farmers.

In Brazil, Getúlio Vargas favoured industry – was he not the friend of all established economic interests? – but he had opposed 'artificial' industries (that is, manufacturing) in his presidential campaign in 1930. Government loans to 'artificial' industries were still prohibited in 1937. Osvaldo Aranha, Vargas's Minister of Finance in 1933, even termed industries

[18] 'The Argentine Industrial Exhibition', *Review of the River Plate*, 22 (December, 1933), pp. 11, 13, 15.
[19] Diego Masón, Introduction to Mariano Abarca, *La industrialización de la Argentina* (Buenos Aires, 1944), p. 5.

'fictitious' if they did not use at least 70 per cent domestic raw materials.[20] Vargas only became committed to rapid industrial expansion during his Estado Novo dictatorship (1937–45). Although he said in 1939 that he could not accept the idea of Brazil's remaining a 'semi-colonial' economy, as late as 1940, when the coffee market was still depressed after a decade of attempts to revive it, Vargas wanted to 'balance' industrial and agricultural growth. In 1941 a division for industrial development of the Bank of Brazil began to make significant loans, but from 1941 through 1945 the Bank only disbursed an annual average of 17.5 per cent of its private sector loans to manufacturing concerns.[21] In Mexico, industrialization in the 1930s made impressive advances even while agrarian reform was at the top of Lázaro Cárdenas' agenda. It was not, however, the result of government policy. Nacional Financiera, a partly government-owned development bank, had been established in 1934, but only became seriously committed to manufacturing after its reorganization at the end of 1940, when the new pro-industry administration of Avila Camacho took office. During the Second World War, the pace quickened.[22] In Chile, nominal government support for industrial development began with the creation of an Institute of Industrial Credit in 1928. Ten years later the Popular Front government of Pedro Aguirre Cerda established Corporación de Fomento de la Producción, the government development corporation. But in 1940 the sum budgeted for the development of manufacturing was less than each of those for agriculture, mining, energy and public housing.[23]

All the same, government attitudes were changing, as were the views of economists both inside and outside Latin America. Even the economists of the League of Nations, champions of free trade in the twenties and thirties, had begun to doubt the advisability of full agricultural specialization for the world's poorer countries. As early as 1937, the League's economic

---

[20] Getúlio Vargas, *A nova política do Brasil*, I (Rio de Janeiro, 1938), pp. 26–7; *O Estado de São Paulo*, 8 March 1933.

[21] Getúlio Vargas, *A nova política*, VI (Rio de Janeiro, 1940), p. 91; VIII (Rio de Janeiro, 1941), p. 179; Annibal Villela and Wilson Suzigan, *Política do governo e crescimento da economia brasileira: 1889–1945* (Rio de Janeiro, 1973), p. 352.

[22] Stephen Haber, *Industrialization and Underdevelopment: The Industrialization of Mexico, 1890–1940* (Stanford, Cal., 1989), pp. 176–7; René Villareal, *El desequilibrio externo en la industrialización de México (1929–75): um enfoque estructuralista* (Mexico, D.F. 1976), pp. 43–5; Calvin S. Blair, 'Nacional Financiera: Entrepreneurship in a Mixed Economy', in Raymond Vernon (ed.) *Public Policy and Private Enterprise in Mexico* (Cambridge, Mass., 1964), pp. 210, 213; Rafael Izquierdo, 'Protectionism in Mexico', in ibid., p. 243; Alfredo Navarrete R., 'The Financing of Economic Development', in Enrique Pérez López et al., *Mexico's Recent Economic Growth: The Mexican View*, trans. Marjory Urquidi (Austin, Tex., 1967), p. 119.

[23] Presidente de la República [de Chile, Pedro Aguirre Cerda], *Mensaje . . . en la apertura . . . del Congreso Nacional 21 de Mayo de 1940* (Santiago, 1940), pp. 21–2, 95.

section stated a preference for a modicum of industrialization for agricultural countries, on the practical ground that factor flows remained substantially blocked, seven years after the onset of depression. A League study at the end of the War argued that the poorer agricultural countries had to industrialize to some degree, because of their lack of sufficient agricultural surpluses 'to ensure them a plentiful supply of imported manufactures'.[24]

In 1943 Paul Rosenstein-Rodan, in an article often considered the point of departure for modern development theory, called for the industrialization of agrarian countries, as did the trade theorist Charles Kindleberger. At a policy level, the Hot Springs conference of the Allied Nations the same year favoured a degree of industrialization for the 'backward' countries. More boldly, the economist Colin Clark had written in 1942 that future equilibrium in world trade depended on the willingness of Europe and the United States 'to accept a large flow of . . . exports of manufactured goods' from India and China.[25]

The somewhat 'unintended' industrialization of the larger Latin American countries and a partial acceptance of it by the United States government was reflected at the Chapultepec conference of the Pan American Union (1945). The meeting's resolutions gave a qualified benediction to the industrialization process in Latin America.[26] At the end of war, therefore, it was clear that industrialization had greatly advanced in Latin America; the process was characteristically import-substitution industrialization (ISI) – the replacement of imported goods with domestic manufactures, based on existing patterns of demand. Economists in several countries were noting the trend and searching for a theory to legitimate it.[27] That theory – and concomitant policies – would be provided by the United Nation's Economic Commission for Latin America in the years immediately after the Second World War.

---

[24] S[ergei] Prokopovicz, *L'industrialisation des pays agricoles et la structure de l'économie mondiale après la guerre*, trans. N. Nicolsky (Neuchatel, 1946), p. 276; League of Nations: Economic, Financial and Transit Department, *Industrialization and Foreign Trade* (N.p., 1945), p. 34.

[25] Paul Rosenstein-Rodan, 'Problems of Industrialization of Eastern and Southeastern Europe', in A. N. Agarwala and S. P. Singh (eds) *The Economics of Underdevelopment* (London, 1958 [orig., 1943]) pp. 246, 253–4; Charles Kindleberger, 'Planning for foreign investment', *American Economic Review*, 33, 1 (March, 1943), Supplement: 347–54; Prokopovicz, *L'industrialisation*, 278–9; Colin Clark, *The Economics of 1960* (London, 1942), p. 114.

[26] *Revista Económica* (Mexico, D. F.), 8, 1–2 (28 February 1945): 30.

[27] Sergio Bagú, '¿Y mañana, Qué?', *Revista de Economía* (Mexico, D. F.), 7, 5–6 (30 June 1944): 37; Heitor Ferreira Lima, "Evolução industrial de São Paulo', *Revista Industrial de São Paulo*, ano 1, 7 (June, 1945), p. 17; 'Monetary Developments in Latin America', *Federal Reserve Bulletin*, 31, 6 (June, 1945), p. 523; Gonzalo Robles, 'Sudamérica y el fomento industrial', *Trimestre Económico*, 14, 1 (April–June, 1947), p. 1.

PREBISCH AND CENTRE-PERIPHERY

The Economic Commission for Latin America was dominated in its early years by the ideas, personality, and programmes of Raúl Prebisch. We must therefore consider Prebisch's early career and formative experiences during the Depression of the 1930s and war years to learn how the ECLA theses of 1949 crystallized, for much of Prebisch's reasoning was apparently based on empirical observation and learning from failed policies.

Born in the city of Tucumán in 1901, Prebisch studied at the University of Buenos Aires, whose Department (Facultad) of Economics at the time was probably the best school for economic theory in Latin America.[28] Prebisch gave early promise of a distinguished career within Argentina's economic establishment. At the age of twenty he published his first professional study in economics. In 1923, upon completing a master's degree in that discipline, he was asked to join the staff at the University.[29] Although Prebisch the student was an assistant of Alejandro Bunge, the foremost promoter of Argentine industrialization in his day, the young man's career followed the more direct route of success, in an early and intimate association with the leaders of the pastoral industry. In 1922, that is, before Prebisch's graduation, Enrique Uriburu, on behalf of the elite Sociedad Rural Argentina, the powerful stockbreeders' association, appointed the young man director of the Sociedad Rural's statistical office. Two years later the Sociedad Rural sent Prebisch to Australia, where he studied statistical methods related to stockraising, and where, presumably, he also obtained a broader perspective on Argentina's position in the international economy.[30] By 1925 he was both a teacher at the University and an official in the Argentine government's Department of Statistics. In 1927 he published a Sociedad Rural-sponsored study that became the basis for government action on behalf of stockbreeders in the foreign meat market.[31]

Leaders of the Sociedad Rural were apparently impressed by the need for

[28] In 1918, Luis Gondra introduced South America's first course in mathematical economics at the University of Buenos Aires. Luis Gondra et al., *El pensamiento económico latinoamericano* (México, D. F., 1945), p. 32.

[29] Raúl Prebisch, 'Planes para estabilizar el poder adquisitivo de la moneda', Universidad Nacional de Buenos Aires: Facultad de Ciencias Económicas (hereafter UBA: FCE), *Investigaciones de Seminario*, II (Buenos Aires, 1921), pp. 459–513; interview of Prebisch by author, Washington, D.C., 10 July 1978.

[30] Prebisch, 'Planes', p. 459 (on Bunge); Prebisch, *Anotaciones demográficas a propósito de los movimientos de la población* (Buenos Aires, 1926), p. 3.

[31] Prebisch's study offered statistical proof that the meat pool's interference in the market had been beneficial for the British packing-houses, but not for the Argentine cattlemen. See Raúl Prebisch, 'El régimen de pool en el comercio de carnes', *Revista de Ciencias Económicas* (hereafter RCE) 15 (December, 1927): 1302–21.

good statistical data, by the need for economic analysis, and by Prebisch. In 1928 he was again working part time for the Sociedad Rural, compiling a statistical yearbook for the organization. Thus, from the outset of his career, Prebisch was interested in policy issues, set in the context of the international trading system. In 1928 he launched the publication of the *Revista Económica,* the organ of the government-directed Banco de la Nación Argentina, for which Prebisch established a research division.[32] The journal was concerned not only with pressing monetary matters, but also with the problems of stockraising, agriculture, and international trade – not with theoretical issues in economics.

In the early 1930s Prebisch served as an economic advisor to the Argentine government's ministries of finance and agriculture, and proposed the creation of a central bank (with powers to control interest rates and the money supply) to the government of General José Uriburu, who had seized power in 1930. After several years of study and parliamentary debate, in 1935 the Banco Central became the nation's first true central bank, and from its inception until 1943, Prebisch served as its Director-General. In addition, the Bank functioned as the government's economic 'brain trust', as a member of Prebisch's group put it.[33] In many respects, Prebisch and his colleagues in the 1930s were treading in theoretical terra incognita. Before the Depression of the 1930s it was considered axiomatic that Argentina had prospered according to the theory of comparative advantage. The benefits of export-led growth, based on an international division of labour, made comparative advantage a near-sacrosanct doctrine.

The twenties were a period of disequilibrium as well as expansion in world trade, and though Argentina prospered, the country experienced the same problems as a number of other primary-producing nations in the final years before the October 1929 crash – namely, falling export prices, rising stocks, and debt-payment difficulties. Argentina and Uruguay were, in fact, the first nations in the world to abandon the gold standard in the Depression – before the end of 1929. Following Britain's departure

---

[32] Banco de la Nación Argentina, *Economic Review,* 1, 1 (August, 1928): 2. Duhau, the president of the Sociedad Rural, had a hand in these events as a member of the Bank's governing board: Interview of Ernesto Malaccorto by Leandro Gutiérrez, Buenos Aires, Aug. 1971 (Inst. Torcuato di Tella), p. 7 [copy at Columbia University, Oral History Collection].

[33] *Who's Who in the United Nations and Related Agencies* (New York, 1975), pp. 455–56; Raúl Prebisch, "Versión taquigráfica de la conferencia de prensa . . . 15 de noviembre de 1955', pp. 23–4 (Prebisch file, Economic Commission for Latin America (hereafter ECLA), Santiago, Chile); Carlos F. Díaz-Alejandro, *Essays on the Economic History of the Argentine Republic* (New Haven, Conn., 1970), p. 97; Banco Central de la República Argentina, *La creación del Banco Central y la experiencia monetaria argentina entre los años 1935–1943* (Buenos Aires, 1972), 1: 267 *et seq.;* Malaccorto interview, p. 40 ('brain trust').

from the gold standard, in October 1931 Argentine authorities introduced exchange controls to try to stem the outflow of capital and facilitate the repayment of loans negotiated in hard currencies. Prebisch later wrote that 'Exchange control was not the result of a theory but was imposed by circumstances'.[34] The Depression thus brought the abandonment of many hallowed economic doctrines and practices.

In the crisis, Great Britain exploited her monopsonistic position against her many suppliers. As a rule she attempted to purchase less abroad, and thereby got her imports cheaper. In the case of Argentina, Britain's trading power was magnified by the South American nation's loss of dollar investments. The United States had become a major supplier to Argentina in the mid-1920s, but Argentina had chronic difficulties in paying directly for U.S. imports with her own non-complementary exports. Therefore Argentina had depended on U.S. capital exports, but during the Depression, North American lenders disinvested in Argentina. Excluded from the U.S. market by high tariffs and other regulations, and cut off from continental markets as well in the early thirties, Argentina feared above all the loss of British market; indeed, it was already partly closed by the Ottawa Conference agreement (1932) among Great Britain and her dominions, several of which were Argentina's export competitors. Britain's trading power was further enhanced by the fact that in these years she bought much more from Argentina than she sold to that country. In the four years 1930–33, Britain took over 40 per cent of Argentina's exports, but supplied only about 20 per cent of Argentina's imports.

Consequently, Argentine statesmen and government economists – among them Raúl Prebisch – were willing to enter into the Roca–Runciman Pact of 1933, an arrangement more to Britain's advantage than Argentina's, whereby the United Kingdom agreed to keep up a certain level of meat purchases in exchange for regular debt service payments and tariff reductions for British manufactures. Thus beef exports, the traditional preserve of the Argentine oligarchy, were favoured over wheat. A bilateral agreement in 1936 was even more favourable to British interests. After war broke out in 1939, the British government played its monopsonistic position to yet greater advantage, in negotiations between the Bank of England and Argentina's Central Bank, led by Raúl Prebisch. One can easily surmise that Argentina's protracted and notorious dependency on her major trading

[34] ECLA, *The Economic Development of Latin America and its Principal Problems* (Lake Success, N.Y., 1950), p. 29.

partner left a lasting impression on Prebisch. Furthermore, the Argentine government made great sacrifices to retain its credit rating by paying its debts; perhaps Argentine statesmen were overly influenced by the manifest success, before the Depression, of export-driven growth.[35]

The Depression of the 1930s not only brought about bilateral negotiations, but a series of international economic meetings as well. In 1933 Prebisch, as an invitee of the Council of the League of Nations, attended a gathering of the Preparatory Committee of the Second International Monetary Conference in Geneva. From Switzerland Prebisch reported to the *Revista Económica* that the assembled monetary experts believed that one basic blockage in the international economic system derived from the facts that the United States had replaced Great Britain as the world's chief creditor country, and that high American tariff schedules (especially the Smoot-Hawley Act of 1930) did not permit other countries to repay U.S. loans with exports. Consequently, the rest of the world tended to send gold to the United States, and the bullion was not recirculated in the international monetary system.[36] Prebisch soon went to London to help negotiate the Roca–Runciman Pact as a technical advisor. Later in 1933, he attended the World Monetary Conference in the same city. But the Conference broke up in failure, and the tendency toward bilateralism in world trade continued.

In Argentina, Prebisch sought to understand another vexing problem wrought by Depression – declining terms of trade. In 1934 he published an article pointing out that 'agricultural prices have fallen more profoundly than those of manufactured goods', and that in 1933 Argentina had to sell 73 per cent more than before the Depression to obtain the same quantity of (manufactured) imports. In the same article Prebisch attacked as 'scholastic' the orthodox equilibrium theories of his senior colleague at the University of Buenos Aires, Professor Luis Gondra, because such doctrines ignored the stubborn fact of sustained depression.[37]

---

[35] On the Argentine economy in the 1930s, see Javier Villanueva, 'Economic Development', in Mark Falcoff and Ronald H. Dolkart (eds), *Prologue to Perón: Argentina in Depression and War: 1930–1943* (Berkeley, Cal., 1975), pp. 57–82; Jorge Fodor and Arturo A. O'Connell, 'La Argentina y la economía atlántica en la primera mitad del siglo XX', *Desarrollo Económico*, 13, 9 (April–June, 1973); Vicente Vásquez-Presedo, *Crisis y retraso: Argentina y la economía internacional entre las dos guerras* (Buenos Aires, 1978).

[36] Prebisch, 'La conferencia económica y la crisis mundial', in [Banco de la Nación Argentina], *Revista Económica* 6, 1 (January, 1933), pp. 1, 3. Another reason for U.S. absorption of the world's gold supply was the overvaluation of the pound sterling, when Britain returned to the gold standard in 1925.

[37] Prebisch, 'La inflación escolástica y la moneda argentina', *Revista de Economía Argentina*, año 17, 193 (July 1934), pp. 11–12; 194 (August, 1934), p. 60. Later it was discovered that the purchasing

Prebisch was a member of an economic 'team' groping with the crisis, and recent research has emphasized that the policies of Federico Pinedo (Finance Minister, 1933–5 and 1940–1) and his collaborators, including Prebisch, involved extensive governmental intervention in the economy; such innovation occurred despite the oligarchic political cast of the regime from 1930 to 1943 (the 'infamous decade' of political history).[38] Not only did the state reform the monetary and banking system through the creation of a central bank and the introduction of exchange controls, but it also intervened in the processing and marketing of Argentina's main exports, that is, beef and grain. This novel and vigorous activity by the state may have had corporatist sources of inspiration or not, but in the endeavour Argentina was clearly in step with her neo-protectionist trading partner, Great Britain.

The return of severe depression in 1937–8, a problem originating in the United States, had its major spread effects in the less developed agricultural- and mineral-exporting areas of the world, because Europe and Japan were 'pump priming' through their armaments programmes. Wheat was one of the commodities for which prices fell sharply in 1937.[39] As other countries introduced new trade controls, so did Argentina, in 1938, in the form of quantitative restrictions on imports. In the next two years, Argentina's banking officials, among them Raúl Prebisch, were trying to keep international credits and debts in balance 'in the strictest short-run sense'. Thus trade policy was not yet consciously used to foster industrialization.[40]

Yet manufacturing in Argentina grew impressively in the 1930s and early 1940s, a fact which was recognized by contemporaries at home and abroad. In particular, the Central Bank's *Revista Económica* noted an increase in output of 85 per cent (by value) between the industrial census of 1913 and that of 1934–5.[41] In its annual report for 1942 (published in 1943), the Bank followed through on its changing economic emphases by

power of Argentina's exports fell by about 40 per cent between 1925–9 and 1930–4. Between these two periods the capital flow was also temporarily reversed, so in 1930–4 Argentina's capacity to import fell to 46 per cent of what it had been in the preceding five years. Aldo Ferrer, *The Argentine Economy*, trans Marjory M. Urquidi (Berkeley, Cal., 1967), p. 162.

[38] On Raúl Prebisch's role, see interview of Federico Pinedo by Luis Alberto Romero, Buenos Aires, June 1971 (Inst. Torcuato di Tella), esp. pp. 64–7 [copy at Columbia University, Oral History Collection].

[39] Charles P. Kindleberger, *The World Depression: 1929–1939* (London, 1973), pp. 278–9.

[40] Walter Beveraggi-Allende, 'Argentine foreign trade under exchange control' (Ph.D thesis, Harvard University, 1952), p. 219 (quotation), p. 246; Malaccorto interview, p. 64.

[41] Phelps, 'Industrial Expansion', p. 274; *Economic Review* [Eng. tr. of *Revista Económica*], series 2, 1, no. 1 (1937): 69.

championing industrialization. The report, reflecting Prebisch's views, argued that exports and industrial development were by no means incompatible; rather, the issue was to change the composition of imports from consumer to capital goods.[42]

Prebisch the policy-maker interests us less than Prebisch the emerging economic theorist, though the two can hardly be separated. In the latter capacity he was beginning to formulate a theory of unequal exchange by 1937. In that year the *Revista Económica* noted that agricultural production was inelastic compared to industrial output, and that its products' prices tended to rise and fall faster than industrial prices in the trade cycle. The *Revista* also noted the related problem of the lack of organization of agricultural producers, and concluded: 'In the last depression these differences manifested themselves in a sharp fall in agricultural prices and in a much smaller decline in the prices of manufactured articles. The agrarian countries lost part of their purchasing power, with the resultant effect on the balance of payments and on the volume of their imports.'[43] The emphasis was thus on the elasticity of supply of industrial production, and implicitly on monopoly, and not on wage contracts in the industrial countries, which was later to be a focal point of Prebisch's analysis.

In the same comment the *Revista* noted that Argentina's industrial complex made its greatest gains in two periods, the First World War, and during 'the world wide recrudescensce of the policy of economic self-sufficiency during the years 1929–1936'.[44] Thus Prebisch seemed to be considering the possibility that export-led growth was no longer a viable path to economic development.

Prebisch was also intensely interested in the trade cycle in Argentina. The Central Bank began its effort to conduct counter-cyclical monetary policy in 1937, by decreasing the public's purchasing power through the sale of bonds in that boom year; in the following period of contraction, it would attempt to expand purchasing power by lowering the rediscount rate.[45] In 1939, in its annual report for the previous year, the Central Bank – representing Prebisch's thinking on the matter – argued that the nation's trade cycles were primarily a reflection of those of its principal (industrialized) trading partners. It held that Argentina's internal credit expansion began with an export surplus, which led to additional demand for foreign goods, because of exporters' high propensities to import; when

[42] Banco Central de la República Argentina, *Memoria . . . 1942* (Buenos Aires, 1943), pp. 30–31.
[43] *Economic Review,* series 2, 1, 1 (1937): 26–7.
[44] Ibid., p. 69.
[45] Rafael Olarra Jiménez, *Evolución monetaria argentina* (Buenos Aires, 1968), p. 13.

combined with heavy import requirements, the process repeatedly produced a balance-of-payments crisis in the national business cycle.[46]

After his dismissal from the Central Bank in 1943, apparently because the coup makers associated him with the ranching oligarchy, Prebisch began to read widely in the recent economic literature.[47] Returning for the moment to teaching, he prepared a series of lectures in 1944 in which he referred, for the first time, to 'Centre' and 'Periphery', terms he would later make famous.

Prebisch developed a historical argument, with Britain as the nineteenth-century 'Centre' of the trading and monetary systems based on the gold standard. (Clearly, this was a better model for the first half of the century than the second half, but Britain as Centre for the whole period fit Argentina's situation well enough.) Under Britain's leadership as the cycle-generating Centre, Prebisch argued, the world's economic system had equilibrated gold flows and the balance of payments over the course of the cycle for both Centre and Periphery. 'Gold tended to leave Great Britain, the Center of the system, and to enter countries of the Periphery in the upswing of the cycle'. Then it returned in the downswing. A problem for peripheral countries was that when gold departed in the downswing, 'there was no way to diminish the gold flow except by contracting credit . . . No one could conceive of . . . the possibility of raising the rediscount rate in competition with the monetary Center in London'. Thus overall monetary stability was only maintained at the cost of economic contraction of the 'Periphery'. 'The gold standard was therefore an automatic system for the countries of the Periphery, but not for the Center', where the rediscount rate could be adjusted for domestic needs. In the Periphery, the gold standard had the effect of exaggerating rather than offsetting the cycle.[48]

Passing on to the post-First World War years, Prebisch concluded that New York bankers in the 1920s and 1930s did not have the knowledge or experience of the 'British financial oligarchy', though of course the world situation was dramatically different after the War. By 1930 the United States had sucked up the world's gold. Consequently, 'the rest of the world, including our country, [is] forced to seek a means of inward-directed development (*crecer hacia adentro*)'[49] – a phrase that ECLA would later make famous.

[46] Banco Central, *Memoria . . . 1938* (Buenos Aires, 1939), pp. 5–8; Prebisch to author, Washington, D.C., 9 November 1977.

[47] Prebisch interview.

[48] Prebisch, 'La moneda y los ciclos económicos en la Argentina' [class notes by assistant, approved by Prebisch], 1944, pp. 61–5, mimeo. [Located at UBA: FCE.]

[49] Ibid., p. 65.

The Argentine business cycle, Prebisch continued, had depended on exogenous factors operating through the balance of payments. In the upswing, exports and foreign investment produced an influx of gold and exchange credits, creating new money and therefore imports. Such changes also expanded credit to agricultural industries; but because of inelastic supply, during the downswing, credit was immobilized in the rural sector. Additional imports were paid for with reserves, producing a monetary crisis.[50]

In seeking a solution to Argentina's problems, Prebisch began to think in more general terms about Latin America and its relation with the United States; his first concern in that area had involved the previously mentioned plan in 1940 – probably drafted by Prebisch, but presented to Congress by Finance Minister Pinedo – to link the Argentine economy to the United States and to expanding Latin American markets, in part by exporting manufactures.[51]

Freed from his duties at the Central Bank, Prebisch was twice in Mexico during the mid-forties at the invitation of Mexico's central bank (Banco de México). On both occasions he participated in international meetings: once in 1944 at a gathering of intellectuals from Latin America at the Colegio de México on problems the region would face in the post-war era,[52] and again in Mexico City at an inter-American meeting of central bankers in 1946.

Prebisch's interest in industrialization as a solution to Latin America's economic problems originally arose from the desire, shared by many Argentine contemporaries, to make Argentina less economically 'vulnerable', a vulnerability painfully evident for the whole period 1930–45. As noted above, the Argentine Central Bank, under Prebisch's leadership, had begun to advocate industrialization in its 1942 report. By implication Prebisch was recommending similar policies to other Latin American governments in his Colegio de México lecture of 1944.[53] In his 'Conversations' at the Banco de México in the same year, Prebisch again noted that the period of greatest industrial development in Argentina had been the

---

[50] Summary of 'La moneda', in Olarra Jiménez, *Evolución*, p. 76.

[51] See Javier Villanueva, 'Economic Development', in Falcoff and Dolkart, (eds), *Prologue to Perón*, p. 78. On Prebisch as probable author of the Pinedo plan, see Díaz-Alejandro, *Essays*, p. 105, note 37.

[52] At the same time Prebisch gave a series of lectures at the Banco de México on 'the Argentine monetary experience (1935–1943)', that is, covering the period in which he was the Director-General of the Central Bank. See Banco Central, *La creación*, 1:249–588; 2:599–623.

[53] Raúl Prebisch, 'El patrón oro y la vulnerabilidad económica de nuestros países' [a lecture at the Colegio de México], *Revista de Ciencias Económicas*, año 32, serie 2, no.272 (March, 1944), p. 234; Banco Central, *Memoria . . . 1942*, p. 30.

Great Depression and the times of war, periods in which the nation had to produce for itself what it could not import.[54] Later, ECLA theorists would explore the implications of this observation, as they elaborated the concept of 'inward-directed development'.

In a 1944 article in Mexico's *Trimestre Económico,* Prebisch noted that the United States, unlike Argentina, had a low propensity to import (defined as the change in the value of imports generated by a given change in the national product). Since other countries, he implied, had high propensities to import, and the U.S. had replaced Britain as the chief industrial trading partner of the Latin American states, Prebisch expanded on the League experts' argument in 1933, and warned that the postwar international trading system faced the danger of permanent disequilibrium.[55]

Prebisch first used the terminology 'Center-Periphery' in print in 1946, at the second meeting mentioned above, that of the hemisphere's central bankers, who convened at the invitation of the Banco de México. Prebisch now identified the United States as the 'cyclical Center' and Latin America as the 'Periphery of the economic system'. The emphasis, as indicated, was on the trade cycle, whose rhythms the U.S. economy set for the whole international system. Fiscal and monetary authorities in the United States could pursue a policy of full employment without producing monetary instability, Prebisch argued; furthermore, such authorities did not need to be especially concerned about the impact of full employment policies on the exchange rate of the dollar in other currencies. By contrast, Prebisch asserted, the nations of the Periphery could not apply the same monetary tools as the Centre did. Extrapolating from his 1944 argument with reference to Argentina, Prebisch contended that the money supply in peripheral countries not be expanded in pursuit of full employment, because, with a high propensity to import, any expansion of income would quickly exhaust foreign exchange, assuming no devaluation.

This 1946 statement and previous writings of Prebisch implied that peripheral countries faced three options, all with undesirable consequences: they could have strong currencies and maintain high levels of imports at the cost of high unemployment; they could fight unemployment with an expansionary monetary policy, but would thereby create

---

[54] Raúl Prebisch, 'Análisis de la experiencia monetaria argentina (1935–1943)', in Banco Central, *La creación,* 1, p. 407. See the similar judgements by Adolfo Dorfman, *Evolución industrial argentina* (Buenos Aires, 1942), p. 74 (on First World War and Great Depression); Heitor Ferreira Lima, 'Evolução industrial', p. 17 (on São Paulo, Second World War).

[55] Raúl Prebisch, 'Observaciones sobre los planes monetarios internacionales', *Trimestre Económico,* 11, 2 (July–September, 1944), pp. 188, 192–3.

inflation and put pressure on the exchange rate, thus raising the cost of repaying foreign debts; or, if they used monetary policy to maintain high levels of employment, but failed to devalue, their reserves would disappear. When prices of the Periphery's products fell during the downswing of the cycle, furthermore, governments of peripheral countries, at least in isolation, could not affect world prices for their goods as the Centre could for its goods. Thus equilibrium theories in international trade were not acceptable.[56] This was an assault on the policy prescriptions of neo-classical economics. Prebisch's message in Mexico City was in tune with the pessimism then prevailing in Latin America regarding international trade as a long-term engine of growth. Even the improving terms of trade of the early post-war years was widely viewed as transient.

In the classroom in Buenos Aires in 1948, Prebisch specifically attacked the theory of comparative advantage, and noted that its precepts were repeatedly violated by the industrialized nations, whose economists none the less used neo-classical trade theory as an ideological weapon. He also implied that industrial countries acted as monopolists against agricultural countries in the trading process. Prebisch then asserted that historically, in both the United States and Britain, technological progress did not result in a decrease in prices, but in an increase in wages. 'The fruit of technical progress tended to remain in Great Britain' in the nineteenth century; yet because Britain had sacrificed its agriculture, part of the benefits of technological progress had been transferred to the 'new countries' in the form of higher land values. Britain's nineteenth-century import co-efficient (defined as the value of imports divided by real income) was estimated by Prebisch as 30–35 per cent, whereas that of the United States in the 1930s was only about 5 per cent. All of this implied a blockage to growth for the agricultural-exporting Periphery under the new largely self-sufficient Centre.[57]

This Centre-Periphery framework implied a single system, hegemonically organized.[58] To appreciate the significance of the concept, we should

---

[56] Raúl Prebisch, 'Panorama general de los problemas de regulación monetaria y crediticia en el continente americano: A. América Latina', in Banco de México, *Memoria: Primera reunión de técnicos sobre problemas de banca central del continente americano* (Mexico, D. F., 1946), pp. 25–8; 'Observaciones', p. 199.

[57] Raúl Prebisch, 'Apuntes de economía política (Dinámica económica)' [class notes], 1948, pp. 88–97 (quotation on 97), mimeo. [Located at UBA: FCE]

[58] Though the term 'hegemony' did not appear in this early use of Centre-Periphery terminology, Prebisch himself, years later, would specifically employ the word to characterize relations between the two elements of the world economy. Prebisch, 'A Critique of Peripheral Capitalism,' *CEPAL Review*, January–June 1976, p. 60.

bear in mind that the idea that there was something fundamentally different about the economies of the underdeveloped areas was still novel in the
1940s. The concept of 'underdevelopment' as a syndrome was only elaborated in that decade, chiefly after the creation of specialized United Nations agencies in 1947–48. The euphemisms 'developing countries' and
'less developed countries' were still in the future.[59] While a few Marxists
and others preferred to employ 'backward' rather than 'underdeveloped',
even 'backward' among these non-Centre-Periphery terms did not in itself
imply hegemony; nor did 'backward' necessarily put the central emphasis
on the international capitalist system. Rather, such a term could imply
that the problem was largely one of the leads and lags – the modernization
thesis in its ahistorical setting.

Despite the fact that some of the key ideas of Prebisch's later analysis were set forth in international meetings in 1944 and 1946, there
were no discussions on these occasions of an Economic Commission for
Latin America, the U.N. agency that was subsequently to be Prebisch's
principal theoretical and ideological vehicle. Rather, it resulted from a
Chilean initiative in 1947 at U.N. headquarters in Lake Success, New
York. The agency was approved by the U.N. Economic and Social Council in February 1948, and ECLA held its first meeting in Santiago,
Chile, in June of that year. Alberto Baltra Cortés, the Chilean Minister
of the Economy, presided at the occasion. At the opening session Baltra,
who was familiar with Prebisch's ideas, stressed Latin America's need to
industrialize, an attitude to which representatives of the United States
and the European colonial powers professed not to object. For the future
of ECLA, or at least its most famous thesis, the chief outcome of the
meeting was a resolution calling for a study of Latin America's terms of
trade.[60]

Without Prebisch's leadership, ECLA was not yet ECLA. His personality, theses, and programmes so dominated the agency in its formative
phase that it stood in sharp relief to the Economic Commission for Asia
and the Far East (established in 1947) and the Economic Commission for
Africa (1958), agencies with more purely technical orientations. The year
of ECLA's founding, 1948, seemed propitious for obtaining Prebisch's
services: in Juan Perón's Argentina he was excluded from official posts,

[59] See Gunnar Myrdal, 'Diplomacy by Terminology', in *An Approach to the Asian Drama: Methodological and Theoretical* (New York, 1970), pp. 35–6.
[60] UN ECOSOC E/CN.12/17 (7 June 1948), p. 2; E/CN.12/28 (11 June 1948), p. 6; E/CN.12/71 (24 June 1948).

perhaps because of his long and close association with the nation's traditional economic elite. Meanwhile, his reputation as an economist in Latin America had been enhanced by the publication in Mexico of his *Introducción a Keynes* (1947).

Prebisch in fact turned down the first offer to direct the Santiago-based ECLA in 1948, because he feared an international organization like the U.N. would not permit underdeveloped countries to analyse economic problems from their own perspectives; in this regard, he had in mind the League of Nations' lack of interest in underdeveloped areas.[61] Meanwhile, this concern was apparently justified by the failure of the U.S. Congress to take action on a U.N.-sponsored International Trade Organization (ITO), proposed in 1948 as a third leg – along with the World Bank and the International Monetary Fund (IMF) – of an international economic system. The ITO was to have dealt with an issue of great concern to the Latin Americans, commodity price stabilization.

In any event Prebisch was again invited to go to Santiago to work on special assignment as editor and author of the introduction to an economic report on Latin America, authorized at the initial ECLA meeting. In Santiago he elaborated his thesis on the deterioration of the terms of trade in *El desarrollo económico de América Latina y sus principales problemas,* published in May 1949 (English translation: *The Economic Development of Latin America and its Principal Problems,* 1950), an essay termed the 'ECLA Manifesto' by Albert Hirschman.[62] Prebisch had already formed his opinions about the direction of Latin America's long-range terms of trade, since he had argued in the classroom in 1948 that the benefits of technological progress were absorbed by the Centre. Now, a new study, *Relative Prices of Exports and Imports of Underdeveloped Countries,* by Hans Singer of the U.N. Department of Economic Affairs, provided an empirical foundation for Prebisch's thesis. This work was an examination of long-term trends in relative prices in the goods traded by industrialized and raw materials-producing countries, and concluded that the terms of trade from the late nineteenth century till the eve of the Second World War had been moving against the exporters of agricultural goods and in favour of the exporters of industrial products: 'On the average, a given quantity of primary exports would pay, at the end of this period, for only 60% of the

---

61 Prebisch interview. For support on the League's lack of interest in underdeveloped areas, see H. W. Arndt, *Economic Development: the History of an Idea* (Chicago, 1987), p. 18.

62 Albert O. Hirschman, 'Ideologies of Economic Development in Latin America', in Albert O. Hirschman (ed.), *Latin American Issues: Essays and Comments* (New York, 1961), p. 13.

quantity of manufactured goods which it could buy at the beginning of the period'.[63]

ECLA explained this finding in part by arguing that gains in productivity over the period in question were greater in industrial than in primary products, thus challenging basic assumptions of the theory of comparative advantage. If prices of industrial goods had fallen, this development would have spread the effects of technical progress over the entire Centre-Periphery system, and the terms of trade of agricultural goods would have been expected to have improved. They did not do so; and the significance of this fact had to be understood in terms of trade cycles. During the upswing, the prices of primary goods rise more sharply than those of industrial goods, but they fall more steeply during the downswing. In the upswing the working class of the Centre absorbs real economic gains, but wages do not fall proportionately during the downswing. Because workers are not well organized in the Periphery (least of all in agriculture), the Periphery absorbs more of the system's income contraction than does the Centre.[64] Thus in current jargon, Prebisch focussed on the 'double factorial terms of trade' – domestic labour's compensation vs. that of its foreign counterpart.

In the *Economic Survey of Latin America: 1949* (Spanish edition, 1950; English edition, 1951), Prebisch expanded on these arguments. He held that there were two distinct sources of the potential deterioration of the terms of trade, namely, those from technological productivity gains in the Centre, and those in the Periphery. He assumed the Centre's gains would be greater, and if the system worked normally, these would, to some extent, spread to the Periphery. In that case, over the long run the Centre's terms of trade would deteriorate, and the periphery's would improve. If the Periphery's terms deteriorated, such fact would indicate that it was not only failing to share in the Centre's presumably larger gains, but was transferring some of its *own* productivity gains to the Centre.[65] Since *Relative Prices* had established a deterioration in the Periphery's terms, protection for industry was a sine qua non to arrest the concentration of the fruits of technological progress in the Centre.

The basic cause of the deterioration was the surplus labour supply and

---

[63] United Nations: Department of Economic Affairs, *Relative Prices of Exports and Imports of Under-Developed Countries: A Study of Postwar Terms of Trade between Under-Developed and Industrialised Nations* (Lake Success, N.Y., 1949), p. 7.

[64] ECLA, *Economic Development*, pp. 8–14.

[65] ECLA, *Economic Survey of Latin America: 1949* (New York, 1951), p. 47.

the underlying population pressure in the precapitalist, largely agricultural, sector of the Periphery's economy. As modern agricultural technique penetrates and reduces the size of the precapitalist sector, the *Survey* stated, a labour surplus develops. It then adduced historical data to show that the export sector in Latin America could not absorb this surplus. Industrialization, in part to absorb the labour surplus, was the centrepiece of a policy of economic development, the *Survey* contended. Even when protection was needed, industries were 'economical in so far as they represent a net addition to real income'. National income could be increased by selectively lowering components of the import coefficient.[66]

Another initial ECLA argument grew out of Prebisch's observations on Argentina's import problems in the 1930s. The United States, the principal cyclical Centre, had a much lower import co-efficient than export co-efficient, and the former was also much lower than those of the Latin American countries. The U.S. tended to sell more to Latin America than it bought from the region, exhausting Latin American reserves, and creating a tendency toward permanent disequilibrium. Such a tendency had not existed, ECLA averred, during the time in which import-hungry Great Britain had been the principal Centre.[67] The U.S. economy even grew by closing: ECLA produced statistics showing that the United States' import co-efficient had fallen from the 1920s to the late 1940s. The explanation was that technological progress in some industries was much greater than on average; this allowed such industries to pay much higher wages, driving up wages in general, and in some other industries, above productivity gains. Therefore rising costs led to greater average protectionism and a 'closing' of the Centre.[68]

But Prebisch and the ECLA team he organized were also interested in another dimension of the problem – monopolistic pricing at the Centre. The original analysis in 1949–50 laid much more emphasis on the rigidity of wages in the downward phase of the cycle than on monopolistic pricing as such, but the latter argument was there.[69] In any event, both wage rigidities and monopoly were assumed to be non-existent in neo-classical

---

[66] Ibid., p. 78 (quotation), 79. At that time Prebisch believed that by changing the composition of imports from consumer to capital goods, Latin American countries could reduce their import coefficients. ECLA, *Economic Development*, pp. 44–5.

[67] ECLA, *Economic Development*, pp. 15–16; ECLA, *Economic Survey 1949*, pp. 20, 35–8.

[68] *Economic Survey 1949*, pp. 35, 75.

[69] Ibid., p. 59. More ambiguously, *Economic Development* stated that 'the income of entrepreneurs and of productive factors' in the Centre increased faster than did productivity in the Centre from the 1870s to the 1930s; but in another passage the document placed exclusive emphasis on the role of wages in the Centre (pp. 10, 14).

trade theory. Peripheral countries did not have monopolies on the goods they offered in the world market, with rare and temporary exceptions, just as they lacked well-organized rural labour forces that would resist the fall in wages during the downswing of the cycle.

The preceding analysis, taken as a whole, pointed to negative features in the Periphery's economy: structural unemployment, external disequilibrium, and deteriorating terms of trade – all of which a properly implemented policy of industrialization could help eliminate.

In 1950, the year after the appearance of the original Spanish version of the 'ECLA manifesto', another United Nations economist independently made a case related to the ECLA theses. Hans W. Singer, who had directed the U.N. study *Relative Prices* – the data base for ECLA's terms-of-trade argument – alleged that technological progress in manufacturing was shown in a rise in incomes in developed countries, while that in the production of food and raw materials in underdeveloped countries was expressed in a fall in prices. He explained the differential effects of technological progress in terms of different income elasticities of demand for primary and industrial goods – an extrapolation of Ernst Engel's law that the proportion of income spent on food falls as income rises – and in terms of the 'absence of pressure of producers for higher incomes' in underdeveloped countries. Since consumers of manufactured goods in world trade tended to live in underdeveloped countries, and the contrary was true for consumers of raw materials, Singer continued, the latter group had the best of both worlds while the former had the worst.[70] This idea was linked to Prebisch's, and quickly termed the Prebisch–Singer thesis, though both economists later stated that there was no direct exchange of views at the time the related sets of propositions, based on the same U.N. data, were developed.[71] (Prebisch was then in Santiago, and Singer in New York.)

In fact Prebisch had made *two* arguments, of which one was better stated by Singer. (Singer in turn had touched on Prebisch's theme of contrasting degrees of labour organization in Centre and Periphery.) Prebisch's central argument related to differential productivities in Centre and Periphery. His other argument dealing with disparities in import

---

[70] H[ans] W. Singer, 'The distribution of gains between investing and borrowing countries', *American Economic Review: Papers and Proceedings*, 40, 2 (May 1950): 473–85 (quotation on 479). Income elasticity of demand for a good refers to the relative response of demand to a small percentage change in income, $\Delta q/q/ \Delta y/y$, where q is the quantity demanded, and y is disposable income.

[71] Prebisch to author, 29 June 1977; Singer to author, Brighton, England, 21 August 1979.

coefficients was rougly analogous to Singer's more elegant argument on differential income elasticities. Since Prebisch's *Economic Development*, ECLA's 'manifesto', appeared in print in May 1949, more than six months before Singer presented his paper to the American Economic Association (published in the *American Economic Review* in May 1950), Prebisch seems to have reached his position earlier than Singer; in fact, Singer's *Relative Prices* simply bolstered conclusions he had already drawn.

By 1951, the year that ECLA became a permanent organ of the United Nations, the agency was referring less to import coefficients than to disparities in income elasticities of demand at the Centre for primary products, and those at the Periphery for industrial goods.[72] This adoption of Singer's terms was significant, because it dealt with the Centre countries as a group and not just the United States, which had unusually low import requirements because of its tremendous agricultural output. Though ECLA first emphasized differential productivities, by the late fifties it was tending to emphasize differential income elasticities of demand, possibly as a result of perceived export stagnation in Argentina and Chile.[73]

Such were the main lines of Prebisch's and ECLA's early development. Yet it seems useful to digress briefly on other possible, and sometimes specifically alleged, influences on Prebisch. If these were not genetically related, comparing such propositions and theories with ECLA's will serve to highlight the distinctive features of the ECLA model.

One obvious possibility is the work of Alejandro Bunge, Argentina's leading advocate of industrialization in the 1920s, and Prebisch's former teacher at the University of Buenos Aires. Like *ancien régime* mercantilists, Bunge defended industrialization not in theoretical but in policy terms, and saw it as a means of reducing imports to relieve pressure on the balance of payments; yet he viewed industrialization as a complement to export-driven growth more than a substitute for it.[74]

A Latin American who anticipated a more important element in the Prebisch model was Víctor Emilio Estrada, the director of Ecuador's central bank in the 1920s. In 1922 he wrote that his country's terms of trade for its traditional exports would deteriorate indefinitely. Estrada attrib-

[72] E/CN.12/221 (18 May 1951), p. 30.

[73] For example, see Raúl Prebisch, 'Commercial policy in the underdeveloped countries', *American Economic Review: Papers and Proceedings*, 49, 2 (May, 1959): 251–73.

[74] Alejandro E. Bunge, *La economía argentina* (Buenos Aires), 2 (1928), pp. 229–31; 4 (1930), p. 131. Also see Tulio Halperín Donghi, 'Argentina: ensayo de interpretación' in Roberto Cortés Conde and Stanley J. Stein (eds), *Latin America: A Guide to Economic History, 1830–1930* (Berkeley, Cal., 1977), pp. 67, 115.

uted the price-scissors problem principally to rising labour costs in manufacturing in the United States, Ecuador's chief trading partner; this fact owed to trade-union activity, a pressure which was lacking in the price-formation of Ecuadorian exports. But Estrada did not generalize beyond his own country, nor associate his idea with the trade cycle; he was only groping for measures to offset the falling prices of cacao, Ecuador's leading export at the time.[75]

Another possible influence is Werner Sombart, whose *Der moderne Kapitalismus* was the first work to distinguish between Centre and Periphery in the world economic system. Specifically, Sombart wrote, 'We must . . . distinguish a capitalist Center – the central capitalist nations – from a mass of peripheral countries viewed from that Center; the former are active and directing, the latter, passive and serving. England constituted the capitalist Center in the first half of the nineteenth century; later, in the longer period of High Capitalism, Western Europe [joined England] . . . Finally, in the last generation, the eastern part of the United States has moved up [to the Center]'. Sombart also wrote of the 'dependency' of peripheral countries, and even of the servitude of the peasantry of the Periphery, in part caused by western European capitalism.[76] But he did not provide any theory of relations between Centre and Periphery; in particular, he offered no analysis of the relation between business cycles and the international distribution of income. Later Prebisch did not recollect acquaintance with Sombart's passage at the time of his initial use of the terms 'Centre' and 'Periphery', but even if he was inspired indirectly, Prebisch would owe little more than an arresting phrase, since Sombart only used 'Centre' and 'Periphery' in a few scattered paragraphs.[77]

More plausible as a theoretical influence than the writings of Bunge or Sombart, however, is the work of the aforementioned Rumanian, Mihail Manoilescu. The Canadian-American trade theorist Jacob Viner linked the

[75] Víctor Emilio Estrada, *Ensayo sobre la balanza económica del Ecuador* (Guayaquil, 1922), p. 77. (I am grateful to Paul Drake for bringing this work to my attention.)

[76] Werner Sombart, *Der moderne Kapitalismus* (München, 1928), III [2 vols. bound as 1], Vol. 1, pp. xiv–xv (quotation), 64; Vol. 2, p. 1019.

[77] Prebisch to author, Washington, D.C., 26 June 1979. Still another possible source of inspiration for the Centre-Periphery terminology was the work of Ernst Wagemann, the German economist born in Chile. In *Struktur und Rhythmus der Weltwirtschaft* (Berlin, 1931), Wagemann, a specialist in business cycles, used 'central cycle' [*zentrische Konjunktur*] to designate money income movements *within* a given country, and 'peripheral cycle' [*periphere Konjunktur*] to designate capital movements at the international level (pp. 70–1). Thus Wagemann employed a Centre-Periphery scheme in connection with a cyclical movement, but not in the sense which Prebisch shared with Sombart. In 1977 Prebisch did not recall how he came to use the terms 'Centre' and 'Periphery.' Prebisch to author, 29 June 1977.

theses of Manoilescu with those of ECLA as early as 1950.[78] Over the next twenty years, others in Latin America, the United States and Rumania would concur in Viner's judgement.

During the thirties and forties, Manoilescu was in fact well known in certain parts of the Iberian world: several of his economic and political works had been published in those years in Spain, Portugal, Brazil and Chile. The most likely sources of inspiration were two articles appearing in Chile, one about Manoilescu and the other by him, in 1945 and 1947, respectively. They were published in *Economía,* the economics journal of the University of Chile, later to be edited by Aníbal Pinto Santa Cruz, one of ECLA's leading figures. In Argentina, however, Manoilescu seems to have had less influence than in Chile and Brazil.[79] Clearly, there were broad similarities between the two theories of unequal exchange which converged in the same policy prescription of industrialization. It is notable that Prebisch's focus on productivities within Centre and Periphery paralleled Manoilescu's. And both shared a common theoretical perspective: the separation of the critique of imperialism from that of capitalism.[80]

Prebisch was probably not directly influenced by Manoilescu, and there are no references to the Rumanian economist's works in Prebisch's early writings. Prebisch in 1977 confirmed the absence of such an influence, though he may have been familiar with Manoilescu from the brief discussions the latter's ideas received in the *Revista de Ciencias Económicas* in the late thirties. Nevertheless, Manoilescu's ideas – in the Latin American circles where they were known – probably helped pave the way for the acceptance of ECLA doctrines when they appeared in 1949.

Another source of possible inspiration for Prebisch in the latter forties was François Perroux's theory of the 'dominant economy' (1948).[81] His analysis focused on different elasticities of demand of the United States and 'the rest of the world', a perspective similar to one Prebisch was employing in the mid-1940s. Perroux was principally interested in 'dominated' econo-

---

[78] Jacob Viner, *International Trade and Economic Development* (Glencoe, Ill., 1952) [lectures delivered in 1950], pp. 61–4.

[79] See Edgar Mahn Hecker, 'Sobre los argumentos proteccionistas de List y Manoilesco' [sic], *Economía* (Chile), no. 17 (December, 1945): 59–70, Mihail Manoilesco, 'Productividad del trabajo y comercio exterior', *Economía,* no. 22–3 (September, 1947): 50–77. In the late 1930s Manoilescu's works had been discussed in the *Revista de Ciencias Económicas,* the journal of the UBA: FCE, where Prebisch had been a professor.

[80] Moreover, Manoilescu in 1940 and the structuralists Hans Singer and Celso Furtado in the 1950s independently worked out models of what is now called 'internal colonialism'. See Joseph L. Love, 'Modeling internal colonialism: history and prospect', *World Development,* 17, 6 (1989): 905–22.

[81] François Perroux, 'Esquisse d'une théorie de l'économie dominante', *Economie Appliquée,* 2–3 (August–September, 1948): 243–300.

mies of pre-Marshall Plan Europe, but he also argued that agricultual exporters had deteriorating terms of trade, owing to the import patterns of the dominant economy.[82] It seems unlikely that any genetic connection exists between Perroux and Prebisch, and it is notable that Perroux's emphasis on differential elasticities of demand is closer to Singer than Prebisch. Perroux in the 1930s, like Manoilescu, had explicitly espoused corporatism, and we may note that both share with ECLA a focus on monopoly relations (e.g., in labour and capital markets). But Manoilescu believed there was no necessary connection between his economic and political theories, and it seems inappropriate to label ECLA's economics 'neo-corporatist'.[83]

In fact, Prebisch's sources of inspiration were eclectic, as shown by his debt to the American neo-classical trade theorist Charles Kindleberger. In 1943 Kindleberger had published two articles calling for the industrialization of agricultural and raw material producers on the basis of long-term deterioration of the terms of trade, and Prebisch was familiar with at least one of them.[84] In 'International Monetary Stabilization', Kindleberger argued that the terms of trade moved against agricultural products 'because of the institutional organization of production' in industry, a references to internal and external economies and possibly to monopoly elements, and also because of differences in the elasticity of demand for agricultural and industrial products.[85]

Kindleberger pointed out that an agricultural country's increased productivity in primary activities under these conditions could only raise real income if the labour freed from agriculture were permitted to emigrate or found employment in industry – a proposition he borrowed from Colin Clark.[86] Otherwise, the terms of trade would move against the country, and it would have realized no benefit from the increased output of primary

---

[82] Ibid., p. 297.

[83] François Perroux, *Capitalisme et communauté de travail* (Paris, [1938]); Mihail Manoilescu, 'Doctrinele şi teoriile noastre in lumina criticei (răspuns D-lui Prof. Gh. Tasca)' *Anale Economice şi Statistice*, 20, 3–5 (March–May, 1937): 27. On ECLA's doctrines as neo-corporatism, see Charles W. Bergquist (ed.), *Alternative Approaches to the Problem of Development: A Selected and Annotated Bibliography* (Durham, N.C., 1979), p. xiii.

[84] Kindleberger, 'Planning for foreign investment', *American Economic Review*, 33, 1 (March, 1943), Supplement: 347–54; and 'International monetary stabilization', in Seymour E. Harris (ed.), *Postwar Economic Problems* (London, 1943), pp. 375–95. Prebisch cited the latter article in 'Observaciones sobre los planes monetarios internacionales', *Trimestre Económico*, 11, 2 (July–September, 1944): 195–6, though he did so in order to contest the American's references to the behaviour of the Argentine economy.

[85] Kindleberger, 'International monetary stabilization', p. 378.

[86] Ibid., p. 377, citing Clark, *The Economics of 1960* (1942).

goods. But domestic industry need not be as efficient as that abroad: an agricultural country's real income would be increased if, 'at some level of costs, labor displaced from agriculture can produce industrial products previously imported to enable part of the proceeds of an unchanged volume of exports to be spent upon other types of imports', Kindleberger wrote, thereby endorsing import-substitution industrialization.[87]

Looking ahead to the post-war era, Kindleberger foresaw disequilibria in the international trading system. A specific instance was the case of two countries with differing marginal propensities to import. For the country heavily dependent on exports and having a high propensity to import, a rise in exports could eventually produce an unfavourable balance of trade. 'It may be suggested that the United States has a comparatively low propensity to import and a low ratio of exports to national income, whereas the rest of the world has a relatively high elasticity of demand for United States exports of manufactured goods and a relatively high ratio of exports to income'.[88] One may infer the external imbalance was, potentially at least, a structural problem. In fact, at Prebisch's seminar on central banking in Mexico in 1944, he cited Kindleberger's thesis that the U.S. would have a persistent trade imbalance with the rest of the world because of disparities in demand elasticities. At the time, Prebisch was not certain the thesis was valid,[89] but later decided it was. Kindleberger's contribution to Prebisch's original structuralism thus seems large.

In any case, ECLA's theses, from their initial appearance in 1949, were hotly contested by neo-classical trade theorists, such as Viner. The economics profession in 1948–9 had just been treated to a formal demonstration by Paul Samuelson that, under certain conventional (but unrealistic) assumptions, trade could serve as a complete substitute for the movement of factors of production from one country to another, indicating that international trade could potentially equalize incomes among nations. Thus the less rigorous, but much more realistic, arguments of Prebisch and Singer burst upon the scene just after Samuelson had raised neoclassical trade theory to new heights of elegance, and against this theory new ideas would have to struggle.[90] In particular, the terms-of-trade thesis came

---

[87] Kindleberger, 'International Monetary Stabilization', pp. 378–9.
[88] Ibid., p. 381. The writer was referring both to income- and price-elasticity (p. 380).
[89] Prebisch, in Banco Central, *La creación*, I, pp. 530–1.
[90] Albert O. Hirschman, 'A Generalized Linkage Approach to Development, with Special Reference to Staples', *Economic Development and Cultural Change* 25, 1977 supplement, p. 68. Samuelson's articles were 'International Trade and the Equalisation of Factor Prices', *Economic Journal*, 58 (June, 1948): 163–84 and 'International Factor-price Equalisation once again', in ibid., 59 (June, 1949): 181–97.

under severe attack, as the validity of the data was challenged on a variety of grounds.[91]

ECLA: THE HALCYON YEARS

Despite the disputations that ensued, the terms-of-trade argument was a point of departure for a structuralist school which would seek to restrict the applicability of neo-classical economics to Latin America, and by extension to all underdeveloped countries. In this endeavour Prebisch was able to attract to, or retain in, his agency a pleiad of talented economists in the early years, including Aníbal Pinto, Jorge Ahumada, and Pedro Vuscovic, all of Chile; Aldo Ferrer of Argentina; Juan Noyola Vázquez and Víctor Urquidi of Mexico; and Celso Furtado of Brazil. These men were entering economics just as the field was becoming a profession in a number of Latin American countries.

Furtado, who joined the ECLA staff shortly before Prebisch officially took over, quickly drew further conclusions from Prebisch's analysis of the business cycle and high import co-efficients. Arguing that income tended to concentrate in Brazil during the upswing of the cycle, owing to a highly elastic labour supply, he then hypothesized that much of the effect of the Keynesian multiplier 'leaked' abroad, owing to the high propensity to import. Furtado anticipated, by four years, W. Arthur Lewis's famous analysis of an infinitely elastic labour supply as the source of wage 'stickiness' in underdeveloped countries. Such analysis, of course, pointed again to the importance of an industrialization policy.[92]

According to a study of ECLA's theoretical innovations by Octavio Rodrí-

---

[91] The principal arguments and sources in this long debate have been summarized and evaluated by John Spraos, who concludes that Prebisch was right about long-term deterioration of net barter terms of trade for 1870–1939, but that the trend was weaker than Prebisch thought. Furthermore, for 1900–75, Spraos concludes the data were trendless. Yet Prebisch would still argue, one assumes, that anything less than a *favourable* trend for primary products would show that the Centre was benefiting more than the Periphery in the trading process (assuming greater technological productivity gains in the centre). See Spraos, 'The statistical debate on the net barter terms of trade between primary commodities and manufactures', *Economic Journal*, 90 (March, 1980): 107–28, esp. p. 126. More recent studies of long-term data have tended to support Prebisch and Singer. For an extensive review of the literature, generally supporting Spraos's findings, see Dimitris Diakosavvas and Pasquale L. Scandizzo, 'Trends in the terms of trade of primary commodities, 1900–1982: the controversy and its origins', *Economic Development and Cultural Change*, 39, 2 (January, 1991), p. 237 (on Spraos).

[92] Celso Furtado, 'Características gerais da economia brasileira', *Revista Brasileira de Economia*, 4, 1 (March, 1950), p. 11; W. Arthur Lewis, 'Economic Development with Unlimited Supplies of Labour', *Manchester School*, 22 (May, 1954): 132–91. ECLA was also referring to highly-elastic labour supplies in 1950, and it is not clear whether Furtado introduced this concept.

guez, a former staff economist, its major theoretical contributions, beyond its analysis of the terms of trade, have fallen in the areas of problems of industrialization; the analysis of structural obstacles to development; and the related problem of the causes of inflation. Rodríguez further argues, in a work which is far from uncritical, that ECLA's period of greatest originality was from 1949 through the latter sixties, after which few new theses were presented.[93] Other contributions cited in ECLA publications were the promotion of Latin American economic integration, implicit in the agenda of the 1949 'manifesto'; 'programming' or planning economic development; and helping to create the Inter-American Development Bank (IDB) and the U.N. Conference on Trade and Development (UNCTAD).[94] Although some governments in the 1950s, notably Brazil's, openly acknowledged ECLA as a source of their developmentalist policies, Argentina's *desarrollistas* were quick to distance themselves from ECLA, possibly because of Prebisch's previous activity in national policy formation.[95] In any event, such activities of ECLA were in applied fields, not theory, and many policy prescriptions had little success, as noted below, when implemented by Latin American governments. Yet regional integration, part of ECLA's strategy from 1958, began to produce complementary industrial structures by the late 1960s. Intra-regional trade, and that in manufactures in particular, grew faster than extra-regional trade overall and that in manufactures between 1965 and 1979.[96]

Of the theoretical endeavours, the 'structuralist' explanation of inflation, a challenge to 'monetarism', is sometimes viewed as only second in importance to the terms-of-trade thesis.[97] Despite the fact that a number of ECLA economists helped develop it, it was never accorded recognition from ECLA as part of its official doctrine, though at times Prebisch himself endorsed it in the agency's publications.[98]

---

[93] Octavio Rodríguez, 'On the Conception of the Center Periphery System', *CEPAL Review*, January–June 1977, p. 196; Rodríguez, *La teoría del subdesarrollo de la CEPAL* (Mexico, D.F., 1980), p. 297. More strictly, Rodríguez believes ECLA's best years for theory ended with the 1950s: *La Teoría*, p. 15.

[94] CEPAL, *El aporte de las ideas-fuerza* (Santiago, 1978); CEPAL, *XXV años de la CEPAL* (Santiago, 1973), p. 34.

[95] For an instructive comparison of Argentine *desarrollismo* and Brazilian *desenvolvimentismo* in the 1950s and 1960s, analysing the greater success of the latter, see Kathryn A. Sikkink, *Ideas and Institutions: Developmentalism in Brazil and Argentina* (Ithaca, N.Y., 1991).

[96] Werner Baer, 'Import Substitution and Industrialization in Latin America: experiences and interpretations', *Latin American Research Review*, 7, 1 (1972) p. 104; Inter-American Development Bank, *Economic and Social Progress in Latin America: Economic Integration. 1984 Report* (Washington, D.C., n.d.), p. 98.

[97] For example, Ignacy Sachs, *The Discovery of the Third World* (Cambridge, Mass., 1976), p. 137.

[98] Raúl Prebisch, 'Economic Development or Monetary Stability: the false dilemma', *Economic Bulletin*

Inflation was more rampant in Latin America during most of the post-war decades than in all other areas of the world. The basic structuralist proposition was that *underlying* inflationary pressures derive from bottlenecks produced by retarded sectors, especially agriculture, whose backward state yields an inelastic supply, in the face of rapidly rising demand by the burgeoning urban masses. In Chile, where the analysis was first applied, the stagnation of the export sector was also recognized as a structural cause. Repeated devaluations to raise export earnings automatically boosted the price of imports. A related cause in this view was deteriorating terms of trade, fuelled by a demand for imports that rose faster than the demand for exports. Also associated with the foreign trade problem was a shift in the fiscal system: as exports stagnated, the relative weight of revenues provided by regressive domestic taxes tended to rise, allowing more income for the already import-orientated upper classes. To a lesser degree the ECLA economists noted as a cause of inflation national industrial monopolies and oligopolies, shielded by high tariffs, which could raise prices quickly.[99]

The several 'structural' features of inflation were distinguished from 'exogenous' or adventitious causes (for example, natural disasters, changes in the international market), and 'cumulative' causes (action by government and private groups to raise wages and prices in a climate of inflationary expectations). It is important to recognize that the thesis did not deny that orthodox 'monetarist' explanations of inflation had some validity – for example, that some supply inelasticities were caused by distortions in exchange rates and prices, following an inflationary spiral.

In a broad sense, 'structuralism', which received its name in the context of the analysis of inflation, owed something to the 'doctrine of market failure' that led to Keynesianism in Britain in the 1930s. More directly, Michál Kalecki, who had been at Oxford in the thirties and forties, published a seminal article on inflation in Mexico's *Trimestre Económico* in 1954; its influence on the structuralist school was acknowledged by Juan Noyola and the Chilean economist Osvaldo Sunkel.

for Latin America, 6, 1 (March, 1961): 1–25, esp. 3, where agriculture is cited as a structural cause of inflation (because of antiquated land-tenure systems). Rodríguez stresses personal, rather than official, contributions of *cepalistas* in *La Teoría del subdesarrollo*, pp. 4, 190. ECLA's *Aportes* and *XXV años* do not mention any contribution by ECLA as such on inflation.

[99] See Juan Noyola Vázquez, 'El desarrollo económico y la inflación en México y otros países latinoamericanos', *Investigaciones Económicas*, 16, 4 (1956): 603–18; Osvaldo Sunkel, 'Inflation in Chile: an unorthodox approach', *International Economic Papers*, no. 10 (1960): 107–31 [orig. in *Trimestre Económico* (1958)]; Rodríguez, *Teoría*, chapter 6.

Kalecki emphasized the 'inelasticity of agricultural supply and monopolistic tendencies in industry' in inflationary patterns in underdeveloped countries. Since inflation was due to 'basic disproportions in productive relations', it could not 'be prevented by purely financial [monetary] devices'.[100]

For the Latin Americans, this was not the whole story, for among other things the fact that Chile experienced major inflationary pressures while Mexico did not, had to be explained. Part of the answer for Noyola was that Mexico's agrarian reform had produced a more elastic supply of farm goods than latifundia-dominated Chile, but Noyola also emphasized that Chile had 'propagating mechanisms', while Mexico lacked them. The latter country had a large labour surplus which tended to depress the wage level, whereas Chile had a well-organized working class which sought to protect its share of national income.[101] Finally, one might argue that the structuralist interpretation of inflation was implicit in Prebisch's early observation that a given rise in income produced a more than proportional rise in imports, since imports were identified as a source of inflationary pressure, assuming, as ECLA did, that Latin America's terms of trade tend to deteriorate.

A number of ECLA economists, especially those concerned with Chile, developed the structuralist interpretation of inflation in the mid- and late fifties. The contributors were so numerous and the contributions so nearly simultaneous that attribution is difficult; but the Mexican Juan Noyola may have been the first in print to emphasize the role of the backward agrarian sector. He and the Chilean Aníbal Pinto in 1956 were the first to distinguish between 'structural' causes and 'propagating mechanisms' – fiscal policies, credit, and the wage-price spiral.[102]

The inherent weakness of the structuralist thesis on inflation as a policy guide is that any increase in economic efficiency – even if agriculture is the most notorious offender – will diminish 'basic' inflationary processes; 'it is therefore always possible to claim that inflation is due to the failure to carry out one particular improvement', and it can be associated with a

---

[100] Michál Kalecki, *Essays on Developing Economies* (Atlantic Highlands, N. J., 1976 [orig. Spanish edn, 1954]), pp. 50, 62.

[101] Noyola, 'El desarrollo', pp. 605, 608–612.

[102] Noyola, 'El desarrollo'; Aníbal Pinto in *La intervención del Estado* . . . (Santiago, 1956). On their priority, see Rodríguez, *Teoría,* p. 190. Furtado puts Noyola first in his memoir *A fantasia organisada* (Rio de Janeiro, 1985), p. 185. Other contributors include Osvaldo Sunkel, Jorge Ahumada, Jaime Barros, and Luis Escobar, all from Chile. Hirschman independently developed an analogous approach. See Albert O. Hirschman, 'Inflation in Chile', in his *Journeys toward Progress: Studies of Economic Policy-Making in Latin America* (New York, 1963), p. 213, note 1.

variety of social problems.[103] Therefore, the emphasis on 'underlying' or 'structural' causes could be interpreted in different ways: it could be used as a rationale either for government-sponsored reform, or, in the absence of reform, to explain government powerlessness to stem an inflationary tide. Structuralism became the dominant interpretation of inflation – and a stimulus for reform – in two Latin American administrations in the 1960s – those of João Goulart in Brazil (1961–4) and Eduardo Frei in Chile (in his first eighteen months of office, 1964–6). Though the structuralist view of inflation has seen its heyday, economists are still debating its merits, and econometric testing is cited for and against it, as in the case of the terms-of-trade thesis.[104] Structuralists seemed to have lost their influence on the inflation issue because of their relative neglect of monetarist measures necessary in times of hyperinflation.[105]

The reformist views implicit in structuralism were part of an increasing concern with social issues by the ECLA staff, a concern that quickened with the growing radicalism of the Cuban Revolution after 1959. More dramatic than ECLA's contribution to the Alliance for Progress (for which it helped win acceptance for the goals of agrarian reform, commodity price stabilization, and economic integration) was Prebisch's call for social reform in his 1963 essay, *Toward a Dynamic Development Policy for Latin America*. Here he appealed for specific reforms in agrarian structure, income distribution, and education.[106] Beyond this, he wrote that Latin American industrialization was based on the technology appropriate to the labour-saving needs of the developed countries, and that the consumption patterns of Latin America's upper strata exacerbated the problem through their preferences for capital-intensive consumer goods. It was 'absolutely necessary [*ineludible*] for the state to deliberately compress the consumption of the upper strata'. Given the sharply skewed pattern of income

[103] Hirschman, 'Inflation in Chile', p. 216.

[104] See, for example, Susan M. Wachter, 'Structuralism vs. Monetarism: Inflation in Chile', in Jere Behrman and James Hanson (eds), *Short-term Macroeconomic Policy in Latin America* (Cambridge, Mass., 1979), pp. 227–55, esp. 247 (qualified support for structuralism); Raouf Kahil, *Inflation and Economic Development in Brazil: 1946–1963* (Oxford, 1973), p. 330 (against structuralism). Luis Cáceres and F. J. Jiménez have concluded that two structuralist variables, the dynamism of investment and the elasticity of agricultural supply, are basic causes of Latin American inflation. Cáceres and Jiménez, 'Estructuralismo, monetarismo e inflación en Latinoamerica', *Trimestre Económico* (May–June, 1983): 151–68.

[105] See Albert O. Hirschman, 'The Social and Political Matrix of Inflation: Elaboration of the Latin American Experience', in Albert O. Hirschman, *Essays in Trespassing: Economics to Politics and Beyond* (Cambridge, 1981), p. 183.

[106] Raúl Prebisch, *Hacia una dinámica del desarrollo latinoamericano* (Montevideo, 1967 [orig., 1963]), pp. 41, 52.

distribution and the upper classes' high propensity to consume, deteriorating domestic terms of trade between agriculture and industry had their explanation 'in the insufficient dynamism of development, which does not facilitate the absorption of the labor force [because such absorption is] not required by the slow growth of demand [for agricultural products] and the increase of productivity in primary activities. This insufficient dynamism prevents a rise of wages in agriculture parallel to the increase in productivity, and . . . [thus] primary production loses in part or in whole the gains from its technological progress'. Prebisch further denounced the actual pattern of industrialization in Latin America, pointing out that the exaggerated pattern of protection had allowed grossly inefficient industries to arise. Latin America had, on average, the highest tariffs in the world, depriving it of economies of scale and opportunities to specialize for export.[107] In retrospect this 1963 statement anticipates the somber Prebisch of *Capitalismo periférico* (1981).

In the same period Prebisch acknowledged that 'social' as well as economic forces had to be 'influenced' if reforms were to be achieved.[108] To this end, in 1962 ECLA established an annex called the Latin American Institute for Economic and Social Planning (ILPES). Meanwhile, ECLA's long-standing proposals for restructuring the international trading system were largely shifted in 1963 to a new U.N. agency, UNCTAD, which, under Prebisch's leadership as its first executive secretary, was clearly the international body most appropriate for such efforts.

ECLA's reformism had definite limits, however, since it was an international agency whose constituent members were western hemisphere states and disengaging European colonial powers. At a theoretical level, it always assumed that the state was an exogenous factor in the economic and social system. In the latter 1960s its reformist efforts were still focussed on pressuring governments of developed countries to liberalize their trade policies, thus assisting the new UNCTAD, and persuading Latin American states to accept a greater degree of regional integration. Furthermore, ECLA had always welcomed foreign investment in Latin America, under certain conditions, and this attitude patently ruled out a number of radical strategies.[109]

The reformism of the sixties was conditioned by, and for an increasing

---

[107] Ibid., pp. 21, 41, 90, 99.
[108] Prebisch, 'Economic Development or Monetary Stability', p. 24.
[109] Girvan, 'Development of Dependency Economics', p. 8; ECLA, *International Cooperation in a Latin American Development Policy* (New York, 1954), p. 15.

number of structuralists, made irrelevant by, a long evolution of ECLA's views on its initial key policy recommendation – import-substitution industrialization (ISI). An ISI policy had seemed a brilliant success, especially in Brazil in Mexico, during the 1950s, but success owed in part to unusually high commodity prices during the Korean War. In the latter fifties, ECLA began to consider the complexities of ISI. By 1957 the organization had distinguished between two types, which in the 1960s would be seen as phases, of import substitution. The first involved the relatively easy substitution of simple domestically produced consumer goods for previously imported items. The second, more difficult, type involved the production of intermediate goods and consumer durables, a shift from 'horizontal' to 'vertical' ISI – so denominated because of the substitution of simple goods on a broad front in the first phase, and in the second, an integrated line of production of fewer final goods and their inputs. A third phase, the production of capital goods, would ensue at a later date.[110]

In 1956 ECLA had still assumed the existence of a threshold in structural changes in the economy, beyond which 'dependence on external contingencies' would diminish. Yet the following year the agency first suggested that dependence on 'events overseas' might even increase as ISI advanced; all the same, it still held that 'import substitution' consisted of lowering 'the import content of supplies for the home market'.[111]

Argentina was Latin America's most industrialized country, and despite its unique political phenomenon of *peronismo,* ECLA tended to view it in 1957 as a trendsetter for other Latin American nations. Argentina, ECLA noted, had reduced its imports of finished goods to one-third the total dollar amount. Yet its declining capacity to import had meant that reducing the importation of consumer goods was not sufficient to contain balance-of-payment difficulties; capital goods and fuels also had to be reduced, and this fact was reducing the rate of growth. Chile was seen as facing similar though less dire problems. ECLA seemed to wonder aloud whether the Argentine experience was the future of Latin America. Two conclusions followed: that primary exports and food production for domestic consumption had to be increased (the latter to relieve pressure on

[110] ECLA, *Economic Survey of Latin America: 1956* (New York, 1957), p. 116; ECLA, *The Process of Industrial Development in Latin America* (New York, 1966), pp. 19–20; Rodríguez, *Teoría,* pp. 202–3.

[111] 'The Situation in Argentina and the New Economic Policy', *Economic Bulletin,* 1, 1 (January, 1956): 30; ECLA, 'Preliminary Study of the Effects of Postwar Industrialisation on Import Structures and External Vulnerability in Latin America', in *Economic Survey 1956,* p. 115.

imports), and that a region-wide common market must be developed to assure the future development of efficient manufacturing industries.[112]

Why should industrialization bring rising import requirements in its train? Using a simple two-sector model, Furtado in 1958 explained the problem as one in which, by assumption, the advanced sector, A, had a larger import coefficient than the backward sector, B. As the economy developed, A's co-efficient grew ever larger as a share of the whole economy's coefficient, and *pari passu* the average import co-efficient tended to rise.[113] If the terms of trade were deteriorating, the pressures on the balance of payments became even more acute.

Thus, for ECLA economists in the mid- and late fifties, the import requirements in the later stages of ISI, unless offset by capital inflows or rising exports, could cause 'strangulation' – a favourite ECLA metaphor for stagnation caused by insufficient imports of capital goods and other industrial inputs. As a partial solution to stuttering ISI, ECLA in 1957–8 formally appealed to its sponsoring states for a Latin American common market, which, ECLA held, would provide incentives (through economies of scale) for the production of capital and intermediate goods.[114]

Yet in its early years the Latin American Free Trade Area, established in 1960, was only an expression of hope for alleviating the ills associated with ISI. Already in 1959 Prebisch had observed that the more economically advanced Latin American countries were becoming increasingly the hostages of external events, because they had compressed their imports to the absolute essentials for the maintenance of growth. Two years later he wrote, 'It remains a paradox that industrialization, instead of helping greatly to soften the internal impact of external fluctuations, is bringing us a new and unknown type of external vulnerability.'[115]

The agonizing reappraisal of ISI came in 1964. In that year an ECLA study, though blaming Latin America's declining rates of growth on deteriorating terms of trade in the 1950s, also noted that 80 per cent of regional imports now consisted of fuels, intermediate goods, and capital equipment. Consequently, there was little left to 'squeeze' in the

---

[112] ECLA, 'Preliminary Study', pp. 128, 150, 151.

[113] Celso Furtado, 'The External Disequilibrium in the Underdeveloped Economies', *Indian Journal of Economics* 38, 151 (April, 1958), p. 406.

[114] 'Bases for the Formation of the Latin American Regional Market', *Economic Bulletin*, 3, 1 (March, 1958): 4. The seventh session of ECLA in 1957 adopted a resolution calling for steps toward the creation of a region-wide common market.

[115] Prebisch, 'Commercial Policy', p. 268; Prebisch, 'Economic Development or Monetary Stability', p. 5.

region's import profile to favour manufacturing.[116] Meanwhile, two monographs highly critical of ISI appeared in the agency's *Economic Bulletin* – one on the Brazilian experience in particular, and the other on Latin America in general.[117] These articles pointed to problems that by the 1960s were beginning to affect other parts of the Third World as well.

Examining the Brazilian case in the fifties and early sixties, Maria da Conceição Tavares argued that ISI had failed because of the lack of dynamism of the export sector, coupled with the fact that ISI had not diminished capital and fuel import requirements. Other problems were the apparent ceilings on the domestic market, owing in part to highly-skewed income distribution, which also determined the structure of demand; the constellation of productive resources – for example, the lack of skilled labour; and the capital-intensive nature of industrialization in more advanced phases of ISI, which implied little labour absorption. In the advanced stages of ISI, Tavares contended, the low labour absorption of manufacturing tended to exaggerate rather than to terminate the dualism of Brazil's economy. Among other things, she argued that bottlenecks in the food supply, partly due to the antiquated agrarian structure, put unsustainable pressures on the import bill. Tavares recommended agrarian reform as a partial solution.[118]

In the same number of the *Bulletin,* Santiago Macario wrote a blistering critique of the way in which ISI had actually been practised in Latin America, following up Prebisch's observation the previous year, 1963, that the region had the highest tariffs in the world. Macario observed that the governments of the four most industrialized countries – Argentina, Brazil, Mexico and Chile – had used ISI as a deliberate strategy to counteract a persistent lack of foreign exchange, and to create employment for expanding populations. But in those four countries, and in most of the others of the region, protectionism, primarily in the form of tariff and exchange policies, had been irrational, in that there was no consistent policy to develop the most viable and efficient manufacturing industries. On the contrary, the most inefficient industries had received the greatest protection; there had been over-diversification of manufacturing in small

---

[116] ECLA, *The Economic Development of Latin America in the Postwar Period* (New York, 1964), pp. 14, 21.

[117] Maria da Conceição Tavares, 'The Growth and Decline of Import Substitution in Brazil', and Santiago Macario, 'Protectionism and Industrialization in Latin America', in *Economic Bulletin for Latin America,* 9 (1964): 1–59, and 61–101, respectively.

[118] Tavares, 'Growth and Decline', pp. 7–8, 11, 12, 55.

markets in the 'horizontal' phase; and these factors had contributed, in some instances, to real dissavings.[119]

Nor did Latin American manufactures hold their own in international markets, continued Macario, at a time when exchange earnings had become critical for the future of industrialization. On the positive side, there were tendencies in the early sixties to abolish exchange controls, quantitative restrictions, and multiple exchange rates, and a related tendency to begin tariff reduction; yet Macario asserted that Latin American tariffs were still being built on a makeshift basis, resulting in a gross misallocation of scarce resources.[120]

Rational criteria were needed to develop industries – such as the use of factors in greatest abundance (e.g. labour), or the promotion of industries that could earn foreign exchange. Equally important, thought Macario, was the establishment for each country of a 'uniform level of net protection'. Overall, his thesis was less that ECLA's policy prescriptions had initially been wrong – which Tavares's analysis in some ways showed – than that the region's governments had flagrantly ignored ECLA's technical advice, pursuing, in Macario's words, 'import substitution at any cost'.[121] Though Hirschman suggested four years later that Tavares and Macario had issued the death certificate of ISI somewhat prematurely, other scholars soon added new charges, such as ISI's having increased the concentration of income with regard both to social class and to region (within countries).[122]

FROM STRUCTURALISM TO DEPENDENCY

ECLA had voiced its first doubts in 1956 whether industry, in the world region with the fastest growing population, could absorb surplus labour from agriculture; nine years later its survey of ISI showed that non-agricultural employment in Latin America had increased from 13 to 36 million persons between 1925 and 1960, but that only five of the 23

---

[119] Macario, 'Protectionism', pp. 65–7, 77, 81.

[120] Ibid., pp. 67, 78, 81.

[121] Ibid., pp. 67 (quotation), 84 (formula for 'uniform level of net protection'), 87.

[122] *Inter alia*, Hirschman argued that the failure of ISI was not inevitable, but depended on the interaction of social and political factors with economic elements. See his 'The Political Economy of Import-substituting Industrialization in Latin America' [orig., 1968] in Albert O. Hirschman, *A Bias for Hope* (New Haven, Conn., 1971), pp. 85–123, esp. 103. On ISI failures, see the discussion of Sunkel and Furtado in the following section, and the literature surveyed in Baer, 'Import Substitution', pp. 95–122, esp. 107.

million additional employees were absorbed in industrial activities.[123] Furtado, writing over his own signature, contemporaneously noted that while Latin America's industrial output in the 1950s had risen 6.2 per cent a year, industrial employment had risen only 1.6 per cent annually, about half Latin America's average population growth rate. The problem in part was the labour-saving technology which the Periphery had imported from the Centre.[124]

Furtado explained that ISI was fundamentally different from European industrialization in the eighteenth and nineteenth centuries. In the classic phase, technology continually cheapened the relative cost of capital goods, creating the possibility of solutions to social problems. In twentieth-century Latin America, unlike nineteenth-century Europe, technology was exogenous to the regional economy, and was specifically designed for the requirements of the developed countries. Factor absorption, therefore, did not depend on the relative availability of factors, but on the type of technology used, and over this matter Latin Americans could exercise little choice.[125] Among other things, they had to compete in their own national markets with high-technology, multinational corporations.

This tendency by the mid-sixties to take the longer view and seek lessons in history was partly the result of the fact that, from ECLA's perspective, Latin America now had thirty-five years of import-substituting experience; but it was also due in part to the inclination to take a long-term perspective that was part of ECLA's original style. Prebisch's 1949 *Survey* had tried to view the sweep of economic history from the 1880s to the mid-twentieth century for the region, and in more detail for the four most industrialized nations. In some ways this volume was a model for country case studies to be carried out between 1959 and 1963 – Furtado on Brazil, Pinto on Chile, Aldo Ferrer on Argentina, and later, Osvaldo Sunkel and Pedro Paz on the whole region.[126] Furtado's study, however, derived principally from his pre-

---

[123] ECLA, 'The Situation in Argentina', p. 42; ECLA, *The Process of Industrial Development* (New York, 1966 [Sp. orig., 1965]), p. 38.

[124] Celso Furtado, *Subdesenvolvimento e estagnação na América Latina* 2nd edn (Rio de Janeiro, 1968) [orig., 1966]), pp. 9–10. As noted above, Prebisch had previously made this point in *Hacia una dinámica*, p. 38.

[125] Ibid., pp. 9–11. A later perspective permits a slightly more sanguine view of industrial employment than that ECLA and Furtado faced in the mid-sixties: Although industry in Argentina and Chile absorbed a smaller percentage of the labour force in 1981 than in 1965, in 1981 it employed a larger share in Brazil, Mexico, Colombia and Venezuela. But in no Latin American country in 1981 did industry account for as much as a third of the labour force. International Bank for Reconstruction and Development, *World Development Report: 1985* (New York, 1985), pp. 214–15.

[126] Celso Furtado, *Formação econômica do Brasil* (Rio de Janeiro, 1959); Aníbal Pinto Santa Cruz, *Chile, un caso de desarrollo frustrado* (Santiago, 1959); Aldo Ferrer, *La economía argentina: las etapas de su*

ECLA interests in the defining features of colonial Brazil. In fact, more than anyone else at ECLA, Furtado was responsible for 'historicizing' structuralist analysis, and departing from cyclical concerns.[127]

Explicit in the 1949 *Survey* was the thesis that industrialization in Latin America had historically occurred in periods of world crisis; that is, ECLA viewed development as occurring through the agency of 'external shocks', in Celso Furtado's phrase.[128] For the Brazilian case, Furtado pointed to rapid industrial growth in the Depression, partly due to 'the socialization of losses' through exchange devaluation, which none the less helped maintain domestic demand.[129] In Brazil, Furtado viewed expansionary fiscal and monetary policies during the Depression of the 1930s as a form of unwitting Keynesianism. His views on Brazilian industrialization touched off a long debate. Yet it now seems clear for Brazil, as for the other most-industrialized countries, that the two world wars and the Depression were less important in producing 'inward-directed growth' than was believed by some contemporaries to these events, and by ECLA economists later. A now widely held view is that investment in industry (capacity) grew in line with export earnings for the period 1900–45, while output (but not capacity) tended to rise during the 'shocks', when imports had to be curtailed. Capacity could not grow appreciably during the Depression for lack of exchange credits to buy capital goods and inputs, nor during the world wars because of the unavailability of capital goods and fuels from the belligerent powers.

Thus the perceived failure of ISI as a historical process – and perhaps the growing suspicion that industrial growth had varied directly and not inversely with export earnings – was a leading cause of pessimism among structuralists in the mid- and late sixties. There were reasons for pessi-

desarrollo y problemas actuales (Mexico, D. F., 1963); Osvaldo Sunkel and Pedro Paz, *El subdesarrollo latinoamericano y la teoría del desarrollo* (Mexico, D. F., 1970). Later a more specialized structuralist work appeared on Mexico: Villareal's *El desequilibrio externo*, in note 22. Villareal argues, however, that structuralism accounts more adequately for Mexico's external disequilibrium in the period 1939–58 than in 1959–70.

127 Furtado's pre-ECLA dissertation does not contain much formal economic analysis of any kind. Celso Furtado, 'L'économie coloniale brésilienne (XVIe et XVIIe siècles): Eléments d'histoire economique appliqués' (Ph.D. thesis, Faculté de Droit, U. de Paris, 1948); but *A economia brasileira* (Rio de Janeiro, 1954) offers a structuralist analysis of Brazil's economic history.

128 See ECLA, *Economic Survey 1949* (Sp. orig., 1950), p. 97, citing the case of Argentina; Furtado, 'Características gerais', p. 28.

129 See Furtado, 'Características gerais'. For a similar thesis about the socialization of losses through exchange depreciation and government maintenance of aggregate demand, see ECLA, *Economic Survey 1949*, pp. 60, 171–72. For a summary of Furtado's arguments, best developed in *Formação econômica do Brasil*, and the subsequent debate, see Wilson Suzigan, *Indústria brasileira: origem e desenvolvimento* (São Paulo, 1986), pp. 21–73.

mism as well in a variety of other areas, both immediate and long-term. ECLA's efforts at 'programming' – calculating required savings and inputs to meet government-specified development targets – had had some success in the 1950s (notably in Brazil during the presidency of Juscelino Kubitschek, 1956–61), but were increasingly seen as futile exercises in the 1960s. ECLA publications were now criticizing the agency's own earlier efforts in the field for failing to take into account 'social and political viability' as an essential criterion in the attempt to set and meet realistic development targets. Another problem, perceived in 1966 and having an obvious social dimension, was the rising degree of income inequality among social classes in Argentina, usually viewed as the pacesetter.[130] The problem of increasing income concentration was already observable in Mexico, and would be so in Brazil after the census of 1970.

Meanwhile Sunkel, writing in his own name in 1966, revealed a new pessimism characteristic of structuralist thinking in the mid-sixties.[131] Among the problems he identified as without apparent solution were the decline in the (perceived) rate of growth of Latin America's domestic product from 1950 to 1965; the persistent, rather than diminishing, dependency on the foreign sector, with its deteriorating terms of trade, as the key to growth; the concentration of income in the upper income brackets; and the falling share of industry in non-agricultural employment, as population climbed higher. The last observation seemed to show the failure of the structuralist programme of industrialization as the cornerstone of development. Sunkel wrote that 'the record of development policy in Latin America with respect to the area of employment opportunities is very poor indeed, and the long-term prospect is frightening'.[132]

Other structuralist criticisms of the Latin American economies in the latter sixties included the perception of a sustained balance-of-payments disequilibrium and a 'debt spiral' for the most industrialized countries, and of high rates of inflation, with consequent social tensions and political instability. For ECLA, these problems were chiefly structural problems – the agrarian pattern of latifundium and minifundium; industrial structure

---

[130] Rodríguez, *Teoría*, p. 223 (on planning); 'Income Distribution in Argentina', *Economic Bulletin for Latin America*, 11, 1 (1966): 106–31.

[131] Sunkel, 'The Structural Background of Development Problems in Latin America' in Charles T. Nisbet (ed.), *Latin America: Problems in Economic Development* (New York, 1969 [Sp. orig., 1966]), pp. 3–37. For an indication of a more generalized pessimism at the time, see the essays by Aníbal Pinto, Víctor Urquidi, Celso Furtado, Hélio Jaguaribe, Osvaldo Sunkel, and Jacques Chonchol, in Claudio Véliz (ed.), *Obstacles to Change in Latin America* (London, 1965).

[132] Sunkel, 'Structural Background', pp. 7, 11, 13, 23.

(indivisibilities of scale, tending to produce under-utilization of capital, and high capital density, with the implication of low labour absorption); the rigidly stratified social structure; and the consequent maldistribution of income.[133]

On the political front, another source of pessimism was the end of the 'developmentalist' experiment in Brazil, where the populist regime of Goulart was ousted by military coup in 1964; two years later, a coup in Argentina installed a conservative and authoritarian government. Though less dramatic, the inability of the Frei government in Chile to carry through major economic and social reforms was likewise a disappointment. Furthermore, the diminished interest of the United States under Lyndon Johnson in the reform and development goals of the Alliance for Progress, coupled with the U.S. invasion of the Dominican Republic in 1965 – the first such action in Latin America since the twenties – was a blow to reformism.

More broadly, the intellectual and political climate in which dependency analysis would be received was radicalized by the international resistance to the U.S. war in Vietnam, of which the Dominican intervention was a consequence – to prevent a 'second Cuba' and the danger of two simultaneous long-term military engagements. Resistance to the Viet Nam War interacted with anti-establishment protest in a variety of countries, often led by students, and reached a peak in the demonstrations and repressions of 1968–70.

Yet there was a tendency, if not yet a dominant one, for official economic policy in Latin America to move in a contrary direction from the radicalism of the streets. Anti-ECLA orthodoxy made its reappearance during the mid-1960s in the programmes of 'monetarists' who set policy in the anti-populist, anti-inflationary, and authoritarian regimes of Generals Humberto Castelo Branco in Brazil and Juan Carlos Onganía in Argentina. In Brazil, at the end of the decade, it was a professedly neo-classical economist – though hardly an orthodox one, because of his use of state intervention – Antônio Delfim Neto, who implemented ECLA's earlier calls for the export of manufactures.[134] Liberal orthodoxy would assume the dominant position at the policy level under most military regimes in the 1970s, though in Brazil the state's role in the economy expanded. The

---

[133] Rodríguez, *Teoría*, pp. 187–88, 214–17.
[134] In 1957 ECLA had still denied that Latin America could compete in manufactured exports on the world market, but in the 1960s the agency viewed the export of manufactures as a requirement for continued development. ECLA, *Economic Survey 1956*, p. 151; Rodríguez, *Teoría*, p. 222.

rising star of neo-classical orthodoxy and associated policies in the late 1960s, even if less distant from structuralist policy in practice, as in the Brazilian case, probably contributed to a frustration in intellectual circles which prepared the way for the acceptance of dependency analysis.

In this regard, Chile's experience under its first Christian Democratic administration was probably even more important than that of Brazil, though Chile's military coup was still several years away. The host country for ECLA, Chile was the site of a major reformist experiment under the administration of Eduardo Frei for the six years beginning in November, 1964. Jorge Ahumada, Frei's chief economic advisor and a former ECLA analyst, in the economic plan of 1965 wanted concurrently to achieve faster growth, a redistribution of income (in part through agrarian reform), and the elimination of the structural causes of inflation. After an initial success in stimulating economic growth through expansionary policies, the Frei government saw the growth rate fall from an average of 6.0 per cent in 1965–6 to 3.2 per cent in 1967–70. The rate of investment also dipped in the Frei years, as employers became wary of the government's social experiments, and unemployment rose. To contain inflation, from late 1966 Frei cut government expenditures, but without notable success: the rate of inflation, held to 17.0 per cent in 1966, averaged 28.5 per cent in 1967–70. The foreign sector, so important in structuralist analysis, was not responsible for these difficulties, as copper prices remained high, along with exports and imports in general.[135] Consequently, the Frei experience revealed the enormous political difficulties of implementing ECLA-inspired reforms as envisioned in Prebisch's *Toward a Dynamic Development Policy* and other structuralist writings of the 1960s.

Ironically, in the retrospect of the 1990s, a rather favourable economic climate in Latin America can be seen in the 1960s, the years in which dependency analysis emerged. The rate of population growth in Latin America, highest among the world's major regions, had peaked in the early 1960s, and had begun a long-term decline – something Sunkel could not have known in the middle of the decade. The international economy was more dynamic in the period 1960–73 (ending with the OPEC oil price shock) than in any other period in the post-war era,

---

[135] Sergio Bitar, *Transição, socialismo e democracia: Chile com Allende*, trans. by Rita Braga (São Paulo, 1980), pp. 49–50; Aníbal Pinto, 'Desarrollo económico y relaciones sociales', in Aníbal Pinto, Sergio Aranda and Alberto Martínez, *Chile, hoy* (Mexico, D. F., 1970), p. 47; Enrique Sierra, *Tres ensayos de estabilización en Chile: Las políticas aplicadas en el decenio 1956–1966* (Santiago, 1970), pp. 91–4, 183–5.

permitting diversification of Latin American exports, including manufactures. Perhaps most ironical was the fact that the post-war economic growth rate for the region reached a peak in 1965–73, and in the same years, industrial output in the region averaged 8.0 per cent annually, a higher rate than in any other period before or since.[136] But analysts of the mid-sixties, in the midst or on the cusp of these developments, had no way of knowing Latin America was beginning its most successful period of economic growth and diversification.

At all events ECLA's theories and policy prescriptions were not only challenged by the neo-classical right, but also by a heterodox left, some of whose members had been leading figures in ECLA itself, notably Furtado and Sunkel. This new left would quickly make 'dependency theory' famous. Although ECLA itself had produced nothing if not a kind of dependency analysis, the new variety was set off by its more clear-cut 'historicizing' and 'sociologizing' tendencies in both its reformist and radical versions.

Not only had Furtado and Sunkel in the mid-sixties adopted an explicitly historical view of development, noted above, but Furtado now elaborated on an earlier contention that development and underdevelopment were linked. As early as 1959 he had written that there was a 'tendency for industrial economies, as a result of their form of growth, to inhibit the growth of primary economies', and he expanded on the idea in *Development and Underdevelopment* two years later. In 1966 he argued that because the two processes were historically associated, underdevelopment could not be a phase in the passage to development.[137]

[136] See chapter by Ricardo Ffrench-Davis, Oscar Muñoz and José Gabriel Palma, 'The Latin American economies, 1950–1990', in *Cambridge History of Latin America*, vol. VI, part 1 (1994).

[137] Celso Furtado, *A operação Nordeste* (Rio de Janeiro, 1959), p. 13; Furtado, *Desenvolvimento e subdesenvolvimento* (Rio de Janeiro, 1961), p. 180 and passim; Furtado, *Subdesenvolvimento*, pp. 3–4. These statements lend credence to a claim of priority for Furtado as the first theorist of dependency, but I believe H. W. Arndt has exaggerated in tracing Furtado's dependency position back to *The Economic Growth of Brazil* (Berkeley, Cal., 1963 [Portuguese orig., 1959]), which in my view is more correctly described as the full historicization of structuralism. (See Arndt, *Economic Development*, p. 120.) In any event, in a recent retrospective Furtado dates his major contributions to dependency analysis in books and articles published between 1970 and 1978. In these works, Furtado views as a central feature of underdevelopment the adoption of the consumption patterns of the developed West by the upper strata of underdeveloped areas, as these regions entered the international division of labour. This process was the 'result of the surplus generated through static comparative advantages in foreign trade. It is the highly dynamic nature of the modernized component of consumption that brings dependence into the technological realm and makes it part of the production structure'. Novel items of consumption require increasingly sophisticated techniques and increasing amounts of capital. But capital accumulation is associated with income concentration, so industrialization 'advances simultaneously with the concentration of income'. Celso Furtado, 'Underdevelopment: to conform or reform', in Gerald Meier (ed.), *Pioneers in*

In his analysis of economic history, Furtado also introduced the element of social class. He argued in 1964 that class struggle had historically been the engine of economic growth in the West: workers 'attack' through organization in order to raise their share of the national product and capitalists 'counterattack' by introducing labour-saving technology. Since labour is unorganized in the Periphery, above all in the rural sector, he asserted, the process fails to work there. These *marxisant* propositions are perhaps less surprising than they appear at first glance, since they are an extrapolation of Prebisch's initial explanation of declining terms of trade.[138] Furtado's several essays in the latter sixties, written largely in exile in Paris, pointed to the need for an analysis of the whole capitalist system, Centre and Periphery together.

Another Brazilian, Fernando Henrique Cardoso, played a major role in moving the dependency perspective toward an analysis of social relations during his association with ECLA (through its sociological annex, ILPES) in the latter sixties. Indeed, Santiago, with its various research institutions through which structuralists and their leftist critics moved, was the crucible of dependency analysis.[139] Independently of ECLA, Cardoso had arrived at a pessimistic view of the 'national bourgeoisie' through his empirical studies of industrialists in Brazil and Argentina; and his view that Latin America lacked what Charles Morazé has called a 'conquering bourgeoisie' was shared by other sociologists who had studied the matter.[140] Cardoso had reached his position before the presence of multinational corporations became so prominent, and native industrialists less conspicuous, in the more open economies of the Argentine and Brazilian dictatorships of the latter 1960s.

Development, second series (New York, 1987), pp. 210–211. A full statement of Furtado's mature views on dependency is *Accumulation and Development: The Logic of Industrial Civilization*, trans. by Suzette Macedo (Oxford, 1983 [Port. orig., 1978]), in which he relates accumulation to power and social stratification. Thus the evolution of Furtado's thought on this matter was similar to Prebisch's between *Hacia una dinámica* (1963) and *Capitalismo periférico* (1981).

138 Furtado, *Subdesenvolvimento*, p. 7; Furtado, *Diagnosis of the Brazilian Crisis*, trans. by Suzette Macedo (Berkeley, Cal., 1965 [Port. orig., 1964]), pp. 48–51.

139 For example, note the Brazilian contributors to dependency who were in Santiago in the years following the 1964 coup in their country: Furtado, Fernando Henrique Cardoso, Theôtonio dos Santos, Rui Mauro Marini, and José Serra (still a student).

140 See Fernando Henrique Cardoso, *Empresário industrial e desenvolvimento econômico no Brasil*, (São Paulo, 1964); Cardoso, 'The Entrepreneurial Elites of Latin America', *Studies in Comparative International Development*, 2 (1966): 147; Cardoso, *Ideologías de la burguesía industrial en sociedades dependientes (Argentina y Brasil)* (Mexico, D. F., 1971) [data collected in 1963, 1965–6], pp. 1, 103, 146, 158, 215; Dardo Cuneo, *Comportimiento y crisis de la clase empresarial* (Buenos Aires, 1967), pp. 129, 172, 192; and Claudio Véliz, 'Introduction', in Véliz (ed.), *Obstacles to Change in Latin America*, pp. 2, 7–8.

While Sunkel spoke of the international capitalist system as 'a determining influence on local processes', and one which was 'internal' to the Periphery's own structure, Cardoso and his Chilean collaborator, Enzo Faletto, preferred to speak of two sub-systems, the internal and the external, and emphasized that the international capitalist system was not solely determining. There was a complex internal dynamic to the system, they asserted.[141]

Beyond this, Cardoso and Faletto stressed the mutual interests among social classes *across* the Centre-Periphery system. The interests of the bourgeoisie of the Centre, and by implication, those of its proletariat, overlapped those of the bourgeoisie of the Periphery; these links became all the more intimate as multinational corporations loomed ever larger in Latin America.[142] Cardoso and Faletto analysed the development of the 'populist' coalition of national and foreign capital with the working class, corresponding to the successful phase of ISI, and linked the failure of import substitution with the demise of the populist political style. In the current phase of capital accumulation, they believed, authoritarian regimes were needed to assure a political demobilization of the masses.[143]

Their treatment of dependency, despite its early appearance, was more nuanced than others, emphasizing contradiction, shifting alliances, and a range of historical possibility. Cardoso and Faletto distinguished between simple enclave economies and those controlled by local bourgeoisies. For the latter, they entertained the possibility of significant manufacturing sectors. In a scheme they called 'associated development' or 'development with marginalization [*marginalidad*]' and which Cardoso would later term 'associated-dependent' development, they noted that contemporary foreign capital was focusing its investment in manufacturing operations. Furthermore, the public sector, multinational capital, and the 'national' capitalist sector were joining hands under authoritarian rule. Like Furtado, Cardoso and Faletto pointed to the international system as a whole as the proper unit of analysis; and like Furtado, they saw development and underdevelopment not as stages, but as locations within the international

[141] Osvaldo Sunkel, "The Pattern of Latin American Dependence', in Victor L. Urquidi and Rosemary Thorp (eds), *Latin America in the International Economy* (London, 1973), p. 6; Fernando Henrique Cardoso and Enzo Faletto, *Dependencia y desarrollo en América Latina: Ensayo de interpretación sociológica* (Mexico, D. F., 1969), pp. 17, 28, 38.

[142] In 1965 Hélio Jaguaribe had already specified a 'consular' bourgeoisie, with distinct interests from the 'national' or 'industrial' variety: 'The Dynamics of Brazilian Nationalism', in Véliz (ed.), *Obstacles*, p. 182.

[143] Cardoso and Faletto, *Dependencia*, pp. 27, 143, 154, 155.

economic system, for which they offered a schematic historical analysis of the Periphery's class dynamics.[144]

Concurrent with the efforts of Cardoso and Faletto, another researcher in Santiago was producing a radical version of dependency that was almost as widely, and perhaps more hotly, debated. This was the German-born, U.S.-educated André Gunder Frank, whose *Capitalism and Underdevelopment in Latin America* has sold 100,000 copies in nine languages, compared to an equal number in the Spanish edition alone by Cardoso and Faletto.[145] Because Frank borrowed from a Marxist tradition – probably without being decisively influenced by it – it is necessary to consider the history of Latin American Marxism, which, like structuralism, was undergoing a fundamental reassessment in the 1960s.

The crisis of Marxism in Latin America in the 1960s revolved around one of the issues that had most troubled structuralists, namely, the role of the local or national bourgeoisies. Since the twenties, the Communist parties of Latin America had vacillated – in truth, oscillated – between the view that the local bourgeoisie was progressive, and the view that it was reactionary, depending largely on the varying position of the Communist International (Comintern) and the Soviet Union. In 1929 the Peruvian José Carlos Mariátegui, usually regarded as the most original Latin American Marxist writing before the Second World War, had argued that capitalism had reached Latin America too late for the local bourgeoisies to emulate the historic role of their European forebears.[146] Yet the prevailing doctrine in most Latin American Communist Parties, from the Popular Front period, beginning in 1934, until the early sixties, was that the local bourgeoisie was a progressive force: contending that their continent had large feudal residues, Party spokesmen argued that proletarians and bour-

---

[144] Cardoso and Faletto, *Dependencia*, pp. 28, 32–3, 135 (quotation), 142, 147, 155. For Cardoso's views on dependency in the early 1970s, see his 'Associated-dependent Development: theoretical and practical implications', in Alfred Stepan (ed.), *Authoritarian Brazil: Origins, Policies and Future* (New Haven, Conn., 1973), pp. 142–78. This feature of Cardoso's dependency analysis, emphasizing the possibilities of growth, against the theses of Furtado, Frank, and Marini, became more prominent in the midst of the 'Brazilian miracle'. The role of the multinationals became the subject of a major research agenda in the 1970s for students of dependency and for ECLA as such; in the absence of a 'European' bourgeoisie, the multinational corporations would dominate the new phase of industrialization in Latin America.

[145] Andre Gunder Frank, 'The Underdevelopment of Development' [a memoir], *Scandinavian Journal of Development Alternatives* 10, 3 (September, 1991), p. 35; interview with F. H. Cardoso by author, São Paulo, 8 June 1990.

[146] José Carlos Mariátegui, 'Point de vue anti-imperialiste' [1929] in Michael Lowy, *Le marxisme en Amérique latine de 1909 à nos jours: Anthologie* (Paris, 1980), p. 113.

geois must struggle in concert, at the present phase of history, to eliminate feudal residues and to contain imperialist penetration. They agreed
with Mariátegui that capitalism was relatively recent in Latin America; it
had made its first appearance there in the nineteenth century.[147] But
unlike Mariátegui, they concluded that capitalism could and must, by
grim necessity, be developed in the region.

Support for the national bourgeoisie and capitalist industrialization was
the position, for example, of the Communist Party of Brazil, an organization effectively part of Brazil's 'developmentalist' and populist coalition for
much of the period 1945–64. In Cuba, as late as August 1960, just two
months before Castro's sweeping nationalization of the economy, the Communist leader Blas Roca announced that the Cuban Revolution was not
socialist, but 'bourgeois-democratic'.[148] Yet the issue that the Cuban Revolution posed after October 1960 was the viability of 'the uninterrupted path
to socialism', a thesis long defended by Latin American Trotskyists, but
more audibly proclaimed as viable policy by Ernesto 'Che' Guevara the same
year. After Fidel Castro's public adherence to Marxist-Leninism in December, 1961, the thesis that contemporary Latin America could only sustain
bourgeois-democratic regimes would have to be reappraised.[149]

A pre-existing historiography was now discovered – beginning with
Sergio Bagú's *Economía de la sociedad colonial* in 1949, an essay which
argued that Latin America had never had a feudal past at all, but in broad
outline had evinced fundamental features of capitalism since the sixteenth
century. The Spanish and Portuguese empires in the New World, Bagú
and others alleged, were basically commercial enterprises, for which 'feudal' titles and trappings were but a veil.[150] This school, composed chiefly
of non-conformist Marxists, would oppose Communist orthodoxy on the
role of the bourgeoisie *not* by asserting that capitalism had arrived too late

---

147 For example, V[olodia] Teitelboim, 'El desarrollo del capitalismo en Chile', in Alexei Rumiantsev
(ed.), *El movimiento contemporaneo de liberación y la burguesía nacional* (Prague, 1961), p. 156. On
feudal residues in contemporary Latin America, see Rodney Arismendi, 'Acerca del papel de la
burguesía nacional en la lucha anti-imperialista', in ibid., pp. 134, 136.

148 Lowy, *Le marxisme*, pp. 223–6 (Brazil), 47 (Cuba).

149 [Ernesto] Che Guevara, *Guerrilla Warfare* (New York, 1961 [Sp. orig., 1960]), p. 15; Lowy, *Le
marxisme*, p. 269.

150 Sergio Bagú, *La economía de la sociedad colonial: Ensayo de la historia comparada de América Latina*
(Buenos Aires, 1949). Bagú's work was not explicitly Marxist, unlike those of four other contributors to this thesis: Marcelo Segall and Luis Vitale of Chile, Milcíades Peña of Argentina, and Caio
Prado, Jr. of Brazil, whose writings on this matter are anthologized in Lowy, *Le marxisme*, pp. 243–
53, 413–22. From a non-Marxist perspective, Roberto Simonsen had denied that Brazil had known
anything other than capitalism in its colonial history, well before the Marxist debate. Simonsen,
História econômica do Brasil (1500–1820), 4th edn (São Paulo, 1962 [orig. 1937]), pp. 80–3.

in Latin America, as Mariátegui had contended, but that, on the contrary, capitalism had already prevailed too long in the region; consequently there was nothing to hope from the local bourgeoisie. This class, rather than overseas imperialists, would constitute the 'immediate enemy', as Frank put it, for Cuba-inspired groups.

In Brazil, for instance, between 1960 and 1966 Caio Prado Jr. elaborated the argument that from the outset his country's agriculture had been capitalist in its essential features, that is, that the Portuguese colony was a mercantile enterprise in which there existed (at a theoretical level), legal equality among the settlers. In *A revolução brasileira* (1966), a work which influenced a generation of urban guerrillas and was the unstated reason for his incarceration in 1969, Prado reviewed the course of Brazilian history to show that his country, as fully 'capitalist', was ripe for revolution, contrary to the official position of the nation's Communist Party, of which he had long been a member. Prado's thesis seems to have had a major influence on Andre Gunder Frank, who expanded Prado's argument on capitalism in Brazilian agriculture in Prado's journal, *Revista Brasiliense,* in 1964.[151]

Frank's work forms the most obvious point of contact between the revisionist Marxists who emphasized relations of exchange and the structuralists. In the mid-sixties he would in fact rework ECLA's theses to yield a radical conclusion.[152] Frank was explicit about at least some of his sources: from Sergio Bagú – whose work was not cast in Marxist terms – he borrowed the proposition that Latin America's economy had been essentially capitalist from the colonial era. From the economist Paul Baran, a Russian-born U.S. Marxist, Frank took the proposition that capitalism simultaneously produces underdevelopment in some areas as it produces development in others.[153] Frank briefly worked on commission for ECLA,

---

[151] Caio Prado, Jr., *A revolução brasileira* (São Paulo, 1966). Prado's articles of the early 1960s are collected in his *A questão agrária* (São Paulo, 1979). Andre Gunder Frank's essay reflecting Prado's influence was 'A agricultura brasileira: capitalismo e o mito do feudalismo', in *Revista Brasiliense,* 51 (January–February, 1964), published in English in Frank, *Capitalism,* pp. 219–77. Frank acknowledges Prado's influence in 'Underdevelopment of Development', p. 26. Fernando Henrique Cardoso in 1977 viewed Prado as one of a group of Brazilian scholars trying to identify a colonial mode of production. See Cardoso, 'The Consumption of Dependency Theory in the United States', *Latin American Research Review,* 12, 3 (1977), pp. 11–12. I do not believe Prado saw the problem in that way in the early 1960s: his category was capitalism.

[152] Frank's model has the force and crudity of W. W. Rostow's 'stages of growth' model, to which it has been compared. See Aidan Foster-Carter, 'From Rostow to Gunder Frank: conflicting paradigms in the analysis of development', *World Development,* 4, 3 (1976): 167–80, esp. 175.

[153] Despite Frank's attribution of Baran, H. W. Arndt has pointed out that Frank went beyond Baran, who had held that capitalism was an obstacle to the underdeveloped world's progress, to argue that underdevelopment was *caused by* capitalism: *Economic Development,* p. 127.

from which he presumably took his thesis of deteriorating terms of trade, though he was to emphasize monopoly elements in the process much more than ECLA had. Frank's antinomy 'metropolis-satellite' is surely derived from 'Centre-Periphery', and his notion of 'involution' — the development of the satellite in periods of crisis in the metropolis — is directly analogous to ECLA's historical analysis of 'inward-directed' growth.

From the Mexican political scientist Pablo González Casanova, Frank borrowed the thesis of 'internal colonialism', whereby industrial and political centres within the satellite exploit their dependent regions through fiscal and exchange policies, and by draining off capital and talent.[154] Frank linked transnational exploitation with internal colonialism, hypothesizing a concatenation of metropolis-satellite relations from Wall Street down to the smallest Latin American village, in which only the end points of the continuum would not stand in both relationships.[155]

Frank, perhaps more than any other writer except the Mexican sociologist Rodolfo Stavenhagen,[156] hammered away at the theme that dualism did not exist in Latin America: all areas were linked by an unequal exchange of goods and services, consequent to underdeveloped capitalism. Thus Frank attacked the traditional Communist positions on 'feudal residues' and non-Marxist dualism as well.[157] Frank's polemical essay paralleled the simultaneous but less didactic and less explicit efforts of Furtado and Sunkel to find causal links between development and underdevelopment.

Frank the synthesizer was also an effective wordsmith, and he termed the plight of Latin America and, by extension, that of the Third World, the 'development of underdevelopment'. For Frank, Latin America had been 'underdeveloping' for more than four centuries, a process which he divided into four phases, each defined by the principal form of monopoly

---

[154] Andre Gunder Frank, *On Capitalist Underdevelopment* (Bombay, 1975), p. 11 (on Prebisch), 26 (on Bagú), 68 (terms of trade), 73 (González Casanova); Frank, *Capitalism and Underdevelopment in Latin America* (New York, 1967), pp. xi, xviii (on Baran), xii (association with ECLA). On Frank's professional development, see his memoir, 'Underdevelopment of Development'.

[155] This was an independent 'rediscovery', I believe, of a model Manoilescu had developed a generation earlier, and one Singer and Furtado had worked out in a structuralist framework in the 1950s. (See note 80 above.)

[156] Rodolfo Stavenhagen, 'Seven Fallacies about Latin America', in James Petras and Maurice Zeitlin, (eds), *Latin America: Reform or Revolution?: A Reader* (Greenwich, Conn., 1968 [Sp. orig., 1965]), pp. 15–18.

[157] The non-Marxist dualism Frank and Stavenhagen attacked was less that of ECLA than that of the Dutch colonial economist J. H. Boeke, who had first developed the concept of virtually unrelated modern and peasant subsistence sectors in the Indonesian economy. Although ECLA had hypothesized the existence of a dual economy in the 1949 *Survey*, in its model the surplus labour force passed from subsistence to modern sectors, assuming a highly wage-elastic labour supply. ECLA in any event preferred the term 'heterogeneous' to 'dualist'.

exercised from the metropolis: commercial monopoly, in the age of mercantilism; industrial monopoly, during the age of classical liberalism; monopoly of capital goods, 1900–50; and monopoly of technological innovation, 1950 to the present.[158]

It is notable that the stages developed by Frank, the Brazilian Theotônio dos Santos, and the Norwegian Johan Galtung (who had extensive contacts in Santiago)[159] were stages in the development of the entire capitalist system, not stages in the sense of W. W. Rostow, in which the underdeveloped countries would repeat the unilinear trajectory of the advanced capitalist nations.[160] A similar emphasis on the development of the whole system was also implicit in the work of Furtado, and Cardoso and Faletto.

For Frank, exit from the system in a revolutionary struggle, following the Cuban example, was the path to development. Only in that manner could 'involution', a partial and temporary exit, be transformed into continuous development. There was an urgency in Frank's voluntarist view that the continued underdevelopment inherent in capitalism would make the breakthrough all the more difficult.[161] He argued that the gap between metropolis – the United States – and satellite – Chile, a case study – was widening 'in power, wealth, and income'; and that the 'relative and absolute' income of the poorest classes in Chile was decreasing.[162] Frank agreed with Cardoso and other dependency writers on the existence of a single Centre-Periphery system, developing historically; on the consequent error of a Boekean dualist approach (see note 157); on the failure of national bourgeoisies to provide leadership in capitalist development; and on the existence of unequal exchange. But he differed with Cardoso on the political inferences to be drawn, and on the extent of unequal exchange, interpreting it in 'drain' terms rather than as unequal gains between Centre and Periph-

[158] Frank, *Capitalism*, p. 211.

[159] Galtung was in Santiago in 1962–63, and maintained contact with Santiago-based personnel later. His model of imperialism cites the dependency literature, and Sunkel criticized the essay in manuscript. See Johan Galtung, 'A Structural Theory of Imperialism', *Journal of Peace Research*, 2 (1971): 81–117.

[160] Theotônio dos Santos, 'The Structure of Dependence', *American Economic Review: Papers and Proceedings*, 60, 2 (May, 1970), pp. 231–36, esp. 232; Johan Galtung, in preceding note; W. W. Rostow, *The Stages of Economic Growth: A Non-Communist Manifesto* (Cambridge, 1960).

[161] Revolution would be more costly in human terms because of the strengthening of capitalist institutions in the development-underdevelopment process. Frank, *On Capitalist Underdevelopment*, p. 110.

[162] Frank, *Capitalism*, pp. 47–8. A writer who took a similar position on the 'superexploitation' of workers in dependent countries was Rui Mauro Marini, in *Dialéctica de la dependencia* (Mexico, D.F. 1973). In 1974 F. H. Cardoso argued that Frank and Marini were repeating an error of the *narodniki* in denying the possibility of capitalist development in the Periphery. Cardoso, *Autoritarismo e democratização* (Rio de Janeiro, 1975 [orig., 1974]), pp. 27–30.

ery. Frank clearly disagreed with Marx and Prebisch, who, holding that rising productivity was the essence of capitalist development, did not believe that the development of the Centre had to be *primarily* at the expense of the Periphery.[163]

Just as we examined the roots of Prebisch's Centre-Periphery model, so it is necessary to ask about the origins of the dependency school. This is important, since Marxist roots have been ascribed to dependency analysis by one of its best students, José Gabriel Palma, and by the man with one of the best claims to be the school's founder, Fernando Henrique Cardoso. Many other contributors to, and students of, dependency have agreed with its derivation from a Marxist or Leninist tradition.[164] This interpretation has been reinforced by the English edition of *Dependency and Development* (1979) by Cardoso and Faletto, in which preface, postscript, and parts of the text show a strong Marxist orientation. By contrast, the first Spanish edition (1969) is far less obviously influenced by Marxism, and the original draft (1965) is recognizably an ECLA product. In this first version the authors challenge the Parsonian categories of modernization theory, and they are pessimistic about the reformism of local bourgeoisies, but from an eclectic perspective. No Marxist studies were cited in the draft, and Marxist categories are almost completely lacking. The theme receiving most attention in the 1965 version was the inadequacy of the bourgeois-directed project of development, partly resulting from increasing market domination by multinational corporations.[165]

The issue is clouded, however, by elements in Cardoso's 1964 study of

---

[163] Frank's use of Marxist analysis was quickly challenged. Ruggiero Romano and Ernesto Laclau charged him with 'circulationism' – putting primary emphasis on relations of exchange rather than relations of production, whereas for Marx, as Laclau emphasized, capitalism was defined by a (free) wage labour market: Only when labour power had become a commodity could relative surplus value be maximized, and this process occurred in the Centre long before it appeared in the Periphery. Romano, review of *Capitalism and Underdevelopment* in *Desarrollo Económico*, 10, 38 (July–September, 1970), p. 287; Laclau, 'Feudalismo y capitalismo en América Latina' [orig., 1971], in Carlos Sempat Assadourian, (ed.), *Modos de producción en América Latina* (Mexico, D.F. 1973), pp. 28–37, 43.

[164] José Gabriel Palma, 'Dependency: a formal theory of underdevelopment or a methodology for the analysis of concrete situations of underdevelopment?', *World Development*, 6, 7–8 (1978), p. 882 (while Palma acknowledges ECLA as a contributor to dependency analysis, he gives far more attention to Marxism); Cardoso, 'Consumption', pp. 10, 14; Heraldo Muñoz, 'Cambio y continuidad en el debate sobre la dependencia y el imperialismo', *Estudios Internacionales*, 11, 44 (October–December, 1978): 104; Sheldon B. Liss, *Marxist Thought in Latin America* (Berkeley, Cal., 1984), p. 25; José Aricó, *La cola del diablo: itinerario de Gramsci en América Latina* (Buenos Aires, 1988), p. 106.

[165] See Cardoso and Faletto, *Dependencia y desarrollo* (1969); and the original draft, 'Estancamiento y desarrollo económico en América Latina: Condiciones sociales y políticas (Consideraciones para un programa de estudio)', mimeo., late 1965, located in ILPES files, at the Santiago headquarters of the U.N.

Brazilian entrepreneurs. That work adumbrates one of his most important contributions to the dependency tradition – namely, his denial of the adequacy of the modernization paradigm, although in the limited context of the role of entrepreneurs.[166] In that work, Cardoso, though eclectic in methodology, cast his major conclusions within a Marxist paradigm.[167] Thus the sources of Cardoso's contribution were various, and a safe conclusion would seem to be that he could make his statement in either a structuralist or a Marxist idiom. Yet it was initially made in the former, as dependency emerged in Santiago.

As the decade of the sixties developed, many writers on dependency adopted an exclusively Marxist perspective, and dependency analysis matured as a 'region' of Marxism: It offered a perspective on imperialism which the classical Marxist theorists of the subject had ignored, namely, the view from the Periphery.[168] A respectable Marxist pedigree was apparently required to validate the dependency perspective after its radicalization, and after it was challenged by those claiming to represent an orthodox Marxist tradition. Yet most of the dependency propositions were initially derived from structuralism, rather than Marxism, even when compatible with the latter school.[169] In any event, dependency became influential outside Latin America in the 1970s. The best-known historical model of world capitalism developing the implications of dependency was Immanuel Wallerstein's *Modern World System*. As Wallerstein had a major impact on Anglophone scholars, so Samir Amin extended dependency perspectives in Francophone areas, and to Africa more broadly.[170]

While 'orthodox' Marxists attacked dependency for focussing on relations in the international market and neglecting class analysis – a charge only partly justified in the case of Cardoso – the dependency school was attacked by non-Marxist social scientists, especially in North America, for

---

[166] Cardoso denied that the roles played by Europe's historical bourgeoisies in economic development could be replicated by Brazilian entrepreneurs in the 1960s. Cardoso, *Empresário*, pp. 41, 44, 183.

[167] Ibid., pp. 181–7.

[168] Though a critic of the dependency literature, one of the few writers on dependency who worked within a framework of formal Marxist economics, as opposed to historical materialism, was the Colombian Salomón Kalmanovitz. He sketched a theory of dependent reproduction, accounting for the incomplete accumulation process in the Periphery. See his *El desarrollo tardío del capitalismo: Un enfoque crítico de la teoría de la dependencia* (Bogotá, 1983).

[169] Cf. a fuller argument in Joseph L. Love, 'The Origins of Dependency Analysis', *Journal of Latin American Studies*, 22, 1 (1990): 143–68.

[170] Wallerstein's main project, *The Modern World System*, a history of capitalism from the late middle ages to modern times, has yielded three volumes to date (New York, 1974, 1980, 1989). Amin's major works were *Accumulation on a World Scale*, 2 vols (1974 [Fr. orig., 1970]) and *Unequal Development* (1976 [Fr. orig., 1973]), both published in New York and translated by Brian Pearce.

its vagueness, inconsistencies, and alleged inability to generate propositions which could be falsified (in Karl Popper's sense). Cardoso's affirmation that the school did not offer a body of theory, but a perspective for
contextual and historical analysis, was seen as elusive. Its inability to
provide unambiguous solutions or programmes, in the Cardoso version,
also weakened its appeal.

THE MODES OF PRODUCTION DEBATE

For economic policy in the late 1960s and 1970s, neo-classical orthodoxy,
not structuralism nor dependency, provided the signposts for most of Latin
America. The neo-classical counter-attack dismissed dependency and challenged structuralist interpretations of the capital-intensive bias in Latin
American industry. Orthodox economists argued that the *actual* cost of
labour was greater than that of capital (relative to respective shadow
prices). Capital costs in Latin America were kept artificially low by liberal
depreciation allowances, low or even negative real interest rates (in periods
of inflation), low tariffs on capital imports, overvalued exchange rates, and
institutionally induced high wages. Therefore, according to this reasoning, choices of labour-saving techniques had been rational, in the face of
distortions of relative prices. Furthermore, the neo-classical school argued
that low productivity in agriculture was not necessarily caused by a lack of
rural entrepreneurship – as a result, for example, of a traditional *lati-
fundista* mentality – but derived in great measure from government programmes of import-substitution. By this analysis, ISI, resulting in high-
cost manufactured goods, had turned the domestic terms of trade against
agriculture. Furthermore, exchange policies designed to assist industrialization had given agricultural exporters less than the full value of their
foreign sales, and thereby discouraged production.

Economic orthodoxy was frequently introduced by repressive regimes,
if for no other reason than to reduce wages in an effort to restore profits
after ISI had faltered, and to control inflation. Four countries in which the
military held power for long periods – Brazil, Argentina, Chile, and
Uruguay – were particularly influenced by the monetarist economics of
the Chicago school.[171] It was in this economic climate – and in a political
context of repression and the failure of urban guerrilla movements in the

---

[171] See Alejandro Foxley, *Latin American Experiments in Neo-Conservative Economics* (Berkeley, Cal., 1983),
esp. on Chile, where monetarism was applied most rigorously. Juan Gabriel Valdés offers a scholarly
but equally unsympathetic study in *La escuela de Chicago: Operación Chile* (Buenos Aires, 1989).

late sixties and early seventies – that Marxist intellectuals in Latin America began to move in more abstract and theoretical directions, and to experience the impact of the modes of production debate in France, particularly concerning an 'African' mode.

For the historical development of the West, Marx had defined five 'modes of production', which were complex assemblages of the relations of production between producer and non-producer, and of the forces of production. These were the primitive collective, slave, feudal, capitalist, and socialist modes, which corresponded to past, present, and future of the West. He had also written of an Asiatic mode, in which a despot skimmed all but a negligible surplus. Therefore, this mode included no investment nor technological change; it was cyclical and history-less. Stalin directed Soviet ideologues to strike the Asiatic mode from the catalogue in 1931, and proclaimed the inevitability of the sequence of the five others in the 1930s. All existing societies were reinterpreted by Communist theorists as falling into the Western stages, even though it was obvious to specialists that such sequential 'stages' for many societies were inadequate. The Comintern's linear view of national histories was, in fact, a counterpart to modernization theory. Thus the rehabilitation of the Asiatic mode in the 1950s was an element in the revitalization of Marxist research in Europe. It was in this context that Marxist students of Africa in France, influenced by the recent translation and diffusion of Marx's *Grundrisse,* began to search for modes of production unknown, and unknowable, to Marx and Engels.[172]

The modes-of-production debate in Latin America was conditioned not only by French writings specifically directed to the issue, but by the broader current of structuralist Marxism associated with the work of Louis Althusser and Etienne Balibar. On the modes problem, Balibar had written in *Reading Capital* (1965) that two or more modes could be articulated in a single 'simultaneity', during a period of transition from one mode to another, provided that one was dominant.[173] Althusser's rereading of *Capital* and his defense of the mature 'Leninist' Marx against the young 'humanist' Marx inspired seminars on Marx's magnum opus in several Latin American cities during the mid-sixties. The most important of these

---

172 Maurice Godelier, Jean Suret-Canale, and Catherine Coquery-Vidrovich were the principal participants in the debate, which took place in the Marxist journal *La Pensée* over the decade of the 1960s.
173 Etienne Balibar, 'Elements for a Theory of Transition', in Louis Althusser and Balibar, *Reading Capital,* trans. by Ben Brewster (London, 1970 [French orig., 1965]), p. 307. A Spanish edition of Althusser's *Pour Marx* was published in Mexico in 1967.

was held in Santiago, already mentioned as the locus of the dependency school; many of this group participated in the *Capital* seminar.[174] Also among the participants was Marta Harnecker, who probably did more than anyone else in Latin America to diffuse the work of Althusser, with whom she had studied in Paris. Harnecker's Althusserian primer, *Los conceptos elementales del materialismo histórico,* was first published in 1969 and had reached its thirty-fifth edition eight years later.[175] Many other Latin Americans, of course, were in direct contact with French Marxist ideas through study in Paris or acquaintance with *La Pensée* and other French Marxist publications.

Yet for Latin Americans, French Marxism was not the only source; indigenous forces were also at work. In some respects the modes of production debate was a response to the dependency school, in that it questioned the uses to which Marxist theory was put. Viewed from a different perspective, the 'modes' debate was an extension of an increasingly formally Marxist dependency literature. It dealt with the same basic problem, namely, how 'backward' structures are related to an advancing capitalist order.

Dependency might even be seen as the opening phase of the modes-of-production debate, since the conventional thesis of 'feudal residues' was challenged by Frank in his polemic in 1965 with Rodolfo Puiggrós, a former leader of the Argentine Communist Party. Among other things, Frank argued that Latin America's so-called feudal estates were not related to a subsistence economy, but were the decadent result of a previous phase of capitalist expansion. The exchange resonated especially in Argentina and Mexico.[176]

The issue was reframed when the Argentinian Ernesto Laclau attacked Frank in two articles in 1969 and 1971. Laclau, who had read the debate on the 'African' mode in *La Pensée*,[177] argued that students of the Latin American economy, a congeries of disparate elements, did not have to choose between capitalism and feudalism: The region could have more than one mode of production, as long as a dominant, structuring mode –

[174] Interview with Theotônio dos Santos by author, Rio de Janeiro, 22 July 1985.
[175] Marta Harnecker, *Los conceptos elementales del materialismo histórico* (Mexico, D. F., 35th rev. edn, 1977 [orig. 1969]).
[176] The debate, originally in *El Gallo Ilustrado,* a Sunday supplement of the Mexican daily *El Día,* was twice published in both Mexico, D.F. and Buenos Aires. Puiggrós's essay was 'Los modos de producción en Iberoamérica', and Frank's counterthesis, '¿Con qué modo de producción convierte la gallina maíz en huevos de oro?' See *El Gallo Ilustrado* (no. 173 of 17 October 1965).
[177] Interview of Ernesto Laclau by author, Urbana, Ill., 12 November 1984.

capitalism – established the laws of motion for the whole system. Feudal elements were intensified, or even invented, by the international market, but were subordinated to it. [178]

In 1973 a collection of studies by Carlos Sempat Assadourian and others, *Modos de producción en América Latina,* reflected the influence of French Marxism and revealed that Latin America, like Africa, offered fertile ground for theorizing. Laclau's essay, 'Feudalism and Capitalism', was republished there. The introductory essay by Juan Carlos Garavaglia, another Argentinian, argued that Latin America had experienced several analytically distinguishable modes of production in the colonial era. Ciro F. S. Cardoso, a Brazilian, called for an effort, to which he contributed, to build a theory of a slave-based 'colonial' mode. Other contributors to the collection identified highly specific modes, such as Garavaglia's 'despotic village' mode in the Jesuit missions of Paraguay. Yet in the view of the contributors, the proliferation of types did not pose the danger of historicism – the view that all historical patterns are unique – because, as Garavaglia put it, the main proposition of the group was that the dominant mode, capitalism, was exterior to the 'dominated space' of colonial Latin America. Or, as Ciro F. S. Cardoso formulated the proposition more in accord with French thinking, dominant and dominated modes coexisted in the same 'social formation'. [179] The latter term was understood as a concrete historical whole, defined by specific economic, political, ideological, and theoretical processes of production. Yet as more and more researchers 'discovered' new modes of production, the prospect loomed that every case study would produce its own mode; where, then, was Marxist science, if every instance was unique?

In 1973 a seminal article appeared in *La Pensée,* in which Balibar revised his views on conceptualizing modes of production. The philosopher now argued that 'mode of production' was necessarily an ahistorical abstraction, and that class struggle determined the mode. Since class struggle only occurred in a given social formation, the latter, in effect, determined the mode, not vice-versa, as the contributors to the Sempat Assadourian volume had posited. [180]

[178] Ernesto Laclau, 'Modos de producción, sistemas económicos y población excedente: Aproximación a los casos argentino y chileno', *Revista Latinoamericana de Sociología,* 5, 2 (1969), pp. 305–11; 'Feudalismo y capitalismo'.

[179] Carlos Sempat Assadourian et al., *Modos de producción en América Latina,* pp. 14, 94, 161, 212.

[180] Etienne Balibar, 'Sur la dialectique historique: Quelques remarques critiques a propos de *Lire le Capital',* *La Pensée* (August, 1973), p. 47. Also see Enrique Tandater, 'Sobre el análisis de la dominación colonial', *Desarrollo Económico,* 16, 61 (April–June 1976), p. 154.

This reformulation apparently affected the thinking of participants at an international symposium on modes of production held the following year in Mexico City, which now replaced Santiago as the chief venue of radical intellectual exchange.[181] One participant was the Ecuadorian Agustín Cueva, who contended that there could be no colonial mode, because colonialism and 'mode of production' were concepts at different levels of abstraction. In other words, a concept at the level of theory, mode of production, was being fused with an empirical category, colonialism. The symposium revealed a growing dissensus on the utility and proper use of the concept of precapitalist modes.[182] Other problems with any sort of colonial mode are the issues of who constitutes the ruling class – local or overseas groups – and how class struggle under such conditions can be specified.

A more fruitful form, perhaps, of theorizing about articulated modes concerned contemporary urban underemployment, for which the category 'marginality' was the subject of academic debate among students of dependency in the decade after 1965. Francisco de Oliveira, Lúcio Kowarick, Paul Singer, as well as Fernando Henrique Cardoso – all researchers at the Centro Brasileiro de Planejamento e Análise (CEBRAP) in São Paulo during the early 1970s – took issue with Aníbal Quijano of Peru and José Nun of Argentina, who had worked at CEPAL and other Santiago-based institutions. Quijano and Nun viewed marginality, in the sense of huge numbers of urban un- and under-employed, as a specific deformity of dependent capitalism, something distinct from Marx's 'industrial reserve army', the unemployed workers who served the purpose of holding down wages. Nun held that marginality as a Latin American social phenomenon exceeded the dimensions of a reserve army, in an age of monopoly capitalism and labour-saving technology. Though some marginals directly con-

---

[181] General Augusto Pinochet's coup in September 1973 prompted Marxists to flee Chile, and Mexico, D.F. became the home of many exiles. The Puiggrós-Frank polemic had occurred in the Mexican capital in 1965, and the new journal *Historia y Sociedad* published the modes-of-production papers of the 1974 Congress of Americanists, as well as later contributions on the problem. For the development of Latin American Marxism in general, the prominence of Mexico, D.F. owed significantly to the writing, editing, and publishing José Aricó, an Argentine national and Latin America's leading scholar of Marxism. He transferred his Pasado y Presente operations, which had first published the Sempat collection on modes of production, from Argentina to Mexico, D.F. in the mid-1970s.

[182] Roger Bartra et al., *Modos de producción en América Latina* (Lima, 1976); in particular, see Cueva, 'El uso del concepto de modo de producción en América Latina: Algunos problemas teóricos', p. 28. José Roberto do Amaral Lapa provides a list of sixty works on modes of production in Brazil, divided into four types of interpretation – feudal, capitalist, uniquely Brazilian modes, and works revising the others, in his introduction to *Modos de produção e realidade brasileira* (Petrópolis, 1980), pp. 29–33.

tributed to capitalist accumulation, for example, in the construction industry, Nun's 'marginal mass' was partly dysfunctional for the capitalist
system because of its overwhelming strain on urban services.[183]

The CEBRAP group denied that marginality constituted a social problem for which classical Marxian categories were inadequate.[184] Accusing
Nun and Quijano of introducing a new dualism, CEBRAP researchers saw
marginality as a phenomenon which was linked to dependent capitalist
accumulation through the articulation of capitalist and precapitalist
modes, or the precapitalist relations of production derived from them; this
articulation was dominated by the logic of the former system, locating the
precapitalist elements largely in the service sector.[185] Not only did newly
urbanized peasants hold down the wage level as an 'unlimited supply of
labour',[186] but poorly paid hawkers helped realize profits on industrial
goods with their intensive sales techniques; moreover, urban services such
as car-washing, or, one could add, even shoe-shining, indirectly contributed to the realization of surplus value in the industrial sector by distribut-
ing and maintaining its products at low cost. Workers furthermore diminished the cost of wage goods for employers by constructing their own
housing.[187] Thus CEBRAP analysts tended to identify marginality with
the economic contributions of the informally employed or underem-
ployed, whereas Quijano and Nun had a less sanguine view of their productivity, and emphasized the precarious nature of marginal employment.
Whether influenced by the articulation approach or otherwise, the issue of
marginality generated a variety of empirical and theoretical studies of the
informal sector, contributions which questioned the adequacy of the concept of underemployment in Third World countries.[188]

But this was the only avenue of the modes debate that seemed to open
new doors. In Brazil and elsewhere, although participants in the debate
frequently appealed to the authority of Marx, the issue was vexed by the
lack of a general definition of 'mode of production' in Marx's own writ-

[183] For a summary of Quijano's and Nun's positions and a critique, see Cristóbal Kay, *Latin American Theories of Development and Underdevelopment* (London, 1989), pp. 100–24. Kay also discusses the CEBRAP group in this context, and I draw upon his work.

[184] Fernando Henrique Cardoso, 'Participação e marginalidade', in *O modelo político brasileiro e outros ensaios* (São Paulo, 1972), p. 184.

[185] Lúcio Kowarick, 'Capitalismo, dependência e marginalidade urbana na América Latina: Uma contribuição teórica', *Estudos CEBRAP* 8 (April–June, 1974), pp. 79–80; Francisco de Oliveira, 'A economia brasileira: Crítica a razão dualista', *Estudos CEBRAP* 2 (October, 1972), p. 27.

[186] In W. Arthur Lewis's sense. Kowarick, 'Capitalismo, dependência e marginalidade', pp. 92, 96.

[187] Oliveira, 'A economia brasileira', pp. 29, 31.

[188] See Kay, *Latin American Theories*, ch. 4.

ings, and by his use of 'society' and 'social formation' interchangeably.[189] An indication of the general barrenness of the modes-of-production controversy in Latin America was that most of the early enthusiasts, at least those who contributed to the Sempat Assadourian volume, simply dropped the issue — overarching as it was — in their later monographic studies, though subsequently the theoretical effort probably helped produce some major economic studies of the colonial period, focussing on relations of production, the production process, and the circulation of commodities.[190] One of the few general results was the modest conclusion that precapitalist relations of production after the Conquest gained their significance from their *relation* to capitalism, not from any inherent 'feudalism'; another was the refutation of the thesis of an omnipresent and sempiternal capitalism. A final contribution was the CEBRAP group's work on marginality, but researchers outside the modes-of-production debate were also beginning to study the 'informal sector'.

STRUCTURALIST REPRISE

As we have seen, ECLA's theories and policy recommendations were out of favour with most of the governments of Latin America throughout the 1970s; meanwhile ECLA marshalled persuasive arguments that industrialization was still critical for social reasons. In 1979 ECLA's demographic annex had calculated that in 1990 Latin America would need 37 million more jobs than in 1980, the vast majority of them urban. In this situation, industry, broadly interpreted, was far from an unambiguous failure, in the opinion of ECLA economist Aníbal Pinto: in 1980 27 per cent of Latin America's economically active population was involved in manufacturing, power, construction, and transport; manufacturing employment alone grew faster than the region's general population growth rate from 1950 to 1980. Thus, implied Pinto, Prebisch's call for industrialization in the forties was still relevant in the eighties.[191] Furthermore, Víctor Tokman, an economist at an ECLA-associated agency, demonstrated that, compared to the historical experience of the developed countries, the

---

[189] Harnecker, *Conceptos elementales*, p. 137; Tom Bottomore, 'social formation', in Bottomore (ed.), *A Dictionary of Marxist Thought* (Cambridge, Mass., 1983), p. 444.

[190] For example, Sempat's own *El sistema de la economía colonial: El mercado interior, regiones y espacio económico* (Mexico, D. F., 1983); and Garavaglia, *Mercado interno y economía colonial* (Mexico, D. F., 1983).

[191] Aníbal Pinto, 'Centro-periferia e industrialización: Vigencia y cambios en el pensamiento de la CEPAL', *Trimestre Económico*, 50, 2 (April–June, 1983), pp. 1063–4.

problem of insufficient employment opportunities in Latin America owed less to excessive population growth and a low rate of expansion in industry than to a failure of the service sector to absorb the 'informally' employed into activities of higher productivity.[192]

Nor had the terms-of-trade thesis disappeared from the scene. The British economist John Spraos revived Prebisch's argument in a more sophisticated form. The net barter terms of trade used by Prebisch is a 'one-dimensional concept' for Spraos, because a policy that resulted in deterioration of net barter terms of trade might nevertheless have merit if offsetting gains in employment and labour productivity occurred. Thus Spraos proposed a measure which takes into account (net barter) terms of trade, employment, and productivity – the 'employment-corrected double factorial terms of trade'. Applying econometric tests to world trade data for 1960–77, he found substance in the arguments that disparities exist in elasticities of both income and supply between agricultural commodities and manufactures, coupled with pressure for increasing the supply of commodities, owing to the excess supply of labour in agriculture.[193] The Prebisch–Singer thesis of unequal exchange, thus transformed, survived into the 1990s. Furthermore, although Prebisch received not a little blame for the excesses of Third World industrialization, it may be argued that, *without* significant industrialization, terms of trade would have deteriorated much more than they actually did for primary-exporting countries.

Prebisch's own activity as economic theorist and policy advisor continued until his death at eighty-five in 1986. Though he did not associate himself directly with the dependency school, his book *Capitalismo periférico*, written in his final years, shows strong affinities with the dependency tradition, and incorporates social and political elements into his economic analysis. It dealt by implication with Brazil and Southern Cone, where military regimes were in power as the seventies ended, though the problems he treated were Latin America-wide in most respects.

The capitalism of the Periphery, Prebisch contended, was structurally different from that in the central industrialized countries, in that it was insufficiently dynamic. Prebisch focussed on the 'surplus', a concept pre-

---

[192] Víctor Tokman, 'Unequal Development and the Absorption of Labour: Latin America 1950–1980', *CEPAL Review*, 17 (August, 1982), p. 126.

[193] John Spraos, *Inequalising Trade* (Oxford, 1983), pp. 15, 33, 113, 118. Though the term did not yet exist, Prebisch was interested in the double factorial terms of trade from his earliest concern with labour costs in the industrial and agricultural trading nations, and Singer was implicitly so.

sumably inspired by classical economics: the surplus was 'the productivity increment, which, not being transferred to the labor force . . . is appropriated by the owners of the means of production.' Prebisch's surplus differed from Marx's surplus value in that it excluded compensation of entrepreneurial and managerial services.[194] The owners of the means of production appropriated productivity gains such that labour got less than a proportional share, according to Prebisch, but much of the surplus was wasted in unwarranted consumption rather than being applied to productive investment. The upper classes' interests, as well as their tastes and life styles, were closely bound up with those of the Centre. Though the Centre itself, because of its technological and economic superiority, helped generate increasing productivity in the Periphery, it also siphoned off part of these productivity gains through the activities of multinational corporations and through market and extra-market 'power relations': the Centre was 'hegemonic' for Prebisch.[195]

In peripheral capitalism new production techniques, always more capital-intensive, replaced older ones before the latter were fully amortized, because the newer ones produced the goods demanded by the Periphery's 'privileged consumer society'. Thus there was a conflict between the rationality of the firm, especially of the multinational, which would replace physical capital through amortization funds and reduce the labour force to increase efficiency, and 'collective rationality, which would choose to prolong the working life of physical capital and use the amortization funds for new investment that would provide more employment'.[196]

In the course of the struggle within the Periphery for the benefits of technological progress, there was a conflict between democratization of polity and economy and the 'serious socioeconomic bias of the mechanism for income distribution and capital accumulation in favor of the higher social strata'.[197] Conflicts between the two tended to result in the emergence of authoritarian regimes in order to restore the threatened system of income distribution and accumulation, while the population excluded from the privileged consumer society was continually increasing. Prebisch re-

---

[194] Raúl Prebisch, 'Power Relations and Market Laws', Working Paper no. 35, Kellogg Institute (University of Notre Dame, 1984), p. 22; also see Prebisch, *Capitalismo periférico: Crisis y transformación* (Mexico, D.F. 1981), p. 40.

[195] Prebisch, *Capitalismo periférico*, pp. 203–10.

[196] Raúl Prebisch, 'A Critique of Peripheral Capitalism', *CEPAL Review*, January–June 1976, p. 30.

[197] Raúl Prebisch, 'Five Stages in my Thinking on Development', in Gerald M. Meier and Dudley Seers (eds), *Pioneers in Development* (New York, 1984), p. 189. For a summary of Prebisch's views on 'peripheral capitalism', see pp. 183–92.

tained his faith in the state as an exogenous actor to bring about the socio-economic changes he thought imperative: 'The state must regulate the social use of the surplus, to increase the rhythm of accumulation and progressively to correct the distributive disparities of a structural character'. [198]

This theoretical *envoi* was not regarded as sacrosanct by ECLA and other U.N. agencies in Santiago, where Tokman's finding of parallel experiences between the history of developed countries and the contemporary Latin American experience in industrial employment – published a year after *Capitalismo periférico* – clearly implied an excessive pessimism by Prebisch on the secondary sector.

The wave of dictatorships in the 1970s, government rejection of structuralist policies, and the expanded dependence of foreign borrowing no doubt made Prebisch and others more pessimistic about development within democratic contexts, but the economies of Latin America were still growing. From 1950 to 1981 per capita income in the region grew, in constant 1970 dollars, from US$420 to 960. The eighties, however, were the 'lost decade' for Latin American growth: of the years through 1990, per capita income for the region never attained the level of 1980, and a net outflow of capital occurred, as Latin American nations sacrificed investment to repay foreign debt. The degree to which monetarist-inspired policies can be blamed for this failure is debatable, but the 'lost decade' and the collapse of the Soviet model in 1989–91 seemed to open new vistas for the debate on development.

Structuralism during the eighties yielded to 'neo-structuralism'. The new version would avoid the mistakes of ISI and incorporate lessons from neoliberalism, seeking, for example, export opportunities, in a flexible policy to develop both internal and external markets: 'inward-directed development' would be replaced by 'development *from* within'. The state would remain interventionist, seeking to collaborate with the private sector, but would concern itself as well with social development, equity issues, and environmental problems. [199] A counter-trend emphasizing privatization, focussed on the waste of 'rent-seeking' behaviour within state bureaucracies and supported by such powerful ideological statements as the Peruvian Hernando de Soto's *El otro sendero*, [200] proved the stronger force.

[198] Raúl Prebisch, 'Centro y periferia según Prebisch', *Revista Idea* año 7, no. 71 (November, 1983), p. 22. For the similar evolution of Furtado's views on dependency, see note 137.

[199] See the essays in Osvaldo Sunkel (ed.) *El desarrollo desde dentro: Un enfoque neoestructuralista para la América Latina* (Mexico, D. F., 1991).

[200] Hernando de Soto, *El otro sendero: La revolución informal* ([Lima], 1986). Published in English as *The Other Path: the Invisible Revolution in the Third World* (London, 1989).

CONCLUSION

The preceding pages have traced the development of economic ideas and ideologies, and especially those concerning industrialization, from a largely pre-theoretical phase in the 1930s through the rise and fall of structuralism and dependency analysis to the dominance of neo-liberalism in the 1980s. In essence, there were two phases in this story, corresponding to perceived failures in economic performance, which both implied inadequacy in analysis. The first was the failure of export-led growth, giving rise to the Prebisch–Singer thesis, which is still the subject of debate more than forty years later. The second was the failure of import-substitution industrialization, begetting in succession a dependency school on the fringes of the ECLA camp, and a Marxist riposte to dependency, a modes-of-production literature. A broader attack on the perceived failures of structuralism by neo-classical theorists, contemporaneous with that of dependency, resulted in the wave of privatization that coincided with, and was reinforced by, the failure of socialism in the Soviet Union and Eastern Europe.

In the earlier phase, Prebisch formulated his thesis of unequal exchange between Centre and Periphery over the course of two decades of direct involvement in economic and financial policy. He came to reject the thesis of comparative advantage via his partial rejection, in the context of peripheral economies, of the monetary and banking policies of Keynes. Prebisch was an eclectic, however, and also drew on the writings of Kindleberger and others. He had formulated the elements of his thesis before the appearance, in 1949, of the empirical base on which the thesis would rest in its first published form – Singer's U.N. study, *Relative Prices*. 'Structuralism' had been present in embryonic form in Prebisch's institutional arguments as to why neo-classical economics did not apply to the Periphery without modification. The analysis contained some historical elements from the outset (e.g. the decisive shift, in Prebisch's view, of the principal centre after the First World War), and a young group of ECLA economists subsequently employed structural analysis in formal historical studies.

Structuralism, in tune with international trends after 1930, gave the state a key role in the development process, in contrast with the dependency school, whose members viewed the state as less autonomous of social forces and more bound to particular class interests. In its assumption of government action as an independent variable, ECLA had perhaps approached a Hegelian position wherein the state, possessing a monopoly on objective consciousness, was the demiurge of development and the protagonist of the historical process.[201] At all events, structuralism distinguished itself from neo-classical analysis in its emphasis on macroeconomics, institutions, and interdisciplinary approaches to economic issues, as well as in treating long-term (trans-cyclical) changes.[202]

'Dependency' as a body of doctrine grew out of the perceived inability of the Latin American states to surmount the difficulties ECLA had identified – above all, the alleged dead-end of ISI, but also inflation and other problems rooted in institutional rigidities. Much of the contribution of ECLA, and its theorists writing in their own names, in this period was 'negative'. Explanations of the failure to transform the Latin American economy provided material for dependency analysts, who widened their focus from the historical development of the economy to embrace society and politics as well. Furtado and Sunkel bridged the gap between structuralism and dependency, because their examination of Latin American issues was based on a critique of international capitalism. Furtado had first raised the issue of the relation between development and underdevelopment in his study of internal colonialism, using a model derived from structuralism.

Prebisch's terms-of-trade thesis and other pro-industrialization arguments had initially provided ideological support – intentionally or not – for Latin America's national bourgeoisies.[203] Yet by the latter 1960s it was

---

[201] Guido Mantega, *A economia política brasileira* (São Paulo, 1984), p. 43.

[202] The relationship between French structuralism, which ranged across a wide spectrum of disciplines in the post-war era, and the structuralism of ECLA economists was in part coincidental. To some degree, however, the French school did have an impact on the ECLA economists, largely through the work of François Perroux, whose work on the 'dominant economy' paralleled Prebisch's, and whose subsequent work on growth poles did influence Latin American structuralism. Of the early ECLA group, Furtado, having trained in Paris, was closest to the French tradition, which defined wholeness, transformation, and self-regulation as basic features of social structures. French structuralism informed the Marxism of the Althusserians as well, leading to a possible terminological confusion for the uninitiated: one writer calls the followers of Althusser 'the Latin American structuralists'. See Richard Harris, 'Structuralism in Latin America', *The Insurgent Sociologist,* 9, 1 (Summer, 1979): 62–73.

[203] There can be little doubt that early ECLA writings did define a project for the national bourgeoisies of Latin America. Yet ECLA's 'representation' of these groups was necessarily indirect, since it was an agency answerable to member states, not to social classes or corporate groups. The degree to which the several national bourgeoisies 'embraced' ECLA's theses is a much more difficult issue, since many businessmen were not versed in economic analysis and were often unsympathetic toward state planners' designs for development. A look at the business journals in the period under examination offers some clues. But the issue is clouded by the fact that there was as yet little distinction between 'business' and 'economics' periodicals. It was perhaps to be expected that such economics journals as *Trimestre Económico* (Mexico), *Revista de Economía* (Mexico), *Revista Brasileira de Economia,* and *Economía* (Chile) – all 'academic' publications – would give ECLA a favourable hearing. Yet it is interesting to note that some journals with a substantial readership of industrialists and other businessmen also occasionally or frequently published ECLA materials or com-

questionable whether that class could achieve the historical project which Prebisch had envisioned. Frank attempted to expose the exploitative nature of the national bourgeoisies, while Fernando Henrique Cardoso emphasized their diminished relevance.

Before the sixties had ended, Frank's version of dependency was challenged by claimants to a Marxist orthodoxy, theorists who saw themselves restoring relations of production to their rightful primacy. Yet the modes-of-production controversy which ensued was European-derived and scholastic, though it had Latin American features, since it began, in part, as a critique of dependency. For example, the anti-dualism of the dependency school almost necessitated an 'articulation' explanation of local relations of production. The repercussions of the Latin American modes-of-production debate were far weaker than those of structuralism and dependency, which in the late work of Prebisch tended to converge. Whether neo-structuralism is merely an epigonal phenomenon remains to be seen, but the tradition of state intervention in the economies and societies of Latin America – and therefore of an interventionist doctrine of some sort – is not likely to disappear quickly.

mented favourably on them, for example, *Revista de Economía Argentina, Economía y Finanzas* (Chile), *Industria* (Chile), *Industria Peruana, Estudos Econômicos* (Brazil), and *Desenvolvimento e Conjuntura* (Brazil). Some other businessmen's journals, however, tended to ignore ECLA, and the issue of how widely and in what ways Latin American industrialists supported the agency awaits further research. (For Brazil, in any event, Kathryn Sikkink notes that 'industrial leaders in Rio de Janeiro and São Paulo already had adopted CEPAL terminology in their speeches by the early 1950s'. Sikkink, *Ideas and Institutions*, p. 155.)

4

A NOTE ON LIBERATION THEOLOGY*

The Catholic Church dominated the religious and cultural life and was a major influence in the political and economic life of Latin America during 300 years of colonial rule. In the nineteenth century, following independence from Spain and Portugal, freemasons, liberals and positivists in the new states challenged the Church's exclusive ideological claims and forced it on to the defensive. The secularization of the State and its absorption of liberal and anti-clerical influences, together with the confiscation of Church properties and the introduction of lay education, civil marriage and burial weakened the power of the Catholic Church, economically and socially as well as politically. As the State shed much of its conservative and Catholic past, so the Church was compelled to diminish its hitherto heavy reliance on the State and to look to its own resources and institutions. New challenges were posed in the first decades of the twentieth century by explicitly atheistic versions of anarchism and socialism. Freethinking was a powerful force among urban intelligentsias; and the process of urbanization was frequently accompanied by a growth of religious indifference among all social classes.

During the papacies of Pius XI (1922–39) and Pius XII (1939–58) – and it is important always to remember that the Catholic Church is an international institution organized from Rome – the Church began to establish connections with new socio-political forces – industrial, bureaucratic, nationalist and popular – which, for lack of power, themselves needed allies. The Church, for the most part antiliberal and also now fiercely anti-communist, abandoned the defensive posture acquired during the liberal ascendancy, and placed its relationships with the state and civil society on a new basis. Thus after 1930 the Church again became a major

* The editor wishes to acknowledge the help of Dr. Christopher Abel, University College London, in the final preparation of the chapter from which this note is drawn.

actor in Latin American politics, whether governments were conservative and authoritarian, populist and developmental, liberal, or even revolutionary socialist.

At the same time, twentieth-century Roman Catholicism inherited traditions of popular religiosity that were strong among peasants, rural-urban migrants, and urban workers – native Americans, Blacks, people of mixed blood or poor immigrants from Mediterranean countries. The official Church was frequently divided over whether it should confront and try to eliminate religious syncretisms that ran contrary to the official theology proclaimed at the First Vatican Council (1870–1) and embodied in papal encyclicals, or whether it should accommodate them. If the bishops tried to purge popular religious practices and impose a uniform theology, they risked the defection of genuine believers at a time when religious disbelief was growing; if, however, they accommodated 'folk' variants, the bishops were open to accusations of diluting and betraying the mission of the Church and even of appeasing paganism. The result of these debates was usually an uneasy compromise. Numerous syncretic religious beliefs survived, often in conjunction with syncretisms in curing and healing practices; native Americans in the Andean republics and Central America blended Catholic and Amerindian beliefs; people of African descent, especially in Brazil and Cuba, worshipped at the shrines of Catholic virgins and saints who, in their eyes, were simultaneously African deities; poor Spanish immigrants in major cities conserved Hispanic folk beliefs. Important as an element of resistance to liberalism, popular religion co-existed uneasily with official Catholicism. In the second half of the twentieth century and especially from the 1960s, however, popular religion was increasingly acknowledged as having a place within the Church's pastoral mission. Yet the institutional adoption of popular religion was ambiguous: in some hands it was manipulative, in others a justification for revolution.

The Catholic Church of the 1930s and 1940s has frequently been misrepresented by conservative and radical theologians alike as uniform and monolithic. It was neither. The victory of General Francisco Franco in the Spanish Civil War encouraged the authoritarian elements in the Church who identified with the ultra-montanism associated with the First Vatican Council to press for an intransigent rejection of all manifestations of 'modernism' and liberalism; and, in particular, to interpret and denounce all worker organizations, even those sponsored by the Church, as containing a potential for communism and subversion. At the same time, more conciliatory elements, influenced by the papal encyclicals *Rerum Novarum* (1891) and *Quadragessimi Anno* (1931) assumed the more flexible posture of Pius XI and XII, who argued that in a world where communism, fascism and Nazism endangered the Catholic faith, cautious concessions should be made to liberal and populist governments, so long as they abandoned anti-clerical policies, especially in education, refrained from further assaults upon property ownership by the Church, and undertook welfare measures that promoted class harmony in the cities. The cumulative impact of minor changes in the Church between the 1920s and 1950s, for the most part ignored by historians, was considerable.

Belatedly recognizing that Latin America was the largest constituency of the Roman Catholic Church (and, as the population of Latin America entered a period of rapid expansion, that with most growth potential – in 1960 Latin America already had 35 per cent of the world's Catholic population compared with Europe's 33 per cent) Pius XII designated Latin America as a region urgently requiring re-evangelization. There followed a large influx of missionaries from western and southern Europe, the United States and Canada. The presence of foreign-born clergy had a significant impact. Shocked by the conditions of the poor in the Latin American cities, they and their Latin American peers pressed vigorously for ecclesiastical resources to be allocated both to welfare programmes and to sociological analyses of poverty and welfare conditions. At the same time, a small number of young clergy, carefully selected as potential bishops, was sent by its superiors on scholarships to study at such institutions as the University of Louvain in Belgium. Here they were introduced to the social sciences in an environment shaped by usually cordial relationships between Catholics and laymen including socialist intelligentsias and activists, that were established in moments of trade union solidarity and consolidated in the Resistance to the Nazi occupation during the Second World War.

At the same time there was a shift from control by the Church hierarchy to greater lay participation. Between the 1920s and 1950s the Catholic bishops and their allies in the religious orders, answered lay, free-thinking and atheistic challenges by over-hauling the networks of Catholic primary and secondary schools, expanding their range of publications, and by opening Catholic universities. Pious groups of Catholic youth, women, artisans and students were co-ordinated under the umbrella of Catholic Action (Acción Católica). Furthermore, the official Church both sponsored Catholic trade unions which in Colombia, for example, were to merge after the Second World War in the Unión de Trabajadores de Colombia (UTC), and gave its blessing and encouragement to the formation by Catholic lay intellectuals of Christian Democratic parties which propagated a non-violent 'revolution in liberty' that was rooted in the social doctrines of the Church and in assumptions of class collaboration. Promising businessmen and the middle classes sustained development, and wooing urban workers and peasants with policies of redistribution and income growth, the Christian Democrats came to power in the 1960s in freely held elections in both Chile and Venezuela. Through class collaboration they aimed to achieve a peaceful 'middle way' that simultaneously limited the impact of an atheistic, materialistic communism that preached class warfare and of an unbridled, egoistic capitalism that exploited labour and upon which communism flourished.

By institutionalizing its lay movements, the Church, it could be argued, strengthened and reaffirmed pre-existing patterns of authority. In the late 1960s, however, the emergence of Christian Base Communities in Brazil and some parts of Hispanic America signified a return to much earlier traditions of active Christian believers, whose commitments and priorities were not defined exclusively by the Catholic hierarchy. Many of these Base Communities were connected with popular religious movements that had antecedents in the sixteenth century. They were also responses to the processes of reform during the papacies of John XXIII (1958–63) and Paul VI (1963–78) that were catalysed by the Second Vatican Council in Rome (1962–5), the encyclicals *Mater et Magistra* (1961) and *Pacem in Terris* (1963) stressing the social obligations of the Church to the poor, and the adoption by Pope John XXIII at the Vatican Council of the phrase *Iglesia de los pobres*.

Many of the Council's decisions and recommendations that were considered particularly appropriate to Latin American conditions were clarified at the Second General Conference of Latin American Bishops, held ironically at the Catholic conservative citadel of Medellín in 1968. The Catholic Church declared its 'preferential option for the poor'. The vernacular was adopted in the mass; the liturgy was revised and made more accessible to the poorly educated; the clergy was encouraged to identify more closely with the everyday tribulations of their poor parishioners; and the laity, male and, later and more cautiously, female, was encouraged to take a more active role in the ceremonies and daily life of the Church. Furthermore, the Medellín meeting redefined the concept of sinfulness. Whereas, conventionally, 'sin' was regarded as an individual matter, a direct consequence of the Fall, which might be absolved by the priest in the confessional when the sinner repented sincerely, now sin was reinterpreted as a collective matter. Structures of power and wealth that exploited the oppressed and dispossessed and that prevented them from enjoying the fullness of God's riches and the opportunity to prepare in dignity for the afterlife were defined by a new generation as sin-laden. The redemption of the poor would be achieved only when society itself achieved redemption.

The scene was set for the advocates of a prophetic, scripture-centred Church to denounce the alleged inadequacies of tradition-centred orthodoxies. Most controversially, Catholic radicals argued the need to adopt non-violent techniques of protest and resistance and to enter into pragmatic alliances with agnostics and atheists that were committed to radical social change; a minority contended that Catholics had a right to resort to violence to overthrow tyranny and that violent revolution could be successful in combatting the violence that shored up inequalities of power and wealth. The Church had a duty to break its over-identification with entrenched interests, and an obligation both to propagate social justice and to abandon the practices of preaching a saintly obedience and an unthinking fatalism to the poor. The poor were indeed to inherit the earth; and it was incumbent upon the Church as an institution to empower the poor so that oppressive structures might be destroyed. The 'Final Document' of the Medellín Conference came to be a manifesto for many priests, monks and lay-persons committed to the struggle for justice and to political, and in some cases revolutionary, action. It crystallized divisions in the Latin American church, polarizing the conservative and radical factions for a generation.[1]

For four years (1968–72) the progressive elements in the Church encountered little opposition within the Latin American Council of Bishops (CELAM). The conservative and traditional sectors held their fire. They continued to be supported by certain elements in the Vatican such as, for example, Cardinal Sebastiano Baggio, but the Vatican bureaucracy was crucially divided. At its fourteenth meeting in Sucre, Bolivia in 1972, however, CELAM underwent a change in its orientation and leadership. Traditional groups, led by a new conservative Executive Secretary, Mons. Alfonso López Trujillo, auxiliary bishop of Bogotá before becoming archbishop (and later Cardinal) of Medellín, were strongly critical of and opposed to the stances adopted by CELAM since Medellín. And from around

---

[1] *Iglesia y liberación humana,* edited by José Camps (Barcelona, 1969), pp. 76–7.

1973, but more especially under Pope John Paul II (1978–   ), circumstances became more generally propitious for a reassertion of the Right against liberals and radicals in the Catholic Church. The particular target of its criticism and opposition was liberation theology.

It was in this context of ecclesiastical reform in the aftermath of the Second Vatican Council (1962–65) and the Medellín Conference of Latin American Bishops (1968), of the existence of prophetic and progressive groups within the Church committed to the poor, of social convulsions on the continent (and even in Cuba of revolution), and keeping in mind the advance in the academic social sciences of the so-called 'theory of dependence', which offered analyses of the structural causes of poverty in Latin America, that a Christian theological response arose in the form of 'liberation theology'. It was one of the major developments in the history of the Catholic Church in Latin America.

The history of Latin American theology remains to be written.[2] From 1930, an implicit theology of Catholic Action defined a vision of the 'two kingdoms' (the temporal, or the State, and the spiritual, or the Church, and both institutions as 'perfect societies'). From about 1955 theologians began to reflect on the problems of development and from this arose a 'development theology'.[3] It was as a critique of development theology and as a consequence of the deepening of the 'theology of revolution'[4] that liberation theology began. All this was defined by the historic discovery of the 'poor', of the 'people', as a social bloc of the oppressed, in the history and life of the Church as a prophetic institution of evangelization and installation of the 'Kingdom of God'. Liberation theology has gone through four stages. The years from 1959 to 1968 constituted the incubation period; 1968 to 1972 represented a period of creativity and hegemony; 1972 to 1984 was a time of confrontation throughout Latin America; and since 1984 liberation theology has been exported and, indeed, universalized.

As the Second Vatican Council opened in 1962 a small Christian com-

---

[2] For a brief survey, see Enrique Dussel, *Hipótesis para una historia de la teología en América Latina* (Bogotá, 1986). See also CEHILA, *Historia de la Teología en América Latina* (San José, 1981) and Pablo Richard (ed.), *Raíces de la Teología Latinoamericana* (San José, 1985).

[3] See V. Cosmao, *Signification et théologie du dévelopment* (Paris, 1967); Rubem Alves, 'Apuntes para una teología del desarrollo', in *Cristianismo y Sociedad,* 21 (1969); F. Houtart and O. Vertrano, *Hacia una teología del desarrollo* (Buenos Aires, 1970).

[4] See Hugo Assmann, 'Die Situation der unterentwickelten Lander als Ort ainer Theologie der Revolution', in *Diskussion Sur Theologie der Revolution* (Munster, 1969).

munity in Nazareth (Israel) posed the problem of the 'poor' from a perspective that was both social (in a co-operative of Arab manual labourers) and
biblical (rereading the text of Isaiah 61, 1 and Luke 4, 18 that Jesus read in
Nazareth: 'The spirit of the Lord has consecrated me to preach to the
poor').[5] This movement came to the attention of Pope John XXIII, who
spoke in 1963 of a 'Church of the poor'. At the same time, as we have
seen, the Catholic youth movements (JUC in Brazil, Argentina and Peru)
became radicalized and increasingly influenced by and identified with
socialism. Thus a crisis arose in which it was necessary to clarify the
question of 'faith and politics'. Simultaneously, and in various Latin
American countries, Catholic theologians (and an occasional Protestant)
took moves towards what was soon to be called liberation theology.

Richard Shaull in his articles 'Consideraciones teológicas sobre la
liberación del hombre' and 'La liberación humana desde una perspectiva
teológica' (1968),[6] Rubem Alves in his book *Towards a theology of liberation* (1968),[7] and Gustavo Gutiérrez in *Hacia una teología de la liberación*
(1969)[8] explicitly initiated the movement. It would be necessary, however, to wait for the epistemological clarifications of Hugo Assmann in
Teología de la liberación (1970)[9] for liberation theology to be distinguished
clearly from the theology of revolution, the political theology of J. B.
Metz and the theology of hope of J. Moltmann. At meetings, congresses
and symposia liberation theology expanded and spread all over Latin
America. Especially important were a meeting held in Mexico in November 1969 on 'Faith and development', which ended as 'Faith and liberation theology'; and meetings in Bogotá (March 1970), Buenos Aires
(August 1970) and Oruro, Bolivia (December 1970). The meeting at the
Escorial in Spain (July 1972) had special relevance, because the movement was introduced to Europe with more than 500 participants from
numerous European countries.[10] Magazines like *Víspera* (Montevideo),

---

[5] See Paul Gauthier, *Jésus, l'Eglise et les pauvres* (Tournai, 1963). It was at Nazareth that Enrique
Dussel (the author of this note) conceived of writing *Hipótesis para una historia de la Iglesia en América
Latina* (Barcelona, 1967). See also Gustavo Gutiérrez, *La Pastoral de la Iglesia en América Latina*
(Montevideo, 1968).

[6] *IDOC* (Bogotá), 43 (1968), 242–8; *Mensaje*, 168 (1968), 175–9.

[7] Rubem Alves, *Toward a Theology of Liberation* (Princeton, N.J., 1968).

[8] Gustavo Gutiérrez, *Hacia una teología de la liberación* (Montevideo, 1969); published in English as
Notes for a Theology of Liberation (1970). See also his influential *A Theory of Liberation. History, Politics,
Salvation* (Sp. orig. 1971; Maryknoll, N.Y. 1973).

[9] See Hugo Assmann, *Teología de la Liberación* (Montevideo, 1970). See also his *Theology for a Nomad
Church* (Maryknoll, N.Y., 1976).

[10] See *Fe cristiana y cambio social en América Latina*, Instituto de Fe y Secularidad (Salamanca, 1973);
this meeting produced a special issue of the international journal of theology, *Concilium*, on
Liberation Theology, 96 (1974).

Pastoral Popular (Santiago de Chile), *Diálogo* (Panama), *Servir* (Mexico), *Sic* (Caracas), and later *Páginas* (Lima) and *Puebla* (Petrópolis) became the organs of the theological movement.

During the years 1972–84, liberation theology grew steadily: the number of its exponents and of their publications expanded, together with its influence. It was an intellectual movement rooted in the poor masses, suffering under the persecution of the national security dictatorships and the ire of many conservative clergymen. Liberation theology, moreover, made a strong impact in the United States at the Detroit meetings (1975); it spread through the Third World with the founding of the Ecumenical Association of Third World Theologians (EATWOT) in Dar es Salaam (1976). There followed a period of profound maturation in which liberation theology developed in many directions; for example, on the question of Afro-American culture and problems of racial discrimination; on the condition of the indigenous peoples of Latin America; on feminism; on the problem of popular religion; and on the writing of Church history – an area developed by both the Commission on Historical Studies of the Latin American Church (Comisión de Estudios de Historia de la Iglesia, CEHILA)[11] and the newly founded Working Commission of Church History of the Third World. But perhaps the most strategic aspect was the redefinition of the function of religion in the process of social change.

Serious criticism of liberation theology in Latin America had first surfaced, as we have seen, at the meeting of CELAM in Sucre in 1972. It was elaborated at meetings such as those held in Bogotá in 1973[12] and Toledo, Spain in 1974.[13] Liberation theologians were now excluded from CELAM institutes by policy directives clearly emanating from certain groups in the Roman Curia. And not one liberation theologian was invited to attend the Third General Conference of Latin American Bishops finally held in Puebla, Mexico in 1979, although 42 went to Puebla at the invitation of individual bishops and participated in the Conference from outside.

---

[11] The Commission, founded in Quito in 1973, has held annual symposia and published numerous books on the history of the Church in Latin America. In addition to the *Historia General de la Iglesia en América Latina* (*HGIAL*), it publishes material on the history of theology in Latin America, the religious orders and communities, a *Historia Mínima* of the Church by country (this collection includes the work by Jean-Pierre Bastian on Protestantism), history of the Church at the popular level (supplemented by audiovisual material on the history of the Church published in Bogotá), and monthly and quarterly studies published in São Paulo, Mexico City and elsewhere in Latin America.

[12] See CELAM, *Liberación: diálogos en el CELAM* (Bogotá, 1974), which contains the following chapters of special interest: B. Kloppenburg, 'Las tentaciones de la teología de la liberación' (pp. 401–515), J. Mejía, 'La liberación, aspectos bíblicos' (pp. 271–307) and Mons. Alfonso López Trujillo, 'Las teologías de la liberación' (pp. 27–67).

[13] Papers published under the title *Teología de la liberación. Conversaciones de Toledo* (Burgos, 1974).

The appearance of the 'Documento de consulta' in 1978, in advance of the Puebla Conference, started a theological polemic of a kind never seen on the continent in all its history.[14] However, only the Vatican's 'Instruction on some aspects of Liberation Theology', the confrontation between the Brazilian theologian Leonardo Boff and the Congregation for the Doctrine of the Faith in Rome, and the judgement of Cardinal Josef Ratzinger against Boff, all in 1984, brought liberation theology to the attention of the public at large, in Latin America and internationally. A second 'Instruction' of 1986 and Pope John Paul II's letter to the Brazilian episcopate (9 April 1986), in which he stated that 'liberation theology is not only timely, but useful and necessary', signified an important climacteric.

[14] See Enrique Dussel, *De Medellín a Puebla: una década de sangre y esperanza* (Mexico, D.F., 1979), pp. 477–97. See also Leonardo Boff, *Iglesia: carisma o poder* (Petrópolis, 1981), and P. Richard and S. Croatto (eds.), *La lucha de los dios* (San José, 1980).

Part Three

5

SCIENCE IN TWENTIETH CENTURY
LATIN AMERICA

INTRODUCTION

The development of science as an organized activity in Latin America has rarely been smooth or lineal. Rather it has been replete with false starts, with periods of consolidation followed by periods of fragmentation and reverse, often for political reasons.[1] Moreover, the considerable national variation both in the organization of science and the level of achievement of different disciplines makes any homogeneous synthesis problematical at best. This chapter treats the history of selected scientific disciplines – biology, biomedicine, psychoanalysis, physical and exact sciences, and geology – in Latin America in the twentieth century. Because of substantial gaps in the secondary literature coverage must necessarily be incomplete. The chapter focusses on the formative years of these sciences, primarily before the Second World War but with some attention of developments during the two decades after the war. Science in the second half of the twentieth century is then treated in a more general sociological mode, reflecting the bias of the secondary literature, which is supplemented by materials from the author's own collection of internal documentation of scientific institutions. Here we will follow the institutionalization of science, the emergence of a scientific ethos and changing relationships between scientists, government and society. If this leaves us with an imperfect view, we are content at least to advance some working hypotheses and provide an armature for future research.

---

[1] For example, on the trauma of independence which ruined the hopes and confirmed the anxieties of those, especially the naturalists, who at the end of the eighteenth century were beginning to conceptualize a science that was distinctly American and that could mature without a constant infusion of energy, materiel and information from European expeditionaries, see Thomas F. Glick, 'Science and Independence in Latin America', *Hispanic American Historical Review*, 71,2 (1991): 307–34.

An important chronological break came in 1939 when Spanish refugee scientists, joining other specific, mainly Jewish, refugees from Nazism, began acting as catalysts of an institutional transformation whose first phase was completed in the 1950s when substantial numbers of young scientists trained mainly in the United States began to make their presence felt. This transformation had both institutional and cognitive foci and was accompanied by a value change involving the implantation – socially selective and politically incomplete – of a scientific ethos.

At the beginning of the Civil War in July 1936 Spain was more advanced scientifically and producing scientific research at a higher level than any Latin American nation, although Argentina's science establishment was perhaps marginally larger. Spain's success was mainly due to the ability of her scientists to mobilize government support for science in the wake of neurohistologist Santiago Ramón y Cajal's winning the Nobel Prize for medicine in 1906. Cajal headed the Junta para Ampliación de Estudios, founded soon after, an institution which provided scholarships for study abroad and established laboratories in the most promising biomedical fields, including neurohistology and physiology. In the 1920s, attracted by the Junta's programme and congruent value structure the Rockefeller Foundation made substantial investments in Spanish medicine and physics. The Spanish Junta itself became a model that was explicitly emulated by more than a few countries of Latin America as they attempted to expand their scientific capabilities in the 1920s and after.[2]

Spanish scientists left the country in great numbers after the Republic's defeat in 1939. Five hundred medical doctors went to Mexico alone where they constituted 10 per cent of that country's medical community. But many Latin American countries that received far fewer refugees were the beneficiaries of a scientific stimulus not measurable in numbers alone. They arrived there just as their Latin American colleagues were gaining self-awareness of their collective professional and social roles as scientists.

The implantation of a scientific ethos in Latin America was strongly conditioned by attitudes laid down by the positivists of the nineteenth century. Arturo Ardao has argued that European positivism appeared as the culmination of one hundred years or more of scientific revolution, but

---

[2] See J. M. Sánchez Ron (ed.), *La Junta para Ampliación de Estudios e Investigaciones Científicas: 80 años después,* 2 vols (Madrid, 1988).

that in Latin America the relationship was more nearly the inverse: there 'positivism anticipated and precipitated scientific culture, instead of resulting from scientific thought as in Europe'.[3] In Latin America, scientific positivism did not have its origins in science but rather in the political philosophy and educational programmes – national 'diagrams' – of leading positivists.[4] In the nineteenth century, as put into practice by positivist political leaders like Domingo Sarmiento, in Argentina the scientific programme of positivism centered on the description of natural resources with an eye towards their exploitation in the interest of modernization. But the rest of the diagram(s) related to science materialized only at the rhetorical level in the nineteenth century and emerged in a programmatic way in the twentieth as, for example, in the creation of scientific institutions in the wake of the Mexican Revolution, or in the scientific programmes of specific ministries, such as the Brazilian Ministry of Agriculture, both a hotbed of positivism and a fecund generator of scientific projects in the first four decades of the century.

If positivism preceded rather than followed the development of science in Latin America, the same is true of science policy and the discussion and evaluation of the place of science in society. Different groups formed attitudes about science prior to the inception of national scientific institutions, producing in the process a very interesting body of discussion of the role of science in society. Concomitant with the inception of modern scientific institutions the ethos informing modern science had also to take root. These two processes took place in politically charged atmospheres, such as the continuing institutionalization of the Mexican revolution under Cárdenas in the late 1930s or the transition from the Pérez Jiménez dictatorship to democracy in Venezuela of the late 1950s. As a result the social and political study of science has both an immediacy and a sensitivity to social and cultural issues that it lacks in the developed countries. There is greater attention to the 'high tradition' in the sociology of science in Latin America than we are accustomed to in the Anglo-American academic world, as sociologists of science, observing scientific culture in the act of creation, routinely work through the great themes of science/society interaction as defined by Robert Merton, Derek Price, Thomas Kuhn and others.

[3] Arturo Ardao, 'Assimilation and Transformation of Positivism in Latin America', *Journal of the History of Ideas*, 24 (1963), p. 517.
[4] The notion of positivist diagrams is that of Oscar Terán, *Positivismo y nación en la Argentina* (Buenos Aires, 1987), p. 12.

Two considerations of a theoretical nature underlie the discussion that follows. The first is that in general science has been generated from the metropoli – that is Europe and the United States – by a process of diffusion (a cognitive process) that has a number of concomitant components. Diffusion curves show that ideas spread by contagion and that the process is self-generating, once initiated. But reception is shaped by a specific context, that of peripherality, with respect to the 'mainstream' science of the metropolis, which produces characteristic reactions. The parameters of such reaction to scientific ideas can be grouped under two modal types, called active and passive.[5] Passive receptions are limited to assimilation of scientific ideas with ability to further diffuse them but without the ability to add creatively to the set of ideas in question. Active reception involves the capacity to carry the paradigm further in original research programmes. Although both modes assume dependence, the dependent variables of each also reflect the differential ability of recipient groups to generate original responses to the stimulus diffused. Clearly, such modes reflect different institutional features prevailing in the disciplinary groups in the recipient societies that receive and rework the ideas. Groups that have achieved a 'critical mass' of highly trained personnel have the ability to carry new paradigms further. Both the training of such personnel and their ability to assimilate new ideas critically depends in turn on issues of cultural congruence and a variety of educational and communication factors.

The implantation of institutional models also can be described in terms of the metropolitan experience and the specific contours of the recipient society. The Pasteur Institute provided a universal model for the implantation of microbiology, both pure and applied. Its success or failure relates to the conditions prevailing in local settings. Finally, although many modern scientific disciplines were born in Latin American countries under situations of 'scientific imperialism' with mentors sent out, rather like apostles, from the scientifically developed countries, the motives of those missionaries, as Lewis Pyenson shows, were frequently far from imperialistic or self-seeking.[6] Many of the foreign scientists who played such a large role in the institutionalization of science in twentieth-century Latin Amer-

---

[5] See Thomas F. Glick, 'La transferencia de las revoluciones científicas a través de las fronteras culturales,' *Ciencia y Desarrollo* (Mexico, D.F.), 12, no. 72 (1987), pp. 77–89.

[6] Lewis Pyenson, 'Functionaries and Seekers in Latin America; missionary diffusion of the exact sciences, 1850–1930,' *Quipu*, 2 (1985): 387–420. See also Thomas F. Glick, 'Crítica a N. Stepan y L. Pyenson,' ibid., pp. 437–42.

ica had no metropolitan connections whatever when they arrived (e.g., Spanish republicans and Jewish refugees from Nazism). How then can they be portrayed as serving imperialist interests? Actors must be accorded some autonomy. To insist on arguing that such persons were acting as mere unconscious agents of imperialism is either to miss the point of their personal career patterns and objectives or else to reduce an intellectual process to a purely transactional one in a wider and impersonal movement of power politics. The two interpretations are not mutually exclusive by any means, but generalization runs the risk of misreading as political, scientific processes that had in themselves little or no political content or, at worst, converts the antinomy of international science/local interests into an exercise in special pleading. *Mutatis mutandis,* phenomena with overtly economic overtones, such as invasion of mining countries by legions of U. S. Geological Service geologists, may well have had politically neutral outcomes, such as the generation of university instruction in such fields.

BIOLOGY

Darwinism

The reception of Darwinism, which put an end to the old Natural History and created modern biology, was, in most Latin American countries, a phenomenon of the 1880s. However that reception was characterized by a debate among positivist lawyers, doctors and social thinkers; only in Argentina were there any researchers actively engaged in biological research programmes that could directly incorporate the orientation of evolutionary biology, although in other countries evolutionary perspectives were assimilated in some medical school theses. In Brazil the preeminence of philosophers among historians of ideas has led to the exaggeration of the impact of Comtean positivists and the neglect of Spencerians and Darwinians whose impact was just as great.[7] Darwinists were particularly powerful in the Bahia Medical School and in the Recife Law School. Medical doctors were characteristically Darwinian in science and republican in politics. In Chile, there was a kind of mute assimilation of Darwinian ideas, especially in applied areas such as agronomy and field geology,

---

[7] On Brazilian Spencerianism, see Richard Graham, *Britain and the Onset of Modernization in Brazil, 1850–1914* (Cambridge, 1958), ch. 9; on Darwinism, Therezinha Alves Ferreira Collichio, *Miranda de Azevedo e o darwinismo no Brasil* (São Paulo, 1988).

no doubt because of the pre-eminence of Comteans in the academic world.[8] The reception of Darwinism in Cuba was marked by the variegated philosophical discussion accompanying it. Not only was there a Spencerian contingent composed mainly of medical doctors (the Spencerianism of doctors was marked throughout Latin America), but also the group of neo-Hegelian lawyers who wrote in the *Revista de Cuba*, also staunchly Darwinian.[9] In Mexico, Justo Sierra introduced Darwin's ideas in 1875 and by the end of the decade they had entered official curricula. But the leading Mexican positivist, the French-trained Comtean Gabino Barreda was a Lamarckian and followed the French line on Darwin, whose frequently metaphorical language seemed at odds with the canons of positivist science.[10]

In Uruguay, positivists – as much Darwinian as they were Spencerian – controlled the educational system in the 1870s and 1880s and Darwinian professors controlled both the faculties of medicine and law. Catholics took their futile complaints of a 'positivist dictatorship' to the floor of the congress. But even before the positivist/Catholic debate, Darwin's ideas had already been debated by cattlemen, perhaps as early as the mid-1860s. In the polemic over how best to upgrade the herds of creole cattle, some *estancieros* asserted that natural selection had already acted upon native herds to adapt them to local conditions of pasture and climate; they argued against crossing with imported Durham bulls on the grounds that Darwin did not believe that such admixtures would be permanent.[11]

In Argentina, Darwinism was well entrenched by 1875 when Eduardo Holmberg began teaching evolutionary theory in the Escuela Normal de Maestras; two years later the English naturalist was elected to membership in the Argentine Scientific Society.[12] Argentina produced the only 'classical' evolutionist in Latin America, the paleontologist Florentino Ameghino (1854–1911). A prodigious field worker, Ameghino discovered more than 6,000 species of fossil mammals. He accepted 'the laws of

[8] Bernardo Márquez Bretón, *Orígenes del darwinismo en Chile* (Santiago, 1982).

[9] Pedro M. Pruna and Armando García González, *Darwinismo y sociedad en Cuba: Siglo XIX* (Madrid, 1989).

[10] Roberto Moreno, *La polémica del darwinismo en México: Siglo XIX* (Mexico, D.F., 1984); Rosaura Ruiz Gutiérrez, *Positivismo y evolución: Introducción del darwinismo en México* (Mexico, D.F., 1987); Charles A. Hale, *The Transformation of Liberalism in Late Nineteenth-Century Mexico* (Princeton, N.J., 1989), pp. 206–10.

[11] Thomas F. Glick, *Darwin y darwinismo en el Uruguay y en América latina* (Montevideo, 1989), chs 5 and 6.

[12] Marcelo Montserrat, 'La mentalidad evolucionista: Una ideología del progreso', in Ezequiel Gallo and Gustavo Ferrera (eds), *La Argentina del Ochenta al Centenario* (Buenos Aires, 1980), pp. 785–818.

evolution' as undisputed principles and devised a natural classification system in his *Filogenia* (1884) based on morphological features. His achievement was vitiated by his obsession with proving the American origin of man, a fallacy resulting from his misdating of South American strata. He was a rhetorical Darwinian, his notions of the mechanisms of evolution being closer to those of the neo-Lamarckians he had met in France. In the early decades of the twentieth century, Ameghino became a political symbol, defended by the left and opposed by the Jesuit biologists who led the Catholic crusade against Darwin.[13]

By the turn of the century the controversy had died down in most places, but in Venezuela it erupted anew, revealing the unresolved antagonism between evolutionary biology and traditional Catholicism. There, the comparative anatomist and evolutionist Luis Razetti, while acknowledging that evolution, either in its neo-Lamarckian or Darwinian form, was established officially in Venezuelan education, still sought to have the Academy of Medicine of Caracas, the nation's highest scientific authority, proclaim it to be the basis of scientific biology. In order to accomplish this, he proposed in 1904 that the Academy adopt three conclusions: that life has its origin in inorganic matter; that present-day organisms derive by descent from that primitive living matter; and that man is one organism more, subject to the same natural laws as the others. By a deft parliamentary manoeuvre Razetti further insisted that the Academy had to accept his conclusions if members were unable to prove their falsity without straying from the bounds of experimental science; those who voted against did so at the risk of exposing themselves as retrograde ideologues. The Academy accepted Razetti's proposals, but not before bowing to pressure from the archbishop of Caracas who insisted on the insertion of a qualifying phrase. The promotion of Darwinism thus became a matter for political action. In 1906 Razetti's materialist book, *What is Life?* was published with a government subvention: it was in the interest of the positivist dictator Cipriano Castro to promote evolution, inasmuch as his political enemies, the traditionalist 'Goths' were as much opposed to him as to Darwin.[14]

[13] Julio Orione, 'Florentino Ameghino y la influencia de Lamarck en la paleontologia argentina del siglo XIX,' *Quipu*, 4 (1987): 447–71; Justo Garate, 'Florentino Ameghino', *Dictionary of Scientific Biography*, I, 129–32; 'Hablan los hombres de ciencia del país sobre las asendereadas teorías de Ameghino', *Estudios*, 22 (1922): 428–45.

[14] For an account of the Razetti polemic, see Thomas F. Glick, 'Perspectivas sobre la recepción del darwinismo en el mundo hispano', in *Actas, II Congreso de la Sociedad Española de Historia de las Ciencias*, 3 vols (Zaragoza, 1984), I: 49–64, on pp. 53–7.

Around the turn of the century, the leading Mexican biologist was Alfonso L. Herrera (1868–1942). The rubrics of his *Recueil de lois de la Biologie Générale* (Paris, 1897) are Darwinian (e.g., differentiation, variation, adaptation, selection, distribution, struggle for life, evolution). Two years later in *La vie sur les hauts plateaux* (Mexico, D. F., 1899) he argued that flora and fauna alike adapt to the harsh conditions of high altitude and that certain mechanisms of adaptation are most likely hereditary. Herrera was such a materialist and evolutionist that he proposed an experimental crossing of a human and an ape to demonstrate the animal nature of man.[15] Herrera was best known for his pioneering speculations on the origins of life. In 1942 he explicated his concept of 'sulphobes', microstructures within cells which he claimed to have replicated chemically. Herrera's work was significant because he explained the origin of organisms by alluding to inorganic polymers, whereas contemporary origin theorists focused on organic macromolecules.[16]

Social Darwinism

Social Darwinism in general is better called Social Spencerism, because it stressed the struggle for life (a term Darwin picked up from Spencer) and competition, rather than attempting to extend the Darwinian sense of selection into the social sphere. In Latin America, much of the writing in this vein had to do with distinctions between Europeans, Blacks and Indians.

Brazilians, in particular, were much concerned with what was perceived as biological differentiation between various racial and ethnic groups. An extreme social Spencerian was Euclides da Cunha. This is apparent in the sociological sections of his great book *Os Sertões* (1902) (translated into English as *Rebellion in the Backlands*) which is an account of a revolt of mestizo *sertanejos,* brutally put down by the government in 1897. Mestizos were racially degenerate, a 'hyphen' (he says) between three races, the Indo-European, the Negro and Indian which 'represent evolutionary stages in confrontation'. 'According to the conclusion of the evolutionist,' da Cunha asserted, 'even when the influence of a superior race has reacted

---

[15] Alfonso L. Herrera, *El híbrido del hombre y el mono* (Valencia, 1933). Herrera was prescient on the closeness of apes and humans; see 'Redrawing the Ancestral Tree: genetics changes traditional ideas about chimpanzees and gorillas', *Harvard Alumni Gazette,* (February 1990): 17–18.

[16] See Sidney W. Fox and Klaus Dose, *Molecular Evolution and the Origin of Life* (San Francisco, Cal., 1972), pp. 6–8.

upon the offspring, the latter show vivid traces of the inferior one. Misce-genation carried to an extreme means retrogression.'[17] The result of this hereditary degeneration, though not an evolutionary result in itself, has evolutionary consequences, because such groups are disadvantaged in the struggle for existence: 'The fact is that in the marvelous competition of peoples, all of them evolving in a struggle that knows no truce, with selection capitalizing those attributes which heredity preserves, the mestizo is an intruder. He does not struggle.'[18]

The mestizo thereby violates the laws of nature. Although the genetic tendency is regression towards the primitive race (the Negro in this case), mestizos despise Negroes and avoid mating with them. They seek inter-marriages, by force, with whites who will extinguish the despised traits: 'This [social] tendency is significant. In a manner of speaking it picks up the thread of evolution which miscegenation has severed.' The superior race becomes the biological objective and in seeking it the mestizos are obeying the instinct of self-preservation, an instinct with evolutionary implications. 'The laws of the evolution of species are inviolable ones.' The missionaries proved unable to civilize the Indians, who will nevertheless civilize themselves through miscegenation.

Not all social Darwinians, however, reached the conclusion that Indians were evolutionarily or biologically degenerate. The exact opposite conclu-sion, in fact, was reached by Vicente Riva Palacio (1832–96), a Mexican politician and amateur naturalist. In 1884 he asserted in a history of colonial Mexico that if the Indians were judged from an evolutionist perspective, it would have to be concluded that they were superior to all other known races. For example, Mexican Indians lacked body hair; they also lacked wisdom teeth and had an extra molar in place of the rudimen-tary canine tooth that Europeans have. Such traits indicated that they were more highly evolved than Europeans.[19] Riva Palacios' theory was picked up by Andrés Molina Enríquez in his great social critique of 1909, *Los grandes problemas nacionales,* a work which had a tremendous influence on the Mexican revolutionary generation. Molina quotes Riva Palacios at length and then adds a long 'scientific note' on selection, comparing its action upon individuals with that upon groups.[20] He distinguishes be-

[17] Euclides de Cunha, *Os Sertões;* Eng trans, *Rebellion in the Backlands* (Chicago, Ill., 1964), pp. 84–85.
[18] Ibid., p. 86.
[19] Roberto Moreno, 'Mexico', in Thomas F. Glick (ed.), *The Comparative Reception of Darwinism,* 2nd edn (Chicago, Ill., 1988), pp. 366–68.
[20] Andrés Molina Enriquez, *Los grandes problemas nacionales* [1909] (Mexico, D.F., 1978), pp. 346–8.

tween groups in more densely settled areas who, because of constant conflict, have evolved a kind of collective strength, and those from less densely settled areas upon whom selection acts at the individual level. For this reason, the indigenous peoples of America had a number of highly evolved individual traits but could not stand up collectively to the Europeans. Social evolution, therefore, is portrayed as a biological process.

Social Darwinism continued well into the twentieth century as a force to be reckoned with in Latin American social science. A representative figure is the Cuban anthropologist Fernando Ortiz who, in the early part of his career, was a biological determinist and social Darwinist, who viewed Blacks as primitive and lustful. In 1914 he wrote that 'Evolutionism is today the law of life in all of its manifestations . . . Perhaps our national future could in the end be nothing more than a complex problem of ethnic selection. [Humanity] continues abandoned to the most elementary socio-physical laws, struggling against the general biological promiscuity of inferior species.'[21]

Genetics

The rediscovery of Mendel was appreciated early in Argentina where, in 1908, the biologist Angel Gallardo published a short book on modern research on heredity in biology, whose bibliography demonstrates his acquaintance with European genetics. Articles followed on practical applications of Mendel's law to agriculture and cattle breeding and on the polemic between Mendelians and Galtonian biometricians, a topic of interest in Argentina where Galton's work had been followed in the 1880s. Teaching of genetics was introduced by Miguel Fernández, trained in Germany, at the University of La Plata in 1915. Fernández was the teacher of Salomón Horovitz and Francisco Alberto Sáez who built a tradition in genetics in Argentina. Horovitz's early research, on chromosomes in plant meiosis, appeared in 1927, antedating his doctoral dissertation at Cornell on segmented interchange in plants. His research, as professor of genetics at the Faculty of Agronomy in La Plata (1938–47) was mainly on applied problems. An opponent of Perón's dictatorship, he emigrated to Venezuela in 1947. Sáez (1898–1976), Uruguayan by birth, directed the cytology laboratory in the same faculty from 1938 to 1947, when he also

---

[21] Cited by Roberto González Echevaría, *Alejo Carpentier: The Pilgrim at Home* (Ithaca, N.Y., 1977), p. 47 n. 26.

departed to join the Institute of Biological Research in Montevideo. Sáez introduced cytogenetics in Latin America in 1925. A pronounced evolutionist, he asserted in a 1929 article the value of cytology and genetics for the future of systematics, which should be based on the behavior of chromosomes from a phylogenetic perspective. When Clarence McClung visited Argentina in 1930, he stimulated Sáez's future research both in sex chromosomes and in the genetics of grasshoppers. In 1935 Sáez and his student Eduardo De Robertis made the striking discovery that amphibians have no morphologically differentiated sex chromosomes. In 1946 Sáez and de Robertis published the first edition of their influential textbook on general cytology. In the late 1940s and 1950s a number of Argentinians went to Berkeley to study with G. Ledyard Stebbins. One of Stebbins' disciples, Juan Hunziker, performed research on the evolution of the karyotype in various genera of gymnosperms with large chromosomes.[22]

Drosophila research was introduced by Arturo Burkart in his Buenos Aires thesis of 1931. Burkart had studied in Germany with Curt Stern and his account of the methodology of fruit-fly research was influential in Argentinian biology. Nevertheless, fruit flies were used primarily for instruction. Systematic research did not begin until 1957 when two disciples of Herman Muller, Juan I. Valencia and his wife Ruby Allen returned from Indiana (Valencia to the University of Buenos Aires, Allen to the genetics laboratory of the Nuclear Energy Commission). Their work on the genetic effects of ionizing radiation led to the International Symposium of Genes and Chromosomes, held in Buenos Aires in 1964 under the aegis of the American Atomic Energy Commission and the Oak Ridge Laboratory. In 1966 the Valencias returned to the United States.[23]

Mendelism was introduced in Brazil through the agricultural schools. Carlos Teixeira Mendes, professor at Piracicaba, is generally regarded as the first Brazilian Mendelian for the treatment of genetics in his 1917 book on improvement of agricultural varieties.[24] Teixeira Mendes began teaching genetics and evolution there in 1918. A real research effort, however, was

[22] Luis B. Mazoti and Juan H. Hunziker, 'Los precursores de la genética en la Argentina', in Mazoti and Hunziker (eds), *Evolución de las ciencias en la República Argentina, 1923–1972: Genética* (Buenos Aires, 1976), pp. 5–12; and Hunziker and Francisco A. Sáez, 'Citogenética y genética evolutiva vegetal y animal', ibid., pp. 33–75.

[23] Beatriz Mazar Barnett, 'Genética de Drosophila', in Luis B. Mazoti and Juan H. Hunziker (eds), *Evolucíon de la ciencias en la República Argentina, 1923–1972: Genética* (Buenos Aires, 1976), pp. 219–27.

[24] Thomas F. Glick, 'Establishing Scientific Disciplines in Latin America: genetics in Brazil, 1943–1960', in A. Lafuente, A. Elena and M. L. Ortega (eds), *Mundialización de la ciencia y cultural nacional* (Aranjuez, 1993), pp. 364–5.

not mounted until the arrival of the German Friedrich Brieger as professor of cytology and genetics in 1936. Brieger built an important research programme in plant genetics with Rockefeller Foundation aid and a programme of interchange with foreign scholars. Brieger himself wrote important studies on the origins of corn. He also worked on the evolution of plants in the tropics, a major theme of genetics in Brazil, showing the Orchids to be in a phase of explosive evolution. Genetics at the Campinas agricultural school was of a more applied nature, centring on diseases of coffee and other cultigens.[25]

A critical moment for Brazilian genetics came in 1943 when Theodosius Dobzhansky arrived at André Dreyfus's genetics department at the University of São Paulo for the first of a number of visits. Dobzhansky had just concluded a series of studies on the genetics of natural populations, in which he had studied the distribution of native populations of *Drosophila* in temperate zones; now he wanted to extend his research programme by comparing temperate to tropical populations. The research he conducted over a fifteen-year period with Brazilian colleagues and disciples revealed the greater genetic variety and plasticity of tropical species and had important implications for evolutionary biology. From the Drosophilists trained by Dobzhansky came the future leaders of Brazilian genetics. The success of Brazilian genetics was due in large part to the Rockefeller Foundation, which consistently supported the entire Drosophila programme, enabled numerous Brazilians to study in Dobzhansky's laboratory at Columbia University, and which then broadened its support to encompass human genetics in the 1950s.[26]

In the 1970s the Multinational Genetics Project of the Organization of American States facilitated research in human genetics in a number of countries by standardizing biochemical techniques important in medical genetic research. This was the origin of the biochemical genetics programme in the Institute of Human Genetics (founded 1972) of the University of San Andrés medical school in Bolivia.[27]

[25] Ernesto Paterniani, 'Genética vegetal', in Mario Guimaraes Ferro and Shozo Motoyama (eds), *História das ciências no Brasil,* 3 vols (São Paulo, 1979), I: 219–40.
[26] Glick, 'Establishing Scientific Disciplines in Latin America', pp. 365–75; A. Brito da Cunha, 'The Seventy Years of Life of C. Pavan and Science', *Revista Brasileira de Genética,* 12 (1989), pp. 691–9; C. Pavan et al., 'Departamento de Biologia Geral da Faculdade de Filosofia, Ciências e Letras da Universidade de São Paulo', *Atas do Primeiro Simpósio Sul-Americano de Genética* (São Paulo, 1961), pp. 61–95; Simon Schwartzman, *Formação da comunidade científica no Brasil* (São Paulo, 1979), pp. 274–80; and the symposium, 'A genética no Brasil: passado e futuro', *Ciência e Cultura,* 41 (1989): 439–66.
[27] Universidad Mayor de San Andrés, Facultad de Medicina, Instituto de Genética Humana, 'Breve reseña histórica del Instituto de Genética Humana' (typescript).

Eugenics

Eugenics, a socially constructed application of genetics, was, in part, the application of social Darwinian constructs in an attempt to preserve the predominance and 'racial purity' of whites, in countries where miscegenation was in evidence, and to encourage the immigration of socially favoured groups in predominantly European countries. As in Europe, eugenics was an attempt to biologize social problems and propose 'scientific' solutions for them.[28]

In Europe eugenics found its scientific roots in Mendelian genetics informed by a harsh selectionism inherited from social Darwinism. The congenitally infirm, the psychopath and other 'unfit' elements were to be selected out of the body politic, using sterilization as the instrument of eugenic policy. The Nazi racial programme was, of course, the apotheosis of selectionist eugenics, whose terrible implementation had the effect of discrediting the scientific pretensions of eugenics.

Latin American eugenics in general was not selectionist, since its base in biological theory was neo-Lamarckian, rather than Darwinian and Mendelian, and, in its public health aspect was pro-natalist rather than Malthusian (promoting the medicalization of pregnancy and birth rather than birth control). Inasmuch as the Church opposed (and in the encyclical *Casti Connubi* of 1930) officially banned eugenics as a challenge to the Church's authority in matrimonial and sexual matters, attempts to promote sterilization of the undesirable were muted in Latin America. Emphasis was laid on 'puericulture', the hygienic treatment of infants and on maternal health care. Alcoholism, criminality, tuberculosis and other conditions thought to be inheritable were viewed, under the ethos of neo-Lamarckian meliorism, to be responsive to public health measures, the improvements being passed on to succeeding generations.

It is in the area of race, however, that Latin American eugenics most reflected ideological influence. As Nancy Stepan has demonstrated, all Latin American eugenics movements were, to a greater or lesser degree, about race.[29] In Argentina, eugenics became intertwined in the discussion of national identity and post First World War agitation to limit immigration in order to exclude Jews, Arabs and other peoples whose ability to assimilate was questioned. Victor Delfino, founder of the Argentine Eu-

---

[28] Nancy Stepan, *The Hour of Eugenics: Race, Gender and Nation in Latin America* (Ithaca, N.Y., 1991), pp. 1–14.
[29] Ibid., ch. 5: 'National Identities and Racial Transformations', pp. 135–70.

genics Society, argued for control of immigration and against racial crossing. In accord with the norms of 'biotypology', race as well as family
history entered into the biological monitoring of society.[30] The Argentine
Association of Biotypology and Eugenics, whose intellectual roots originated in Italian Fascism, was able to associate Latin civilization with
eugenic superiority and in that way create a different criterion for assessing
races than that associated with German or English eugenics. Argentinian
eugenists fretted that Argentinian society was still too racially heterogeneous to establish strong institutions.

Brazilian social Darwinians, like Francisco José de Oliveira Vianna,
proposed to solve the racial problem by 'aryanizing' or whitening
the racially inferior groups by encouraging their intermarriage with
Europeans – immigrants to be imported for that purpose.[31] Further
north, 'whitening', retread to eugenic specifications, came up again in
Guatemala, in an unlikely source: Miguel Angel Asturias's law thesis of
1925. According to Asturias the Indians had fallen into 'physiological
decadence' to which there was but one solution, a biological one: 'only
inheritance is strong enough to combat inheritance.' Social palliatives
such as converting Indians into small landholders didn't work. The
Indians needed new blood; European immigrants must come and biologically mix with the indigenous population. 'The laws of society,' Asturias
concluded, 'resolve themselves inexorably; mortally wounded organisms,
like our population, are destined to disappear.'[32]

In Mexico, as already indicated with respect to social Darwinism, racial
eugenics was given a progressive twist. There miscegenation was viewed
positively, as the origin of a distinctively Mexican race – a 'cosmic race' in
José Vasconcelos' term – the biological underpinning of political and intellectual *indigenismo* in the 1920s. It is also true, however, that to identify
Mexican nationality with the *mestizo* was to depreciate the worth of the
Indian as a race.[33]

The 'soft' nature of eugenics in Latin America, in contrast to the hard
selectionism of Germanic and English versions, calls into question what is

[30] Biotypology had been introduced in Argentina by Nicolo Pende in a 1930 visit. Its central concept
    was that human populations could be broken down into analytical types based on characteristic
    illnesses, personality and racial origin. The inventory of biotypes was a prerequisite to rational
    organization of the biological resources of the state (ibid., p. 65).
[31] On whitening in Brazilian sociology, see the discussion by Oracy Nogueira, 'A sociologia no
    Brasil', in Guimaraes and Motoyama (eds), *História das ciências no Brasil,* III: 181–234, on pp.
    191–2.
[32] Jesús J. Amurrio, *El positivismo en Guatemala* (Guatemala City, 1966), pp. 80–87 (mimeo).
[33] Ibid., p. 256.

normative in science. In general the original version of any scientific idea or tradition is taken as normative and departures from the norm are measured against it. Comparative study reveals patterns of reception – such as that of eugenics in the Latin world – which display pervasive systemic differences from the original cognitive system (in this case Galtonian selectionism) to a degree where the relationship of the transferred idea with its 'hearth' loses much of its significance.

BIOMEDICINE

The new microbiology that resulted from the discoveries of Pasteur and Koch transformed medical research and public health everywhere from the 1880s. Latin Americans went to the Pasteur Institute in Paris soon after its founding (1885) to master the new techniques and theories. Among the first was the Brazilian Augusto Ferreira dos Santos who studied there in 1886 and inaugurated a Pasteur-style institute to treat rabies in Rio de Janeiro soon after. In São Paulo, the Frenchman Félix Le Dantec arrived to found a Pasteur Institute in 1892 but left the country precipitously and the facility, the first modern research laboratory in Brazil, was directed by Adolfo Lutz, highly regarded for his research on cholera and yellow fever.[34] In Venezuela a Pasteur Institute was founded in 1895 by Santos Aníbal Dominici; it closed in 1902 when Dominici ran afoul of the dictator Cipriano Castro. Another Pasteur Institute was established in Maracaibo in 1897.[35] In Paraguay, Miguel Elmassian, an Armenian graduate of the Pasteur Institute, was from 1900–5 first director of the National Institute of Bacteriology. With his disciple and successor Luis E. Migone, he produced important research on equine flagellosis and various amoebic diseases.[36]

At the turn of the century, yellow fever was the burning issue in what had come to be called 'tropical medicine'. Since its cause turned out to be a virus, Koch's bacteriological methodology only occasioned repeated false starts in identifying the pathogen. But, as early as 1881 the Cuban Carlos

---

[34] On bacteriology in Brazil, see Nancy Stepan, *Beginnings of Brazilian Science: Oswaldo Cruz, Medical Research and Policy, 1890–1920* (New York, 1976). Lutz's Bacteriological Institute was the antecedent of Butantan Institute, established by Lutz with Vital Brasil as director in 1899; see Jandira Lopes de Oliveira, 'Cronologia do Instituto Butantan (1888–1981), Vol. 1: 1888–1945', *Memorias do Instituto Butantan*, 44/45 (1980–81): 11–79.

[35] Marcel Roche, *Rafael Rangel: Ciencia política en la Venezuela de principios de siglo* (Caracas, 1978), p. 43.

[36] Arquimedes Canese, 'La microbiología y parasitología en el Paraguay,' *Anales de la Facultad de Ciencias Médicas de la Universidad Nacional de Asunción*, 15 (1983): 395–7.

Finlay had correctly identified the vector of the disease, the mosquito eventually named *Aedes aegypti*. Finlay's discovery, however, had no impact until after the War of 1898 when Reed Board in the United States performed further experiments, along lines laid out by Finlay, and quickly confirmed his hypothesis.[37] The U.S. Army's public health effort, led by General William Gorgas, quickly wiped out yellow fever first in Cuba and later in Panama. Then in 1914 the recently-founded Rockefeller Foundation decided to make a major effort to locate endemic foci of yellow fever and destroy the mosquitos. It established a commission to identify such foci in Ecuador, Peru, Colombia, Venezuela and Brazil. The Commission had only one Hispanic member, Juan Guiteras, a Cuban who, like Finlay, had served as a doctor in the U.S. Army during the Cuban war of independence against Spain, and indeed the Foundation's efforts in Ecuador and Peru, although successful in conquering yellow fever, made no contribution to national medical science.[38] The most glaring case was Peru where Henry Hanson, a member of the Rockefeller Foundation's Yellow Fever Commission, was actually named the country's Director of Public Health in 1919–22. Hanson wiped out yellow fever by placing fish in home cisterns to eat mosquito larvae. The Rockefeller's take-over of Peruvian public health resulted in the virtual cessation of local bacteriological research.[39]

The Serum Therapy Institute founded at Manguinhos near Rio de Janeiro in 1900, was also in the Pasteurian mold, particularly after Oswaldo Cruz, himself trained in Paris, became director in 1903. In a letter to the Brazilian congress the same year, Cruz made clear what kind of establishment he had in mind: 'an institute for the study of infectious and tropical diseases, along the lines of the Pasteur Institute of Paris'. The facility was to prepare sera and vaccines, of course, but also would give instruction in bacteriology and parasitology and would, as a result, 'transform itself into a nucleus of experimental studies that would greatly enhance the name of our country abroad'. Cruz rode a yellow fever campaign based on the Finlay Doctrine to success in transforming a serum institute into a great research organism, renamed the Institute of Experimental Pathology in 1906. The original staff was wholly Brazilian, alumni of the Rio de

[37] Nancy Stepan, 'The Interplay between Socio-economic Factors and Medical Science: yellow fever research, Cuba and the United States', *Social Studies of Science*, 8 (1978): 397–423.

[38] See Wilbur A. Sawyer, 'A History of the Activities of the Rockefeller Foundation in the Investigation and Control of Yellow Fever', *American Journal of Tropical Medicine*, 17 (1937): 35–50.

[39] Marcos Cueto, *Excelencia científica en la periferia: Actividades científicas e investigación biomédica en el Perú, 1890–1950*, (Lima, 1989), pp. 144–8.

Janeiro medical school, and included such future leaders of Brazilian medicine as Henrique de Rocha Lima and Artur Neiva; Cruz taught them microbiology in a course patterned after a famous one given in Paris by Emile Roux. As research activities increased medical students in Rio de Janeiro soon became aware that 'a new kind of science' was being practised in Manguinhos.[40] Interestingly, Cruz's 1904 campaign to make smallpox vaccination obligatory was opposed by Brazilian positivists who styled it 'hygienic despotism' while attacking the germ theory as 'fantasy'.[41]

The most famous discovery of the Institute's early years was that of American sleeping sickness (*Trypanosomiasis americana*), or Chagas's Disease, by Carlos Chagas in 1908. Chagas made the discovery serendipitously while on an anti-malaria campaign in Minas Gerais. The disease, which induced multiple symptoms in its victims, had eluded classification before. Once described, a wealth of studies ensued, on the pathology, incidence and geography of the disease, making it one of the most closely studied of all human diseases.[42] Many of these studies were published in the *Memorias* do Instituto Oswaldo Cruz, which began publication in 1909.

The initiation of bacteriology in Peru was associated with Carrión's disease, which had long confused researchers because its pathogen causes two discrete illnesses: one is Oroya fever and it usually precedes the second, called *verruga peruana* after the tumour-like skin eruptions that it causes. It receives its name from a medical student named Daniel Carrión who in 1885 inoculated himself with the infection, proved that the two diseases had the same origin, and died. The disease was described in 1898 in a classical clinical monograph by Manuel Odriozola but not until 1909 was the pathogen isolated by Alberto Barton. Barton's discovery stimulated the growth of bacteriology in Peru, including the establishment of a first-rate laboratory at the Municipal Institute of Hygiene in Lima under the direction of the Italian Ugo Biffi and a scholarship programme to send promising researchers to Europe for training.[43]

Between 1916 and the late 1920s the Rockefeller Foundation commissioned a series of reports assessing medical education in virtually all Latin American countries. The reports are remarkable for the uniformity of the pattern revealed throughout the region. In particular, the Rockefeller leg-

[40] Stepan, *Beginnings of Brazilian Science,* ch. 5.

[41] Angela Porto, 'Positivismo e seus dilemas', *Ciência Hoje,* 6, no. 34 (August 1987), 55–61.

[42] Stepan, *Beginnings of Brazilian Science,* pp. 118–19.

[43] Cueto, *Excelencia científica en la periferia,* ch. 4; Myron G. Schultz, 'A History of Bartonellosis (Carrión's Disease)', *American Journal of Tropical Medicine and Hygiene,* 17 (1968): 503–15.

ates were looking for what they termed 'didactic' instruction methods (that is, lectures unaccompanied by demonstrations or laboratory assignments), for a deficient university structure, characterized by semi-autonomous chairs headed by clinical practitioners rather than departments with full-time research professors. And they were looking for talent: scientists in whom they could invest in order to 'make the peaks higher' and who would act like 'young Turks' in promoting institutional reform.

In the University of Bogotá, Alan Gregg found a medical school under the domination of the Catholic Church, whose laboratories were under-equipped (ten microscopes in bacteriology, six in pathological anatomy), or completely lacking (neither internal pathology nor general surgery offered laboratory work), with French textbooks used in all courses. 'A "young Turk" party of graduates who had had experience abroad would in ten years do the most to improve the teaching, the relations and the influence of the medical school of Bogotá,' Gregg concluded.[44]

In Brazil (surveyed first in 1916, and then again on three separate occasions), the Rockefeller assessors found both a defective institutional structure and signs of hope that the 'new science' championed by Oswaldo Cruz was diffusing through the system. In the medical school of Bahia, which had been a bastion of Darwinism in the 1880s, R. A. Lambert found that defective organization was subverting the utilization of the laboratories: only a fraction of the students could work in the laboratory at any one time. The pathological anatomy laboratory had only twelve micro-scopes, that of histology, fifteen. On the other hand, the total amount of apparatus was quite large. If the current chairs were brought together into eight departments, the number of microscopes would be sufficient. Teach-ing was found to be 'didactic' and one student reported never having seen an autopsy in the department of pathological anatomy and only occasional slide demonstrations. Research judged worthwhile was found only in parasitology and legal medicine.[45]

In Belo Horizonte, bacteriology was taught in 1916 by Ezequiel Dias of the Cruz Institute. 'His working tables were well outfitted with Zeiss microscopes and practically every useful instrument found in a well-equipped laboratory was on hand.' Chemistry was taught by Alfred Schaeffer, a German, 'and is a fine course . . . His department was the largest and best equipped in the school'.[46] Another Cruz product, Pereira

[44] Stepan, *Beginnings of Brazilian Science*, p. 95.
[45] Rockefeller Archives Center, Record Group 1.1, series 305, folder 15.
[46] Ibid., p. 91.

Filho, had a laboratory in the Pasteur Institute of Porto Alegre which the Rockefeller assessor found to be 'the best of this type we have seen anywhere'.[47] But in 1925 when Lambert visited Dias' laboratory, conditions had already deteriorated: 'it has only seven microscopes and no suitable desks for students. It is my impression that in this department, as in physiology, physics and parasitology, the teaching is largely didactic.' He then counted microscopes ('the common measure of equipment') and found only thirty-eight in the entire faculty.[48] Later, in Paraná Lambert found only a half dozen microscopes, all for histology.[49] Two years later, Lambert reported from the medical school in Rio that the situation in pathological anatomy illustrates 'the present hopeless inadequacy of space and other shortcomings'. Only nine microscopes could be found, including one in the professor's office, with six students at each table sharing a microscope in an overcrowded class of 500. Carlos Chagas's son, referring to this school as it was in the 1930s, described it as 'a cemetery of scientific vocations (cemitério de vocações científicas)'.[50]

Richard M. Pearce filed a gloomy assessment of laboratories at the University of Buenos Aires in 1916: physiology had but seven tables; anatomy had eighty, but the class size was eight hundred. The situation in the analytical chemistry and pharmacology laboratories was even worse, 'while that devoted to physiological chemistry has such poor equipment that our guide apologized for it on the ground that the essential practical work in biological chemistry was given in connection with the various clinical courses. Still, he ranked laboratory instruction as superior to that in Brazil. Instruction in anatomy, bacteriology and pathology approached that of United States medical schools but was far inferior in physiology or chemistry. Entire systematic courses in physiology, chemistry and embryology were lacking. 'As in Brazil, the fault lies with the system which permits the appointment of clinicians as heads of laboratory departments and denies the advantage of full-time men to encourage teaching and research in the laboratory branches'.[51]

In 1925, R. A. Lambert received a negative impression of Houssay's physiology laboratory (where work that would bring Houssay the Nobel

[47] Ibid., p. 276.
[48] Ibid., p. 123. Twenty of the microscopes were in the pathology laboratory, eight in bacteriology, six in natural history and parasitology and four in the clinical labs of the hospital.
[49] Ibid., p. 146.
[50] Ibid., p. 252; Maria Clara Mariani, 'O Instituto de Biofísica da UFRJ,' in Simon Schartzman (ed.), *Universidades e instituicoes científicas no Rio de Janeiro* (Brasilia, 1982), pp. 199–208, on p. 200.
[51] Rockefeller Archives Center, Record Group 1.1, Series 301, Box 2, folder 18, pp. 135–7.

Prize was already underway): 'I got the impression that the disorder was probably chronic and that B. H. [sic] is one of those laboratory workers to whom housekeeping is a bore. The departmental library showed the lack of method evident elsewhere.'

Interpretation of the Rockefeller reports raises the issue of conflicting scientific cultures. The North Americans were unused to the economy of scarcity and deprivation that reigned throughout Latin American laboratories. There, researchers were accustomed to make the best with what they had; resourcefulness in designing experiments was perhaps the key to the best Latin American science of the period. Still, one must give the Foundation's men credit for identifying scientists of talent. Houssay, of course, was the prime example.

Born in 1887, Bernardo Houssay earned degrees in pharmacy and medicine and by 1912 was professor of physiology at the University of Buenos Aires Veterinary School.[52] There he developed a method for removing the pituitary gland from experimental animals in order to study that organ's function. In the 1920s, as professor of physiology in the medical school and director of its Institute of Physiology he performed a series of experiments to test the effects of injections of insulin (recently discovered) on animals from whom various glands had been removed. One series of experiments produced the astounding finding that the anterior lobe of the pituitary inhibited the utilization of glucose, implicating the pituitary in the etiology of human diabetes. Related research, on the role of the pituitary in the metabolism of carbohydrates, won him the Nobel Prize in 1947.

The Rockefeller Foundation began backing Houssay's research in 1929. By 1941, when the foundation established a regional office in Buenos Aires, Houssay's laboratory was already a world-class institution and was training physiologists from other Latin American countries. Then in 1943, he was dismissed from the University along with other academics following the military coup that eventually brought Péron to power. The dismissal forced Houssay to create a private research institute, the Institute of Biology and Experimental Medicine, free from governmental interference. The Institute opened in March 1944, staffed mainly by others who had been dismissed

---

[52] On Houssay, see Frank Young and Virgilio G. Foglia, 'Bernardo Alberto Houssay (1887–1971)', *Biographical Memoirs of Fellows of the Royal Society*, 20 (1974): 247–70; Foglia, 'The History of Bernardo A. Houssay's Research Laboratory, Instituto de Biología y Medicina Experimental: the first twenty years, 1944–1963', *Journal of the History of Medicine and Allied Sciences*, 35 (1980): 380–96; Foglia and Venancio Deulofeu, (eds) *Bernardo A. Houssay, su vida y su obra, 1887–1971* (Buenos Aires, 1981); and Marcos Cueto, 'La política médica de la Fundación Rockefeller y la investigación científica latinoamericana: El caso de la fisiología', in *Anais do Segundo Congresso Latino-Americano de História da Ciência e da Tecnologia* (São Paulo, 1989), pp. 366–75.

(Juan T. Lewis, Oscar Orias) or who had resigned in protest (Eduardo Braun Menéndez, Virgilio Foglia). Such an Institute fulfilled two of the Rockefeller Foundation's desiderata: its researchers held full-time appointments and the Institute was free of traditional university bureaucratic structures. A stream of young researchers was sent abroad, many on Rockefeller fellowships, and the result was research on a high level: Braun Menéndez on renin; Luis Leloir on the biochemistry of carbohydrates (which won him Latin America's second Nobel in 1970).[53] Houssay's Institute produced three related laboratories, an index of its success: Lewis's Institute of Medical Research in Rosario, Orias's laboratory in Córdoba, and Leloir's Institute of Biochemical Research (the Campomar Foundation).

Houssay's laboratory was part of an international physiology network whose nerve centre was Walter Cannon's laboratory in Boston and whose research programmes (hormonal action) and methodologies (piqûre, organ extirpation) were closely linked. Others in this network were Arturo Rosenblueth and José Joaquín Izquierdo in Mexico, Franklin Augusto de Moura Campos in Brazil, Joaquín V. Luco and Fernando Huidobro in Chile, and, after 1940, Rossend Carrasco Formiguera in Venezuela, all trained by Cannon, and others influenced but not trained directly by Cannon: August Pi-Sunyer in Venezuela, his son Jaume and Alexander Lipshutz in Chile.[54]

This network was the one Houssay and Braun Menéndez relied on to organize a journal, *Acta Physiologica Latinoamericana* which began publishing in 1950 to diffuse the results of Latin American physiology. From its inception the journal published mainly in English (never less than 69 per cent of its articles, reaching 100 per cent in 1971), with Argentinian authors predominating. The journal illustrates the difficulty that high-quality Latin American researchers had (and have) in diffusing their results: the leading figures in physiology chose mainly to publish in mainstream journals, leaving the *Acta*'s author pool skewed towards Argentinians and second-line researchers.[55]

Rosenblueth, returning to Mexico in 1944 after fourteen years with Cannon to head the physiology laboratory in the Cardiology Institute (a

---

[53] On Leloir, see César Lorenzano, 'La ciencia paradigmática de Luis Leloir', in *Anais do Segundo Congresso Latino-Americano da História da Ciência e da Tecnología* (São Paulo, 1989), pp. 164–72, and bibliography cited.

[54] See Cueto, 'Política médica de la Fundación Rockefeller', p. 372. Cueto sees this network as a medium for the diffusion of Argentinian influence in Latin American physiology.

[55] Hebe Vessuri, 'Una estrategia de publicación científica para la fisiología latinoamericana: *Acta Physiologica Latinoamericano*, 1950–1971', *Anais do Segundo Congresso Latino-Americano de História de Ciência e da Tecnologia* (São Paulo, 1989), 232–40.

new institution, outside of the university structure, heavily funded by the Rockefeller Foundation), had performed a classic series of experiments with Cannon, extirpating the sympathetic nerve chains of cats in order to demonstrate the regulatory function of the autonomic nerve system. This research drew Rosenblueth into collaboration with Norbert Wiener on the functional analysis of the nervous system, whose results were crucial in the foundation of cybernetics.[56]

One other group of physiologists, not in the Cannon-Houssay network, also performed high-quality research in the 1930s and 1940s. This was a distinctive group of high-altitude or environmental physiologists working in the Institute of Andean Biology founded by Carlos Monge in 1934. Monge had previously described a kind of chronic mountain sickness now known as Monge's Disease. The Rockefeller Foundation (and later the United States Air Force) provided laboratory equipment and fellowships for study abroad. Monge's later research was related to the acclimatization of cattle at high altitudes, while his colleague and successor Alberto Hurtado studied pulmonary edema and other problems of human physiology in the mining districts of the high Andes.[57]

The work of Monge and Hurtado provided a model for centres of Andean biology and medicine established later, for example, the Institute of High-Altitude Pathology (Clínica IPPA), in La Paz, Bolivia (founded 1970) and the Veterinary Institute of Tropical and High-Altitude Research of the University of San Marcos (Lima), founded in 1985, which has a unique Information Centre on South American Camelidae.

Historians of Mexican medicine all stress the role of Spanish republican researchers in training students and founding distinctive research 'schools' in various specialties. Four figures were of particular significance. Isaac Costero, trained in neurohistology by Pío del Río-Hortega joined the Institute of Cardiology where he developed a distinctive approach to pathological anatomy; he is recognized as the founder of the Mexican school of pathology. Rafael Mendez, a pharmacologist, who before arriving in Mexico was chairman of pharmacology at the University of Chicago, was head of the pharmacology department of the Institute of Cardiology where he developed a working group in cardiovascular pharmacology. Dionisio Nieto, a German-trained psychiatrist, led the department of neuroanatomy and neuropathology at the Laboratory (later Institute) of

---

[56] See A. M. Monnier, 'Arturo Rosenblueth', *Dictionary of Scientific Biography*, 16 vols (New York, 1970–80), 11: 545–7.

[57] On high altitude physiology in Peru, see Cueto, *Excelencia científica en la periferia*, ch. 5, and *idem*, 'Andean Biology in Peru: scientific styles on the periphery', *Isis*, 80 (1989): 640–58.

Biomedical Research (a unit established at The Universidad Nacional Autónoma de México (UNAM) by the Rockefeller Foundation to provide a research facility for exiled Spaniards[58]) as well as the department of neurobiology at UNAM where he strove to create a Mexican neurological school in the mold of that of Cajal. José Puche continued in Mexico the root concerns of August Pi-Sunyer's Catalan school of physiology, in research on trophic sensitivity, physiological correlation, and an inventive programme in the metabolism of crustaceans.[59]

Among other Spaniards who contributed to Mexican medical research was the gynaecologist Alejandro Otero who stimulated gynaecological research in the Laboratory of Medical Research of the General Hospital in Mexico, D.F. and was instrumental in the formation of the Medical Association for Sterility Studies.[60] Spanish physicians also revitalized provincial medicine in Mexico. Two founded provincial medical journals: Luis Fumagallo (*Monterrey Médico*) and Antonio Aparicio Sánchez Covisa (*Acta Médica Hidalguense*).[61]

Spanish exiles also played a significant role in Mexican biology. In entomology were Cándido Bolívar (who became president of the Mexican Society of Natural History), Gonzalo Halffter Salas (who became director of the Museum of Natural History), and Federico Bonet. In oceanography came the de Buen family: the aged Odón, a pioneer Spanish Darwinian, and his sons Rafael, who held posts at UNAM and at the University of Michoacán, and Fernando, appointed to the limnological station at Pátzcuaro (he subsequently left the country to become director of fisheries in Uruguay); Enrique Rioja; and Bibiano Osorio Tafall. Among botanists was Faustino Miranda, founder of UNAM's botanical garden.[62]

Although the density of republican scientists was considerably less marked in other countries, it is worth reviewing some representative figures and contributions. In Cuba, the parasitologist Gustavo Pittaluga

[58] Larissa Lomnitz, 'Hierarchy and Peripherality: the organization of a Mexican Research Institute', *Minerva*, 17 (1979): 527–48.
[59] José Cueli, 'Ciencias médicas y biológicas', in *El exilio español en México, 1939–1982* (Mexico D.F., 1982), pp. 495–528, especially pp. 503–8; Augusto Fernández Guardiola, 'Semblanza de cuatro médicos españoles', in María Luisa Capella, (ed.) *El exilio español y la UNAM* (*coloquio*) (Mexico D.F., 1987), pp. 43–48; Rafael Mendez, *Caminos inversos: Vivencias de ciencia y guerra* (Mexico, D.F., 1987); José Luis Barona Vilar and María Fernández Mancebo, *José Puche Alvarez (1896–1979). Historia de un compromiso* (Valencia, 1989), pp. 57–73, 95–111,
[60] José Fernández Castro, *Alejandro Otero, el médico y el político* (Barcelona, 1981), p. 204.
[61] *Exilio español*, p. 514. See also Germán Somolinos d'Ardois, *25 años de medicina española en México* (Mexico D.F., 1966), p. 20 (for republican doctors in Matehuala, Culiacán, Ciudad Valles, Veracruz and Jalapa); and Patricia W. Fagen, *Exiles and Citizens: Spanish Republicans in Mexico* (Austin, Tex., 1973), pp. 70–4.
[62] *Exilio español*, pp. 526–8.

(Spain's leading malariologist), became head of the Department of Experimental and Clinical Hydrology in the Ministry of Health. There he trained a distinctive Cuban school of epidemiology.[63] In Venezuela, August Pi-Sunyer transferred from Barcelona his distinctive approach to experimental physiology in the Institute of Experimental Medicine at the Central University. There, along with Rossend Carrasco Formiguera, a Catalan colleague who had performed with Walter Cannon the crucial experiment establishing Cannon's 'emergency theory' of adrenaline, he not only trained a group of Venezuelan physiologists but participated in a broader movement of scientific professionalization.

PSYCHOANALYSIS

The reception of psychoanalysis in Latin America makes an interesting comparison with that of relativity (see below). Popular and intellectual diffusion was a certainty due to the notoriety of Freud and Einstein. But more profound reception depended on the presence of professional groups with appropriate training. Both psychologists and physicists were in short supply in Latin American countries in the 1920s. Thus the reception of psychoanalysis by psychiatrists is in some sense parallel to that of relativity by engineers. Psychiatrists in the Latin world, although trained in a wholly somatic approach to mental illness, had traditionally adopted an eclectic stance with regard to medical theory and this pronounced eclecticism strongly coloured the reception of Freud in the period before the establishment of 'orthodox' psychoanalytical groups in the 1940s and 1950s. Inasmuch as most 'histories' of psychoanalysis are written from within the movement, the 'prehistory' has been derogated, when not ignored completely, resulting in a deformed picture of Freud's impact on Latin American culture.[64] Yet Freud's influence was already enormous in the 1920s, when his collected works, in Luis López Ballesteros' Spanish translation, were read in all the capitals of the region.[65]

---

[63] Leonard Jan Bruce-Chwatt and Julian de Zulueta, *The Rise and Fall of Malaria in Europe* (Oxford, 1980), p. 126; Victor Santamaria, 'El Prof. Gustavo Pittaluga', *Archivos Médicos de Cuba*, 7 (1926): 221–27; Concepción Carles Genovés and Thomas F. Glick, 'Gustavo Pittaluga Fatorini', in J. M. López Piñero (ed.), *Diccionario Histórico de la Ciencia Moderna en España*, 2 vols (Barcelona, 1983), II: 187–7.

[64] The terms 'psychoanalysis' and 'Freudian psychology' are used interchangeably. The second term avoids the bounded cognitive and professional structures that the first implies, particularly for its practitioners. With respect to the reception of Freudian psychology, the fidelity of the receivers to orthodox canons is not the most significant aspect.

[65] For the history of the Spanish translation of Freud's works, see Thomas F. Glick, 'The Naked Science: psychoanalysis in Spain, 1914–1948', *Comparative Studies in Society and History*, 24 (1982): 533–71.

The first sustained interest in psychoanalysis in Latin America dates from Honorio Delgado's first writings on the subject in 1915. Delgado, a Peruvian psychiatrist was, as a young man, very enthusiastic about the therapeutic possibilities of psychoanalysis although from the outset he had reservations regarding its theoretical underpinnings, in particular the concept of libido. His 1919 volume *El psicoanálisis* was the first volume in Spanish on the subject and the beginning of his correspondence with Freud himself which led to Delgado's becoming the institutional representative of psychoanalysis in Latin America. In 1922, he attended the psychoanalytic congress in Berlin, meeting Freud and his lieutenants in person, and an intellectual biography of Freud followed in 1926. Delgado's objective, however, was not to become a psychoanalyst but simply to assimilate Freudian therapeutic methods in his clinical practice. His psychological ideas were, in fact, an amalgam (rather typical in the world of Latin psychiatry), of Freud, Jung and Adler, a theoretical promiscuity which brought Delgado a mild rebuke from Freud. Even in his therapy, however, Delgado's methods were quite unique: he claimed to have cured psychotic patients simply by having them attend seminars he organized for them on the Freudian explanation of their symptoms. By 1927, when he attended the Innsbruck psychoanalytical congress his enthusiasm had cooled, and over the next decade his position moved from sceptical to overtly antagonistic.[66]

After 1929 Delgado used his chair of psychiatry to oppose Freud in Peru, thereby retarding the emergence of professional analytic groups. But his activity in the 1920s had been influential in the diffusion of Freudian ideas. It was through him that Peruvian intellectuals like José Carlos Mariátegui learned of Freud. (Mariátegui, however, noted in 1927 that 'the Latin spirit seems the least apt to understand and accept psychoanalytic theories which French and Italian critics reproach for their Nordic and Teutonic content, when not for their Jewish origins'.) In Ecuador Julio Endara based his understanding of personality in part on Freudian ideas gleaned from Delgado's early articles. The emergence of orthodox psychoanalysis in Peru is associated with Carlos A. Seguín, who had undergone analysis at the New York Psychoanalytic Institute in the 1940s

[66] Alvaro Rey de Castro, 'Freud y Honorio Delgado. Crónica de un desencuentro', *Hueso Humero* (Lima), nos. 15–16 (1983): 5–76; José Carlos Mariátegui, "El 'freudismo' en la literatura contemporánea," *Sagitario* (La Plata), 2 (1927): 205–210, on p. 209; Julio Endara, 'Notas acerca de la evolución de la personalidad' (1922), Leopoldo Zea (ed.), *Pensamiento positivista latinoamericano* (Caracas, 1980), pp. 529–58. See also Javier Mariátegui's edition of Delgado, *Freud y el psicoanálisis: Escritos y testimonios* (Lima, 1984).

and returned to Peru to practice psychosomatic medicine. The first group of orthodox analysts were his students. The Peruvian Society of Psychoanalysis was founded in 1980.[67]

The first Brazilian, probably the first Latin American, to speak publicly of Freud was Juliano Moreira in his chair of psychiatry in Bahia in 1899. Later, when he was director of the psychiatric hospital in Rio de Janeiro he supported the establishment there by Carneiro Ayrosa of a laboratory of psychoanalytic diagnosis in 1929. From as early as 1914 the psychiatrist Henrique Roxo was recommending psychoanalysis as a diagnostic method and this approach to Freud was characteristic of his reception. There were also examples of self-taught analysts in the 1920s, such as Júlio Porto-Carrero in Rio de Janeiro and Durval Marcondes in São Paulo. (Marcondes provided the link between the early reception and introduction of normative psychoanalytic methods, when he recruited the Jewish refugee Adelheid Koch to begin orthodox training in 1937.) At the end of the 1920s Marcondes and Francisco Franco de Rocha (who had been lecturing on Freud in the medical school since 1918) in São Paulo together with Porto-Carrero and Moreira in Rio founded a short-lived Brazilian Psychoanalytical Society, not as a professional association but rather to diffuse the ideas of Freud among the Brazilian elite. In the wake of the Revolution of 1930, many of Freud's supporters (including Ayrosa, Porto-Carrero, Inaldo Neves-Manta and Arthur Ramos) weighed in with books addressing the relevance of psychoanalysis to Brazilian culture and society generally, an indication of the successful diffusion of Freudian ideas among the intellectual class.[68]

In Argentina, there was ample commentary on Freud in the 1920s, especially in academic journals. A series of lectures on the theory and methods of psychoanalysis by Spanish psychiatrist Gonzalo R. Lafora in 1923 was influential in establishing the significance of Freudian ideas among the medical community of Buenos Aires.[69] Medical students who

[67] Alvaro Rey de Castro, 'El psicoanálisis en el Perú: Notas marginales', *Debates en Sociología*, 11 (1986): 229–310, on p. 236.

[68] On the early reception of Freud in Brazil, see Silvia Alexim Nunes, 'Da medicina social à psicanálise', in Joel Birman (ed.), *Percursores na história da psicanálise* (Rio de Janeiro, 1988), pp. 61–122; Marialzira Perestrello, 'Primeros encontros com a psicanálise. Os precursores no Brasil (1899–1937)', in Sérvulo Figueira (ed.) *Efeito PSI: A influência da psicanálise* (Rio de Janeiro, 1988), pp. 151–181; Gilberto S. Rocha, *Introduçao ao nascimento da psicanálise no Brasil* (Rio de Janeiro, 1989); and Roberto Sagawa, 'A psicanálise pionera e os pioneiros da psicanálise em São Paulo', in Figueira, ed., *Cultura de psicanálise* (São Paulo, 1985), pp. 15–34.

[69] Gonzalo R. Lafora, 'La teoria y los métodos del psicoanálisis', *Revista de Criminología, Psiquiatria y Medicina Legal* (Buenos Aires), 10 (1923): 385–408.

read Freud's works in López Ballesteros' translation in the 1920s wrote extensively on psychoanalytic theory and therapy in medical journals in the 1930s as they integrated them into their clinical practice. Gregorio Bermann said that he had practiced psychoanalysis in the 1920s (such reminiscences are a leitmotiv in autobiographies of psychiatrists), meaning most likely that dream interpretation, free association and other Freudian techniques were worked into his clinical practice. Others who wrote about Freud in this period were Gonzalo Bosch, Jorge Thenón, Emilio Pizarro Crespo and two future analysts Federico Aberastury and Enrique Pichón-Riviere.[70]

The 'official' history of Argentinian psychoanalysis begins in 1942 with the foundation of the Argentinian Psychoanalytical Association by the Spanish refugee Angel Garma, Celes Cárcamo, Arnaldo Rascovsky and Pichón-Riviere. Garma, trained in Berlin and a specialist in psychosomatic medicine, had been the first practicing psychoanalyst in Spain. Cárcamo had read Freud in the late 1920s and practised psychotherapy, as a doctor, in the 1930s. Rascovsky had discovered Freud around 1935, when he began clinical research on the psychosomatic background of endocrinological problems like obesity. He convened a Freudian discussion group in his house from 1937 and, when Garma arrived, underwent a didactic analysis with him. In the same period Pichón-Riviere was conducting classes of psychoanalytic psychiatry in the Hospicio de las Mercedes; he also was analysed by Garma.[71] Also involved in the early APA was Marie Langer, an Austrian Jewish refugee analyst.

The APA shortly began to offer professional seminars through its teaching arm, the Institute of Psychoanalysis, organized along German lines, although contact was lost with the German-speaking analysts. The APA analysts read Freud in English, or in the López Ballesteros version, corrected against James Strachey's standard English translation.[72] The early interests of Pichón in the psychoanalytic theory of psychosis and of

---

[70] Jorge Balán, *Profesión e identidad en una sociedad dividida: La medicina y el origen del psicoanálisis en la Argentina* (Buenos Aires, 1988; Documento Cedes, 7), pp. 11–16.

[71] Arminda Aberastury, Fidias R. Cesio, Marcelo Aberastury, *Historia, enseñanza y ejercicio legal del psicoanálisis* (Buenos Aires, 1967), pp. 24–45. This is very much the officialist APA view of the introduction of psychoanalysis in Argentina. An entertaining, but equally myopic, Lacanian view of the same events is Germán L. Garciía, *La entrada del psicoanálisis en la Argentina* (Buenos Aires, 1978). See also Antonio Cucurullo, Haydée Faimberg and Leonardo Wender, 'La psychanalyse en Argentine', in Roland Jaccard (ed.), *Histoire de la psychanalyse*, 2 vols (Paris, 1982), pp. 453–511. The national studies in the Jaccard volumes are narrowly focussed studies by movement insiders, largely bereft of sociological and cultural perspective.

[72] According to Garma (personal communication, 1979).

Aberastury in the psychology of children shaped the future involvement of psychoanalysis in public health.[73] The first thirteen years of the APA, until the fall of Perón in 1955, were a period of hibernation. In the intellectual effervescence following Perón's fall the first Argentinian intellectuals underwent psychoanalysis, initiating a boom in the field's popularity. Also in 1956, Garma and Rascovsky organized the Second Iberoamerican Congress of Medical Psychology in which Argentinian analysts displayed their Freudian wares. Foreign students, notably from Brazil and Mexico, came to Argentina for training and didactic analysis.[74] Inasmuch as there had been practically no clinical psychology at all in the country, 'this empty space was filled by psychoanalysts' trained by the APA. As psychology was added to university curriculum, its first teachers were psychoanalysts. This led to a real boom in psychoanalysis in the 1960s, coinciding with the graduation of the first university-trained psychologists. The psychoanalysts rode out the coup of 1966 and the ensuing university crisis by retreating to their private practices. Then in the 1970s there was a new expansion. At the same time the APA lost its monopoly over accreditation and numerous new analysts emerged. The coup of 1976, however, brought on a severe repression of Freudian psychology, now portrayed by the regime as anti-Christian, and there was a mass migration of Freudians to other Latin American countries (Marie Langer for example, went to Mexico) and Spain.

In Colombia, Freud appeared in medical theses as early as 1922 and J. B. Montoya lectured on Freud's concept of hysteria in Medellín in 1923. Analytic therapy did not begin until 1948 and the Colombian Psychoanalytical Society was not founded until 1961.[75] The early reception of Freud in Mexico has not been studied. His work was amply diffused there in the 1920s and 1930s. And in 1938 there was a movement – originating in Yucatan – to offer Freud a refuge in Mexico. This idea was backed by five influential labour unions, suggesting that Freud's ideas had diffused well beyond the 'groves of academe' and the medical community.[76] At the end

---

[73] The following section is based on Emiliano Galende's lucid contribution to 'El psicoanálisis argentino: Un cuestionamiento', *Vuelta 16*, II, 16 (1987): 25–40, 32–6.

[74] Marie Langer, Jaime del Palacio y Enrique Guinsberg, *Memoria, historia, y diálogo psicoanalítico* (Mexico, D.F., 1981), p. 89, where Langer also gives an interesting account of the sociology of the early analysands.

[75] Humberto Roselli, 'Evolución de la psiquiatría en Colombia', in Fondo Colombiano de Investigaciones Científicas, *Apuntes para la historia de la ciencia en Colombia*, I (Bogotá, 1971), pp. 69–100, on p. 98.

[76] Archivo Histórico Genaro Estrada, Secretaria de Relaciones Exteriores, Mexico, D.F., III-423-3, III-425-4.

of the 1940s the first Mexicans professionally interested in psychoanalysis went abroad to study. When they returned in the early 1950s they were already affiliated with the international analytic movement and in 1955 a Mexican group was accepted in the International Association under the supervision of the Argentinian APA.[77]

In Brazil, the Spanish psychiatrist Enrique Mira y López was the founding father of applied psychology as director of the Institute of Testing and Professional Orientation of the Vargas Foundation from 1947 until his death in 1964. Mira, who had introduced the Rorschach test in Spain and given the first course there on psychoanalysis, brought to Brazil psychodiagnostic tests and methods of his own invention (the myokinetic test), founding the Brazilian Psychotechnic Association and editing its *Arquivos Brasileiros de Psicotécnica.* Mira trained an entire generation of Brazilian psychologists at his institute,[78] another example of a Spaniard filling an empty professional niche and creating a new national disciplinary group. But Mira also travelled widely and was influential in the modernization of psychology in Argentina and Uruguay, where he lived briefly, and in Venezuela.[79]

In Mexico, the Spanish neurologist Gonzalo R. Lafora joined Dionisio Nieto at Laboratory of Medical Research where he continued his research on neuropathology. In 1942 Lafora wrote a series of articles examining the case of a serial murderer, Gregorio Cárdenas, based on interviews with the killer, which included free association and Rorschach tests, on the basis of which Lafora rejected a psychogenic etiology of the criminal's actions in favour of a neurological one (epilepsy). Lafora was subsequently accused by the criminal's family of having revealed privileged information publicly and the affair was debated in the Mexican Neurological Society. The public furor was a measure of Lafora's great prestige in the Mexican psychiatric community.[80]

---

[77] Ramón Parrés and Santiago Ramírez, 'Historia del movimiento psicoanalítico en México', *Cuadernos de Psicoanálisis* (Mexico, D.F.), 2 (1966): 19–29.

[78] Franco LoPresti Seminério, 'Emilio Mira y López e a psicologia contemporanea – uma interpretaçao', *Arquivos Brasileiros de Psicologia Aplicada,* 30 (1978): 21–36; Alice Madeleine Galland de Mira, *PMK: Psicodiagnóstico miocinético* (São Paulo, 1987), pp. 9–12; Thomas F. Glick, 'Emilio Mira y López', in López Piñero, (ed.), *Diccionario Histórico de la Ciencia Moderna en Espana,* II: 63–4.

[79] On the influence of Mira in Latin America, see Gregorio Bermann, 'In Memoriam: Dr. Emilio Mira y López', *Acta Psiquiatrica y Psicológica de América Latina* (Buenos Aires), 10, 1 (March 1964): vi–xi; articles by and about Mira in *Revista de Psiquiatria del Uruguay,* no. 28 (July–August 1940); and J. F. Reyes Baena, *Emilio Mira y López: Ensayo biográfico* (Caracas, 1975).

[80] Raquel Alvarez Peláez and Rafael Huertas García-Alejo, *¿Criminales o locos? Dos peritajes psiquiátricos del Dr. Gonzalo R. Lafora* (Madrid, 1987), pp. 225–311; 145–60.

PHYSICAL AND EXACT SCIENCES

Physics

In Latin America there was virtually no independent discipline of physics until the twentieth century. The subject matter of theoretical physics was traditionally the province of mathematics. Mechanics was taught in departments of mathematics until well into the twentieth century. Nor was it uncommon for astronomers to teach physics. Until the emergence in this century of modern faculties of science, the experimental side of physics, on the other hand, was domiciled in the special schools, especially those of engineering and mining. (Indeed, military engineers were the carriers of the high tradition in mathematics and physics from colonial times through to the end of the nineteenth century.)

In Argentina, Maxwellian physics was introduced only in 1892, by the engineer Jorge Duclout.[81] Substantial change did not come until the University of La Plata was reorganized in 1904 by Joaquín V. González, who was determined to introduce modern physical sciences in the country. This he did by contracting with the German physical chemist, Emil Bose, who arrived to assume the directorship of the Institute of Physics at the end of 1909.[82] Bose was soon able to attract two first-rate colleagues, Jakob Laub, a pioneer in the theory of relativity as Einstein's first collaborator, for the chair of geophysics, and, as head of electrical engineering, Konrad Simons. Bose quickly built the best physics library in Latin America, using his personal collection as the core, and the government came through with promised funds for laboratory equipment. A visiting U.S. physicist remarked that he had never seen 'so much apparatus together in one place'. When Bose died in 1911 he was replaced by Richard Gans who became the dominant figure in Argentinian physics during the first quarter of the century.

La Plata was the first university in Argentina with authority to grant doctorates in physics and astronomy. Students were quickly recruited, the number of those in degree programmes rising from 67 in 1911 to 126 in 1914. Most of these students, however, were candidates for engineering degrees; only a handful were physicists. Instruction was of the highest calibre: Walter Nernst gave a short course on thermodynamics in 1914,

---

[81] Ramón G. Loyarte, *La evolución de la física* (Buenos Aires, 1924), p. 64.
[82] The story of the implantation of German physics in Argentina is told by Lewis Pyenson, *Cultural Imperialism and Exact Science: German Expansion Overseas, 1900–1930* (New York, 1985), ch. 3.

Laub's lectures on relativity were surely the first on the subject in the New World, and Simons' electrical engineering textbook 'defined a discipline in Ibero-American cultures'.[83] Argentinian physicists trained at La Plata included Teófilo Isnardi, who worked with Nernst in Berlin and produced some important research in atomic theory and Ramón Loyarte, Gans' successor as director of the Institute.

No episode marked the coming of age of Argentinian physics, while at the same time demonstrating both its strengths and its limitations, than Albert Einstein's visit to Argentina in 1925. As did Einstein's trips to other countries, the visit stimulated an avalanche of popular books and articles on the theory of relativity as well as the realization that such high interest was in part a reflection of the general level of scientific activity in the country. 'It is clear,' *La Prensa* commented, 'that had there not existed a scientific sentiment, Einstein would not have awakened intense and strongly felt interest in so great a mass of people.'[84] Much was made in the press of the capacity shown by Argentinian scientists by their very ability to direct questions at the visiting physicist in a public meeting at the Academy of Sciences: 'If half the population of Argentina finds itself disorientated and trying only to gain an approximate idea of the theory of relativity, a group of Argentinian professors has demonstrated its profound knowledge of it.'[85] Einstein, unfortunately, was not as impressed, noting in his travel diary: 'Was asked a lot of stupid scientific questions so that it was difficult to keep a straight face.'[86] Einstein's reservations notwithstanding, the reception of relativity in Argentina was notable for the lack of conflict it generated; since Maxwellian physics had been incompletely assimilated, there was no entrenched group of physicists wedded to mechanistic principles to oppose relativity on physical grounds.

Einstein's theory was widely commented upon in Argentina: by Georg Friedrich Nicolai (a German physiologist at the University of Córdoba and the only German professor other than Einstein who had refused to sign the notorious Manifesto of German professors supporting the Kaiser's war aims), by engineers like Enrique Butty and José Galli, and by the physicists Loyarte and Isnardi.[87] In Uruguay, where Einstein made a short visit,

[83] Ibid., p. 206.
[84] *La Prensa*, 31 March 1925.
[85] *La Prensa*, 17 April 1925; Einstein was questioned by Loyarte, Isnardi and others. See also a transcription of a private exchange between Isnardi and Einstein, *La Prensa*, 20 April.
[86] Einstein Travel Diary, 1925, Einstein Papers, Princeton Duplicate Archive.
[87] Jorge F. Nicolai, 'La base biológica del relativismo científico y sus complementos absolutos', *Revista de la Universidad Nacional de Córdoba*, 12 (1925): 1–378; José Galli, *Einstein explicado* (Buenos Aires,

relativity was likewise explained in popularizations addressed by engineers to engineers. There too he met with the philosopher Carlos Vaz Ferreira, probably the first Latin American to lecture on relativity.[88]

In all the countries which Einstein visited (Brazil, Argentina and Uruguay, in Latin America) he and his ideas were heralded as symbols of modernization, and the mastery of his ideas as indicative of the will to modernize. In all these countries where the scientific community was thinly populated, engineers, standing in for non-existent physicists, were eager to associate themselves with this particularly abstract idea. Among engineers (and it is well to recall that the leading Brazilian mathematicians during Einstein's visit to Rio de Janeiro, were professors at the Escola Politécnica), the capacity (either individually or in a collective sense) to understand relativity stood for the capacity to do modern science. Note that this is the same class of people who in Europe and the United States opposed relativity as excessively abstract and scientifically regressive! Engineers, typically a conservative group in Latin countries, by associating themselves with relativity were able to contest leadership of the professions with medical doctors, traditionally liberal. This was a standard pattern in the reception of relativity in Latin countries (including Spain and Italy): relativity is mainstream, it is practical, engineers should at least understand the special theory, and one cannot expect to implant modern science in a country whose mathematicians are incapable of teaching it.

Scientific and academic politics aside, relativity, because of its connotations of philosophical relativism, was commonly appropriated for direct application to politics. Spanish anarchists, for example, were quick to point out that they espoused economic relativism and the relativity of political institutions, just as Einstein espoused the relativism of time and space. It is hardly surprising that Latin America, that laboratory of politics, should have produced perhaps the most original political embroidery of relativity: *El espacio-tiempo histórico* of Víctor Raúl Haya de la Torre. Haya was almost certainly informed of the relativity revolution from

1925); Ramón G. Loyarte, 'La obra de Einstein', *Revista de Filosofía*, 21 (1925): 475–8; Teófilo Isnardi, 'En torno a la relatividad', *La Nación*, 20 April 1925. On Einstein's visit to Córdoba and his pallid reaction to Nicolai's treatise, see Wolf Zuelzer, *The Nicolai Case* (Detroit, Mich., 1982), pp. 379–82.

[88] A. Geille Castro, 'La teoría de la relatividad', *Revista de la Asociación Politécnica del Uruguay*, 18 (1924): 132–43 and following; José Llambías de Olivar, 'Consideraciones sobre la teoría de Einstein', 19 (1925): 177–88 and following. On Vaz Ferreira and Einstein, Sara Vaz Ferreira de Echevarria, 'Carlos Vaz Ferreira con Alberto Einstein' (Montevideo, 1965), typescript.

around 1923 and between 1935 and 1945 elaborated a coherent *americanista* political philosophy for APRA (Alianza Popular Revolucionaria Americana) using Einsteinian relativity as a convenient source of political analogies.

According to Haya, the Hegelian and Marxian dialectic suffered the handicap of having been elaborated under the constraints of pre-Einsteinian physics characterized by Newtonian absolutes and a circumscribed (Galilean) concept of relativity. Hegelian and Marxian views of the new world are hopelessly Eurocentric, but in post-Einsteinian history there can be no privileged observers. Because of the immobility of the observer, Marxism is dogmatic, and dogmatism is anti-dialectical. Marxism, in Haya's view, cannot be held to be a fixed and absolute entity and there can be no standard evolutionary cycle that all societies pass through, as Marx had posited. There is no absolute parallelism in the vastness of historical space-time, just as there is none in the Einsteinian universe. Each historical society constitutes its own distinctive space-time and proceeds according to its own rhythms, not strictly comparable with those of any other society. Capitalism may be a late form of economic organization in European societies, not necessarily elsewhere.[89]

Two promising theoretical physicists trained at La Plata, Enrique Gaviola and the Uruguayan Enrique Loedel, emerged in the 1920s. Loedel's specialty was general relativity (he was the only Argentinian scientist able to pose an interesting question to Einstein during his visit). Gaviola published research on the atomic spectrum of mercury (with R. W. Wood) and then, in 1931, an important paper on wave-particle duality. Indeed, in the 1920s Gaviola was the only Argentinian physicist (besides Gans, of course) who attained 'citation visibility' in Europe (in German publications above all). Argentina was the only Latin American nation whose production in physics registers in the Citation Index for this period.[90]

Although the accomplishments of the Institute of Physics were considerable, in the long run the effort was a failure. The German professors were unable to establish a local research market or to transplant the research ethic so closely identified with German excellence in physics. Pyenson suggests that Argentinian students may well have had difficulty identifying with the authoritarian disciplinary style of German physicists and

[89] V. R. Haya de la Torre, *El espacio-tiempo histórico* (Lima, 1986).
[90] Pyenson, *Cultural Imperialism and Exact Science*, pp. 237–8 (Loedel), 240–6 (Gaviola); Pyenson and M. Singh, 'Physics on the Periphery: A world survey, 1920–1929', *Scientometrics*, 6 (1984): 301.

their upper class manners. European chemistry, more democratically organized, won more adherents.[91]

Other countries were considerably less fortunate in physics in the 1920s than was Argentina. In Cuba, for example, Manuel Gran, professor of physics at the University of La Habana from 1923 until he was named ambassador to France in 1960, left an evocative memoir of the desolate state of Cuban physics in the 1920s when university instruction in the subject was inferior to that imparted in the better secondary schools. The laboratory had not been restored to use after its destruction in the cyclone of 1906 and the apparatus was broken or dispersed. The mathematics education of the students was so deficient that 'it was necessary first to explain a point of higher mathematics before getting to the physics topic that depended on it'.[92] In Venezuela, there were virtually no physicists before the 1950s. Relativity, for example, was received and commented on by a fine mathematician, Francisco J. Duarte.[93]

In Brazil, systematic instruction in physics dates from the creation of the Escola Politécnica in 1893, and instruction mainly in applied physics by Francisco Ferreira Ramos (who demonstrated x-rays in his laboratory in 1896, within a year of their discovery) and, later, by Luiz Adolfo Wanderly.[94] At the time of Einstein's visit there in 1925, however, only astronomers, mathematicians and engineers could comment on his theory. Of the astronomers Henrique Morize, director of the Brazilian National Observatory, had planned the English expedition to view the solar eclipse at Sobral in 1919, when the general theory was confirmed. He and Lélio Gama, a member of the Sobral commission, wrote popularizing articles in the press during Einstein's visit.

Among Brazilian mathematicians Einstein's visit drew attention to a deep division in their ranks between entrenched Comtean positivists (Licinio Cardoso was the leading figure) and a younger generation more attuned to European mathematics and mathematical physics. The Com-

[91] Lewis Pyenson, 'The Incomplete Transmission of a European Image: physics at Greater Buenos Aires and Montreal, 1890–1920', *Proceedings of the American Philosophical Society,* 122 (1978): 114.

[92] Luis Felipe LeRoy y Gálvez, *Profesores de física de la Universidad de la Habana desde su secularización en 1842 hasta Manuel F. Gran* (Havana, 1979), pp. 24–33.

[93] Luis Urbina Luigi, 'Reseña histórica y bibliográfica de la ciencias físicas y matemáticas en Venezuela', in IVIC, *La ciencia, base de nuestro progreso* (Caracas, 1965), pp. 93–103. See also *Hemenaje al Dr. Francisco J. Duarte, 1883–1972: Personalidad y correspondencia* (Caracas, 1974).

[94] For general accounts of the history of modern physics in Brazil, see José Goldemberg, *100 años de física* (Rio de Janeiro, Centro Brasileiro de Pesquisas Físicas, 1973; Ciência e sociedade, vol.2, no. 2); Shozo Motoyama, 'A física no Brasil', in Guimaraes and Motoyama (eds), *História das ciências no Brasil,* I: 61–91; and J. Costa Ribeiro, 'A física no Brasil', in Fernando de Azevedo (ed.), *As ciências no Brasil,* 2 vols (São Paulo, n.d.), I, pp. 163–202.

teans clung dogmatically to regressive ideas long ago promoted by Comte which impeded the reception of both non-Euclidean geometry and the Maxwellian concept of fields, both decried as metaphysical abstractions. Accordingly, Einstein's appearance in Rio de Janeiro precipitated a fierce debate in the Brazilian Academy of Sciences in which a group of relativists led by the mathematician Manoel de Amoroso Costa and the engineer Roberto Marinho were able successfully to discredit Cardoso and the old-line Comtean positivists in noisy sessions held on 10 June and 8 July, 1925.[95] Once the Comteans were defeated, there were none to oppose Einstein's theories and opposition was notably weak. Einstein flattered his Brazilian hosts by noting 'The problem conceived in my head had to be solved by the luminous sky of Brazil.'[96] In his diary, Einstein was less than charitable: of his lecture on relativity at the Engineering Club he noted 'Little understanding for science. To them, I am a kind of white elephant, and for me they are fools.'[97]

Even in the provinces, Einstein was a beacon of modern science. In Recife, Luiz de Barro Freire explained Einstein's theory and defended it against a well-known traditionalist attack by Henri Bouasse. Freire, engineer, mathematician and physicist, was largely self-taught in contemporary science. He imparted his enthusiasm to a gifted generation of students, including physicists Mario Schenberg and José Leite Lopes and mathematician Leopoldo Nachbin.[98]

Profound understanding of theoretical physics had to wait until the 1930s when two important research groups were founded, each by a European immigrant. In Rio de Janeiro, the German Jewish physicist Bernard Gross performed a series of important experiments in 1934–7 at the Instituto Nacional Tecnológico measuring the intensity of cosmic rays in an ionization chamber.[99] Gross trained J. Costa Ribeiro who discovered the thermodialectric effect in 1944. At the University of São Paulo the Russian-born Gleb Wataghin, who arrived from Turin in 1934, was also

[95] Antonio Paim, 'O neopositivismo no Brasil. Período de formação da corrente', in M. Amoroso Costa, *As idéias fundamentais da matemática e outros ensaios*, 3rd edn (São Paulo, 1981), pp. 41–63, p. 58. Some short articles on relativity by Amoroso Costa are reproduced in the same volume, pp. 101–19. See also, Paim, 'Indicadores do término do ciclo positivista,' *Revista Brasileira de Filosofía*, 30 (1980): 335–49.

[96] For a chronicle of Einstein's trip to Brazil, see Roberto Vergara Caffarelli, 'Einstein e o Brasil,' *Ciência e cultura*, 31 (1979), 1437–55.

[97] Einstein Travel Diary, 6 May 1925. Einstein Papers, Princeton Duplicate Archive.

[98] Ivone Freire de Mota e Albuquerque and Amélia Império Hamburger, 'Retratos de Luiz de Barros Freire como pioneiro da ciência no Brasil', *Ciência e Cultura*, 40 (1988): 875–81.

[99] L. Jánossy, *Cosmic Rays*, 2nd edn (Oxford, 1950), p. 139.

interested in cosmic rays. This proved to be an appropriate field on which to found Brazilian experimental physics in view of the low cost of experiments. It also had the advantage of stimulating a number of interconnected fields such as astrophysics, nuclear physics and the physics of elementary particles. In the late 1930s, Wataghin's group, joined by the Italian Giuseppe Occhialini, performed experiments on cosmic ray showers, with two young Brazilians, Marcello Damy de Souza and Paulus Aulus Pompéia, discovering the penetrating or 'hard' component of cosmic radiation. This research programme was consolidated by the International Conference on Cosmic Rays, held in Rio de Janeiro in 1941. Another disciple of Wataghin, Mario Schenberg, collaborated with George Gamow in 1941 on the neutrino theory of stellar collapse, a phenomenon associated with the tremendous production of light associated with novae and supernovae. The following year, Schenberg co-authored an important paper with Subrahmanyan Chandresakhar on the growth of helium nuclei in the evolution of stars.

In the mid-1940s Occhialini and a Brazilian student César Lattes joined in collaborative research with Cecil Powell of the University of Bristol in England who had developed a method of detecting elementary particles by exposing photosensitive plates to cosmic radiation at mountain altitudes. The Brazilians induced Bolivian colleagues to refit a meteorological observatory high in the Bolivian Andes at Chacaltaya for cosmic ray research. There in 1947 they discovered the pi meson, or pion (a highly unstable particle which decays forming a muon and a neutrino) whose existence had been predicted by H. Yukawa. The following year, Lattes and E. Gardner produced an artificial pi meson in the cyclotron of the Berkeley Radiation Laboratory.[100] The discovery of the pi meson was the starting point of modern elementary particle physics. In the next step of meson research, the Brazilian Jayme Tiomno and J. L. Wheeler of Princeton, in a famous paper delivered at the AAAS meeting in 1948, explained the one-half spin of muons in terms of a weak 'Fermi' interaction.[101]

The institutional fall-out from pi meson research was of considerable

---

[100] On pi meson research, see Alfredo Marques, *24 años da descoberta do meson*, 2nd edn (Rio de Janeiro, CBPF, 1985; Ciência e sociedade, vol. I, no. 12), and Bruno Rossi, *Cosmic Rays* (New York, 1964), pp. 133–6. This research brought Powell the Nobel Prize in 1950.

[101] José Leite Lopes, 'Point-counterpoint in Physics: theoretical prediction and experimental discovery of elementary particles', *Fundamenta Scientiae*, 6 (1984): 165–77. On Tiomno, see A. Luciano L. Videira, *Da relatividade as particulas (ida-e-volta): Cuarenta anos de física de Jayme Tiomno* (Rio de Janeiro, CBPF, 1980, mimeo) and José Maria Filardo Bassalo, *Jayme Tiomno, os mésons e a física paraense* (Rio de Janeiro, CBPF, 1987, mimeo).

significance for the future of Latin American physics: first, Chacaltaya was developed into an outstanding research facility, the Laboratory of Cosmic Physics of San Andrés University. Under its first director, the Spaniard Ismael Escobar, and later, Gastón R. Mejía, the range of research was broadened to include meteorology, solar radiation, the ionosphere, glaciology, and so forth. The success of the Laboratory was reflected in other sections of the university, stimulating, for example, the foundation of the University Computing Centre, directed by a member of the Laboratory, where Bolivia's first computer was installed in 1965.[102] Secondly, the success of the pi meson research programme led directly to the establishment of the Centro Brasileira de Pesquisas Físicas (CBPF), in Rio, which became the nerve center of Brazilian physics.

The Rockefeller Foundation had backed the physics effort at the University of São Paulo, allowing it to produce world-class research in the 1940s. But the department at the Universidade do Brasil in Rio de Janeiro could not attain the same grant level because there were no full-time research positions (a key Rockefeller requirement) in that university. Therefore, the CBPF was conceived as a private institute, with some links to the university, where original research in physics would proceed under the direction of José Leite Lopes in theoretical and Lattes in experimental physics.[103]

After the Second World War a school of nuclear physics built upon the prior accomplishments in theoretical and particle physics. In São Paulo experimental nuclear physics began when Damy de Souza acquired a Betatron (a kind of particle accelerator) in 1951 and Oscar Sala, an electrostatic generator in 1954, giving the São Paulo group two different ways of bombarding atomic nuclei. Pompéia and others worked on the detection of elementary particles and Sala, in the United States, investigated nuclear reactions induced by neutrons. In theoretical physics Schenberg ranged over a host of topics from general field theory and electrodynamics to the theory of elementary particles and astrophysics. The Brazilian school never lost its interest in elementary particles. In 1949, Richard Feynman, then working on meson theory, began a long relationship with Brazilian physicists which took him to Brazil frequently over the next fifteen years. He and José Leite Lopes collaborated on studies of weak particle interactions,

---

[102] Ismael Escobar, *Anteproyecto para el Observatorio de Física Cósmica en Chacaltaya* (La Paz, 1950); Gastón R. Mejia, *El rol del Laboratorio de Física Cósmica en el desarrollo de la ciencia y tecnología boliviana* (La Paz, 1969).

[103] José Leite Lopes, 'A física nuclear no Brasil', *Ciência e Cultura*, 8 (1956), 14–21 and *idem*, 'Trinta años de física no Brazil: Evocações', *Revista Brasileira de Tecnología*, 16 (1985): 25–33.

publishing a joint paper on weak pseudoscalar coupling in 1952. A few years later, Leite, stimulated by Feynman and Gell-Mann's research, predicted the existence of another elementary particle, the neutral vector boson (z_0) which was subsequently discovered experimentally in 1983.[104]

The phenomenal growth of Brazilian physics from its formative period in the 1930s (when virtually all of the future leaders of the discipline were recruited from the engineering schools) is attributable to the success of the cosmic radiation research programme. By 1960 there were approximately one hundred Brazilian research physicists, a number which grew to eight hundred by 1977.

Cosmic radiation research was introduced in Argentina by a number of the leading figures in physics: Gaviola, Guido Beck, Isnardi. The lead institution was the Jesuit Observatory of San Miguel, established in 1935 under the direction of the Catalan Ignasi Puig (1887–1961). Puig was succeeded in 1943 by Juan Bussolini who inaugurated a department of solar physics. In 1968–9 the observatory was reorganized and its director Mariano Castex became president of the National Geoheliophysical Research Commission, established to coordinate solar research in Argentina, including the solar observatory of La Rioja and the Patagonian Centre of Geoheliophysics. It was also in the mid-1940s that cosmic physics was established at the Laboratory of Cosmic Radiation of the University of Buenos Aires. In 1952 this group moved to the Atomic Energy Commission (DNEA, later CNEA) which sent the future director of its cosmic radiation laboratory, Juan Roederer, to finish his doctorate at Göttingen. The DNEA, which tended to absorb all nuclear-related research-front physics during this period, also sponsored a new cosmic studies center at the University of Tucumán (1961). In 1964, Roederer was named director of the National Center of Cosmic Radiation which installed neutron supermonitors in Buenos Aires and Antarctica. Argentine research in cosmic radiation has been more observational than theoretical in focus.[105]

In Mexico, modern physics dates to the career of Manuel Sandoval Vallarta.[106] Sandoval was trained at MIT (1917–29) where he was a profes-

[104] Leite Lopes, 'Point-counterpoint in Physics', pp. 176–7, and *idem, Richard Feynman in Brazil: Recollections* (Rio de Janeiro, 1988).

[105] José Federico Westerkamp, *Evolución de las ciencias en la República Argentina, 1923–1932: Física* (Buenos Aires, 1975), pp. 161–70; Otto Schneider, *Evolución de las ciencias en la República Argentina, 1923–1972: Geofísica y geodesia* (Buenos Aires, 1980), pp. 36–9. On Puig, see *Escriptors jesuïtes catalans. Bibliografia 1931–1976* (Barcelona, 1977), pp. 233–49.

[106] The following section is based on Regis Cabral, 'Sandoval Vallarta, as condições de validade da macromecânica, e a estructura conceitual de mecânica', *Quipu*, 5 (1988), 327–37; Héctor Cruz Manjarrez, 'Reseña histórica del Instituto de Física, Primer etapa 1938–1953' (Mexico, D.F.,

sor from 1926 (teaching the first course there on electromagnetic theory) until he returned to Mexico in 1949. His early research interest in relativity and quantum mechanics (in particular the application of relativity to atomic models) yielded, from 1932 on, to a dedication to cosmic rays (the nature of the particles forming them and the effect of the earth's magnetic field upon them). He was an influential pedagogue: the American Nobel laureate Richard Feynman and the Mexicans Carlos Graeff and Luis Enrique Erro were among his students.

Here too, the Spanish republicans made a mark. Mexico welcomed Spain's leading physicist, Blas Cabrera, the only Spanish member of the Solvay Institute, and the astronomer, Pedro Carrasco, both nearing the end of their careers. Cabrera installed a machine shop in his Laboratory of Precision Electrical Measurement at the Institute of Physics (UNAM) for use in his own magnetism research and to build instruments, not only for the Institute, but for the rest of the University.[107] Cabrera must have modelled his shop after Leonardo Torres Quevedo's famous automation laboratory in Madrid which supplied Cabrera's Institute there with instruments and built equipment for all scientific disciplines in the 1920s. The many exiled Spanish mathematicians made their mark primarily in secondary schools, particularly by writing text books, thereby influencing future generations of Mexican mathematicians.[108] Prior to 1930 there had been practically no organized higher mathematics in Mexico; therefore the Spaniards filled a particularly useful niche.

In the late 1940s Mexican theoreticians elaborated upon aspects of George Birkhoff's theory of gravitation in flat space-time, a model consistent with Einstein's special relativity but which avoided the general theory's curvilineal coordinates, which Birkhoff 'always considered to be unnecessary and difficult to interpret experimentally'.[109] Indeed, Birkhoff had expounded his idea in a 1944 lecture in Mexico, D.F.,[110] and a group of Mexican physicists were working on Birkhoffian relativity or on comparisons between Einstein's and Birkhoff's cosmologies, including Jaime Lifshitz (Birkhoff's student), Fernando Alba Andrade, Graeff and Sandoval.

1975) and 'Reseña histórica del Instituto de Física, Segunda etapa 1953–1970' (Mexico, D.F., 1976) (mimeo); and Juan Manual Lozano et al., 'Historia de la Sociedad Mexicana de Física', *Revista Mexicana de Física*, 3 (1982): 277–93.

[107] Cruz Manjarrez, 'Reseña histórica del Instituo de Física. Primera etapa 1938–1953,' pp. 24–5.
[108] José Cueli, 'Matemáticas, física y química', in *Exilio español*, pp. 531–43, on pp. 532–3.
[109] Marston Morse, 'George David Birkhoff', *Dictionary of Scientific Biography*, II: 143–6.
[110] George D. Birkhoff, 'El concepto matemático de tiempo y la gravitación', *Boletín de la Sociedad Matemática Mexicana*, 1 (1944): 1–24.

By 1950 the Mexican physics community consisted of three Ph.Ds, one M.S. and a licenciate. Still, two years later there was enough interest to found the Mexican Physics Society, with Graeff as president, which by 1982 had grown to 1400 members. This exponential growth is in part explained by the dynamism that nuclear physics imparted to the discipline beginning with the acquisition of a Van de Graaf accelerator in 1950–52. Three young physicists sent to MIT to learn how to use it became the nucleus of an experimental physics research group. Virtually all physics research in Mexico has concentrated in the National University (UNAM) and it has been difficult to establish viable centres elsewhere in the country.

After the Second World War physics research in Argentina, Brazil, Chile and Mexico became increasingly focussed on atomic physics. In Argentina, there was a politically charged debate among physicists as to the degree to which research in physics should be linked to the armed forces. Enrique Gaviola argued that the hierarchical and disciplinary structure of the military was at odds with the keystones of scientific training which were 'intellectual rebelliousness, dissatisfaction with existing theories and methods and a rejection of hierarchical authority in science and technology'.[111] Gaviola's argument was found persuasive by the Argentinian Senate which, in November of 1946, was considering a draft law establishing the Institute of Physical and Chemical Research.

In 1949 Perón hired a refugee German physical chemist named Ronald Richter to direct an ambitious project of nuclear science. Richter convinced Perón that he could produce controlled nuclear fusion with cheap materials in a process that could underwrite a vast expansion of the nation's industrial capacity by supplying cheap energy in huge quantities. Perón's reasons for backing Richter were wholly in line with the ideology of modernization that informed his concept of the 'New Argentina'; he had no interest in the military uses of atomic energy but saw it as a way to expand iron and steel production quickly and cheaply. In February 1951 Richter made the sensational announcement that he had achieved controlled nuclear fusion under laboratory conditions (a claim ultimately proven false; Richter was a charlatan who had simply exploded hydrogen in a voltaic arc). Even so, the announcement had important, though unforeseen consequences: the news

---

[111] From a letter from Gaviola to General Savio, 28 September 1946), cited by Mario Mariscotti, *El secreto atómico de Huemul* (Buenos Aires, 1985), p. 63. The following section is based on Mariscotti's fascinating account. See also, Regis Cabral, 'The Perón-Richter fusion program, 1948–1953', in Juan José Saldaña (ed.), *Cross-Cultural Diffusion of Science; Latin America* (Mexico, D.F., 1987; Cuadernos de Quipu, 2), pp. 77–106.

from Argentina stimulated the United States to begin a fusion programme and, at the same time, the Argentinian government purchased a syncho-cyclotron from the Netherlands. Not long after Richter had been exposed (by a series of committees that included Richard Gans and José Antonio Balseiro) the cyclotron became the central element in training a distin-guished generation of Argentine nuclear scientists who early on produced internationally recognized results in the field of radioisotopes. The Dirección Nacional de Energía Atómica (DNEA) became the focus of a rapid institutionalization of physics around 1953 (the multiplication of sub-specialties, large expenditures on instrumentation, grants established to send young scientists abroad, were some of the signs). In 1950, the year of DNEA's founding, the Dirección Nacional de Investigaciones Técnicas (DNIT − antecedent of CONICYT) was also established. Hence, atomic research was the stimulus that led to the crystallization of a general scientific research structure. Balseiro had been a disciple of Guido Beck, an Austrian emigré quantum physicist whom Gaviola had hired at the Córdoba Observa-tory.[112] With Beck, Balseiro cut his teeth as a theoretical physicist in research on the quantum structure of magnetic fields. After study abroad (in Liverpool), Balseiro returned to Argentina to head the theoretical section of the Atomic Energy Commission. Then in 1950, he was named director of the Bariloche laboratory which he promptly removed from politics, recruit-ing the best Argentinian talent (Gaviola organized a high-temperature laboratory there in 1953) for faculty and sixty students in its initial class.[113] The depoliticization of nuclear physics promoted its rapid institutionaliza-tion in the 1950s: subdisciplinary groups multiplied and ample funds were spent both on the purchase of instruments and on fellowships for foreign study. The success of the DNEA had no precedent in Argentina; its budget under Enrique P. González exceeded that of any other Argentinian univer-sity or institute scientific programme.

Numerous other atomic physics centres were established in Latin Amer-ica. In 1954, for example, a Nuclear Physics Group was established in the Physics Department of the University of Chile; the group acquired a Dutch particle accelerator and Chileans were trained by a team of Dutch physi-

[112] According to Gaviola, Beck's stimulus was crucial for the program of Argentine physics. The year after Beck's arrival in 1943, Gaviola and others at Córdoba founded the Asociación Física Argen-tina (Gaviola, 'La Asociación Física Argentina: su historia hasta', 1965) (mimeo). See also H. M. Nussenzveig, *Guido Beck: 1903−1988* (Rio de Janeiro, 1989).

[113] On Beck and Balseiro, see Alberto Maiztegui, 'Un investigador que actuó en una época tan difícil como la de hoy,' *La Voz del Interior*, 16 June 1985; Guido Beck, 'José Antonio Balseiro (1919−1962), *Ciencia e Investigación*, 18 (1962), 145−9.

cists.[114] In 1956 an Atomic Energy Commission was established in Guatemala, which developed a sizeable atomic physics research establishment (the National Institute of Nuclear Energy, founded 1970, and the Dirección General de Energía Nuclear, a bureau of the Ministry of Energy and Mines). Mexican nuclear physics expanded rapidly with the acquisition of four reactors between 1960–70. A dynamitron accelerator and financial support from the Rockefeller Foundation and other U.S. bodies underlay the growth of research beginning around 1965. The Mexican National Institute of Nuclear Research, like the Guatemalan effort, is highly applied in nature, focussing on agriculture, medicine and metallurgy.

Astronomy, Astrophysics and Geophysics

The status of astronomy in Latin America at the beginning of the century can be appreciated from the composition of the astronomical commissions witnessing the solar eclipse of 10 October 1912, which was visible only in Brazil. The Chilean and two Argentinian delegations were led by foreign astronomers: the German F. W. Ristenpart and the North Americans William Joseph Hussey and Charles D. Perrine, directors of the observatories of Santiago, La Plata and Córdoba respectively. Only the two Brazilian commissions led by Henrique Morize and composed mainly of Brazilian personnel were Latin American in the true sense.[115]

Latin American astronomy throughout the century, but particularly in the first half, was closely tied to European and U.S. astronomy as a source both of technical know-how and of research programmes. The most advanced countries like Argentina, Mexico and Brazil developed dual observatory structures, with the older, more urban observatories performing the tasks of classical astronomy (charting the stars of the southern hemisphere and measuring their magnitudes) and newer, usually more outlying, dependencies initiating the study of astrophysics (cosmology, spectroscopy, galactic astronomy).

In Mexico the National Observatory of Tacubaya in Mexico City, founded in 1878, devoted much of its labors to the unification of time, the country being a hodge-podge of different time zones (which interfered, logically, with the efficient functioning of the incipient railroad system). The staff was duly concerned with the elaboration of the Mexican zone of the celestial map and photographic star catalogue as well as other classical

---

[114] J. Mir Dupont, *Evolución de la energia nuclear en Chile* (Santiago, 1985), p. 2.
[115] Roberto Vergara Caffarelli, 'O eclipse solar de 1912', *Ciência e Cultura*, 32 (1980): 561–73.

endeavours such as the observation of solar eclipses.[116] A Mexican team had gone to Spain in 1905 to view the solar eclipse there. The solar eclipse of 1923 was visible in Mexico, and mindful of the ambiguous results of the 1919 Sobral eclipse, the Mexican government had invited Einstein himself to direct the eclipse observations.[117]

In 1942 the Astrophysical Observatory of Tonantzintla (Puebla) was inaugurated under the direction of Luis Enrique Erro. Its Schmidt telescope was one of the largest of the period and similar to Harvard Observatory's where its mechanical parts were made. Erro was in close contact with Harvard astronomers, notably Leon Campbell and his American Association of Variable Star Observers, and the observatory's early research programme was just a descriptive hand-me-down from Harvard. MIT-trained Carlos Graeff was the theoretical physicist on Erro's team; he gave an early seminar on quantum mechanics and wrote on Birkhoff's relativistic cosmology while Paris Pismis conducted original research on galactic kinematics. A fresh round of original research ensued when Guillermo Haro returned from Harvard to take up the direction of both Tacubaya and Tonantzintla. Under his direction, theoretical work was concentrated at Tacubaya and observational work, including his own research on nebulae in Andromeda, at Tonantzintla, air pollution having made the older facility almost useless for observation.[118] As pollution worsened Tacubaya was closed as its equipment moved to Tonantzintla whose own utility was increasingly jeopardized by deteriorating air quality. The observatory was integrated into an Institute of Astronomy established at the National University in 1967 even as the search was underway for a site for a new national observatory. In 1970 construction began on a facility in Baja California in close collaboration with the University of Arizona. The new national observatory, used mainly for photometric observation, became the axis of a new scientific research centre (CICESE) designed to complement its own activities.[119]

---

[116] On the history of modern classical astronomy in Mexico, see Marco Arturo Moreno Coral, 'El origen de la investigación astronómica en México,' *Actas de las Sociedad Mexicana de Historia de la Ciencia y de la Tecnología,* 1 (1989), 79–94, and *idem,* 'El Observatorio Astronómico Nacional y el desarrollo de la ciencia en México (1878–1910)', *Quipu,* 5 (1988), 59–67, and Joaquín Gallo Sarlat, 'Entre eclipses y cometas: Reminiscencias de la vida de Joaquín Gallo,' in Moreno Corral (ed.), *Historia de la astronomía en México* (Ensenada, 1983), pp. 245–66.

[117] *New York Times,* 9 June 1923.

[118] Bart J. Bok, 'Astronomía mexicana, 1930–1950', in Moreno Corral, *Historia de la astronomía en México,* pp. 267–80; Paris Pismis, 'El amanecer de la astrofísica en Mexico,' ibid., pp. 281–97.

[119] Manuel Alvarez and Eduardo López, 'Los últimos diez años del Observatorio Astrónomico Nacional', in *Historia de la astronomía en México,* pp. 311–36.

In Argentina the two major observatories were founded in the late nineteenth century – Córdoba in 1871, La Plata in 1882. The North American Benjamin Gould, the first of a succession of foreign directors at Córdoba, published a number of important star catalogues beginning with the famous *Uranometría Argentina* in 1879.[120] Córdoba continued this work under two more North American directors, John M. Thome who replaced Gould in 1885 and Charles D. Perrine who replaced Thome in 1909 and served until 1936. By the end of Perrine's term the effort of Córdoba was widely viewed as out of touch with the ambient culture. As an investigation of 1927 noted, 'After more than a half century's existence, the Observatory still preserves its basic original character as a foreign mission in Argentina. With its foreign personnel, its total disconnectedness with the technical and cultural problems of our country, this National Observatory remains alien to the life of the nation.'[121] In particular it was perceived as playing no role in the training of Argentinian scientists. Although astrophysics had begun under Perrine, its real impulse resulted from the transition to Argentinian leadership, under the directorships of Juan José Nissen (1937–40) and Enrique Gaviola (1940–47), the founding of an astrophysical station at Bosque Alegre, and the melding of astronomical research interests with those of theoretical physics under the leadership of Gaviola and Guido Beck, as already described. The research programme at Bosque Alegre included stellar spectography (e.g., Jorge Sahade's research on spectroscopic binaries) and direct photography.

The La Plata Observatory had a more varied programme. It owned a geodesic station at Oncativo where important studies on the variation of latitude in the southern hemisphere were conducted in the nineteenth century. Systematic astronomy (in the form of star catalogue work) began only under the North American director William J. Hussey (who served 1911–15). Hussey brought two other North Americans with him: Bernhard Dawson, who discovered numerous double stars in collaboration with Hussey and later became director and Paul Delavan, who in 1913 rediscovered Westphal's comet (which since has borne his name). Astrophysics began in earnest in the 1930s with the arrival as refugees from Germany of Alexander Wilkens, former director of the Breslau observatory with re-

---

[120] For exhaustive descriptions of the southern star catalogues produced at the Córdoba Observatory, see Enrique Chaudet, *La evolución de la astronomía durante los últimos cincuenta años (1862–1922)* (Buenos Aires, 1926).

[121] Félix Aguilar and Norberto B. Cobos, 'Informe sobre el Observatorio Nacional de Córdoba', in Simón Gershanik and Luis A. Milone (eds), *Evolución de las ciencias en la República Argentina, 1923–1972: Astronomía* (Buenos Aires, 1979), pp. 173–6 (Appendix 3).

search on the spectroscopic temperatures of double stars, and his son Herbert.[122]

The National Observatory of Brazil in Rio de Janeiro, under the long directorship of Henrique Morize was another Observatory of the old school with a classical metrological function and descriptive research programme. Perhaps its great accomplishment was directing the logistics of the 1919 expedition to view the solar eclipse at Sobral, confirming the theory of general relativity. Around the same time Amoroso Costa, the astronomer-mathematician who was Einstein's leading supporter in the Brazilian scientific community, was investigating double stars and worked out the evolution of a binary system following a theory of George Darwin on the formation of the earth/moon system. Like its counterpart at La Plata, the Brazilian Observatory maintained a geodesic station at Vassouras for the study of terrestrial magnetism. There were also observatories at São Paulo (the Observatorio da Avenida, founded in 1903, which moved, because of air pollution, to a park south of the city in 1941 and later became the Astronomical and Geophysical Institute of the University of São Paulo) and Porto Alegre (1908).

Theoretical astrophysics, as we have noted above, was another result of Wataghin's efforts in physics; Schenberg's collaborations of the 1940s with Gamow and Chandrasakhar represented a new direction in Brazilian theoretical astronomy. Modernization in observational astronomy and geodesy dates to the appointment of Lélio Gama as director of the National Observatory in 1951. A new geomagnetic observatory was established near the magnetic equator. In the 1970s a new astrophysical observatory was established at Brasópolis (Minas Gerais) and the National Center of Radio Astronomy and Astrophysics was founded in São Paulo.[123]

In Peru, efforts in astronomy were subordinated to geophysics. For some years early in the century, Harvard ran an observatory there, called Boyden Station, for photographing variable stars. Later on the Carnegie Institution built (between 1919–22) a magnetic observatory at Huancayo, a site determined to be equidistant between the Córdoba Observatory and a U.S. facility in Panama. The research programme at Huancayo was to measure the magnetic field and to make meteorological observations. In

[122] On the La Plata Observatory, see Pyenson, *Cultural Imperialism and Exact Sciences*, pp. 185–205, and Simón Gershanik, 'El Observatorio Astronómico de La Plata', in *Evolución de las Ciencias . . . Astronomia*, pp. 5–122.

[123] For surveys of astronomy in Brazil, see Abraão de Morais, 'A astronomía no Brasil', in Azevedo (ed.), *As ciências no Brasil*, I: 81–161, and Ronaldo Rogério de Freitas Mourão, 'A astronomía no Brasil', in Guimarães and Motoyama (eds), *Historia das ciências no Brasil*, II: 409–41.

1932 a seismograph was installed and, the following year, a spectrohelio-scope was contributed by the Mount Wilson Observatory. As a result the research programme was broadened to include cosmic radiation and obser-vation of the ionosphere. The Huancayo facility was transferred to the government of Peru in 1947 and was renamed the Geophysical Institute of Peru in 1962. During the 1960s a number of dependent stations were founded, including a radio observatory at Jicamarca (established under contract with the U.S. National Bureau of Standards for ionospheric stud-ies), an ionospheric station at Talosa, and seismological station at Ñaño. Finally, in the 1970s the Cosmos Station, an installation purely for moni-toring solar activity, was built at Huancayo by Kyoto University. It is interesting to note that although the Geophysical Institute has become one of the major physical science units in Latin America, contacts with foreign institutions have been crucial and the financial contribution of the Peruvian government minimal.[124]

The San Calixto Seismographic Observatory in La Paz, Bolivia, is an example of an institution with scant funding and inadequate instrumenta-tion which preserved and made a significant contribution.[125] The observa-tory was founded in 1911 by Esteban Tortosa, a Spanish Jesuit who had worked at the Observatory of Cartuja in Granada, Spain, with Manuel Navarro Neumann. The director, who arrived in 1912, was the French Jesuit, Pierre M. Descotes. In May 1913 he began publishing a bulletin of seismic data which has continued uninterrupted to this day. The instru-ments, patterned after those in Granada, were home made in a rudimentary shop. Nevertheless, the data was so good that a standard American seismo-logical text stated that 'La Paz at once became, and still remains, the most important single seismological station of the world. This is a consequence of its isolated location, the sensitive instruments, and the great care with which records were interpreted and reports issued under the direction of Father Descotes.' With the passage of time an astronomical section was added and the Bolivian government awarded Descotes a salary (which the Jesuit applied to new instrumentation). In 1960, when Descotes retired, the observatory joined in a program directed by the Department of Terres-trial Magnetism of the Carnegie Institution. Under the new director, Ra-

[124] Gustavo Estremadoyro, 'Historia de la astronomía en el Perú', in Ernesto Yepes (ed.), *Estudios de historia de la ciencia en el Perú*, 2 vols (Lima, 1986), I: 37–62, and Alberto Gisecke Matto, 'El desarrollo de la geofísica', ibid., I: 115–26.
[125] Pierre M. Descotes, S. J., *Le nouvel observatoire sismologique de la Compagnie de Jésus a La Paz, Bolivie* (La Paz, 1913); Ramón Cabré, S. J., 'Datos históricos del Observatorio San Calixto, en La Paz, Bolivia' (typescript).

món Cabré five subsidiary stations were installed, all communicating data to La Paz electronically. A variety of geophysical phenomena were studied, including anomalies of gravity and electric conductivity.[126]

Another Jesuit seismology station is the Geophysical Institute of the Colombian Andes, in Bogotá. Seismology in Colombia dates to 1923 when Simón Sarasola, the Spanish director of the National Meteorological Observatory, introduced the nation's first seismograph. At the same time, Enrique Pérez Arbeláez and Carlos Ortiz Restrepo were trained in seismology in Spain by Navarro Neumann, ordering for Bogotá a seismographic of his design constructed in Automotation Laboratory of the great inventor Leonardo Torres Quevedo. Finally, a new geophysical observatory was established in 1941 with Sarasola in charge of meteorology and seismology under the direction of Emilio Ramirez who had just completed graduate work in the seismology programme of the University of St. Louis. In 1945 an accelerograph was obtained from the U.S. Coast and Geodetic Service in whose observational network the Institute participated.[127]

In 1966 a regional centre for the study of seismic phenomena (CERESIS) was established with Ramon Cabré as its first president.[128] This is a consortium of nine South American countries operating under UNESCO auspices to exchange technical data and train personnel for seismographic observatories. Among its numerous publications are a multi-volume catalogue of earthquakes, a book on historical earthquakes, studies of economic effects of quakes, and a series of maps. If the origins of CERESIS can be traced to Descotes' modest observatory, then the lesson is that persistence, vision and adeptness at attracting the support of foreign institutions can eventually pay off.

Mathematics

Advanced research in physics and astronomy presupposes a pool of scientists trained in higher mathematics. Although mathematics is the most basic of sciences Latin American dependence upon Europe – particularly Italy – and the United States in this field well into the second half of the present century was notable.

---

[126] Ramón Cabré, S. J., 'Geophysical Studies in the Central Andes', *Geodynamics of the Eastern Pacific Region*, 9 (1983), 73–6.
[127] J. Emilio Ramírez, *Historia del Instituto Geofísica*, 2 fascicles (Bogotá, 1977).
[128] Alberto A. Giesecke, 'Centro Regional de Sismología para America del Sur: CERESIS' (mimeo, 1986).

The Italian Hugo Broggi of the University of La Plata, where he taught between 1912 and 1927, was associated with the modernization of mathematics in Argentina, but the Spaniard Julio Rey Pastor of the Faculty of Sciences in Buenos Aires was more influential, creating a distinctive Argentinian school of mathematical research. The Faculty of Sciences (which early in the century was an engineering school) had a doctoral programme in mathematics and physics but no courses had been given since 1900. From then until Rey Pastor's arrival some improvement had occurred in mathematics instruction for engineers, but higher mathematical study was in full decadence. Operationally, Rey Pastor's task was to convince engineering professors of the utility of any mathematics other than what appeared in elementary textbooks.

In his first course in 1917 Rey Pastor introduced, as he had already in Madrid, Felix Klein's famous 'Erlangen Program', a course of geometry instruction based on the theory of groups, whose method is to establish the invariants of each one, topology being the most general. His next course, the following year, was a specialized course for engineering students. His impact was immediate and profound, in that among this early group of advanced students were the future leaders of Argentinian mathematics. The topics he covered – e.g. functions of a complex variable, conformal mapping – were standard in Germany and Italy, but completely new in Argentina.[129]

Rey Pastor received a six-year contract (followed by a permanent appointment) and restructured mathematics instruction at the Faculty of Sciences by offering courses on advanced (including non-Euclidean) geometry, mathematical analysis and mathematical methodology. Mathematicians of the old school, whose instruction was based on outmoded French manuals, were incensed at what they regarded as a usurpation by a foreigner.[130] Rey Pastor taught mainly engineering students among whom he recruited prospects for pure mathematics. This implied no contradiction, because he believed both that engineering school mathematics courses, which stressed the techniques of calculation, were good preparation for pure mathematicians and also that pure mathematicians should never lose touch with applications.

---

[129] Sixto Ríos, Luis A. Santaló and Manuel Balanzat, *Julio Rey Pastor, matemático* (Madrid, 1979), pp. 59–61, 71, 89. On Rey Pastor and the renewal of mathematics in Spain, see Thomas F. Glick, *Einstein in Spain* (Princeton, N.J., 1988), pp. 17–26.

[130] See Claro Cornelio Dassen, *Las matemáticas en la Argentina* (Buenos Aires, 1924), especially the sarcastic comments on pp. 69–70.

After his permanent appointment in 1927, Rey Pastor held two chairs, those of Mathematical Analysis and Higher Geometry, and, in 1928, founded an influential Mathematical Seminar patterned after one he had established in Madrid in the previous decade. Its shortlived *Boletín* published the first modern research in Argentinian mathematics. By the end of the decade, his first disciples were presenting papers in scholarly meetings abroad. As he had in Spain, Rey Pastor brought a succession of important foreign mathematicians to give short courses, including the Italians Federigo Enriques (1925), Francesco Severi (1930) and Tullio Levi-Civita (1937), and the Frenchmen Emile Borel (1928) and Jacques Hadamard (1930).

In the 1940s his best students began to make their mark in international research. Among these were Alberto González Domínguez (who became an important figure in Argentine quantum physics), Alberto Calderón (future chairman of mathematics at the University of Chicago whose specialty was singular integrals), Roque Scarfiello (theory of distributions), Emilio Roxin (control systems and optimal controls) and Misha Cotlar. At the same time, Spanish exiles including Esteban Terradas, Luis Santaló, Manuel Balanzat, and Pedro Pi Calleja, and the Italian Beppo Levi at the Mathematics Institute of Rosario, considerably enhanced the collective teaching capacity of the mathematical community.

By the time Rey Pastor retired in 1952 Argentinian mathematics had been transformed. Virtually every engineering student at the University of Buenos Aires between 1921 and 1952 had studied with him and, in other institutions and through his textbooks, he influenced generations of secondary school teachers as well. He had laid the foundation for the great Argentinian 'Generation of 1961'.

Rey Pastor had not taught the members of the Generation of 1961 (mathematicians born between 1937–40). They were more directly influenced by Mischa Cotlar. Of the ten most important members of this group[131], all studied in the United States and eight earned doctorates there (three at New York University and three at the University of Chicago). Three of this group – Beatriz Margolis (differential equations), Cora Sadowski (singular integrals) and Víctor Pereyra (numerical analysis) – ended up at the Central University in Caracas in the 1970s where they participated in the modernization of mathematics there.

---

[131] As listed by Luis A. Santaló, 'La matemática en Buenos Aires y La Plata (Período 1943–1972', in Luis A. Santaló (ed.), *Evolución de las ciencias en la República Argentina, 1923–1972: Matemática* (Buenos Aires, 1972), pp. 54–103, on pp. 85–8.

The Central University's School of Physics and Mathematics had been founded in 1958 with a largely foreign faculty (including five Spanish mathematicians, three Brazilians and a number of Argentinians including Rodolfo Ricabarra who energized students in geometry and topology in the 1960s). Towards the end of the 1960s, Mischa Cotlar and Cora Sadowski arrived to stimulate research in harmonic analysis and integral equations. This was the moment of the awakening of Venezuelan mathematics, associated with the leadership of Luis Baez first at the Central University and then at the Instituto Venezolana de Investigaciones Científicas (IVIC), and was quickly followed by the creation of institutions: the Caracas Mathematical Colloquium (1976), the first Venezuelan Mathematical Congress (1977), the Seminar of Mathematical Logic (1978), and the Foundation of the Venezuela Mathematical Society (1980). The 1970s saw a diversification of topics of research, which had hitherto centred on analysis.[132]

Uruguay developed a fine school of mathematicians in the 1950s and 1960s, also under the stimulation of contact with Argentinian mathematics, and in this case, with Rey Pastor directly. At the end of the 1930s, Rey Pastor began to give regular weekend seminars on general topology in Montevideo to a group which included José Luis Massera, Mischa Cotlar, and Rafael Laguarda. The Institute of Mathematics and Statistics (IME), established in the Engineering School in 1942, became the center of an emergent school of Uruguayan mathematics. The research programmes of both Massera and Laguarda were set in the course of fellowships in the United States, Massera's on differential equations and Laguarda's on integral transformations. By 1960, with the maturation of the 'third generation' of Uruguayan mathematicians, the identity of a distinctive school had emerged and research interests broadened considerably (into probability, differential topology and so forth). Cotlar returned from Argentina after the military coup of 1966 had paralyzed the University of Buenos Aires. The military intervention in Uruguay in 1973 brought, in turn, the ruin of Uruguayan mathematics: Massera was imprisoned, virtually the entire staff of the IME emigrated and, in the early 1980s, twenty-five Uruguayan mathematicians of high quality were employed in other countries.[133]

[132] Carlos A. Di Prisco and Lorenzo Lara, 'Comentarios sobre la investigación matemática en Venezuela,' in Hebe M. C. Vessuri (ed.), *Ciencia académica en la Venezuela moderna* (Caracas, 1984), pp. 237–77.

[133] Rodrigo Arocena and Gonzalo Pérez, 'Matemática', in Ministerio de Educación y Cultura, *Ciencia y tecnología en el Uruguay* (Montevideo, 1986), pp. 71–9, y José Luis Massera, 'Los orígenes y el desarrollo de la escuela uruguaya de matemáticas', *Interciencia*, 13 (1988): 177–82. A memoir of the Institute in the 1950s can be found in Paul R. Halmos, *I Want To Be a Mathematician* (New

In Brazil, Oto de Alencar (1874–1912) was an important precursor of modern mathematics, a student of non-Euclidean geometry who, as professor at the Politécnica of São Paulo introduced Painlevé on differential equations. His student and follower, Manoel de Amoroso Costa (1885–1928) continued to teach modern mathematics which brought him into conflict with positivists of the old school, as we have noted. Another benchmark was the 1918 thesis of Teodoro Ramos (1895–1935) on real variables; he too continued a tenuous modern tradition as professor of rational mechanics at the Politécnica of São Paulo. A relativist, he gave notable courses on vectorial calculus and quantum mechanics. To São Paulo he invited the Italian Luigi Fantappié who introduced functional analysis, a line continued by Omar Catunda and, in some early articles, Mario Schenberg. Lélio Gama was the first great mathematics professor in Rio de Janeiro where visiting Italians (Gabrielle Mammana and Achille Bassi), introduced modern analysis, combinatory topology and similar subjects in the 1940s. The foundation of the Conselho Nacional de Pesquisa (CNPq) in 1951 had a decisive influence on Brazilian mathematics with the establishment in 1952 of the Institute of Pure and Applied Mathematics (IMPA) through which most senior Brazilian mathematicians of the 1970s and 1980s passed in the 1950s and 1960s. IMPA sponsored a biennial Colloquium of Brazilian Mathematics which instilled an unusual cohesiveness in the Brazilian mathematics community. The number of participants in this Colloquium grew dramatically from fifty at the first (1957), to 250 at the sixth (1967), to 700 at the eleventh (1977).[134]

Chemistry

Throughout Latin America chemistry was traditionally associated with pharmacy and the preponderance of chairs were in medical schools well into the present century. At the point at which local chemical industries required a research establishment, institutes and schools were established for that purpose. In many cases the two traditions merged, forming unified departments or faculties of chemistry. In others, pharmacy remained autonomous. The institutional patterning of today's national chemistry

York, 1985), pp. 167–99. Halmos, lecturing to the Institute's 'second generation' in 1950 noted (p. 190) that his audience was 'unfamiliar with the language and attitude of modern mathematics'.
[134] F. M. de Oliveira Castro, 'A matemática no Brasil', in Azevedo (ed.) *As ciências no Brasil*, I: 41–77; Chaim S. Hönig and Elza F. Gomide, 'Ciências matemáticas', in Guimaraes and Motoyama (eds), *História das ciências no Brasil*, I, 35–60.

disciplines therefore reflects the previous balance established between pharmaceutical and biochemists, on the one hand, and industrial chemists, on the other.

We can observe this bimodal pattern in Mexico where, during the Revolution, Juan Salvador Agraz, the first Mexican member of the International Commission on Atomic Weights, secured the creation of a National School of Industrial Chemistry in the village of Tacuba near Mexico, D.F.[135] The pharmacists, meanwhile, wanted to leave the Medical School where they felt themselves treated like poor relations, and soon they were folded into the Tacuba school, which continued however to concentrate on chemical engineering. No less than ten of its graduates were sent to Germany (in part, to lessen French influence on Mexican scientific culture) in 1921 for advanced study; when they returned most were employed by the government in various ministerial laboratories, because no one knew what a chemical engineer was supposed to do.

During the directorship of Fernando Orozco, one of the German-trained chemists, the civil engineering component of instruction was reduced and emphasis on biochemistry increased at the same time as Spanish republican refugees were integrated into Mexican chemistry. In 1941 a research unit, the Institute of Chemistry, was founded at the National University with Orozco as director and the Spanish republican Antonio Madinaveitia as director of research. The Institute soon became the centre of chemical research in Mexico, aided by the financial support of the Rockefeller Foundation (which continued to 1963) and the establishment in it of a doctoral programme.[136] Meanwhile, instruction in chemical engineering assimilated the pedagogical model of unitary operations brought from MIT by Estanislao Ramírez. The success of Mexican chemical engineering was proven in the saga of Syntex and the domination of the world market in synthetic steroids by Mexico in the late 1940s and 1950s on the basis of research carried out in Madinaveitia's laboratory at the behest of a company founded by Hungarian and German refugees from Nazism together with the North American Russell Marker who identified a plant source of progesterone.[137] The Tacuba School was converted into the Autonomous

---

[135] For the history of the Tacuba School, based on extensive interviews with graduates, see Horacio García Fernández, *Historia de una Facultad: Química, 1916–1983* (Mexico, D.F., 1985).

[136] Pilar Rius, 'Los exiliados españoles y la creación del Instituto de Química de la UNAM', in María Luis Capella (ed.), *El exilio español y la UNAM (coloquio)* (Mexico, D.F., 1987), pp. 35–41; Alberto Sandoval L., 'Cinco lustros de existencia', *Boletín del Instituto de Química*, 17 (1965): 83–121.

[137] On Syntex see García Fernández, *Historia de una Facultad*, pp. 186–8; Ingrid Rosenbleuth, 'Dependencia tecnológica e evolución profesional: La industria y la ingeniería química en México',

University's Faculty of Chemistry and moved to the new University City (1957–63). There, chemistry enrolments increased precipitously from 1620 in 1967 to 5420 in 1971 (with 621 professors).

Uruguay presents a similar case of the fusion of industrial and pharmaceutical chemistry.[138] An Institute of Chemistry had been established in Montevideo in the Faculty of Medicine in 1908, housed in a grandiose building modelled after the Chemistry Institute of the University of Berlin and whose first director was the professor of medical chemistry, José Scoseria. He was succeeded by Domingo Giribaldo who struggled to implant modern chemistry against entrenched resistance by old-school pharmacologists. In 1917 he inaugurated a chair of physical chemistry with a course on electrochemistry.

Meanwhile in 1912 an Institute of Industrial Chemistry had been founded under the directorship of the North American Latham Clarke, with the mission of training a small number of industrial chemists. The first members of the staff had been trained in pharmacology or mineralogy. Like Tacuba, the Institute had a production section designed to support the Institute's research and instruction in applied chemistry which commenced in 1915. In 1918 a degree programme in industrial chemistry was instituted; this was precocious in Latin America, inasmuch as chemical engineering had only been created (at MIT) in the first decade of the century. In 1929 a new Faculty of Chemistry and Pharmacy was founded, combining pharmaceutical chemistry with the teaching functions of the Industrial Chemistry Institute. In 1950 the national research effort was restructured in the Laboratory of the Division of Scientific Research of the National Commission of Combustibles, Alcohol and Cement, with five sections (organic, inorganic and physical chemistry, industrial microbiology and experimental biology).

Prior to the establishment of a School of Chemistry at the Central University in the 1940s the only advanced training available in the field in Venezuela was in a small school run since 1912 in the Development Ministry. The new School was initially housed in the Faculty of Pharmacy, then moved to engineering and finally was folded into a faculty of sciences in 1958. The first professors in the 1950s were mainly foreigners, central Europeans and Spanish republicans, who in general were not researchers but who performed the instrumental role of transmitting classical chemis-

---

Relaciones. Estudios de Historia y Sociedad (Michoacán), 1 (1980): 35–90; and Gary Gereffi, *The Pharmaceutical Industry and Dependency in the Third World* (Princeton, N.J. 1983).

[138] Jorge Grünwaldt Ramasso, *Historia de la química en el Uruguay (1830–1930)* (Montevideo, 1966).

try. In the late 1950s and 1960s several hundred Venezuelans went abroad to study, mainly to the United States but also to England and France and in 1966–70 several dozen Argentinian chemists, including a number of already established working groups, migrated to Venezuela en masse, fleeing military oppression. The Argentinians in general moved on without leaving disciples behind, having perceived Venezuela as infertile ground for chemical research.[139] But here too the growth in chemistry enrolments was astounding, with matriculations in 1955–75 growing at double the rate of the rest of the sciences combined, a phenomenon obviously related to the Venezuelan oil boom.

In Brazil, pharmacology and biochemistry were established in medical schools and institutes. In particular, biochemists of the first half of the century were almost all medical doctors who studied the chemical composition of blood or other tissue. Two biochemists trained by Otto Folin at Harvard rose to distinction in the 1930s: A. A. Cavalcanti (1899–1976) in São Paulo and João Baeta Vianna (1894–1967) in Belo Horizonte. Baeta Vianna worked on the biochemistry of Chagas' Disease. Maurício de Rocha e Silva at the Biological Institute of São Paulo, discovered bradykinin, a pharmacologically important polypeptide. Biochemists at the Oswaldo Cruz Institute worked on vitamins, the action of drugs of enzymes and other topics of medical application in the 1940s and 1950s, while at Butantan Thales Martins (1896–1979) studied the pharmacology of hormones.

Industrial chemistry got under way in 1918 perhaps in response to a famous article, 'Façamos Químicos', written the previous year by José de Freitas Machado, calling for a major school of chemistry modelled on that of Paris. (Freitas Machado organized the first Brazilian Chemistry Congress in 1922 and was the first president of Brazilian Chemistry Society, founded in 1923.) Hence in 1918 the Institute of Agricultural Chemistry was established under the direction of Mário Saraiva. In 1919 the Brazilian Congress established courses of industrial chemistry in eight state capitals, in association with local engineering schools. The Porto Alegre course was taught by Otto Rothe and another German, Erik Schirm, was hired to head a new Institute of Industrial Chemistry. Rothe introduced both

---

[139] Hebe M. C. Vessuri, 'Scientific immigrants in Venezuela: national identity and international science', in Arnaud F. Marks and Hebe Vessuri (eds), *White Collar Migrants in the Americans and the Caribbean* (Leiden, 1983), pp. 171–97, and Vessuri and Elena Díaz, 'El desarrollo de la química científica en Venezuela', in Vessuri (ed.), *Ciencia académica en la Venezuela moderna* (Caracas, 1984), pp. 237–7.

physical chemistry and experimental physics there. The Belo Horizonte course was taught by Alfred Schaeffer, a German who had directed the State Analysis Laboratory there since 1911. An Institute of Chemistry was likewise organized there in 1921. In its laboratories, Schaeffer introduced 'methods analogous to those used in the majority of advanced European schools'. Schaeffer was followed as director by Rothe. The course in Pará was directed by Paul Le Cointe with an entire teaching staff recruited in France. In 1934 the Ministry of Agriculture, long a backer of positivist projects, organized a National School of Chemistry in Rio de Janeiro at the same time as the first real effort in basic chemistry was begun in the newly inaugurated Faculty of Philosophy and Sciences at São Paulo under the direction of Heinrich Rheinboldt. Rheinboldt had been a chemistry professor in Bonn. His specialties were the chemistry of co-ordination complexes and organic compounds, the latter also the specialty of his assistant Heinrich Hauptmann. Physical chemistry was not introduced until 1946. The major research effort in this area, Hans Stammreich's programme in molecular spectroscopy, was begun in the physics department and later incorporated into the Department of Basic Chemistry.[140]

Finally in Argentina, the pharmacy/chemistry split was handled differently in different universities. At the University of Buenos Aires (where a doctorate in pharmacy had been in place since 1875 and in chemistry from 1897) a single curriculum was introduced for basic and industrial chemistry, in the faculty of sciences, while pharmacy was taught in the medical school. La Plata, of more recent foundation, was not bound by the traditional autonomy of pharmacy and offered three parallel programmes (housed in the same building from the 1930s) in pharmacy, basic chemistry and industrial chemistry. The National University of El Litoral had a doctorate in chemical engineering (1919), the first such degree programme in Latin America. In Córdoba, the School of Pharmacy and Biochemistry split from the medical school in 1950 and became the Faculty of Chemical Sciences.[141]

As a result of the precocious establishment of university degree programmes Argentina, in contrast to all other Latin American countries, produced a sizeable number of native chemists. As a result, reliance upon

[140] On chemistry in Brazil, see Heinrich Rheinboldt, 'A química no Brasil', in Azevedo (ed.), *As ciências no Brasil*, II: 9–89; Simao Mathias, 'Evoluçao da química no Brasil', in Guimaraes and Motoyama (eds), *História das ciências no Brasil*, 1: 93–110; J. Leal Prado, 'A bioquímica no Brasil', ibid., 1, 111–50; and José Ribeiro do Valle, 'A farmacologia no Brasil', ibid., 175–89.

[141] Noemí G. Abiusso (ed.), *Evolución de las ciencias en la República argentina: Química* (Buenos Aires, 1981), 6–18.

foreign chemists was diminished. Chemical activities have been so numerous that it is not feasible to summarize them here. However, one area of development in the field is worthy of comment. As a result of government backing of nuclear research, two important chemistry laboratories were organized within the Atomic Energy Commission in 1951–2.[142] These were the radiochemistry laboratory, whose first director Walter Seelmann-Eggebert had been a doctoral student of Otto Hahn, and the general chemistry laboratory under the Argentinian Arturo Cairo. Seelmann worked on radionucleids while Cairo's group began a research programme in inorganic chemistry, centred mainly on uranium. Both laboratories trained many Argentinian chemists. In 1953, Alfred Maddock of Cambridge made the first of a series of visits in order to impart his first-hand knowledge of nuclear chemistry acquired in the atomic projects of the Second World War. That same year the Commission acquired a pilot plant for uranium production to make metallic uranium for reactors. This step led to increased activity in the general chemistry laboratory which by now had several working groups, including a metallurgy group under the physicist Jorge Sábato. At the same time two Phillips particle accelerators stimulated research on artificial radioactivity and chemists discovered fifteen new radionucleids. Finally, so much chemistry activity had been fostered that a Chemistry Department was established within the DNEA in 1954. In 1955, thirty-seven Argentinian papers were presented at the first Conference on the Peaceful Uses of Atomic Energy in Geneva, of which twenty four were by chemists. Among these were reports on the radioactive isotopes of ten different elements, some of them discovered in Argentina. When Argentinian nuclear research burst upon the world after some years of work in secret it caused a sensation internationally, and in the United States in particular, fear of nuclear proliferation.

Geology

Perhaps the most salient element of geological research in those Latin American countries where it was organized early in the century was the influence of the U.S. Geological Survey as an organizational model. In Brazil, the founders of geology were North Americans. The ephemeral Imperial Geological Commission (1875–77) did not survive the death of its

---

[142] Martín B. Crespo, 'La química en la Comisión Nacional de Energía Atómica en el período 1950–1972', in ibid., pp. 167–72.

founder Charles F. Hartt but nevertheless provided a fecund institutional model for future development. Hartt had recruited three young North Americans, Orville A. Derby, Richard Rathburn and the future president of Stanford University, John C. Branner. Derby (1851–1915), now considered the first Brazilian geologist, was made director of the Geographical and Geological Commission of the State of São Paulo, which he led until resigning in 1906 to lead a geological study of Bahia. In São Paulo, Derby mapped the state on a scale of 1:100,000 using the methodology of the U.S. Coast and Geodetic Survey. The Geological Service of São Paulo was organized along the lines of the U. S. Geological Survey, producing an important series of maps and stimulating a similar effort in Minas Gerais. Then in 1907 Derby became first head of the Brazilian Geological and Mineralogical Service, where he trained the first generation of Brazilian geologists. During the early years of the Service, Derby located huge iron reserves in Minas Gerais while Branner carried out a series of structural and stratigraphic studies which were the basis of the first geological map of Brazil when he published in 1919. He also wrote an elementary geology textbook for Brazilian students (*Geologia elementar,* 1915).

The educational centre of Brazilian geology (as well as physical geography and geomorphology) was the School of Mines at Ouro Preto. (University geology instruction was initiated only in the 1930s.) At Ouro Preto was trained Eusebio Paulo de Oliveira, author of the second geological map of Brazil and a student of the geology and paleontology of Rio Grande do Sul. Another graduate was Djalma Guimarães, named petrographer of the Geological Service in 1923. Guimarães was noted for his theory of hyperstenization which explained the origin of certain rocks by magmatic differentiation.

The 1923 visit of the South African Alex du Toit was important for raising broader issues in geological theory. Du Toit was interested in the geological relationship between Africa and South America and stimulated a discussion of general geological theory among Brazilian naturalists.

Geology in São Paulo, moribund since Derby's departure, was revived by two foreigners. Ettore Onorato, an Italian who had mastered X-ray analysis of crystalline formations in Leipzig and at Sir William Bragg's physics laboratory in Manchester, was chairman of the department of mineralogy and petrography at the University of São Paulo, a model department which trained a new generation of Brazilian researchers. At the same time, the German Viktor Leinz was invited by Guimarães to direct the petrographical laboratory of the National Department of Mineral Production (the successor institution of the Geological and Mineralogical Service). Later he joined the geological division of the National Museum and headed the geology department at the University of São Paulo.[143]

Beginning in 1913 the Geological and Mineralogical Service published the results of paleontological studies by Brazilian, North American, German and English scholars. By the 1940s, however, Brazilians dominated this specialty (e.g, Carlos de Paulo Couto on Cenozoic mammals). In the 1950s, emphasis shifted from fossil mammals and marine life to micropaleontology. The Micropaleontological Laboratory of Petrobrás was the center of paleontological research in the 1960s and 1970s, where paleopalinological methods were used to establish biostratigraphic zones.[144]

Engineering geology, the inception of which is associated with a famous textbook, Ries and Watson's *Engineering Geology* (1914), has a variety of applications from mining geology to soil mechanics and engineering problems related to highway and railway construction. Brazilian soil mechanics date from the 1920s and Alberto Ortenblad's MIT thesis on consolidation mud deposits. In 1947 Karl Terzaghi, one of the pioneers of soil mechanics, came to Brazil to solve a rockslide problem in a hydroelectric project in São Paulo; his lectures in applied geology at the Polytechnic School opened a new era in Brazilian geotechnology.[145]

In Peru the first organized instruction in geology was included in the curriculum of the School of Mines, founded in 1876. At the governmental level, the Development Ministry's corps of mining engineers began publishing a series of bulletins in 1902 which diffused geological research nationally. José Balta, a former director of the corps of mining engineers, became minister in 1904, emphasizing the ministry's close association with mining. The corps, which had been founded in 1902, undertook a series of hydrological surveys lasting until 1920 which were designed in consultation with the U. S. Geological Survey.

A number of foreigners were instrumental in the implantation of modern geology, in particular the German Gustav Steinmann who, in the first

---

[143] Viktor Leinz, 'A geologia e a paleontologia no Brasil', in Azevedo, ed., *As ciências no Brasil,* I: 243–63; Othon Henry Leonardos, 'A mineralogia e a petrografia no Brasil', ibid., 265–313; José Verissimo de Costa Pereira, 'A geografia no Brasil', *ibid.,* pp. 315–412; Rui Ribeiro Franco, 'A mineralogia e a petrologia no Brasil', in Guimarães and Motoyama (eds), *História das ciências no Brasil,* III: 1–42.

[144] Josué Camargo Mendes, 'A pesquisa paleontológica no Brasil', in Guimarães and Motoyama, *História das ciências no Brasil,* III: 43–71.

[145] Milton Vargas, 'A geotecnologia no Brasil', *Quipu,* 2 (1985): 263–79.

decade of the century, performed the geological and paleontological research that led to his monumental *Geología del Perú*. Another founder, Carlos Lissón, was the author of the country's first geological map. In 1935 he founded the school of geology at the University of San Marcos and was the first Peruvian to teach modern stratigraphy. In the next generation the important figures were Fernando de las Casas, founder of the geology department in the National Engineering University and author of the first metalogenetic map of Peru, and Ulrich Petersen who succeeded H. Mckintry as professor of mining geology at Harvard in 1963. Mckintry had been a geologist with the Cerro del Pasco corporation and was one of a number of U.S. mining geologists who trained Peruvian disciples. George Petersen, Ulrich's father, was a German-born petroleum geologist who spent his entire career in Peru, engaged in research, teaching and applied work. Beginning in the 1950s the U.S. Geological Survey sent a series of geologists to collaborate with Peruvian geologists on surveys of mineral deposits, including lead, zinc, iron, mercury and tungsten.[146] Because of the economic importance of mining in Peru, mining engineering was the leading engineering field and the formation of a national school of geologists was closely linked to the international community of mining geology.

As in Peru, geology in Chile was linked to mining as evidenced by the early institutions which cultivate it: the Corps of Mining engineers (1854), the Mining, Geography and Geodesy Service (1888), the Geological and Mining Service (1918), Department of Mines and Petroleum (1930), and so forth. Academic geology in this period was practiced primarily by foreign specialists. In Chile too, the U. S. Geological Survey played an instrumental role in the modernization of geology, particularly in the geological mission of 1954–60 led by George Eriksen, whose systematic mapping led to the Geological Map of Chile. The resulting interchange between U.S. geologists and their Chilean counterparts and geological study in the United States by Chileans transformed Chilean geology and promoted its professionalization. The Institute of Geological Studies was founded in 1957 to co-ordinate the geological map and direct exploration related to the mining sector.[147]

In Venezuela modern geology was linked to petroleum prospecting. In

---

[146] Pedro Hugo Tumialán, 'El desarrollo de la geología en el Perú', in *Estudios de historia de la ciencia en el Perú*, I: 105–14; Mario Samamé Boggio, 'Historia: Del Cuerpo de Ingenieros de Minas as INGEMMET', *De Re Metallica: Revista del Instituto Geológico Minero y Metalúrgico*, No. 1 (May–June 1984), 25–32.

[147] Servicio de Minas del Estado, 'Los servicios de minas del estado desde su fundación hasta la actualidad' (mimeo); *Instituto de Investigaciones Geológicas* (Santiago, n.d.).

1912 Ralph Arnold led a team of young geologists from Stanford who prepared a geological map in 1914. The first comprehensive geology of the country was published in 1928 by Ralph A. Little, a Standard Oil Company geologist. Ten years later the school of geology, later incorporated into the Central University, was founded.[148]

The Spanish republican geologist José Royo Gómez played a role in two countries. He first became director of the Geological Museum of Bogotá which he fashioned into the best museum of its kind in Latin America. He also played an instrumental role in the execution of the Geological Map of Colombia. In 1951 he moved to Caracas where he founded another geological museum.[149]

SCIENCE AND SOCIETY IN THE SECOND HALF OF THE TWENTIETH CENTURY

In the 1940s, conditions favouring the institutionalization of science occurred simultaneously in several countries of Latin America. At the same time the inaccessibility of European scientific centres in wartime provoked a decisive shift to the United States not only as the pre-eminent provider of scientific education and know-how but also as an increasingly attractive job market for Latin American scientists.

In Brazil, when in 1947 Adhemar de Barros, a populist governor of São Paulo state, pressed the scientific community to produce more applied research, biologists – the largest basic research group – moved to organize scientists to protect their own interests. A meeting held of the São Paulo Medical Association in July 1948 led to the founding of the Brazilian Association for the Progress of Science (SBPC), whose leading spirit was the pharmacologist Mauricio Rocha e Silva.[150] In common with its European and North American prototypes, the SBPC saw science as the basis of social progress[151] and sought to diffuse the scientific ethos and promote solidarity among scientists through a journal – *Ciência e Cultura* – and through annual meetings. The Brazilian Association, perhaps more than most, viewed

[148] Pedro I. Aguerrevere, 'Historia de la investigación geológica en Venezuela', in IVIC, *La ciencia base de nuestro progreso* (Caracas, 1968), pp. 104–10.
[149] Thomas F. Glick, 'José Royo Gómez', in López Piñero (ed.), *Diccionario de Historia de la Ciencia Moderna en España*, II: 267–8.
[150] Antonio José J. Botelho, 'The Professionalization of Brazilian Scientists, the Brazilian Society for the Progress of Science (SBPC), and the State, 1948–60, *Social Studies of Science*, 20 (1990): 473–502.
[151] According to Rocha e Silva himself, 'Vinte años de SBPC', *Ciência e Cultura*, 20 (1968): 581–5, on p. 581.

its role as pre-eminently political and did not hesitate to bring pressure upon different levels of government to respond to its demands.

Although the Brazilian Academy of Science had recommended the establishment of a national research council as early as 1931, no such entity was formed until 1951 when the government, responding to pressure from scientists and from the technical sector of the military interested in developing atomic energy, established the Conselho Nacional de Pesquisa [CNPq], whose first members were predominantly military men and engineers centred mainly in Rio de Janeiro.[152] The initial action of CNPq in the early 1950s was to back nuclear physics (and physics in general) and atomic energy projects. We have already observed some of the projects undertaken by experimental physicists in this period. In its first four years nearly ninety travel grants were given in physics. There were many more in biology, reflecting that field's deeper institutionalization, but the two fields were nearly equal in the total amount of money awarded. After 1955, CNPq's influence diminished: in a time of budgetary retrenchment technical research was favoured over pure science and awards were made more with the objective of training personnel rapidly than with developing the country's research capability. And in the early 1960s, with a political shift to the left, scientists were increasingly called upon to justify themselves in terms of their contribution to the social welfare of the nation.[153]

The relationship between organized scientists and governmental science planning was similar in Venezuela. There, Marta Ardila associates the *prise de conscience* of scientists with the assimilation of European norms instilled in the early 1940s by three European refugees: August Pi Sunyer, founder of the Institute of Experimental Medicine, Martin Meyer, in the Institute of Tropical Pathology, and Rudolph Jaffe in his department of pathological anatomy. Together the three 'established discipline in research and a mystique with respect to the practice of science which they transmitted to their students', the future leaders of the Venezuelan scientific establishment.[154] A student of Pi Sunyer, Francisco de Venanzi, conceived the idea for a scientific association in 1949, having identified about eighty scientists in various fields (no more than ten of whom were full-time research-

---

[152] Jacqueline Pitangui Romani, 'O Conselho Nacional de Pesquisa e institucionalizaçao de pesquisa científica no Brasil', in Simon Scwartzman (ed.), *Universidades e instituições científicas no Rio de Janeiro* (Brasilia, 1982), pp. 137–67, and Botelho, op. cit.

[153] Botelho, 'The Brazilian Society for the progress of Science,' p. 27.

[154] Marta Ardila, 'Origen y evolución histórica de la Asociación Venezolana para el Avance de la Ciencia,' undergraduate thesis (Caracas, 1981), p. 117.

ers). Accordingly, he convened a meeting in Pi Sunyer's Institute in August 1949. This was the origin of the Venezuelan Association for the Progress of Science [AsoVAC], founded with 150 members in 1950. AsoVAC, in its journal, *Acta Científica Venezolana* and in its annual meetings, laboured insistently to diffuse scientific norms and values and to instill a sense of solidarity among scientists, stressing the importance of free scientific research and of the publication of results. In its editorials the journal pictured science as the key to modernization. The leadership of AsoVAC included the organizers of the Venezuelan Institute of Scientific Research (IVIC), established in 1959 on the campus of an institute established under the patronage of the dictator Pérez Jiménez which had oddly conjoined neurology with atomic science (again, an important motor of government interest). At the same time AsoVAC campaigned for the establishment of a national research council run by scientists. In 1962 the Association's leaders occupied key positions in Venezuelan science and met at IVIC to formulate plans for the council, which was not however established until 1969. In the 1970s, CONICIT replaced AsoVAC as the chief institutional spokesman for science and scientists (its leaders were the former activists of AsoVAC including the council's first president, Marcel Roche). With the oil boom of the 1970s, science policy became increasingly orientated to technology, providing AsoVAC an opportunity to reassert its role as promoter of basic science. By 1980 AsoVAC's membership had reached 3,000.

In both Brazil and Venezuela the science associations were instrumental in organizing political support for research efforts at the national level. Once the science councils were established, the associations were either weakened or forced into an adversarial role as state planners stressed practical results. Nevertheless, and in spite of the pure versus applied science debates, the research councils inevitably had a positive effect on the scientific research base.

Scientific research councils were established in virtually all the other Latin American countries between the late fifties and the late seventies, e.g., Argentina (CONICET, 1958), Uruguay (CONICYT, 1961), Chile (CONICYT, 1967), Colombia (CONCYT, COLCIENCIAS, 1968), Peru (CONCYTEC, 1968), Mexico (CONACYT, 1970, although its antecedent organization was founded in 1942), Costa Rica (CONICIT, 1972), Ecuador (CONACYT, 1979).[155] All these organisms were similar in objectives and

---

[155] *Normas orgánicas del CONCYT y COLCIENCIAS* (Bogotá, 1986); *EL CONACYT hoy* (Mexico, D.F. 1984); *CONICIT in Science and Technology* (San José, Costa Rica, 1983); Guillermo Ramírez and

structure and most had co-ordinate semi-autonomous Foundations which dispersed funds. In addition, various regional and supraregional organizations became significant in science policy co-ordination, for example, the Andean Science and Technology Council (1983) of the Junta del Acuerdo de Cartagena, and the Interamerican Development Bank (which has supplied infrastructural aid to the Scientific Research Councils.[156]

Studies of published output of scientific research in Latin America in the 1970s and 1980s have shown remarkable consistency. Over those two decades, five countries (Argentina, Brazil, Mexico, Chile and Venezuela) have accounted for most of the region's publications; by the mid 1980s, Brazil had replaced Argentina as the top producer, with Argentina falling to second place and no change in the rest of the top five.[157] The percentage of Latin American contributions to mainstream publications was quite low (1.1 per cent in 1973–5), with a marked emphasis on clinical medicine (Latin American publications in this area were 21 per cent above the world norm in the 1970s while, by comparison, production in physics was 29 per cent below it).[158] In terms of citations of Latin American articles in mainstream publications, the most favored fields are geosciences, psychology and biology (in that order).[159]

The Brain Drain

The 'brain drain', that is, the flight of scientific researchers from their country of origin, has been studied primarily with respect to Argentina, the country in which the phenomenon was most marked. Argentina was an exporter of professionals from the beginning of the twentieth century. The migration of scientific and technical professionals became noteworthy in the early 1950s when groups of engineers migrated to the United States. In 1966 the Ongania coup and subsequent 'intervention' in the University of Buenos Aires provoked mass resignations of faculty. Particularly hard hit was the Faculty of Exact Sciences, which lost 215 faculty (71.4 per cent of all the

Alfredo Recalde, 'Institucionalización de la política de desarrollo científico y tecnológico en el país,' in *Preinversión y desarrollo* (Quito, n.d.; Cuadernos de Fonapre, 6), pp. 20–5; ¿*Qué es el Concytec?* (Lima, n.d.).

[156] See in particular, 'Enfoque y contribuciones del Banco Interamericano de Desarrollo (BID) en ciencia y tecnología' (Washington, D.C., 1985), mimeo.

[157] Patricia McLauhlan de Arregui, *Indicadores comparativos de los resultados de la investigación científica y tecnológica en América Latina* (Lima, 1988).

[158] J. Davidson Frame, 'Mainstream Research in Latin America and the Caribbean,' *Interciencia*, 2 (1977), p. 144.

[159] McLauchlan de Arregui, *Indicadores comparativos*, p. 27.

University's emigrants and 55 per cent of the total of resignées). These scientists were anti-Peronist, members of the generation of 1955, who subscribed to the general notion of scientific ethos and basic science that we have been discussing. Of the 215 who resigned in 1966, seventy-three (including many physicists and chemists) went to Chile (where the Ford Foundation helped the University of Chile pay their salaries), forty-four to Venezuela (mainly biologists and mathematicians), seven to Uruguay and sixty-four to the United States. In the Faculty of Sciences, the physics, inorganic chemistry and mathematics departments were devastated, and only two departments had no emigrants. Interestingly, a younger, more militantly leftist generation of scientists opposed resignation as a tactical error.[160] The emigration of 1966 was one largely of intellectuals, with scientists forming a particularly prominent contingent. The emigration of the mid-1970s covered a broader social spectrum but also included many scientists; psychoanalysts were especially prominent. One newspaper headlined in 1978 'Nos quedamos sin científicos' [We are being left without scientists].[161]

Among those countries in Latin America which welcomed Argentinian scientists, Mexico stands out. Moreover, Mexico lost relatively few of its own scientists to the brain drain of the 1960s because of the capacity of its National University (UNAM) to absorb large numbers of them.[162] Venezuela, as noted above, received a contingent of Argentinian chemists in the 1970s, including entire working groups, but seemed unable to hold them there. Engineers, however, moved there in large numbers (318 counted in 1981).[163]

Although the absolute number of scientists emigrating from Latin America as a whole has been small, they represent a substantial portion of the region's scientific manpower pool.

The Debate Over Science

The model of excellence in basic science promoted by the Rockefeller Foundation and by Latin American scientists of the generations of Houssay

---

[160] On the brain drain in Latin American science, see H., Moysés Nussenzveig, 'Migration of Scientists from Latin America', *Science*, 165 (1969): 1328–1332. On the Argentinian brain drain see, Nilda Sito and Luis Stulhman, *La emigración de científicos de la Argentina* (San Carlos de Bariloche, 1970); Marta Slemenson, et al., *Emigración de científicos argentinos: Organización de un éxodo a América Latina* (Buenos Aires, 1970); and Alfredo E. Lattes and Enrique Oteiza (eds), *The Dynamics of Argentine Migration (1955–1984)* (Geneva, 1987).

[161] Lattes and Oteiza, *Dynamics of Argentine Migration*, p. 127.

[162] Romeo Flores Caballero, 'Cerebros, talentos y subdesarrollo en México', *Diálogos*, 5, no. 5 (Sept.–Oct., 1969), 21–4.

[163] Lattes and Oteiza, *Dynamics of Argentine Migration*, p. 100, table 36.

and the leaders of AsoVAC was related to the general theory of modernization which held that cultural factors and values determined social change. Such a conceptualization fits perfectly with the campaign to implant the scientific ethos, which was the specific ideology promoted by scientists during the key phase of professionalization extending from 1940 into the early 1970s. The fact that the newly founded CONICTs and supraregional science organizations were called upon less to co-ordinate pre-existent scientific capacity than to create and foster such capacity had the effect of focussing attention on the role of science in Latin American society. This produced in the late 1960s and 1970s an interesting body of sociological literature centering not on the content of science policy but on its objectives and on the capacity of societies to operationalize them.[164]

A key document in this debate was an article written by Amílcar Herrera in 1972 which drew a distinction between 'explicit' and 'implicit' science policies.[165] The central notion, which subsequently became a reiterated theme of dependency theory comment on science, is that scientific research in Latin America has been unconnected to the organization of the societies in which it is carried out and lacks social relevance. More is invested on basic research than on applied, reversing the pattern of industrialized countries, an investment that has failed to produce any substantial economic or social dividends.[166] The reason is that investment in research is made not on the basis of explicit science policy, as expressed in official documents of science planning agencies, but rather on implicit policies that embody the social objectives of elites, which are to maintain themselves in power. On this view, explicit science policy is only a brilliant façade.

What does this imply for the practice of science? If elites are content to practice import substitution using imported technology, then obviously there will be no interest in supporting either basic or applied research. 'If society, and in particular its productive system, is a dependent structure merely copying other societies', wrote Osvaldo Sunkel, 'scientific research is unnecessary, dysfunctional and without practical utility'. University efforts in promoting scientific research are, in this view, doomed to isolation and unable to ensure their own continuity: 'No disciples are left, as

---

[164] See Hebe M. C. Vessuri, 'The Social Study of Science in Latin America', *Social Studies of Science*, 17 (1987): 519–54.

[165] Amílcar Herrera, 'Social Determinants of Science Policy in Latin America', *Journal of Development Studies*, 9, (1972–73): 19–36. See also his influential book, *Ciencia y política en América Latina*, 9th edn (Mexico, D.F., 1985).

[166] *Ibid.*, pp. 21–2.

they must go abroad at some stage of their training; if they return, they are either persecuted and expelled by the government or emigrate soon afterwards, when they realize the futility of their isolated efforts.'[167]

To Sunkel and other commentators of the period the perceived failure of science was the inevitable result of a deficient social structure. In a scheme popularized by Jorge Sábato, science and technology were pictured as a part of a triangular model in which the points corresponded to (1) the state, (2) the productive or industrial structure and (3) science and technology research capability. The triangular model provided a context for analysing the relationships in each vertex as well as those among all three (in other work-ups, a fourth point representing the financial sector was added).[168] The assertion by Herrera, Sunkel and others that the industrial sector had been particularly remiss in its backing of scientific and technical research was soon corroborated empirically by statistical studies showing that Latin American countries place less emphasis than the world norm on basic research bearing on industrialization.[169]

The heart of the *dependentista* thesis as it relates to science is that, given the unequal power relation between developed and developing countries, implanted or transferred science becomes a means of cultural domination and causes the disappearance of local knowledge as a possible alternative construction. This critique was popular in Venezuela in the mid-1970s when the scientific generation that founded CONICIT was displaced by a new group of bureaucrats, mainly leftist social scientists, who questioned the social utility of basic, as opposed to applied, research. At the same time, an analogous critique of the academic model of science which dominated the main Venezuela research institution, IVIC, produced a hegira of applied scientists who founded their own research institute, INTEVEP.[170] The problem with the applied science critique of pure science is that it failed to recognize that scientists were not passive actors in the transfer of

---

[167] Osvaldo Sunkel, 'Underdevelopment, the Transfer of Science and Technology, and the Latin American University,' *Human Relations*, 24 (1970): 1–18.

[168] Sábato's model was first presented at the The World Order Models Conference held in Bellagio, Italy, in September 1968, and widely published thereafter, e.g. Jorge Sábato and Natalio Botana, *La ciencia y la tecnología en el desarrollo futuro de América Latina* (Lima, 1970; Instituto de Estudios Peruanos, Documentos teóricos, 11). Sábato reworked the model on numerous subsequent occasions, e.g., in 'Situación actual del desarrollo científico y tecnológico: Implicaciones al nivel de política y de estrategia' (Washington, D.C., CECIC, 1969; mimeo), a paper presented to an OAS meeting on strategy for technical development held at Viña del Mar, Chile in May 1969.

[169] See Frame, 'Mainstream Research in Latin America', pp. 143–7.

[170] Yajaira Freites, 'La institucionalización del *ethos* de la ciencia: el caso de IVIC,' in Vessuri (ed.), *Ciencia académica en la Venezuela moderna*, pp. 351–86, on pp. 375–6.

mainstream science from Europe or the United States, but in fact participated actively in the process, on the basis of ideological motives associated with both the scientific ethos and that of development and modernization. As Hebe Vessuri has observed, in developing countries the flow of scientific information tends to become hopelessly entangled with economic and power relations, all of which are conflated and confused by contemporary analysts.[171]

The social relevance critiques of the 1970s fell wide of the mark because they failed to realize that national science could not function except as part of an international network. The attack on basic science was misplaced: the applied scientists who left IVIC soon had to apply to their former teachers for the solutions to basic research problems; mathematicians who had stressed applied fields like statistics soon saw that problems in hydrology or petroleum engineering required differential geometry for their solution, and so forth.[172]

Finally let us return to a *leitmotiv* of the history of science in recent Latin America: the constant intrusion by political elites in the institutionalization of science. We have noted repeated repression of scientists to the detriment of their institutions (although in some cases, the same repression stimulated the foundation of institutions designed to be autonomous and thereby somewhat protected from arbitrary interference): for example, Cipriano Castro and the closure of the Pasteur Institute in Caracas, Perón and Argentinian physiology, Pérez Jiménez and Venezuelan bio-medicine.

These intrusions are the consequences of a built-in relationship between the practice of science and the objectives of national elites. As Amílcar Herrera expressed it at the beginning of the 1970s: 'The objective of the ruling classes is not to create R. & D. systems which will make the countries scientifically autonomous . . . Their objectives are mainly to create a scientific and technological system which will help to solve minor problems without putting the system itself in question. It has become apparent, however, that it is extremely difficult to circumscribe scientific activity in this very rigid manner. The more or less autonomous scientific centres, particularly in universities, tend to become discussion centres where the fundamental values of the prevailing order are questioned. The political leadership does not realize that this critical or 'subversive'

---

[171] Hebe Vessuri, 'Introducción: La formación de la comunidad científica en Venezuela', in Vessuri (ed.), *Ciencia académica en la Venezuela moderna* (Caracas, 1984), p. 33.

[172] Carlos A. Di Prisco and Lorenzo Lara, 'Comentarios sobre la investigación matemática en Venezuela', in Vessuri (ed.), *Ciencia académica en la Venezuela moderna*, pp. 237–77, pp. 269 and 272.

attitude – to use the stereotyped official terminology – has its origins in free discussion of ideas in an atmosphere of scientific objectivity. They become alarmed because they cannot tolerate serious analysis of the system. Consequently they try to neutralize criticism by repressing free expression, by ideological persecution, by selecting scholars for their ideology rather than their intellectual ability, and so on. The result is that the scientific structure, submitted to a régime which is incompatible with genuine intellectual creation, is degraded, until it becomes incapable of satisfying even the limited demand of an essentially static system which only aspires to maintain itself'.[173]

The modernizing rhetoric promoted by scientists in the 1940s and 1950s praising the scientific ethos and basic research had the effect of creating cohesive scientific groups with enough atonomy to launch an effective critique of the societies that refused to back their efforts or which only gave them lip service. Part of this ethos is that science is (in Robert Merton's phrase) 'organized scepticism' and that civil, non-ideologized discourse is required for its advancement (hence, the association, among modernizing scientists, of science, democracy and academic freedom). But scepticism, organized or not, is not a value likely to win praise from authoritarian elites and thus civil discourse may become impossible, polarization inevitable. This is the ultimate dilemma of science in modernizing countries.

Not unexpectedly, scientists in Latin America ran afoul of military regimes in the 1960s and 1970s. An example is the fate of research at the Oswaldo Cruz Institute at Manguinhos in Rio de Janeiro under the directorship of a mediocre doctor, Francisco de Paula Rocha Lagoa, appointed by the Castelo Branco regime that came to power in April 1964. The Health Minister Raymundo de Britto immediately announced that 'exotic ideas that infiltrated Manguinhos would be banned'. Accordingly, Rocha Lagoa began to threaten his enemies and in January 1966 had sixteen scientists investigated for 'conspiring in their laboratories'. One of the accusations was that all favoured the creation of a Science Ministry. Rocha Lagoa systematically ruined the laboratory of Walter O. Cruz, Oswaldo Cruz's son, diverting from him and others monies they had won from U.S. foundations and giving the proceeds to his supporters. Finally in 1970 ten researchers were fired, having their civil rights suspended for ten years. The so-called 'Manguinhos Massacre' summarily extinguished the research programme of those cashiered, virtually shut down all collaborative re-

173 Herrera, 'Social Determinants of Science Policy', p. 33.

search of the Institute with foreign and Brazilian institutions, and resulted in capricious depredation such as the dispersal or liquidation of important insect collections deemed not of medical interest.[174]

An extreme case of the entanglement of pure science and political ideology is afforded by the infamous vector affair, in Córdoba, Argentina, in 1978. This was a period of great repression when, for example, all fifty psychoanalysts practicing in that city were dismissed from their public posts at once. (The ideological vulnerability of Freudian psychology under traditional authoritarian rule is obvious.) The provincial authorities outlawed the 'new math' on the grounds that, 'Modern mathematics introduces procedures different from those taught by Aristotle . . . This makes doubts arise on this [Aristotelian] logic and promotes lack of confidence in our guiding and traditional figures, and therefore encourages and gives comfort to subversion . . . Some themes of mathematics use words such as vector and matrix, which are typical of a Marxist or typically subversive vocabulary. The same happens with set theory which evidently tends to massify [*masificar*] and to evolve multitudes.'[175]

Like their anti-Darwinian forebears who held that under a Christian system of values, science must produce certainty, the critics of the new math held that mathematics must produce palpable, easily recognizable truth or else it was subversive. This kind of attack on mathematical abstraction in Argentina can be linked to the attacks on Einstein from various members of the military hierarchy, including the later jailed Admiral Massera who in a 1977 speech observed that 'in 1905 Einstein enunciated his Theory of Relativity in which he threw into crisis the inert and static condition of matter, as if something more were needed to confuse a system which was protected by the immutable solidity of its values'. Others alleged that Einstein had destroyed the 'Christian concepts of space and time'.[176]

CONCLUSION: PERIPHERAL SCIENCE

Peripherality in science has been described with respect to a number of distinct parameters: (1) difficulty of insertion in networks of scientific communication, which causes problems of accessibility to research-front

---

[174] See the chronicle of the affair by one of those affected, zoologist Herman Lent, *O massacre de Manguinhos* (Rio de Janeiro, 1978).

[175] Mauricio Schiojet, 'Who's Afraid of a Vector', *Bulletin of the Atomic Scientists*, June 1980, pp. 60–2, on p. 61. See also anon., 'Polémica con Euclides', *Confirmado*, 30 November 1978, p. 11, and 'Matemática sin polémica', ibid., 21 December pp. 8–10.

[176] Quoted by Anthony Lewis, *New York Times Book Review*, 10 May 1981.

science; (2) smallness of the scientific community, which has both cognitive (lack of inter-criticism) and institutional effects; (3) lack of resources, related to the country's level of economic development: to which is appended in the Latin American discussion, a lack of fit between the 'scientific ethos' and local needs. One problem with the conceptualization of peripherality is that it cannot explain how pockets of 'central' science emerge on the periphery. Cueto's studies of Andean high-altitude biology have shown how in spite of problems of communication, smallness and lack of resources a research-front scientific group emerged nevertheless.[177]

Communication factors are crucial. In Latin America this has meant difficulty of access (whether physical, cognitive or linguistic) to scientific publications and to mainstream science centres. Lack of English skills in part explains the low incidence of Latin American publications in world science statistics, and Derek Price has made the point that there has been a tendency 'for Spanish-speaking countries to be low in science perhaps because of the inadequacy of international scientific literature in what is nevertheless a major world language'.[178]

Smallness conveys another set of problems. With few institutions in place, it is difficult to establish the characteristic structure of modern science with sufficient institutional differentiation to permit career mobility (including positions for young scientists), a viable peer review system, or to accommodate the establishment of new specialties. As Richard Feynman observed of Brazilian science in 1956, 'There are not enough people involved or rather [not enough] separate institutions involved [so] that the thing is stable against statistical fluctuation. You can't go off and get a job at another Centro if the one you are working at is unsatisfactory.'[179]

Looking at discipline formation the large number of what might be termed *unipersonal disciplines* is striking, that is to say, disciplines formed by only one person which then grow as the founder's disciples mature and join him. Carlos Chagas's son's biophysics group in Rio de Janeiro has been described as a family, with researchers 'raised' by him.[180] These disciples typically appear as co-authors of papers with the founder or with each other and they go off to other universities or institutions to found

[177] On peripherality in Latin American science, see Elena Diaz, Yolanda Texera, and Hebe Vessuri, *La ciencia periférica: Ciencia y sociedad en Venezuela* (Caracas, 1983), and comment by Marcos Cueto, 'Andean Biology in Peru', p. 658.

[178] Derek J. de Solla Price, *Little Science, Big Science . . . and Beyond* (New York, 1986), p. 192.

[179] Feynman to Leite Lopes, February 15, 1956, in Leite, *Richard Feynman in Brazil*, p. 25.

[180] Maria Clara Mariani, 'O Instituto de Biofísica da UFRJ', p. 208.

satellite disciplinary groups.[181] Such patterns are typical of small countries. Founders, moreover, are frequently viewed as *isolated geniuses*. Isolated genius myths are typically autogenerated and reflect the difficulty of
the scientist (characteristically a founder of a specialty) in establishing a
research programme in the absence of any national tradition in his field.

The presence of foreigners in the formation of disciplines has been a
trademark of modern science in Latin America, as has the practice of
sending students abroad.[182] In general, both processes are patterned: scientific traditions of specific countries are preferred. Thus, Brazilian engineering students throughout the nineteenth century and well into this century
were partial to study in Belgium,[183] as Mexican chemists were to Germany. France played a formative role in the conceptualization of science in
Brazil,[184] Italy and France in Argentina.[185] Julio Rey Pastor had a practical rationale for sending his Argentinian disciples to Italy: 'It would be
desirable,' he wrote in 1927, 'for Argentinian students, for whom Paris is
Europe, to share their preferences with Italian universities, where the most
intimate contact with professors makes the work more positive.'[186] For
Rey Pastor, there was an implicit comparison to be made with the generous and open pedagogical style of Italian mathematicians and the authoritarian and distant styles of German and French professors. Certain national
disciplines became so linked to foreign institutions that those planning to
enter the field did so with the presumption of completing their doctorate
there, and only there: in contemporary Mexican mathematics, for example, this is the 'Princeton o nada' – 'Princeton or nothing' – syndrome.[187]
The perception of cultural congruity has clearly been a major factor informing such patterns of cultural influence. Such attachments may be dysfunctional: Schwartzman points out that the structure of French professions

[181] Cf. Thomas F. Glick, 'On the Diffusion of a New Specialty: Marañón and the "crisis" of endocrinol-
ogy in Spain', *Journal of the History of Biology*, 9 (1976): 287–300.

[182] An excellent study of the phenomenon in one country is Humberto Ruiz Calderón, 'Una vieja
historia: Los becarios de Venezuela en el exterior (1900–1954)', *Interciencia*, 15 (1990): 8–14.

[183] Eddy Stols, 'Les étudiants brésiliens en Belgique (1817–1914), *Revista de Historia* (São Paulo), 50
(1974): 653–91, on p. 662.

[184] Michel Paty and Patrick Petitjean, 'Sur l'influence scientifique française au Brésil aux XIXe et
XXe siècles,' *Cahiers des Ameriques Latines*, new series, 4 (1985), 31–47.

[185] Marcelo Montserrat, 'La influencia italiana en la actividad científica argentina del siglo XIX,' in
Francis Korn (ed.), *Los italianos en la Argentina* (Buenos Aires, n.d.), pp. 105–23; Miguel J. C.
de Asúa, 'Influencia de la Facultad de Medicina de Paris sobre la de Buenos Aires', *Quipu*, 3
(1986): 79–89.

[186] Quoted by Thomas F. Glick, 'Einstein, Rey Pastor y la promoción de la ciencia en España,' in
Actas, I Simposio sobre Julio Rey Pastor, (Logroño, 1985), pp. 79–90, p. 82.

[187] See Gilberto Calvillo Vives and Diego Bricio Hernández, 'La actividad matemática en México',
mimeo, p. 92.

was too rigid and did not generate first-rate research facilities like the Cavendish Laboratory.[188] European models had to be reinvented at home.

When scientists return home from abroad, having experienced mainstream science first-hand, many find it difficult to adjust. Yajaira Freites found that in spite of many positive achievements in building an infrastructure for science in Venezuela in the 1970s, scientists persisted in viewing the country as possessing an unfavourable environment for science. There is a lack of fit between the reality of scientific activity and scientists' expectations, a result of the general phenomenon of the implantation of the *style* of big science in peripheral countries independent of whether such countries may have the infrastructure to sustain that syle of science.[189] Larissa Lomnitz found the same phenomenon in Mexico, 'a subtle, pervasive feeling that it is futile to do scientific research in Mexico under these general conditions'.[190] Gómezgil, surveying the image of scientists held by Mexican teenagers, found that the adolescents knew who Pasteur, Einstein and Newton were but could not name any Mexican scientists.[191] Both stereotypical images of the scientist and scientific ethos and a negative conclusion regarding the capacity of Mexicans to perform science had been transmitted.

One of the values that Latin American scientists seem to have acquired is to associate high prestige with publication in 'mainstream' journals, to the detriment of regional scientific publications. Indeed the struggle to have a journal recognized as 'mainstream' (by virtue of inclusion in the *Science Citation Index*) is a phenomenon of international politics that impacts upon Latin American science.[192] Nevertheless, the rage for international publication conceals local networks of scientific communication, more informal (e.g., circulation of preprints), in part oral, which represents a higher degree of institutionalization than perhaps has been suspected.[193]

---

[188] Schwartzman, *Formaçao da comunidade científica no Brasil*, pp. 213–14.

[189] Yajaira Freites, '¿Es la sociedad venezolana un ambiente favorable a la investigación?' (typescript).

[190] Larissa Lomnitz, 'Hierarchy and Peripherality: the organisation of a Mexican Research Institute,' *Minerva*, 17 (1979): 527–8, p. 540. Entrepreneurial scientists, like Carlos Chagas (son), explicitly set out to dispel this kind of myth as they form working groups (Mariani, 'O Instituto de Biofisica da UFRJ,' p. 200).

[191] Maria Luisa Rodríguez Sala de Gómezgil, *El científico en México: su imagen entre los estudiantes de enseñanza media* (Mexico, D.F., 1977), pp. 166–73; and summary, 'Mexican Adolescents' Image of the Scientist', *Social Studies of Science*, 5 (1975): 355–61.

[192] Vessuri recounts the political play over the de-listing of *Acta Científica Venezolana* from SCI; 'La revista científica periférica: El caso de *Acta Científica Venezolana*,' *Interciencia*, 12 (1987), 124–34. Some twenty Latin American science journals are listed in SCI; see the list provided by Marcel Roche and Yajaira Freites, 'Producción y flujo de información científica en un país periférico americano (Venezuela)', *Interciencia*, 7 (1982): 279–90, on p. 286.

[193] Ibid., p. 283, and McLauchlan de Arregui, *Indicadores comparativos*, p. 15.

Regarding the cognitive nature of science on the periphery, Alfonso L. Herrera noted in 1911 that 'we are relatively distant from foreign scientific centres, from official science and from the somnolent and orthodox academies, for which reason we think with absolute freedom, inasmuch as we have been educated in isolation and do not carry stereotyped in our brain certain maxims repectfully gathered from the lips of some dogmatic professors, who have imposed themselves as advisors to humanity and who deftly insinuate their dogmas and errors in foreign academies'.[194] Such a conclusion may have some truth, though it is contrary to the common wisdom that lack of critical mass in a given discipline makes it difficult for peripheral scientists to assess the value of specific research. Isolation more normally causes defensiveness, though in some, like Herrera and Alberto Monge, it may produce an exuberant sense of discovery. Herrera's conclusion was attacked some years later by Eliseo Ramírez, referring to Herrera's theory of plasmogeny: 'In our rachitic environment lack of education is conjoined, as a consequence of it, with confusion between true scientific work and pseudo-work, as a series of provincial disquisitions demonstrate their protection by official elements but which are nothing more than dissimulation in scientific research.'[195]

Herrera clearly viewed his origin of life theory as an ingenious concept that cut through a dogmatic received view, whereas Ramírez viewed it as contrary to scientific common sense as expressed by a majority of scientists. The polemic highlights the fact that what is normative in mainstream science may not necessarily be so perceived on the periphery. To accept mainstream views is safe but not necessarily relevant to one's cognitive or social environment; to reject them is to run the risk of exaggerated isolation.

Finally, there appears to be, in Latin America as in most developing regions, a structurally based lack of fit between the ideology of science as it appears within the subculture of national scientific communities, and the various political ideologies which share a high value for economic development. The latter will portray those involved in basic science as shirking the needs of the society, while the former assert that basic science is a prerequisite for competent application.

---

[194] Alfonso L. Herrera, 'Una ciencia nueva: la plasmogenia,' *Boletín de Ciencias Médicas* (Mexico, D.F.), I (1910–11): 309–22, 360–73.

[195] Eliseo Ramírez, 'La simulación en la investigación biológica', cited by Fernando Ocaranza, *La tragedia de un vector,* (Mexico, D.F., 1943), pp. 91–2. I am indebted to Adolfo Olea for this reference, as well as that to Herrera in note 194 above.

BIBLIOGRAPHICAL ESSAYS

I. THE MULTIVERSE OF LATIN AMERICAN IDENTITY, C. 1920 – C. 1970

A deeply imaginative reflection on the character of cultural expression in the Americas, presented by historical eras, is *La expresión americana* by the noted Cuban writer José Lezama Lima, first published in Havana in 1957. The sole critical edition is the Portuguese version, *A expressão americana* (São Paulo, 1988), translated with a highly competent introduction and notes by Irlemar Chiampi. In his essays 'Visión de América' and 'Conciencia e identidade de América' in *La novela latinoamericana en vísperas de un nuevo siglo* (Mexico, D.F., 1981), 59–158, Alejo Carpentier addressed continental Americanism. Leopoldo Zea expands the barbarism-civilization theme to global proportions in *Discurso desde la marginación y la barbarie* (Barcelona, 1988). See also his *Filosofía de la historia americana* (Mexico, D.F., 1978). The role of intellectuals is examined in Juan F. Marsal (ed.), *El intelectual latinoamericano* (Buenos Aires, 1970).

Studies of Latin American thought include two classics by the Spanish philosopher José Gaos, *El pensamiento hispanoamericano* (Mexico, D.F., 1944) and *Pensamiento de lengua española* (Mexico, D.F., 1945). Gaos's Mexican disciple Leopoldo Zea produced a volume which, although controversial, remains seminal for the nineteenth century: *The Latin-American Mind*, trans. J. H. Abbott and L. Dunham (Norman, Okla., 1963). See also Harold Eugene Davis, *Latin American Thought: A Historical Introduction,* 2nd ed. (New York, 1974); and W. Rex Crawford, *A Century of Latin-American Thought,* rev. ed. (New York, 1966).

Historical analyses of culture include Germán Arciniegas, *Latin America: A Cultural History* (New York, 1967) and Jean Franco, *The Modern Culture of Latin America: Society and the Artist,* rev. ed. (Harmondsworth,

1970). Two well-illustrated studies of art since independence emphasize historical context: Stanton L. Catlin and Terence Grieder, *Art of Latin America since Independence* (New Haven, Conn., 1966) and Dawn Ades, *Art in Latin America: The Modern Era, 1820–1980* (London, 1989). *La nueva novela hispanoamericana,* 6th ed. (Mexico, D.F., 1980) by the Mexican novelist Carlos Fuentes is a concise study of how modern narrative fiction can 'give form, fix goals, set priorities, and elaborate criticism for a determinate style of life: to say all that cannot otherwise be said.' A study of how language itself yields clues to social experience is the essay 'Language in America' in Richard M. Morse, *New World Soundings* (Baltimore, 1989), 11–60.

Useful for the background of modernism (i.e., Spanish-American vanguardism) are: José Ortega y Gasset, *The Dehumanization of Art and Other Writings on Art and Culture* (New York, 1956); Renato Poggioli, *The Theory of the Avant-garde,* trans. Gerald Fitzgerald (Cambridge, Mass., 1981); Frederick R. Karl, *Modern and Modernism: The Sovereignty of the Artist, 1885–1925* (New York, 1985); R. P. Blackmur, 'Anni Mirabile, 1921–1925: Reason in the madness of letters', in *A Primer of Ignorance* (New York, 1967), 1–80; Malcolm Bradbury and James McFarlane (eds.), *Modernism, 1890–1930* (Harmondsworth, 1976); Richard Kostelanetz (ed.), *The Avant-garde Tradition in Literature* (Buffalo, N.Y., 1982), which acknowledges Brazilian poets; and Meyer Schapiro, *Modern Art, 19th and 20th Centuries* (New York, 1978).

For broad perspectives on Latin American vanguardism, see Guillermo de Torre, *Historia de las literaturas de vanguarda,* 3rd ed., 3 vols. (Madrid, 1974); Oscar Collazos, *Los vanguardismos en la América Latina* (Barcelona, 1977); Saúl Yurkiévich, *A través de la trama: sobre vanguardismos literarios y otras concomitancias* (Barcelona, 1984); Hugo J. Verani et al. (eds.), *Las vanguardas literarias en Hispano-américa* (Rome, 1986); Mário de Andrade, 'O movimento modernista,' in *Aspectos da literatura brasileira,* 4th ed. (São Paulo, 1972), 231–55; and Raúl Antelo, *Na ilha de Marapatá (Mário de Andrade lê os hispano–americanos)* (São Paulo, 1986).

Earlier criticism held that the 'naturalist novels' or 'novels of the land' of the 1930s were derivative, that they fell into the realist or naturalist vein of previous European novels. Since the 1970s, critics have been more tolerant. They no longer draw a sharp line between the esthetically 'elegant' fiction of the 'boom' and the 'worn-out' naturalism and *costumbrismo* of the 1930s and 1940s. They now warn us of 'the dangers of a conception of literary history that perceives progress in literary developments, thereby sanctioning the relegation of certain texts to oblivion.' See Carlos J. Alonso, *The Spanish American Regional Novel, Modernity and Autochthony* (Cambridge, Eng., 1990). For rehabilitation of the fiction of the 1930s, see also Roberto González Echevarría, *Voice of the Masters: Writing and Austerity in Modern Latin American Literature* (Austin, Tex., 1985), and Doris Sommer, *Foundational Fictions, the National Romances of Latin America* (Berkeley, 1991). On the other hand, Flora Süssekind, *Tal Brasil, qual romance?* (Rio de Janeiro, 1984) traces naturalism as a recurrent authorial device of positivist origin from the 1890s to the 1970s, with deeper roots in the eyewitness 'natural history' of the early chroniclers; she makes no resolute attempt to link the Brazilian equivalent to the 'realistic' *novelas de la tierra* with the supposed 'magic' of the narratives that were to follow.

Books that shed light on the transition from the 1930s and 1940s to the 1960s and 1970s include: Emir Rodríguez Monegal, *Narradores de esta América*, 2 vols. (Montevideo, 1969) and *El boom de la novela latinoamericana* (Caracas, 1972); José Donoso, *The Boom in Spanish American Literature* (New York, 1977); Angel Rama, *La novela latinoamericana, 1920–1980* (Bogotá, 1982); and Fernando de Ainsa, *Identidad cultural de Iberoamérica en su narrativa* (Madrid, 1986).

On more specialized subjects, see Antonio Cornejo Polar, *La novela indigenista* (Lima, 1981); Efraín Kristal, *The Andes Viewed from the City: Literal and Political Discourse on the Indian in Peru, 1848–1930* (New York, 1987); Adalbert Dessau, *La novela de la Revolución Mexicana,* trans. Juan José Utrilla (Mexico, D.F., 1972); José Maurício Gomes de Almeida, *A tradição regionalista no romance brasileiro* (Rio de Janeiro, 1981); José Hildebrando Dacanal, *O romance de 30* (Porto Alegre, 1982).

General introductions to identity in Latin America include Martin S. Stabb, *In Quest of Identity: Patterns in the Spanish American Essay of Ideas, 1890–1960* (Chapel Hill, N.C., 1967) and Dante Moreira Leite, *O caráter nacional brasileiro,* 4th ed. (São Paulo, 1983). The following may also be consulted for the national-character essayists: Alberto Zum Felde, *Indice crítico de la literatura hispanoamericana, los ensayistas* (Mexico, D.F., 1954); Juan F. Marsal, *Los ensayistas socio-políticos de Argentina y México* (Buenos Aires, 1969); Peter Earle and Robert Mead, *Historia del ensayo hispanoamericano* (Mexico, D.F., 1973); Isaac J. Lévy and Juan Loveluck (eds.), *El ensayo hispánico* (Columbia, S.C., 1984); and Horacio Cerutti Guldberg (ed.), *El ensayo en nuestra América para una reconceptualización* (Mexico, D.F., 1993).

In the field of philosophy, the Peruvian philosopher Francisco Miró Quesada published two books that follow the technical development of the discipline in Latin America through four generations and stress the regional accents they gave it: *Despertar y proyecto del filosofar latinoamericano* (Mexico, D.F., 1974) and *Proyecto y realización del filosofar latinoamericano* (Mexico, D.F., 1981). Other broad treatments with distinctive emphases include Leopoldo Zea, *El pensamiento latinoamericano* (Barcelona, 1976); Francisco Larroyo, *La filosofía iberoamericana,* 2nd ed. (Mexico, D.F., 1978); Abelardo Villegas, *Panorama de la filosofía iberoamericana actual* (Buenos Aires, 1963); and Arturo A. Roig, *Filosofía, universidad y filósofos en América Latina* (Mexico, D.F., 1981). The Argentine Francisco Romero, one of the region's most distinguished twentieth-century philosophers, outlined his views on New World philosophizing in *Sobre la filosofía en América* (Buenos Aires, 1952). A collection of studies by foremost practitioners that have implications well beyond the book's restrictive title is Luis Recaséns Siches et al., *Latin American Legal Philosophy* (Cambridge, Mass., 1948). For the important impact of exiled Spanish philosophers after 1936, see José Luis Abellán, *Filosofía española en América, 1936–66* (Madrid, 1967), and the chapter 'Filosofía' by Raúl Cardiel Reyes in Salvador Reyes Nevares (ed.), *El exilio español en México, 1939–1982* (Mexico, D.F., 1982), 205–34. A leading interpretation for Brazil is João Cruz Costa, *A History of Ideas in Brazil,* trans. Suzette Macedo (Berkeley, 1964). For an important polemic on the identity question by two leading philosophers, see Augusto Salazar Bondy, *¿Existe una filosofía de nuestra América?* (Mexico, D.F., 1968), and Leopoldo Zea, *La filosofía americana como filosofía sin más* (Mexico, D.F., 1969). A highly competent book of both intellectual and practical interest is Horacio Cerutti Guldberg, *Filosofía de la liberación latinoamericana* (Mexico, D.F., 1983). Anthologies include Aníbal Sánchez Reulet, *La filosofía latinoamericana contemporánea* (Mexico, D.F., 1949); Jorge J. E. Gracia et al. (eds.), *Philosophical Analysis in Latin America* (Dordrecht, 1984); and Jorge J. E. Gracia (ed.), *Latin American Philosophy in the Twentieth Century* (Buffalo, N.Y., 1986).

2. POLITICAL IDEAS AND IDEOLOGIES IN LATIN AMERICA, 1870–1930

The principal sources for the study of political and social ideas in Latin America in the century after independence are the writings of the *pensadores,* those Latin American intellectual leaders who were in part men of letters, in part journalists, in part social or political theorists, and most often also politicians or bureaucrats. They were rarely professional academic scholars, in the present-day sense, and they lacked the leisure, the library resources and the training to engage in extensive empirical research. Thus, the *pensadores* were not isolated thinkers; they were usually respected and influential public figures. Though spokesmen for the establishment receive most attention in the chapter 'Political ideas and ideologies in Latin America, 1870–1930' in this volume, dissenters, both inside and outside the governing group, are also treated. Moreover, since Latin American thought cannot be considered in isolation from Europe, frequent reference is made to European intellectual and political currents. Limitations of space dictate that only the secondary literature on Latin America be discussed in this essay.

Three principal bibliographical problems were encountered in preparing this essay. The first is the paucity of general, and particularly comparative, studies which go beyond national boundaries and/or which treat the years 1870 to 1930 as a whole. Especially scarce are studies that compare ideas in Spanish America and Brazil. The second problem is the lack of bio-bibliographical studies, even on major figures. To analyse ideas in context, it is essential to establish the genesis and publication history of specific texts, which can be complex. Books usually appeared first as articles or speeches and often reappeared several times in slightly revised form. One welcomes such painstaking works as José Ignacio Mantecón Navasal et al., *Bibliografía general de don Justo Sierra* (Mexico, D.F., 1969), Peter J. Sehlinger, 'El desarrollo intelectual y la influencia de Valentín Letelier: Un estudio bibliográfico', *Revista Chilena de Historia y Geografía*, 136 (1968), 250–84, and Guillermo Rouillon, *Bio-bibliografía de José Carlos Mariátegui* (Lima, 1963), just as one laments the lack of similar works for other figures, such as Ingenieros, Molina Enríquez, or Oliveira Vianna.

The third bibliographical problem is that the analysis of political and social ideas does not fall into an established category of scholarship. It must draw on both the study of the literary and philosophic essay by humanists, and of political elites, social movements and ideologies by social-science-oriented historians. Not only do the two groups often emphasize different intellectuals, but the former tend to be less concerned with political and social context and the latter less concerned with the analysis of ideas themselves. Moreover, their respective inquiries are often guided by distinct questions and methodological assumptions.

Probably the two best general studies of ideas, both by humanists who *do* have a sense of historical context, are Alberto Zum Felde, *Índice crítico de la literatura hispanoamericana: Los ensayistas* (Mexico, D.F., 1954), and Martin S. Stabb, *In Quest of Identity: Patterns in the Spanish American Essay of Ideas, 1890–1960* (Chapel Hill, N.C., 1967). It is lamentable that neither work has been reprinted. For the nineteenth century, Leopoldo Zea, *Dos etapas del pensamiento en hispanoamérica* (Mexico, D.F., 1949), Eng. trans., *The Latin American Mind* (Norman, Okla., 1963), is valuable, despite the author's philosophical opposition to historical detachment. The only general synthesis that treats Brazil and Spanish America is Jean Franco, *The Modern Culture of Latin America: Society and the Artist* 2nd ed. (Harmondsworth, 1970). François Bourricaud, 'The adventures of Ariel', *Daedalus*, 101 (1972), 109–36 offers numerous insights. The standard manual of *pensadores* is William R. Crawford, *A Century of Latin American Thought* (Cambridge, Mass., 1961; rev. ed., New York, 1966); also useful is Harold E. Davis, *Latin American Thought: A Historical Introduction* (Baton Rouge, La., 1972; 2nd ed., New York, 1974). A superb, comprehensive essay treating educational ideas from the sixteenth to the twentieth century is Mario Góngora, 'Origin and philosophy of the Spanish American university', in Joseph Maier and Richard W. Weatherhead (eds.), *The Latin American University* (Albuquerque, N.Mex., 1979), 17–64. Several penetrating essays by Tulio Halperín Donghi that treat ideas are reprinted in *El espejo de la historia: Problemas argentinos y perspectivas latinoamericanas* (Buenos Aires, 1987). No student of ideas can overlook the challenging essay by Benedict Anderson, which touches occasionally on Latin America, *Imagined Communities: Reflections on the Origin and Spread of Nationalism* (London, 1983).

Other comparative studies that touch tangentially on ideas include Carl Solberg, *Immigration and Nationalism in Argentina and Chile, 1890–1914* (Austin, Tex., 1970), Hobart A. Spalding, Jr., *Organized Labor in Latin America* (New York, 1977), and Thomas E. Skidmore, 'Workers and soldiers: Urban labor movements and elite responses in twentieth-century Latin America', in Virginia Bernhard (ed.), *Elites, Masses, and Modernization in Latin America, 1850–1930* (Austin, Tex., 1979). Though not explicitly comparative, J. Lloyd Mecham, *Church and State in Latin America* (Chapel Hill, N.C., 1934), remains a standard guide. The work of Claudio Véliz, most recently *The Centralist Tradition of Latin America* (Princeton, N.J., 1980), has proved valuable despite his one-dimensional view of liberalism. On corporatism, see the essays by Philippe C. Schmitter and Ronald C. Newton in Frederick B. Pike and Thomas Stritch (eds.), *The New Corporatism* (Notre Dame, Ind., 1974), and James

M. Malloy's introduction to Malloy (ed.), *Authoritarianism and Corporatism in Latin America* (Pittsburgh, Pa., 1977).

Substantive national coverage in this essay is limited to Argentina, Brazil, Chile, Mexico and Peru. Among the few national studies that are general in scope, see, for Argentina, José Luis Romero, *Las ideas políticas en Argentina*, 3rd ed. (Buenos Aires, 1959), Eng. trans. *Argentine Political Thought* (Stanford, Calif., 1963), and more particularly *El desarrollo de las ideas en la sociedad argentina del siglo xx* (Mexico, D.F., 1965). Alejandro Korn, *Influencias filosóficas en la evolución nacional* (Buenos Aires, 1936) is a primary source that can also be used as an authority. Academia Nacional de la Historia, *Historia argentina contemporánea, 1862–1930*, 2 vols. (Buenos Aires, 1963) is a valuable reference work for the non-specialist. David Rock, *Politics in Argentina, 1890–1930: The Rise and Fall of Radicalism* (Cambridge, Eng., 1975) is fundamental. Since most Argentine intellectual expression took place in the capital, James R. Scobie, *Buenos Aires: From Plaza to Suburb, 1870–1910* (New York, 1974) is invaluable. On Brazil, see T. E. Skidmore's *Black into White: Race and Nationality in Brazilian Thought* (New York, 1974), João Cruz Costa, *A History of Ideas in Brazil* (Berkeley, 1964), Richard Graham, *Britain and the Onset of Modernization in Brazil, 1850–1914* (Cambridge, Eng., 1968), and more recently Emília Viotti da Costa, *The Brazilian Empire: Myths and Histories* (Chicago, 1985). For Chile, Frederick B. Pike, *Chile and the United States* (Notre Dame, Ind., 1963) treats ideas and politics comprehensively and includes prolific notes for further study. Also an essential work is Mario Góngora, *Ensayo histórico sobre las noción de estado en Chile en los siglos xix y xx* (Santiago, Chile, 1986). On Peru, *La literatura política de González Prada, Mariátegui y Haya de la Torre* (Mexico, D.F., 1957) by Eugenio Chang-Rodríguez is a thorough study of ideas. F. B. Pike, *The Modern History of Peru* (New York, 1967) is a good reference, as is Jorge Basadre's monumental *Historia de la república del Perú*, 5th ed., 6 vols. (Lima, 1961–2).

More specific works that are useful include, for Argentina, the studies of university reform by Richard J. Walter, *Student Politics in Argentina* (New York, 1968) and 'The intellectual background of the 1918 university reform in Argentina', *Hispanic American Historical Review*, 49/2 (1969), 233–53. H. Spalding's brief 'Sociology in Argentina', in Ralph L. Woodward (ed.), *Positivism in Latin America, 1850–1900* (Boston, 1971), makes some interesting points. Sandra McGee Deutsch, *Counterrevolution in Argentina, 1900–1932: The Argentine Patriotic League* (Lincoln, Nebr., 1986) breaks new ground in treating the political Right of the 1920s. For the Uruguayan, José E. Rodó, Gordon Brotherston's introduction to his edition of *Ariel* (Cambridge, Eng., 1967) is excellent.

On Brazil Fernando Azevedo, *Brazilian Culture* (New York, 1950) is valuable for positivist educational thought. See also Robert G. Nachman, 'Positivism, modernization, and the middle class in Brazil', *Hispanic American Historical Review*, 57/1 (1977), 1–23. Robert Conrad's English edition of, and commentary on, Joaquim Nabuco, *Abolitionism* (Urbana, Ill., 1977), is a boon to the non-expert. Richard Graham, 'Landowners and the overthrow of the empire', *Luso-Brazilian Review*, 1 (1970), 44–56 places abolitionist ideas in social and political context, and his 'Joaquim Nabuco, conservative historian', *Luso-Brazilian Review*, 17 (1980), 1–16 is valuable, despite some doubts about his use of the label 'conservative'. W. Douglas McLain, Jr., 'Alberto Torres, ad hoc nationalist', *Luso-Brazilian Review*, 4 (1967), 17–34, is a useful précis of ideas, though the best study is now Adalberto Marson, *A ideologia nacionalista em Alberto Torres* (São Paulo, 1979).

Chilean sources are varied. Alejandro Fuenzalida Grandón, *Lastarria y su tiempo* (Santiago, Chile, 1893) and Luis Galdames, *Valentín Letelier y su obra* (Santiago, Chile, 1937) are intellectual biographies by disciples. Ricardo Donoso, *Las ideas políticas en Chile* (Mexico, D.F., 1946) covers the pre-1891 period. Simon Collier, 'The historiography of the "Portalian" period (1830–1891) in Chile', *Hispanic American Historical Review*, 57/4 (1977), 660–90, is an excellent guide. Allen Woll treats several facets of the change in ideas in *A Functional Past: The Uses of History in Nineteenth-Century Chile* (Baton Rouge, La., 1982), and Iván Jaksič, *Academic Rebels in Chile: The Role of Philosophy in Higher Education and Politics* (Albany, N.Y., 1989) focuses on the special significance of formal philosophy. A good reference for political events of the pre-1891 era is Francisco A. Encina, *Historia de Chile* 20 vols. (Santiago, Chile, 1941–52). Harold Blakemore, *British Nitrates and Chilean Politics, 1886–1896: Balmaceda and North* (London, 1974) is indispensable for its period, as is Julio Heise González, *Historia de Chile. El período parlamentario, 1861–1925,* 1 (Santiago, Chile, 1974), for the twentieth century. On the important topic of German influence in Chile, see Jean-Pierre Blancpain, *Les Allemands au Chile, 1816–1945* (Cologne, 1974) and William W. Sywak, 'Values in nineteenth-century Chilean education: The Germanic reform of Chilean public education, 1885–1910' (unpublished Ph.D. dissertation, University of California, Los Angeles, 1977). Arnold J. Bauer provides a valuable characterization of the Chilean elite around 1910 in *Chilean Rural Society from the Spanish Conquest to 1930* (Cambridge, Eng.,

1975). Brian Loveman's *Chile: The Legacy of Hispanic Capitalism* (New York, 1979), gives the non-specialist a good sense of the social bases of politics in the twentieth century. Frederick M. Nunn properly stresses the role of the military in *Chilean Politics, 1920–1931: The Honorable Mission of the Armed Forces* (Albuquerque, N.Mex., 1970). Julio César Jobet, *Luis Emilio Recabarren* (Santiago, 1955) is a sympathetic treatment. James O. Morris, *Elites, Intellectuals, and Consensus. A Study of the Social Question and the Industrial Relations System in Chile* (Ithaca, 1966), is an authoritative study of the Labour Code of 1924.

For late nineteenth-century ideas in Mexico, see Charles A. Hale, *The Transformation of Liberalism in Late Nineteenth-Century Mexico* (Princeton, N.J., 1989). Leopoldo Zea, *El positivismo en México*, 3rd ed. (Mexico, D.F., 1968) is a standard work, but should be completed by W. Dirk Ratt, *El positivismo durante el Porfiriato* (Mexico, D.F., 1975). Moisés González Navarro, *Sociología e historia en México* (Mexico, D.F., 1970) is a ready summary of the ideas of several leading intellectual figures. On Justo Sierra, see Claude Dumas, *Justo Sierra et le Mexique de son temps*, 3 vols. (Lille, 1975). M.S. Stabb, 'Indigenism and racism in Mexican thought: 1857–1911', *Journal of Inter-American Studies and World Affairs*, 1 (1959), 405–23 elucidates the subject. Daniel Cosío Villegas et al., *Historia moderna de México* (9 vols. in 10; Mexico, D.F., 1955–72) is an indispensable reference. Among the many essential works of Alan Knight, one particularly relevant to this essay is 'El liberalismo mexicano desde la reforma hasta la revolución (una interpretación),' *Historia Mexicana*, 35 (1985), 59–91. Several important essays on Mexican political culture can be found in David Brading, *Prophecy and Myth in Mexican History* (Cambridge, Eng., 1984), and approached quite differently in the major work by François-Xavier Guerra, *Le Mexique de l'ancien régime à la révolution*, 2 vols. (Paris, 1985; Spanish ed., 2 vols., Mexico, D.F., 1988). On the Ateneo group, Juan Hernández Luna's introduction to *Conferencias del Ateneo de la Juventud* (Mexico, D.F., 1962) and Patrick Romanell's philosophical *The Making of the Mexican Mind*, 2nd ed. (South Bend, Ind., 1967) are useful. Enrique Krauze, *Caudillos culturales en la revolución mexicana* (Mexico, D.F., 1976) illuminates the intellectual generation of 1915 and Henry C. Schmitt, *The Roots of Lo Mexicano: Self and Society in Mexican Thought, 1900–1934* (College Station, Tex., 1978) highlights the ambiguous relation between social reform and humanism. John Womack's *Zapata and the Mexican Revolution* (New York, 1969) is unsurpassed. James D. Cockroft, *Intellectual Precursors of the Mexican Revolution, 1900–1913* (Austin, Tex.,

1968) and John M. Hart, *Anarchism and the Mexican Working Class, 1860–1931* (Austin, Tex., 1978), are complementary works on anarchism and the P.L.M. Ramón E. Ruíz, *Labor and the Ambivalent Revolutionaries: Mexico, 1911–1923* (Baltimore, 1976) elucidates government policy, as does Barry Carr, 'The Casa del Obrero Mundial, Constitucionalismo and the Pact of February 1915', *El trabajo y los trabajadores en la historia de México* (Mexico, D.F., and Tucson, Ariz., 1979), 603–32. On the development of social thought after 1910, see Alan Knight, 'Racism, revolution, and *indigenismo:* Mexico, 1910–1940,' in Richard Graham (ed.), *The Idea of Race in Latin America, 1870–1940* (Austin, Tex., 1990), 71–113; David Brading, 'Manuel Gamio and official indigenismo in Mexico,' *Bulletin of Latin American Research*, 7 (1988), 75–89; and Cynthia Hewitt de Alcántara, *Anthropological Perspectives on Rural Mexico* (London, 1984). Jean Meyer revises much of the history of the 1910–30 era in *La révolution mexicaine* (Paris, 1973), emphasizing the growth of the revolutionary state. Arnaldo Córdova, *La ideología de la revolución mexicana* (Mexico, D.F., 1973) is a stimulating interpretation from the Left. Another approach to the authoritarian state is Peter H. Smith, *Labyrinths of Power: Political Recruitment in Twentieth-Century Mexico* (Princeton, N.J., 1979).

Besides the general works on Peru, J. Basadre's essay on Francisco García Calderón in the anthology *En torno al Perú y América* (Lima, 1954) is superb. Jesús Chavarría, *José Carlos Mariátegui and the Rise of Modern Peru, 1890–1930* (Albuquerque, N.Mex., 1979), illuminates the national context for Mariátegui's thought; John M. Baines, *Revolution in Peru: Mariátegui and the Myth* (Tuscaloosa, Ala., 1972), the European sources. Peter F. Klarén, *Modernization, Dislocation, and Aprismo: Origins of the Peruvian Aprista Party, 1870–1932* (Austin, Tex., 1973) is a model study, emphasizing Aprismo's tie with the Trujillo region. Thomas M. Davies, Jr., 'The indigenismo of the Peruvian Aprista party: A reinterpretation', *Hispanic American Historical Review*, 51/4 (1971), 626–45, is a critical analysis, as is François Chevalier, 'Official *indigenismo* in Peru in 1920', in Magnus Mörner (ed.), *Race and Class in Latin America* (New York, 1970), 184–96. Steve Stein, *Populism in Peru: The Emergence of the Masses and the Politics of Social Control* (Madison, Wis., 1980) provides excellent context for understanding Haya de la Torre. Robert J. Alexander (ed.), *Aprismo. The Ideas and Doctrines of Victor Raúl Haya de la Torre* (Kent, Ohio, 1973) is a useful English version of the key texts, together with an uncritical study of Haya.

On the ideas of the Latin American Left in the early decades of the twentieth century, see the chapter 'The Left in Latin America since c.1920' (and bibliographical essay) by Alan Angell in *The Cambridge History of Latin America*, volume VI, part 2 (1994).

3. ECONOMIC IDEAS AND IDEOLOGIES IN LATIN AMERICA SINCE 1930[1]

For general surveys of the development of economic thought in Latin America since the Second World War, see Albert Fishlow, 'The State of Latin American Economics', in Inter-American Development Bank, *Economic and Social Progress in Latin America: 1985 Report* (Washington, D.C., [1986]), pp. 123–48; republished in Christopher Mitchell (ed.), *Changing Perspectives in Latin American Studies: Insights from Six Disciplines* (Stanford, Cal., 1988). Fishlow covers the rise and decline of the several schools of thought, based on their policy outcomes. Also valuable is Cristóbal Kay, *Latin American Theories of Development and Underdevelopment* (London, 1989), which offers a sympathetic but critical review of structuralism and dependency and related works on marginality and internal colonialism. A briefer survey which gives particular attention to policy issues is Felipe Pazos, 'Cincuenta años de pensamiento económico en la América Latina', *Trimestre Económico*, 50, 4 (October–December, 1983): 1915–1948. An old but still useful survey of Latin American adaptations of extra-continental ideas is Juan Noyola Vázquez, 'La evolución del pensamiento económico del último cuarto de siglo y su influencia en la América Latina', *Trimestre Económico*, 23, 3 (July–September, 1956): 269–83.

Three works may serve to indicate the impact of Latin American ideas on development theory at large. H[einz] W. Arndt, *Economic Development: the History of an Idea* (Chicago, Ill., 1987), esp. pp. 119–30, places structuralism and dependency in broad historical context. Björn Hettne, *Development Theory and the Three Worlds* (Harlow, 1990), attempts to address underdevelopment and development in a non-Eurocentric and interdisciplinary framework, and in this context Latin American ideas play a prominent role. Dieter Senghaas, *The European Experience: A Historical Critique of Development Theory* (Dover, N.H., 1985), incorporates structural-

---

[1] This brief survey excludes the large North American and European literatures inspired by dependency analysis. It offers English versions of relevant works where they exist. Original versions can be found in the footnotes to the chapter 'Economic Ideas and Ideologies in Latin America since 1930' in this volume, where the reader will also find citations of primary sources. For more on the economic context in which ideas and policies were developed, consult the chapters on the economic history of Latin America since 1930 in *The Cambridge History of Latin America*, vol. VI, part 1 (1994).

ist and dependency perspectives in a comparative treatment of European and non-European economic development, emphasizing 'selective de-linking' as a historically proven development strategy.

On the 'pre-theoretical' justifications of industrial development in Latin America, a documentary collection for Brazil, representative in many respects of nations of the Southern Cone, is Edgard Carone (ed.), *O pensamento industrial no Brasil (1880–1945)* (São Paulo, 1971). A debate on the role of industrialization in the development process at the end of that period is Roberto Simonsen and Eugênio Gudin, *A controvérsia do planejamento na economia brasileira* (Rio de Janeiro, 1977).

On the U. N. Economic Commission for Latin America (ECLA, and from 1985, ECLAC, to include the Caribbean), see the agency's anthology, *Development Problems in Latin America: An Analysis by the UN ECLA* (Austin, Tex., 1970). Fundamental structuralist statements include the ECLA documents *The Economic Development of Latin America and Its Principal Problems* (Lake Success, N.Y., 1950) and *Economic Survey of Latin America: 1949* (New York, 1951). Raúl Prebisch was the exclusive author of the first study, and the principal author of the second. Another important work was his *Toward a Dynamic Development Policy for Latin America* (New York, 1963). The classic statement of the structuralist thesis on inflation is Osvaldo Sunkel, 'Inflation in Chile: an unorthodox approach', *International Economic Papers,* No. 10 (1960): 107–31. In *La teoría del subdesarrollo de la CEPAL* [Sp. acronym for ECLA] (Mexico, D.F., 1980), Octavio Rodríguez – a former ECLA economist – surveys, evaluates and critiques the organization's doctrines. Joseph Hodara, *Prebisch y la CEPAL: Sustancia trayectoria y contexto internacional* (Mexico, D.F., 1987), is an exposition of ECLA's doctrines, largely in non-technical terms, combined with an institutional history.

On the European antecedents of structuralism, see H. W. Arndt, 'The Origins of Structuralism', *World Development,* 13, 2 (February, 1985): 151–9. For more on the context of the formulation of Prebisch's first thesis in 1949, see Joseph L. Love, 'Raúl Prebisch and the Origins of the Doctrine of Unequal Exchange', *Latin American Research Review,* 15, 3 (1980): 45–72.

On neostructuralism, a representative collection is Osvaldo Sunkel (ed.), *El desarrollo desde dentro: Un enfoque neoestructuralista para la América Latina* (Mexico, D.F., 1991; Eng. trans. 1993), containing essays by Sunkel, Joseph Ramos, Ricardo Ffrench-Davis, Winston Fritsch, José Antonio Ocampo, Víctor Tokman, Oscar Muñoz, Adolfo Figueroa, and others. A brief introduction to the doctrine, comparing it to neo-liberalism, can be found in Ricardo Ffrench-Davis, 'An Outline of a Neo-structuralist Approach', *CEPAL Review*, no. 34 (April, 1988): 37–44.

Structuralist and neostructuralist thought can be followed not only in *CEPAL Review* (since 1976), and its predecessor, the *Economic Bulletin for Latin America*, but also in *Pensamiento Iberoamericano*, published by ECLA and the Instituto de Cooperación Iberoamericana in Madrid since 1982.

A frequent commentator on Latin American structuralism whose own structuralist writings have often paralleled developments in the Latin American school is Albert O. Hirschman. A survey and critique of ECLA's theses through 1960 is Hirschman, 'Ideologies of Economic Development in Latin America', in Albert O. Hirschman (ed.), *Latin American Issues: Essays and Comments* (New York, 1961), pp. 3–42. On the Structuralist Interpretation of Inflation in Chile, set in a historical context, see 'Inflation in Chile', in Hirschman, *Journeys Toward Progress: Studies of Economic Policy-Making in Latin America* (New York, 1963), pp. 161–223. An explanation of why the structuralist thesis on inflation lost out at the policy level is 'The Social and Political Matrix of Inflation: elaborations of the Latin American experience', in Albert O. Hirschman, *Essays in Trespassing: Economics to Politics and Beyond* (Cambridge, 1981), pp. 177–207. On the crisis of import-substitution industrialization and its implications for structuralism, see 'The Political Economy of Import Substituting Industrialization in Latin America', in Albert O. Hirschman, *A Bias for Hope* (New Haven, Conn., 1971), pp. 85–123; and Werner Baer, 'Import Substitution and Industrialization in Latin America: experiences and interpretations', *Latin American Research Review*, 7, 1 (1972): 95–122.

In the vanguard of the neo-classical counterattack on structuralism and dependency was the Chicago School, which was most influential in Chile. Juan Gabriel Valdés offers a scholarly but highly critical study of its ideology and practice in *La escuela de Chicago: Operación Chile* (Buenos Aires, 1989). See also Alejandro Foxley, *Latin American Experiments in Neo-Conservative Economics* (Berkeley, 1983) which deals principally with Chile.

On 'developmentalism' (*desarrollismo* in Spanish, *desenvolvimentismo* in Portuguese), an ideology and set of policies associated with structuralism in Argentina and Brazil, see Kathryn Sikkink, *Ideas and Institutions: Developmentalism in Brazil and Argentina* (Ithaca, N.Y., 1991). That Argentine *desarrollistas* ignored Prebisch himself, possibly because of his earlier role in forming government policies in Argentina, is shown in Julio G. Nosiglia, *El desarrollismo* (Buenos Aires, 1983). Ricardo Bielschowsky, *Pensamento econômico brasileiro: O ciclo ideológico do desenvolvimentismo* (Rio de Janeiro, 1988) not only considers in detail the relationship between developmentalism and structuralism, but surveys all other major schools of thought in Brazil from the end of the Second World War to the coup d'état of 1964.

A collection of readings of Marxist thought, including contributions by writers who emphasized relations of exchange rather than relations of production and thereby influenced dependency analysis, is Michael Lowy, *Le marxisme en Amérique latine de 1909 à nos jours: Anthologie* (Paris, 1980, Eng. trans. 1992). On Marxism through the 1960s, also see Sheldon B. Liss, *Marxist Thought in Latin America* (Berkeley, Cal., 1984). For the influence of Antonio Gramsci, indirectly important in some versions of dependency through his notion of hegemony, consult José Aricó, *La cola del diablo: itinerario de Gramsci en América Latina* (Buenos Aires, 1988).

A study of dependency analysis should begin with Fernando Henrique Cardoso and Enzo Faletto, *Dependencia y desarrollo en América Latina* (Mexico, D.F., 1969) [the English version, *Dependency and Development in Latin America* (1979), is much revised]; and Andre Gunder Frank, *Capitalism and Underdevelopment in Latin America* (New York, 1967). Later works in the dependency tradition by the evolving structuralists Prebisch and Furtado are important and similar to one another, in their employment of the classical concept of surplus. See Raúl Prebisch, *Capitalismo periférico: Crisis y transformación* (Mexico, 1981) and Celso Furtado, *Accumulation and Development: the Logic of Industrial Civilization*, tr. by Suzette Macedo (Oxford, 1983 [Port. orig., 1978]).

A review of the dependency literature through the mid-1970s can be found in two critical but sympathetic studies: José Gabriel Palma, 'Dependency: a formal theory of underdevelopment or a methodology for the analysis of concrete situations of underdevelopment?', *World Development*, 6, 7–8 (1978): 881–924; and Heraldo Muñoz, 'Cambio y continuidad en el debate sobre la dependencia y el imperialismo', *Estudios Internacionales*, 11, 44 (October-December, 1978): 88–138. For likenesses and differences in Latin American and Caribbean versions of dependency, see Norman Girvan, 'The Development of Dependency Economics in the Caribbean and Latin America: review and comparison', *Social and Economic Studies*, 22, 1 (March, 1973): 1–33. Jorge Larraín offers a defence of dependency as a legitimate Marxist enterprise in *Theories of Development: Capitalism, Colonialism and Dependency* (Cambridge, 1989). On the relationship between Marxism and dependency analysis, also see Ronald H. Chilcote (ed.), *Dependency and Marxism: Toward a Resolution of the Debate* (Boulder,

Colo., 1982). For an assessment of the relative importance of Marxism and structuralism, the two traditions from which dependency drew, see Joseph L. Love, 'The Origins of Dependency Analysis', *Journal of Latin American Studies*, 22, 1 (1990): 143–68. Robert A. Packenham, in *The Dependency Movement: Scholarship and Politics in Development Studies* (Cambridge, Mass., 1992), argues that dependency is non-scientific and ideological, including the much-praised work of F. H. Cardoso, though much of his criticism is directed against North American, rather than Latin American, dependency analysts. An extensively annotated bibliography chiefly concerned with dependency is Charles W. Bergquist (ed.), *Alternative Approaches to the Problem of Development: A Selected and Annotated Bibliography* (Durham, N.C., 1979). The volume also deals with structuralism and Third World Marxist contributions.

Though a critic of the dependency literature, one of the few writers on dependency who worked within the tradition of formal Marxist economics, as opposed to historical materialism, is the Colombian Salomón Kalmanovitz, who sketched a theory of dependent reproduction and accounted for the incomplete accumulation process in the Periphery. See Kalmanovitz, *El desarrollo tardío del capitalismo: Un enfoque crítico de la teoría de la dependencia* (Bogotá, 1983).

For the flavour of the modes-of-production debate, see two collections: Carlos Sempat Assadourian (ed.), *Modos de producción en América Latina* (Mexico, D.F., 1973); and Roger Bartra et al., *Modos de producción en América Latina* (Lima, 1976). On the articulation of pre-capitalist relations of production with capitalism in the informal economy, see Lúcio Kowarick, 'Capitalismo, dependência e marginalidade urbana na América Latina: uma contribuição teórica', *Estudos CEBRAP* 8 (April–June, 1974), pp. 79–96; and Francisco de Oliveira, 'A economia brasileira: Crítica à razão dualista', *Estudos CEBRAP* 2 (October, 1972), pp. 3–82.

On individual writers, including biographical and autobiographical materials, the following may be consulted:

On Prebisch, see Comisión Económica para América Latina y el Caribe [CEPAL], *Raúl Prebisch: Un aporte al estudio de su pensamiento* (Santiago, 1987), which contains the Spanish version of his 'Five Stages' (in next item) and an annotated list of 466 of his publications from 1920 to 1986; Gerald M. Meier and Dudley Seers (eds), *Pioneers in Development* (New York, 1984), which includes Prebisch's retrospective, 'Five stages in my thinking on development' (pp. 175–91) and H{ans} W. Singer's 'The terms of trade controversy and the evolution of soft financing: early years in the U. N.' (pp. 275–303); Mateo Magariños, *Diálogos con Raúl Prebisch* (Mexico, D.F., 1991), which offers episodic reminiscences by Prebisch through the 1960s; and a brief survey of Prebisch's career in Joseph L. Love, 'Raúl Prebisch (1901–1986): his life and ideas', in Abraham Lowenthal (ed.), *Latin American and Caribbean Record,* Vol. V: 1985–1986 (New York, 1988), pp. A143–A150. A book-length biography of Prebisch is being prepared by David Pollock, a former ECLA official, and Edgar J. Dosman.

On Furtado, a wide-ranging anthology of his writings with a biographical sketch by the editor is Francisco de Oliveira (ed.), *Celso Furtado: Economia,* (São Paulo, 1983). Furtado's memoirs (still in process) consist of three volumes: *A fantasia organizada* (1985); *A fantasia desfeita* (1989); *Os ares do mundo* (1991), all published in Rio de Janeiro; and a brief autobiographical statement in English, 'Adventures of a Brazilian Economist', in *International Social Science Journal,* 25, 1–2 (1973): 28–38. Furtado's and Singer's work on the implications of structuralism for the domestic economy is examined in Joseph L. Love, 'Modeling Internal Colonialism: history and prospect', *World Development,* 17, 6 (June 1989): 905–22. Other aspects of Furtado's work are considered in Love, *Crafting the Third World: Theorizing Underdevelopment in Rumania and Brazil,* ch. 10 (forthcoming). Two studies that place Furtado's work in the context of postwar Brazilian economic thought are Guido Mantega, *A economia política brasileira* (São Paulo, 1984) and Ricardo Bielschowsky, *Pensamento econômico brasileiro* (above). The former also treats dependency.

On Noyola, see Carlos Bazdresch Parada, *El pensamiento de Juan F. Noyola* (México, 1984), which reviews the work of the Mexican economist, one of the earliest structuralist writers, on industrialization, external disequilibrium, and inflation.

On Cardoso, see Fernando Henrique Cardoso, 'The consumption of dependency theory in the United States', *Latin American Research Review,* 12, 3 (1977), pp. 7–24, which contains autobiographical elements, and Joseph L. Kahl, 'Fernando Henrique Cardoso', a biographical interview with critical commentary, in Kahl, *Modernization, Exploitation and Dependency in Latin America: Germani, González Casanova and Cardoso* (New Brunswick, N.J., 1976), pp. 129–94.

On Frank, see Andre Gunder Frank, 'The Underdevelopment of Development', in the *Scandinavian Journal of Development Alternatives,* 10, 3 (September, 1991): 5–72, an autobiographical statement which treats his intellectual development before, during, and after his dependency period.

An appendix contains a complete bibliography of Frank's works, 1955–90 (pp. 133–50).

4. LIBERATION THEOLOGY

A standard introduction to liberation theology is Gustavo Gutiérrez, *A Theology of Liberation: History, Politics and Salvation* (Maryknoll, N.Y., 1973) and, more briefly, 'Liberation, Theology and Proclamation', in Claude Geffre and Gutiérrez (eds), *The Mystical and Political Dimensions of the Christian Faith* (New York, 1974), pp. 53–77. See also Hugo Assmann, *Opresión-liberación desafío a los cristianos* (Montevideo, 1971) and *Theology for a Nomad Church* (Maryknoll, N.Y., 1976); Enrique Dussel, *History of Theology of Liberation* (New York, 1976) and *Hipótesis para una historia de la teología latinoamericana* (Bogotá, 1986); Roberto Oliveros Maqueo, *Liberación y teología. Génesis y crecimiento de una reflexión* (1966–1976) (Mexico, D.F., 1977); Roger Vekemans, *Teología de la liberación y Cristianos por el socialismo* (Bogotá, 1976); Samuel Silva Gotay, *El pensamiento cristiano revolucionario en América Latina y el Caribe* (Salamanca, 1981); Pablo Richard, *Materiales para una historia de la teología latinoamericana* (San José 1984); Leonardo and Clodovis Boff, *Introducing Liberation Theology* (New York, 1987); Phillip Berryman, *Liberation Theology* (New York, 1987) and 'Latin American Liberation Theology', *Theological Studies*, 34, 3 (1973): 357–95; Paul Sigmund, *Liberation Theology at the Crossroads: Democracy or Revolution?* (New York, 1990); Alfred Hennelly (ed.), *Liberation Theology: A Documentary History* (New York, 1990); Michael Novak (ed.), *Liberation Theology* (Washington, D.C., 1987); Michael Dodson, 'Liberation Theology and Christian Radicalism in Contemporary Latin America', *Journal of Latin American Studies*, 11, 1 (1979), pp. 203–22; W. E. Hewitt, 'Myths and Realities of Liberation Theology: the case of the basic Christian communities in Brazil', in Richard Rubinstein and John Roth (eds), *The Political Significance of Liberation Theology* (Washington, D.C., 1988); Deane William Ferm, *Profiles in Liberation. 36 Portraits of Third World Theologians* (Mystic, Conn. 1988), pp. 114–193 and *Third World Liberation Theologies. An Introductory Survey* (New York, 1986), pp. 3–58.

5. SCIENCE IN TWENTIETH-CENTURY LATIN AMERICA

To synthesize the history of science in twentieth-century Latin America is to explore a largely uncharted territory. The first great generation of Latin

American historians of science, whose representative figures were Juan B. Lastres in Peru, Alfredo Bateman, Enrique Pérez Arbeláez and Guillermo Hernández de Alba in Colombia, Enrique Beltrán and Germán Somolinos in Mexico, worked preeminently on the science of the Enlightenment, when scientific activity in Latin America reached a level of brilliance still unsurpassed. Another group of historians domiciled mainly in Argentina (Aldo Mieli, Cortés Plá, José Babini and Desiderio Papp) wrote on mainstream European science, although Babini provided a useful synthesis of science in Argentina, *Historia de la ciencia en la Argentina* (Buenos Aires, 1949; 1986 edition with a perceptive historiographical introduction by Marcelo Montserrat).

Beside's Babini's primer, there are few other single-country histories of science. Of these, by far the most analytical is Simon Schwartzman, *Formação da comunidade científica no Brasil* (São Paulo, 1979; Eng. trans. *A Space for Science. The Development of the Scientific Community in Brazil,* University Park, PA, 1991). Although the entire twentieth century is covered, the book's strength is its description of the *prise de conscience* by Brazilian scientists of the 1930s through 1950s, based on interviews with sixty-nine scientific leaders; their biographies are given in a satellite volume, *História da ciência no Brasil: Acervo de depoimentos* (Rio de Janeiro, 1984). Marcos Cueto's study of high-altitude physiology in Peru, *Excelencia científica en la periferia: Actividades científicas e investigación biomédica en el Perú, 1890–1950* (Lima, 1989), is also a study of a nascent scientific elite. Much less useful are Ramiro Condarco Morales, *Historia del saber y la ciencia en Bolivia* (La Paz, 1978) which, like too much history of Latin American science, is little more than a list of people and institutions, and Eli de Gortari, *La ciencia en la historia de México,* 2nd edn (Mexico, D.F., 1980) which devotes too much space to a defense of Aztec science and not enough on the achievements of the twentieth century.

In an attempt to cover nineteenth and twentieth century science in Argentina by disciplines, the Sociedad Científica Argentina published two series of studies, one in the 1920s, the other in the 1970s. Although the volumes vary in coverage and style, the earlier series is, on the whole, better. Among the most distinguished and interesting disciplinary histories are those of Ramón G. Loyarte, *La evolución de la física* (Buenos Aires, 1924) and Cristóbal M. Hicken, *Los estudios botánicos* (Buenos Aires, 1923). Less objective is Claro Cornelio Dassen, *Las matemáticas en la Argentina* (Buenos Aires, 1924), which in part is a polemic against modern mathematics. The more recent series consists of multi-authored volumes, in which sub-fields have been delegated to specialists (scientists, not historians) in those areas. As a result most of the volumes are chaotic compilations of names, dates and institutions with scant analysis or synthesis. However, some of the volumes may be mined for their rich lode of information; see, in particular, Luis A. Santaló (ed.), *Matemática* (1972), José Federico Westerkamp, *Física* (1975), Luis B. Mazoti and Juan H. Hunziker, *Genética* (1976), and Noemi G. Abiusso, *Química* (1981). A somewhat parallel treatment can be found for Brazil. First are two volumes published in the 1950s under the editorship of Fernando de Azevedo, *As ciências no Brasil* (São Paulo, 1955), characterized by chapters, again written mainly be scientists who had participated in the institutionalization of their own disciplines, of uniformly high quality. Of particular interest are the chapters on astronomy (Abraão de Morais), physics (J. Costa Ribeiro), geology and paleontology (Viktor Leinz) and chemistry (Heinrich Rheinboldt). A more recent work, *História das ciências no Brasil,* Mário Guimarães Ferri and Shozo Motoyama, eds, 3 vols (São Paulo, 1979–81), suffers by comparison. Most of its chapters are unenlightening lists of names and research projects, compiled by scientists in the various disciplines. The same can be said of multi-authored *Estudios de historia de la ciencia en el Perú,* 2 vols (Lima, 1986). Possibly the best collection of disciplinary articles from a single country is Hebe M. C. Vessuri (ed.), *Ciencia académica en la Venezuela moderna* (Caracas, 1984), a collection of mature studies, mainly by social scientists, of discrete disciplines, always within the framework of larger issues of the institutionalization of academic science. In 1993 the Instituto Colombiano para el Desarrollo de la Ciencia (Bogotá) published a nine-volume *Historia Social de la Ciencia en Colombia,* with volumes on Methodology (I), Mathematics, Astronomy and Geology (II), Natural History (III), Engineering and History of Technology (IV–V), Physics and Chemistry (VI), Medicine (VII–VIII), and Social Science (IX).

The Sociedad Latinoamericana de Historia de las Ciencias y la Tecnologia has published since 1984 a distinguished journal, *Quipu* (Mexico, D.F., 1984–), in which appear a variety of studies, by historians, of modern Latin American science. The Society also publishes an occasional series called *Cuadernos de Quipu,* of which two have appeared, *El perfil de la ciência en América* (1987), and *Cross Cultural Diffusion of Science: Latin America* (1987). The acts of the Society's second congress, with many articles on 20th-century science was published as *Anais do Segundo Congresso Latino-Americano de História da Ciência e da Tecnologia* (São Paulo, 1989).

Few Latin American scientific institutions have had proper histories. For Brazil, Nancy Stepan, *Beginnings of Brazilian Science* (New York, 1976) is a model account of the foundation and early years of the Oswaldo Cruz Institute at Manguinhos, the country's most important bio-medical institution. The more recent history of the Cruz Institute and its political problems under the military dictatorship in the 1960s is chronicled by Herman Lent, *O massacre de Manguinhos* (Rio de Janeiro, 1978). On scientific institutions in Rio de Janeiro, see Simon Schwartzman (ed.), *Universidades e Instituções Científicas no Rio de Janeiro* (Brasília, 1982). On botany, see João Conrado Niemeyer de Lavôr, *História do Jardim Botânico do Rio de Janeiro* (Rio de Janeiro, 1983) and F. C. Hoehne et al., *O Jardim Botânico de São Paulo* (São Paulo, 1941).

For Mexico, Horacio García Fernández's account of the Faculty of Chemistry, *Historia de una facultad: Química 1916–1983* (Mexico, D.F., 1985) is a model study of a university science department based in part on interviews with its own alumni. On the related Institute of Chemistry, see Alberto Sandoval L., 'Cinco lustros de existencia', *Boletín del Instituto de Química*, 17 (1965): 83–121. On Mexican physics, there is Héctor Cruz Manjarrez, *Reseña histórica del Instituto de Física*, 2 vols (mimeo) (Mexico, D.F., 1975–6), and Juan Manuel Lozano, et al., 'Historia de la Sociedad Mexicana de Fisica', *Revista Mexicana de Fisica*, 28 (1982): 277–93. A broader study of university science, for Argentina, is Horacio H. Camacho, *Las ciencias naturales en la Universidad de Buenos Aires* (Buenos Aires, 1971).

Astronomical institutions have fared better than most. For Brazil, Henrique Morize, *Observatório Astronômico: Um século de história (1827–1927)*, new edn (Rio de Janeiro, 1987) deals mainly with the nineteenth century; the new edition includes two biographical articles about Morize. For Chile, see Philip C. Keenan et al., *The Chilean National Astronomical Observatory (1852–1965)* (Santiago, 1985). Marco Arturo Moreno Corral, ed. *Historia de la astronomia en México,* (Ensenada, 1983) has an institutional focus.

The few disciplinary histories written tend to be highly institutional in focus; see, for example, Jorge Grünwald Ramasso, *Historia de la Química en el Uruguay (1830–1930)* (Montevideo, 1966). A thrilling institutional and political history of atomic physics in Argentina is Mario Mariscotti, *El secreto atómico de Huemul* (Buenos Aires, 1985).

Hebe Vessuri wrote two pioneering studies of the scientific press: 'La revista cientifica periférica. El caso de *Acta Científica Venezolana*', *In-*

terciencia, 12 (1987): 124–34; and 'Una estrategia de publicación científica para la fisiología latinoamericana: *Acta Physiologica Latinoamericana,* 1950– 1971', in *Anais do Segundo Congresso,* pp. 232–40.

There is no tradition of biographical memoirs in Latin American science and, as a result, this kind of literature is scant. Of the great figures in biomedicine, see the commemorative volume *Bernardo A. Houssay, su vida y su obra 1887–1971* (Buenos Aires, 1981), and Ricardo Archila, *Luis Razetti, síntesis biográfica* (Caracas, 1973). For Brazil, see Miguel Osório de Almeida, *Carlos Chagas* (mimeo) (Rio de Janeiro, 1988); Ivone Freire de Mota and Amélia Império Hamburger, 'Retratos de Luiz de Barros Freire como pioneiro da ciência no Brasil', *Ciência e Cultura,* 40 (1988): 875–81, and the biographical essays in M. Amoroso Costa, *As idéias fundamentais da matemática e outros ensaios* (São Paulo, 1981). An unusually informative autobiography is that of the Chilean agronomist Manuel Elgueta Guerin, *Memorias de una vida 1902–1983* (Santiago de Chile, n.d.). See also Enrique Beltrán, *Medio siglo de recuerdos de un biólogo mexicano* (Mexico, D.F., 1977). Interviews are perhaps the most distinctive form of scientific biography in Latin America, especially in Brazil. See, for example, Lourdes Cedran (ed.), *Dialogos com Mário Schenberg* (São Paulo, 1985) and another collection of interviews *about* Schenberg with his students and colleagues in Brazilian physics, Gita K. Guinsburg and José Luiz Goldfarb (eds), *Mário Schenberg: Entre-Vistas* (São Paulo, 1984).

There is a considerable literature of the contributions of foreigners to Latin American science. See, for example, Lewis Pyenson's discussion of the German contribution to physics, physical chemistry and astronomy in Argentina in *Cultural Imperialism and Exact Science: German Expansion Overseas, 1900–1930* (New York, 1985). See also, Marcelo Montserrat, 'La influencia italiana de la actividad científica argentina del siglo XIX', in Francis Korn (ed.), *Los italianos en la Argentina* (Buenos Aires, n.d.), pp. 105–23; H. M. Nussenzveig, *Guido Beck* (mimeo) (Rio de Janeiro, 1989); and J. Leite Lopes, *Richard Feynman in Brazil: Recollections* (mimeo) (Rio de Janeiro, 1988). More analytical is Miguel J. C. de Asua, 'Influencia de la Facultad de Medicina de París sobre la de Buenos Aires', *Quipu,* 3 (1986): 79–89, which raises the issue of European versus American disciplinary and institutional identities. There is a complementary literature on Latin American science students abroad; see, for example, Eddy Stols 'Les étudiants brésiliens en Belgique', *Revista de História* (São Paulo), 50 (1974):

653–91; and Humberto Ruiz Calderón, 'Una vieja historia: Los becarios de Venezuela en el exterior (1900–1954)', *Interciencia*, 15 (1990): 8–14.

There is a considerable literature on Spanish scientific exiles, particularly in Mexico. See two articles by José Cueli in *El exilio español en Mexico 1939– 1982* (Mexico, D.F., 1982): 'Ciencias médicas y biológicas' (pp. 495–528) and 'Matemáticas, física y quimica' (pp. 531–43). Biographies of Spanish figures can be culled for the chapters on exile; e.g., José Luis Barona Vilar and María Fernanda Mancebo, *José Puche Alvarez (1896–1979): Historia de un compromiso* (Valencia, 1989) ['El exilio mexicano (1939–1979)', pp. 57– 73]; L. Valencia Gayá, *El doctor Lafora y su época* (Madrid, 1977) ['Nueve años de exilio de México', pp. 145–60]. On Lafora and Mexican criminology, see Raquel Alvarez Peláez and Rafael Huertas Garcia-Alejo, *¿Criminales o locos? Dos peritajes psiquiátricas del Dr. Gonzalo R. Lafora* (Madrid, 1987). On Julio Rey Pastor and Latin American mathematics, see Sixto Rios, et al., *Julio Rey Pastor, matemático* (Madrid, 1979) ['Rey Pastor y la matemática en la Argentina', pp. 49–134]; and Mario Otero, 'Las matemáticas uruguayas y Rey Pastor', in Luis Español González (ed.), *Estudios sobre Julio Rey Pastor* (Logroño, 1990), pp. 181–93.

Scientific culture has been thin enough in Latin America to discourage studies of the reception or development of specific ideas there. Those ideas that have had culture-wide repercussions have attracted the most attention. On Darwinism (mainly a nineteenth-century topic, but with tremendous repercussions on popular perceptions of science that extended well into the twentieth century) there are a number of national studies, e.g. Eduardo L. Ortiz, 'La polémica del darwinismo y la inserción del la ciencia en Argentina', in *Actas II Congrso de la Sociedad Española de Historia de la Ciencias*, 3 vols (Zaragoza, 1984), I, pp. 89–108; Marcelo Montserrat, 'La presencia evolucionista en el positivismo argentino', *Quipu*, 3 (1986): 91– 101; Terezinha Alves Ferreira Collichio, *Miranda Azevedo e o darwinismo no Brasil* (São Paulo, 1988); Bernardo Marquez Bretón, *Origenes del darwinismo en Chile* (Santiago, 1982); Pedro M. Pruna and Armando Garcia González, *Darwinismo y sociedad en Cuba* (Madrid, 1989); Roberto Moreno, *La polémica del darwinismo en México* (Mexico, D.F., 1984); Rosaura Ruiz Gutiérrez, *Positivismo y evolución: Introducción del darwinismo en México* (Mexico, D.F., 1987); and Thomas F. Glick, *Darwin y el Darwinismo en el Uruguay y en América Latina* (Montevideo, 1989).

On eugenics, see Nancy Stepan, 'Eugenesia, genética y salud pública: el movimiento eugenésico brasileño y mundial', *Quipu*, 2 (1985): 351–84, and the fuller treatment in her book, *The Hour of Eugenics: Latin America and the Movement for Racial Improvement, 1918–1940* (Ithaca, N.Y., 1991).

On the reception of psychoanalysis, the Brazilian case is the best studied. See Gilberto S. Rocha, *Introdução ao nascimento da psicanálise no Brasil* (Rio de Janeiro, 1989); Marialzira Perestrello, 'Primeiros encontros com a psicanálise. Os precursores no Brasil (1899–1937)', in Sérvulo Figueira (ed.), *Efeito Psi: A influência da psicanálise* (Rio de Janeiro, 1988), pp. 151–81; Roberto Yutaka Sagawa, 'A psicanálise pioneira e os pioneiros da psicanálise em São Paulo', in Sérvulo Figueira (ed.), *Cultura da Psicanálise* (São Paulo, 1985), pp. 15–34; and Ana Cristina Figueiredo, 'O movimiento psicoanalítico no Rio de Janeiro na década de 70', in Joel Birman (ed.), *Precursores na história da psicanálise* (Rio de Janeiro, 1988), pp. 123–47. 'Precursors' in this literature refers to early commentators on Freud who were not canonically trained analysts. An important work on Peru is Honorio Delgado, *Freud y el psicoanálisis. Escritos y testimonios,* Javier Mariategui (ed.), (Lima, 1989). Garmán García's *La entrada del psicoanálisis en Argentina* (Buenos Aires, 1978) is a perceptive 'intrahistory' from a Lacanian perspective. More balanced are Jorge Balán's sociologically perceptive *Cuéntame tu vida: Una biografía colectiva del psicoanálisis argentino* (Buenos Aires, 1991) and Hugo Vezzetti (ed.), *Freud en Buenos Aires* (Buenos Aires, 1989), an anthology of texts.

An excellent introduction to contemporary policy debates can be found in Hebe M. C. Vessuri, 'The social study of science in Latin America', *Social Studies of Science,* 17 (1987): 519–54. Two standard documents are Amílcar O. Herrera, *Ciencia y política en América Latina,* 9th edn (Mexico, D.F., 1985), and J. Leite Lopes, *Ciência e libertação,* 2nd edn (Rio de Janeiro, 1978). On the sociology of science in Mexico, see María Luisa Rodríguez Sala-Gomezgil and Adrián Chavero González, *El científico en México: Su formación en el extranjero, su incorporación y adecuación al sistema ocupacional mexicano* (Mexico, D.F., 1982). For a survey of recent Brazilian science, see the special section on 'Science in Brazil', *Nature,* 342 (1989): 355–74.

INDEX

Aberastury, Federico, 313, 314
Abolicionismo (Nabuco), 147
Academy of Medicine of Caracas, 293
Acta Científica Venezolana (journal), 348
Acta Physiológica Latinoamericana, 307
Adán Buenosayres (Marechal), 31
Adler, Alfred, 65, 311
Africa, 261, 265
African culture, 55–6
African mode of production, 263
Afro-American culture, 55, 282
Afro-Americans, 7, 8, 9, 60, 76
Afro-Cuban culture, 49
Afro-Puerto Ricans, 69
Agassiz, Louis, 167
agrarian reform, 60, 195, 215, 240, 241, 245
agrarianism, 192–9, 200
Agraz, Juan Salvador, 338
Agricultura nacional (Rebouças), 147
agricultural countries, 211, 216, 222, 235–6
agricultural production, 222
agricultural specialization, 215–16
agriculture/agricultural sector, 212, 214; and in-
   flation, 240; productivity in, 262; surplus
   labour in, 211, 230
Águila y la serpiente, El (Guzmán), 40–1
Aguirre Cerda, Pedro, 215
Ahumada, Jorge, 237, 251
Ainsi parla l'oncle (Price-Mars), 53, 55, 56, 58
ajiaco, 68, 69, 84
Alba Andrade, Fernando, 325
Alberdi, Juan Bautista, 99, 111, 135, 147,
   159, 171, 178, 188, 196; and constitu-
   tionalism, 139–40, 141
Alegría, Ciro, 15, 47, 48
Aleijadinho (Antônio Francisco Lisboa), 83, 86
Alem, Leandro, 157, 159
Alencar, Oto de, 337
Alessandri, Arturo, 191–2, 203
Alianza Popular Revolucionaria Americana

(APRA), 196, 197, 199, 200, 201, 319; *see
   also* Aprismo
Allen, Ruby, 297
Alliance for Progress, 241
Almeida, Guilherme de, 18, 21
Almeida, José Américo de, 15, 47
Althusser, Louis, 263, 264
Alves, Rubem, 281
Amado, Jorge, 15, 51
Ameghino, Florentino, 170, 292–3
America, 61, 62, 87
América, La (Lastarria), 136
América en peligro (Bilbao), 136
American Association of Variable Star Observ-
   ers, 329
American Economic Association, 232
American Economic Review, 232
American "spirit', republicanism and, 135–8
Americanism, 135, 137, 182–3, 185, 186,
   191
Amin, Samir, 261
anabatic recovery, 43, 90, 91
anarchism, 9, 193, 194, 195, 275
Andean Science and Technology Council, 349
Andrade, Mário de, 13, 14, 16, 18, 19, 22,
   23–6, 27, 45, 59, 109; esthetic orientations
   of, 20; linguistic-literary priority of, 21
Andrade, Oswald de, 14, 18, 22–4, 26, 35,
   43, 45, 50, 59; Brazilwood Manifesto, 20–
   1, 30, 44
Anta movement (Brazil), 21
anthropology, 77; and racism, 162–3
Anthropophagy, 20, 21, 23–4, 39
anticlericalism, 151–2, 277
anti-mysticism, 83–4
anti-positivism, 93, 99, 198
apocalypticism, 36
Aprismo, 202; see also APRA
Aragón, Augustín, 150
Aranha, Osvaldo, 214–15

Parra, Porfirio, 151
Partido Autonomista Nacional (PAN) (Mexico), 159, 160, 187
Partido dos Trabalhadores (PT) (Brazil), 80
Partido Liberal Mexicano (PLM), 194–5
Partido Obrero Socialista (POS) (Chile), 193
Partido Socialista Brasileira, 79
Pasteur, Louis, 301, 358
Pasteur Institute(s), 290, 301, 302, 305, 353
Pastoral Popular (magazine), 282
Patagonian Centre of Geoheliophysics, 324
pathetic fallacy, 45–52
patriarchalism, 74–5, 77–8, 79
patriarchs, 91, 93, 98–9, 112
Paul VI, Pope, 278
Paulicea desvairada (Hallucinated City) (Mário de Andrade), 24
Paulo de Oliveira, Eusebio, 343
Paz, Octavio, 13, 38, 39, 44–5, 52, 59–70, 83, 127–9
Paz, Pedro, 247
Pearce, Richard M., 305
Pedreira, Antonio S., 69n95
Pedro II, Emperor of Brazil, 134, 158
Peixoto, Floriano, 156, 158
Pellegrini, Carlos, 157, 159–60, 187
Pellicer, Carlos, 37
Peña, Milciades, 256n150
pensadores, 7–8, 9, 52, 90, 96, 126, 127, 171, 172; search for identity, 96
Pensée, La, 264, 265
Pereyra, Victor, 335
Pérez Arbeláez, Enrique, 333
Pérez Firmat, Gustavo, 67–8
Pérez Galdós, Benito, 39
Pérez Jiménez, Marcos, 289, 348, 353
Pérez-Marchand, Monelisa Lina, 106
Pérez Rosales, Vicent, 147
peripheral science, 355–9
peripherality, 290
Periphery: capitalism of, 269–71; *see also* Centre-Periphery
Perón, Juan, 227, 306, 326, 353; dictatorship of, 214, 296; fall of, 314
peronismo, 243
Pérou contemporaine, Le (García Calderón), 182
Perrine, Charles D., 328, 330
Perroux, François, 234–5, 273n202
perspectivism, 94, 97, 98
Peru, 9, 27, 54, 58, 60, 302; astronomy in, 331–2; Catholic youth movement in, 281; corporatism in, 200; economic exploitation in, 53, 54–5; geology in, 344–5; ideology in, 192; new idealism in, 181–3; psychoanalysis in, 311–12; radical ideology in,

195–7; science in, 348; social consciousness of, 185; university reform in, 188, 189; War with Chile, 196
Perú en la historia (Riva-Agüero), 182
Peruvian Society of Psychoanalysis, 312
Peruvian Student Federation (FEP), 196
pessimism: economic, 249, 253, 271; racial, 164–6, 167; in social thought, 178, 183
Petersen, George, 345
Petersen, Ulrich, 345
petty bourgeoisie, 27, 34–5
pharmacy/pharmacology, 337–9, 340, 341
phenomenology, 15, 43, 93–6, 97–8, 99, 106, 108
philosophical idealism, 187, 195; and determinism, 179–80
philosophical project, 89, 91; in Mexico, 104–10
philosophical system(s), 91, 92
philosophy, 11–12, 15, 43, 80, 112; Argentina, 188; generations in renaissance of, 91–3, 98–9; German, 127; and identity question, 15–16, 89–111
Philosophy of History, The (Hegel), 88
physical and exact sciences, 287, 316–46
physics, 316–28, 330, 333, 349
physiology, 307, 309
Pi Calleja, Pedor, 335
pi meson (pion), research, 322–3
Pi-Sunyer, August, 307, 309, 310, 347–8
Pi-Sunyer, Jaume, 307
Picabia, Francis, 20
Picasso, Pablo, 87, 88, 113, 125
Picchia, Menotti del, 18, 21
Pichón-Riviere, Enrique, 313–14
Picón Salas, Mariano, 108
Piérola, Nicolás, 182
Pierson, Donald, 115
Pimentel, Francisco, 168
Pinedo, Federico, 214, 221, 224
Pinto Santa Cruz, Aníbal, 234, 237, 240, 247, 268
Pismis, Paris, 329
Pittaluga, Gustavo, 309–10
Pius IX, Pope, 144
Pius IX, Pope, 275, 277
Pius XII, Pope, 275, 277
Pizarro Crespo, Emilio, 313
Plan of Ayala (1911), 195
Pleiad poets, 21
poetry, 14–15, 20, 38, 62, 119
Poincaré, Jules Henri, 183
Politécnica of São Paulo, 337
Política científica y política metafísica (García), 153
political consensus, 156, 161